Rhetorical Argumentation
in Biblical Texts

Emory Studies in Early Christianity

General Editor
Vernon K. Robbins

Associate Editor
David B. Gowler

Editorial Board
L. Gregory Bloomquist, St. Paul University, Ottawa
Peder Borgen, University of Trondheim, Norway
H. J. Bernard Combrink, University of Stellenbosch, South Africa
David A. deSilva, Ashland Theological Seminary
Anders Eriksson, Lund University, Sweden
Thomas H. Olbricht, Pepperdine University, Emeritus
Russell B. Sisson, Union College
Duane F. Watson, Malone College

Original cover design by Gina M. Tansley
(adapted from Rick A. Robbins, *Mixed Media*, 1981)

The cover design introduces an environment for disciplined creativity. The seven squares superimposed over one another represent multiple arenas for programmatic research, analysis, and interpretation. The area in the center, common to all the arena, is like the area that provides the unity for a volume in the series. The small square in the center of the squares denotes a paragraph, page, or other unit of text. The two lines that extend out from the small square, perpendicular to one another, create an opening to territory not covered by any of the multiple squares. These lines have the potential to create yet another square of the same or different size that would be a new arena for research, analysis, and interpretation.

EMORY STUDIES
IN EARLY CHRISTIANITY

Volumes in this series investigate early Christian literature in the context of Mediterranean literature, religion, society, and culture. The authors use interdisciplinary methods informed by social, rhetorical, literary, and anthropological approaches to move beyond limits within traditional literary-historical investigations. The studies presuppose that Christianity began as a Jewish movement in various geographical, political, economic, and social locations in the Greco-Roman World.

1. David B. Gowler, *Host, Guest, Enemy and Friend: Portraits of the Pharisees in Luke and Acts*, 1991.
2. * H. Wayne Merritt, *In Word and Deed: Moral Integrity in Paul*, 1993.
3. * Vernon K. Robbins, *New Boundaries in Old Territory: Form and Social Rhetoric in Mark*, 1994. Edited and introduced by David B. Gowler.
4. Jan Botha, *Subject to Whose Authority? Multiple Readings of Romans 13*, 1994.
5. Kjell Arne Morland, *The Rhetoric of Curse in Galatians: Paul Confronts a Different Gospel*, 1995.
6. Peder Borgen, Vernon K. Robbins, and David B. Gowler, eds., *Recruitment, Conquest and Conflict: Strategies in Judaism, Early Christianity, and the Greco-Roman World*, 1998.
7. Mark D. Given, *Paul's True Rhetoric: Ambiguity, Cunning, and Deception in Greece and Rome*, 2001.
8. Anders Eriksson, Thomas H. Olbricht, and Walter Übelacker, eds., *Rhetorical Argumentation in Biblical Texts: Essays from the Lund 2000 Conference*, 2002.

* The second and third volumes were published by and are available from Peter Lang Publishing, Inc., 272 Seventh Avenue, 28th Floor, New York, NY 10001-6708; (212) 647-7700; FAX (212) 647-7707; customer service (800) 770-5264, (212) 647-7706; *www.peterlang.com*.

All other volumes are available through Trinity Press International.

Rhetorical Argumentation in Biblical Texts

Essays from
the Lund 2000 Conference

edited by
Anders Eriksson,
Thomas H. Olbricht,
Walter Übelacker

TRINITY PRESS INTERNATIONAL
Harrisburg, Pennsylvania

This publication of this volume was made possible by a grant from
The Swedish Research Council.

Copyright © 2002 Emory University

All rights reserved. No part of this book may be reproduced, stored in a
retrieval system, or transmitted, in any form or by any means, electronic,
mechanical, photocopying, recording, or otherwise, without the written
permission of the publisher, Trinity Press International.

Trinity Press International, P.O. Box 1321, Harrisburg, PA 17105
Trinity Press International is a division of The Morehouse Group.

Cover design: Laurie Westhafer

A catalog record for this book is available from the Library of Congress.

ISBN 1-56338-355-1

Printed in the United States of America

02   03   04   05   06   07   10   9   8   7   6   5   4   3   2   1

Contents

Preface	xi
Abbreviations	xiii
Contributors	xvii
Introduction *Thomas H. Olbricht*	1

Part One: Rhetorical Argumentation and Method

1. Argumentation Theory: An Overview of Approaches and Research Themes
   Frans H. van Eemeren   9

2. Argumentative Textures in Socio-Rhetorical Interpretation
   Vernon K. Robbins   27

3. The Use and Abuse of Lausberg in Biblical Studies
   R. Dean Anderson   66

4. Is There Biblical Argumentation?
   Lauri Thurén   77

Part Two: Historical Background

5. Theories and Practice of the Enthymeme in the First Centuries B.C.E. and C.E.
   Manfred Kraus   95

6. The Economy of Letter Writing in Graeco-Roman Antiquity
   Carol Poster   112

Part Three: Rhetorical Argumentation in the Hebrew Bible

7. The Strategic Use of Enthymeme and Example in the Argumentation of the Books of Chronicles
   Rodney K. Duke   127

8. Should Ahab Go to Battle or Not? Ambiguity as a Rhetorical Device in 1 Kings 22
   Alan J. Hauser — 141

Part Four: Rhetorical Argumentation in the Gospels

9. The Role of the Audience in the Determination of Argumentation: The Gospel of Luke and the Acts of the Apostles
   L. Gregory Bloomquist — 157

10. Instructions for "Broker" Apostles: A Socio-Rhetorical Analysis of Matthew's Mission Discourse
    Russell B. Sisson — 174

11. Argumentation in John 5
    Harold W. Attridge — 188

12. The Question at the Center: A Specific Device of Rhetorical Argumentation in Scripture
    Roland Meynet — 200

Part Five: Rhetorical Argumentation in the Pauline Letters

13. "To Make the Weaker Argument Defeat the Stronger": Sophistical Argumentation in Paul's Letter to the Romans
    Johan S. Vos — 217

14. The Tongues of Men: Understanding Greek Rhetorical Sources for Paul's Letters to the Romans and 1 Corinthians
    C. Jan Swearingen — 232

15. Enthymemes in Pauline Argumentation: Reading between the Lines in 1 Corinthians
    Anders Eriksson — 243

16. Paul's Boasting in 2 Corinthians 10–13 as Defense of His Honor: A Socio-Rhetorical Analysis
    Duane F. Watson — 260

17. Re-reading 2 Corinthians: A Rhetorical Approach
    J. David Hester (Amador) — 276

18. Galatians: Red-Hot Rhetoric
    Michael R. Cosby — 296

19. Rhetorical Argumentation in the Letter to the Ephesians
    Roy R. Jeal — 310

20. Living and Dying, Living Is Dying (Philippians 1:21):
    Paul's Maxim and Exemplary Argumentation in Philippians
    Rollin A. Ramsaran — 325

21. The Argument of Colossians
    Jerry L. Sumney — 339

Part Six: Rhetorical Argumentation in Hebrews

22. Anticipating and Presenting the Case for Christ as High Priest in Hebrews
    Thomas H. Olbricht — 355

Part Seven: The Rhetoric of Apocalyptic and Romance

23. Revelation and Romance: Genre Bending in the *Shepherd of Hermas* and the *Acts of Peter*
    John W. Marshall — 375

Bibliography — 389

Index of Ancient Texts — 421
Index of Subjects and Authors — 425

PREFACE

This volume contains the edited proceedings from the Lund 2000 conference on Rhetorical Argumentation in Biblical Texts, which took place in July 24–27. The scholars met in the historic Old Bishop's Palace of Lund University, within walking distance from the medieval parts of the city, and stayed at the stately Grand Hotel. The renewed interest in rhetorical criticism is an international phenomenon and the conference saw forty-six participants from eleven countries; Canada, Denmark, Finland, Germany, Italy, Japan, The Netherlands, Norway, South Africa, Sweden, and the United States.

The conference was the sixth in a series on rhetorical analysis of Scripture. The proceedings from the previous conferences have been published by Sheffield Academic Press in volumes entitled *Rhetoric and the New Testament: Essays from the 1992 Heidelberg Conference; Rhetoric, Scripture and Theology: Essays from the 1994 Pretoria Conference; The Rhetorical Analysis of Scripture: Essays from the 1995 London Conference; The Rhetorical Interpretation of Scripture: Essays from the 1996 Malibu Conference*; and *Rhetorical Criticism and the Bible: Essays from the 1998 Florence Conference.*

The Lund Conference focused on rhetorical argumentation, a part of *inventio,* the important first part of the *partes artis.* A century ago rhetorical analysis was known as a study of rhetorical figures, *elocutio.* When James Muilenburg, Hans Dieter Betz, and Wilhelm Wuellner brought back the illustrious rhetorical tradition to the attention of biblical scholars, the focus of scholars tended to be on the arrangement of the texts, *dispositio.* During the last ten years, however, interpreters have increasingly come to study the rhetorical argumentation in the texts. What many seek to do is to come to a better understanding of how various biblical authors present their arguments, support their claims and attempt to persuade their readers.

Several scholars from fields other than biblical studies were especially invited. Professor Frans van Eemeren, from the Department of Speech Communication and Argumentation Theory and Rhetoric at the University of Amsterdam, gave an introductory lecture on the wide field of argumentation. Four classical scholars presented papers, Dean Anderson from the Netherlands, Manfred Kraus from Tübingen, Carol Poster from Montana State University, and professor Joachim Classen from Göttingen, whose contribution is published in *Rhetorical Criticism of the New Testament* (WUNT

128; Tübingen: Mohr Siebeck, 2000). Rhetorical critic Jan Swearingen, professor of English at Texas A & M. University, was due to illness unable to attend the conference, but her paper was instead read by Carol Poster. Several papers at the conference had adopted the socio-rhetorical model of interpretation developed by professor Vernon Robbins of Emory University, who had been invited to give the initial address entitled "Rhetorical Argumentation in Socio-Rhetorical Interpretation." Following the format from the previous conferences the papers were available beforehand, which facilitated a frank and lively discussion in a warm and friendly atmosphere. Results of these interactions have now been incorporated in the papers, which we invite you to read.

The theme for the conference was chosen in connection with organizers' research project "Early Christian Letters in the Light of Ancient Rhetoric and Epistolography." We, as organizers of the conference, would like to take the opportunity to express our sincere gratitude to the Swedish Research Council for the Humanities and Social Sciences and the Wenner-Gren Foundations for making the conference possible. We would like to extend our thanks to Lund University and especially the Faculty of Theology for their contributions in making the conference so successful. We would also like to thank Professor Vernon K. Robbins for accepting the conference volume in the Emory Studies in Early Christianity and Trinity Press International for publishing these proceedings.

Anders Eriksson and Walter Übelacker

ABBREVIATIONS

Sources

Acts Pet.	Acts of Peter
Aristides, *Or.*	Orationes
Aristotle, *Rhet.*	Rhetorica
Aristotle, *Soph. elench.*	Sophistici elenchi
Aristotle, *Top.*	Topica
Cicero, *Part. or.*	Partitiones oratoriae
Cicero, *Inv.*	De inventione
Cicero, *Or. Br.*	Orator ad Brutum
Cicero, *De or.*	De oratore
Demetrius, *Eloc.*	De elocutione
Dio Chrysostom, *Disc.*	Discourses
1 En.	1 Enoch (Ethiopic Apocalypse)
Epictetus, *Diss.*	Dissertationes
Heliodorus, *Aeth.*	Aethiopica
Herm. *Sim.*	Shepherd of Hermas, *Similitudes*
Herm. *Vis.*	Shepherd of Hermas, *Visions*
Josephus, *A.J.*	Antiquitates judaicae
Origen, *Comm. Rom*	Commentarii in Romanos
Origen, *Philoc.*	Philocalia
Philo, *Her.*	Quis rerum divinarum heres sit
Philostratus, *Vit. soph.*	Vitae sophistarum.
Plato, *Apol.*	Apologia
Plato, *Euthyd.*	Euthydemus
Plato, *Phaedr.*	Phaedrus
Plutarch, *Mor.*	Moralia
Quintilianus, *Inst.*	Institutio oratoria
Rhet. Alex.	Rhetorica ad Alexandrum
Rhet. Her.	Rhetorica ad Herennium
Seneca the Elder, *Controv.*	Controversiae
Sextus Empiricus, *Math.*	Adversus mathematicos
Tertullian, *Marc.*	Adversus Marcionem
T. Reu.	Testament of Reuben

Journals and Series

AB	Anchor Bible
ABR	*Australian Biblical Review*
ANRW	*Aufstieg und Niedergang der römischen Welt*
ANTC	Abingdon New Testament Commentaries
ASP	*American Studies in Papyrology*
BASPSup	Bulletin of the American Society of Papyrologists: Supplement
BBR	*Bulletin for Biblical Research*
BETL	Bibliotheca Ephemeridium Theologicarum Lovaniensium
BHT	Beiträge zur historischen Theologie
BibInt	*Biblical Interpretation*
BNTC	Black's New Testament Commentaries
BSac	*Bibliotheca Sacra*
BTB	*Biblical Theology Bulletin*
BZAW	Beihefte zur Zeitschrift für die alttestamentliche Wissenschaft
CBQ	*Catholic Biblical Quarterly*
CBQMS	Catholic Biblical Quarterly Monograph Series
CCC	*College Composition and Communication*
ConBNT	Coniectanea Biblica New Testament Series
ESEC	Emory Studies in Early Christianity
ExpT	*Expository Times*
FRLANT	Forschungen zur Religion und Literatur des Alten und Neuen Testaments
GBS	Guides to Biblical Scholarship
GRBS	*Greek, Roman, and Byzantine Studies*
GTA	Göttinger theologische Arbeiten
HAT	Handbuch zum alten Testament
HDR	Harvard Dissertations in Religion
HNT	Handbuch zum neuen Testament
HNTC	Harper's New Testament Commentaries
HSCP	Harvard Studies in Classical Philology
HUT	Hermeneutische Untersuchungen zur Theologie
ICC	International Critical Commentary
JAC	Jahrbuch für Antike und Christentum
JBL	*Journal of Biblical Literature*
JJP	*Journal of Juristic Papyrology*
JNSL	*Journal of Northwest Semitic Languages*

JSNT	*Journal for the Study of the New Testament*
JSNTSup	Journal for the Study of the New Testament: Supplement Series
JSOT	*Journal for the Study of the Old Testament*
JSOTSup	Journal for the Study of the Old Testament: Supplement Series
JTS	*Journal of Theological Studies*
LCL	Loeb Classical Library
LEC	Library of Early Christianity
Neot.	*Neotestamentica*
NICNT	New International Commentary on the New Testament
NIGTC	New International Greek Testament Commentary
NovT	*Novum Testamentum*
NovTSup	Novum Testamentum Supplements
NTFF	New Testament Foundations and Facets
NTS	*New Testament Studies*
NTTS	New Testament Tools and Studies
OCT	Oxford Classical Texts
OTL	Old Testament Library
PG	Migne, Patrologiae Cursus, series Graeca
PhAnt	Philosophia Antiqua
QJS	*Quarterly Journal of Speech*
RSR	*Religious Studies Review*
SBLDS	Society of Biblical Literature Dissertation Series
SBLSP	Society of Biblical Literature Seminar Papers
SBLTT	Society of Biblical Literature Texts and Translations
SESJ	Suomen eksegeettisen seuran julkaisuja
SEÅ	Svensk Exegetisk Årsbok
SFEG	Schriften der finnischen exegetischen Gesellschaft
SJT	*Scottish Journal of Theology*
SNTSMS	Society for New Testament Studies Monograph Series
SPhil	Studia Philonica Monographs
StPatr	*Studia patristica*
TAPA	*Transactions of the American Philological Association*
ThViat	*Theologia viatorum*
TLG	Thesaurus Linguae Graecae
TS	*Theological Studies*
VTSup	Vetus Testamentum Supplements
WBC	Word Biblical Commentary

WdF	Wege der Forschung
WMANT	Wissenschaftliche Monographien zum Alten und Neuen Testament
WTJ	*Westminster Theological Journal*
WUNT	Wissenschaftliche Untersuchungen zum Neuen Testament
ZAW	*Zeitschrift für die alttestamentliche Wissenschaft*
ZBK	Zürcher Bibelkommentare
ZNW	*Zeitschrift für die neutestamentliche Wissenschaft*
ZPE	*Zeitschrift für Papyrologie und Epigrafik*

CONTRIBUTORS

Dr. J. David Hester (Amador)
Center for Rhetoric and Hermeneutics, Santa Rosa, California

Dr. R. Dean Anderson
Valkenburg, The Netherlands

Prof. Harold W. Attridge
Yale Divinity School, New Haven, Connecticut

Prof. L. Gregory Bloomquist
St. Paul University, Ottawa, Canada

Prof. Michael R. Cosby
Messiah College, Grantham, Pennsylvania

Prof. Rodney K. Duke
Appalachian State University, Boone, North Carolina

Prof. Frans H. van Eemeren
University of Amsterdam, Amsterdam, The Netherlands

Dr. Anders Eriksson
Lund University, Lund, Sweden

Prof. Alan J. Hauser
Appalachian State University, Boone, North Carolina

Prof. Roy R. Jeal
William and Catherine Booth College, Winnipeg, Canada

Dr. Manfred Kraus
Eberhard-Karls-Universität, Tübingen, Germany

Prof. John W. Marshall
University of Toronto, Toronto, Canada

Prof. Roland Meynet
Pontificia Università Gregoriana, Rome, Italy

Prof. Thomas H. Olbricht
Pepperdine University emeritus, South Berwick, Maine

Prof. Carol Poster,
Florida State University, Tallahassee, Florida

Prof. Rollin A. Ramsaran
Emmanuel School of Religion, Johnson City, Tennessee

Prof. Vernon K. Robbins
Emory University, Atlanta, Georgia, and
University of Stellenbosch, South Africa

Prof. Russell B. Sisson
Union College, Barbourville, Kentucky

Prof. Jerry L Sumney
Lexington Theological Seminary, Lexington, Kentucky

Prof. C. Jan Swearingen
Texas A & M University, College Station, Texas

Doc. Lauri Thurén
University of Joensuu, Finland

Dr. Johan S. Vos
Vrije Universiteit, Amsterdam, The Netherlands

Prof. Duane F. Watson
Malone College, Canton, Ohio

INTRODUCTION

Thomas H. Olbricht

Conferences on rhetoric, argumentation, and rhetorical criticism exploded in the last half of the twentieth century. Many such conferences include papers on all aspects of rhetoric. The Lund University conference on Rhetorical Argumentation in Biblical Texts was unique in that the focus was upon an analysis of argumentation located in biblical or religious texts. Biblical critics are now deeply indebted to Professors Anders Eriksson and Walter Übelacker for their organizing the conference and securing the necessary funds, as well as for making the arrangements for the printing of the essays collected in this book.

Ancient rhetoricians came to agree upon five divisions or canons: (1) invention, (2) arrangement, (3) style, (4) memory, and (5) delivery. Invention was divided into three aspects: (1) logos, (2) ethos, and (3) pathos. Logos focused upon arguments and proofs. Through the centuries rhetoricians have emphasized one or the other of these divisions. The Lund conference specifically centered upon argumentation. In order to explore more fully perceptions on rhetorical argumentation as they have developed over the centuries, persons with communication backgrounds were invited to reflect upon argumentation along with biblical critics who scrutinized specific texts.

The first section of essays focuses upon method in argumentation. Professor Frans H. van Eemeren of the University of Amsterdam has been at the forefront of international scholars concerned with argumentation in discourse. In his paper he discusses the history of informal logic in the last half of the twentieth century beginning with Toulmin and Perelman, and extending through radical and modern dialectical theorists. He champions a methodology which he labels pragma-dialectics. It remains to be seen whether biblical critics will use his approach, but it is suggestive as a means of analyzing the argumentative features of discourse. Certainly, the arguments in biblical documents do not exhibit the standard features of formal logic. Vernon Robbins, in his essay, has pushed in a new direction beyond the three ancient rhetorical genres, in a sense devising a rhetorical version of form critical categories: wisdom, miracle, prophetic, persecution-death, apocalyptic, and pre-creation. The manner in which Robbins' methodology relates to argumentation is that in each case, the text under consideration is subjected, along with other matters, to enthymemic analysis. Biblical critics influenced by Robbins have employed his socio-rhetorical interpretation, launching a new "school" of criticism that shows promise. R. Dean Anderson, who in other publications has expressed reservations as to whether Paul was influenced by ancient rhetoric, as well as the value of ancient rhetoric in analyzing Paul's letters, in his essay in this volume proposes that the use of Heinrich Lausberg's *Handbuch der literarischen Rhetorik,* while helpful in assaying ancient rhetoric, nevertheless is not designed as a starting point for the rhetorical criticism of biblical documents. He suggests that if one wishes to employ ancient rhetoric a better approach is to use the *Rhetorica ad Herennium* or Theon's *Progymnasmata.* Anderson's reservations in regard to rhetorical analysis are shared by various New Testament scholars but disputed by numerous others who employ a "synoptic" ancient rhetoric. Lauri Thurén in his essay argues that biblical documents are to be subject to the same sort of analysis as other texts. He further argues that biblical critics should not be limited to the dictates of ancient rhetoric but should use contemporary argumentation theory. He looks with special favor upon the model of Stephen Toulmin, an approach that a few other biblical critics have used. As can be seen, there is no unanimity as to argumentation analysis, and it is doubtful that there ever will be. The ancient rhetoricians declared that rhetoric was more of an art than a science. For this reason a plethora of approaches to criticism will likely persist and be of help for differing purposes.

Two essays give attention to the history of argumentation. Manfred Kraus explores changing perspectives on the enthymeme extending from Aristotle through the first century C.E. He concludes that from the beginning of the first century B.C.E. to the end of the first century C.E. the characteristics of the enthymeme get far more intricate and complicated than before or after. He then proceeds to demonstrate how the three major understandings of the enthymeme may have impacted argumentation in the New Testament. His essay is especially crucial for those seeking to resurrect enthymemic analysis. Carol Poster in her essay argues that a neglected aspect of letter writing in the ancient world is the socio-economic and employment status of those who constructed or transcribed the letters. The training at the various levels differed and determined whether the letter writers had advanced training in rhetoric, which in turn may have influenced the characteristics of their letters. It is possible that different approaches to argumentation occurred at the divergent levels, but Poster did not explore that possibility. While much energy has been expended on the history of ancient rhetoric, many aspects are still unexplored, especially for the time period of the New Testament.

Not many scholars have undertaken rhetorical criticism of the Hebrew

Bible in the past thirty-five years, even though James Muilenburg in a presidential address (1968) to the Society of Biblical Literature recommended such a move. Muilenburg especially focused upon stylistics with additional attention to structure. One reason for the paucity of rhetorical studies on the Old Testament is that the observations of the ancient rhetoricians are more applicable to letters and discourses than to the types of materials found in the Old Testament. One finds even fewer studies focused upon argumentation. Rodney Duke in his essay identifies the enthymemes and examples in the Chronicler as a means of tracking the argumentation. Since the argumentative presuppositions of narrators permeate their historical writings, such analyses disclose insight into the basic arguments, as Duke demonstrates. Alan J. Hauser focuses on the use of rhetorical ambiguity in 1 Kings 22. He traces the trajectory in the narrative from earlier in 1 Kings and concludes that ambiguity keeps the reader in suspense as to God's intentions until the end of the story. Argument in narrative therefore may often be implicit rather than explicit, so as to evoke the interest of readers, reminding us that arguments take different forms because of divergent literary and communicative purposes.

Because of the narrative contours of the Gospels, efforts at rhetorical criticism have likewise been few. The focus has been more on materials embedded within the Gospels than the larger structures. L. Gregory Bloomquist argues in his essay that the audience is the critical determinant in the assessment of argument. Several critics in recent years have proposed that audiences may be reconstructed from textual analysis. Bloomquist's claim is more limited and I think more realistic, that is, that it is the presuppositions of the audience that may best be mined from discourses. Bloomquist focuses on wisdom and apocalyptic in Luke-Acts, in the manner of Robbins's socio-rhetorical analysis. Russell B. Sisson sets out to analyze rhetorically the Matthean mission discourse (9:35–10:42). In his socio-rhetorical analysis he employs the roles of broker, patron, and client, and concludes that the argumentative trajectories of this address contribute a thread that runs throughout the five Matthean discourses. Role analysis is in some sense new, however. *Redaktionsgeschichte* also explored in depth threads running through narratives. Harold W. Attridge focuses his paper on the argumentation ensconced in John 5. He concludes that ancient recommendations about forensic rhetoric may be of some help in assessing the accusations against Jesus and his responses, as well as the persuasive strategies of the chapter. But he observes that the rhetoricians do not explore the phenomena of irony, and this is an important feature of John 5. It is my view, too, that limiting rhetorical analysis to those aspects touched upon by the ancients is much too narrow, especially in regard to religious discourse. Roland Meynet argues in his paper that questions at the center of documents provide a means for determining structure, especially in biblical rhetoric. The answers to these central questions are the bases upon which the rest of the discourse is fleshed out. He uses examples from Luke and Amos. Meynet further contends that the questions are often enigmatic and invite the reader to discover his own self as sinner, so as to convert, avoid death, and live. Meynet's approach shares certain presuppositions with reader-response criticism, not so much so as to understand, but to turn and be converted. While I have reservations about analyses of this sort, it is an interesting way of tracking arrangement and argument.

In the latter decades of the twentieth century the most extensive efforts at ancient rhetorical analysis of biblical documents have been of the epistles, especially those of Paul. Johan S. Vos has drawn upon classical reflections on fallacious argumentation to comment upon Paul's arguments, some of which he claims are sophistical while others are ambiguous or obscure. Jan Swearingen comments upon sections of Romans and 1 Corinthians to show that Paul employed rhetorical terms, concepts, and argumentative genres. So whether or not Paul was himself trained in rhetoric, he employed forms that were commonplace in contemporary discourse, and recognized by rhetoricians and Hellenistic Jews. Paul himself, so Swearingen thinks, may have influenced future discourse with some of his own creative employment of prior forms. Both these essays show at minimum that Paul spoke and wrote in a world of discourse which to some extent the rhetoricians reflected upon. This conclusion is becoming increasingly clear at the beginning of this new millennium as countless studies explore the ancient contexts and rhetorical reflections. Anders Eriksson contends in his essay that by locating the enthymemes in 1 Corinthians, one better discerns the social and cultural characteristics endemic in the argumentation. He concludes that argumentation in Paul's letters is similar to that in any other forms of human communication, but that Paul employs special Christian topics or beliefs to substantiate his assertions. A growing recognition seems to be emerging among biblical critics that while various features of ancient rhetoric may be located in biblical documents, the presuppositions upon which the proofs are drawn are different. Aristotle himself declared that special topics are employed in divergent subject areas such as medicine or physics. Duane F. Watson in his essay has shifted from his former use of the George Kennedy model to a socio-rhetorical analysis through tracking first century conventional appeals to honor and shame and challenge and riposte in 2 Corinthians 10–13. As I have already noted Vernon Robbins has taken the lead in this sort of analysis and much rhetorical analysis in commentaries published in the last decade have used aspects of such analysis. Watson concludes that while Paul employed creatively the conventions of the day, he countered with non-conventional values grounded in Christian perspectives on weakness and servanthood. David Hester Amador argues that through rhetorical analysis a good case can be made for the unity of 2 Corinthians. He and others taking the same position are reacting against the consensus view that 2 Corinthians consists of three or more letters, not for older conventional reasons, but because they believe that rhetorical analysis provides the best solution as to why the letter takes the form it does. Michael R. Cosby argues that Galatians is not so much a reasoned treatise as it is a fiery hyperbole directed against his opponents who have challenged his honor. He thinks the dictates of Greco-Roman rhetoric, even in regard to the strong ethos and pathos, do not provide adequate insight into the manner in which Paul proceeded. While arguments may be found in Galatians, they must be examined in the light of Paul's antagonism toward those he perceived to have gone on to another gospel. Cosby's observations are worthy of consideration. The question might be whether a less wooden vision and a non-synoptic approach to ancient rhetoric might not account for some of the characteristics of Galatians. Roy Jeal contends that Ephesians does not employ direct argumentation. Rather, the approach is to impress, and to create a sense of identification with the Christian message so as to foster growth and maturity and move on to the moral exhortation of the paraenesis, that is, the last half of the discourse. Ephesians has not been subjected to rhetorical criticism to the extent of other New Testament epistles. Rollin Ramsaran argues that a general consensus is emerging as to the structural details of Philippians. The micro rhetorical features, however, have not attained a consensus as yet. One aspect requiring further exploration is Paul's rhetorically effective employment of the maxim. After scrutinizing what the classical rhetoricians have written about the maxim, Ramsaran identifies certain maxims in Philippians and analyzes in some detail 1:21, "For me to live is Christ and to die is gain." Jerry L. Sumney observes that the argument in Colossians uses the persuasive features of Hellenistic rhetoric, but when the visionaries are directly confronted, the author mostly referred to traditions surrounding baptism rather than employing enthymemes. The purpose of the rhetoric of the letter is to encourage the readers to remain faithful to the apostolic gospel of the author.

Thomas H. Olbricht in his essay declares that some of the most closely argued discourse in the New Testament may be found in Hebrews. He focuses upon the argument for Christ as high priest and notices that though the gist of the argument is located in 5–7, various statements from the first chapter anticipated the importance of the argument, and furthermore, that the exhortation sections in the treatise are integral to the overall argument. He concludes that in the theological sections the author argued from Old Testament passages and their standard interpretations, but that in the exhortation materials he depended more on the commonplaces set out by rhetoricians.

John W. Marshall examines the Shepherd of Hermas and the *Acts of Peter* in respect to the larger genres of apocalyptic and romance. He concludes that the standard genres are helpful for a beginning, but that a more perceptive approach is to use modern accounts of these genres so as to flush out the power of the rhetorical features. The thread of argument in these discourses emerges with a creative employment of these two genres.

The essays in this book are focused on argument, some more specifically and others only tangentially. No common approach to argumentation characterizes these essays. Methods run all the way from modern views on argumentation and proof, through literary perspectives, to the insights of the rhetoricians, both modern and ancient. I am pleased to conclude that all these methods yield results, but in my opinion some more than others. Classical rhetoric provides a useful insight into the fundamental characteristics of oral and written arguments in public discourse. But texts must be scrutinized for their own distinctive features and means of proof rather than forced into a formalized straight jacket of ancient rhetoric. It is becoming increasingly clear that it is also helpful to incorporate insights from more recent reflections on argumentation.

PART ONE

**RHETORICAL ARGUMENTATION
AND METHOD**

CHAPTER 1

ARGUMENTATION THEORY: AN OVERVIEW OF APPROACHES AND RESEARCH THEMES

Frans H. van Eemeren

Subject-Matter and Aims of the Study of Argumentation

We can describe the subject matter of the study of argumentation in the following way:

> *Argumentation* is a verbal, social and rational activity aimed at convincing a reasonable critic of the (in)acceptability of a standpoint by advancing a certain constellation of propositions which is designed to justify (or refute) the standpoint.

This definition does justice to the "process-product ambiguity" inherent in the word "argumentation": it not only refers to the activity of advancing reasons but also to the shorter or longer oral or written text that results from it.

The study of argumentation concentrates on the analysis, evaluation, and presentation of the "point of departure" and the "organization" of argumentation. The *point of departure* consists of all explicit and implicit premises and assumptions that are taken as the starting point in argumentation. The *organization* of the argumentation comprises the way in which the various reasons are connected with each other and the standpoint at issue to justify or refute this standpoint.

In the study of the point of departure and the organization of argumentation both "logical" and "pragmatic" considerations play a part. Logicians are not generally concerned with argumentation as it is put forward in natural circumstances by somebody who attempts to convince someone else of a certain standpoint, but with abstract "argument forms" or "patterns of reasoning" in which a conclusion is derived from a particular set of formalized premises with the help of various sorts of "logical constants." To be able to clearly distinguish between "valid" argument forms and the "invalid" argument forms underlying specific specimens of reasoning, they leave pragmatic aspects of argumentative reality outside consideration that are indispensable for developing an adequate theory of argumentation. A whole constellation of verbal, contextual, situational and other pragmatic factors influencing the course and outcome of the communication process are left unexamined: the way in which the premises concerned are exactly phrased in ordinary discourse, who is addressing whom, the precise situation in which this happens, all the things that occurred before, et cetera.[1]

The general aims pursued in the study of argumentation can be summarized as follows:

> The study of argumentation aims at determining which soundness criteria a reasonable critic applies when evaluating the point of departure and the organization of argumentation and making clear how these criteria are to be applied in the analysis, evaluation, and presentation of argumentative discourse.

Components of a Research Program

In argumentation there is always an implicit appeal to reasonableness, but this does, of course, not mean that each argumentation is indeed reasonable. In practice, an argumentation can be lacking in all kinds of respects. It is the task of argumentation theorists to determine which soundness criteria should be satisfied for the argumentation to be called "reasonable." Many argumentation theorists inspired by logic study argumentation for normative purposes. There are also argumentation theorists, however, who have a descriptive goal. Linguistically oriented scholars in textual and discourse analysis are only interested in describing how, with varying degrees of success, language users make use of argumentation to convince others. Although in current research practice both extremes are represented, nowadays most argumentation theorists take a middle position. Their starting point is that the study of argumentation has a normative as well as a descriptive dimension. In *Argumentation, Communication, and Fallacies,*[2] Eemeren and Grootendorst propose a research program in which the normative and the descriptive dimensions are integrated.[3] This program has a philosophical, a theoretical, an empirical, an analytic, and a practical component.

The *philosophical* component involves reflection on the ideals of reasonableness underlying the theorizing about argumentation. The outcome of this

---

1. Frans H. van Eemeren, Rob Grootendorst, A. Francisca Snoeck Henkemans, J. Anthony Blair, Ralph H. Johnson, Erik C. W. Krabbe, Christian Plantin, Douglas N. Walton, Charles A. Willard, John Woods, and David Zarefsky, *Fundamentals of Argumentation Theory* (Mahwah, N.J.: Lawrence Erlbaum, 1996), 5–12.
2. Frans H. van Eemeren and Rob Grootendorst, *Argumentation, Communication, and Fallacies* (Hillsdale, N.J.: Lawrence Erlbaum, 1992).
3. Frans H. van Eemeren, Rob Grootendorst, Sally Jackson, and Scott Jacobs, *Reconstructing Argumentative Discourse* (Tuscaloosa: University of Alabama Press, 1993); Frans H. van Eemeren, Rob Grootendorst, Sally Jackson, and Scott Jacobs, "Argumentation," in *Discourse as Structure and Process. Discourse Studies* (ed. Teun A. van Dijk; London: Sage, 1997), 1:208–29.

reflection is pertinent to the question of when argumentation may be considered sound or not. According to the formal "geometrical" conception, sound argumentation is equal to a valid argument with true premises. According to the rhetorical "anthropological" conception, it amounts to a way of persuading that is successful in a certain cultural environment. According to the dialectical "critical" conception, soundness comes down to a constructive contribution to the resolution of a difference of opinion.

The *theoretical* component of the research program, starting from a certain conception of reasonableness, indicates more precisely what reasonable argumentation consists of. Which ways of arguing are acceptable to a reasonable critic? Geometrical logicians will answer this question differently from anthropological rhetoricians or critical dialecticians. The theoretical ideal models of reasonable argumentation will therefore vary in these three cases.

In the *empirical* component of the study of argumentation descriptions and explanations are given of the factors and processes involved in producing, interpreting, and evaluating argumentative discourse. As a consequence of the different theoretical angles of approach, the emphases are put differently. The geometric-logical approach has only recently led to an interest in empirical research; so far the experiments have been almost exclusively restricted to deductive reasoning. The empirical investigations connected with the anthropological approach have been dominated by "persuasion" research aimed at determining the effectiveness of the various means of persuasion that are brought to bear. In empirical studies starting from the critical approach it is systematically investigated to what extent ordinary arguers' argumentative normative conceptions agree with the theoretical procedural conception.

In the *analytic* component of the study of argumentation an attempt is made to create a bridge between the ideal model of argumentative discourse and argumentative reality. The central question is how a text or discussion can be reconstructed in such a way that only those aspects are illuminated that are relevant in the light of the theoretical perspective that is chosen as the starting point. Depending on the approach, the reconstruction can vary from formalizing the logical elements to identifying the persuasive aspects of the discourse or making explicit the contributions to the resolution of the difference of opinion.

In the *practical* component of the study of argumentation the insights gained in the philosophical, theoretical, empirical, and analytic components are used for developing methods to improve argumentative practice in a variety of institutionalized and non-institutionalized contexts. The practical component examines how, from a certain perspective, argumentative practice can be positively influenced and how the individual skills in presenting, analyzing, and evaluating argumentation can be enhanced.

I shall give an overview of some important approaches to the study of argumentation.[4] All modern approaches of argumentation are strongly influenced by classical and post-classical rhetoric and dialectic.

Influential Approaches to Argumentation

Toulmin's Model of Analysis and Perelman's New Rhetoric

The study of argumentation, and particularly the teaching of argumentation, has for a long time been dominated by the theoretical contributions of Toulmin and Perelman (with his collaborator Olbrechts-Tyteca). Both contributions were published in the fifties and are intended to offer an alternative for formal logic that makes it possible to carry out an adequate analysis of ordinary argumentative discourse. Another commonality is that the rational procedure of legal reasoning is taken as the point of departure.

Toulmin's *The Uses of Argument,* which appeared in 1958, is mainly known for the model of argumentation presented in this book.[5] This model represents the "procedural form" of argumentation: the various steps that can be distinguished in the defense of a standpoint. According to Toulmin, the soundness of argumentation is primarily determined by the degree in which the *warrant,* which connects the *data* adduced in the argumentation with the *claim* that is defended, is made acceptable by a *backing.* The following analysis is an example of a description of argumentation in terms of the Toulmin model:

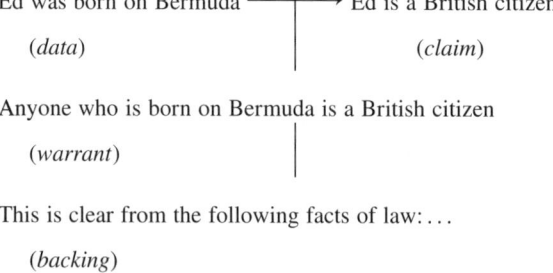

---

4. Together with other approaches with a more limited scope or a less developed research program, these approaches are discussed in more detail in Eemeren et al., *Fundamentals of Argumentation Theory.*

5. Stephen E. Toulmin, *The Uses of Argument* (Cambridge: Cambridge University Press, 1958).

The procedural form of argumentation is in Toulmin's view "field-independent." This means that the steps that are taken, and which are represented in the model, are always the same, irrespective of the kind of subject the argumentation refers to. What kind of backing is required, however, is dependent on the field to which the question at issue belongs. An ethical justification, for instance, requires a different kind of backing from a legal justification. Toulmin concludes from this that the evaluation criteria for determining the soundness of argumentation are "field dependent."

A variety of serious theoretical objections have been raised against Toulmin's views of argumentation and his model. In addition, in concrete cases the model often appears hard to apply. Toulmin's definitions, which combine functional and formal features, are such that the distinction between data and warrants is usually only really clear in carefully selected examples. And without this distinction the model is in fact nothing more than a newly clad reasoning scheme from classical antiquity, the "epicheireme."

In *La nouvelle rhétorique*, which appeared in an English translation in 1969, Perelman and Olbrechts-Tyteca provide an inventory of frequently used "argumentation techniques."[6] They regard argumentation as sound if it adduces (more) assent with the standpoint that is defended among the audience the argumentation is aimed at. Thus in the new rhetoric the soundness of argumentation is measured against its effect on the target group. This target group may consist of a "specific audience," but it can also be the "universal audience": the people who are for the speaker or writer the embodiment of "reasonableness."

Perelman and Olbrechts-Tyteca's theory consists first of all of an extensive list of elements which can serve as point of departure or as argument scheme when constructing the argumentation that should convince or persuade the audience.[7] With the help of a "quasi-logical" argument scheme, for instance, which resembles a logically valid argument form, one can sometimes achieve the effect that the audience considers the standpoint defended in a reasonable way:

> The club is held to maintain certain regulations and therefore its members are also committed to these regulations.

Another way of justifying a standpoint is the use of an argument scheme, such as analogy, that "structures reality," so that the audience will conclude

---

6. Chaim Perelman and Lucie Olbrechts-Tyteca, *La nouvelle rhétorique: traité de l'argumentation* (Bruxelles: l'Université de Bruxelles, 1958). English translation: *The New Rhetoric: A Treatise on Argumentation* (Notre Dame, Ind.: University of Notre Dame Press, 1969).

7. Eemeren et al., *Fundamentals of Argumentation Theory,* ch. 4.

that the standpoint defended is in a similar way acceptable as a different standpoint that was already accepted:

> It is clear from the current lack of discipline and the tolerance with respect to immoral conduct in modern western society that this society is about to come to an end, because the Roman empire too was near to destruction when people lost their sense of order and discipline and allowed immoral conduct to take place.

Unfortunately, the descriptions of the various categories distinguished in Perelman and Olbrechts-Tyteca's catalogue of points of departure and argument schemes are not always so clear. In some cases they also strongly overlap. These and other problems make it difficult to achieve an unequivocal analysis of argumentation in the new rhetorical sense.

The approaches of Toulmin and of Perelman and Olbrechts-Tyteca both start from the assumption that logic has nothing to offer for the analysis and evaluation of argumentation, whereas certain logical insights are indispensable for analyzing and evaluating argumentation adequately. Because both models also concentrate exclusively on isolated arguments and ignore all contextual and situational pragmatic aspects, their approaches do not offer a real alternative to the formal-logical approach of argumentation.

Informal Logic

Dissatisfaction with the way in which argumentation was treated in introductory logic textbooks in Canada and the United States from the beginning of the seventies led to the propagation of an approach to argumentation known as *informal logic*. The main theoretical sources of inspiration were the studies by Toulmin and by Perelman and Olbrechts-Tyteca. Since 1978 the journal *Informal Logic,* edited by Blair and Johnson, has been the mouthpiece of the informal logic movement.

In spite of its name, informal logic is not a new kind of logic, but an approach to the normative study of argumentation in ordinary language which remains closer to the practice of argumentation than formal logic.[8] Informal logicians would like to develop norms and procedures for interpreting, assessing, and construing argumentation. Their starting point is that argumentation should be sound in a logical sense. It is not yet clear what this means apart from the fact that something else is meant than that the arguments used must be valid in a formal-logical sense. It is clear though that informal logicians are primarily interested in the relations between premises and conclusions

---

8. Eemeren et al., *Fundamentals of Argumentation Theory,* ch. 6.

in arguments, and that their interest is not restricted to reasoning aimed at convincing.

Blair and Johnson have indicated what they have in mind when they speak of an informal logical alternative for the formal criterion of deductive validity.[9] In their view, the premises of an argument have to meet three criteria: (1) relevance, (2) sufficiency, and (3) acceptability. These criteria are introduced by Johnson and Blair in *Logical Self-defense* (1977).[10]

They are adopted, sometimes under different names, by other informal logicians, such as Govier.[11] "Relevance" is concerned with an adequate (substantial) relation between the premises and the conclusion of an argument. "Sufficiency" asks whether the premises provide enough evidence for the conclusion. "Acceptability" considers whether the premises themselves are true, probable, or in some other way trustworthy. Unfortunately, none of the three criteria has been more clearly defined and informal logicians have not paid much attention to the linguistic problems of interpretation and reconstruction.

Radical Argumentativism

Starting at the beginning of the seventies, Ducrot and Anscombre have developed in a number of (almost exclusively French) publications a linguistic approach to language use and argumentation.[12] Because Anscombre and Ducrot are of the opinion that every form of language use has an argumentative aspect, they refer to their rather extreme theoretical position as *radical argumentativism*.[13]

Ducrot and Anscombre's descriptive approach is characterized by a great interest in words such as "almost," "nearly," "only," "but," "even," "still," "because," and "so," which can serve as argumentative "operators" or "connectors" and give the utterances a certain *argumentative force* and *argumentative direction*. In a certain context, the sentence "The ring costs only one hundred Euro" can point in the direction of a conclusion such as "Buy that ring." The sentence "The ring costs no less than one hundred Euro" points rather in the direction of a conclusion such as "Do not buy that ring."

---

9. J. Anthony Blair and Ralph H. Johnson, "Argumentation as Dialectical," *Argumentation* 1 (1987): 1:41–56.
10. Ralph H. Johnson and J. Anthony Blair, *Logical Self-defense* (1st ed.; Toronto: McGraw-Hill Ryerson, 1977; 3rd ed. 1993).
11. Trudy Govier *A Practical Study of Argument* (Belmont, Calif.: Wadsworth, 1985).
12. Eemeren et al., *Fundamentals of Argumentation Theory*, 312–22.
13. Jean-Claude Anscombre and Oswald Ducrot, *L'argumentation dans la langue* (Brussels: Mardaga, 1983).

According to Ducrot and Anscombre, sentences that express a standpoint always involve an argumentative relation.

According to Ducrot and Anscombre the opposite standpoints that are suggested by "but" in sentences such as "Paul is rich, but he is married" select two different "argumentative principles" which are on a par with the *topoi* from classical rhetoric.[14] In the context assumed by Nølke in this example these are, "The more someone has the property of being rich, the more attractive it is for a woman to get to know him better," and "The more someone is tied to another woman, the less attractive it is for a woman to get to know him better."[15] In this case the latter *topos* has a bigger argumentative force than the first, which is as it were put aside, overruled, by the latter. Thereby the last *topos* determines the eventual argumentative direction of the sentence, which leads to an implicit conclusion such as "It is no use trying to get to know Paul better."

Modern Rhetorical Approaches

In recent years a powerful revaluation of rhetoric has taken place. The irrational and even anti-rational image of rhetoric that has come into being during the past centuries has now been revised. And the sharp division between rhetoric and dialectic made in the past appears to require weakening. Several argumentation theorists have become aware that rhetoric as the study of persuasive techniques is not per se incompatible with maintaining a critical ideal of reasonableness.

It is remarkable that the rehabilitation of rhetoric in the study of argumentation has started in various countries at about the same time. A considerable time after the pioneering work by Perelman and Olbrechts-Tyteca several argumentation scholars in the United States have defended the rational qualities of rhetoric. Wenzel, for one, would like to give rhetoric full credit, but then emphatically in relation with logic and (more in particular) dialectics.[16] In France, Reboul wanted to give rhetoric a satisfactory position in the study of argumentation beside dialectics.[17] Reboul regarded rhetoric and

---

14. Eemeren et al., *Fundamentals of Argumentation Theory*, ch. 11.1–11.2. See Jean-Claude Anscombre and Osward Ducrot, "Argumentativity and Informativity," in *From Metaphysics to Rhetoric* (ed. Michel Meyer; Dordrecht: Kluwer, 1989), 80.

15. Henning Nølke, "Semantic Constraints on Argumentation: From Polyphonic Micro-structure to Argumentative Macro-structure," in *Argumentation Illuminated* (ed. Frans H. van Eemeren, Rob Grootendorst, J. Anthony Blair, and Charles A. Willard; Amsterdam: Sic Sat/ISSA, 1992), 189–200.

16. Joseph W. Wenzel, "Perspectives on Argument," in *Proceedings of the 1979 Summer Conference on Argument* (ed. Jack Rhodes and Sarah Newell; Falls Church, Va.: SCA, 1980).

17. Olivier Reboul, "Rhétorique et dialectique chez Aristote," *Argumentation* 4 (1990): 1:35–52.

dialectic as different disciplines which also display some overlap: rhetoric applies dialectic to public discussions while dialectic is at the same time a part of rhetoric because dialectic provides rhetoric with intellectual tools. In Germany, Kopperschmidt took a step further: he argued that, viewing things from a historical perspective, rhetoric is the central concern of argumentation theorists.[18] In the Netherlands, Eemeren and Houtlosser aimed for an integration of insight from rhetoric into their "pragma-dialectical" method for analyzing argumentative discourse.[19] In their view, there is a rhetorical goal corresponding with each of the dialectical stages of the process of resolving a difference of opinion. They think that an argumentative text or discussion can be reconstructed with more subtlety, and more fully accounted for, if in each dialectical stage the strategic maneuvering is investigated regarding the selection from the "topical potential" (the possible discussion moves) available in the discussion stage concerned, the adaptation to the wishes of the audience, and the use of presentational devices.

Modern Dialectical Approaches

To modern dialecticians argumentation is part of a procedure to resolve a difference of opinion by means of a regulated discussion. They attempt to formulate "problem-sound" rules that are instrumental in resolving a difference of opinion. To be of practical value, these rules must also be "conventionally valid" in the sense that they are intersubjectively acceptable.[20] When designing a procedure for language users who would like to resolve a dispute by means of a critical dialogue, the "new dialecticians" make use of the ideas propounded by Crawshay-Williams and Naess, and ideas of Lorenzen, Lorenz, and other members of the Erlangen School.[21]

The first initiatives toward a new dialectic are worked out by Barth and Krabbe. In *From Axiom to Dialogue* (1982) they described a "formal-dialectical" procedure to determine whether a standpoint can be maintained in the light of certain starting points or "concessions." The name *formal dialectics* was earlier introduced by Hamblin.[22] The indication "formal" refers to the strictly regimented character of the dialogue games. In dialogue logic

18. Josef Kopperschmidt, *Methodik der Argumentationsanalyse* (Stuttgart-Bad Cannstatt: Frommann-Holzboog, 1989).
19. Frans H. van Eemeren, and Peter Houtlosser, "Strategic manoeuvering in argumentative discourse," *Discourse Studies* 1 (1999): 4:479–97.
20. Else M. Barth and Erik C. W. Krabbe, *From Axiom to Dialogue* (Berlin: Walter de Gruyter, 1982), 21–22.
21. Eemeren et al., *Fundamentals of Argumentative Theory*, ch. 3.3, 3.4, 9.2.
22. Charles L. Hamblin, *Fallacies* (London: Methuen, 1970), 253–82.

an argument is presented as a dialogue game between a "proponent" and an "opponent" of a thesis. Together these two parties try to establish whether the thesis can be defended successfully against critical attacks. In the defense the proponent can make use of the propositions the opponent is committed to uphold ("concessions"). The proponent attempts to bring the opponent in a contradictory position by skillfully exploiting the concessions. If the proponent succeeds, the thesis has been successfully defended given the concessions (*ex concessis*).[23]

In *Speech Acts in Argumentative Discussions* (1984) Eemeren and Grootendorst developed a theory of argumentation, *pragma-dialectics,* which connects immediately with formal dialectics, but is also different.[24] The agreement is expressed in the term *dialectics;* the replacement of *formal* by *pragma* (for "pragmatic") refers to the differences. The pragmatic elements in pragma-dialectics are primarily inspired by insights of "ordinary language philosophers" concerning speech acts and discourse analysis; the dialectical elements are inspired by insights from the work of "critical rationalists" such as Popper.

The metatheoretical starting points of pragma-dialectics manifest themselves in four methodological principles.[25] The first principle is "functionalization": argumentation is conceived as a *complex speech act.* The second principle is "socialization": argumentation is put into an interactional context. The third principle is "externalization": argumentation is immediately connected with the commitments created by the performance of this speech act. And the fourth principle is "dialectification": argumentation is viewed as part of a "critical discussion" aimed at resolving a difference of opinion.

In the pragma-dialectical ideal model of a critical discussion four stages are distinguished.[26] In the *confrontation* stage a participant in the discussion puts forward a standpoint and another participant expresses doubt concerning the acceptability of the standpoint or contradicts it. In the *opening* stage, which is in practice often largely implicit, the point of departure of the discussion is determined. Here the question becomes what are the common starting points and which rules are being observed. Then the "protagonist" advances argumentation in the *argumentation* stage to defend the standpoint; if neces-

---

23. Eemeren, *Fundamentals of Argumentation Theory,* 1996, ch. 9.
24. Ibid., ch. 10.
25. Frans H. van Eemeren and Rob Grootendorst, *Speech Acts in Argumentative Discussions* (Berlin: Walter de Gruyter, 1984), 7–18.
26. Eemeren and Grootendorst, *Argumentation, Communication,* 35.

sary, he or she adduces new arguments to answer further critical reactions. If the arguments that are advanced lead to the acceptance of the standpoint by the "antagonist" in the *concluding* stage, the difference of opinion has been resolved; this is also the case if the protagonist withdraws the standpoint because of the critical reactions of the antagonist.

Besides an ideal model of the speech acts performed in the various stages of a critical discussion by a protagonist and an antagonist who make an attempt to resolve their difference of opinion in a reasonable way, the pragma-dialectical discussion procedure includes a series of basic rules which together constitute a code of conduct for reasonable discussants.[27] Each violation of a rule amounts to an incorrect discussion move that is an impediment to the resolution of a difference of opinion. This can happen in each stage of the discussion. The incorrectness involved generally resembles one or more of the well-known fallacies or a similar offense against reasonableness.[28] An example is the violation of the "freedom rule" that the parties are not allowed to prevent each other from advancing standpoints or expressing doubt by discrediting the other party in the way that is known as the fallacy *argumentum ad hominem.*[29]

Specific Areas of Interest in the Study of Argumentation

Reconstructing Implicit Reasons

The crucial problems of analyzing argumentative discourse pertain to "implicit reasons," "argument schemes," and the "structure of argumentation." Before they can be properly dealt with, it must first be clear exactly which standpoints are being defended and which reasons are given in their defense. This raises the fundamental question of how utterances can be identified as standpoints or as argumentation.

"Implicit reasons," or unexpressed premises, constitute a central problem in the reconstruction of argumentation. How can argumentative elements that

---

27. Eemeren and Grootendorst, *Speech Acts,* 151–75; Eemeren and Grootendorst, *Argumentation, Communication,* 107–207.

28. Eemeren and Grootendorst, *Argumentation, Communication,* 102–207; Frans H. van Eemeren and Rob Grootendorst, "The Pragma-dialectical Approach to Fallacies," in *Fallacies: Classical and Contemporary Readings* (ed. Hans V. Hansen and Robert C. Pinto; University Park, Pa.: Pennsylvania State University Press, 1995), 130–44.

29. Frans H. van Eemeren and Rob Grootendorst, "*Argumentum ad Hominem:* A Pragma-dialectical Case in Point," in: Hansen and Pinto, eds, *Fallacies,* 223–28.

have not been expressed explicitly be systematically detected? Only after 1975 this problem really started to catch the attention of modern argumentation theorists. As long as the formal logical approach was still dominant, it did not play a meaningful role. In logic the starting point is that arguments have explicit premises and an explicit conclusion, but argumentation in ordinary language also contains all kinds of implicit elements.

Eemeren and Grootendorst argued that the problem can best be approached by viewing implicit reasons (or unexpressed premises) as "conversational implicatures" and using Grice's derivation scheme for making them explicit. It is clear that this approach has not yet answered all the questions. No watertight method for determining systematically *the* (or even *a*) correct reconstruction of an implicit reason is available yet. So much is clear that the goal should not be to find out what the speaker or writer "really had in mind," but to determine (1) to which proposition in the context and situation concerned the speaker or writer can be held committed to that not only (2) makes the underlying argument of the argumentation valid, but also (3) adds something informative to the explicit argumentation. Eemeren and Grootendorst then speak of looking for the "pragmatic optimum."[30]

> Shawn loves singing, because he is Irish.
> (Irish people love singing)
> [pragmatic optimum that constitutes the *implicit reason*]

Each of the three requirements just mentioned has its own problems. In the current literature the authors are usually mainly concerned with the question whether "validity" should be taken exclusively as deductive validity, and how implicit reasons can be distinguished from other implicit elements in argumentative discourse.

The Role of Deductive Validity

The role of formal logic is discussed with regard to the criteria for evaluating the soundness of argumentation. This discussion focuses on the logical soundness criterion of "deductive validity": an argument is valid if and only if it is a substitution instance of a formally valid argument form, which is such that it cannot be the case that true premises lead to a false conclusion, as in the following argument based on the valid argument form know as *modus ponens:*

---

30. Eemeren and Grootendorst, *Argumentation, Communication,* 64–68.

Argument:
    Premise 1:   If Peter comes, then Mary comes.
    Premise 2:   Peter comes.
    Conclusion: Mary comes.

Argument form:
    Premise 1: $p \to q$
    Premise 2: p
    Conclusion: q

Apart from the exceptional logical die-hard, no present day argumentation theorist still thinks that "deductive validity" deserves to be in a monopoly position. Following Toulmin and Perelman, argumentation theorists have become ever more convinced that the role of deductive validity is relatively modest.

As a model of argumentation in ordinary language formal logic is most fiercely attacked by the informal logicians. Their criticisms concentrate on the fact that "deductive validity" is too strict a norm for ordinary language, and therefore inappropriate for evaluating arguments in ordinary language. If this criterion were to be maintained without any qualification, almost all argumentation is invalid, if only because in ordinary language always some elements remain implicit. This kind of criticism is most clearly expressed in Govier's *Problems in Argument Analysis and Evaluation*.[31] Nowadays some informal logicians take a more differentiated stance. Johnson, for one, argues that informal logic offers the best framework for evaluating argumentation in ordinary language, but there is still a small role for formal deductive logic when it comes to evaluating implications and inferences.[32]

A strong defender of the "deductivism" so despised by Govier is Groarke, who argues that all good arguments are deductively valid and that this is a fruitful starting point for analyzing and evaluating arguments in natural language. Those who reject every formalism and deductivism throw the baby out with the bathwater. Groarke pleads for "reconstructive deductivism": when making implicit premises explicit one should try to make the argument deductively valid.[33] For practical purposes, Eemeren and Grootendorst advocate the same policy, because validating an argument in this way provides the sim-

---

31. Trudy Govier, *Problems in Argument Analysis and Evaluation* (Dordrecht: Foris, 1987).
32. Ralph H. Johnson, "The Impact of the Continuum Hypothesis on Theories of Evaluation," in Eemeren et al., eds., *Argumentation Illuminated*, 157.
33. Leo Groarke, "In Defense of Deductivism: Replying to Govier," in Eemeren et al., eds., *Argumentation Illuminated*, 117.

plest starting point for determining what the suggested relationship between the explicit reason and the standpoint amounts to.[34]

Distinguishing Argument Schemes

"Argument schemes" are among the concepts that are studied intensively by argumentation theorists to create an alternative to the formal logical model and its deductive validity norm for "argument forms." The point of departure in these studies is that in argumentative discourse, depending on the argument scheme that is used, various types of argumentation can be distinguished. Each type of argumentation calls for the answering of specific critical questions.

Based on the argument schemes that can be employed in attempting to convince the interlocutor or reader, Eemeren and Grootendorst make a distinction between three main types of argumentation: (1) *symptomatic* (or "sign") argumentation, (2) argumentation *by comparison* (or "analogy"), and (3) *causal* (or "teleological") argumentation.[35] By way of illustration I shall present an example in which the argument scheme of a sign relation is used (as is indicated by the expression "is typical of" in the reconstruction of the implicit reason 1.1'):

> *symptomatic argumentation:*
> 1   That restaurant must be expensive. [*because*]
> 1.1   It seems to have three stars. [*and*]
> 1.1' (It *is typical of* restaurants with three stars that they are expensive)
>
> *argument scheme of a sign relation:*
> 1   For X holds Y
> 1.1   *because:* For X holds Z
> 1.1' *and:* Z is typical of Y

The argument schemes of argumentation by comparison and causal argumentation are as follows:

> *argument scheme of a relation of analogy:*
> 1   For X holds Y
> 1.1   *because:* For Z holds Y
> 1.1' *and:* Z is similar as X
>
> *argument scheme of a teleological relation:*
> 1   For X holds Y
> 1.1   *because:* For X holds Z
> 1.1' *and:* Z leads to Y

---

34. Eemeren and Grootendorst, *Speech Acts*, 141–49; Eemeren and Grootendorst, *Argumentation, Communication*, 60–72.
35. Eemeren and Grootendorst, *Argumentation, Communication*, 94–102.

The use of these three types of argumentation leads to three different sets of critical questions. In a critical discussion as envisaged in pragma-dialectics these are the critical questions the other party is supposed to advance. Of course, each type of argumentation comprises a whole series of subtypes that require more, and more specific, critical questions. Kienpointner has made a broad inventory of argumentation (sub)types and argument schemes.[36]

Determining the Structure of Argumentation

A central problem in the analysis of argumentative discourse is the determination of the structure of argumentation. The argumentation structure of a text, speech, or discussion is determined by the way in which the reasons advanced hang together and jointly support the standpoint that is defended. An adequate evaluation of the argumentative discourse cannot take place as long as it is not clear what the structure of the argumentation is. What kind of structural relations can be distinguished?

Initially this problem was only dealt with in practical textbooks. Later it also became an important subject in theoretical publications such as Freeman's *Dialectics and the Macrostructure of Arguments* (1991) and Snoeck Henkemans' *Analysing Complex Argumentation* (1992).[37] In *Practical Reasoning in Natural Language* (1986), Thomas earlier distinguished four different structures: (1) "convergent" argumentation, in which two or more reasons support a standpoint independently, (2) "divergent" argumentation, in which one reason supports two or more standpoints, (3) "serial" argumentation, in which one reason is itself again supported by another reason, and (4) "linked" argumentation, in which two or more reasons depend on each other and support the standpoint only when taken jointly.[38]

In the pragma-dialectical classification of complex argumentation a distinction is made between (1) "coordinative" argumentation (with a combined line of defense), (2) "multiple" argumentation (with separate lines of defense), and (3) "subordinative" argumentation (with a continued line of defense). This classification can be explained with the help of some examples taken from *Argumentation, Communication, and Fallacies:*[39]

---

36. Manfred Kienpointner, *Alltagslogik* (Stuttgart: Frommann-Holzboog, 1992).
37. James B. Freeman, *Dialectics and the Macrostructure of Arguments* (Berlin: Walter de Gruyter; Dordrecht: Foris, 1991); A. Francisca Snoeck Henkemans, *Analysing Complex Argumentation: The Reconstruction of Multiple and Coordinatively Compound Argumentation in a Critical Discussion* (Amsterdam: Sic Sat, 1992).
38. Stephen N. Thomas, *Practical Reasoning in Natural Language,* 3d ed. (Englewood Cliffs, N.J.: Prentice-Hall, 1986; 1st ed. 1973).
39. Eemeren and Grootendorst, *Argumentation, Communication,* 73–89.

We had to dine out, because there was nothing left at home and all shops were closed. (*coordinative* argumentation structure)

It is impossible that you saw my mother last week in Sheringham in Marks and Spencer's, because my mother died two years ago and Sheringham does not have a Marks and Spencer's. (*multiple* argumentation structure)

I need not help you painting next week, because next week I do not have any time because I have to work for an exam then. (*subordinative* argumentation structure)

In spite of the differences in terminology and the descriptions and diagramming of the argumentation structures, the distinctions that are made in the argumentation literature are about the same. A problem in all approaches is, in pragma-dialectical terms, the distinction between coordinative and multiple argumentation. Snoeck Henkemans looks for a solution to the dialogue situation, in which coordinative argumentation fulfills a different function from multiple argumentation. Another problem is the representation of counterarguments and hypothetical or suppositional arguments. Freeman proposes a special notational system for these cases. Snoeck Henkemans also discusses the location of counterarguments and refutations of counterarguments in the argumentation structure. Fisher pays special attention to the analysis of suppositional argumentation.[40]

Detecting Fallacies

Virtually every normative theory of argumentation includes a treatment of the fallacies. In some sense the quality of a normative theory of argumentation can even be judged from the degree to which it makes it possible to provide an adequate analysis of the fallacies. Conversely, it stands to reason that giving an analysis of notorious fallacies can be conducive to the examination of the norms of sound argumentation.

A major source of problems is the logico-centric definition of a fallacy as an argument which seems valid but is not valid, which has been adhered to for a long time in the so-called *standard treatment* of the fallacies.[41] In some cases already the examples given to illustrate this definition are inconsistent with this description. Take for instance the fallacy of *many questions:* "When did you stop beating your wife?" In this example there is no argument. And, viewed logically, circular reasoning, also known as *petitio principii* or *begging the question,* is not invalid: "Rome is the capital of Italy, therefore Rome is the capital of Italy" is a perfectly valid argument. Since Hamblin published

---

40. Alec Fisher, "Suppositions in argumentation," *Argumentation* 3 (1989): 4:401–13.
41. Eemeren et al., *Fundamentals of Argumentation Theory,* 51–74.

Fallacies in 1970 there is a general awareness that the standard treatment suffers from crucial shortcomings.

The Canadian logicians Woods and Walton have continuously attempted to enhance the level of the study of fallacies.[42] Until the beginning of the eighties their efforts were in the first place logically oriented: by exploring advanced logical systems, such as modal and deontic logic, they hoped to arrive at a more satisfactory analysis of a number of fallacies. This is the approach they demonstrate in their textbook *Argument: The Logic of the Fallacies* (1982) and in *Fallacies* (1989), a collection of their joint papers.[43] Around 1985 a pragmatic turn has been made, particularly by Walton, which resulted in logic (in)validity no longer being the only norm. In *Arguer's Position* (1985), *Informal Fallacies* (1987), and later books Walton examines by means of case studies in which contexts and situations a fallacy is really a fallacy and when a certain move is in fact not a fallacy at all but a correct discussion move.[44] His conclusion is that there are various types of dialogues, constituting different types of argumentative contexts. In his opinion, fallacies are incorrect *dialectical shifts* from the one type of dialogue to the other. In *Commitment and Dialogue* (1995) this idea is used by Walton and Krabbe as a point of departure for further theorizing.[45]

Walton's change of vision marks a trend among argumentation theorists to regard fallacies no longer without exception as incorrect moves. Opposing the "moderates," however, who are inclined to take due account of "mitigating circumstances," are the "orthodox," who fear that this will lead to an unsystematic ad hoc approach. The pragma-dialecticians Eemeren and Grootendorst think that any violation of a discussion rule should be viewed as a fallacy that endangers the resolution of a difference of opinion. On the basis of the various discussion rules it can be indicated what exactly went wrong.[46]

A new and different contribution to the study of the fallacies are the experimental empirical tests regarding the extent to which the norms developed on theoretical grounds are in agreement with those favored by ordinary participants in argumentative discourse. Starting from the pragma-

---

42. Eemeren et al., *Fundamentals of Argumentation Theory*, ch. 8.2.
43. John Woods and Douglas Walton, *Argument: The Logic of the Fallacies* (Toronto: McGraw-Hill Ryerson, 1982); idem, *Fallacies* (Dordrecht: Foris, 1989).
44. Douglas N. Walton, *Arguer's Position* (Westport, Conn.: Greenwood Press, 1985); idem, *Informal Fallacies* (Amsterdam: John Benjamins, 1987); idem, *A Pragmatic Theory of Fallacy* (Tuscaloosa: University of Alabama Press, 1995); idem, *Argumentation Schemes for Presumptive Reasoning* (Mahwah, N.J.: Lawrence Erlbaum, 1996).
45. Douglas N. Walton and Erik C. W. Krabbe, *Commitment and Dialogue* (Albany, N.Y.: SUNY Press, 1995).
46. Eemeren and Grootendorst, *Argumentation, Communication;* idem, "The Pragma-dialectical Approach to Fallacies."

dialectical discussion rules, Eemeren and Meuffels have started a series of tests that are aimed at achieving more clarity on this matter. They methodically check whether, and how strongly, different kinds of violations of the various discussion rules are considered "wrong" moves by ordinary critics.[47]

The Infrastructure of the Discipline

The study of argumentation is characterized by its interdisciplinary or, at any rate, multidisciplinary character. Its progress depends on contributions from a great variety of fields: philosophy, logic, (speech) communication, linguistics, psychology, sociology, rhetoric, law, et cetera. Several professional societies promote the study of argumentation. The most important are the International Society for the Study of Argumentation (ISSA) and its associate the Ontario Society for the Study of Argumentation (OSSA), the Association for Informal Logic and Critical Thinking (AILACT), the American National Communication Association (NCA), and its subdivision the American Forensic Association (AFA).

These, and other societies and academic institutions, regularly organize conferences on argumentation, which are usually multidisciplinary and often international. Since 1986 ISSA organizes its general congress every four years in Amsterdam: the "Olympics of argumentation theory." Other kinds of argumentation conferences and colloquia are held all over the world, such as the conferences organized by OSSA, the Alta conferences of the American Forensic Association, the Argumentation Conferences in Venice, the Tokyo Conferences, and the special sessions of the conferences of the International Society for the Study of the History of Rhetoric.

Several journals are exclusively devoted to the study of argumentation. The most prominent are *Argumentation, Informal Logic,* and *Argumentation and Advocacy. Argumentation* has an accompanying book series, Argumentation Library, and publishes annually an extensive annotated bibliography.

---

47. Frans H. van Eemeren, Bert Meuffels, and Mariël Verburg, "The (Un)Reasonableness of *Ad Hominem* Fallacies," *Language and Social Psychology* 19 (2000): 4:416–35.

CHAPTER 2

ARGUMENTATIVE TEXTURES IN SOCIO-RHETORICAL INTERPRETATION

Vernon K. Robbins

A major challenge for interpretation of New Testament literature lies in the multiple ways in which argumentation occurs in the twenty-seven compositions that constitute the corpus. There is no one way in which argumentation proceeds in the New Testament. The thesis of this essay is that New Testament literature exhibits a highly creative rhetorical process at work during the first century, which creates multiple modes of argumentation. This process is characterized by centripetal (inner-directed) rhetorical movement that, at one time and another, places wisdom, miracle, prophetic, suffering-death, apocalyptic, or pre-creation discourse at the center; and centrifugal (outer-directed) rhetorical movement that, at one time and another, drives each rhetorical mode of discourse out into the other five rhetorical modes and into the literary modes of biographical history, epistle, and apocalypse.[1]

The major challenge is to describe not only the literary processes at work in first century Christianity, but also the rhetorical processes. At present, the dominance of the literary paradigm in biblical studies works against this type of rhetorical analysis and interpretation. In order to see the rhetorical processes at work, it is necessary to keep in mind that literary discourse is a particular kind of rhetorical discourse, a kind that has been written according to certain literary conventions. Rhetorical discourse is much broader than written discourse, since it emerges at the moment that sound from the mouth of one person moves another person toward action, or toward a new configuration of feeling, attitude, belief, or understanding.[2]

In his essay entitled "Toward a Hermeneutic of the Idea of Revelation," Paul Ricoeur discusses five kinds of discourse in the Hebrew Bible: prophetic, narrative, prescriptive, wisdom, and hymnic discourse.[3] In each instance there

---

1. Cf. Vernon K. Robbins, "The Dialectical Nature of Early Christian Discourse," *Scriptura* 59 (1996): 353–62. See online: *www.emory.edu/COLLEGE/RELIGION/faculty/robbins/dialect/dialect353.html*.

2. See Patricia Bizzell and Bruce Herzberg, eds., *The Rhetorical Tradition: Readings from Classical Times to the Present* (Boston: Bedford Books of St. Martin's Press, 1990).

3. Paul Ricoeur, *Essays on Biblical Interpretation* (Philadelphia: Fortress, 1980), 75–85. From

are two or more entire books in the Hebrew Bible that contain one kind of discourse. Ricoeur does not list them, but it is easy to see the literary home of prophetic discourse in the major and minor prophets; the literary home of narrative discourse in Genesis through Exodus 19, Joshua through 2 Kings, Ezra-Nehemiah through 1–2 Chronicles, and perhaps Ruth; the literary home of prescriptive discourse in Exodus 20–40, Leviticus, and Deuteronomy; the literary home of wisdom discourse in Proverbs, Ecclesiastes, and Job; and the literary home of hymnic discourse in Psalms and Songs of Solomon. The New Testament presents all of these modes of discourse in the context of three basic literary forms: five biographical histories (Gospels and Acts); twenty-one epistles; and one apocalypse. One might apply two of Ricoeur's kinds of discourse to one or more books in the New Testament, namely, narrative for the Gospels and Acts and wisdom for the Epistle of James. But it becomes evident quite soon in the investigation that a somewhat different discursive process obtains for the New Testament than for the Hebrew Bible. It also becomes clear that Ricoeur's view of discourse is poetic rather than rhetorical. Ricoeur does not show us the rhetorical nature of Hebrew Bible discourse. Rather, he is guided by a literary poetics that identifies all of religious discourse as poetry rather than history.[4] The perspective in this essay is that a literary approach to early Christian discourse is too limited. Early Christians used Hebrew Bible discourse as one major resource within Mediterranean discourse to create their new form of discourse. Through a highly creative process of rhetorical invention during the first century, early Christians interwove Mediterranean wisdom, miracle, prophetic, suffering-death, apocalyptic, and pre-creation discourse into the fabric of three basic literary forms: biographical history, epistle, and apocalypse.

Walter Brueggemann makes a substantive contribution to this discussion in his *Theology of the Old Testament*,[5] where he presents a rhetorical theology of the Hebrew Bible in terms of: (1) core testimony; (2) countertestimony; (3) unsolicited testimony; and (4) embodied testimony. The core testimony of Israel features: (a) verbal sentences (145–212); (b) adjectives (characteristic markings of Yahweh: 213–28); (c) nouns (Yahweh as constant: 229–66); and

---

my perspective, Ricoeur does not give substantive consideration to apocalyptic discourse when he refers to it simply as "subsequently grafted on to the prophetic trunk" (77). His lack of attention results, of course, from his focus on the Hebrew Bible, where there is so much prophetic literature, which also contains the earliest images of destruction during the "last days." Nevertheless, his typology of five kinds of discourses is a good place to begin in an assessment of discourses in the New Testament.

4. Ricoeur, *Essays*, 98–102.

5. Walter Brueggemann, *Theology of the Old Testament: Testimony, Dispute, Advocacy* (Minneapolis: Fortress, 1997).

(d) Yahweh fully uttered (267–303). The countertestimony of Israel features: (a) cross-examining Israel's core testimony (317–32); (b) the hiddenness of Yahweh (333–58); (c) ambiguity and the character of Yahweh (359–72); and (d) Yahweh and negativity (373–99). The unsolicited testimony of Israel features: (a) Israel as Yahweh's partner (413–49); (b) the human person as Yahweh's partner (450–91); (c) the nations as Yahweh's partner (492–527); and (d) creation as Yahweh's partner (528–51). The embodied testimony of Israel features: (a) the Torah as mediator (578–99); (b) the king as mediator (600–621); (c) prophet as mediator (622–79); and (d) the sage as mediator (680–94). This is a rhetorical theology of the Hebrew Bible that contributes directly to the project in this essay. The question for us is how first century Christians appropriated and reconfigured conventional rhetorical discourses in the Mediterranean world, which included the discourses in the Hebrew Bible.

After the New Testament period, second and third century Christian literature built upon the literary forms of biographical history (Gospels and Acts), epistle, and apocalypse of the New Testament.[6] In this context, however, a new configuration of major rhetorical discourses began to emerge. Karen Jo Torjesen displays five major discourses that emerged in second and third century Christian literature. The five modes of discourse she exhibits, which include both analytical categories and community settings, suggest the manner in which New Testament literature functioned as a rhetorical resource for the development of new discourses in the centuries after the New Testament period. Torjesen's five kinds of discourse are: (1) Jesus as divine wisdom (*sophia*), exhibiting the context of worship; (2) Jesus as victor over death, exhibiting the context of martyrdom; (3) Jesus as divine teacher (*didaskalos*), exhibiting the contexts of catechetical instruction and Christian schools; (4) Jesus as cosmic reason (*logos*) exhibiting the context of the Christian scholar's study; and (5) Jesus as world ruler (*pantocrator*), exhibiting the context of the basilica.[7] From the perspective of New Testament discourse, Jesus as victor over death and the powers is a merger of miracle, suffering-death, and apocalyptic discourse; Jesus as divine teacher (*didaskalos*) is an elaboration of paraenetic wisdom discourse; Jesus as cosmic reason (*logos*) is an elaboration of pre-creation wisdom discourse; and

---

6. See James K. Elliott, ed., *The Apocryphal New Testament: A Collection of Apocryphal Christian Literature in an English Translation based on M. R. James* (Oxford: Oxford University Press, 1993); Edgar Hennecke, *New Testament Apocrypha* (ed. W. Schneemelcher; trans. and ed. R. McL. Wilson; 2 vols.; Philadelphia: Westminster, 1963 and 1965).

7. E.g., Karen Jo Torjesen, "You Are the Christ: Five Portraits of Jesus from the Early Church," in *Jesus at 2000* (ed. Marcus J. Borg; Boulder, Colo.: Westview, 1997), 73–88.

Jesus as world ruler (*pantocrator*) is a merger of apocalyptic and pre-creation wisdom discourse.

In other words, socio-rhetorical investigation has yielded six major rhetorical modes of discourse in New Testament literature: wisdom, miracle, prophetic, suffering-death, apocalyptic, and pre-creation. These modes intertwine with one another in different ways in different writings in the New Testament. A major task for rhetorical interpretation is to describe the centripetal-centrifugal interaction of these rhetorical discourses in the five biographical histories, twenty-one epistles, and one apocalypse that constitute the New Testament writings. It is not acceptable to limit the investigation of argumentation simply to the New Testament epistles, or only to include investigation of speeches attributed to Jesus, Peter, Stephen, and Paul in the biographical historical writings. In order for rhetorical interpretation to attain its appropriate place in biblical interpretation, it must describe the centripetal-centrifugal rhetorical movement in every New Testament writing.

Everyone will be aware that I am describing a very large project. The question at the moment is how to begin. This essay gives a preview of some of the argumentative features in each of the six major modes of rhetorical discourse. This approach will leave many legitimate questions unanswered, but it will be a major start. It will give a glimpse of some of the results that have emerged, even though the essay will fall far short of a fully articulated statement of the results of socio-rhetorical investigation of argumentation in the New Testament.

As a result of limitations of space in this essay, my procedure will exhibit only three analytical steps with selected passages either in New Testament literature or in literature that preceded the New Testament:

1. Identification of rhetorical topics in the context of elaboration analysis;

2. Analysis of rhetorical topics in rationales, conditional clauses, and adversative clauses;

3. Enthymemic analysis.

These analytical steps lead to primary insights about the nature of rule/case/result reasoning in each kind of rhetorical discourse.[8] These insights begin to suggest the rhetorical effect of the centripetal-centrifugal interaction of all six kinds of rhetorical discourse in the New Testament.

---

8. Vernon K. Robbins, "Enthymemic Texture in the Gospel of Thomas," *SBL Seminar Papers, 1998* (Atlanta: Scholars Press, 1998) 343–66. Online: *www.emory.edu/COLLEGE/RELIGION/faculty/robbins/enthymeme/enthymeme343.html*.

Argumentation in Early Christian Wisdom Discourse

Wisdom discourse during the Hellenistic period regularly has a triple focus: (1) the relation of the created world to God; (2) the relation of humans to God; and (3) the relation of humans to one another as a result of the relation of God to the created world and to humans.[9] Reasoning about God occurs by means of analogy from human relationships to God. Thus, the primary rule underlying wisdom discourse is that God is Father and Mother of all created things — which means that God is beneficent and just. Human social relationships and well-being set the stage for the primary topics of wisdom discourse: parent/child, patron/client, host/guest, friendship, limited goods, honor/shame, life/death. Therefore, specific enthymemes and syllogisms regularly presuppose general wisdom about one of these topics as its rule or major premise, like: "Hosts must provide food and hospitality for their guests." Cases and results emerge from the specific situations envisioned in the discourse. Since a well-ordered, beneficent, and just world (both divine and human) is the overall context for wisdom discourse, argument from analogy works interactively among all spheres of the universe (God, the heavens, the cosmos, plants, animals, and humans).

The special argumentative power of wisdom discourse is its ability to generalize on the basis of one or more situations. In other words, it thrives on inductive-deductive reasoning. On the basis of one or more specific situations, it offers one or more generalized principles. But on the basis of one or more generalized principles, it may offer any number of specific examples or analogies. These examples and analogies may be brief *meshalim,* or they may be expanded into a short story like a narrative parable, or even a very long story — which we might call a didactic or wisdom narrative.

The *Rhetorica ad Herrennium* and the *Progymnasmata* have taught us that the major forms of argument in wisdom discourse are: thesis, rationale, con-

---

9. James L. Crenshaw, "Prolegomenon," in *Studies in Ancient Israelite Wisdom* (ed. J. L. Crenshaw; New Work: KTAV, 1976), 1–45; idem, "Wisdom and Authority: Sapiential Rhetoric and Its Warrants," in *Congress Volume: Vienna, 1980* (ed. J. A. Emerton; VTSup 32; Leiden: Brill, 1981), 10–29; idem, *Old Testament Wisdom* (Atlanta: John Knox, 1981); idem, *Urgent Advice and Probing Questions: Collected Writings on Old Testament Wisdom* (Macon: Mercer University Press, 1995); Elisabeth Schüssler Fiorenza, *In Memory of Her: A Feminist Theological Reconstruction of Christian Origins* (New York: Crossroad, 1984); idem, *Miriam's Child, Sophia's Prophet* (New York: Continuum, 1994); Leo G. Perdue, *Wisdom and Creation: The Theology of Wisdom Literature* (Nashville: Abingdon, 1992); E. Elizabeth Johnson, *The Function of Apocalyptic and Wisdom Traditions in Romans 9–11* (SBLDS 109; Atlanta: Scholars Press, 1989); idem, *She Who Is: The Mystery of God in Feminist Theological Discourse* (New York: Crossroad, 1992); John J. Collins, *Jewish Wisdom in the Hellenistic Age* (Louisville: Westminster John Knox, 1997).

trary, opposite, analogy, example, and authoritative judgment.[10] These forms of argument are so inherent to wisdom discourse that one finds them already in ancient Near Eastern literature, many centuries before the Hellenistic period. In the terminology of socio-rhetorical interpretation, the presence of many assertions supported by rationales in wisdom discourse gives it a rich enthymemic texture. Enthymemes occur repetitively in wisdom discourse in the context of arguments from the contrary, opposite, analogy, example, and authoritative judgment.

An excellent place to see wisdom argumentation in the context of early Christian biographical history is Luke 11:1–13.[11] When Jesus recites the Lord's Prayer to his disciples in response to their request in 11:1, he introduces the topics of father, holiness, kingdom of God, food, forgiveness, and temptation or testing (11:2–4). After the prayer, Jesus presents an argumentative elaboration of the prayer that builds on Mediterranean social and cultural reasoning. The elaboration begins with an argument based on host/guest, friendship, and family relations. The argument works by analogy to God the Father from a father who gets up at midnight and gives bread to his friend for an unexpected guest (11:5–7). After the analogy, Jesus moves the argument further by introducing honor and shame as the issue, rather than simply friendship (11:8).[12] Then Jesus presents a thesis and rationale based on asking, searching, and knocking on a door (11:9–10), followed by an argument from example based on the relation of parents to their children (11:11–12). The elaboration concludes with an argument from lesser to greater that correlates the knowledge of appropriate social action between parents and their children and the beneficence of God the Father when a human petitions God (11:13).

Jesus' recitation of the Lord's Prayer and his rhetorical elaboration of it give this wisdom discourse a rich enthymemic texture. The prayer and its elaboration contain four rationales and one conditional construction. All of the rationales concern social relationships among people:

---

10. Ronald F. Hock and Edward N. O'Neil, eds., *The Chreia in Ancient Rhetoric* (vol. 1 of *The Progymnasmata;* Atlanta: Scholars Press, 1986); Burton L. Mack and Vernon K. Robbins, *Patterns of Persuasion in the Gospels* (Sonoma, Calif.: Polebridge, 1989); Vernon K. Robbins, "Progymnastic Rhetorical Composition and Pre-Gospel Traditions: A New Approach," in *The Synoptic Gospels: Source Criticism and the New Literary Criticism* (ed. Camille Focant; BETL 110; Leuven: Leuven University Press, 1993), 111–47.

11. Vernon K. Robbins, "From Enthymeme to Theology in Luke 11:1–13," in *Literary Studies in Luke-Acts: A Collection of Essays in Honor of Joseph B. Tyson* (ed. R. P. Thompson and T. E. Phillips; Macon, Ga.: Mercer University Press, 1998), 191–214. Online: *www.emory.edu/COLLEGE/RELIGION/faculty/robbins/Theology/theology191.html.*

12. The RSV and NRSV incorrectly translate the verse as though the issue were persistence rather than shamelessness.

1. For we ourselves forgive every one who is indebted to us (4);
2. For a friend of mine has arrived on a journey, and I have nothing to set before him (6);
3. I tell you, though he will not get up and give him anything because he is his friend, yet because of the shamelessness [of the petitioner] the father will rise and give him whatever he needs (8);
4. For every one who asks receives, and one who seeks finds, and to the one who knocks it will be opened (10).

The first three rationales concern forgiving indebtedness, hosting a friend, and giving bread to a friend because of his shamelessness at asking in the middle of the night. The fourth rationale begins and ends with social actions: asking and receiving, and knocking on someone's door to have it opened. The topic in the middle concerns individual personal action: seeking and finding. The conditional construction at the end of the elaboration moves from social action among parents and their children in the protasis to God the Father in the apodosis: "If you then, who are evil, know how to give good gifts to your children, how much more will the heavenly Father give the Holy Spirit to those who ask him!" (11:13).

A key to the progression of the enthymemes appears when one sees both parts of the five enthymemes in which the rationales and the conditional construction play a role.

1. **Result:** [Father,] forgive us our sins,

   Case: for we ourselves forgive everyone indebted to us (4).

2. **Result:** Friend, lend me three loaves of bread (5);

   Case: for a friend of mine has arrived, and I have nothing to set before him (6).

3. **Result:** I tell you, even though he will not get up and give him anything because he is his friend, he will get up and give him whatever he needs,

   Case: because of the shamelessness [of the friend who petitions at midnight] (8).[13]

4. **Result:** And I tell you, Ask, and it will be given you; seek, and you will find; knock, and it will be opened to you (9).

   Rule: For every one who asks receives, and he who seeks finds, and to him who knocks it will be opened (10).

5. **Case:** If you then, who are evil, know how to give good gifts to your children,

   Abductive Rule: how much more will the heavenly Father give the Holy Spirit to those who ask him (13).

---

13. See Robbins, "From Enthymeme," 203–6 for interpretation of the "shamelessness."

The beginning and ending enthymemes (1. and 5.) present reasoning that sets actions between humans in a dynamic relation to actions between God and humans. Enthymemes (2.) and (3.) ground the argumentation in the social dynamics of host/guest relations, friendship, and honor and shame. Enthymeme (4.) functions as a bridge from human social relations to relations between God and humans, since "asking" can be performed both with other humans and with God. This unit of text gives excellent insight into the manner in which argumentation in wisdom discourse regularly works, setting up an interplay between social relations among humans and the relation of humans to God.

An excellent place to see wisdom argumentation in the context of an early Christian epistle is James 2:1–13. Wesley H. Wachob has investigated this passage with a full form of socio-rhetorical analysis and interpretation.[14] The topics in this passage concern partiality, faith, rich/poor, judging, evil thoughts, kingdom, promise, loving God, honor and shame, law, and mercy.

As Wachob has demonstrated, James 2:1–13 contains the following pattern of rhetorical elaboration:

Introduction 2:1–4

1. Theme 2:1
2. Reason 2:2–4

Probatio 2:5–11

3. Argument from example 2:5
   a. With opposite 2:6a
   b. And social example 2:6b–7
4. Argument with judgment, based on the written law, in four parts: 2:8–11
   a. Proposition based on the written law 2:8
   b. Argument from the contrary 2:9
   c. Rationale for judgment based on law 2:10
   d. Confirmation of the rationale with written testimony 2:11
5. Conclusion 2:12–13

There are four rationales in this unit of text:

1. For if there should enter into your synagogue a gold-fingered man in bright clothes and a poor man in shabby clothes also enters (2), and you look favorably upon the man wearing the bright clothes and say: "You sit here honorably"; and to the

---

14. Wesley H. Wachob, *The Voice of Jesus in the Social Rhetoric of James* (SNTSMS 106; Cambridge: Cambridge University Press, 2000).

poor man you say: "You stand there or sit by my feet" (3); have you not made distinctions among yourselves, and become judges with evil calculations? (4).

2. For whoever keeps the whole law but fails in one point has become guilty of all of it (10).
3. For the one who said, "Do not commit adultery," also said, "Do not commit murder" (11).
4. For judgment is without mercy to the one who has not shown mercy; mercy triumphs over judgment (13).

The first rationale is a conditional construction that concerns the social arrangement of rich and poor people in the formal context of a synagogue. The second rationale concerns the relation of humans to the Torah, which had become a specific manifestation of wisdom by the first century B.C.E. (Sirach), and it contains an adversative clause: "but fails in one point." The third rationale features a recitation of two statements in the Torah. The fourth rationale addresses the relation of mercy to judgment, which became a major topic in prophetic discourse. Thus, in this epistolary context, topics concerning the relation of humans to one another and to God are being taken specifically into the context of discussion of the Torah and the relation of the Torah to the prophets.

In addition to the conditional construction in the rationale in 2:2–4 and the adversative clause in the rationale in 2:10, there are four additional constructions that are either adversative or conditional, or they contain a combination of the two:

1. But you have dishonored the poor (6).
2. If you really fulfill the royal law according to the scripture: "You shall love your neighbor as yourself," you do honorably (8).
3. But if you show partiality, you commit sin and are convicted by the law as transgressors (9).
4. Now if you do not commit adultery but do commit murder, you have become a transgressor of the law (11).

All of these constructions concern actions among humans, and they refer to God through the medium of scripture or law. The topics are honor, the poor, law, scripture, love, neighbor, partiality, sin, adultery, and murder.

The passage has such a rich argumentative texture that every portion of it works together to form four successive enthymemes or syllogisms. James 2:1–4 presents a result/case enthymeme:

> **Result**: My brethren, show no partiality as you hold the faith of our Lord Jesus Christ, the Lord of glory (1).
>
> **Case**: For if a man with gold rings and in fine clothing comes into your assembly, and a poor man in shabby clothing also comes in (2),
>
> and you pay attention to the one who wears the fine clothing and say, "Have a seat here, please," while you say to the poor man, "Stand there," or, "Sit at my feet" (3),
>
> have you not made distinctions among yourselves, and become judges with evil thoughts? (4).

Wachob has reconstructed the underlying syllogistic reasoning of the first four verses accordingly:

> **Rule (unstated)**: Unjust judgings are incompatible with the faith of our glorious Lord Jesus Christ.
>
> **Case**: Acts of partiality are unjust judgings (2:4).
>
> **Result**: Acts of partiality are incompatible with the faith of our glorious Lord Jesus Christ (2:1).[15]

James 2:5–9 presents a complex rule/case/result syllogism filled with contrary, adversative, and conditional constructions:

> **Rule**: Listen, my beloved brothers [and sisters]. Has not God chosen the poor in the world to be rich in faith and heirs of the kingdom which he has promised to those who love him? (5).
>
> **Case**: But you have dishonored the poor. Do not the rich oppress you, and do they not drag you into courts? (6).
>
> Do they not blaspheme the honorable name that was pronounced over you? (7).
>
> **Result**: If you really fulfill the royal law, according to the scripture: "You shall love your neighbor as yourself," you do honorably (8).
>
> But if you show partiality, you commit sin and are convicted by the law as transgressors (9).

In the midst of this syllogism, Wachob has shown, James 2:8 evokes positive syllogistic reasoning in and of itself:

> **Rule [unstated]**: People who fulfill the royal law are people who do honorably.
>
> **Case [unstated]**: People who love their neighbors as themselves are people who fulfill the royal law.
>
> **Result**: People who love their neighbors as themselves are people who do honorably (8).[16]

---

15. Wachob, *Voice*, 77.
16. Ibid., 94.

James 2:10–11 present a rule/case/result syllogism that fulfills the expectations of an epicheireme:

> **Rule**: For whoever keeps the whole law but fails in one point has become guilty of all of it (the whole law; 10).
>
> **Case**: For the one [who gave the whole law] who said, "Do not commit adultery," also said, "Do not commit murder."
>
> **Result**: Now if you do not commit adultery but you do commit murder, you have become a transgressor of the law (=you have become guilty of the whole law; 11).[17]

The final two verses, James 2:12–13, present a result/rule/case syllogism that also fulfills the expectations of an epicheireme:

> **Result**: Thus you should speak and thus you should do as those who are to be judged under the law of freedom (12).
>
> **Rule**: For judgment is without mercy to one who has shown no mercy;
>
> **Case**: but [for one who has shown mercy], mercy triumphs over judgment (13).[18]

All twelve verses, then, present detailed, syllogistic reasoning that correlates the relation of humans to one another with the relation of humans to God. As is characteristic of Hellenistic wisdom discourse, Torah is perceived to be God's wisdom in written form. The final verse (2:12) reaches beyond the Torah into a major topic in prophetic literature, especially in the Septuagint, where "*eleos* [mercy] is demanded by God of those to whom God shows love (Mic 6:8; Zech 7:9–10; LXX Jer 9:23; Hos 12:7...)."[19] In this unit of text, then, we see wisdom discourse playing a centripetal role in the literary mode of epistle and moving centrifugally out into prophetic discourse. In the New Testament, wisdom discourse plays a centripetal role in Matthew and Luke (biographical history); Romans; 1 Corinthians, Galatians, Ephesians, Philippians, 1–2 Timothy, Titus, Philemon, Hebrews, James, 2 Peter, and 1–3 John (epistle); and Revelation, especially in the context of the seven letters in Revelation 2–3 (apocalypse).

Argumentation in Early Christian Miracle Discourse

Miracle discourse places human personal afflictions, ailments, and crises in the position of major topics, rather than human social relationships.[20] A major

---

17. Ibid., 102–3.
18. Ibid., 108.
19. Ibid., 134.
20. Emma J. and Ludwig Edelstein, *Asclepius* (2 vols.; Baltimore: Johns Hopkins Press, 1945); Gerd Theissen, *The Miracle Stories of the Early Christian Tradition* (Philadelphia: Fortress, 1983);

Rule underlying miracle discourse is: "All things are possible with God." A primary form of miracle discourse is the presentation of a case. In these instances, the rhetorical force of the discourse as argument lies in the stasis of fact presupposed for the cases it narrates. The cases concern individual or group affliction, ailment, or crisis. Generalized miracle discourse regularly presents a "summary" of one or more cases. Mark 1:32–34 serves as an example:

> **Case**: That evening, at sundown, they brought to him all who were sick or possessed with demons (32). And the whole city was gathered together about the door (33).
>
> **Result**: And he healed many who were sick with various diseases, and cast out many demons (34).
>
> [**Rule**: Jesus was able to heal people with various diseases or possessed with demons.]

The results are the restoration of a person or a group to well-being. The unexpressed rule is that it was possible for Jesus to heal people who were sick with various diseases or possessed with demons. The cases, naturally, are the individual people who came to Jesus or were brought to him.

While miracle discourse is closely allied with prophetic discourse in the Hebrew Bible, during the Hellenistic period it becomes a close ally of wisdom discourse.[21] By this time, people who engage in miracle discourse regularly reason that if God brought order, well-being, and justice into existence at the beginning of time, then God can restore order in the human and cosmic realm when some kind of disorder emerges as a malfunction in those realms. The shift of major topics from human relationships (wisdom discourse) to human afflictions, ailments, and crises (miracle discourse) shifts the emphasis from the nature of God simply as beneficent and just to the nature of God as "powerful" enough to be beneficent and just in unusual circumstances. Thus, power, rather than beneficence and justice, lies at the center of miracle discourse. The issue, then, becomes the "fact" of God's power. The circumstances of many people living in the human realm of the created order suggest that God is not powerful enough to activate beneficence and justice everywhere. A common topic in miracle discourse becomes "belief." Does a person believe that God miraculously removes illness and crisis, and, if so, what are

---

idem, *The Gospels in Context: Social and Political History in the Synoptic Tradition* (Minneapolis: Fortress, 1991); Wendy Cotter, *Miracles in Greco-Roman Antiquity: A Sourcebook* (London: Routledge, 1999).

21. E.g., Sir 45:3, 19; 48:4–5; 48:12–13.

the conditions in which God does this? This inner reasoning within miracle discourse makes it both conditional and analogical: if certain incredible things happened in the past to correct circumstances of crisis, then a similar thing could happen to a person hearing the story, if the right conditions were present. The right conditions may be the presence of a healer or miracle worker, the appropriate articulation of a prayer, or the right manifestation of faith or hope within the petitioner. Where unusual affliction, oppression, and crisis exists within the human realm, God "may" exercise God's power to restore order and well-being. Thus, miracle discourse works both conditionally and inductively by analogy to other situations that are perceived to be in some way similar.

The interwoven stories of the Woman who Touched Jesus' Garment and Jesus' Raising of Jairus' Daughter are a good place to see both the conditional and analogical dynamics of miracle discourse. The Markan account will serve well in this regard. The overall sequence of Mark 5:21–34 presents the following topics: death, touching to restore, being saved (made well), receiving life, faith (or belief), fear, rising up, and coming to life.[22]

In contrast to the wisdom discourse we analyzed in the previous section, where rationales were frequent, there are only two rationales in Mark 5:21–34. One of the rationales concerns a condition in which the woman might be healed of her disease: "For she said, 'If I touch even his garments, I shall be made well'" (28). A key to the formulation is that the woman does not show doubt in her conditional statement. She asserts in her mind that "if" she is able to touch even his garments, she will be healed.

The second rationale concerns the condition for not making a tumult and weeping over the twelve-year-old daughter of Jairus: "The child is not dead but sleeping" (39). This second rationale contains an adversative formulation, which is one of six adversative formulations beginning with "but" or "yet" in this span of narrative:

1. And there was a woman who had had a flow of blood for twelve years (25), and who had suffered much under many physicians, and had spent all that she had, and was no better *but* rather grew worse (26).

2. And his disciples said to him, "You see the crowd pressing around you, and *yet* you say, 'Who touched me?'" (31).

3. *But* the woman, knowing what had been done to her, came in fear and trembling and fell down before him, and told him the whole truth (33).

---

22. Vernon K. Robbins, "Interpreting Miracle Culture and Parable Culture in Mark 4–11," *SEÅ* 59 (1994): 67–68.

4. *But* ignoring what they said, Jesus said to the ruler of the synagogue, "Do not fear, only believe" (36).

5. And when he had entered, he said to them, "Why do you make a tumult and weep? The child is not dead *but* sleeping" (39).

6. And they laughed at him. *But* he put them all outside, and took the child's father and mother and those who were with him, and went in where the child was (40).

One of the major characteristics of miracle discourse is its inner oppositional nature, which gives it the dynamics of epideictic rhetoric. An underlying rhetorical dynamic of New Testament miracle stories is opposition between disorder and order, unhealed and healed, false healers and true healers, and unbelief and belief. The overall dynamics of a miracle story present praise of the miracle worker, which often includes ridicule or blame of people who will not believe or who could not themselves correct the situation. One of the places in miracle discourse where these dynamics appear is in adversative constructions. In no. 1 physicians receive ridicule and blame for not being able to heal the woman, but for wasting all her resources and making her even more ill. This sets the physicians in opposition to Jesus, whom the story praises for healing her. No. 2 reveals that there is opposition even between Jesus and his disciples over the access of Jesus' power to people who throng around him. No. 3 exhibits the contest between the woman and Jesus. Jesus has the power to heal within him; the woman needs the power to come into her. She fears to confront Jesus directly, so she comes up from behind and touches his garment. In this adversative formulation, she is forced to reveal the manner in which she activated his power for her healing. In no. 4 Jesus stands in opposition to people who ridicule Jairus for bothering Jesus, because his daughter had died. In no. 5 Jesus counters "death" with "sleeping," and in no. 6 he opposes people who ridicule him for thinking he can restore the child to life.

The presence of the two rationales in the context of the six adversatives creates a syllogism followed by an enthymeme. The syllogism is as follows:

Case: She came up behind him in the crowd and touched his garment (27).

Rule: For she said, "If I touch even his garments, I shall be made well" (28).

Result: And immediately the hemorrhage ceased; and she felt in her body that she was healed of her disease (29).[23]

---

23. Vernon K. Robbins, "The Woman who Touched Jesus' Garment: Socio-Rhetorical Analysis of the Synoptic Accounts," *NTS* 33 (1987): 502–15, reprinted in idem, *New Boundaries in Old Territory: Form and Social Rhetoric in Mark* (ESEC 3; ed. David B. Gowler; New York: Peter Lang, 1994): 185–200.

The narrative sequence creates a context in which Jesus' comment to the woman creates an enthymeme:

And he said to her,

Case: "Daughter, your faith has made you well;

Result: go in peace, and be healed of your disease" (34).

[**Rule**: Faith that makes a person well brings peace and healing of disease.]

It is common for miracle discourse to accumulate its implications to a point where a healer, a healed person, or a person who has been delivered safely from a crisis will present enthymemic argumentation about the working of God's power. An unexpressed rule functions in Jesus' speech in Mark 5:34, whereby faith is considered to be a special condition in which God's power works to heal. In Mark 9:23 Jesus asserts that "all things are possible with the one who believes." This creates the context for another syllogism in miracle discourse in Mark:

And Jesus said to him, "If you can!

Rule: All things are possible to him who believes" (23)

Case: Immediately the father of the child cried out and said, "I believe; help my unbelief!" (24)

Result: And when Jesus saw that a crowd came running together, he rebuked the unclean spirit, saying to it, "You dumb and deaf spirit, I command you, come out of him, and never enter him again" (25).

And after crying out and convulsing him terribly, it came out, and the boy was like a corpse; so that most of them said, "He is dead" (26).

But Jesus took him by the hand and lifted him up, and he arose (27).

After this syllogistic reasoning, in 9:29 Jesus tells the disciples that "this kind is not possible for anyone to cast out except by prayer." Jesus completes the argument about prayer and miracle in Mark 11:22–25. His argument contains the following topics: faith, doubt, prayer, and forgiveness. The argument contains no rationales. Rather, it has one adversative clause and one conditional construction. The adversative clause is: "But believes that what he says will come to pass" (23). The conditional construction is: "Forgive, if you have anything against any one" (25).

The adversative clause makes belief a primary condition in which God exercises power in unusual circumstances, and the conditional clause invites wisdom discourse that concerns social relations (forgiving people when you have something against them) centripetally into the miracle discourse.

The overall unit produces a rule/case/result syllogism:

Rule: And Jesus answered them, "Have faith in God" (22).

Case: Truly, I say to you, whoever says to this mountain, 'Be taken up and cast into the sea'

(**Condition**: and does not doubt in his heart, but believes that what he says will come to pass,) it will be done for him (23).

Result: Therefore I tell you, whatever you ask in prayer,

(**Condition**: believe that you have received it,) and it will be yours (24).

And whenever you stand praying,

forgive, (**Condition**: if you have anything against any one;)

so that your Father also who is in heaven may forgive you your trespasses" (25).[24]

Traditional topics of miracle discourse fill the content of the rule and case, and the result centripetally invites topics of prayer and forgiveness, which are characteristic of early Christian wisdom discourse.

Miracle discourse in the context of epistle may take the form of instructions concerning how to pray for healing. James 5:14–17 is an instance. The unit contains a focus on the following topics: sickness, prayer, anointing with oil, name of the Lord, faith, being saved (healed), being raised up, sin, forgiveness, righteousness, power, rain, fruit. Again there are no rationales in this discourse. Also, in this instance there are no adversative clauses. Rather, there are two conditional constructions:

1. Is any among you sick?

   Let him call for the elders of the church, and let them pray over him, anointing him with oil in the name of the Lord (14); and the prayer of faith will save the sick man, and the Lord will raise him up;

2. if he has committed sins, he will be forgiven (15).

The rhetorical effect of 2:14–15 is: "If anyone is sick, then let him...." This conditional construction exhibits the manner in which miracle discourse moves centrifugally from other environments in Mediterranean discourse into Christian wisdom discourse, which is centripetal in James. The protasis, "Is any among you sick?" concerns miracle discourse. The apodosis shows the centripetal force of wisdom discourse in James as instructions emerge that include not only "anointing with oil in the name of the Lord," "saving the sick man," and "the Lord raising him" (miracle discourse), but also calling the

---

24. Cf. Sharyn E. Dowd, *Prayer, Power, and The Problem of Suffering* (SBLDS 105; Atlanta: Scholars Press, 1988).

sages of the church together and prayer (wisdom discourse). Then the conditional construction embedded in the apodosis moves entirely into wisdom discourse as it talks about committing sins and being forgiven.

As in the instance of James 2:1–13, discussed in the previous section, so in James 5:14–17, every verse in the unit produces enthymemic reasoning:

Case: Is any among you sick?

Rule: Let him call for the elders of the church, and let them pray over him, anointing him with oil in the name of the Lord (14);

Result: and the prayer of faith will save the sick man, and the Lord will raise him up; and if he has committed sins, he will be forgiven (15).

Rule: Therefore confess your sins to one another, and pray for one another, that you may be healed.

Argument from Example in Ancient Testimony:

Rule: The prayer of a righteous man has great power in its effects (16).

Case: Elijah was a man of like nature with ourselves and he prayed fervently that it might not rain,

Result: and for three years and six months it did not rain on the earth (17).

Case: Then he prayed again and the heaven gave rain,

Result: and the earth brought forth its fruit (18).

In a context where the rules are wisdom instructions concerning what to do to attain healing, argument from examples in ancient testimony becomes cases governed by the rule that the prayer of a righteous man has great power in its effects. When miracle discourse moves centrifugally into wisdom discourse, individual healers may evoke general premises on the basis of their attributes and actions.

Miracle discourse, then, has a close affiliation with wisdom discourse during the Hellenistic period. One can see this in Sirach 45:3 (Moses); 45:19; 48:4–5 (Elijah); 48:12–13 (Elisha). The emphasis is that God either grants certain individuals the ability to perform miracles "by their word" (Sir 45:3), or God's word performs the miracles (48:5). One sees this emphasis especially in three healing stories in the New Testament (Matt 8:5–13; Luke 7:1–10; John 4:46–54). Yet the social, cultural, and ideological texture of these stories differs significantly. In Matthew and Luke (Q), the Centurion exhibits multiple aspects of the honorable Mediterranean man whom Jesus describes as having "faith" that "he has not found in Israel" (Matt 8:10/Luke 7:9). In John, Jesus emphasizes that the official will not believe unless he has seen "signs and wonders" (4:48). The ideology of the Johannine story exhibits the intertwining of miracle discourse with pre-creation discourse, which will be discussed below. Harold W. Attridge has expertly shown in a paper for this conference how to begin a socio-rhetorical analysis of the miracle story and its elaboration in John 5.[25] Again, in John a major issue is the intertwining of miracle discourse with pre-creation discourse.

Willi Braun has shown how miracle discourse can be used to establish a setting for wisdom discourse about eating at banquets.[26] Eating at banquets is a major topic for wisdom discourse, as can be seen in Sirach 31:12–32:13.[27] In Luke 14, Jesus heals a man with dropsy on the Sabbath in the house of a leader of the Pharisees as a way of beginning an argumentative discourse about the wealthy distributing their benefits to the poor. Miracle discourse plays a centripetal role in Matthew, Mark, Luke, John, and Acts (biographical history). Only miracle discourse is limited to a centripetal role in one literary mode in the New Testament, and in this instance it is biographical history.

Argumentation in Early Christian Prophetic Discourse

Prophetic discourse is a close ally of both wisdom and miracle discourse, since it presupposes that God's word has the power to create and destroy. Prophetic discourse moves beyond either creation or miracle discourse by focusing on special people or groups God has chosen to take leadership in the production of righteousness within the human realm on earth.[28] In other words, prophetic discourse combines the emphasis on the relation of the created world to God, humans to God, and humans to one another as a result of the relation of God to the created world and to humans (wisdom discourse) with the emphasis on the power of God's word to confront malfunction in the human and cosmic realms (miracle discourse). The special emphasis in prophetic discourse lies in God's active role of choosing certain people and groups for special tasks and blessings.

The presupposition within most prophetic discourse is that people whom God previously selected to produce righteousness in the human realm have

---

25. Harold W. Attridge, "Argumentations in John 5," in this volume (pp. 188–99).
26. Willi Braun, *Feasting and Social Rhetoric in Luke 14* (SNTSMS 85; Cambridge: Cambridge University Press, 1995).
27. Collins, *Wisdom,* 32–33.
28. Yehoshua Gitay, *Prophecy and Persuasion* (Bonn: Linguistica Biblica, 1981); idem, "Rhetorical Criticism and the Prophetic Discourse," in *Persuasive Artistry* (ed. D. F. Watson; Sheffield: JSOT Press, 1991), 13–24; idem, "The Realm of Prophetic Rhetoric," in *Rhetoric, Scripture and Theology: Essays from the 1994 Pretoria Conference* (ed. Stanley E. Porter and Thomas H. Olbricht; JSNTSup 131; Sheffield: Sheffield Academic Press, 1996), 218–29.

followed a path of unrighteousness. Therefore, God is choosing someone else (either an individual person or a group) to receive God's blessings, and calling new leaders to accept the responsibility for righteousness in the human realm.

A major rule that underlies prophetic discourse moves beyond an assertion that God is beneficent and just (wisdom discourse), or that God has the power to do all things (miracle discourse), to a twofold assertion that (1) God has chosen certain people to be especially responsible for righteousness in the world, and (2) if they fulfill their responsibility they will be specially blessed, but if they fail to fulfill it they will experience negative consequences. The cases are the individual people and groups that are chosen by God or who do not participate in righteousness. The results are blessings on those who are chosen and fulfill their responsibility, and woes to those who do not fulfill a responsibility of righteousness.

Like both wisdom and miracle discourse, prophetic discourse often features epideictic rhetoric. The polarities in prophetic discourse are a combination of the good and evil, righteousness and unrighteousness of wisdom discourse, and of the ailments and distresses versus healing and restoration in miracle discourse. Thus, prophetic discourse naturally moves centrifugally out into wisdom and miracle discourse, wisdom and miracle discourse naturally move centrifugally into prophetic discourse, and prophetic discourse may work in close alliance with one or both of them.

Two basic categories of topics are regularly the focus of prophetic discourse: (1) God's action of blessing correlated with the opposite result of woe if people do not participate in God's system of righteousness; and (2) people's righteousness or unrighteousness based on a combination of their state of being and the acts they perform.

A good place to see prophetic discourse is in the beatitudes at the beginning of the Sermon on the Mount in Matthew 5:3–12 and in the woes to the scribes and Pharisees in Matthew 23. In Matthew 5:3–12, the topics that emphasize God's action of blessing are: blessedness, receiving the kingdom of heaven, being comforted, inheriting the earth, being satisfied, obtaining mercy, seeing God, being called a child of God, and receiving a heavenly reward. The topics that emphasize people's state of being and the acts they perform are: poor in spirit, mourning, being meek, hungering and thirsting after righteousness, being merciful, being pure in heart, being a peacemaker, being persecuted for righteousness' sake, and being persecuted like the prophets. These topics contain a mixture of personal attributes of righteousness, righteous action toward other humans, right actions and attitudes toward God, and rewards in the future for being righteous.

In Matthew 5:3–12, there are ten rationales in a context of no adversative or conditional statements:

1. For theirs is the kingdom of heaven (3).
2. For they shall be comforted (4).
3. For they shall inherit the earth (5).
4. For they shall be satisfied (6).
5. For they shall obtain mercy (7).
6. For they shall see God (8).
7. For they shall be called sons of God (9).
8. For theirs is the kingdom of heaven (10).
9. For your reward is great in heaven (12),
10. For so men persecuted the prophets who were before you (12).

The topics in the first nine rationales concern states and acts of righteousness, and the nature of blessing that will come as a result of them. The tenth rationale compares those who are righteous now with the prophets in ancient Israel. The difference in topic concerns the different rhetorical function of the tenth rationale. Displaying them in terms of result/case/rule reveals the difference:

1. **Result**: "Blessed are the poor in spirit,

   Case: for theirs is the kingdom of heaven (3).

2. **Result**: "Blessed are those who mourn,

   Case: for they shall be comforted (4).

3. **Result**: "Blessed are the meek,

   Case: for they shall inherit the earth (5).

4. **Result**: "Blessed are those who hunger and thirst for righteousness,

   Case: for they shall be satisfied (6).

5. **Result**: "Blessed are the merciful,

   Case: for they shall obtain mercy (7).

6. **Result**: "Blessed are the pure in heart,

   Case: for they shall see God (8).

7. **Result**: "Blessed are the peacemakers,

   Case: for they shall be called sons of God (9).

8. **Result**: "Blessed are those who are persecuted for righteousness' sake,
   Case: for theirs is the kingdom of heaven (10).
9. **Result**: "Blessed are you when men revile you and persecute you and utter all kinds of evil against you falsely on my account (11).
   Rejoice and be glad,
10. **Case**: for your reward is great in heaven,
    Rule: for so men persecuted the prophets who were before you" (12).

The rationales in the first eight enthymemes present the case, which describes the state or action of people that determines the kind of reward they receive. Prior to each case is a result, which describes the kind of blessing they will receive. What is left unexpressed for each case is the rule that "God has chosen people in various states of righteousness and people who perform certain acts of righteousness to receive special blessing." The ninth instance is a result/case/rule syllogism, and it reveals an important shift in the rule that we also observed when miracle discourse moved centrifugally into wisdom discourse.

In prophetic discourse, "the story of God's chosen people" may supply the "rules" in addition to "God's specific choosing of certain people and groups." To put it another way, not only "God's word that chooses and directs" but also "the story of God's people" begins to become "God's word" (rule) in prophetic discourse. For comparison, in wisdom discourse God's word (rule) can be found in contexts of order in the created human realm (father and son, host with guest, friend with friend), the created natural realm (birds, flowers, trees), and in the nature of God (beneficence, justice). In miracle discourse, God's word (rule) can be found in the conditions (belief, prayer) God establishes for enacting his power in unusual circumstances. When people become "examples," either in wisdom or miracle discourse, they may evoke a rule that governs how a person must imitate their action. Prophetic discourse focuses especially on God's acts of choosing in the rule. However, these "acts" by God extend naturally to "all of God's acts of choosing individuals and groups in the past." This movement increases the uses of "God's acts" as rules.

While blessing is one side of prophetic discourse, "woes" are the other side. Matthew 23 is an excellent example of this other side. To make the analysis manageable in the context of this paper, we will only analyze Matthew 23:1–15, rather than the entire chapter. The topics in this unit of text are: practice, observe, preach, burdens, deeds seen by men, phylacteries, fringes, love, honor, feasts, seats, salutations, market places, rabbi, brethren, father, heaven, masters, Christ, greatest, servant, exalting oneself, humbling oneself, kingdom of heaven, proselyte, child of hell.

There are eight rationales in Matthew 23:1–15:

1. For they preach, but do not practice (3).
2. For they make their phylacteries broad and their fringes long (5),
    and they love the place of honor at feasts and the best seats in the synagogues (6),
    and salutations in the market places, and being called rabbi by men (7).
3. For you have one teacher, and you are all brethren (8).
4. For you have one Father, who is in heaven (9).
5. For you have one master, the Christ (10).
6. Because you shut the kingdom of heaven against men;
7. For you neither enter yourselves, nor allow those who would enter to go in (13).
8. For you traverse sea and land to make a single proselyte, and when he becomes a proselyte, you make him twice as much a child of hell as yourselves (15).

In the context of these rationales, there are two adversative clauses:

1. But they do not practice (3).
2. But they themselves will not move them [heavy burdens] with their finger (4).

These adversatives reveal things that those who have been chosen have "not" done, thus not fulfilling their responsibility for righteousness.

Rule/case/result analysis yields the following sequence:

> Then said Jesus to the crowds and to his disciples (1),

1. [**Rule**: People must follow the teaching of the leaders God has chosen to sit on Moses' seat.]

    Case: The scribes and the Pharisees sit on Moses' seat (2);

    Result: so practice and observe whatever they tell you,

    Contrary Result: but not what they do;

    Contrary Case: for they preach, but do not practice (3).

    They bind heavy burdens, hard to bear, and lay them on men's shoulders; but they themselves will not move them with their finger (4).

2. [**Rule**: God chose the scribes and Pharisees to do all their deeds to be seen by God.]

    Contrary Result: They do all their deeds to be seen by men;

    Contrary Case: for they make their phylacteries broad and their fringes long (5),
    and they love the place of honor at feasts and the best seats in the synagogues (6),
    and salutations in the market places, and being called rabbi by men (7).

3. **Result**: But you are not to be called rabbi,

    Case: for you have one teacher, and you are all brethren (8).

    [**Rule**: God has chosen one teacher for you and made you all brethren.]

4. **Result**: And call no man your father on earth,

   Case: for you have one Father, who is in heaven (9).

   [**Rule**: God in heaven has chosen you to be his children.]

5. **Result**: Neither be called masters,

   Case: for you have one master, the Christ (10).

   [**Rule**: God has chosen one master, the Christ, for you.]

6. **Result**: He who is greatest among you shall be your servant (11);

   Case: whoever exalts himself will be humbled, and whoever humbles himself will be exalted (12).

   [**Rule**: God has chosen to humble the exalted and exalt the humble.]

   Result: But woe to you, scribes and Pharisees, hypocrites!

   Case: because you shut the kingdom of heaven against people; for you neither enter yourselves, nor allow those who would enter to go in (13).

   [**Rule**: God has chosen the scribes and Pharisees to open the kingdom of heaven to people and to enter it themselves.]

   Result: Woe to you, scribes and Pharisees, hypocrites!

   Case: for you traverse sea and land to make a single proselyte, and when he becomes a proselyte, you make him twice as much a child of hell as yourselves (15).

   [**Rule**: God has chosen the scribes and Pharisees to make people into children of heaven.]

In each result/case enthymeme, the unexpressed rule is that God has chosen either specific people or groups of people to fulfill a particular role in the production of righteousness in the human realm on earth. The rule in prophetic discourse, then, naturally moves beyond a generalized sentence characteristic of wisdom discourse into a specific circumstance or event in which God has chosen certain people to be leaders or representatives of righteousness.

An example of prophetic discourse in an epistle occurs in 1 Corinthians 9:16–17. The topics are: preaching the gospel, boasting, necessity, one's own will, reward, and being entrusted with a commission.

There are three rationales in this unit of text:

1. For if I preach the gospel, that gives me no ground for boasting (16).
2. For necessity is laid upon me (16).
3. For if I do this of my own will, I have a reward (17).

Two of these rationales contain a conditional construction. In addition, there is a woe-saying containing a conditional construction and an adversative clause containing a conditional construction, which makes a sequence of four conditional constructions:

1. If I preach the gospel, that gives me no ground for boasting (16).

2. Woe to me if I do not preach the gospel! (17).

3. If I do this of my own will, I have a reward (17).

4. If not of my own will, I am entrusted with a commission (17).

All of this produces an argumentative elaboration containing a case/result/rule syllogism followed by a result/case enthymeme containing a case/result argument from the contrary:

1. **Case**: For if I preach the gospel,

   Result: that gives me no ground for boasting.

   Rule: For necessity is laid upon me [by God's choosing of me].

2. **Result**: Woe to me if I do not preach the gospel! (16).

   Case: For if I do this of my own will, I have a reward;

   Contrary Case: but if not of my own will, I am entrusted with a commission (17).

   [**Rule**: God chose me and entrusted me with a commission to preach the gospel.]

The key to the dynamics of this passage lies in the perception that the nature of the discourse is prophetic. The presupposition for the rules is that at some time in the past God has chosen Paul to perform a particular task in the production of righteousness in the human realm on earth. In each instance, then, the rule is not simply a general characterization of the nature of God or a general presupposition about the relation of humans to one another and to God. Rather, the rule presupposes a specific act of choosing by God as an event in the past for a particular purpose.

Prophetic discourse contains a combination of topics of wisdom and miracle discourse, with a new dimension in the rule that God chooses certain individuals and groups to receive special blessings and to exercise special responsibilities for righteousness on earth. Thus, when prophetic discourse is in a centripetal position, or when it moves centrifugally into wisdom or miracle discourse, specific acts of choosing by God regularly fill the content of the rules in the argumentation. Prophetic discourse plays a centripetal role in Matthew, Mark, Luke, and Acts (biographical history), Galatians, 2 Peter (epistle), and Revelation (apocalypse). In this literature especially, one sees the rules, cases, and results of God's choosing of certain individuals and groups for the production of righteousness in the human realm.

Argumentation in Early Christian Suffering-Death Discourse

Suffering-death argumentation has a significant history both in the Hebrew Bible and in general Mediterranean discourse.[29] In the context of wisdom, miracle, and prophetic discourse, socio-rhetorical investigation has yielded three kinds of suffering-death argumentation in the New Testament. One is basic wisdom argumentation about suffering and death: the one who, choosing righteousness, suffers unjustly receives God's approval. A second is Christian prophetic discourse about suffering and death: one who suffers fulfilling God's calling is following the example of Christ. A third is Christian atonement argumentation about suffering and death: Christ's sinless death removes the sins of those who choose Christ as specially chosen mediator of God's redemption.

The special power of suffering-death discourse lies in its naming of rejection, abuse, or death as the result of actions by fellow members of one's society, or perhaps by neighboring inhabitants. When suffering-death discourse uses specificity, it takes the form of *narratio* and has the power of fact told by an eyewitness. When it takes a more generalized form in Christian discourse it becomes creedal, articulating special forms of belief about God and Christ.

First Peter 2:18–25 presents three kinds of suffering-death argumentation in a sequence. Verses 18–20 present a basic suffering-death argument in the form of a wisdom discourse. Some of the topics of argumentation concern the relation of humans in different social locations: slaves/masters, submission, honor, receiving credit, kindness, gentleness, doing wrong, patiently enduring, doing right, and receiving God's approval. Into these characteristic wisdom discourse topics are embedded the special topics of enduring pain and suffering unjustly. Thus, the topics exhibit a discussion of suffering and death from the perspective of wisdom discourse.

In this suffering-death argumentation there are two rationales containing two conditional constructions and one adversative construction. All of these specifically concern suffering:

---

29. Sam K. Williams, *Jesus' Death as Saving Event: The Origin of a Concept* (HDR 2; Missoula, Mont.: Scholars Press, 1975); Martin Hengel, *Atonement: The Origins of the Doctrine in the New Testament* (Philadelphia: Fortress, 1981); David Seeley, *The Noble Death: Graeco-Roman Martyrology and Paul's Concept of Salvation* (JSNTSup 28; Sheffield: Sheffield Academic Press, 1990); Arthur J. Droge, *A Noble Death: Suicide and Martyrdom among Christians and Jews in Antiquity* (San Francisco: HarperSanFrancisco, 1991); Judith Perkins, *The Suffering Self: Pain and Narrative Representation in the Early Christian Era* (London: Routledge, 1995); Daniel Boyarin, *Dying for God: Martyrdom and the Making of Christianity and Judaism (Figurae: Reading Medieval Culture)* (Stanford: Stanford University Press, 1999); H. Stephen Brown, "The Martyrs on Trial: A Socio-Rhetorical Analysis of Second Century Christian Court Narrative" (Ph.D. diss., Temple University, 1999).

> For one is approved if, mindful of God, he endures pain while suffering unjustly (19).
>
> For what credit is it, if when you do wrong and are beaten for it you take it patiently?
>
> But if when you do right and suffer for it you take it patiently, you have God's approval (20).

The entire context produces a result/rule/case syllogism.

> **Result**: Slaves, be submissive to your masters with all respect, not only to the kind and gentle but also to the overbearing (18).
>
> **Rule**: For one is approved if, mindful of God, he endures pain while suffering unjustly (19).
>
> **Case**: For what credit is it, if when you do wrong and are beaten for it you take it patiently?
>
> But if when you do right and suffer for it you take it patiently, you have God's approval (20).

The rule and the case directly concern suffering, and they work from a generalized conditional statement to a more specific conditional statement and an adversative construction that tests the reasoning through an argument from the contrary. The result is a wisdom sentence directly concerned with relations of humans to one another. Thus, the reasoning about suffering in 1 Peter 1:18–20 leads to instruction in the mode of wisdom discourse.

First Peter 2:21 shifts from suffering-death argumentation in a wisdom mode to suffering-death argumentation in a prophetic mode. Its topics are: being called, Christ's suffering, Christ as example, and following in the steps of the example. The unit contains two rationales, with no adversatives or conditional constructions:

1. For to this you have been called,
2. Because Christ also suffered for you (21).

The entire unit presents a case/rule/result syllogism:

> **Case**: For to this you have been called,
>
> **Rule**: because Christ also suffered for you,
>
> **Result**: leaving you an example, that you should follow in his steps (21).

In this instance the rule is the action of Christ. This is a natural feature in prophetic discourse, where the actions of God or the model of specially selected individuals or groups establish the rule for the reasoning. The case concerns the specific ones called by God for special activity. Once again, the result has the nature of wisdom instruction, but in this instance it focuses specifically on the "example" cited in the rule. Rather than wisdom about action based on a general principle from basic social relations, the wisdom emerges from the action of a specific individual chosen by God to enact righteousness in the human realm, namely, Christ.

First Peter 2:22–25 presents suffering-death discourse in the mode of Christian atonement argumentation. Its topics are: committing sin, guile, being reviled, suffering, threatening, trusting, being judged justly, bearing sins, dying to sin, living to righteousness, wounds, being healed, straying like sheep, and returning to one's shepherd and guardian.

First Peter 2:22–25 contains one rationale:

> For you were straying like sheep (25).

In addition, it contains two adversatives:

> But he trusted to him who judges justly (23).
>
> But have now returned to the Shepherd and Guardian of your souls (25).

The first adversative explains the manner in which Christ countered natural inclinations to return evil with evil in the context of suffering and death. The second adversative explains how the wounds of Christ have reversed the sinful circumstances of those focused on Christ as the mediator of God's beneficence.

The syllogistic argumentation in the sequence is as follows:

> **Case**: He committed no sin; no guile was found on his lips (22).
>
> When he was reviled, he did not revile in return; when he suffered, he did not threaten; but he trusted to him who judges justly (23).
>
> **Rule**: He himself bore our sins in his body on the tree,
> that we might die to sin and live to righteousness.
>
> **Result**: By his wounds you have been healed (24).
>
> **Case**: For you were straying like sheep, but have now returned to the shepherd and guardian of your souls (25).

In Christian atonement argumentation, the actions of Christ are the primary case (the one who suffered and died maintaining integrity with a righteous life), and the responses of people to Christ are the secondary case. The rule that governs the results is a principle that lies within a mysterious process God has devised whereby the righteous action of a particular person whom God has chosen can bring the benefits of righteous life to a group of people God has chosen to bless. In other words, in contexts where suffering-death discourse moves into a centripetal position in Christian literature, there is a potential for suffering-death discourse to move beyond wisdom and prophetic argumentation into an assertion of vicarious atonement. The key lies in the rule, where it is a principle within God's prerogatives that one specially chosen by God can, by acting righteously in a context of suffering and death, "bear" the sins of others in his or her own body. The result is an extension of miracle discourse into atonement discourse: By his wounds you have been healed (1 Pet 2:24). In early Christian discourse, then, suffering-death discourse does not only move centrifugally into wisdom, miracle, and prophetic discourse. Rather, suffering-death discourse becomes centripetal discourse that gathers dynamics of wisdom, miracle, and prophetic discourse into itself. Argumentation about Christ's suffering and death brings together the wisdom of living with integrity in a context of suffering and death, the prophetic blessing that comes upon one who righteously fulfills a task given by God, and the healing that God can offer under certain conditions. Christian atonement argumentation gathers these three modes of discourse together in a manner that produces a process in God's world where a person chosen specially by God can bring healing to many by bearing their sins in his own body in a context of suffering and death.

Suffering-death discourse plays a centripetal role in the four Gospels and Acts (biographical history); 1 Thessalonians, 1–2 Corinthians, Philippians, Colossians, 2 Timothy, Hebrews, and 1 Peter (epistle); and Revelation (apocalypse). Luke's passion narrative appears to present suffering-death discourse in a mode especially characteristic of wisdom discourse. In 1 Thessalonians 1–3, Paul presents suffering-death discourse especially in a mode characteristic of prophetic discourse. Mark 14–15 presents suffering-death narrative in a mode that evokes Christian atonement argumentation. A challenge lies before socio-rhetorical interpretation to produce specific commentary on the centripetal-centrifugal rhetorical movement of suffering-death argumentation in this literature.

Argumentation in Early Christian Apocalyptic Discourse

The special power of apocalyptic discourse lies in its reconfiguration of all time (past, present, and future) and all space (cosmic, earthly, and of personal bodies) in terms of holy and profane, or good and evil. The specificity and concreteness of apocalyptic discourse lies in revelation to specific people, display of very detailed descriptions of beings (God, beasts, evil personages, good personages), display of places (bountiful gardens, beautiful cities, places of punishment, places of worship, altars, temples, walls), and display of procedures (programmatic destruction of portions of the earth, specific procedures of torture, specific processes of journey of the righteous soul into heaven and then into the paradise of jubilation, specific processes of journeys through the heavens and throughout the cosmos).[30]

In the context of specific descriptions of all kinds, rationales appear that summarize the attributes of God, the actions of God in the past, the nature of God's action in the present, and the nature of God's action in the future. Also, the rationales tell the evil actions of humans in the past, present, and future. The effect of these rationales is to make God's actions in all time (past, present, and future) and all space (heaven, earth, Sheol, etc.) into the rule that governs cases and results. In other words, the rule is not limited to God's giving of Torah (wisdom discourse), God's intervention in particular unusual circumstances (miracle discourse), God's choosing of particular individuals or groups (prophetic discourse), or God's giving of a particular effect of healing from sin through suffering and death (suffering-death discourse). Rather, the Rule in apocalyptic discourse evokes all of God's actions at all times. All past, present, and future events (human and divine) are "God's story" that creates a universe where righteousness is preserved and unrighteousness is destroyed. The cases feature the "identification" of those who are righteous and those who are evil. The results feature the manner in which the righteous will be preserved and the unrighteous will be destroyed. The overall result of apocalyptic discourse, then, is that "the entire biblical story" becomes "scripture": God's "word" that produces the rules for being preserved or destroyed. This means that the story of God in the Hebrew Bible is simply the beginning of God's story. God's story continues into the present and into the future. Thus, apocalyptic discourse authorizes post-biblical interpretations of the present and the future as "scripture," since all of God's ongoing story is "rule."

First Enoch 100:1–6 exhibits well a syllogistic structure in which God's actions in the past, present, and future become the Rule which functions as the major premise governing the nature of the result for the cases:

> **Result**: And in those days in one place the fathers together with their sons shall be smitten
> And brothers one with another shall fall in death
> Till the streams flow with their blood (1).

---

30. John J. Collins, ed., *Apocalypse: The Morphology of a Genre* (Semeia 14; Chico, Calif.: Scholars Press, 1979); idem, *Wisdom;* idem, *The Apocalyptic Imagination: An Introduction to Jewish Apocalyptic Literature* (2d ed.; Grand Rapids: Eerdmans, 1998); idem, ed., *The Encyclopedia of Apocalypticism* (vol. 1 of *The Origins of Apocalypticism in Judaism and Christianity;* New York: Continuum, 1998); Adela Yarbro Collins, "Early Christian Apocalyptic Literature," *ANRW* 25.6:4666–4711; Gregory Carey and L. Gregory Bloomquist, *Vision and Persuasion: Rhetorical Dimensions of Apocalyptic Discourse* (St. Louis: Chalice, 1999).

56   *RHETORICAL ARGUMENTATION IN BIBLICAL TEXTS*

Case: For a man shall not withhold his hand from slaying his sons and his sons' sons,
And the sinner shall not withhold his hand from his honored brother:
From dawn till sunset they shall slay one another (2).

And the horse shall walk up to the breast in the blood of sinners,
And the chariot shall be submerged to its height (3).

Rule: In those days the angels shall descend into the secret places
And gather together into one place all those who brought down sin.
And the Most High will arise on that day of judgment
To execute great judgment amongst sinners (4).

And over all the righteous and holy he will appoint guardians
from amongst the holy angels
To guard them as the apple of an eye,
Until he makes an end of all wickedness and all sin,
And though the righteous sleep a long sleep, they have naught to fear (5).

And (then) the children of the earth shall see the wise in security,
And shall understand all the words of this book,
And recognize that their riches shall not be able to save them
In the overthrow of their sins (6).

First Enoch 100:4–6 present the Rule that governs the reasoning in 100:1–3. The major premises for judging all actions of humans on earth reside in the events that will occur "in those days" (100:4–6). The rule speaks about righteousness as well as judgment. If the case in 100:2–3 were about one or more righteous people, the result in 100:1 would talk about the preservation of them through resurrection or some other means. Thus, the rule in the syllogistic reasoning of apocalyptic discourse contains all of God's actions in the past, present, and future.

In a context where all events become "God's story," argument from analogy moves beyond its role of similarity among all spheres throughout the universe (wisdom discourse) or among events where God's power has intervened in an extraordinary manner (miracle discourse) into a role of imagery that exhibits the nature of good and evil, righteousness and unrighteousness. Apocalyptic discourse describes people through analogy with dragons, locusts, cows, bulls, bears, and eagles. Analogy is part of seeing, and seeing, interpreted by a heavenly being, is knowing. The sensory-aesthetic region of the head is central, with special emphasis on seeing and hearing. Seeing is not simply believing, as it is in miracle discourse, but seeing is knowing. This links apocalyptic discourse with wisdom discourse (where seeing and hearing also are knowing). Wisdom discourse places first emphasis on hearing, which starts a process of "learning to see God's ways." Apocalyptic uses hearing as a medium to get people to look beyond the human realm into the heavenly realm, where seeing incredible things becomes "knowing the story of God." In this context, "knowing" is understanding the deepest consequences of good and evil, righteousness and unrighteousness. Thus, one sees "a person in the form of a beast" (Revelation 13) in contrast to "a woman clothed with the sun, with the moon under her feet, and on her head a crown of twelve stars" (Rev 12:1).

Apocalyptic discourse shares with wisdom discourse the belief that God created the earth and heavens and all that are in it. Apocalyptic discourse, however, emphasizes dramatic scenes of seeing and hymns of praise to God. In these contexts, rationales often appear, either making declarations about God or assertions about time. Revelation 4:2–11 presents a scene that shows the relation of apocalyptic discourse to wisdom discourse at the same time it exhibits the remarkable differences.

The topics in Revelation 4:2–11 are: God, thrones, holiness, worship, singing, and creation.

The entire unit of text contains one rationale:

> For thou [God] didst create all things,
> and by thy will they existed and were created (11).

The topic of the rationale is God's action of creating all things. The rationale does not limit itself to the action of creation, however, but extends into the will of God and the existence of things into the present and future. Its rhetorical form is "abbreviation of narrative." The rationale could be expanded to recount any number of God's acts of creating and exercising divine will over the things and beings that exist in the realm of creation.

There are no conditional or adversative constructions in Revelation 4:2–11. The presence of the rationale, however, provides a clue for its overall syllogistic structure.

> **Case**: a throne stood in heaven, with one seated on the throne! (2).
>
> And he who sat there appeared like jasper and carnelian, and round the throne was a rainbow that looked like an emerald (3).
>
> Round the throne were twenty-four thrones, and seated on the thrones were twenty-four elders, clad in white garments, with golden crowns upon their heads (4).
>
> From the throne issue flashes of lightning, and voices and peals of thunder, and before the throne burn seven torches of fire, which are the seven spirits of God (5);
>
> and before the throne there is as it were a sea of glass, like crystal. And round the throne, on each side of the throne, are four living creatures, full of eyes in front and behind (6):
>
> the first living creature like a lion, the second living creature like an ox, the third living creature with the face of a man, and the fourth living creature like a flying eagle (7).

> **Result**: And the four living creatures, each of them with six wings, are full of eyes all round and within, and day and night they never cease to sing,
> "Holy, holy, holy, is the Lord God Almighty,
> who was and is and is to come!" (8).
>
> And whenever the living creatures give glory and honor and thanks to him who is seated on the throne, who lives for ever and ever (9),
>
> the twenty-four elders fall down before him who is seated on the throne and worship him who lives for ever and ever; they cast their crowns before the throne, singing (10),
>
> "Worthy art thou, our Lord and God,
> to receive glory and honor and power,
>
> **Rule**: for thou didst create all things,
> and by thy will they existed and were created" (11).

The description of God, the thrones, and all the other accouterments of heaven present the case which produces the result of worship, and the hymn in the context of worship provides the rule that governs the overall reasoning. Because God created all things and rules over them, the place where God dwells is splendid in every way, and the result of its magnificence is worship and praise. This reasoning establishes a syllogistic structure for apocalyptic discourse in which God's actions in the past, present, and future become the rule which functions as the major premise for all things that occur.

One can see in Revelation 4:6–13 how early Christian discourse nurtured the rule into more and more specific events, featuring additional evil and holy personages and beings. David A. deSilva has explored this unit in detail with socio-rhetorical strategies of interpretation.[31] This unit of text contains an enthymeme at the beginning and the end, and a full syllogism in the middle. The two enthymemes are:

1. **Result**: "Fear God and give him glory, and worship him who made heaven and earth, the sea and the fountains of water."

   Case: for the hour of his judgment has come (7).

2. **Case**: "Blessed are the dead who die in the Lord henceforth." "Blessed indeed," says the Spirit,

   Result: "that they may rest from their labors,

   Rule: for their deeds follow them!" (13).

---

31. David A. deSilva, "The Persuasive Strategy of the Apocalypse: A Socio-Rhetorical Investigation of Revelation 14:6–13," (*SBLSP* 1998; Atlanta: Scholars Press, 1998), 785–806; idem, "A Socio-Rhetorical Investigation of Revelation 14:6–13: A Call to Act Justly toward the Just and Judging God," *BBR* 9 (1999): 65–117.

The full syllogism occurs in 4:8–11:

> (Another angel, a second, followed, saying,)
>
> **Result**: "Fallen, fallen is Babylon the great,
>
> **Case**: she who made all nations drink the wine of her impure passion" (8).
>
> (And another angel, a third, followed them, saying with a loud voice,)
>
> **Rule**: "If any one worships the beast and its image, and receives a mark on his forehead or on his hand (9),
>
> he also shall drink the wine of God's wrath, poured unmixed into the cup of his anger, and he shall be tormented with fire and sulphur in the presence of the holy angels and in the presence of the Lamb (10).
>
> And the smoke of their torment goes up for ever and ever; and they have no rest, day or night, these worshipers of the beast and its image, and whoever receives the mark of its name" (11).

The rule now emerges from a story that not only features people like Enoch in the past and God's angels in the future, but "the beast," its image, the holy angels, and the Lamb. Early Christian apocalyptic discourse nurtures the story further into the future, featuring characters that are not present in preceding apocalypses, and the events around these characters function as rules that govern cases that produce results according to the new rules that emerge.

Apocalyptic discourse plays a centripetal role in Matthew and Mark (biographical history); 1–2 Thessalonians, 1–2 Corinthians, Ephesians, 2 Peter, and Jude (epistle); and Revelation (apocalypse). Socio-rhetorical interpretation has been started on apocalyptic discourse,[32] but a full-scale analysis and interpretation awaits.

Argumentation in Early Christian Pre-Creation Discourse

Pre-creation discourse focuses on the redemptive effect for humans and the cosmos of Christ's relation to God prior to creation. In close alliance with creation discourse, analogy between earthly fathers and their children establishes the dynamics for reasoning about God's relation both to Christ and to humans. Yet the focus of attention is on the attributes and activity of Christ the Son in the past and present. The focus on Christ in pre-creation discourse

---

32. deSilva, "Persuasive Strategy," and "A Call to Act"; Vernon K. Robbins, "Rhetorical Ritual: Apocalyptic Discourse in Mark 13," in *Vision and Persuasion: Rhetorical Dimensions of Apocalyptic Discourse* (ed. Gregory Carey and L. Gregory Bloomquist; St. Louis: Chalice, 1999), 95–121.

places "the story of Christ and the world" in the position of the case, supported by God's story in the background as the rule. The redemptive result emerges from the reasoning from God the Father through the Son to humans and the cosmos.

The reasoning in pre-creation discourse is dynamically abductive rather than primarily inductive-deductive like the five other kinds of discourse. Abductive reasoning proceeds either through invention or discovery that puts "together [metonymy] what we had never dreamed of putting together, which flashes the new suggestion [metaphor] before our contemplation."[33] Pre-creation discourse puts the attributes and actions of Christ together with the attributes and actions of God in the rule, with special focus on the relation of Christ to God prior to creation of the world. From this emerges the insights about Christ in the case as one who is the image of the invisible God (light), the first of all creation (life), the one who came into the world (dwelling in flesh), who is the head of all things, who holds all things together, and who reconciles both humans and the cosmos to God. The result is that light shines in darkness, humans become children of God, and the cosmos becomes reconciled to God.

As a close ally of creation discourse, pre-creation discourse coheres naturally with miracle and prophetic discourse, and through its coherence with prophetic and suffering-death discourse, it invites Christian atonement reasoning centripetally into pre-creation reasoning. Colossians 1:11–20 exhibits pre-creation reasoning in an epistle very well. Its syllogistic structure is as follows:

> May you be strengthened with all power, according to his glorious might, for all endurance and patience with joy (11),
> giving thanks to the Father.
>
> **Result**: The Father has qualified us to share in the inheritance of the saints in light (12).
>
> He has delivered us from the dominion of darkness and transferred us to the kingdom of his beloved Son (13),
>
> in whom we have redemption, the forgiveness of sins (14).
>
> **Case**: He is the image of the invisible God, the first-born of all creation (15);
>
> **Rule**: for in him all things were created [by God], in heaven and on earth, visible and invisible, whether thrones or dominions or principalities or authorities — all things were created through him and for him [by God] (16).

---

33. Charles S. Peirce in Richard L. Lanigan, "From Enthymeme to Abduction: The Classical Law of Logic and the Postmodern Rule of Rhetoric," in *Recovering Pragmatism's Voice: The Classical Tradition, Rorty, and the Philosophy of Communication* (ed. Lenore Langsdorf and Andrew R. Smith; Albany, N.Y.: SUNY Press, 1995), 66, Lanigan's insertions.

> **Case**: He is before all things, and in him all things hold together (17).
>
> He is the head of the body, the church; he is the beginning, the first-born from the dead, that in everything he might be pre-eminent (18).
>
> **Rule**: For in him all the fullness of God was pleased to dwell (19),
>
> and through him to reconcile to himself all things, whether on earth or in heaven, making peace by the blood of his cross (20).

One of the keys is to see the references to the action of God in the Rules. As in apocalyptic discourse, the actions of God create the rule for the reasoning. In contrast to apocalyptic discourse, pre-creation discourse focuses all of its attention on the action of God "through Christ." God created all things "in Christ, through Christ, and for Christ" (1:16). In addition, all of God's fullness took the pleasure of dwelling in Christ, of reconciling all things in earth and heaven to himself, and of making peace by the blood of Christ's cross (1:19–20). In the rules, then, God is active in the background working through Christ. In contrast to apocalyptic discourse, there is no reference in Colossians to God's sending of angels or other cosmic beings to perform certain tasks. The cases focus on the attributes and actions of Christ. He is "the image of the invisible God, the first-born of all creation" (1:15). He is also "before all things," "in him all things hold together," and he is "the head of the body, the church" (1:17). The results then describe what God the Father has done for humans through Christ: "qualified us to share in the inheritance of the saints of light" (1:12), "delivered us from the dominion of darkness," and "transferred us to the kingdom of his beloved Son" (1:13), in whom we have redemption, the forgiveness of sins" (1:14). Colossians 1:12–14 focuses on humans as the blessed recipients of the action both of God and Christ.

John 1:1–18 also exhibits pre-creation discourse in an exemplary manner. Its syllogistic structure is as follows:

> **Rule**: In the beginning was the Word, and the Word was with God, and the Word was God (1).
>
> He was in the beginning with God (2);
>
> all things were made through him [by God], and without him was not anything made that was made [by God] (3).
>
> **Case**: In him was life, and the life was the light of men (4).
>
> **Result**: The light shines in the darkness, and the darkness has not overcome it (5).
>
> **Case**: There was a man sent from God, whose name was John (6).
>
> He came for testimony, to bear witness to the light, that all might believe through him (7).
>
> He was not the light, but came to bear witness to the light (8).

62   *RHETORICAL ARGUMENTATION IN BIBLICAL TEXTS*

> **Case**: The true light that enlightens every man was coming into the world (9).
>
> He was in the world, and the world was made through him, yet the world knew him not (10).
>
> He came to his own home, and his own people received him not (11).
>
> **Result**: But to all who received him, who believed in his name, he gave power to become children of God (12);
>
> who were born, not of blood nor of the will of the flesh nor of the will of man, but of God (13).
>
> **Case**: And the Word became flesh and dwelt among us, full of grace and truth;
>
> **Result**: we have beheld his glory, glory as of the only Son from the Father (14).
>
> **Case**: John bore witness to him, and cried, "This was he of whom I said, 'He who comes after me ranks before me, for he was before me' " (15).
>
> **Result**: And from his fullness have we all received, grace upon grace (16).
>
> **Rule**: For the law was given [by God] through Moses; grace and truth came [from God] through Jesus Christ (17).
>
> **Contrary Case**: No one has ever seen God;
>
> **Case**: the only Son, who is in the bosom of the Father, he has made him known (18).

The rule is that Christ the Word was in the beginning with God, they were inseparable, and God made all things through Christ the Word (1:1). In addition, God gave grace and truth through Jesus Christ; in contrast, God gave the law through Moses (1:17). The case is that there was life in Christ, and this life was the light of humans (1:4). Also, there was a man named John, also sent by God, who bore witness to the light as it came into the world and was rejected by the world (1:6–11). By this process, the only Son of God has made God known to humans (1:15, 18). The result is that "the light shines in the darkness, and the darkness has not overcome it" (1:5); to all who received him he gave power to become children of God (1:12–13); and from his fullness all humans who believe have received grace upon grace (1:16). Both the rule and the case, then, are "stories" about Christ embedded in a story about God. Since Christ came to earth, all the things that happened on earth around Christ are part of the case. The result exhibits how the stories about Christ and God are the medium for benefits to come from God to humans. Those who focus their lives in accordance with this story about God and Christ receive God's redemption.

In pre-creation discourse, then, the story of Christ's relation to God prior to and during creation provides the rule for Christ's attributes and actions. The result of the attributes and actions of both God and Christ are redemption of both humans and the cosmos. Pre-creation discourse plays a centripetal role in the Gospel of John (biographical history), Philippians, Colossians, Hebrews, and 1 John (epistle), and Revelation (apocalypse).

Conclusion

Each New Testament writing has its own particular centripetal-centrifugal rhetorical movement and interaction. The result of this rhetorical dynamic in New Testament literature is a powerful inductive-deductive-abductive rhetorical environment of argumentation. Wisdom discourse highlights inductive-deductive reasoning that leads to an understanding of the ways of God, whose beneficence brought forth an ordered, just world. Analogies throughout all spheres of the universe support this reasoning and leave the hearer in a position of deciding to live according to the way of life or the way of death, which is built into the created order. Miracle discourse, featuring topics of human ailment, disease, or crisis, presupposes the existence of God's power to intervene in the human and cosmic realms. Presenting arguments that imply a stasis of "fact," miracle discourse exhibits and discusses the conditions in which God's power counters opposing forces to produce well-being and order through extraordinary means. Prophetic discourse features God's choosing of people to oversee righteousness, in a context where there are negative consequences for people who do not participate in righteousness. While abductive reasoning surrounds the assertion of God's choice (the rule) in prophetic argumentation, inductive-deductive reasoning about God's righteousness produces results that apply to various individuals and groups in God's world. Suffering-death discourse occurs in a wisdom mode, a prophetic mode, and a Christian atonement mode. In its atonement mode it brings dynamics of wisdom, miracle, and prophetic discourse centripetally into its own discourse and evokes abductive results concerning death's miraculous removal of sin and guilt. In apocalyptic discourse, the entire story of God and the world in the past, present, and future provides the rules that govern the case and the result. In pre-creation discourse, the story of the relation of Christ to God prior to and during creation provide the rule, the attributes and actions of Christ provide the case, and what God has achieved through Christ for humans and the cosmos is the result.

A major challenge for socio-rhetorical interpretation is to gather New Testament literature into groups that exhibit their relationships on the basis of these six kinds of discourse. First, it is notable that some writings begin with a similar kind of discourse. For example, Galatians, Romans, 1 Timothy, 1–2 Peter, Mark, Matthew, and Luke begin with a significant presence of prophetic discourse that is not intertwined with pre-creation discourse. In contrast, Ephesians, Colossians, 2 Timothy, Titus, Hebrews, and the Gospel of John exhibit a significant presence of pre-creation discourse as they begin. Second, many New Testament writings contain shifts in argumentation that transform the discourse into "instruction," Christian *paideia*. In the overall inductive-deductive-abductive rhetorical environment of early Christian discourse, these instructions attain the status of "natural guidelines" grounded in "common sense reasoning" about living in God's world. For example, 1 Thessalonians, introducing topics of suffering-death discourse as early as 1:6, shifts to a combination of suffering-death and apocalyptic topics in 4:13–17 and negotiates them toward wisdom discourse in 4:18–5:28, with the assistance of an apocalyptic statement in 5:3. 2 Thessalonians, introducing topics of suffering-death discourse as early as 1:4, shifts into apocalyptic topics in 1:5–2:12 and negotiates them toward wisdom discourse in 2:13–3:17. The Gospel of Luke establishes prophetic and miracle discourse centripetally in chapters 1–5 and shifts periodically to wisdom, suffering-death, and apocalyptic discourse to interweave its guidelines for living in God's world. The Epistle of James, which features wisdom discourse centripetally from beginning to end, invites apocalyptic discourse (5:7–9) and miracle discourse (5:14–18) into its argumentation as it brings its overall wisdom guidelines to a conclusion. Third, a group of New Testament writings introduces pre-creation discourse as a means of offering "the fullest reasons" why its discourse is "reasonable." The Gospel of John, for example, establishes pre-creation discourse centripetally in the prologue, in close alliance with suffering-death discourse ("He came to his own, and his own did not receive him": 1:11). As the story proceeds, it shifts periodically to prophetic, miracle, and wisdom discourse to interweave its guidelines for living in God's world. Fourth, the rhetorical function of miracle discourse in NT writings needs substantive attention from rhetorical interpreters. On the one hand, miracle discourse functions centripetally only in the biographical histories in the New Testament (Gospels and Acts), in contrast to the five other forms of discourse, which have a centripetal function at one time or another in each literary mode. On the other hand, emphasis on God's extraordinary power circulates centrifugally throughout most of the New Testament corpus, and emphasis on Christ as victor over death and ruler over the world plays a substantive role in second and third century Christian discourse.[34] Peter Brown and Jonathan Z. Smith in particular have argued that a major dynamic in Late Antiquity was

---

34. Torjesen, "You Are the Christ."

to present the Holy Man as a site of the divine.[35] Another way to formulate this might be to focus on the presence, absence, accessibility, and inaccessibility of God's extraordinary power in special humans. In many ways, then, the dispute is over the manner in which miracle discourse is an appropriate or inappropriate dialect (in our terms "rhetorolect"[36]) for talking about the power of God.

Many challenges stand before rhetorical criticism as interpreters face the centripetal-centrifugal rhetorical interaction both within each New Testament writing and among all New Testament writings. Since this interaction evokes the richly complex social, cultural, ideological, and religious environment of thought and action intrinsic to early Christianity, exhibitions of its dynamics can give substantive clues to some of the rhetorical effects of early Christian discourse in Mediterranean society and culture, and potential effects of this kind of discourse in contemporary society and culture.

---

35. Peter Brown, *The Making of Late Antiquity* (Cambridge: Harvard University Press, 1978); idem, *Power and Persuasion in Late Antiquity: Towards a Christian Empire* (Madison: University of Wisconsin Press, 1992); Jonathan Z. Smith, *To Take Place: Toward Theory in Ritual* (Chicago: University of Chicago Press, 1987).

36. Robbins, "Dialectical Nature," 355–57.

CHAPTER 3

THE USE AND ABUSE OF LAUSBERG IN BIBLICAL STUDIES

R. Dean Anderson

In approaching a topic on the use and abuse of a particular textbook, we do well first to pay attention to the purpose and intended audience of such a book.[1] Only then can we begin to assess how such a book may be used by a particular group of scholars who do not, perhaps, fall within the original purview of the author.

In this essay we shall therefore begin by considering the purpose of Lausberg's textbook, and then consider of what use it may be to biblical scholars interested in rhetorical studies. At this point we will be ready to look more closely at the nature of Lausberg's synopsis of ancient rhetoric as we consider several historical problems and distinctions, and finally discuss a number of concrete examples of Lausberg's work to illustrate its inadequacy as a textbook for historical rhetorical criticism.

The Purpose of Lausberg

Lausberg himself was not in the first place a scholar of rhetoric, nor of classical studies, but a philologist of Romance languages. It was his interest in French literature (which began with his appointment to the university in Münster in 1949) which stimulated his interest in rhetoric. Lausberg saw that French classical literature could not properly be studied apart from a knowledge of classical rhetorical theory. Already in 1949 he had published a short work on the elements of literary rhetoric subtitled *eine Einführung für Studierende der romanischen Philologie*. The first edition of the handbook discussed here appeared in 1960 with the subtitle *eine Einführung*

---

1. Heinrich Lausberg, *Handbuch der literarischen Rhetorik: Eine Grundlegung der Literaturwissenschaft*, 2d ed. (Munich: Max Hueber, 1973). There is now also an English translation available, *Handbook of Literary Rhetoric: A Foundation for Literary Study* (ed. David E. Orton and R. Dean Anderson; trans. Matthew T. Bliss, Annemiek Jansen, and David E. Orton; Leiden: E. J. Brill, 1998).

für Studierende der klassischen, romanischen, englischen und deutschen Philologie.[2]

This background is reflected in his own statements in the foreword to the *Handbook* regarding his purpose in writing.[3] Lausberg posits a twofold purpose for the work: first to help the beginner find his way to a phenomenologically and historically meaningful study of literary art; second, to function as an orientation for philologists[4] involved in the practice of the interpretation of texts.

Lausberg's purpose is concerned with providing an aid to those engaged in the study of literature, a very broad target audience indeed. The textbook is not specifically targeted at those studying *ancient* literature. In fact, Lausberg is clearly thinking of literature from the Middle Ages, and more particularly from the modern era, as is clear from what he says in his defense for not writing a *history* of rhetoric from either of these periods.

If Lausberg is thinking of the interpretation of modern literature, why then does he write a textbook which primarily concerns itself with giving an overview of rhetoric from Graeco-Roman antiquity? Precisely because ancient rhetoric functions as the foundation or basis upon which medieval and modern rhetorical theory traditionally rest. In this sense Lausberg is consciously providing a description of the *foundation* for modern literary study (or "rhetoric"). His textbook is to be considered as the starting point (*Ausgangsbasis*) for scholars of literature. The purpose of the book is to clarify this starting point for these scholars of (medieval or modern) literature. That is why he describes it as an *auf das Mittelalter und die Neuzeit hin geöffnete Darstellung der antiken Rhetorik* ("an open-ended presentation of ancient rhetoric with the Middle Ages and the modern era in mind").

For this reason Lausberg offers a number of important disclaimers. It is not his intention to treat the historical development of rhetorical theory within the period of classical antiquity, nor is it his intention to provide an exhaustive description of ancient rhetorical phenomena and terminology. Such matters are of minor relevance to his intended audience. Literary scholars need a general foundational knowledge of ancient rhetoric in order to understand its use and development in later ages. The target period for the audience post-dates the period of classical antiquity, and for this reason the internal

---

2. For an overview of Lausberg's life and scholarly endeavors see further Arnold Arens, "In memoriam Heinrich Lausberg," in *Archiv für das Studium der neueren Sprachen und Literaturen* 230 (1993):1–5.

3. *Handbuch*, 7–8.

4. The term "Philologe" is obviously given a fairly wide meaning here.

development of rhetorical theory within the classical period itself is of little consequence.

The Usefulness of Lausberg in Biblical Studies

When we come to the question of rhetorical criticism in biblical studies it is incumbent upon us to make an important distinction, namely, that between a modern rhetorical critical approach, and an historical rhetorical approach.

The distinction is important because at root a different purpose is at play in these two approaches. An approach from modern rhetorical criticism seeks to understand the communicative structure and methodology of the text (at both macro and micro levels) and its effectiveness in communicating, especially to a modern audience. The rhetorical system or tools which are applied seek to clarify the way in which this communication is achieved regardless of whether the biblical author himself would have analyzed or considered his own work in this way or with these tools. To some extent this kind of rhetorical analysis may also tell us something about the way in which the document studied will have communicated to its first audience(s). Nevertheless such analysis is generally not historically conditioned.

An historical rhetorical approach has other purposes in mind. This approach seeks to analyze the New Testament[5] literature in terms of the rhetorical methods and systems current in its own day. The results of this kind of analysis may help us determine the extent to which a given author was consciously working with rhetorical theory. They may help us to assess the communicative value of a document to a first-century audience, particularly a rhetorically educated one. By studying historical rhetorical theory and practice we attempt to attune our ears to those primarily of the educated class in antiquity in order to reflect, from their perspective, upon the literary and argumentative methods used in the New Testament writings.[6] In this respect, the results of this approach may also help us to unveil literary techniques

---

5. Obviously it is not possible to subject the Old Testament to a rhetorical analysis of this nature, although it is conceivably possible to analyze the Septuagint in terms of its reception to a rhetorically educated or influenced audience in ancient times.

6. We need to distinguish between historical theory and historical practice. An historical rhetorical approach needs to take into account the fact that theory and practice were not always the same thing. It is precisely this point that Jan Swearingen seems to miss when she criticizes my claim that Paul departs from rhetorical theory in his use of showy figures in serious contexts, and in his emotional rebukes; J. Swearingen, "The Tongues of Men"; see below p. 232. The fact that Paul departs from the *theory* at these points is not the same as saying that there are no historical parallels in terms of contemporary *practice*. In the second edition of my book *Ancient Rhetorical Theory and Paul* (rev. ed.; Leuven: Peeters, 1999), 283–88, I attempt to show something of the background of Paul's use of showy figures.

and methods, no longer completely obvious to the modern reader, which aid a correct understanding of the message of the text. An historical rhetorical analysis may also help us to understand the communicative structure of the text generally (as a modern rhetorical analysis seeks to do), but the historical analysis has definite limitations in this area, not in the least in that ancient rhetorical theory was severely underdeveloped in terms of analyzing the communicative effect of rhetorical methodology. In addition there is the fact that ancient rhetorical theory and methodology too often proves an inadequate tool for general rhetorical analysis. The theory behind a particular methodology may be faulty (cf. Dionysius of Halicarnassus' theories on the analysis of poetical prose), or simply too rigid and regulative to be applied in practice.

Although consciousness of this distinction among biblical scholars is now more widespread than it was twenty years ago, there is still not infrequently an element of confusion as to what purpose a given rhetorical study has in mind, and what methods are used to achieve this.

Of course it is possible to use an ancient rhetorical theory (such as Aristotle's) for ostensibly modern rhetorical purposes, i.e., to analyze the communicative effect of a given document. Such an analysis from an Aristotelian perspective is provided by Rodney Duke in his paper on Chronicles. It is not Duke's contention that the Chronicler was influenced by an Aristotelian kind of rhetorical theory. This theory is merely used as a tool of analysis.[7] In principle there is nothing against such an approach if it is made clear to the reader that what is being attempted is not an historically conditioned rhetorical analysis. For myself, even where Aristotle is concerned, there remains the question of how far his work is a viable rhetorical tool for (modern) rhetorical analysis. The recent history of scholarship on Aristotle's Rhetoric (I am thinking of the last century) shows how vague, and at points self-contradictory, this treatise is. In this respect I would be more inclined to agree with Lauri Thurén that, for the analysis of communication in general, modern theories are far more highly developed than any ancient theory, Aristotle included.[8] The debate between Thurén and Eriksson on the adequacy of ancient theory and terminology in the analysis of the New Testament needs, in my opinion, to pay more attention to the specific purposes in view with respect to such analysis.[9]

---

7. A good example of how Aristotle's theory ought not to be considered to have been current in the school rhetoric of the first centuries of the common era and before may be seen from Manfred Kraus's paper on the enthymeme in this volume (pp. 95–111). See also my brief note on the period below (in relation to Lausberg's text) and further my *Ancient Rhetorical Theory and Paul*, 41–49.

8. See his paper in this volume (pp. 77–92).

9. See their respective papers in this volume (pp. 77–92; 243–59).

Bearing in mind the original purpose of Lausberg's textbook, we can readily see that it is most obviously an aid to those engaged in the practice of modern rhetorical criticism. And yet its helpfulness is not, in the first place, as a textbook for the practice of such criticism. Among biblical scholars interested in modern rhetorical criticism a textbook such as Ch. Perelman and L. Olbrechts-Tyteca's *La Nouvelle Rhétorique: Traité de l'Argumentation* (also in English translation) has often been used. Frans van Eemeren's paper in this same volume provides a helpful overview of various more recent modern approaches.[10] Lausberg's book is intended as a *foundation* for modern rhetorical criticism. The rhetorical methods of such modern criticism will often have been built upon this foundation, and it is incumbent upon the modern rhetorical critic to have some kind of understanding of the foundation underlying his own approach, whatever that approach might be.

In this sense it must be considered a *misuse* when Lausberg's work is used as a systematic textbook for the direct application of rhetorical criticism to the New Testament. The work functions inadequately as a textbook for either modern rhetorical criticism or historical rhetorical criticism. It is a very handy reference work for modern rhetorical criticism which can provide depth and understanding for the application of various (modern) rhetorical tools by means of the historical perspective it supplies. But it was never Lausberg's intention to supply the reader with those modern tools themselves. Historical rhetorical critics may initially think that they have more direct use for Lausberg's textbook, but even this proves to be a mirage as we hope to show below.

Historical rhetorical criticism involves a complex interplay between contemporary theory and practice in the context of developing traditions which at any one time can vary considerably from author to author even within different legitimately defined schools of thought. Around the beginning of the Christian era we may, for example, legitimately distinguish philosophically influenced rhetorical theory (i.e., theory influenced in some way by Aristotle's *Rhetoric*),[11] e.g., Cicero's later treatises and the genuine treatises of Dionysius of Halicarnassus, and Greek school rhetoric best represented in the two Latin treatises, the *Rhetorica et Herennium* and Cicero, *De inventione*. And yet whilst there is a great deal of agreement between the two latter treatises (so much so that most scholars postulate some kind of common documentary source), they are not always in agreement in their rhetorical methodology.

---

10. See his paper in this volume (pp. 9–26).
11. By this time no philosophical school we know of was attempting to describe rhetorical theory. The only clear example, besides Aristotle some centuries before, was the first-century B.C. Academician Philo of Larissa whose ideas may, perhaps, be embodied in Cicero, *Part. or.* (see my *Ancient Rhetorical Theory and Paul*, 55–59).

And there is, of course, a world of difference between the rhetorical theory of the late Cicero and that of Dionysius of Halicarnassus even though both are attempting to synthesize school rhetoric with a more philosophical approach (particularly Aristotelian "philosophical" rhetoric).

The question which must be asked is what kind of rhetorical "system" it is that Lausberg attempts to summarize in his textbook.

Lausberg's Rhetorical Synopsis

Although Lausberg's systematic summary of ancient rhetorical theory is, as he himself admits, eclectic, the general structure of the system follows Quintilian's *Institutio Oratoria* fairly closely. For Lausberg's aim, this was a sensible choice. Quintilian provides us with a monumental systematic work which is itself extremely eclectic, taking much from the school rhetoric of the day, but also attempting to incorporate the main ideas of Cicero's late philosophically conceived treatises (e.g., the *De or.* and the *Orator*). Lausberg fills in this structure with a myriad of quotations and details from other, mostly later, treatises. Many of the details with which Lausberg pads out Quintilian's system are in fact methods and theories of late antiquity, or at least late outworkings of earlier methods and theories, which would have been unknown to Quintilian himself. This is, of course, unimportant to Lausberg's own purpose, but of great significance to the biblical scholar wishing to pursue an historical rhetorical approach.

A biblical scholar wishing to dabble in historical rhetorical analysis may easily be mislead into thinking that Lausberg's systematic presentation provides him or her with a suitable rhetorical system for historical rhetorical analysis of the New Testament. Nothing could be further from the truth. Not only did such a monolithic system not exist in antiquity, this system is so eclectic that it cannot be said to represent any individual school of rhetorical thought at any time in antiquity.[12]

A few examples of particularly misleading problems may be cited.

Stasis Theory in Deliberative and Epideictic Rhetoric?

In the first place there is Lausberg's rather strange decision to discuss the deliberative and epideictic (=demonstrative) genres in conjunction with *stasis*

---

12. That is to say, it cannot even represent a typical rhetorical system of late antiquity. For one thing, late antiquity very rarely had anything to do with the later philosophically influenced treatises of Cicero which form the foundation of Quintilian's (and thus also Lausberg's) system.

theory. This is highly misleading. No extant treatise I am aware of applies *stasis* theory to these genres. Hermagoras (whose treatise is not extant) may have done this, although it is clear that his emphasis in the working out of *stasis* doctrine was on judicial rhetoric.[13] It seems probable that Lausberg's detailed working out of *stasis* doctrine with respect to these genres was based on a comment which Quintilian makes in *Institutio oratoria* 3.6.1 where he defends this concept.[14] But not even Quintilian himself applies this in the working out of his own treatise.

We might ask what the practical effect of such an approach is. Whatever Lausberg may have had in mind, it unfortunately gives a skewed idea of how the ancients would have gone to work in preparing, for example, the proof section of a deliberative speech. And this is the whole point of stasis doctrine. It is a method whereby one can classify the kind of judicial case that needs to be argued and then scan through his rhetorical textbook to see the kinds of arguments (loci) which may be applicable to his case.[15] But this was not the procedure in preparing a deliberative speech. For a deliberative speech was considered to be a separate category altogether which, generally speaking, relied upon a set of totally different kinds of arguments, namely, those which in late antiquity came to be known as the *telika kephalaia* ("arguments of purpose"), e.g., arguments related to such concepts as justice, legality, advantage, etc.[16] These were the loci for building a deliberative speech, and not those associated with stasis theory, even if it is theoretically possible to classify deliberative propositions into one or other stasis. Similarly, at least in Hellenistic and early imperial rhetorical theory, epideictic speeches were considered to have their own set of relevant loci. In late antiquity various different kinds of epideictic speeches were often isolated and treated separately.

Now Lausberg does indeed discuss such matters as the deliberative *telika kephalaia*, but this discussion is hidden in his introductory section on argumentative *loci* which he has chosen to discuss in connection with the proof section of a speech, and thus structurally within the discussion of the *partes orationis*. A quite false impression is left to the reader who quickly consults Lausberg to discover how the ancients set about writing deliberative, or epi-

---

13. See Hermagoras, *Fragmenta*, Bibliotheca Scriptorum Graecorum et Romanorum Teubneriana (ed. D. Matthes; Leipzig: B. G. Teubner, 1962), *Fr.* 3, and further A. D. Leeman and A. C. Braet, *Klassieke retorica: haar inhoud, functie en betekenis* (Groningen: Wolters-Noordhoff/Forsten, 1987), 78–79.

14. See Lausberg, *Handbook,* 43 (§83).

15. See my *Ancient Rhetorical Theory and Paul*, 96–107, for a discussion of the methodologies implied by the extant treatises in preparing the different kinds of speeches.

16. See my *Glossary of Greek Rhetorical Terms Connected to Methods of Argumentation, Figures and Tropes from Anaximenes to Quintilian* (Leuven: Peeters, 2000), s.v. *kephalaion* III.

deictic, speeches. For he will then turn to the section on deliberative speeches and only be confronted with the application of stasis theory.

Amplificatio Methodology

A second problem which is also related to the reliance upon Quintilian concerns the methodology for the important and, in the ancient treatises, much discussed concept of *amplificatio,* i.e., expanding upon what one has argued or proven by variously promoting, or conversely, denigrating it.[17] Almost all the extant theorists deal with this topic by providing a list of the kinds of arguments (loci) which can be used to promote or denigrate any given matter. The arguments provided tend to vary in terms of their abstractness, but are frequently very similar from treatise to treatise. Amplificatio was frequently dealt with in conjunction with epideictic rhetoric, which does not first have to *prove* anything, or with the *peroratio* of a speech, that section of a speech where nothing more needs to be proven, but the urgency and importance of the matters need to be amplified.

Quintilian's handling of *amplificatio* is, however, quite different. He provides a rather atypical presentation and methodology.[18] In the first place Quintilian chooses to place his discussion of amplificatio not under the section on the invention of arguments, whether for judicial or epideictic rhetoric, but under one of the headings associated with *elocutio* (use of language), namely, ornatus (i.e., the ornamentation of one's language). It is then further placed under a subdivision of *ornatus* which lists stylistic virtues. The reason for placing amplificatio here is clearly related to Quintilian's enormous respect for Cicero, who also discussed amplificatio in this context,[19] although Cicero referred back to the loci which had been mentioned in connection with the discussion on *inventio.* Whilst Quintilian's placement of the discussion of amplificatio under elocutio follows Cicero, his discussion of the subject is quite original.[20] He identifies only four kinds of argument (loci) by which matters may be amplified, and discusses these with examples. This is quite different from the multiplication of loci normally presented in the rhetorical treatises of antiquity.

---

17. For an overview of the way in which the theorists from Anaximenes to Quintilian deal with amplificatio see my *Glossary,* 26–29.
18. Quintilian, *Inst.*, 8.4.
19. Cicero, *de Orat.* 3.104–8.
20. At least there are no extant treatises which deal with the matter in quite the same way. It may, perhaps, be suspected that Quintilian "borrowed" this discussion from somewhere else (as with much of his work), but this cannot be proven.

With respect to the placement of the discussion of amplificatio it is noteworthy that Lausberg chooses *not* to follow Quintilian, but to treat the discussion as one of the headings under argumentatio in the proof section of a speech. This is, indeed, the place which it most frequently has in the extant treatises, and Lausberg has made a sensible choice here.[21] But Lausberg's brief discussion of amplificatio is simply a summary of Quintilian's unique fourfold methodology followed by a brief and rather messy presentation of *loci communes*. Nowhere are we informed of the uniqueness of this fourfold approach and the fact that the normal way of dealing with amplificatio is to provide a very much longer list of possible loci. In fact, we get the (false) impression that this fourfold treatment is a standard abbreviated form (see §400 and §259). The loci communes that are discussed by Lausberg are placed in the context of the philosophically oriented distinction between *quaestiones infinita* and *finita,* which is not really relevant to amplificatio in the treatises. They are also organized according to the various staseis — a complete *novum* as far as is known to me.

This is unfortunate both because of the importance of amplificatio in ancient rhetorical theory, and because the all-pervasiveness of the loci-method of dealing with such subjects is lacking. By this I mean the idea that the speech-writer would check his textbook under amplificatio and find a long list of possible arguments out of which he would choose the most relevant ones for his subject in hand. This method was ubiquitous in the ancient theorists, from preliminary exercises (*progymnasmata*) to stasis theory to amplificatio.

The Discussion of Periods (Sentence Construction)

Treatment of the period in ancient rhetoric tended to be fairly complex and no two authors are exactly alike in their definitions and presentation. The foremost difference is seen in two distinct ways in which the period was defined, namely, a) as any complete sentence, or b) as a sentence which has been put together in a particular way, i.e., with interweaved connections whereby the total sense of the sentence is really only perceived in the final words. Representatives of the former definition are Aristotle, Quintilian, and probably Alexander (*De figuris*). Representatives of the latter are Demetrius (*Eloc.*), *Rhetorica ad Herennium,* and Cicero.[22] What makes matters confusing is

---

21. Although Lausberg briefly defends the placement of *amplificatio* at this point (§400), he does not mention the fact that Quintilian (following Cicero) chooses a different placement and therefore implies a quite different emphasis as to what amplificatio is all about.

22. Dionysius of Halicarnassus had a rather more peculiar approach essentially defining periods in terms of breath length (which is different to saying, as many theorists did, that the length of a period should be limited by what someone can say in one breath). For a discussion of many of the ancient treatises on the period see my *Glossary,* 94–101.

the fact that many theorists use the same or similar terms with completely different meanings. The "turned down" (*katestrammenee*) style discussed by Aristotle is, for example, something quite different to the "turned down" style discussed by Demetrius, despite the fact that Demetrius is highly influenced by Aristotle's treatise, probably via secondary sources.

Nothing of these problems is mentioned by Lausberg, who defines the period in terms of a particular kind of sentence (i.e., the circularly constructed sentence) and refers to various sources as if they all agree with this definition (including Aristotle and Quintilian), §§923–24.[23] The same problem surfaces in §§941–44. A false sense of agreement among the ancient theorists is created which can cause many a mishap for the unwary scholar wishing to apply "ancient theory" to his documents.

The problem is not so acute for the intended audience of the work, since the definition which Lausberg has chosen to illustrate and expound upon is the one which most pervaded school rhetoric, and this audience is not reading the work so as to directly apply *ancient* rhetorical theory.

Conclusions

In conclusion I would like to suggest that whilst Lausberg's textbook is quite adequate for the purpose and audience of scholars of medieval and modern literature for which it was intended, it proves unsatisfactory for an historical rhetorical approach to the New Testament. Those scholars wishing to take a more modern rhetorical approach to analyzing the New Testament may, of course, use Lausberg's work for the same purpose as that for which he wrote it, namely, as an introduction to that general rhetorical system which underlies much modern rhetorical theory.

The main reasons why Lausberg's work cannot function as a textbook for historical rhetorical criticism are: (1) the fact that it, intentionally, does not provide a history of the development of ancient rhetoric, and thus does not enable the reader to readily distinguish concepts and methods which might be relevant to the first century C.E. from those which are not (either because they are unique, too early, too late, or too philosophical).[24] This limitation can obviously not be blamed on Lausberg himself. (2) The unevenness with which

---

23. At §943 Lausberg does correctly note that Aristotle's "divided style" is defined differently than that of Demetrius. This is, however, but one small detail from a complex mass of distinctions and differences in definition.

24. The reader may gain a small introduction into the kinds of differences in definition and methodology in some of the ancient treatises by making a cursory examination of my *Glossary*. This book is, however, restricted to methods of argumentation, figures, and tropes excluding stasis theory,

Lausberg alerts the reader to problems and differences in interpretation in the sources which he quotes and the definitions which he provides. (3) The presence of several serious problems in Lausberg's own description of rhetorical methodology, of which a few have been illustrated in this paper.[25]

There is really no substitute for personal study of the original treatises themselves. Lausberg may be read with profit as a kind of general introduction to the subject, and even used as a quick reference tool for finding references to take one back to the sources themselves, but it cannot substitute for a study of those sources.

Of course not all biblical scholars wishing to apply rhetorical theory have the time or inclination to take on a detailed study of all the extant rhetorical treatises. But rather than opting for a general summarizing work of the nature of Lausberg, one is far better off choosing a typical treatise embodying the school rhetoric of the time and studying that together with a suitable commentary which should supply any necessary background and collaboratory information. In this respect the treatise that most stands out for suitability for New Testament scholars is the *Rhetorica ad Herennium* which is really nothing more than an adaptation of standard Greek school rhetoric into the Latin language. The Loeb edition of this work provides a satisfactory Latin text with English translation, and there is a very good text and commentary by G. Calboli.[26] This work might be supplemented by a study of Theon's *Progymnasmata*, now available in an excellent edition by M. Patillon in the Budé series, and also available in an English translation by G. Kennedy.[27]

By putting Lausberg's textbook into perspective, the various avenues of rhetorical study of the Bible may be better served. The book cannot be considered to be a standard textbook for all forms of rhetorical study of the Bible. But if Lausberg is used, and not abused, particularly in terms of the purposes which Lausberg himself had in mind, the rhetorical study of the Bible can only be enhanced by his work.

---

and confines itself to the period from Anaximenes to Quintilian (end of the fourth century B.C.E. to the end of the first century C.E.).

25. A few other examples may be found in my *Ancient Rhetorical Theory and Paul*, cf. pp. 185, 191, 252, 291–92.

26. *Cornifici Rhetorica ad C. Herennium* (2d ed.; Bologna: Pàtron, 1993). There is also a Budé edition (G. Achard, ed., *Rhétorique à Herennium* [Paris: Les Belles Lettres, 1989]), which I have not examined.

27. Michel Patillon, *Aelius Théon: Progymnasmata* (Paris: Les Belles Lettres, 1997); George A. Kennedy, *Progymnasmata: Greek Textbooks of Prose Composition Introductory to the Study of Rhetoric. Writings by or Attributed to Theon, Hermogenes, Aphthonius, Nicolaus, Together with an Anonymous Prolegomenon to Aphthonius, Selections from the Commentary Attributed to John of Sardis, and Fragments of the Progymnasmata of Sopatros Translated into English, with Introductions and Notes* (Fort Collins, Colo.: Chez l'auteur, 1999).

CHAPTER 4

IS THERE BIBLICAL ARGUMENTATION?

Lauri Thurén

One cannot really argue with a mathematical theorem.[1]
— Stephen Hawking

In our first international conference on rhetorical studies of biblical texts, in Heidelberg 1992, I read a paper on argumentation theories and New Testament studies.[2] The paper briefly presented the vast development in argumentation studies during recent decades. Simultaneously, research based solely on ancient theories of argumentation was criticized.

It seems that the paper was ahead of its time, for it could well be read even today. Despite the rapidly growing interest in biblical argumentation, most studies are still executed with little knowledge of, or reference to, modern theories of reasoning. Sometimes, however, the pioneers of the late 1950s may represent the most up-to-date development in argumentation theory.[3]

Is our disregard of modern trends in argumentation analysis due to pure negligence? Or does biblical argumentation have such qualities that standard approaches cannot easily be applied? This paper seeks to answer this question, which is not purely rhetorical.

---

1. Stephen W. Hawking, *A Brief History of Time: From the Big Bang to Black Holes* (Toronto: Bantam, 1988), 50.
2. Lauri Thurén, "On Studying Ethical Argumentation and Persuasion in the New Testament," in *Rhetoric and the New Testament* (ed. S. Porter and T. Olbricht; JSNTSup 90; Sheffield: Sheffield Academic Press, 1993), 464–78.
3. Perelman's pioneering study of reasoning (Chaim Perelman and L. Olbrechts-Tyteca, *The New Rhetoric: A Treatise on Argumentation* [trans. J. Wilkinson and P. Weaver; Notre Dame, Ind.: University of Notre Dame Press, 1969]), but not the criticism leveled against it (e.g., Frans van Eemeren and R. Grootendorst, *Handbook of Argumentation Theory: A Critical Survey of Classical Backgrounds and Modern Studies* [Dordrecht/Providence: Foris, 1987], 251–59), is known to many biblical scholars. See especially Folker Siegert, *Argumentation bei Paulus* (WUNT 34; Tübingen: Mohr-Siebeck, 1985), and Wilhelm Wuellner, "Where Is Rhetorical Criticism Taking Us?" *CBQ* 49 (1987), 448–63. Stephen Toulmin, *The Uses of Argument* (Cambridge: Cambridge University Press, 1958); Stephen Toulmin, R. Rieke, and A. Janik, *An Introduction to Reasoning*, 2d ed. (New York: Macmillan, 1984), is rarely mentioned (Thurén, "On Studying Ethical Argumentation"; Lauri Thurén, *Argument and Theology in 1 Peter: The Origins of Christian Paraenesis* (JSNTSup 114; Sheffield: Sheffield Academic Press, 1995); Manuel Alexandre, *Rhetorical Argumentation in Philo of Alexandria* (Brown Judaic Studies 322, SPhil 2; Atlanta: Scholars, 1999).

Sancta Simplicitas?

At a first glance, the use of ancient theorists and neglect of recent studies in argumentation analysis appears to result from ignorance; many of us are unaware of developments in the field. To name but a few examples, Donelson categorically rejects any modern research in the field and argues that Aristotle provides the best tools for analyzing argumentation in the Pastoral Epistles. Nevertheless, he suggests that for analyzing modern debate, as well as the Pastoral Epistles, further development is needed.[4] Correspondingly, Bünker finds some simple syllogisms and enthymemes in 1 Corinthians and concludes: "Die rhetorische Analyse... ist ein durchaus geeignetes Instrument zur Erhellung der argumentativen Struktur der Korintherbriefe.... Die traditionelle antike Rhetorik gibt uns Kriterien an die Hand, mit deren Hilfe eine solche Analyse durchzuführen ist."[5]

According to a simple explanation, the phenomenon is due to biblical scholars' traditional familiarity with antiquity. Consequently, we study biblical rhetoric and biblical argumentation with ancient tools, believing that there is no alternative. This, of course, is an unacceptable excuse. Scientists no longer rely solely on Aristotle, or even on Galileo or Newton, despite recognizing their indebtedness to these great thinkers. Students of history, language, and sociology have likewise proceeded to more refined problems and more adequate methodology, even when studying antiquity.

After World War II, many pioneering studies on modern argumentation theory were written. One of these critical scholars is the famous Norwegian philosopher Arne Næss.[6] R. Crawshay-Williams,[7] S. Toulmin,[8] and C. Perelman[9] paved the way for a new understanding of human reasoning, and are still widely known representatives of modern studies on argumentation. But much has happened in the field of argumentation analysis since Toulmin

---

4. Lewis R. Donelson, *Pseudepigraphy and Ethical Argument in the Pastoral Epistles* (HUT 22; Tübingen: Mohr, 1986), 3–4, 201–2.

5. Michael Bünker, *Briefformular und rhetorische Disposition im 1. Korintherbrief* (GTA 28; Göttingen: Vandenhoeck & Ruprecht, 1984), 75. Yet he refers to some modern studies of rhetoric and text-linguistics. W. Viertel, *The Hermeneutics of Paul* (Waco, Tex., 1976, unpublished) is another example.

6. His first essay, *Om meningsytring*, was published already in 1941. See also Arne Næss *En del elementære logiske emner* (Oslo: Universitetsforlaget, 1947). Perhaps most important was Arne Næss, *Interpretation and Preciseness: A Contribution to the Theory of Communication* (Oslo: Det Norske videnskaps-akademi, 1953).

7. R. Crawshay-Williams, *The Comforts of Unreason* (London: Routledge & Kegan Paul, 1947); idem, *Methods and Criteria for Reasoning: An Inquiry into the Structure of Controversy* (London: Routledge & Kegan Paul, 1957).

8. Toulmin, *Argument*.

9. Perelman and Olbrechts-Tyteca, *New Rhetoric*.

and Perelman. The development and current situation is well illustrated in, for example, Eemeren and others, *Fundamentals of Argumentation Theory* (1996), or other recent publications.[10] Eemeren and others present the history of argumentation analysis and, more thoroughly than its predecessors, also report on different lines in current analysis. Studies in modern rhetoric, informal logic, dialogue logic, formal dialectics, pragma-dialectics, and various language-oriented approaches have expanded our possibilities to study and understand human reasoning, argumentation, and persuasion. Most of these approaches are not bound to a specific culture, but are applicable in any type of communication and interaction. These theoretical discussions and the methods built thereon would greatly benefit studies of biblical reasoning as well.

If the problem were this simple, it could easily be resolved by an introductory textbook on argumentation and some further studies. One could argue that modern theories not only pose more adequate questions than do the ancient ones; they also enable more accurate and sophisticated solutions of the questions. But biblical scholars' rejection of modern methodology cannot be explained by referring only to insufficient homework. For even scholars who are cognizant of modern studies nevertheless rely on ancient ways of analyzing argumentation. How is such a conscious decision justified?

Three types of arguments have been presented: a) If rhetoric is seen as cultural artefact, the choice of "classical conceptions" is historically justified.[11] An ancient text ought to be understood in the light of Greco-Roman rhetorical tradition.[12] But it has also been suggested that ancient modes of reasoning differ essentially from our way of thinking.[13] b) Ancient terminology is more convenient as we are all familiar with it.[14] c) Classical theories suffice for analyzing the Bible, for they are sophisticated enough. This is

---

10. Frans van Eemeren et al., *Fundamentals of Argumentation Theory: A Handbook of Historical Backgrounds and Contemporary Developments* (Mahwah, N.J.: Erlbaum, 1996). Further sources for the current status include papers from a conference on argumentation (e.g., Eemeren et al., eds., *Argumentation Illuminated: Papers from a Conference Organized by the International Society for the Study of Argumentation in Amsterdam, June 1990* [Amsterdam: SICSAT, 1992] or copies of *Argumentation,* a journal on reasoning. All these provide a good start for updating knowledge of this field.
11. George A. Kennedy, *New Testament Interpretation through Rhetorical Criticism* (Chapel Hill: University of North Carolina, 1984) 10; Anders Eriksson, *Traditions as Rhetorical Proof: Pauline Argumentation in 1 Corinthians* (ConBNT 29; Stockholm: Almqvist & Wiksell, 1998) 21, 23.
12. Margaret Mitchell, *Paul and the Rhetoric of Reconciliation* (HUT 28; Tübingen: Mohr-Siebeck, 1991), 6.
13. Eriksson, *Traditions,* 21, 26.
14. Lauri Thurén, *The Rhetorical Strategy of 1 Peter* (Åbo Akademis Förlag, 1990), 54, speaking of rhetorical analysis in general. However, it is emphasized that ancient terminology should be used only insofar as it remains viable.

supported by the fact that even modern theories recognize their dependence on classical ones.[15]

c)

To begin in a chiastic order, the last argument may also be implicit in Alexandre's methodological solution: after a rather well-informed discussion of "recent" studies of argumentation, he nevertheless resorts without further comment to Aristotle's enthymematic reasoning when studying Philo of Alexandria.[16] I have difficulties in following this reasoning. If modern scholars analyzing argumentation, and rhetoric, are familiar with the results of their ancient predecessors and build upon their work, but judge it necessary to replace them with their own models, this implies that they do not regard the ancient approaches as adequate for the analysis of texts. The choice of scholars who are unfamiliar with modern methods and choose ancient ones appears less dependable — unless, as the first argument postulates, ancient rationality was in principle different from ours.

b)

The problems with the third argument also impinge on the second. According to argument b), ancient terminology is currently widely known and thus convenient. Although this is certainly true to some degree, old terminology may also be misleading, insufficient, and not viable. Whereas in general rhetoric[17] much of ancient terminology is still appropriate, when referring to specific phenomena (such as *captatio benevolentiae*), the terms pertinent to argumentation are more problematic, as their use is closely connected with the corresponding theory of argumentation. For example, the Aristotelian concepts of "major premise" and "minor premise" require acceptance of his model of analyzing argumentation, and cannot easily be applied independently. Thus it is not surprising that, for example, Toulmin, well versed in Aristotle, was unable to use his elementary, albeit well-known, terminology.

---

15. Eriksson, *Traditions*, 24–25.
16. Alexandre, *Rhetorical Argumentation*, 23–30.
17. Which is not to be confused with argumentation; see below.

a)

More promising than the third and second argument is the first, historical one. In an exclusively historical research, a comparison with other ancient argumentative texts is certainly justifiable.[18] But this can lead to a further idea, according to which we ought to use not only ancient handbooks, but Aristotle himself when studying the New Testament, since he represents a typical ancient way of reasoning. Yet in my view, at least the latter claim is untenable. Aristotle's theses cannot be used as a description of the mainstream ancient way of reasoning. On the contrary, he acquired his reputation by presenting novel and radical opinions about argumentation and its internal structure. Aristotle was not concerned simply to catalogue and report upon adequate means of reasoning, but attempted to influence the way people reason, and even eradicate bad persuasion.[19] It is unlikely that New Testament authors, who hardly received any higher education in rhetoric or dialectic, were strongly influenced by Aristotle.

Other, more practically oriented rhetoricians, such as Quintilian and his predecessors, might prove more useful. In principle they wanted to train their pupils in the most effective ways of reasoning and persuasion, which were derived not so much from normative prescriptions but from observations of ordinary rhetoric.[20] Yet such an idealistic view is hard to justify. More likely, the techniques of upper class rhetoricians were culturally bound indeed. The biblical authors did not share that sophisticated culture. They lived in a different world from that of the Roman professors of rhetoric.

Just as in rhetoric, only if it can be demonstrated that certain modes of reasoning were something specific in those days, or that the biblical authors had studied a certain type of argumentation, can references to such a system be made. One may wonder whether such specific features or such a dependence can ever be proven.[21] But even then, we would be dealing with *historical* research. The goal would not be to clarify and understand the argumentation

---

18. Mitchell, *Paul*, 6–7.

19. For example, Aristotle's claim that one should not try to affect the judge's emotions, is not an ordinary ancient attitude (*Rhet.*, 1.1.1354a). He further almost omits the "extra-technical means" (*Rhet.*, 1.2.1355b).

20. See George A. Kennedy, "Historical Survey of Rhetoric," in *Handbook of Classical Rhetoric in the Hellenistic Period (330 B.C.–A.D. 400)* (ed. S. E. Porter; Leiden: Brill, 1997), 3–50; 31–32.

21. I believe that most conventions of communication are universal. Professor Robert Thurman, whose special interest is the exploration of the Indo-Tibetan philosophical and psychological traditions, with a view to their relevance to parallel currents of contemporary thought and science, writes in an email-interview (June 2, 2000): "Tibetan conventions of reasoning, like modern western ones are just that, conventions. They are not essentially different from any others." Correspondingly Kennedy (*New Testament Interpretation*, 4, 10–11) argues that the rhetoric of the Far East does not substantially differ from Aristotelian rhetoric. On Jewish reasoning, see Siegert, *Argumentation*.

as such, but to demonstrate the historical connections with a certain type of thinking. If however, Paul or Matthew did not study Aristotle, and if a common way of reasoning of their time is not best described by Aristotle, there is little reason for using his system in modern scholarship.[22]

Argumentation Is Not to Be Equated with Rhetoric

There is, however, another reason why we might rely on ancient models of argumentation when analyzing the Bible. If we are used to the concepts of ancient rhetoric, it is easy to equate rhetoric with argumentation. But although there is no widely accepted agreement about the definition of "argumentation" and "rhetoric" or "persuasion," it is obvious that a simple equation of the two concepts is misleading. A study of almost any form of argumentation analysis shows that argumentation is not identical with rhetoric, reasoning, or persuasion.[23]

In the current discussion of argumentation, there are two basic solutions. The birth of scholarly analysis of argumentation as an independent discipline was attributable to the idea that human argumentation, contrary to logical demonstration, has *some* rhetorical elements: its validity is to a certain degree dependent on the audience.[24] Referring to the quotation by Hawking at the beginning of the paper, in mathematical demonstration all argumentation, persuasion, and rhetoric is superfluous.

To be sure, many recent scholars argue that a distinction between logic and argumentation is actually unnecessary; argumentation can be analyzed with more sophisticated formal logic and dialectic.[25] Yet on both sides, the use of either pure ancient rhetoric or classical formal logic is seen as an unsatisfactory solution. The basic idea in human persuasion is that we cannot just display the absolute logical truth, but only different logical systems within which validity can be sought.[26]

But even without taking any stand in the discussion between "rhetorical" and "logical" forms of argumentation analysis, the debate itself indicates that

---

22. See also Stanley E. Porter, "The Theoretical Justification for Application of Rhetorical Categories to Pauline Epistolary Literature," in *Rhetoric and the New Testament* (ed. Stanley E. Porter and Thomas H. Olbricht; JSNTSup 90; Sheffield: Sheffield Academic Press, 1993), 100–122.

23. Alexandre correctly assesses Perelman's *opus magnum* as a study of argumentation, not of rhetoric in general (Alexandre, *Rhetorical Argumentation,* 24), and discusses the relationship between argumentation, logic, and demonstration (25–29).

24. Perelman and Toulmin belong to this category.

25. See Eemeren et al., *Fundamentals of Argumentation Theory,* 163–311.

26. See, e.g., Else M. Barth and Erik C. W. Krabbe, *From Axiom to Dialogue: A Philosophical Study of Logics and Argumentation* (Berlin/New York: de Gruyter, 1982).

the two cannot be easily identified. I have suggested the following definitions: unlike logical demonstration, both argumentation and persuasion seek the adherence of an audience.

> The substantive "argumentation" and the verb "convince" mean activity aimed at gaining the audience's assent to the author's theses and opinions. The word "persuasion" is used for the process of gaining the audience's volitional, often also intellectual, assent to the speakers' will.... The speaker may (but need not) use argumentation in order to persuade the listener to obey him so that the latter becomes motivated to do something.[27]

Thus, the ultimate goal (consecutive effect) of demonstration is perception, whereas communication results in knowledge, argumentation in opinion, and persuasion in action.

Enthymemes versus Toulmin's Model

I shall now discuss some basic differences between "ancient" and modern perspectives on argumentation. A widely known, simple model by S. Toulmin, from the late 1950s, may serve here as an example of "modern" argumentation analysis, which, however, stays close to Aristotle and thus formally resembles a typical syllogistic model. Thereby the two can be easily compared.[28]

Toulmin's model is a fairly precise tool, which has three basic advantages compared with the three-phase syllogism. First, it does not consist of only three components. Second, each component has a specific function: *claim* (the opinion put forward), *data* (or grounds, specific information which supports the claim in a certain situation), *warrant* (a general rule indicating the relevance of the claim), *rebuttal* (states the circumstances under which the claim is valid), *backing* (general information implicitly included in warrant), and *qualifier* (expresses the probability to which the conclusion is correct).[29] The characterization of the internal functions of the components in argumentation is important especially when searching for its implicit premises: we obtain some specifications of the missing component, which guide the search and reduce the role of the interpreter's own (uncontrollable and misleading) creativity. Third, it enables us to see the open-endedness of

---

27. Thurén, "On Studying Ethical Argumentation," 469.
28. It is, however, good to know that Toulmin's model does not represent the cutting edge of modern argumentation analysis. More sophisticated and, perhaps, useful tools can be found, e.g., in Eemeren's textbook, *Fundamentals of Argumentation Theory*.
29. Toulmin, *Argument;* Toulmin, *Introduction,* 29–77. For a more detailed presentation, see Thurén, *Argument,* 41–46 and Eemeren et al., *Fundamentals of Argumentation Theory,* 129–60.

argumentation: between each component there is always an additional warrant, and behind every claim or backing can be glimpsed an extra train of thought.[30]

To be sure, there are many problems with applying Toulmin's model. People often fail to understand the aim of the analysis and the specific roles of different elements in the structure.[31] The differentiation between data and warrants seems to be especially difficult.[32] In addition the model does not take into account finality[33] or development in argumentative situations. Direct means of validating the argumentation are not provided, and the *pathos* effect is difficult to assess. Therefore the model must often be modified; yet in such a task its philosophical nature must be taken fully into account.

The theories of Perelman and Toulmin have occasionally been applied to biblical texts. Siegert actually claims that both ordinary Jewish and New Testament reasoning do not essentially differ from modern argumentation.[34] In my study of 1 Peter, a modified version of Toulmin's theory was used in order to illuminate the ideological background and structure of the motivation of the paraenesis. Apparently the model proved successful, although also complicated for some readers.[35]

I shall now demonstrate the difference between a syllogistic approach and a greatly simplified form of Toulmin's model. Instead of producing myself some Aristotelian analyses, I refer to two existing, carefully constructed studies of Pauline texts by using Aristotle.

Perhaps the main difference is found in the way implicit material is presented. The Achilles' heel of any mode of analyzing argumentation is the presentation of the statements in the text, viz., the derivation of explicit elements of argumentation. As the statements per se are seldom suited to the analysis, they have to be revised. However, this process easily resembles the

---

30. See Joseph W. Wenzel, "The Rhetorical Perspective on Argument," in Frans H. van Eemeren et al., eds., *Argumentation: Across the Lines* (Dordrecht: Foris, 1987), 101–9; Wenzel, *Perspective,* 106–7. For examples of applying Toulmin to a biblical text, see Thurén, *Argument.*

31. E.g., J. B. Freeman, "Relevance, Warrants, Backing, Inductive Support," *Argumentation* 6 (1992): 219–35; A. F. Snoeck Henkemans, *Analyzing Complex Argumentation: The Reconstruction of Multiple and Coordinatively Compound Argumentation in a Critical Discussion* (Amsterdam: SIC-SAT, 1992). For different applications of Toulmin's model in scholarship, see Thurén, *Argument,* 41 n. 36.

32. So also Eemeren et al., *Fundamentals of Argumentation Theory,* 158. Furthermore, their criticism (1987, 204f.; 1996, 159) on this point is based on a misunderstanding of the term warrant (See Thurén, *Argument,* 45 n. 46; M. Weinstein, "Toward an Account of Argumentation in Science," *Argumentation* 4 [1990]: 269–98).

33. K. Zappel, "Argumentation and Literary Texts," in F. H. van Eemeren et al., eds., *Argumentation: Analysis and Practices* (Dordrecht: Foris, 1987), 217; Thurén, *Argument,* 45.

34. Siegert, *Argumentation.*

35. For John H. Elliott, "Review of Thurén, Argument and Theology in 1 Peter," *CBQ* 59 (1997): 597–98, the presentation was "extremely difficult to follow."

subtle technique of narratio in ancient rhetoric: by a seemingly neutral presentation of the situation, where the author in fact slightly modifies the facts, the hearer is easily manipulated.[36]

Moreover, one of the most fruitful, but also difficult tasks, is to reveal hidden, implicit elements in an argumentative structure. Thereby the nature and possible weaknesses of the reasoning can be easily displayed. But this step is even more vulnerable than the presentation of the explicit statements. The deduction of the implicit elements must be as transparent as possible, so that everybody can see how it is done. Otherwise we cannot speak of a scholarly analysis. In both cases, Aristotle's simple syllogistic model for explicating enthymemes[37] has proven difficult.

1 Timothy 4:6–11

> (6) If you put these instructions before the brothers and sisters, you will be a good servant of Christ Jesus, nourished on the words of the faith and of the sound teaching that you have followed. (7) Have nothing to do with profane myths and old wives' tales. Train yourself in godliness (γύμναζε δὲ σεαυτὸν πρὸς εὐσέβειαν) (8) for, while physical training is of some value, godliness is valuable in every way, holding promise for both the present life and the life to come. (9) The saying is sure and worthy of full acceptance. (10) For to this end we toil and struggle, because we have our hope set on the living God, who is the Savior of all people, especially of those who believe. (11) These are the things you must insist on and teach.

Donelson constructs the following syllogism, which shows that "one should do something because it leads to salvation":

(A) Piety leads to life (salvation).

(B) Training can produce piety.

(C) If you want life, train yourself towards piety.

He then adds: "The...conclusion comes as an imperative. It is, of course, assumed that life or salvation is desirable."

I have difficulties in seeing how elements A, B, and C are derived, for none

---

36. See J. D. O'Banion, "Narration and Argumentation: Quintilian on Narratio as the Heart of Rhetorical Thinking," *Rhetorica* (1987): 325–51.

37. In practice, human reasoning is presented as simplistic formal logic, consisting of a major premise, a minor premise, and a conclusion; George A. Kennedy, *The Art of Persuasion in Greece* (Princeton, N.J.: Princeton University Press, 1963), 97.

of them is actually found in the text. The basic structure can be presented with a simplified Toulminian model (implicit factors in *italics*):[38]

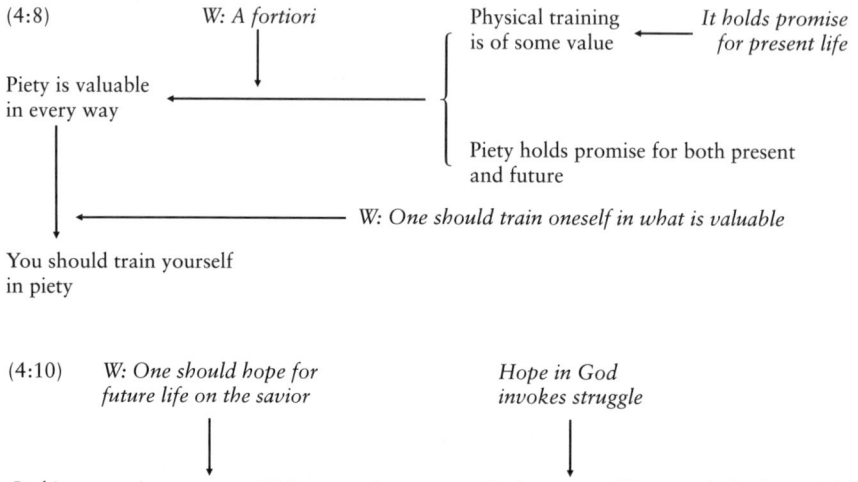

(4:8) W: *A fortiori*

Piety is valuable in every way

You should train yourself in piety

Physical training is of some value ← *It holds promise for present life*

Piety holds promise for both present and future

W: *One should train oneself in what is valuable*

(4:10) W: *One should hope for future life on the savior*

Hope in God invokes struggle

God is our savior → We have our hope set on God → We struggle for future life

How are the two trains of thought combined? Struggling for future life presumably corresponds to training oneself in piety. Then:

(4:8–10) W: *One should follow the example of those who have a savior (=are saved)*

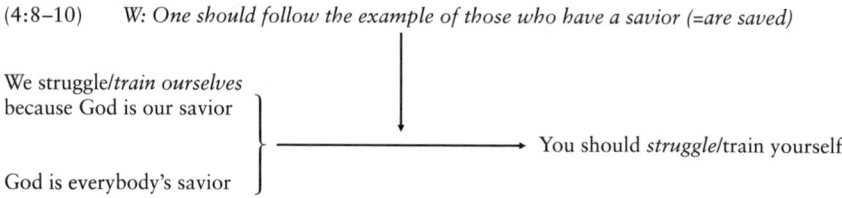

We struggle/*train ourselves* because God is our savior

God is everybody's savior

You should *struggle*/train yourself

The persuasive effect of verse 9 presumably depends on the *auctoritas* of the author. But the connection between training and salvation remains somewhat unclear. Is the motivating factor willingness to obtain salvation or joy in the salvation already bestowed by God? If the expression "God is our savior" can be rephrased "God has saved/will save us," the latter is to be preferred. At least the Aristotelian model hardly suffices for providing the solution.

---

38. In Toulmin's model, Data and Conclusions are connected with a Warrant, which has a different character when compared with the Data: it is a general rule (according to Karl-Heinz Göttert, *Argumentation* [Tübingen: Niemeyer, 1978], 28–29 "Schlussregel"). This characterization makes it easier to explicate the often unexpressed Warrants.

1 Corinthians 8:4–12

A more sophisticated example of applying a syllogistic model on the New Testament is offered by Eriksson. His pioneering study on Pauline argumentation is an important attempt to understand Paul's complex thinking. However, the actual analyses could benefit from further explication, or a methodological adjustment. In 1 Corinthians 8, the theological position of the wise is formulated as follows:[39]

> Major premise: There is only One God, 8:4c.
>
> Minor premise: The pagan gods are not real gods, 8:4b.
>
> Conclusion: Therefore, eating idol sacrifices is allowed.

Unfortunately, I cannot find any of these actual sentences in the text. It is also difficult to perceive the logic that could combine the three elements. Perhaps it is good to stay as close to the existing text as possible and study the theological positions as they are expressed there. Then the following simple structure can be suspected:

There is no idol or god ⟶ *Eating food offered to idols*
(except for one)   *is allowed*

This presentation is not, however, very illuminating. How is the existence of the idols and gods connected with food offered to them? Presumably it would be dangerous, if they existed.

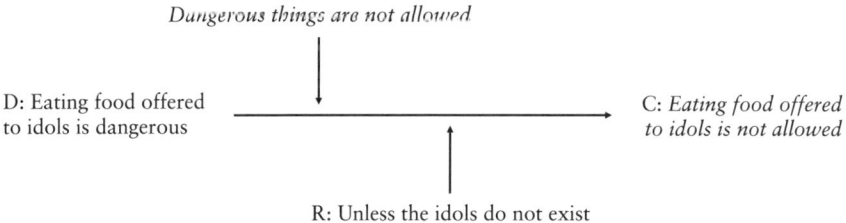

D: Eating food offered to idols is dangerous

Dangerous things are not allowed

C: *Eating food offered to idols is not allowed*

R: Unless the idols do not exist

Paul continues in verse 5–6, according to the syllogistic model:[40]

> Major premise: There are so-called gods, 8:5a
>   and they are in reality daemons.
>
> Minor premise: Eating idol sacrifices leads to fellowship
>   with these daemons.

---

39. Eriksson, *Traditions*, 154.
40. Eriksson, *Traditions*, 155.

Conclusion: Therefore, idol sacrifices should be shunned.

Again, it is difficult to find such a conclusion in the text. Whereas Paul in verse 4 referred to the "wise" Corinthians' thinking, he now only presents his own version. It seems to fit their thinking, but in fact paves the way for Paul's forthcoming reasoning.

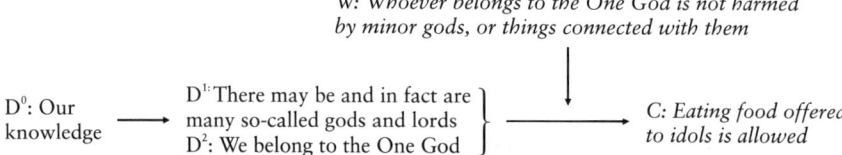

Only in verse 6 do we find the decisive signal "but" (*alla*), which means that Paul no longer agrees with the "wise" but adduces his counterarguments. In Toulmin's terminology, the reasoning in 6–12 could be called a rebuttal: Unless somebody lacks D^0.

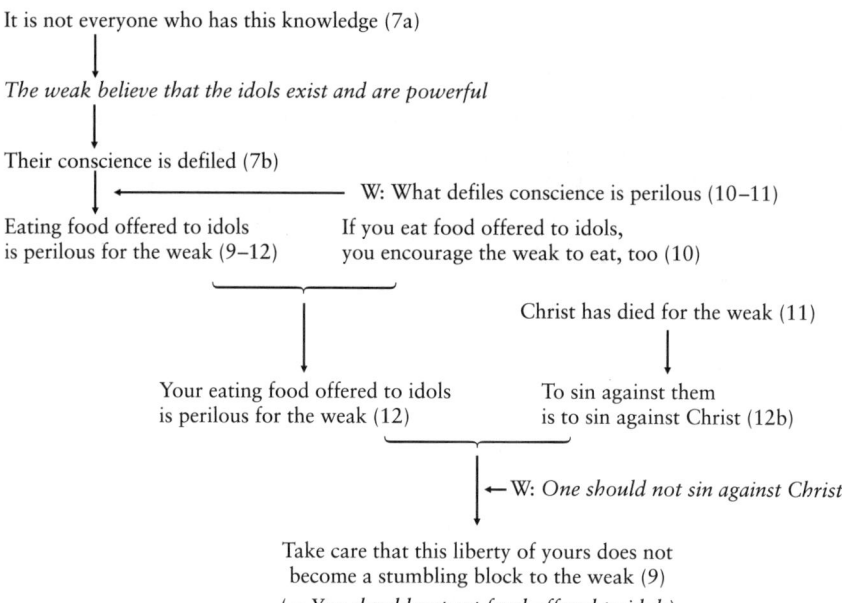

But Paul's chief thrust is not yet revealed: perhaps it is not merely to prevent the wise from eating, but to demonstrate that their knowledge (*gnosis*) and liberty is the main reason for the problems (1 Cor 8:11). The whole case thereby demonstrates the main problem in 1 Corinthians, discussed especially in chapter 13.

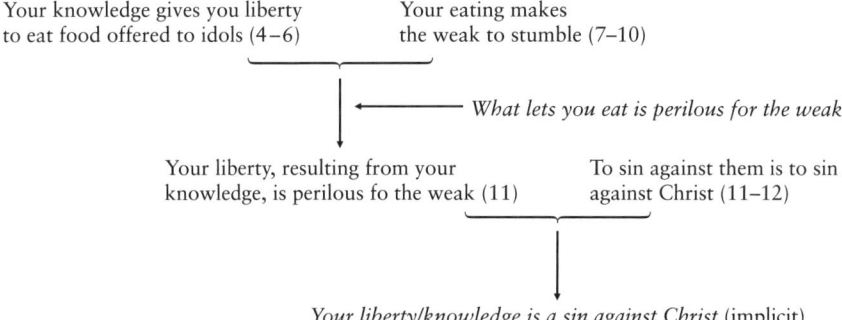

Even these presentations are simplified, for the argumentation is open-ended and implicit elements could be articulated ad infinitum. The main difference from the syllogistic model is, however, that Paul's subtle and careful line of reasoning becomes clearer. Paul cannot directly attack the gnosis, in this case the monotheistic thesis, on which the behavior of the "wise" is based. In fact he shares that gnosis, and perhaps has himself introduced it in Corinth.[41] Instead, he invites his addressees to a three-phased reasoning, where he first shows understanding of the addressees' thinking, but then illuminates its inherent dangers.

Such a technique is in fact typical for most questions discussed in 1 Corinthians. If Paul here states: "We know ... that there is no god," he can also, in just as astonishing a way, say that "all things are lawful for me" (1 Cor 6:12), when countering immorality,[42] or "strive for the greater *charismata*" (1 Cor 12:31) and "strive for the spiritual gifts" (1 Cor 14:1), when moderating the recipients' over-enthusiasm. Without proper analysis, such sentences are either ignored or misunderstood.

Ideological, Religious Reasoning Is *Different*

The question of methodology ultimately depends on the goals. Whereas the only possible reason for using ancient approaches is an historical aim, there are two general objectives for modern argumentation analysis. Eemeren,

---

41. Lauri Thurén, *Derhetorizing Paul* (WUNT 1/124, Tübingen: Mohr, 2000), 102–4.
42. See Thurén, *Derhetorizing,* 104.

Grootendorst, and Kruiger claim that the analysis must always enable us to "differentiate between sound and unsound argumentation," and since both Toulmin and Perelman fail to do so, they are "of no direct practical significance." The Dutch scholars, however, presuppose that the aim of the analysis is "a reasoned improvement in the practice of arguing."[43] When studying historical texts, such a *normative* goal is seldom justifiable, especially if it rules out the *descriptive* alternative, viz., the study of how the biblical authors reasoned, developed their ideas, and manipulated their readers.

To be sure, even when studying the Bible it is interesting to know whether the thinking in a particular text is "logical, rational, civilized, sound," or "happy." Is the reasoning reliable or based on fallacies? But such questions are especially suited to analyzing, for example, juridical decisions or political reasoning. The alternative is descriptive research: the analysis only illuminates the way argumentation proceeds, without taking a stand for or against it.

However, even a primarily descriptive approach à la Toulmin or Perelman provides tools for criticizing argumentation.[44] What makes such a study critical is its potential to explicate and characterize the implicit, unvoiced elements — premises, warrants, backings — which are essential for the reasoning. Thereby the study enables the reader to decide whether he or she is willing to accept even the unexpressed factors and thereby the whole train of thought.

I have argued above that ancient texts deserve the same methods as other texts, unless something specifically culture-bound can be demonstrated. But what are such features in early Jewish or Christian religious persuasion? If they are not attributable to the ancient cultures *per se*, could it be due to the religious nature of such texts?

Religious argumentation, or any ideological argumentation, is not identical with, for example, juridical or modern political reasoning, and this imposes also some methodological requirements. Seen from a normative point of view, much of religious reasoning is problematic indeed. Many chains of thought could be directly classified as fallacies. But this is not due to lacking logical ability, or to the age of the texts, but to their ideological and religious character. Many argumentative techniques in the Bible were disliked by ancient theorists as well as modern scholars.

Burton Mack has pointed out how *appeal to authority* is typical of Early Christian reasoning.[45] Such a reference to authority can be poor reasoning

---

43. Eemeren et al., *Handbook*, 268.
44. *Pace* Eemeren et al., *Handbook*, 267–68.
45. Burton Mack, *Rhetoric and the New Testament* (GBS; Minneapolis: Fortress Press, 1990), 96,

indeed,[46] but it is widely used and often effective argumentation.[47] And if the audience believes that there is an existing, active God, and that the speaker reliably represents God's opinions, what could be a stronger proof than to refer to those opinions? For example: "Anyone who claims to be a prophet, or to have spiritual powers, must acknowledge that what I am writing to you is a command of the Lord" (1 Cor 14:37).

Other examples include such techniques as threats and repetition. Both are common in the New Testament. Thus the following verse threatens with a *passivum divinum* and judgment: "Anyone who does not recognize this is not to be recognized" (1 Cor 14:38).[48] Using *repetitio* is not very civilized either, but it is part of everyday persuasion, also in the Bible. For example, 1 Peter reiterates the same commandments and arguments.[49] Moreover, the use of pompous style, including rare or invented, complicated words and expressions, was also an effective means of manipulating ethos and pathos, as a (misleading) picture of the author's education and professional qualities was thereby conveyed.[50] Many other examples could be mentioned.

Nevertheless, they do not prove that there is any special biblical branch of argumentation, which requires a holy method. Perhaps only appeal to a divine authority is specific for religious argumentation. But such appeals are not recommended by the great teachers of ancient oratory, and in modern normative studies they would usually be labeled as fallacies, which is hardly a value-free label in a neutral study. Yet even such a normative perspective is useful when reading holy texts, for even if no ultimate decisions concerning the validity were made, it is interesting to study the degree to which the argumentation appears sound and reliable.

As an alternative, even the above-mentioned techniques can be conveniently approached with any good *descriptive* method. The first reason for using a descriptive approach is presented by 2 Peter 3:16. The author, speaking of Paul's writings, asserts, "there are some things in them hard to understand." Most of Paul's modern readers may share the ancient critic's experience. To explicate and illuminate the way in which Paul develops his ideas is an important goal in itself.

---

referring to the practice of appealing to external authorities, such as Jesus, the Holy Spirit, or God. This kind of appeal to special authorization was, according to Mack, unusual in Greek argumentation.

46. Perelman, *Rhetoric*, 305–10; Toulmin, *Introduction*, 142–44.

47. Perelman, *Rhetoric*, 306.

48. For the interpretation and textual criticism, see Gordon Fee, *The First Epistle to the Corinthians* (NICNT; Grand Rapids: Eerdmans, 1987), 712.

49. See Thurén, *Argument*.

50. For the functional use of style in 2 Peter, see Lauri Thurén, "Style Never Goes out of Fashion — 2 Peter Re-evaluated," in *Rhetoric, Scripture and Theology* (ed. S. Porter and T. Olbricht; JSNTSup 131; Sheffield: Sheffield Academic Press 1996), 329–47.

The underlying ideological or theological structure can also be better displayed. When studying the motivation of paraenesis in 1 Peter, it soon became clear that scholars have two opposite views of its theological foundation. However, their most important argument was that of (their own) *auctoritas*. Different opinions among scholars, or in 1 Peter, were not refuted, they were merely omitted. And, *mirabile dictu,* both opinions could be well substantiated with the Epistle, when difficult verses were not discussed. However, a modified version of Toulmin's analysis enabled me to study all the motivating expressions in the Epistle and combine them in a single underlying theological system.

But there is more: a modern approach to argumentation lets us excavate implicit factors in Pauline argumentation. This not only clarifies the Apostle's thinking, but also enables a critical view: when the implicit elements are displayed, it is easier to decide whether they are theologically acceptable.

In Defense of Scholarly Exegesis

The analysis of biblical argumentation is still in *statu nascendi*. The most common modern methods used are based on an early phase in developing modern theories of argumentation. It may be presumed that more sophisticated approaches, currently discussed by argumentation theorists, could shed more light in biblical reasoning. This is not just a matter of better results, but of the essence of New Testament scholarship in general. It would be useful for biblical scholars to return to the thesis of the founding fathers of New Testament exegesis. According to Jean Alphonse Turretini, there should be no holy means for studying the Holy Scriptures. The same methods should be applied to the Bible as to any other literature.[51]

---

51. J. A. Turretini, *De Sacrae Scripturae interpretandi methodo tractatus bipartitus* (Dordrecht, 1728).

PART TWO

HISTORICAL BACKGROUND

CHAPTER 5

THEORIES AND PRACTICE OF THE ENTHYMEME IN THE FIRST CENTURIES B.C.E. AND C.E.

Manfred Kraus

"What, then, was an enthymeme? — Oxford! Thou wilt think us mad to ask." This famous sentence, coined in 1828 by Thomas De Quincey in a review of Richard Whately's *Elements of Rhetoric*[1] and aimed at the inveterate Oxonian tradition of sticking unswervingly to the definition of the enthymeme as an incomplete or truncated syllogism, i.e., a syllogism with one premise unexpressed, is quoted by Thomas Conley in his important and in many respects groundbreaking article on the enthymeme.[2] Any definition of the enthymeme, Conley concludes, based upon his research, "depends on whose view you are referring to. By the same token, it appears that one would not be at all mad to ask the question."[3] This conclusion seems all the more true for the first centuries B.C.E. and C.E., in which the theory of the enthymeme gets more complicated and intricate than ever before or after. But most of the many books and articles dedicated to the study of the enthymeme since the beginning of the twentieth century[4] are concerned either with Aristotle's theory of the enthymeme only, or with the medieval and modern interpretation of the enthymeme as an incomplete syllogism. Only very few take any interest at all in what Myles Burnyeat calls "continuing the history,"[5] and Conley refers to as "the later career of the term."[6] Conley therefore is perfectly right to say that here one is "moving into relatively unexplored territory."[7]

On the other hand, if one ventures to trace and analyze enthymemes in

---

1. Thomas De Quincey, "Elements of Rhetoric," *Blackwood's Edinburgh Magazine* 24 (1828): 886.
2. Thomas M. Conley, "The Enthymeme in Perspective," *QJS* 70 (1984): 168.
3. Conley, "Enthymeme," 179.
4. For a survey see Carol Poster, "The Enthymeme: An Interdisciplinary Bibliography," *Journal for the Study of Rhetorical Criticism of the New Testament* (http://rhetjournal.uor.edu/Enth.html).
5. Myles F. Burnyeat, "Enthymeme: Aristotle on the Logic of Persuasion," in *Aristotle's Rhetoric: Philosophical Essays* (ed. David J. Furley and Alexander Nehamas; Princeton, N.J.: Princeton University Press, 1994): 39–46.
6. Conley, "Enthymeme," 174.
7. Ibid. Before Conley and Burnyeat, apparently only James H. McBurney ("The Place of the Enthymeme in Rhetorical Theory," *Speech Monographs* 3 [1936]: 68–71) devoted appropriate attention to this period.

New Testament texts, one is probably well advised first to determine the actual characteristics of an enthymeme in the relevant period, in other words, that which was designated an enthymeme among rhetoricians and ordinary people of the first century C.E.

Quintilian's Summary

If we first turn to Quintilian, whom we might most reasonably expect to provide a reliable survey of the state of the theory of the enthymeme among rhetoricians in the second half of the first century C.E., that is, one contemporary with the corpus of the Pauline letters, we find the following definition (*Inst.* 5.10.1–3):

> "Enthymeme" (which we translate by *commentum* or *commentatio*, there being no alternative, though we had better use the Greek name) has three meanings: firstly, it means anything conceived in the mind (this is not, however, the sense of which I am now speaking); secondly it signifies a sentence with a reason, and thirdly a conclusion of an argument drawn either from consequents (*ex consequentibus*) or from incompatibles (*ex repugnantibus*); although there is some controversy on this point. For there are some who style a conclusion from consequents an epicheireme, while it will be found that the majority hold the view that an enthymeme is a conclusion from incompatibles only: wherefore Cornificius calls it a "contrariety" (*contrarium*). Some again have called it a rhetorical syllogism, others an incomplete syllogism, because its parts are not so clearly distinct or of the same number as those of the regular syllogism, since such precision is not specially required of the orator.

Quintilian apparently is at a loss as to what to declare his own days' mainstream theory. He offers instead a mere summary of different views, which, to say the least, is somewhat inconsistent.

The first meaning Quintilian mentions is the oldest, pre-Aristotelian meaning of "enthymeme." For fourth century orators such as Isocrates or Alcidamas the word very generally refers to thoughts or arguments expressed in a speech, sometimes to especially pointed or pungent remarks.[8] "Thought" is indeed what the word most basically means. Roman rhetoricians are still conscious of this broad and unspecific meaning of "enthymeme."[9]

The second meaning, a sentence (or maxim, γνώμη in Greek) accompanied by a reason, has a long history, too. It is discussed by Aristotle as well as by Roman rhetoricians.[10] It is sometimes regarded as a special case of the

---

8. Isocrates, *Or.*, 9.10; 12.2; 13.16; 15.47; Alcidamas, *On the Sophists*, 3–4; 18–20; 24–25; 33; Aeschines, *Or.*, 2.110; see Conley, "Enthymeme," 172.
9. See Cicero, *Topica*, 55; Quintilian, *Inst.*, 8.5.9.
10. Aristotle, *Rhet.*, 2.21.1394a31–b6; *Rhet. Her.*, 4.24f.; Quintilian, *Inst.*, 8.5.11.

truncated syllogism type, since it consists of two propositions only: the maxim and a reason or rationale, which functions as the explicitly stated premise of an incomplete syllogism.

Quintilian dismisses both these meanings very quickly. The crucial definition for him is the third, the rhetorical meaning proper. But here the problems only just begin, for the various strands of theory that have emerged in the preceding two centuries have grown so divergent that any attempt to merge them into one coherent theory must fail.

Early Roman Rhetoric: The Enthymeme as a Figure of Speech

After Aristotle's outstanding, but also very individual treatment of the subject, there is a long period of complete silence on the enthymeme. The library of Aristotle's school, including the *Rhetoric* and the *Analytics,* got lost temporarily and was thus inaccessible until the first century B.C.E. Of rhetorical treatises from the Hellenistic period not many traces are extant. Theophrastus's book on the enthymeme[11] is lost. The few fragments preserved of Hermagoras of Temnus (second century B.C.E.) say nothing about the enthymeme. And the treatise *On Style* by Pseudo-Demetrius of Phaleron, which does mention it, is now dated to the first rather than the second or third century B.C.E.[12]

Even after these dark ages, when the first documents of Roman rhetoric emerge in the early first century B.C.E., the word "enthymeme" itself is still absent. Neither the anonymous *Rhetorica ad Herennium* (probably around 85 B.C.E.), nor Cicero's *De inventione* (ca. 82 B.C.E.), nor his *De oratore* (55 B.C.E.) say as much as a word about it. To be precise, they never mention *enthymema* (or whatever Latin equivalent) in sections dealing with invention or argumentation and proof.

Instead, in regard to deductive argumentation, both the *Rhetorica ad Herennium* and Cicero in *De inventione* choose to recommend rather lengthy and cumbersome types of argument, each consisting of no less than five parts. What the *Rhetorica ad Herennium* calls a "complete and perfect argument" consists of the thesis of the problem (*propositio*), a reason (*ratio*), the proof of the reason (*rationis confirmatio*), an embellishment (*exornatio*) and a conclu-

---

11. Diogenes Laertius, 5.47.
12. See *Demetrius On Style, together with Aristotle's Poetics and Longinus's On the Sublime* (ed. and trans. Doreen C. Innes; Cambridge: Harvard University Press, 1995), 312–21.

sive summary (*complexio*).¹³ While this argument is definitely rhetorical in character, Cicero's is more of a logical kind. His *ratiocinatio* (deductive argument) is an expanded form of a traditional three part syllogism, i.e., exactly the type of argument that would later be called an epicheireme; it consists of two premises, major (*propositio*) and minor (*assumptio*), their respective proofs or backings (*approbationes*) and a conclusion (*complexio*).¹⁴ Both also allow for four-part or three-part arguments by occasionally dropping parts of secondary importance, but Cicero openly rejects any possibility of arguments with less than three parts.¹⁵

The reason is that Cicero draws upon Stoic rather than Peripatetic sources, and the Stoics would not allow for any logically invalid or formally incomplete argument even in a rhetorical context. For them, the same types of arguments were appropriate for rhetoric as well as for dialectics. They even held that while dialectics had to be short and precise, rhetoric could be lengthy and verbose.¹⁶ This Stoic view is clearly contrary to that of Aristotle, who frequently states that it is the orator who may to his advantage express himself more briefly than the dialectician, who is obliged to present every step of his argument explicitly. On a theoretical basis like this, therefore, for a short and pungent argument like the enthymeme there seems to be no place in rhetoric.

Is early classical Roman rhetoric then totally ignorant of the enthymeme? The answer is no. For in the fourth book of the *Rhetorica ad Herennium,* a book entirely devoted to problems of style, a figure called *contrarium* occurs in a long list of figures of speech.¹⁷ It is described as a form of expression "which, of two opposite statements, uses one so as neatly and directly to prove the other." The author illustrates with several examples, e.g.: "Now how should you expect one who has ever been hostile to his own interests to be friendly to another's?" Or: "Now why should you think that one who is, as you have learned, a faithless friend, can be an honorable enemy?" Or again: "Do we fear to fight them on the plains when we have hurled them down from the hills?" Of course, in each of these examples, one or two pairs of opposites are involved (own interests versus another's; hostile versus friendly; friend

---

13. *Rhet. Her.*, 2.28–30; see Anders Eriksson, *Traditions as Rhetorical Proof: Pauline Argumentation in 1 Corinthians* (Stockholm: Almqvist & Wiksell, 1998), 57–58.
14. Cicero, *Inv.*, 1.57–72. For a graphic description, see Frans H. van Eemeren, Rob Grootendorst, and Tjark Kruiger, *Handbook of Argumentation Theory: A Critical Survey of Classical Backgrounds and Modern Studies* (Dordrecht: Foris, 1987), 75–76; also Eemeren, *Fundamentals of Argumentation Theory: A Handbook of Historical Backgrounds and Contemporary Developments* (Mahwah, N.J.: Lawrence Erlbaum Assoc., 1996), 48–49.
15. *Rhet. Her.*, 2.28; 30; Cicero, *Inv.*, 1.70–75.
16. Sextus Empiricus, *Adversus mathematicos,* 2.7.
17. *Rhet. Her.*, 4.25–26.

versus enemy; faithless versus honorable; plains versus hills). But what is being demonstrated is not simply the stylistic figure of antithesis. The author makes it obvious that the figure in question is generally used for the purpose of proof (*confirmat*).

If we further remember that Quintilian mentions a certain Cornificius who used to call the enthymeme by the name of *contrarium,* we can be confident that here, too, what is really meant is a kind of enthymeme. The argument in question certainly is what one would call a topical enthymeme, i.e., an enthymeme that derives its persuasive force from a certain argumentative topos. It is, however, not identical with the enthymeme "from contraries" that Aristotle has in his list of topical enthymemes in the *Rhetoric* (e.g., "if war is a bad thing, peace must be a good thing"),[18] for in this case the first example would have to run: "Who is hostile to his own interests, will be *friendly* to another's." Here, however, the conclusion is exactly the contrary: that person will be *even less* friendly (= *even more* hostile) to another's interests. So rather another topos, the topos *a maiore ad minus* or *a minore ad maius,* is involved.[19] The other examples are to be analyzed accordingly: Who is a faithless friend, will be an even less honorable (= even more perfidious) enemy. Those defeated easily on the hills, will be even easier to fight on the plains. The rhetorical question, of course, in every case is tantamount to a negation ("How should you expect...?" = "you should not expect..."; "do we fear...?" = "we cannot possibly fear..."). It is important, however, that the author expresses all his examples in the form of a rhetorical question, since this turns out to be a typical predilection of the Romans.

No less important is the fact that the author assigns to the enthymeme a place primarily among figures of speech. He regards it as a special means of embellishment that ought to be briefly and tightly completed within one unbroken period. But at the same time he calls it a "vehement" proof, an inference of what is doubtful from what is not called in doubt.

At all times three main factors have contributed to the concept of the enthymeme: First, a logical factor: The enthymeme is associated with or at least compared to a deductive inference or even a syllogism. It is the rhetorical counterpart to philosophy's deductive syllogism, or, more cautiously put, an "assertion that is expressible as a syllogism."[20] Second, a psychological and audience-oriented factor: An enthymeme pays respect to the socio-cultural

---

18. Aristotle, *Rhet.*, 2.23.1397a7–19.
19. See Aristotle, *Rhet.*, 2.23.1397b12–29.
20. Vernon Robbins, "From Enthymeme to Theology in Luke 11:1-3," in *Literary Studies in Luke-Acts: A Collection of Essays in Honor of Joseph B. Tyson* (ed. R. P. Thompson and T. E. Phillips; Macon, Ga.: Mercer University Press, 1998), 191.

background of its audience. It proceeds not from scientific axioms, but from preconceived opinions shared by the audience or a majority of them. As a consequence, it generally does not attain absolute truth, but still convincing plausibility. Moreover, it leaves to the audience something to think or infer themselves. Thus the inference is successfully drawn as a result of "the joint efforts of speaker and audience."[21] Third, a stylistic factor: An enthymeme will be expressed in a short, pungent, and witty manner, employing strong and powerful figures of speech, of which antithesis is only one. In different periods, however, others of these factors predominated, which at least partly accounts for the complex and manifold history of the term.

In the earliest period of Roman rhetoric in the first half of the first century B.C.E., it is clearly the stylistic element that prevails. Cicero, too, in *De oratore* (55 B.C.E.), lists *contrarium* among figures.[22] Inasmuch as he does not set out any examples, we cannot ascertain whether he, too, is referring to a kind of enthymeme. This, at least, is what Quintilian suspects, judging from the fact that later in the *Orator* (46 B.C.E.) Cicero removes *contrarium* completely from his list of figures, apparently because he has realized that it does not really belong there.[23]

This predominantly stylistic view of the enthymeme might seem a radical break with the tradition of Aristotle, who had most strongly stressed its argumentative character. But not only were Aristotle's works hardly known at that time, but the element of stylistic pungency was already present even in pre-Aristotelian sources such as Isocrates. Aristotle himself, after all, several times mentions antithesis as a characteristic feature of enthymemes or even pseudo-enthymemes, which manage to look like real enthymemes precisely by imitating their typical outward appearance.[24] It may thus well be that the stylistic approach had already gained ground during Hellenistic times without it coming to our attention due to lack of sources.

Cicero's Topica: *The Enthymeme from Incompatibles as a Stoic Syllogism*

We have to wait until Cicero's *Topica* (44 B.C.E.) for the first clear-cut Latin analysis of the enthymeme in terms of argumentation and logic. In a section of this work Cicero expounds a number of "forms of conclusion" the orator

---

21. Lloyd F. Bitzer, "Aristotle's Enthymeme Revisited," *QJS* 45 (1959): 408.
22. Cicero, *De or.*, 3.207.
23. Quintilian, *Inst.*, 9.3.90; cf. Cicero, *Orator*, 135.
24. Aristotle, *Rhet.*, 2.21.1394b20–26; 23.1400b26–29; 24.1401a5–8; cf. 3.9.1410a20–24; see Burnyeat, "Enthymeme," 42.

may use for purposes of proof.²⁵ These "forms of conclusion," of course, are syllogisms, or more precisely Stoic syllogisms. For by Cicero's time Stoic logic, differing from Aristotelian logic in that it is a logic of propositions, not of terms, was by far more popular than its Peripatetic rival, although there were also tendencies to amalgamate the two paradigms. The syllogisms Cicero presents are the so-called "indemonstrables" or basic syllogisms of Stoic logic.²⁶ They were termed so, because according to the Stoic philosopher Chrysippus they did not need demonstration, but were self-evident. Their number varies in different sources; originally there seem to have been only five, but Cicero has seven. They are partly hypothetical, partly conjunctive, partly disjunctive syllogisms, but all of them have a tripartite rule-case-result structure, too.²⁷

Now the third "indemonstrable" consists of the negation of a conjunction of propositions, plus the position of one of the conjunctional members, which results in the elimination of the other member.²⁸ In symbolic language: $\neg (p \wedge q) \wedge p \rightarrow \neg q$ (rule: not at the same time p and q; case: but p; result: therefore not q; for example, rule: not at the same time: it is day and it is night; case: but it is day; result: therefore it is not night). Cicero additionally claims that one of the conjunctional members should be negative; the conclusion will then be positive. And he explicitly adds that this form of argument which (Stoic) logicians refer to as the third type of syllogism, is called ἐνθύμημα by teachers of rhetoric. While basically any expression of thought may be called ἐνθύμημα, the one based on contraries (*ex contrariis*), as it appears to be the most pointed form of argument, has, as it were, appropriated the common name for itself. It is evident that the major premise (rule) in this type of syllogism expresses an incompatibility. So what we have here is a logical analysis of the enthymeme from incompatibles (*ex repugnantibus sententiis*). In fact, the examples of *contrarium* enthymemes in the *Rhetorica ad Herennium* can likewise easily be analyzed in this way. Cicero thus lays a theoretical, logical basis for the type of enthymeme we already met in the earlier work. It may be remarked, incidentally, that the demonstration of some incompatibility already formed the core of the definition of the enthymeme in the so-called *Rhetoric to Alexander* (now generally ascribed to Anaximenes

---

25. Cicero, *Topica,* 53–57.
26. See Diogenes Laertius 7.79–81; Sextus Empiricus, *Pyrrhonian Hypotheses,* 2.157–58; Quintilian, *Inst.*, 5.8.4.
27. On the triad of rule, case, and result, introduced by C. S. Peirce, see Anders Eriksson, this volume p. 248.
28. Cicero, *Topica,* 55–56.

of Lampsacus), which is roughly contemporary to or perhaps even earlier than Aristotle's *Rhetoric*.[29]

Cicero illustrates this pattern of reasoning by four examples:

1. Fear this, and not dread the other!
2. You condemn the woman whom you accuse of nothing?
3. You deserve ill of the woman (or: you say that the woman deserves ill)[30] whom you assert to deserve well?
4. What you know is of no use; is what you do not know then detrimental?

All these examples are in iambic verse and therefore certainly taken from some unknown Roman tragedy or tragedies.[31] The last three are also quoted by Cicero in the *Orator* for their rhythmical qualities.[32] But again we find the rhetorical questions typical of Roman enthymemes, or, in the first example, an indignant exclamation.

These examples are each stated in extremely succinct form. Elaborated in full tripartite length,[33] the first example would read: rule: not at the same time: fear this, and not fear the other; case: but you fear this; result: therefore you should fear the other, too. I do not agree with Burnyeat and others who hold that this example, by virtue of the exclamation mark, should express two contrary commands ("Fear this, but don't dread the other!").[34] Apart from the fact that punctuation in ancient texts is always liable to interpretation, this cannot be the sense of this line; for in a letter to Atticus, Cicero uses the same quotation to illustrate how absurd it is to have been afraid of Caesar, and nonetheless not to fear Antony.[35] No, the indignant exclamation, too, just like a rhetorical question, must amount to the negation of the second conjunctional member. The relationship between "this" and "the other" may be a climax like in many of the examples in *Rhetorica ad Herennium* (e.g., "Fear a dog, and not dread a lion!").

Accordingly, the second example reads: rule: not at the same time: no accusation *and* condemnation; case: no accusation; result: therefore no condemnation either. Here the second member is positive, the result therefore negative. The third example is exactly parallel: rule: not at the same time:

---

29. *Rhetorica ad Alexandrum*, 10.1430a23–36; 14.1431a29–35.
30. The Latin text is slightly uncertain here, depending on whether one reads *merere* or *mereri*.
31. *Tragicorum Romanorum Fragmenta* (ed. Otto Ribbeck; Leipzig: B. G. Teubner, 1871), nos. 110; 107; 108.
32. Cicero, *Orator*, 166.
33. For a thorough logical analysis, see Boethius, *In Ciceronis Topica commentaria*, 5, *Patrologia Latina* 64, 1142C–1144B.
34. See Burnyeat, "Enthymeme," 42, note 110.
35. Cicero, *Epistulae ad Atticum*, 14.21.3.

asserting she deserves well and doing her bad service (saying she deserves ill); case: you assert she deserves well; result: therefore you should not do her bad service (not say she deserves ill). Evidently, in that scene, some mythical woman (Alcmena? Medea?) has been accused by a man who has neither right nor reason to do so.

The fourth example is less clear: It seems to say that if what one knows has no good effects, what one does not know can't have any bad effects either. But without any context, the sense of this statement remains opaque.

From a logical point of view, this type of argument in itself is absolutely sound. The perceptibly probabilistic ring in Cicero's examples derives from the kind of incompatibilities they proceed from. It is here exactly that the audience's preconceived opinions, the ἔνδοξα, come in. It is, for instance, absolutely debatable whether having nothing to reproach a person of is strictly incompatible with condemning him or her (in a sense like its being day is incompatible with its being night); this is neither a fact proven by science nor a logical truism (and many counter-examples from history testify to the contrary). Common sense, however, would probably approve of this maxim. It is only for this reason that the argument works.

The strong and exclusive commitment to the enthymeme drawn from contradictions or incompatibles appears to be a common feature of classical Roman rhetoric of the first century B.C.E. Its interpretation as a primarily stylistic device and its classification among figures rather than arguments because of its markedly antithetical structure is a corollary to that. Quintilian explicitly ascribes the same view to several minor rhetoricians of the first centuries B.C.E. and C.E. (Visellius, Gorgias of Athens, Rutilius Lupus, Cornelius Celsus).[36] And much later writers such as Iulius Victor or Iulius Rufinianus (fourth century C.E.) still testify to this Roman predilection.[37]

The "Ciceronian" Enthymeme in Practice

In his own speeches Cicero only very rarely uses the full five-part epicheireme he recommends in *De inventione*.[38] Instead, in speeches from all periods of his career, he makes ample use of the enthymeme from incompatibles, often long before its formal analysis in the *Topica,* as for instance in *Pro*

---

36. Quintilian, *Inst.*, 10.2.106.
37. Rufinianus, *De figuris,* 30, *Rhetores Latini Minores,* ed. K. Halm, 45.27–33; Iulius Victor, *Ars rhetorica,* 11, *Rhetores Latini Minores,* ed. Halm, 412.22–413.31.
38. Rudolph Preiswerk, *De inventione orationum Ciceronianarum* (Basel: Friedrich Reinhardt, 1905), 101–2, counts only six passages: *Pro Quinctio,* 48–50; *Pro Tullio,* 41–42; *Pro Caecina,* 41–43; *Pro Murena,* 3–5; *Pro Rabirio perduellionis reo,* 29–30; *Pro Archia poeta,* 18–19.

Quinctio (81 B.C.E.): "Who decides that what is fair for Quinctius is unfair for Naevius?... So you demand that I should admit this, so that we may by our own verdict confirm the existence of this possession which we maintain in this case does not exist?"[39] Likewise in *Pro Caecina* (69/68): "Shall not that which is called force in war be called the same in peace? Shall that which is termed vigour in the conduct of a soldier be adjudged as mildness under citizen law?... Can you deny the cause when you admit the effect?"[40] Later still in *Pro Milone* (52): "Was he resolved then to kill to the dissatisfaction of some a man whom he refused to kill to the satisfaction of all?"[41] But also contemporaneously with the *Topica* in *Philippics 2* (44): "What is more shameful than that he who set on the diadem (sc. Antony) should be living, while all confess that he who flung it away (sc. Caesar) was rightly slain?"[42]

Again, we note the typical phrasing in rhetorical questions, which is almost a stereotype.[43] It is remarkable how frequently arguments of this peculiar pattern occur in Cicero's speeches.[44] Compared with their number, straight inferential arguments are definitely a minority. Obviously, in the *Topica* Cicero only describes what he and others have been practicing long since.

On the other hand, the prominent outward features of this kind of argument could easily be exploited for feigning enthymemes. A sentence showing antitheses and rhetorical questions, but not based on an incompatibility, was judged "a worthless and faulty enthymeme" by Cicero's secretary Tiro.[45] Nevertheless, the term "enthymeme" was sometimes also used in a colloquial sense to designate any witty or pungent phrase added as a "cap" or "tag" to the end of a longer chain of reasoning, in the sense of an epiphonema.[46]

By the second half of the first century B.C.E. this "Ciceronian" type of enthymeme appears to have been officially taught in rhetors' classrooms. In the Elder Seneca's *Controversiae* and *Suasoriae*, which collect his memories of the rhetors' schools and famous declaimers of his time, this kind of argument recurs constantly. A few random examples may illustrate this: "Are you a hero's son, you who cannot draw a sword?" "Can we be poor if we have something that rich men ask for?" "Does a father-in-law propose to sever a

---

39. Cicero, *Pro Quinctio*, 45.
40. *Pro Caecina*, 43–44.
41. *Pro Milone*, 41.
42. *Philippics 2*, 86.
43. For a similar argumentative function of questions in a Jewish context, see Roland Meynet, this volume pp. 200–214.
44. For further examples, see e.g., *Pro Quinctio*, 38–39; 62; 76; *Pro Sex. Roscio Amerino*, 113; *Pro Q. Roscio comoedo*, 5; 8; *In Verrem*, 2.3.82; *Pro Balbo*, 12; *Pro Milone*, 79.
45. Gellius, *Noctes Atticae*, 6.3.26–27.
46. Gellius 1.4.2; 12.2.14; 17.20.4–5; see Conley, "Enthymeme," 178.

couple whom even death will not sever?" "Do you suppose that he forgives you, he who is enraged by your genius?"[47]

While handbooks like Cicero's may not have reached the general public, for the popularization of a specific rhetorical device rhetors' schools were an important disseminator. Declamations, attended by large audiences, made oratorial techniques familiar to ordinary people not explicitly trained in rhetoric. The classroom routine also influenced everyday public speech. Persons without rhetorical training would intuitively identify (and employ) a typical pattern of reasoning, even though they could not specify its technical appellation.

It is thus not unreasonable to search for enthymemes of the Ciceronian type even in New Testament texts. And indeed arguments of this kind are not infrequent, for example, in Paul's letters. A particularly fine example is Romans 2:21–23, where five such enthymemes follow in line:

> You, therefore, who teach another, do you not teach yourself? You who preach that one shall not steal, do you steal? You who say that one should not commit adultery, do you commit adultery? You who abhor idols, do you rob temples? You who boast in the law, through your breaking the law, do you dishonor God?

Evidently, Paul's readers are meant to understand that teaching others and not teaching oneself, and urging others not to steal and stealing oneself, and so on, are pairs of incompatibles. So those who commit themselves to one side of the conjunction must needs refrain from the other. Even the phrasing of the argument in the form of a rhetorical question, which is tantamount to a negation or, in this case, a prohibition, closely follows the typically Roman type of enthymeme.

Some further examples from the many in Paul's letters include: "He who did not spare His own son, but delivered Him over for us all, how will He not also with Him freely give us all things?" (Rom 8:32); "You cannot drink the cup of the Lord and the cup of demons; you cannot partake of the table of the Lord and the table of demons. Or do we provoke the Lord to jealousy? We are not stronger than He, are we?" (1 Cor 10:21–22).

Enthymemes from Consequents and from Incompatibles

A peculiar feature of Quintilian's account of the enthymeme is his dichotomy between an enthymeme from consequents and one from incompatibles. Quintilian has not invented this classification himself. He even, in slight ironical

---

47. Seneca maior, *Controversiae*, 1.4.1; 2.1.4; 2.2.1; *Suasoriae*, 7.7.

detachment, refers to it as to the mystical doctrine of persons who treat oratory like a profound mystery.[48] Quintilian is probably hinting here at some unknown Greek rhetors of the first century c.e., upon whom he is drawing.

In fact, we happen to know a few names of minor Greek rhetors, whose theories roughly coincide with Quintilian's, such as Neocles, Valerius Harpocration, Alexander son of Numenius, and Rufus of Perinthus. Unfortunately, with the possible exception of Neocles, these are all slightly younger than Quintilian. But they might, of course, have had predecessors advocating similar positions.

In late Greek sources independent of Quintilian, we actually find reports about a dichotomy among those rhetors between a "deictic" (= demonstrative) and an "elenctic" (= refutative) enthymeme, occasionally expanded by further types.[49] At first sight, it would seem then that the rhetors Quintilian depends upon are simply adopting the dichotomy between deictic and elenctic enthymemes already proposed by Aristotle.[50] On closer inspection, however, it turns out that this cannot be true. For Aristotle states very clearly that for him the difference between a deictic and an elenctic enthymeme is absolutely parallel to that between a συλλογιεμός and an ἔλεγχος.[51] Now an ἔλεγχος for Aristotle is not a refutative argument, but an inference to a negative result, to the opposite of what the opponent in a debate holds.[52] So Quintilian's sources cannot simply be copying Aristotle.

Myles Burnyeat has recently made very plausible that the dichotomy Quintilian and his sources have in mind may first have come about as an attempt at classifying Stoic syllogisms, whereby the first two (hypothetical) types would be categorized as syllogisms from consequents, and all others (conjunctive or disjunctive) as syllogisms from incompatibles.[53] This would also account for a significant difference in terminology between Cicero and Quintilian: When Cicero in the *Topica* speaks of an inference from consequents, he refers to the second Stoic syllogism only (if p, then q; but not q; therefore not p), because in this case one is inferring backwards from consequent to antecedent. The first syllogism (if p, then q; but p; therefore q) he calls an inference from

---

48. Quintilian, *Inst.*, 5.13.60; 14.27.
49. Maximos Planudes, *Scholia in Hermogenis De inventione, Rhetores Graeci*, ed. C. Walz, 5.406.17–410.5; *Scholia anonyma in Hermogenis De inventione, Rhetores Graeci*, ed. Walz, 7.766.4–16.
50. Aristotle, *Rhet.*, 2.22.1396b22–27; 2.23.1400b26–29; 3.17.1418b1–4.
51. *Rhet.*, 2.22.1396b24–25.
52. Aristotle, *Soph. elench.*, 1.165a2–3; 5.167a23–27; 9.170b1–3.
53. Burnyeat, "Enthymeme," 43–44.

antecedents.⁵⁴ For Quintilian, however, both hypothetical types of syllogisms fall under the category of inference from consequents.⁵⁵

Furthermore, it seems that the original Greek terms for this dichotomy were "ἐξ ἀκολουθίας" and "ἐκ μάχης," which would give the exact parallels to "ex consequentibus" and "ex pugnantibus." And indeed, exactly this pair of terms is found in the first century B.C.E. in Pseudo-Demetrius.⁵⁶ Greek rhetors of the first century C.E., however, willfully confounded this Stoic concept with Aristotle's manifestly different division into deictic and elenctic enthymemes.

Quintilian's example for an enthymeme from consequents is: "Virtue is a good thing, because no one can put it to bad use," whereas an enthymeme from incompatibles would run: "Can money be a good thing when it is possible to put it to bad use?"⁵⁷ Clearly, this last example can be analyzed in terms of a Ciceronian enthymeme, while the first one may be interpreted as a first or second type Stoic syllogism, or alternatively as an Aristotelian syllogism lacking the major premise.

The Birth of the Elliptic Enthymeme

This takes us to the last concept of the enthymeme still missing from our survey; its interpretation as a syllogism with one premise (or the conclusio) omitted or suppressed. For convenience we may call it the concept of the elliptic enthymeme. This view predominated in the whole of the Middle Ages and the greater part of the modern era. But it is absolutely clear today that it was not the original Aristotelian concept.

What must concern us here is the question of how, why, and when this concept came into existence and how it even came to be regarded as Aristotelian. The story of the omitted premise argument, however, is highly complicated, and can by no means be explicated here in its entirety. We will thus confine ourselves to sketching selected aspects.

It is currently a matter of much heated debate whether Aristotle, when he first devised his *Rhetoric,* already proceeded from a syllogistic concept of the enthymeme. Probably he did not. Chapters 23 and 24 of the second book, listing topical enthymemes and pseudo-enthymemes, may well reflect a stage when he had not yet even thought of associating the enthymeme with the

---

54. *Topica,* 19–20; 53–54.
55. See Burnyeat, "Enthymeme," 43.
56. Ps.-Demetrius of Phaleron, *De elocutione,* 30.
57. *Inst.,* 5.14.25–26.

kind of syllogistic expounded in the *Analytics.* But beyond reasonable doubt, at least at one (possibly later) stage he brought them together.

Aristotle viewed the enthymeme as the rhetorical counterpart to συλ-λογισμός (deductive inference) and defined it as a συλλογισμός from probabilities or signs.[58] For him it was either (a) a deductive inference proceeding from sentences that are only probable (εἰκότα), i.e., true only for the most part or in general or commonly accepted (ἔνδοξα), or (b) an inference from signs. Any inference of this kind, of course, will not yield truths, but only probabilities. It is in this respect only that an Aristotelian enthymeme is rightly called an imperfect syllogism: It is logically imperfect, not necessarily formally incomplete.

Of course, Aristotle, too, occasionally suggests that an orator may leave unspoken certain elements of an enthymeme, if the audience can readily supply them. But this is not part of its definition.[59] Aristotle also indeed distinguishes between perfect (τέλειοι) and imperfect (ἀτελῖς) syllogisms. But for him, a perfect syllogism is one whose validity is evident in itself, while an imperfect syllogism needs to be proven. There is no hint as to formal deficiency.

But, soon after the rediscovery of Aristotle's works in the first century B.C.E., the word "ἀτελής," evidently originally a gloss, began to creep into the definition of the enthymeme in the *Prior Analytics,* which then read: "An enthymeme is an *imperfect* syllogism from probabilities or signs." This was not even wrong; for, from a logical point of view, an Aristotelian enthymeme indeed is an imperfect syllogism. But sooner or later, the word "ἀτελής" began to be interpreted in terms of formal incompleteness instead. It was misunderstood as referring to a convention that in an enthymeme one of the premises of a syllogism necessarily had to be suppressed.

The answer to the question how and why this happened lay in the dark for a long time. But recently, Myles Burnyeat and Lawrence D. Green have independently proposed the same solution.[60] They both point to the fact that in the first centuries B.C.E. and C.E. Stoic logic had more or less totally absorbed its Peripatetic counterpart. When, in that period, one was talking about syllogisms, it was most certainly Stoic syllogisms. But Stoic logic, as is well known, would never allow for any relaxation in standards of validity in syllo-

---

58. *Analytica priora,* 2.27.70a10; *Rhet.,* 1.2.1357a32.
59. *Rhet.,* 1.2.1357a16–21; 2.22.1395b25–27; 3.18.1419a18–19.
60. Burnyeat, "Enthymeme," 44–46; Lawrence D. Green, "Aristotle's Enthymeme and the Imperfect Syllogism," in *Rhetoric and Pedagogy: Its History, Philosophy, and Practice. Essays in Honor of James J. Murphy* (ed. Winifred Bryan Horner, Michael Leff; Mahwah, N.J.: Lawrence Erlbaum Assoc., 1995): 27–32.

gisms. So the only leeway possible for distinguishing an enthymeme from a genuine syllogism was in standards of expression and style. In fact, the Stoic enthymemes we examined in Cicero and the Elder Seneca all represented such abridged and condensed forms of originally tripartite syllogisms. Once the expression συλλογισμὸς ἀτελής had acquired the sense "incompletely expressed but formally valid syllogism" in a Stoic context, this could easily be applied to Aristotelian syllogisms as well.

Apparently, this momentous shift took place fairly early. Quintilian seems to be perfectly acquainted with the new concept as also his sources such as, for instance, Neocles.[61] Much earlier Pseudo-Demetrius used the expression "συλλογισμὸς ἀτελής."[62] But most conclusively, Quintilian's contemporary Aelius Theon, in his *Progymnasmata,* in explaining how to phrase a chreia "enthymematically," puts it unmistakably: "We need to add in our minds a proposition... which seems to have been omitted in the chreia but is potentially clear."[63] This is ample proof that by the first century C.E. the notion of the elliptic enthymeme was already fully established.

Practicing the Elliptic Enthymeme

This new concept of the elliptic enthymeme had many practical advantages. It was easy to handle and both much more flexible and less emotional than the Ciceronian type. It allowed for affirmative arguments capable of deducing positive results or producing reasons for assertory statements. It was thus preferable to the refutative type, especially in circumstances in which no immediate opponent had to be attacked or refuted. Besides, it analytically describes a type of reasoning that oratory will naturally embrace for reasons of brevity. So the concept may be applicable as an analytical tool even to cases in which it might not have been used deliberately.[64] But its many assets and the ubiquity of rhetoric at the time made for its rapid dissemination anyway.

That the elliptic enthymeme already was in common use around the middle of the first century C.E. is utterly conspicuous, e.g., in the Younger Seneca, who was Paul's contemporary and also productive in the epistolary genre. His *Letters to Lucilius* exhibit a great variety of enthymemic types. But while he

---

61. *Scholia anonyma in Hermogenis De inventione, Rhetores Graeci,* ed. Walz, 7.763.8–10.
62. Ps.-Demetrius of Phaleron, *De elocutione,* 32.
63. Aelius Theon, *Progymnasmata, Rhetores Graeci* (ed. Michel Patillon; Paris: Les Belles Lettres, 1997), 22.
64. For examples from an Old Testament context, see Rodney K. Duke, this volume pp. 127–40.

still occasionally employs enthymemes of the "Ciceronian" kind (e.g., 4.4 or 94.47), these are now clearly outnumbered by the more "modern" elliptic type, examples of which suddenly abound:

For instance, an elliptic enthymeme lacking the major premise (rule) appears at 56.4: "Words seem to distract me more than noises; for words demand attention, but noises merely fill the ears and beat upon them." (Supply: what demands attention, distracts more than what merely fills the ears.)

At 95.33, however, the minor (case) is omitted: "No vice remains within its limits; (supply: luxury is a vice; therefore:) luxury is precipitated into greed."

And last, the conclusion (result) is suppressed at 55.4: "The mass of mankind consider that a person is at leisure who has withdrawn from society, is free from care, self-sufficient, and lives for himself; but these privileges can be the reward only of the wise man." (Conclusion: the mass of mankind consider that the wise man is at leisure.)

If the elliptic concept, whose origins probably lay in the Greek east (where the intrusion of the ἀτελής-gloss would naturally have occurred), was already making such effective impact on Latin oratory and epistolography, it will have had an equally good opportunity to influence Greek New Testament texts. And in fact, rational argumentation in Paul's letters, whether consciously or unwittingly, often surprisingly closely follows those argumentative patterns.[65]

Thus an enthymeme with the major (rule) suppressed is found in 1 Thessalonians 4:9: "Now as to the love of the brethren, you have no need for anyone to write to you, for you yourselves are taught by God to love one another." (Supply: whoever is taught by God has no need for anyone to write to him.)[66]

The minor (case) is omitted in 1 Corinthians 11:29–30: "For he who eats and drinks, eats and drinks judgment to himself if he does not judge the body rightly. (Supply: and many among you have eaten and drunk without judging the body rightly.) For this reason many among you are weak and sick, and a number sleep."[67]

Even the conclusion (result) is left to the readers' imagination in 1 Corinthians 6:9–11: "Or do you not know that the unrighteous will not inherit the kingdom of God? Do not be deceived; neither fornicators, nor idolaters, nor adulterers, nor effeminate, nor homosexuals, nor thieves, nor the covetous, nor drunkards, nor revilers, nor swindlers, will inherit the kingdom of God.

---

65. For more examples, see Eriksson, "Enthememes in Pauline Argumentation," this volume pp. 243–59.
66. Cf. Rom 6:14; 16:17–18; Luke 11:4.
67. Cf. 1 Cor 15:16; Gal 6:8–9; Luke 11:9–10.

Such were some of you." (Conclusion: Therefore they will not inherit the kingdom of God.)[68]

But Paul, as we saw, does not use elliptic enthymemes exclusively. He, rather like the Younger Seneca or Quintilian, appears open to a richer variety of formations. Although the elliptic enthymeme today is certainly better known than any other, it is by no means the only type there ever was. Especially in the first centuries B.C.E. and C.E., different views were still competing. If this were more taken account of in rhetorical analysis of scriptural texts, it might open up new ways to new insights.

---

68. Cf. Rom 8:5–9; 13:8.

CHAPTER 6

THE ECONOMY OF LETTER WRITING IN GRAECO-ROMAN ANTIQUITY

Carol Poster

The topic of epistolary theory, rhetorical theory, and Paul has been widely canvassed.[1] This study attempts to add to the ongoing scholarly conversation by taking a slightly different perspective from the traditional one, beginning from economic utility rather than textual outcome.

Existing work on ancient epistolary theory and its relationship to epistolography (whether concerned with Pauline or pagan works) is primarily literary in both methods and ends. By this I mean that scholars analyze the verbal contents of letters and manuals looking for ways in which they clash or cohere, or examine compositional techniques[2] to understand textual outcomes. The typical questions debated are whether certain recurrent letter formulae match the recommendations of epistolary manuals or whether the overall persuasive strategies of letters seem to be influenced by rhetorical handbooks. This approach, to a degree, presumes the world of written artifacts to be a self-contained and independent one, informed and influenced primarily by itself, rather than external economic constraints. Although lip service is often paid to educational and social context, most of our study of ancient epistolography and epistolary theory has remained surprisingly remote from analysis of the role of letters within the economic functioning of the Roman empire and the ways in which epistolary instruction was conditioned by its necessarily practical outcomes. In this paper, therefore, I will be examining the relationship of Paul to epistolarity quite indirectly, by discussing how the economic role of letter writing in the Graeco-Roman world shaped epistolary theory and instruction.

---

1. See, e.g., R. Dean Anderson, *Ancient Rhetorical Theory and Paul* (Kampen: Kok Pharos, 1996); C. Joachim Classen, "St. Paul's Epistles and Ancient Greek and Roman Rhetoric," in *Rhetoric and the New Testament* (ed. Stanley E. Porter and Thomas H. Olbricht; JSNTSup 90; Sheffield: JSOT Press, 1993), 265–91; and Stanley E. Porter, "The Theoretical Justification for the Application of Rhetorical Categories to Pauline Epistolary Literature," in *Rhetoric and the New Testament* (ed. Stanley E. Porter and Thomas H. Olbricht; JSNTSup 90; Sheffield: JSOT Press, 1993), 100–122.

2. See E. Randolph Richards, *The Secretary in the Letters of Paul* (Tübingen: J. C. B. Mohr, 1990).

I shall begin by making axiomatic one methodological claim, namely that epistolary conventions and the training and theories informing them are shaped by social and economic functions, i.e., that we can explain epistolary texts and handbooks by asking for what purposes they were written and how those manners of writing served to further the personal ends of the letter writers qua letter writers and the official and private economic enterprises in which they were engaged. In the plainest terms, people learned how to write letters in order to make money, and employers, government or private, promulgated letter-writing standards in order to keep their offices functioning smoothly.

The primary obstacles to understanding ancient epistolarity, which term I use to signify both epistolography and epistolary theory, are, paradoxically, a simultaneous over-abundance and absence of information. The overabundance of information is a byproduct of the ubiquity of letter writing throughout Graeco-Roman civilization and the penetration of letters into all areas of economic activity, including private business, contract law, imperial law, the military, and imperial, provincial, and municipal administrations. Any official act, whether government or private, from selling wheat promised for future delivery (e.g., P. Ups. Frid. 5)[3] to issuing imperial edicts (the rescripts collected in the Justinian digest), might take epistolary form. Letters, especially when properly sealed, witnessed, recopied, certified, or archived, became official and legally authoritative documents. Letters also served as the single most important technology of long-distance communication; a soldier requesting warm socks (T. Vindol.) or an agent ordering pickled fish and pigs' food (P. Ryl. 2:229) would do so by letter. In terms of the economic circulation of epistolarity, the immense number of letters being written implies a concomitant mass of people who wrote letters, some as part of more broadly defined economic roles, and some as literate specialists. Their functional tasks might include taking shorthand, taking dictation in other forms, making copies, writing receipt and disposition information on letters, editing letters from general directions (oral or written), composing letters in *aliena persona* for employers (whether as street scribes, or private, or official secretaries), or writing letters in *propria persona* as part of official duties or private business. Each of these tasks might be accomplished by slaves, freedmen, employees, clients (*amici*), officials, elite private individuals, or emperors. Our evidence for such activities is overwhelming. There are literally tens of thousands of letters (both literary, as in the cases of Pliny, Cicero, Cassiodorus, or

---

3. For papyri, I use the standard abbreviations in BASP Suppl. 7 (1992). Unless otherwise cited, Greek texts are available in the *Thesaurus Linguae Graecae* CD ROM.

Symmachus, and documentary, as in the case of numerous papyri) with some economic significance (i.e., representing an activity for which the writer was paid or which might bring economic benefit to one of the correspondents), and mentions of letter writing in historical works (e.g., Suetonius, Ammianus, *Historia Augustae,* Cassius Dio, Diodorus of Sicily), both private and official. While such a plethora of evidence ought to bring joy to the heart of the scholar and illumination to the subject at hand, in fact, it does precisely the opposite. No source (ancient or modern) puts the economics of epistolarity into any sort of coherent scheme. The closest we have to a rationalized account of professional letter writing is John Lydus's description of the Byzantine chancery, a text that is late and specialized. This leads to the second part of our paradox, the absence of evidence concomitant with its overabundance. We don't have anything resembling an ancient equivalent of a pamphlet, or even a matchbook advertisement, entitled "career opportunities for letter-writers," and in our small collection of extant letter-writing manuals, only brief mentions are made of possible future employment of the knowledge gained from the manual ("undertaking such services for men in public office"; Ps. Demetrius 5).[4] It strikes me, therefore, that the most important foundational task to be accomplished in trying to understand ancient epistolarity from an economic perspective is to develop some scheme of categorization for economically significant letter-writing activities. From that starting point, it will be possible to extrapolate the functional necessities, which determine compositional methods, and eventually literary outcomes for epistolarity.

Professional Letter Writing Categories:
Caveats and Restrictions

As has often been pointed out, ancient distinctions between private and public or personal and economic activity were less clear than modern ones. The assistants, or entourage, of a Graeco-Roman emperor, administrator, or aristocrat were his *"amici"* (Greek: *philoi*) and a significant aspect to the conduct of business and administrative activity was maintenance of what Koskenniemi[5] calls philophronetic relationships. The epistolary maintenance of personal networks was a significant part of elite economic life; Russell, for example,

---

4. Ps. Demetrius and other ancient letter-writing manuals are collected in Abraham J. Malherbe, *Ancient Epistolary Theorists* (Atlanta: Scholars Press, 1988).

5. Heikki Koskenniemi, *Studien zur Idee und Phraseologie des griechischen Briefes bis 400 n. Chr.* (Helsinki: Suomalainen Tiedeakatemia, 1956).

points out the degree to which sustaining his "old boy network" dominates Libanius's correspondence.[6] From a functionalist perspective, however, this tremendously significant philophronetic activity can be categorized as simply one genre of elite or subelite quasi-familiar private autograph or secretarial letter, which, for purposes of this study, would be similar to the imperial *epistulae* and elite familiar letters in requiring advanced elite literary skills of either autograph or secretarial writers, as opposed to imperial *libelli* or letters of receipt for merchandise, which would require subelite technical writing skills.

A second type of distinction which must be kept in mind while developing functional epistolary rubrics is that between epistolarity as mechanical and epistolarity as cultural art. Especially since the advent of personal computer technology, composition and mechanical production of documents have become simultaneous and indistinguishable. My "composing" this paper is a mechanical act creating a virtual record in computer memory; a hardcopy is produced by pressing a few additional keys. Sending additional copies across the world can be accomplished almost instantaneously by pressing a few more keys. In antiquity, of course, this was not the case. The mechanical art of making physical letters was often sharply distinguished from the art of composing. In Graeco-Roman Egypt, clerks who could compose were paid more than those who merely copied or took dictation. Composition tended to be an elite or subelite skill; mechanical reproduction (tachygraphy or calligraphy) a slavish or nonelite profession, though the association of tachygraphy with legal studies made this particular mechanical skill important for certain elite and subelite professions at least by the third century C.E.[7] Thus epistolographic functions, such as producing answers to petitions in a provincial chancery, might involve three layers of activity and personnel: (1) a culturally literate secretary/administrator, (2) a tachygrapher (perhaps capable of minor editing), and (3) a copyist. The first might be an equestrian or subelite citizen, and the other two either (1) young citizens being trained for future offices, (2) nonelite free clerks, (3) freedmen, or (4) slaves.

While the functions involved in composing letters and the economic significance of these functions are enormously complex, they can be somewhat simplified when redescribed as remunerated epistolary tasks, and further simplified by restriction to what might be called alienated tasks, namely ones that are done for the benefit of someone else rather than one's self. Since writing one's own letter to arrange a grain sale is part of selling grain, we need only

---

6. D. A. Russell, trans. and intro., *Libanius: Imaginary Speeches* (London: Duckworth, 1996), 4.
7. Discussed in H. C. Teitler, *Notarii and Exceptores* (J. C. Gieben: Amsterdam, 1985).

consider as an economically distinct epistolary activity selling one's epistolary skills to a grain merchant by taking payment for writing a letter *in aliena persona* about a grain sale. With these restrictions, categorizing the economically significant epistolary functions in antiquity becomes, if not easy, at least possible. While the list below is not, and could not be, exhaustive, it should suffice to categorize the functional epistolary tasks sufficiently well that we can then use these rubrics to explain the purposes of epistolary theory and instruction, and the concomitant compositional methodologies.

I will present the major categories of economically significant epistolary tasks in the form of a list, giving for each item a designation and a brief definition, beginning with the simplest, most mechanical, and most poorly remunerated, and moving to the more culturally complex.

1. **Copyists:** Both official and private documents were copied, often multiple times. Authors of letters kept duplicates in case the original went astray. Legal documents were prepared in multiple copies. Most documents received by officials were copied before being answered or forwarded. Slaves normally performed this task of basic copying, though nonelite free literates might also be employed, and freed skilled slaves would normally continue in the professions they had pursued while enslaved.

2. **Calligraphers:** While the vast mass of bureaucratic copying was done in a visually unappealing but extremely efficient chancery cursive,[8] more formal letters or materials meant for wider circulation rather than archival purposes might need to be written in more legible, or even elegant, hands. While calligraphy, as a mechanical art, was also a slave or nonelite activity, a calligrapher had more advanced skills and training than a more basic copyist.

3. **Letter-Cutters:** Certain letters, especially imperial edicts and other official decrees, were carved onto stone by professional letter-cutters. Usually a secretary of some sort would draft the inscription and supervise the inscribing.[9] This implies two professional activities necessary to the production of letters inscribed on stone: a mechanical one, which is sufficiently particular to be outside the realm of this study, and a supervisory one, which falls under related categories of secretarial duties.

4. **Tachygraphers:** That there were numerous stenographers, who could either take dictation verbatim or by abbreviated notes, is overwhelmingly obvious. Cicero's famous secretary Tiro is credited with the invention of Latin shorthand proper (the so-called "Tironian notes"), and Suetonius mentions Caesar and Marcus Aurelius, among others, as dictating letters. We know of slaves trained in tachygraphy (P. Oxy. 724). What makes this skill so complex is that it can occur alone, as a nonelite mechanical skill mastered by slaves or women, or as a stage in the career of an elite

---

8. See G. Cavallo and H. Maehler, *Greek Bookhands of the Early Byzantine Period, A.D. 300–800* (Institute of Classical Studies Bulletin Suppl. 47, 1987), and E. G. Turner, *Greek Manuscripts of the Ancient World* (2d ed.; rev. P. J. Parsons; Institute of Classical Studies Bulletin Suppl. 46; London, 1987).

9. See Richards, *Secretary,* and Stephen W. Tracy, *Attic Letter-Cutters of 229 to 86 B.C.* (Berkeley: University of California Press, 1990).

notarius. Teitler[10] argues, correctly, I think, for a major shift in the role of tachygraphy in the times of Constantine and Domitian, in which tachygraphic skills become not only mechanical functions performed by slaves, but also a prerequisite for entry level positions in chanceries and other administrative offices (a detail described at some length by John Lydus),[11] and thus part of subelite professional qualifications and tasks. Perhaps this was because *notarii* were entrusted with confidential information and important legations — requiring both transcriptional and compositional skills, as well as sufficient rank to serve as legal witnesses (something which could not be done readily by slaves, whose testimony was normally invalid unless given under torture.) Under Constantius II, the number of imperial *notarii* alone reached 520;[12] given the existence of provincial, regional, municipal, and private chanceries, we must conclude that tachygraphy represented a quite significant range of remunerated or economically significant activities.

5. **Letter-Delivery: Messengers and Lectors:** While we normally think of epistolary tasks in terms of composition, we must be aware that reception was also an activity which was conducted through intermediaries. Letters were carried by messenger and often read to their recipients by lectors. A trusted messenger might be charged with conveying additional confidential material, implying that messengers could vary from slaves skilled at running (e.g., the "running slaves" of Roman comedy), to more sophisticated intermediaries, through, at the most elite end of the spectrum, official delegations who would present, e.g., municipal petitions to emperors. The widespread use of lectors does not, *pace* Harris and Ong,[13] imply lack of silent reading ability or absence of widely diffused literacy, but reflects matters of practical convenience.[14] We do not need to presuppose specialized training for lectors, as normal literacy education at all levels involved substantial oral exercises, including pronouncing syllables, word division, and reading aloud, and oral delivery of prepared (dictated by professor, taken from written source, or composed by student) or extemporaneous materials, at levels from basic literacy to sophistic declamation. Professionally, lectors might be specialists chosen for pleasing voices and strong eyes, but the function of lector might have been assumed by a more generally trained clerk, depending on the staff size in a particular situation.

6. **Clerks (basic):** Basic clerical tasks (and thus professions) were diffused through almost every imaginable area of Graeco-Roman life. Even very small private business transactions, such as buying a few donkeys or selling small quantities of oil, were recorded and authenticated by means of letter (see, e.g., the Zenon and Aurelius Isidorus archives for numerous examples), often written by clerks. Illiterates, e.g.,

---

10. Teitler, *Notarii*.
11. Anastastius C. Bandy, Intro., ed., trans., comm., *Ioannes Lydus, On Powers or the Magistracies of the Roman State* (Philadelphia: The American Philosophical Society, 1983).
12. Teitler, *Notarii*, 60.
13. Both William V. Harris, *Ancient Literacy* (Cambridge, Mass.: Harvard University Press, 1989), and Walter Ong, *Orality and Literacy: The Technologizing of the Word* (London: Methuen, 1982), underestimate the amount of ancient literacy and silent reading ability.
14. Discussed very sensibly by Nicholas Horsfall in two articles: "Statistics or State of Mind?" in *Literacy in the Roman World* (*Journal of Roman Archeology* Suppl. 3; Ann Arbor, Mich.: Department of Classical Studies, University of Michigan, 1991), 59–76, and "Rome Without Spectacles," *Greece and Rome* 42 (1995): 49–56.

Petaus and Aurelius Isidorus,[15] might keep substantial written archives, obviously recorded and managed by clerks. Government offices from the local level[16] through the imperial kept elaborate records and copied and logged incoming and outgoing documents. While advanced compositional skills were required at the upper administrative letters, many of the recording functions required only minimal literacy, and administrators were normally assigned one or more clerical assistants.[17] A specifically Egyptian clerical job was necropolis *grammateus,* who in addition to normal scribal tasks marked symbols on newly arrived corpses awaiting mummification.[18]

7. **Street (Freelance) Scribes:** A particularly entrepreneurial form of literacy work was street (or generally, freelance) secretary. Even smaller Egyptian villages would have individuals who sat in the marketplace, writing letters and other documents for hire. There was tremendous variability in the tasks, roles, and talents of these individuals. Some were probably literate individuals (schoolteachers, retired soldiers) who supplemented their income with occasional writing jobs. Others had some scribal training, usually in penmanship as well as composition, and may have relied on literacy work for their livelihoods (numerous records of short-term government contracts for scribal labor imply the availability of regular remuneration). Since scribes normally wrote petitions and other legally authoritative documents for illiterate and uncertain writers, we can assume freelance scribes with training extending to legal letter formulae (the equivalent of the medieval *ars notariae*). Though there is little explicit discussion of this legal-secretarial function in ancient sources, it might be particularly significant as an epistolary career.

8. **Translators:** In the multi-lingual environment of the Graeco-Roman empire outside Italy, letters were written in languages unknown or minimally known to their "authors"; a Greek composed a letter for an Egyptian temple scribe because "he does not know [Greek] letters." Multi-lingual literates could be employed in translingual letter writing as well as oral translation tasks (e.g., in law courts).

9. **Business Managers/Agents:** Writing letters with the authority of their masters was a major task of ancient business managers, who normally had literacy and numeracy

---

15. For Petaus, see *Das Archiv des Petaus* (ed. U. Hagedorn et al.; Cologne and Opladen: Westdeutscher Verl., 1969) and discussion in H. C. Youtie, "Pétaus, fils de Pétaus, ou le scribe qui ne savait pas écrire," *Chronique d'Egypte* 41 (1966): 127–43. For Aurelius Isidorus, see *The Archive of Aurelius Isidorus in the Egyptian Museum, Cairo and the University of Michigan (P. Cair. Isidor.)* (ed. Arthur E. R. Boak and Herbert Chayyim Youtie; Ann Arbor: University of Michigan Press, 1960), and H. C. Youtie, "AGRAMMATOS: An Aspect of Greek Society in Egypt," *HSCP* 75 (1971): 161–76; idem, "Βραδέως γράφων: Between Literacy and Illiteracy," *GRBS* 12 (1971): 239–61; and idem, "Because They Do Not Know Letters," *ZPE* 19 (1975): 101–8.

16. For discussion of the archive of the village secretary, Menches, see A. M. F. W. Verhoot, *Menches, Komogrammateus of Kerkosiris* (Leiden: Brill, 1998). For general discussions of local government in Egypt, see Naphtali Lewis, *Life in Egypt Under Roman Rule* (Oxford: Clarendon Press, 1983), and idem, *The Compulsory Public Services of Roman Egypt* (2d ed.; Florence: Edizioni Gonnelli, 1997).

17. See, inter alia, David Braund, ed., *The Administration of the Roman Empire* (Exeter: University of Exeter Press, 1988).

18. Discussed in Tomasz Derda, "Necropolis Workers in Graeco-Roman Egypt in the Light of Greek Papyri," *JJP* 21 (1991): 13–36.

schooling. Most frequently, due to the Roman liability laws, these managers were slaves or first generation freedmen.[19]

10. **Military Clerks:** Even in the Principate, *litterati milites* formed a nucleus of the civil service. Within the army, clerks were responsible for extensive record keeping, including regular supply and personnel reports and communications to and from outposts. These clerks were exempted from all other military duties. This provides a military career path distinct from that of combat soldier and thus a way for epistolary and literate skills to give access to all the advantages of membership in Roman or auxiliary legions. The combination of the official literacy requirement for officers with the existence of a clerical corps, as it were, partially accounts for the substantial number of military letters and archives extant (e.g., P. Abinn, T. Vindol., P. Mich. 8:464, P. Oxy. 12:1481).

11. **Clerks (skilled):** Skilled clerks, who could compose letters, were paid more than those who merely wrote them. Competition for positions at the upper levels of Graeco-Roman chanceries was intense, and could be quite profitable (either through salaries or bribes). There is no clear demarcation between the most skilled of clerks from nonelite backgrounds and the quasi-elite secretarial positions, although the requirement of rhetorical education for elite chancery posts after the third century C.E. may imply a socio-economic barrier separating lower clerical from upper secretarial posts.[20]

12. **Secretaries (quasi-elite):** Rhetorically trained secretaries were a common feature of elite economic activity. Lucian attests that the rhetorically trained could find ready employment as private secretaries (especially as a Greek employed by Romans). Government offices also employed the rhetorically trained elites for positions that required composing documents or speeches for elite audiences.[21]

13. **Office of *ab epistulis*:** The office of *ab epistulis* (originally one secretary for Greeks and one for Romans, but by the third century a large office) was responsible for composing speeches and writing *epistulae* to the provincial elites (as opposed to the *a libellus,* which dealt with similar tasks for non-elites). It was an elite position, held by members of the Senatorial or equestrian classes. Philostratus, in his *Lives of the Sophists,*[22] cites several sophists who achieved the post of *ab epistulis* (titular head of the office): Celer (574), Alexander (571), Hadrian (590), Antipater (607), and Aspasius (628).[23]

---

19. For a papyrus archive containing managerial correspondence, see *The Zenon Archive* (vol. 7 of *Greek Papyri in the British Museum;* ed. Theodore C. Skeat; London: British Museum Publications Ltd., 1974). For business managers in Italy, see Jean-Jacques Aubert, *Business Managers in Ancient Rome* (Leiden: E. J. Brill, 1994).

20. For discussion of professional qualifications in late antiquity, see Fritz Saaby Pedersen, *Late Roman Professionalism* (Odense, Denmark: Odense University Press, 1976).

21. See Fergus Millar, *The Emperor in the Roman World* (Ithaca, N.Y.: Cornell University Press, 1977), 83–109, 213–27, and 313–40, for discussion of secretaries in Roman administration.

22. Philostratus and Eunapius, *Lives of the Sophists* (trans. Wilmer C. Wright; Loeb Classical Library; Cambridge, Mass.: Harvard University Press, 1989).

23. Glen. W. Bowersock, *Greek Sophists in the Roman Empire* (Oxford: Oxford University Press, 1969), 44, 50–51, 53–57, and 92, discusses the Greek sophists holding the position of Imperial Secretary. For more general discussions on the role of *ab epistulis,* see Hugh Lindsay, "Suetonius

14. **Administrators:** While administrators would have staffs for the mechanical tasks of letter writing, a significant part of their duties involved answering letters or petitions or issuing directives in the form of letters. Thus, rhetorical training (which would provide skill in oral dictation of letters) was not only useful, but in some cases (e.g., a decree of Constantius) required for many administrative posts.

Educational Categories in Light of Professional Outcomes

The professional rubrics for letter writing adumbrated above can be specifically useful for understanding ancient epistolary education. Graeco-Roman education was not regulated, standardized, or publicly supported in the manner of modern western education. Instead, schoolmasters of varying specializations and abilities offered a bewildering variety of educational options for students of various different socio-economic classes, abilities, and interests. Letter-writing skills were scattered among various levels and types of instruction, from basic grammar classes to advanced professional training courses. Certain specific training paths and skills, however, would be advantageous for specific careers. Slaves and women could profitably be trained in the mechanical skills of tachygraphy and calligraphy. Freedmen or nonelite metropolitan Greeks could, by limited literacy and professional letter-writing education, take advantage of plentiful employment opportunities as lower-level clerks, but might not have the social qualifications (or fees) appropriate to elite rhetorical courses. Sophistic education would provide access to elite secretarial positions, both private and official. The following educational rubrics all included some level of epistolary training, appropriate to specific professional and socio-economic outcomes:

> **Basic Literacy Classes:** In quite basic classes, students, while learning declensions of nouns (e.g., from the handbook of Dionysius Thrax), learned the correct forms of salutation: "[to] recipient [in dative] [from] sender [in nominative or genitive depending on letter type], greetings [*chairein*]." This indicates that letter writing

as *ab epistulis* to Hadrian and the Early History of Imperial Correspondence," *Historia* 43:4 (1994): 454–68, and G. B. Townend, "The Post of *ab epistulis* in the Second Century," *Historia* 10 (1961): 375–81. Naphtali Lewis ("Literati in the Service of Roman Emperors: Politics Before Culture," in *Coins, Culture, and History in the Ancient World: Numismatic and Other Studies in Honor of Bluma L. Trell* [ed. Lionel Casson and Martin Price; Detroit: Wayne State University Press, 1981]), argues strongly against the notion that the sole, or even primary, qualifications for this position were literary, but even if the titular head of the office were not rhetorically trained, stylistic evidence indicates that the staff who actually produced rescripts had extensive rhetorical training, as is discussed in Margareta Benner, *The Emperor Says: Studies in the Rhetorical Style in Edicts of the Early Empire* (Göteborg: Acta Universitatis Gothoburgensis, 1975), and Gunhild Vidén, *The Roman Chancery Tradition: Studies in the Language of Codex Theodosianus and Cassiodorus' Variae* (Göteborg: Acta Universitatis Gothoburgensis, 1984).

was of sufficient utility that the basic forms would be taught to students acquiring even minimal literacy skills — something borne out by the frequency of autograph papyrus letters by unskilled writers. These classes could be taught by private tutors (more common among the provincial elites), tutors (including women) who took on small numbers of pupils,[24] or in larger "schools." These classes would be sufficient preparation for lower-level positions as military and civilian basic clerks, unskilled copyists, and street scribes.

Grammatical Classes (Advanced/Elite Literacy): Students who had achieved basic literacy could pursue intermediate studies in reading poetry and written composition with grammarians. Students at this skill level might encounter two sorts of letter-writing instruction. In what one might term "rhetorical preparatory schools," ones training students who were likely to continue on to an elite sophistic education, a standard element in the curriculum was a sequence of *"progymnasmata,"* or preliminary exercises. One of these, *prosopopoieia,* or impersonation, which involved writing in the voice of a fictitious or historical character, was sometimes taught in epistolary form. School papyri also contain evidence of students learning to write simple familiar letters *in propria persona* in both Greek and Latin, but there is little literary evidence to contextualize these within any curricular sequence. Internal evidence of literate competence with occasional syntactic and orthographic errors would place the student writer of the P. Bon. 5,[25] a bilingual (Greek and Latin) exercise in writing common types of familiar letter, at some intermediary educational level. The linguistic and literary formulae taught at this level would be particularly useful for subelite letter writing, but direct professional relevance (other than as preparation for rhetoric) might be limited.

Sophistic/rhetorical schools: Sophistic schools concentrated primarily on the oral skills of declamation. Libanius, however, did read a letter received from a friend to his students as an example of good epistolary style (*Ep.* 128), the letter of Philostratus of Lemnos preserved in the *Epistolimaioi Characteres* of Ps. Proclus[26] and scattered comments in Flavius Philostratus indicate that letter-writing skills were occasionally included in sophistic teaching. Rhetorical education served as preparation for elite administrative and chancery positions (the office of *ab epistulis,* especially), but was not particularly relevant at lower levels of employment.

Law/stenography training: Law and stenography schools providing focused vocational training competed, far too successfully for Libanius's comfort, with sophistic schools for students. Tachygraphy was an important skill by itself, and also, given the oral nature of certain legal proceedings, a useful ancillary skill for a lawyer. The more frequent use of tachygraphic signs in legal than in other types of papyri is evidence for a strong association between stenography and law. Stenography appears from the highest classes (when young, the Emperor Titus would compete with his secretaries in speed and accuracy of stenography) to slaves. There may

---

24. For literacy schooling see Raffaella Cribiore, *Writing, Teachers, and Students in Graeco-Roman Egypt* (American Studies in Papyrology 36; Atlanta, Ga.: Scholars Press, 1996).
25. In Malherbe, *Ancient Epistolary Theorists.*
26. In ibid.

also have been courses available in letter writing itself, for which manuals such as the pseudo-Demetrian *Typoi Epistolikoi*[27] were used as texts. However, there is not sufficient evidence to determine who taught them, whether the teaching was in the form of limited apprenticeships, training contracts, or larger "schools," or whether these were part of more general business or law courses or offered independently. There were probably instances of all these cases. Since even street scribes and basic clerks wrote letters which were legally binding and used legal formulae, somewhere within legal or letter writing training at a subelite level, there must have been opportunities to learn legal formulae without completing full advocacy or juristic training. Questions not answerable within this paper but nonetheless important are whether there existed in antiquity any equivalent of the medieval *ars notariae* and whether such an art might clarify some of the more puzzling aspects of the role of *notarii* (tachygraphers *cum* administrators) in Roman administration.

Scribal training: Papyrus evidence shows specialized training for scribes focused primarily on mastery of various formal hands, and independent of compositional training.

Bureaucratic apprenticeship: Evidence from the Zenon archive and late historians (especially John Lydus) indicates that much of the training for lower level secretarial skills occurred in the form of apprenticeships, either with private households or in larger bureaucratic environments.

Slave schools: Schooling of slaves in literacy was an extensive and potentially lucrative business. Large households, including the imperial household, would often hire teachers or use their own slaves or freedmen to instruct slaves in literacy. A substantial number of the copyists, stenographers, and letter-writers on major estates and in the imperial chancery were slaves and freedmen. There was also a flourishing industry in producing literate slaves. The Elder Cato, e.g., would educate slaves to sell them at a profit. One contract from Graeco-Roman Egypt (P. Oxy. 4.724), for example, specifies that a slave will be put through an eighteen-month stenography course and the teacher paid in three increments. It even notes that if the slave has learned the commentary (probably a stenography text) completely before the stipulated eighteen months were over, the teacher will be paid in full. Vespasian wrote to an Egyptian *strategos* that if teachers with tax exemptions granted for providing liberal education to free children engaged in educating slaves, they would have their exemptions revoked. Much of the training for the lowest level of letter-writing professional skills — taking dictation, making fair copies, becoming a street scribe — was probably oriented towards training slaves or freedmen.[28]

Military literacy schools: Officers in the Roman army were required to be literate. Soldiers' letters among the Vindolanda and Egyptian papyri show a fairly wide-

---

27. In ibid.
28. For slave training, see Alan D. Booth, "The Schooling of Slaves in First Century Rome," *Transactions of the American Philological Association* 109 (1979): 11–20, and Clarence Forbes, "The Education and Training of Slaves in Antiquity," *Transactions of the American Philological Association* 86 (1955): 321–60.

spread practice of letter writing, often autographs, and army clerks were ubiquitous. The evidence for military literacy schools is, however, ambiguous.

Implications for Epistolary Composition

By combining the two rubrics of professional opportunities and training possibilities for letter writers, we can establish a somewhat more nuanced account of epistolarity than is possible when treating the genre as monolithic. Rather than ask whether rhetorical or epistolary theory exerts the greater influence on epistolography (especially Pauline), we can consider which epistolary professions and levels of training are grounded in which traditions. I would like to suggest a tentative hierarchy of compositional techniques and skills, ranging from the most basic to the most elaborate:

1. **Basic literacy:** Marginally literate private individuals, basic clerks, and scribes (e.g., street scribes in very small villages) would know only minimal letter formulae (e.g., proper address and closing) and no rhetorical formulae. When more sophisticated formulae appear in their work, they were often copied from formularies (model letter collections), which were common in all levels of chancery.

2. **Professional subelite or nonelite letter writers:** Professional letter writers in nonelite private employment or government offices would know extensive letter-writing formulae, including appropriate salutations for all ranks and legal signature formulae. At the upper end of this category, we find knowledge of letter types (Ps.-Demetrius) and the appropriate language and approach for each type. Training at this level included preliminary instruction in basic literacy and some mix of tachygraphy, legal formulae, and/or specialized epistolary theory.

3. **Rhetorical/Sophistical Training:** Members of the Graeco-Roman elite (or subelite) employed in very wealthy private houses or major public offices, had advanced rhetorical training, including rhetorical structures and formulae, especially through the late third century C.E., although, as we find lamented frequently by Libanius, Latin and legal training seems to supplant rhetorical training for administrative posts in the fourth century.

The question, therefore, of whether we should expect to find rhetorical or epistolary formulae in letters, depends on the specific training of the letter-writer, and also the use of secretaries.[29] We cannot make generalizations that hold true for all socio-economic strata. Instead we need to look at how the specific economic functions of epistolarity within the Graeco-Roman world resulted in multiple epistolary theories, styles, and pedagogies. When examin-

---

29. See Richards, *Secretary*, for discussion of secretarial influences.

ing a specific epistolary composition, we need to contextualize it adequately within its specific social, economic, and functional surroundings. The appropriate comparanda, therefore, for the Pauline letters, are not the works of the Graeco-Roman elite, but rather works by other subelite writers from the Greek east, perhaps Epictetus or authors of subliterary or documentary papyri.[30]

---

30. Research for this essay was supported in part by a research leave from the English Department and College of Letters and Sciences of Montana State University and a visiting fellowship at the Project on Rhetoric of Inquiry at the University of Iowa. I completed final editing while a Visiting Fellow at the Tanner Humanities Center of the University of Utah. I would like to thank the organizers and participants at the Lund conference, and several people for useful comments and references, including David Amador, Anders Eriksson, John Garcia, Malcolm Heath, and Tom Olbricht.

PART THREE

**RHETORICAL ARGUMENTATION
IN THE HEBREW BIBLE**

CHAPTER 7

THE STRATEGIC USE OF ENTHYMEME AND EXAMPLE IN THE ARGUMENTATION OF THE BOOKS OF CHRONICLES

Rodney K. Duke

Overview

In comparison with the history found in the Former Prophets, the Chronicler[1] took on the task of retelling the history of Israel with a new focus on subject matter and from a new paradigmatic perspective, both influenced by the return from the Babylonian exile. In terms of subject matter, he tells the story of the rise, fall, and beginning restoration of the southern kingdom of Judah with an emphasis on the roles of the Davidic kings and the temple cultus. In terms of paradigmatic perspective, he perceives and illustrates the thesis that each generation could experience the effect of a reversal in its situation based on the cause of seeking or failing to seek Yahweh. The Chronicler faced the rhetorical dilemma of how to present persuasively a new history of Israel to an audience that presumably already knew older traditions of their past. The fact that the Chronicler's work was accepted within the canon of the Jewish community of faith along side another recital of Israel's past, that of the Former Prophets, indicates that the Chronicler was successful in his new re-presentation.

Taking my lead from Aristotle's *Rhetoric*[2] in which he describes how a communicator can demonstrate an argument rhetorically using enthymemes and examples, I examine how the Chronicler's use of enthymeme and example would have had a persuasive effect.[3] I demonstrate: (a) that the

---

1. I am assuming the generally held position that there has been one main hand behind the composition of the books of Chronicles, even though other hands have probably shaped it, and am calling that person the Chronicler. Also, I have adopted the custom of referring to the Chronicler with masculine pronouns.

2. The translation of Aristotle's *Rhetoric* cited in this paper is by W. Rhys Roberts in *The Basic Works of Aristotle* (ed. R. McKeon; New York: Random House, 1941), 1317–1451.

3. This paper is a re-presentation, with new material and other changes, of selections from Chapter 3, "Logos: The Rational Mode of Persuasion," of my work, Rodney K. Duke, *The Persuasive Appeal of the Chronicler: A Rhetorical Analysis* (ed. David M. Gunn; Bible and Literature Series 25; Sheffield: Almond, 1990), 81–104. A synthesis may be found in Rodney K. Duke, "A Rhetorical Approach to Appreciating the Books of Chronicles," in *The Chronicler as Author: Studies in Text and Texture* (ed. M. P. Graham and S. L. McKenzie; JSOTSup 263; Sheffield: Sheffield Academic Press, 1999), 100–135.

Chronicler built his enthymeme on a generally accepted Israelite theological maxim, (b) that the Chronicler skillfully used these two forms of argumentation in two different kinds of narrative, and (c) that the Chronicler ordered and balanced his use of enthymemes and examples in a strategic manner.

The Application of Greek Rhetorical Theory to the Books of Chronicles

First, one might ask what justifies the application of Greek rhetorical theory to an ancient Hebrew text such as Chronicles. The decision to be dependent on Aristotle is grounded on the fact that, in the modern era, his writings have been among the most influential **descriptive** works on rhetoric. In regard to Aristotle's work, George Kennedy states, "If one looks back over the first hundred and fifty years of rhetorical theory, Aristotle's *Rhetoric* seems to tower above all the remains.... Its influence has been enormous and still continues."[4] The emphasis above on "descriptive" is essential. Aristotle did not write *Rhetoric* as a prescriptive work, although it was used for training rhetors. Neither did he write it merely to be descriptive of Greek rhetoric. He sought to describe the universal characteristics of persuasive/effective communication engaged in by all people.[5] As such, the system as set forth in the *Rhetoric* may be applied to verbal acts of communication in which the communicator seeks to address matters over which people deliberate. Certainly stylistic features vary from culture to culture, but some of the elements of an effective rhetorical strategy will be universal (e.g., construction of arguments, selection and arrangement of material, employment of the modes of persuasion, expectations regarding the audience, etc.).

Second, one might ask what justifies applying ancient rhetorical theory to historical narrative, which is certainly not one of the types of speech Aristotle

---

4. George Kennedy, *The Art of Persuasion in Greece* (Princeton, N.J.: Princeton University Press, 1963), 123.

5. Aristotle stated in *Rhet.*, 1.1.1354a:

> Rhetoric is the counterpart of Dialectic. Both alike are concerned with such things as come, more or less, within the general ken of all men and belong to no definite science. Accordingly all men make use, more or less, of both; for to a certain extent all men attempt to discuss statements and maintain them, to defend themselves and to attack others. Ordinary people do this either at random or through practice and from acquired habit. Both ways being possible, the subject can plainly be handled systematically, for it is possible to inquire the reason why some speakers succeed through practice and others spontaneously; and every one will at once agree that such an inquiry is the function of an art.

See also George Kennedy, *New Testament Interpretation Through Rhetorical Criticism* (Chapel Hill: University of North Carolina, 1984), 10–11; and Charles Sears Baldwin, *Ancient Rhetoric and Poetic: Interpreted from Representative Works* (New York: Macmillan, 1924), 8.

addressed.[6] I would argue that all acts of communication over which people deliberate function rhetorically. Hayden White defines historical narrative as "a verbal structure in the form of a narrative prose discourse that purports to be a model, or icon, of past structures and processes in the interest of *explaining what they were by representing* them."[7] Historical narratives are representational depictions of the world composed for the purpose of conveying meaning to the intended audience. The addresser wishes to persuade the audience to accept her or his story as true, that is, to accept it with its inherent presuppositions, worldview, and ideology. Each historical narrative not only informs an audience about the past, but also confronts it with the need to make a variety of decisions: to judge a past act, to assess praise or blame, to accept certain laws of coherence among events, to believe there is a teleology to history. The degree to which the audience accepts the story as "true" depends on the rhetorical effectiveness of the narrative. The effectiveness of a historical work, that which makes it acceptably real to one's audience, is, therefore, rhetorical in nature.[8]

Rhetorical Purposes of the Books of Chronicles

On a general level, I would suggest that the rhetorical purposes of the genre "historical narrative" in the Hebrew Bible are: (1) to preserve the traditions of Israel, and consequently to shape its identity; (2) to respond to the needs and questions of the intended audience; and (3) to present and inculcate a worldview, a description of how the world operates. In particular I would like to focus on the third purpose. A primary reason for doing history is for the "why" questions that it answers, viz., what it tells us about the way the world works. Ancient historians such as Livy and Thucydides recognized this rhetorical function.[9] Moreover, since the Israelites viewed their God as active in history, historical narrative became a means of inculcating theology.

---

6. Aristotle originated a classification of three genres of speech: (1) deliberative or political, (2) legal or forensic, and (3) epideictic or ceremonial (*Rhet.*, 1.3.1358a–1358b). For examples of categories of classical rhetoric applied to other biblical narratives, see Kennedy, *New Testament Interpretation*, 39–96.
7. Hayden White, *Metahistory: The Historical Imagination in Nineteenth-Century Europe* (Baltimore: Johns Hopkins University Press, 1973), 2.
8. Hayden White, "Rhetoric and History," in *Theories of History* (ed. H. White and F. E. Manuel; Los Angeles: University of California, 1978), 3.
9. Livy discusses how one may learn moral lessons through history in the "Preface" of his *History of Rome* (trans. D. Spillan and C. Edmonds; 2 vols.; Harper's Classical Library; New York: Harper & Brothers, 1875–81). Thucydides saw his work as having abiding value, since human nature, being what it is, would cause events of the past to be repeated in the future in *History of the Peloponnesian War* (trans. R. Warner; Penguin Classics 139; Baltimore: Penguin Books, 1954), 1.1.

Specifically, in order to clarify the Chronicler's view of how the world works, I am working with the thesis set forth by G. E. Schaefer that one of the primary purposes of the Chronicler was to move his audience to seek Yahweh through the proper forms of the Jerusalem cult. Schaefer's thesis reconciles a variety of proposals regarding the Chronicler's purposes that recognize the Chronicler's emphases on the Davidic kings, the temple cultus, Judah, the return from exile, the value of religious orthodoxy, the mechanism of divine retribution, etc.[10] Schaefer states:

> The primary aim of the Chronicler was to demonstrate from history that a faithful adherence to the "God of the fathers" results in happiness and blessing and that forsaking the LORD will lead the nation and individual to ruin and curse. His highlighting of the reigns of David and Solomon was to demonstrate that one is to seek the LORD through the temple cultus that was established in Jerusalem by them and honored by subsequent kings. The Chronicler's emphasis on "seeking the LORD" is to be understood as an invitation extended to the people to experience life on its highest plane. His desire was to see the theocracy realized in Israel, with the people giving themselves completely to the LORD and looking to him to meet all their needs.[11]

"Seeking Yahweh" meant a total response of the worshipper to God. The Davidic king and all Israel were to turn to, pray to, inquire of, trust, praise, and worship Yahweh and no other god. Most importantly, they were to do so through the proper cultic form in the proper cultic place as established and modeled by David and Solomon. The opposite of seeking was not so much the commission of a sinful action, but unfaithfulness demonstrated by failing to turn to Yahweh and by neglecting the temple cultus.[12] The resultant blessing or cursing, although often centered on the king, had an impact on the well-being of the whole nation. Blessing took a variety of forms: victory in battle, rest from one's enemies, united support of the people, prosperity, wisdom, healing, the ability to execute building projects or to increase one's army and fortifications. Cursing or retribution took the opposite forms: military defeat, illness or death, rebellion of the people, etc.[13]

---

10. For a list of some of these proposals and their proponents, see Duke, *Persuasive Appeal*, 47–51.

11. Glenn Edward Schaefer, "The Significance of Seeking God in the Purpose of the Chronicler" (Th.D. diss., Southern Baptist Theological Seminary, 1972), 17–18. Sara Japhet seems to be making much the same point when she summarizes Chronicles as "a comprehensive expression of the perpetual need to renew and revitalize the religion of Israel" (*I & II Chronicles: A Commentary* [London: SCM, 1993], 49).

12. Schaefer, "Seeking God," Chapter 3.

13. So, too, Wilhelm Rudolph, *Chronikbücher* (HAT 21; Tübingen: J. C. B. Mohr [Paul Siebeck], 1955), xviii–xx; Roddy L. Braun, "The Significance of 1 Chronicles 22, 28, and 29 for the Structure and Theology of the Work of the Chronicler" (Th.D. diss., Concordia Seminary, 1971), 169–81, 204; Raymond B. Dillard, "Reward and Punishment in Chronicles: The Theology of Immediate Retribution," *WTJ* 46 (1984): 165–70; Peter Welten, *Geschichte und Geschichtsdarstellung in den*

The Chronicler's paradigm of seeking explained the exile and the return from exile to his audience as well as defended their cultic institutions. Moreover, it gave them an identity that connected them to the promises of God and to the institutions of their past. It focused and guided their present actions. It gave them reason to hope for a better future. As Sara Japhet has said, "For the Chronicler, 'the history of Israel' is the arena in which God's providence and rule of his people are enacted. By unveiling the principles which govern its history, a firm foundation is laid for the future existence of Israel."[14]

*The Development of the Seeking Argument and
the Complementary Use of Enthymemes and Examples in Chronicles*

In rhetorical argumentation there are two forms of demonstration, the enthymeme and the example.[15] The enthymeme, a "consideration," is a reasonable inferential argument from a likelihood or sign to the best explanation.[16] The example is a form of argument by which a parallel is drawn between things of the same class.[17]

In the historical narrative of Chronicles, enthymemes occur in material in which an opinion or evaluation is stated either in a speech of one of the characters or in the form of explanatory narrative comments. Examples occur in the kind of material that might be called "straight narrative," narrative material that simply reports an event, as opposed to various kinds of explanatory comments from the narrator. Also, in some cases, evaluative comments of an enthymemic nature may be woven into a narrative example.

The nature and style of the rhetorical presentation determines the manner in which one uses enthymemes and examples. Aristotle observed that when examples precede enthymemes, the argument takes on an inductive air. For such an argument to be convincing, one must give a large number of examples. On the other hand, when examples follow enthymemes, they function much like the testimony of witnesses. In the latter case a single example

---

Chronikbüchern (WMANT 42; Neukirchen-Vluyn: Neukirchener Verlag, 1973). See also the chart of the indications of blessing and cursing in Duke, *Persuasive Appeal,* 78–79.

14. Japhet, *I & II Chronicles,* 44.
15. Aristotle, *Rhet.*, 1.2.1356a36–1356b17.
16. For a fuller treatment, see Eugene E. Ryan, *Aristotle's Theory of Rhetorical Argumentation* (Montreal: Bellarmin, 1984), 95–96; and Myles Fredric Burnyeat, "Enthymeme: Aristotle on the Logic of Persuasion," in *Aristotle's Rhetoric: Philosophical Essays* (ed. D. J. Furley and A. Nehamas; Princeton, N.J.: Princeton University Press, 1994), 3–55.
17. For a fuller description of the example, see Ryan, *Aristotle's Theory,* 117–27.

might be sufficient, if it is a good one.[18] So, how did the Chronicler employ enthymemes and examples?

The Chronicler's history of Israel offered a new interpretation of his audience's traditions; that is, he interpreted much of Israel's story as shaped by the "seeking God" paradigm. He faced a rhetorical challenge of how to present this new interpretation convincingly. On the one hand, an attempt to offer this new interpretation deductively by using enthymemes at the beginning of his work would have increased the likelihood of its rejection, unless he wielded the authority necessary to demand that the audience reject the old traditions and accept the new. On the other hand, to present a new interpretation inductively through examples would create less of a demand on the speaker's authority. However, to offer a string of historical examples without explicit and interpretive enthymemes would also increase the possibility that the audience would fail to see the argument. One finds that to solve this rhetorical problem the Chronicler presented a skillful and delicately balanced employment of examples and enthymemes. The Chronicler's demonstration through enthymemes moves: (1) from infrequent use to frequent use, (2) from being presented in unobtrusive material to more obtrusive material, and (3) from being related to traditionally accepted signs to being related to more specific signs connected to the concept of seeking. His demonstration through example moves from the creation of a whole David-Solomonic paradigm, which in itself contains several examples of seeking Yahweh, to a succession of examples found in the account of the following Davidic kings.

From Adam to Saul (1 Chronicles 1–9):
Anticipation of the Seeking Argument

In the genealogical lists of the first nine chapters, a basic form of the Chronicler's argument appears proleptically five times in enthymemes. These "argue" a maxim of divine blessing/punishment and are based on traditionally accepted signs and relationships: Judah's son Er was "wicked" and put to death (2:3); certain Israelite tribes were victorious in battle because they cried out to God and trusted him (5:20, 22); exile occurred because Israel "played the harlot" after other gods (5:25–26) and because Judah was "unfaithful" (9:1). In the midst of various lists, such narrative comments stand out and begin to direct the thinking of the audience to the principles operative in the narrative world and, therefore, in the real world.

---

18. Aristotle, *Rhet.*, 2.20.1394a9–17.

Saul (1 Chronicles 10): Introduction of the Seeking Argument

Once the narrative proper begins at Chapter 10, the seeking argument is first clearly and blatantly stated in enthymemic form in the connection with an example, Saul's death (1 Chr 10:1–12):

> And Saul died for his sin, which he sinned against Yahweh, on account of the word of Yahweh which he did not keep, and even by asking the medium to seek. But he did not seek Yahweh, so he killed him and he turned over the kingdom to David the son of Jesse (1 Chr 10:13–14).

The enthymeme in this narrative comment is expressed in its negative form: Saul died and lost his kingdom because he did not seek Yahweh. Although the enthymeme is complete in this form, this one can be restated in syllogistic form:

> The one who does not seek Yahweh will be cursed/punished.
>
> Saul did not seek Yahweh.
>
> Therefore, Saul was punished (lost his kingdom and his life).

The above enthymeme regarding Saul's death is constructed on one of the common topics, a maxim. A maxim is a commonly accepted opinion about a generally applicable principle.[19] The maxim here is, "Yahweh blesses those who act in the manner he prescribes and forsakes or curses those who do not." The strength of this maxim was that it was not new. One finds this idea of divine retribution in the Samuel-Kings narrative, in legal material, in wisdom literature, and in the prophets. The Chronicler built his enthymeme on a concept he could safely assume his audience accepted. According to Aristotle, building an enthymeme on such generally accepted principles invests the act of communication with moral character and gains the audience's favor.[20] The maxim used by the Chronicler is related causally to a specific event by a connecting "sign" that reveals that the principle is in effect. Saul died in battle; Saul lost his kingdom. Here is a sign that the negative corollary of the maxim is in effect. The logical structure behind this kind of enthymeme may be expressed as follows:

> If A is a sign of B, and A has occurred, then one can predicate B.

An enthymeme based on this structure is formally non-genuine or not "valid," but still may present the best explanation and convince the audience.[21] The persuasive appeal of the Chronicler's enthymeme, therefore, rested upon

---

19. Aristotle, *Rhet.*, 2.21.
20. Ibid., 2.21.1395b–17.
21. See the description of the fourth non-genuine enthymeme in Aristotle, *Rhet.*, 2.24.1401b9–13.

the degree to which his audience believed the maxim and accepted the relationship between the signs and the maxim.[22]

The enthymeme is stated "blatantly" because it occurs in a narrative comment; that is, in material which "breaks frame" with the action of the narrative and provides an interpretation or explanation. The Chronicler as narrator becomes most visible to his audience in such material and leaves himself and his argument open to challenge by the audience. Such blatant presentations of the enthymeme are rare in the first half of Chronicles. Only twice in the following material about David and Solomon (comprising 28 chapters) are there enthymemes about God's intervention in the form of narrative comments. These exceptions concern the proper cultic procedure for the transportation of the ark (1 Chr 13:10; 15:25-26), two occasions that were used to define the Chronicler's particular concept of "seeking." His general argument is not again demonstrated by an enthymeme in narrative comment material until one reaches the accounts of the Davidic monarchy. By then the argument has been well established by the use of examples and by presenting the enthymeme in other types of material.

This first enthymemic comment, regarding Saul's death, reveals some persuasive subtlety. As a narrative explanation it carries the risk of leaving the Chronicler as narrator open to challenge. As an enthymeme based on a sign topic, it is also open to refutation by counter example. Still, the Chronicler has minimized the risks in a couple of ways. First, because enthymemes built on the same maxim occurred in the lists of the first nine chapters, the evaluation fits in with a train of thought already introduced, thus lessening its obtrusiveness. Second, the Chronicler is careful not to stray far from tradition. Virtually the whole chapter (with the exception of the unique tradition about the disposal of Saul's head [v. 10b]) through v. 13 is equivalent to the tradition of 1 Samuel 31:1-13.[23] Then begins this narrative comment, which also draws on tradition. The cause of Saul's demise in the older tradition was primarily regarded as Saul's failure to obey the commands of Yahweh (1 Sam 13:13-14; 15:23). This event is what the Chronicler alludes to when he states, "Saul died... because of the word of Yahweh which he did not keep" (v. 13). He then adds to this general reason another specific transgression of Saul's,

---

22. One problem the Chronicler faced while recounting the traditions of Israel was that of providing the audience with a counter example, the exception to the rule that would weaken his argument. I would suggest that this is the primary reason that the Chronicler presents traditions of the life of David that support his argument and in virtually all cases omits those that could call the paradigm into question.

23. I have argued elsewhere that although one should not presuppose that the Chronicler's audience had in hand the parallel account of Samuel-Kings that there is evidence that the Chronicler expected his audience to be familiar with its traditions (Duke, *Persuasive Appeal,* 36-37).

which also belonged to older tradition: Saul also failed to obey Yahweh when he inquired of the medium at Endor, the event at which his defeat was announced (1 Sam 28:8–19). The Chronicler, making a play on Saul's name for heightened effect, includes Saul's (*sh'wl*) act of asking (*sh'l*) the medium as the specific cause of Saul's death (v. 13). This conclusion, while not stated explicitly in the Book of Samuel, would have followed by analogy. Here was another transgression of Saul and the particular one at which his defeat was prophesied.

However, at this point the Chronicler begins to introduce a new concept. He sums up his evaluation, adding a new element: "Now he did not seek (*drsh*) Yahweh, so he put him to death" (v. 14). The new element is that the maxim of blessing/punishment is connected to the action of seeking or not seeking Yahweh. Here "seeking" occurs with the same technical nuance found in its use in Samuel-Kings, that of prophetic inquiry or consultation, so that its occurrence here is quite appropriate.[24] The audience is prepared to accept the identification of "not seeking" with "not keeping the word of Yahweh." However, by the end of Chronicles, "seeking" will have been used some thirty-five times in a redefined sense, such as establishing the cult (1 Chr 28:9), keeping the Torah (2 Chr 14:3), walking in God's commandments (2 Chr 17:4), and destroying Asherahs (2 Chr 19:3).[25] As a result, the maxim of divine retribution becomes applied to a new range of actions and events. In short, the Chronicler introduced his enthymeme in a rather obtrusive form of material while he lessened the chance of rejection by building on a safe example from the tradition of the audience. At the same time he began a program to move the audience to accept a transformed understanding of the process of blessing/punishment by using a key term with an accepted range of meaning ("seek"), which he would later redefine in more specific cultic terms.

David and Solomon (1 Chronicles 11–2 Chronicles 9):
Development of the Seeking Argument

Development through Examples. The period of history that received the most attention from the Chronicler was that of David and Solomon. Their stories make up about one third of the book. At first thought one might suppose that the personal characters of David and Solomon were of particular importance

---

24. Mark A. Throntveit, *When Kings Speak: Royal Speech and Royal Prayer in Chronicles* (SBLDS 93; Atlanta: Scholars, 1987), 116–18. See also Schaefer, "Seeking God," 62–66, on the use of *drsh* in a religious context.

25. Throntveit, *When Kings Speak,* 116–18; Schaefer, "Seeking God," 62–66; Roddy L. Braun, "The Significance of 1 Chronicles 22, 28, and 29 for the Structure and Theology of the Work of the Chronicler" (Th.D. diss., Concordia Seminary, 1971), 172–74.

to the Chronicler. Yet, in this material there is little interest shown in their personalities. In contrast to the account in Samuel-Kings, little is learned about their thoughts and feelings.[26] Rather, in contrast to Saul, who becomes a foil, David and Solomon are presented typologically through several examples as persons who properly sought Yahweh and received blessing. For instance: Saul inquired (*sh'l*) of a medium (10:13), but David inquired (*sh'l*) of God (14:10, 11); Saul was defeated by the Philistines and his head was placed in the temple of Dagon (10:1, 9–10), but Yahweh gave David victory over the Philistines and their gods (ch. 14); all of Saul's house perished (10:6; note that Mephibosheth is never mentioned in Chronicles), but David's lineage and claim to the kingdom were secured by God (ch. 17); the ark was not sought in the days of Saul (13:3), but David's first official act was to try to bring the ark to Jerusalem (ch. 13). In short, Saul was put to death because he did not keep the word of God and seek God, but David's rule was secured because he properly sought God. The following narratives are rhetorically structured in various ways (i.e., using key words, inclusio, alternating repetition, chiasmus, etc.) in order to emphasize the point that as these key characters sought God and established the things of God, God established them.[27] As a result, this account consists primarily of examples which redefine the maxim of blessing/punishment and which establish the Chronicler's major historical paradigm by which the actions of the succeeding Davidic kings are measured.

Development through Enthymemes. Only twice in this material does the enthymeme occur in narrative comments (1 Chr 13:10; 15:25–26), and these instances are related to the correct transportation of the ark. They explain that when improper cultic procedures are used, disaster follows; but when proper cultic procedures are heeded, success occurs. However, the enthymemic form of the Chronicler's argument does appear thirteen more times in this section, but in a particular type of material. Rather than in the more obtrusive form of narrator comment, it occurs in the speeches of authoritative characters: Yahweh, David, and Solomon.[28] The vehicle of speech material allows the Chronicler as narrator to remain in the background and yet communicate the enthymeme through the ethos of authoritative characters. Therefore, the

---

26. So, too, observed W. Johnstone, "Guilt and Atonement: The Theme of 1 and 2 Chronicles," in *A Word in Season* (ed. J. D. Martin and P. R. Davies; JSOTSup 42; Sheffield: JSOT, 1986), 113.
27. See Duke, *Persuasive Appeal*, 56–66.
28. These instances are: 1 Chr 17:4–14; 17:16–27; 21:8; 21:17; 22:7–16; 22:18–19; 28:2–8; 28:9–10; 28:20–21; 29:10–19; 2 Chr 1:7–12; 6:14–42; 7:12–22. In some instances the enthymeme is more implicit than explicit.

persuasive appeal of the argument rests less on his authority and more on the authority of those speaking. In these instances, too, the argument becomes increasingly defined and more boldly phrased.

The first two illustrations of this communication of the enthymeme are found in the section in which the Davidic dynasty is secured (1 Chr 17). The enthymeme is communicated by implication in an expression of the reciprocal principle of "establishing," that is as David establishes Yahweh's house, Yahweh establishes David's. Yahweh, via Nathan, promises:

> He [Solomon] will build for me a house, and I will establish [*kwn*] his throne forever (1 Chr 17:12).

David responds in a lengthy prayer:

> And now, Yahweh, let [your] word ... concerning his house be established [*'mn*]....
> And let your name be established [*'mn*] and magnified forever, saying, "Yahweh of hosts is the God of Israel...." " and the house of David your servant is established [*kwn*] before you (1 Chr 17:23–24).[29]

Although it is not explicitly stated, the context of events should lead the audience to see that David has "sought God" by desiring to build the temple, and Yahweh consequently has blessed David by promising to found his dynasty. The application of the Chronicler's maxim is implied. Again, this expression of the maxim is based on tradition found in synoptic material (2 Sam 7).

One finds the negative expression of divine retribution in the next two instances of the enthymeme, 1 Chronicles 21:8 and 17. These instances also occur in a synoptic passage and again demonstrate the argument rather implicitly in two prayers of David. Having sinned by ordering a census, David incurred punishment on himself and his people. Praying to Yahweh (i.e., an expression of seeking), David confesses his responsibility and asks that the judgment on the people be diverted.

At the close of David's life, in two sets of parallel speeches that bracket cultic-list material, David proclaims the enthymeme with increasing specificity. In chapter 22, in a charge to Solomon, David repeats the promise about the reciprocal relationship of establishing and adds further:

> Now, my son, may Yahweh be with you, so that you may succeed and build the house of Yahweh your God just as he promised concerning you. Only may Yahweh give you discretion and understanding, when he gives you command over Israel, to keep the law of Yahweh your God. Then you will prosper, if you are careful to do the statutes and the judgments (1 Chr 22:11–13).

---

29. The second occurrence of *'mn* in vv. 23–24 is not found in the parallel material in 2 Sam 7. It is possible that the Chronicler has added it to his source in order to highlight this reciprocal relationship.

And to the leaders he charges:

> Is not Yahweh your God with you, and has given you rest from all sides?... Now set your heart and your soul to seek Yahweh your God; and arise and build the sanctuary of Yahweh God (1 Chr 22:18–19).

Then in the parallel speeches in chapter 28, which invert the order of those addressed, David, quoting the promise of Yahweh, first gives a charge to the leaders:

> And I will establish [*kwn*] his kingdom forever, if he resolutely performs my commandments and my ordinances, as at this day. So now... observe and seek after all the commandments of Yahweh your God in order that you may possess the good land (1 Chr 28:7–8).

And David charges Solomon, stating the enthymeme explicitly;

> Serve Yahweh with a whole heart. If you seek him, he will let you find him; but if you forsake him, he will reject you forever (1 Chr 28:9b).

Some observations are called for in regard to these parallel speeches. First, the above speeches are not found in synoptic tradition but are unique to Chronicles. It is possible that the Chronicler has gone beyond the range of known tradition. If so, the type of material again reduces the risk of the argument being rejected. It is not found in obtrusive narrative comments, but in speeches by an authoritative person, speeches which are "in character" for the Chronicler's presentation of David. Second, at the same time there is a special force to the argument because it is in the form of speech. Not only does the king address the audience within the narrative, but also the actual audience of the Chronicler is likely to hear and feel the force of direct speech. As David speaks to Solomon and the Israelite leaders, he speaks to the Chronicler's audience. Third, these speeches, which are in inverted order and form an inclusio, bracket material consisting primarily of lists of cultic personnel appointed by David. This rhetorical structure emphasizes further David's vital role in establishing the temple cultus (see 1 Chr 23:5a, 6, 25–27; 24:3, 31; 25:1, 6; 26:30–32).[30] Finally, the causal relationship between blessing and seeking Yahweh through proper cultic practice is fully and explicitly argued in these speeches.

In the following account of Solomon, the same pattern is followed. The events chosen by the Chronicler give examples of Solomon seeking Yahweh and receiving blessing in return. The enthymemic clarification of this relationship is stated directly only in speech material found in the mouths of

---

30. Chapters 23–26 consist of personnel who did service either for the temple or for the temple and the king (26:29–32), while chapter 27 consists of personnel who served the king only.

Yahweh and Solomon. By the end of the account of David and Solomon the causal relationship of seeking Yahweh to blessing has been forcefully argued by a well-constructed interplay of examples and enthymemes.

The Davidic Kings (2 Chronicles 10–36): Application of the Seeking Argument

Once the Chronicler's argument had been well demonstrated in the construction of the Davidic-Solomonic paradigm, the events in the following lives of the Davidic kings further exemplified the Chronicler's fuller maxim of blessing/punishment that he saw at work in the nation's history. The accounts of the kings of Judah are presented in quick succession. Jehoshaphat, Ahaz, Hezekiah, and Josiah are explicitly compared to David and/or Solomon (17:3; 28:1; 29:2; 34:2, 3). Other comparisons are implicit. If a king "does right in the sight of Yahweh," "walks in the ways" of a righteous predecessor, humbles himself, preserves the Jerusalem cult (i.e., engages in some form of seeking God), then the king is blessed with deliverance from defeat, with military success, wealth, building projects and so forth. If the king "walks in the ways" of an unrighteous predecessor, is proud, relies on an idolatrous king or nation, ignores cultic concerns, (i.e., some expression of forsaking God), then he and the people meet with a reversal of fate.[31]

A significant change in pattern occurs in this section on the succeeding Davidic kings. In this section the enthymeme now occurs more frequently and in more blatant form. It is stated twenty-three times in speech material.[32] Moreover, now that the Chronicler has demonstrated his argument he states the enthymeme twenty times in the more obtrusive form of narrative-explanatory comments.[33]

Summary and Conclusion

The Chronicler used a supportive balance of demonstration through enthymeme and example. His argument is first stated by an example with an accompanying enthymeme in a "high-risk" form of narrative comment ex-

---

31. See also the chart of the indications of blessing and cursing in the reign of each king in Duke, *Persuasive Appeal*, 78–79.

32. 2 Chr 12:5, 7–8; 13:4–12; 14:7, 11; 15:2–7; 16:7–9; 19:2–3; 20:6–12, 15–17, 20, 37; 21:12–15; 24:20, 22; 25:7–9, 15–16; 28:9–11; 29:5–11; 30:6–9, 18–19; 33:7–8; 34:23–28. In some cases the enthymeme is stated implicitly and in others more explicitly.

33. 2 Chr 13:18, 20; 14:5 (6); 15:15; 17:3–4; 20:30; 21:10; 22:7; 24:24; 25:20, 27; 26:5; 27:6; 28:6, 19, 25; 32:22, 26, 33:12–13; 36:15–16. Again, in some cases the enthymeme is stated implicitly and in others more explicitly.

plaining the death of Saul. The Chronicler decreased the risk by basing what he said on an appeal to tradition and a common maxim regarding the divine principle of blessing/punishment. This principle is then expanded to include a broader range of actions related to the cult, and is supported inductively by many examples taken from the lives of David and Solomon. In the material on David and Solomon (1 Chr 11–2 Chr 9) the enthymeme is infrequently stated. However, where it is found is in the mouths of authoritative characters, so that its weight of authority rests on those characters and not on the ethos of the narrator. The accounts of the succeeding kings (2 Chr 10–36) are structured so as to serve as series of examples further demonstrating the results of seeking or forsaking Yahweh. In this section the Chronicler proceeded with greater boldness. The enthymeme is more frequently stated, not only in the speeches of authoritative characters, but now in the form of narrative comments. This is to say that the Chronicler started with a primarily inductive and safe demonstration of his argument while establishing his Davidic-Solomonic paradigm. He then moved to a more deductive demonstration in the lives of the Davidic kings, employing more explanatory statements and using examples as supportive "witnesses." He made his case subtly and cautiously and then argued it more forcefully once he felt it had been sufficiently established.

In conclusion, a good communicator knows that in the demonstration of an argument to a general audience one must present one's case in an appealing manner and must repeat the argument several times in different ways. The Chronicler did just that. In effect, through his re-presentation of the story of Judah, one of the Chronicler's arguments might be paraphrased as follows:

> As you know, there is a principle operating in this world, a principle of retribution according to which Yahweh blesses or curses. Blessing is contingent on seeking Yahweh through establishing and maintaining the cult of Yahweh. Surely you will want to take this course of seeking God, because it results in what is good and advantageous for you and virtuous. See the examples from our past, make the comparison, and judge for yourselves. Look at David and Solomon. They sought Yahweh and were blessed. Look at those who were without such virtue. You certainly do not desire for yourselves what happened to them. What course of response, then, will you choose?

The Chronicler made a strategic and persuasive appeal as he represented the traditions of his audience's past in order to move them to understand the way God works in their world and to respond accordingly.

CHAPTER 8

SHOULD AHAB GO TO BATTLE OR NOT? AMBIGUITY AS A RHETORICAL DEVICE IN 1 KINGS 22

Alan J. Hauser

Introduction

The writer of the narrative in 1 Kings 22 uses ambiguity as an effective rhetorical device to argue that Ahab is very wicked and Yahweh, therefore, urgently desires his death. This argument is carefully developed through the words and actions of Ahab and Micaiah. Before analyzing this account, we need to compare the nature of argumentation in Old Testament narrative literature to argumentation in other types of Old Testament literature. We begin by briefly describing argumentation in Old Testament texts other than narrative, using several examples, and then comparing these to narrative argumentation.

Argumentation

Argumentation in wisdom literature is often presented tersely, as in the series of pithy sayings at the beginning of Proverbs 13, wherein each verse contains a complete argument. Even when argumentation in wisdom literature is more extensive, small, closely knit units are frequently clustered to build a larger argument, as in Job 3:20–23, which itself forms one piece within the broader context of Job's opening soliloquy. In legal literature, argumentation is often presented in short units, perhaps not as tightly focused as in wisdom literature, but often vividly descriptive of particular problems or practices, as in Leviticus 19:5–8 and Deuteronomy 24:1–4. Clarity and succinct argumentation prevail. In prophetic literature, the words typically concentrate vividly-drawn pictures and tightly-woven arguments into short units that drive home an argument with caustic precision, as in Amos 1:3–5, and 4:1–3. In one last sample, the Psalms, argumentation may be developed in a longer framework, as in Psalm 124, which employs numerous images and metaphors from Israel's life to show why the reader should bless the Lord, or Psalm 137, which uses two vivid scenes to plead with the Lord to requite Babylon and Edom.

In contrast, argumentation in Old Testament narrative normally employs a lengthier format as the writer guides the reader toward particular conclusions, although the words chosen are, nevertheless, very carefully focused. Narrative argumentation often is less explicit, relying on the subtleties of story line and dialogue to make its case. For example, in the narrative poetry of Judges 5, which never once directly *curses* the Canaanites, the writer, through succinct characterization, heavily laden but terse dialogue, and a series of skillfully constructed vignettes which have a cumulative effect, devastatingly excoriates the Canaanites.[1] In Genesis 22 the writer argues effectively that Abraham is a man of great faith without ever saying so explicitly, choosing instead to use sharply honed dialogue, pregnant silence, a sparse but precisely articulated story line, suspense, carefully focused development of characters, and phrases laden with implication to concentrate the reader's attention on the enormous sacrifice which Abraham is prepared to make. What is unspoken can be as important as what is said openly in moving the writer's argument forward.[2] This is not to say that narrative cannot be direct and forceful in presenting a point: it certainly can, as in 1 Kings 21:17–26. Nevertheless, narrative argumentation tends, overall, to be less direct, more implicit, more complicated, more nuanced, and more dependent on the writer's use of skilled narrative tools to develop in the reader's mind the essence of the writer's argument.[3]

Source Criticism and Narrative Criticism

In the late nineteenth century and throughout most of the twentieth century, the text of 1 Kings 22 has been treated in either of two ways. Some scholars have divided the text into two or more sources.[4] This approach, unfortunately,

---

1. See Alan J. Hauser, "Judges 5: Parataxis in Hebrew Poetry," *JBL* 99 (March 1980): 23–41, and Robert Alter, *The Art of Biblical Poetry* (New York: Basic Books, 1985), 43–49.
2. See Erich Auerbach's excellent discussion in *Mimesis: The Representation of Reality in Western Literature* (Princeton, N.J.: Princeton University Press, 1968), 8–23.
3. Due to space limitations, this discussion of the difference between argumentation in OT narrative and argumentation in other types of OT literature is of necessity couched in generalizations. They all have exceptions, but the basics hold true.
4. Friedrich Schwally, "Zur Geschichte der historischen Bücher," *ZAW* 12 (1892): 159–61; John Gray: *I and II Kings; A Commentary* (OTL; Philadelphia: Westminster, 1963), 371–72, 394–95; Georg Fohrer, *Introduction to the Old Testament* (trans. D. Green; Nashville: Abingdon, 1968), 232; Simon De Vries, *Prophet Against Prophet: The Role of the Micaiah Narrative (I Kings 22) in the Development of Early Prophetic Tradition* (Grand Rapids: Eerdmans, 1978); Ernst Würthwein, "Zur Composition von I Reg. 22:1–38," in *Das ferne und nahe Wort: Festschrift L. Rost* (ed. F. Maass; BZAW 105; Berlin: A. Töpelmann, 1967), 245–54.

slices up the text, thereby obscuring the rich texture of its narrative.[5] Other scholars have viewed the text as a single unit, with perhaps a few glosses.[6] While this approach does retain the basic integrity of the text, it is typically more concerned with historical rather than rhetorical or narrative issues. My own approach will treat the text as a unity, following the methods of recent narrative criticism.

In the past three decades, narrative criticism has come to mean, in Old Testament studies, careful attention to all the details and subtleties of the given text, such as character, plot development, the use of repetition and convention, and the tightly focused use of discourse. Most readers will be familiar with the numerous works that have articulated recent narrative criticism, but let me cite the works of Fokkelman, Sternberg, Alter, Berlin, Bar-Efrat, Gunn and Fewell, and Trible.[7] Sternberg, especially, presents an extensive development of Old Testament narrative theory, and Berlin and Alter[8] provide excellent analyses of character development in biblical narrative. Crucial to my paper, which focuses on ambiguity as a key means of argumentation in 1 Kings 22, are the discussions of the use of ambiguity in biblical narrative argumentation presented by Sternberg,[9] Alter,[10] Berlin,[11] Gunn and Fewell,[12] and Fokkelman.[13]

---

5. For example, De Vries's comment that 1 Kings 22 "exhibits a meaninglessly complex and disjointed structure," *Prophet,* 25, reveals a profound insensitivity to the writer's carefully nuanced development of this narrative. De Vries dissects the narrative into "two simple and internally consistent accounts" (*Prophet,* 29).

6. Julius Wellhausen, *Die Composition des Hexateuchs und der historischen Bücher des Alten Testaments* (4th ed.; Berlin: Georg Reimer, 1963), 283–87; Hugo Gressmann, *Die älteste Geschichtsschreibung und Prophetie Israels.* Vol. 2.1 of *Die Schriften des Alten Testaments in Auswahl* (2d ed.; Göttingen: Vandenhoeck & Ruprecht, 1921), 279–80; Norman Snaith, "Introduction and Exegesis on Kings," in *The Interpreter's Bible* (New York: Abingdon Press, 1954), 13; and James A. Montgomery, *A Critical and Exegetical Commentary on the Books of Kings* (ICC; Edinburgh: Clark, 1967), 336.

7. Robert Alter, *The Art of Biblical Narrative* (New York: Basic Books, 1981); Shimon Bar-Efrat, *Narrative Art in the Bible* (Sheffield: Almond Press, 1989); Adele Berlin, *Poetics and the Interpretation of Biblical Narrative* (Sheffield: Almond Press, 1983); Jan P. Fokkelman, *Narrative Art and Poetry in the Books of Samuel: A Full Interpretation Based on Stylistic and Structural Analysis* (4 vols.; Assen: Van Gorcum, 1981, 1986, 1990, 1993); David M. Gunn and Dana Nolan Fewell, *Narrative in the Hebrew Bible* (Oxford: Oxford University Press, 1993); Meir Sternberg, *The Poetics of Biblical Narrative* (Bloomington: Indiana University Press, 1985); Phyllis Trible, *Texts of Terror: Literary Feminist Readings of Biblical Narrative* (Philadelphia: Fortress Press, 1984).

8. Berlin, *Poetics,* chs. 2, 3, and 4; and Alter, *Narrative,* ch. 6.

9. Sternberg, *Poetics,* 186–229.

10. Alter, *Art,* 114–30.

11. See Berlin's discussion of point of view (*Poetics,* 43–82), and especially dissonance, pp. 71–73.

12. Gunn and Fewell, *Narrative,* passim.

13. Fokkelman, *Narrative Art,* passim.

The Definition of Ambiguity

Ambiguity results when the writer purposely has two or more significantly different options which vie with one another during a portion of the narrative. This can be at the micro level, where short scenes develop brief ambiguities which are quickly resolved, or at the macro level, where ambiguity often forms a key element driving the main story line.[14] As Lotman notes, the interactions between the options "contribute[s] additional layers of meaning."[15] Thus, every vying option "makes claims to be the truth and struggles to assert itself in the conflict with opposing ones."[16]

Skillful use of ambiguity requires careful structuring of the text, and therefore must be carefully distinguished from vagueness. Vagueness indicates a lack of precision on certain points, as when a writer's terse style emphasizes important matters and inadvertently leaves other matters unattended.[17] Ambiguity is intentional rather than inadvertent, structuring opposing systems whose incompatibility will clash until they are resolved when the writer's point is made.[18] Thus, ambiguity keeps the reader guessing until the key moment, when things are suddenly made clear and the desired point is driven home most effectively.

Ambiguity in 1 Kings 22

The writer of 1 Kings 22 deftly employs ambiguity to cause the reader to vacillate between the possibility that Yahweh will be on Ahab's side in the battle against Syria and will give Ahab the victory (e.g., vv. 6, 11–12), and the possibility that Ahab and his military expedition are doomed. Although the latter point is never explicitly voiced until Micaiah speaks it in verses 17 and 19–23, the writer repeatedly hints at it throughout the story, thereby keeping the reader torn between the two scenarios. The numerous and dramatic twists and turns in the plot push the reader first in one direction, then in the other. The ambiguity is clarified only when Ahab is killed in battle (vv. 34–36). Then, the blunt words of Micaiah in verse 17 and the description of Yahweh's

---

14. See, for example, Berlin's discussion of the multiple ambiguities in Genesis 37, which go unresolved until ch. 42; *Poetics*, 48–53.
15. J. M. Lotman, *The Structure of the Artistic Text* (Ann Arbor: University of Michigan, 1977), 341.
16. Lotman, *Structure*, 352.
17. See Shlomith Rimmon, *The Concept of Ambiguity — the Example of James* (Chicago: University of Chicago Press, 1977), 19–20.
18. Rimmon, *Ambiguity*, 13–21.

plot against Ahab in verses 20–23 serve to emphasize Yahweh's powerfully negative assessment of Ahab. The reader can reflect on these words and say, "I should have seen it coming. All the signs were there."

The Literary Context for 1 Kings 22

The earlier condemnation of Ahab by the disguised prophet in 1 Kings 20:42 is unequivocal: "Thus says the Lord, 'Because you have let go from your hand the man [Ben-hadad] whom I had devoted to destruction, therefore your life shall take the place of his life, and your people shall take the place of his people.'" Likewise, the condemnation of Ahab by Elijah in 1 Kings 21 is very blunt: "Thus says the Lord, 'In the place where the dogs licked up the blood of Naboth, the dogs will also lick up your blood, even yours'" (v. 19); "I will bring disaster on you; I will consume after you, and I will cut off from Ahab every male, slave or free, in Israel" (v. 21). Yet, despite these strong words, the story of Naboth's vineyard concludes with the decidedly ambiguous scene (21:27–29) wherein the contrite Ahab elicits from Yahweh the response, spoken to Elijah, "Have you seen how Ahab has humbled himself before me? Because he has humbled himself before me, I will not bring the disaster in his days; rather, in the days of his son I will bring the disaster on his house." Does this reverse the previous negative prophetic words anticipating Ahab's death, even though the dynasty is still clearly doomed? Does "the disaster" which will be postponed until the time of Ahab's son include the violent end typically inflicted on the reigning king when a dynasty falls, thereby exempting Ahab from this fate? Or, will Ahab still suffer his violent end, but under circumstances that will not yet bring down the dynasty? The reader is left wondering, and therefore approaches chapter 22 with no clear sense of direction concerning Ahab. Furthermore, the reader is not told whether the words of Yahweh concerning Ahab are ever conveyed *to* Ahab, or whether Ahab still knows only the previous highly negative words spoken by the bandaged prophet and by Elijah. Does Ahab assume forgiveness by Yahweh as he plans for the battle at Ramoth-Gilead, or does he assume that the prophets' sentences of death still hang over his head? This ambiguity regarding the meaning of Yahweh's words to Elijah in 21:29 prepares the way for further development of the ambiguity concerning Ahab's fate in 1 Kings 22.

Jehoshaphat and the 400 Prophets (1 Kings 22:1–8)

From the outset, Jehoshaphat's role underlines the ambiguity about Ahab's situation. When Ahab asks Jehoshaphat if he will go to war with him (v. 4), Jehoshaphat answers with resolve: "We are as one. My people are as your people, my horses are as your horses." However, the writer immediately makes Jehoshaphat's commitment appear ambiguous by having Jehoshaphat ask Ahab to inquire of Yahweh before they go to battle (v. 5: "Please inquire [imperative], today").[19] The reader wonders why Jehoshaphat, so recently committed to fighting at Ramoth-Gilead (v. 4), is now wavering. This is the writer's first hint that perhaps all is not well.

Ahab calls together 400 prophets, who assert (v. 6), "Go up! [in the imperative] The Lord will give it into the hand of the king." The number of prophets and the decisiveness of their words convey a tone of certainty, suggesting that Yahweh's words in 21:28–29 had postponed any disaster initially intended for Ahab. Yet, the 400 prophets remind the reader of the 450 prophets of Ba'al[20] and the 400 prophets of Asherah (18:19) whom Elijah had confronted on Mount Carmel. There, the many voices had been wrong. This allusion to the earlier story casts into doubt the dependability of the many voices in chapter 22. Jehoshaphat also undercuts the 400 by asking whether there is not *another* prophet of whom they may inquire (v. 7: "Let us inquire" [cohortative]). Jehoshaphat's request seems ludicrous, until one recalls the earlier errors of the large groups of prophets. Thus, the writer has introduced ambiguity both by having Jehoshaphat's previous resolve (v. 4) dissolve into skepticism (vv. 5, 7), and by having the words of the 400 prophets fail to restore Jehoshaphat's confidence. The wisdom of Ahab's decision to fight the Syrians therefore comes more and more into question, and the reader is led to wonder whether Yahweh's words to Elijah in 21:29 really meant that Ahab would be spared.

The king of Israel's response in verse 8 is hardly reassuring, even to himself: "There is still one man through whom to inquire of the Lord, but I hate him, because he never prophesies good to me, but only evil, Micaiah the son of Imlah." Jehoshaphat's skepticism now appears especially well founded. Ahab is playing with a stacked deck, carefully omitting the one prophet certain to speak a negative word against him. The ambiguity about Ahab's situation therefore deepens, as the writer shows that not only is Jehoshaphat skeptical: the king of Israel is also trying to convince *himself* that all will be well. Furthermore, Ahab's entrenched fear of negative words from Micaiah sets the stage for Micaiah's surprisingly positive words to Ahab in verse 15, and these in turn set the stage for the dramatic shift when Micaiah reverses himself (v. 17) and presents Yahweh's plot against Ahab (vv. 19–23).

---

19. Würthwein misunderstands the ambiguity, and sees Jehoshaphat's reversal as evidence that we have two narratives in 1 Kings 22, vv. 1–4 and 29–37 being originally independent of 5–28; *Composition*, 250.

20. Gray, *I and II Kings*, 399.

Ahab's fears (v. 8) about Micaiah's words ultimately turn out to be true, but the writer keeps the reader guessing, both about Yahweh's purpose and about Micaiah's, until verses 19–23. Thus, in verses 2–8 the ambiguity concerning Ahab's fate grows as the plot twists and turns.

Zedekiah and the 400 Prophets (1 Kings 22:9–12)

The writer increases the ambiguity by reintroducing a positive note after the negative words of Jehoshaphat and the haunting doubts of Ahab. While the officer goes for Micaiah (v. 9), the 400 repeat their earlier words about Yahweh giving Ramoth-Gilead into the hand of the king of Israel, even using a symbolic pantomime with horns of iron, performed by Zedekiah, to reinforce their words. The "pomp and circumstance" of the situation, with the two kings arrayed in their robes, sitting on their thrones, and with the prophets in full ecstasy, strengthens the prophets' words, which seem to be carrying the day. The addition in verse 12 of the words "Go up [in the imperative] to Ramoth-Gilead and triumph" when the earlier words of the 400 (v. 6) are repeated, adds assurance to the prophets' message.

The writer alternates between positive words supporting Ahab's enterprise (vv. 3–4, 10–12) and negative words undermining that enterprise (vv. 5, 7–9). This alternating pattern will continue even beyond the crucial words in verse 23.

Micaiah (1 Kings 22:13–23)

The brief exchange between Micaiah and the officer (vv. 13–14) intensifies the ambiguity. The officer's careful, pleading words, urging Micaiah to go along with the 400, indicate that he fears Micaiah's word will be negative. Thus, the officer echoes Ahab's concern about what Micaiah will say. Micaiah's tart oath in verse 14, "By the life of Yahweh, I can only speak what Yahweh says to me," reinforces the fears of Ahab and his officer, for the prophet appears unwilling to "join the crowd" and speak a favorable word.

When Ahab questions Micaiah, the prophet surprises everyone by giving exactly the message Ahab wanted to hear: "Go up and triumph. Yahweh will give it into the hand of the king" (v. 15), reinforcing the words of the 400 prophets in verses 6 and 12.[21] Micaiah follows the request of the officer meticulously, assertively repeating the positive words of the 400. For now,

---

21. See Sternberg's discussion of the use of repetition (and variation) in vv. 12, 15, and 20 to heighten the ambiguity in this narrative; *Poetics*, 407, 409, 411, and 438.

the cloud over Ahab seems to have been lifted. The reader is left wondering, however, why the usually negative prophet so readily endorses Ahab's plan.

The writer springs another surprise with Ahab's response (v. 16). He tells Micaiah not to lie, but to speak "only the truth in the name of Yahweh." That Ahab does not rejoice in Micaiah's words, but instead accuses Micaiah of lying, suggests once again that Ahab fears that he and his war effort are doomed. Otherwise there would be no reason to challenge this positive word from Micaiah.[22] Ahab appears to have joined Jehoshaphat (cp. v. 7) in doubting the words of the 400. As we shall see, Ahab's demand that Micaiah speak the truth opens a whole new agenda of ambiguities regarding the "truth" that Yahweh wishes to have spoken.

Ahab threatens to order Micaiah to take an oath to ensure that he speaks the truth. It is most unusual for a king to distrust a positive word spoken about him by a prophet, and to threaten the prophet with an oath in order to receive a different word. Ahab's insistence on hearing the truth accentuates his innermost doubt about the words of the 400 prophets and Micaiah's initial word, and sets the stage for the stunning words of Yahweh and the lying spirit in verses 20–23. As will be seen, Micaiah is indeed lying to Ahab in verse 15, but is doing so *at the command of Yahweh.* Ahab senses only that Micaiah is lying on his own recognizance, but will soon discover a much more devastating lie directed against him. In the powerfully ironic twist in verses 22–23 Yahweh, the very one in whose name Ahab commands Micaiah to swear he is telling the truth, in fact *sanctions* the lie that Micaiah tells Ahab in verse 15. In verses 16–18 neither the reader nor Ahab knows this. Hence, the ambiguity grows, since the reader is left wondering why the normally negative prophet at first lies and speaks a positive word about the king. Only in verses 20–23 does it become clear why Micaiah initially lied: Yahweh wants all prophets to lie to Ahab, so that Ahab may fall in battle.

By verse 16, the ambiguity in the narrative has become intense. Zedekiah and the 400 prophets are the only ones who are not ambiguous, consistently urging Ahab to go up and triumph. Jehoshaphat waffles increasingly in two successive steps (vv. 5, 7). Ahab, who seemingly wants to hear only positive words about the battle, and therefore initially avoids Micaiah (v. 8), somehow suspects that the true word about him may be negative, and consequently bristles when Micaiah surprisingly speaks a positive one. Even Micaiah is decidedly ambiguous, insisting that he will speak only the true word Yahweh

---

22. I agree with De Vries (*Prophet,* 38) that Micaiah's comment is not to be taken as sarcastic, or "tongue in cheek." Contrast the opinion of Bar-Efrat, *Narrative Art,* 210–11.

tells him (v. 14), but then falling completely in line with the positive words of the 400 (v. 15).

Micaiah's response to Ahab's directive to speak the truth quickly plumbs Ahab's worst fears, presenting a frightening vision (v. 17) in which all Israel is scattered about the mountains (cf. 20:42). Micaiah does not describe Israel's defeat, nor does he say directly that Ahab will be killed, but rather that all Israel will be scattered like sheep without a shepherd.[23] The writer's use of indirection effectively forces the reader to conclude that Israel will be defeated and Ahab will be killed. The indirection contrasts strongly with the much more assertive "Go up and triumph: the Lord will give it into the hand of the king" uttered by the 400 prophets and initially by Micaiah (vv. 6, 12, and 15). That confidence now appears foolish in light of the picture of the fleeing Israelites, which is followed by a surprisingly low-key word from Yahweh, who says that Israel should be allowed to go home in peace, since it has no leader. This indirect, somber presentation of "the truth" adds considerable power to the devastating message Micaiah speaks.

Verse 18 again points to Ahab's ambivalence toward the prospects of the battle. He wants to believe that he will be successful, yet his own doubts have also surfaced (vv. 8, 16). Now, when he hears the "true" word extracted from Micaiah under threat of an oath, Ahab is also displeased, not wanting to confront the possibility of a horrible defeat. Micaiah's vivid vision strikes a raw nerve, and leads to Ahab's second complaint (v. 18; cf. v. 8) about Micaiah's negativism. Clearly, Ahab is torn, and cannot be happy with either message from Micaiah.

The writer has numerous ambiguities at work. Why does Micaiah reverse himself, knowing that the king's anger might be aroused? Why does he not deliver the negative message the first time he speaks? How will the 400 prophets respond to Micaiah? Which word will Ahab accept as true? Which word will in fact prove true?

Some of these ambiguities are directly addressed when Micaiah describes the earlier scene in the heavenly council (vv. 19–24). The key to these verses, and indeed to the whole chapter, comes in verse 20 when Yahweh asks, "Who will entice Ahab that he may go up and fall at Ramoth-Gilead?" The verb *pth*, in the Piel, commonly refers to deceiving someone or making someone appear to be a fool, especially by entrapping them. The verb is used three times in verses 20–22, emphasizing Yahweh's intention to entrap Ahab and lead him to his death. The entrapment motif is strengthened by the twofold

---

23. The shepherd is frequently used in the ancient Near East as a figure for the king, as in Zech 13:7. See Gray, *I and II Kings,* 402.

use of "lying spirit" in verses 22–23 to describe the devious means Yahweh will use to destroy Ahab, placing deceptive words in the mouths of Yahweh's own prophets.[24] Furthermore, in verse 20, for the first time in chapter 22, the writer introduces the name "Ahab." Heretofore, the king has consistently been called "the king of Israel" or simply "the king." The writer's sudden introduction of Ahab's personal name at precisely that point in the narrative where Yahweh's plot to entice and kill Ahab is clearly described for the first time adds considerable impact to the negative words spoken against him. He is "the king of Israel" as long as the account is ambiguous about whether he enjoys God's favor and support in the upcoming battle, but he becomes the much more personal "Ahab" when Yahweh makes it unmistakably clear that he wants this wicked king to die on the battlefield. The name "Ahab" is not used again until verses 39 and 40, which summarize Ahab's reign and burial. Thus, in this chapter Ahab's personal name is used only twice, once when Yahweh indicates his desire that Ahab fall, and then after Ahab's life has ended.

Up to verse 20, the writer has kept the reader in suspense regarding Yahweh's intentions toward Ahab, and has not clearly addressed the issue of whether Yahweh's words in 21:29 meant that Ahab would be allowed to die in peace. The writer periodically provides hints that all might not be well with Ahab's battle plan, as in Jehoshaphat's unwillingness to accept the word of the 400 prophets, or in Ahab's own vacillation (as in v. 8). Now, however, this ambiguity appears to have been lifted, as Micaiah's words claim that Yahweh intends for Ahab to die, and is prepared to launch a deceitful plot to destroy Ahab.

At this point, much that has happened in the chapter appears to have been caused by the actions of the lying spirit (vv. 21–23). Thus, in verses 19–23 the writer has used a flashback technique to make the point emphatically that Yahweh wished for Ahab to die, revealing Yahweh's earlier decision at the point in the narrative calculated to have the maximum impact. Had the writer opened the chapter with the scene in verses 19–24, there would have been no ambiguity and suspense in the events of verses 1–18. The revelation of the will of Yahweh toward Ahab would not have carried the impact that it now carries by having kept the reader in the dark for so long.

The devious manner Yahweh uses to lead the king to his downfall adds considerable emphasis to the negative words spoken against Ahab. The prophetic corpus is filled with occasions when Yahweh has negative words to

---

24. As De Vries notes, the evil spirit here serves as a clear expression of Yahweh's will, not as "a semi-independent principle of evil"; *Prophet*, 44.

speak about a particular king, but Yahweh typically has a prophet deliver an unmistakably negative word to or about the king. Rarely is there much subtlety or equivocation. In this instance, however, Yahweh is anything but forthright, deliberately speaking a false word to entrap the king. Yahweh wants Ahab to die thinking that Yahweh will give him the victory. The shock effect on the reader of this unusual manner of Yahweh's bringing about a king's death adds great power to Yahweh's negative assessment of Ahab. Yahweh does not simply lead Ahab to his death: he toys with him, suckering him into his deceitful web, as if Ahab no longer deserves a direct and clear sentence of death from Yahweh.

The words of Micaiah in verses 19–23 appear to have resolved a number of ambiguities. Jehoshaphat's anxiety about the battle now seems reasonable, and his desire to hear from yet another prophet (v. 7) seems appropriate in light of his suspicion that something is wrong with the word of the 400 prophets. The unanimity of the 400 prophets in supporting Ahab's venture at Ramoth-Gilead, and Zedekiah's strong words and pantomime, now appear understandable since, if Micaiah is correct, both Zedekiah and the 400 have been unknowingly infected by a lying spirit.[25] Even Micaiah's initial words to Ahab now make sense as those of a prophet obedient to Yahweh's command to lie to Ahab.

Response to Micaiah (1 Kings 22:24–28)

This flash of clarity lasts, however, for only a moment. Just as Zedekiah's blow to Micaiah's cheek brings Micaiah abruptly back to the dangerous situation in which he finds himself, so also the clarity brought about by Micaiah's words is struck down in an instant. Zedekiah and the 400 prophets do *not* see themselves as being led by a lying spirit, as Zedekiah's hand painfully and emphatically tells Micaiah. Micaiah alone has witnessed the scene in the heavenly council, and his entire interpretation is therefore called into question. Thus, the reader and Ahab must once again ask whether the word of the 400 prophets is not the correct word from Yahweh.

His interpretation vehemently challenged, Micaiah warns Zedekiah that he will have to hide in shame and fear after his positive words have proven wrong (v. 25), but Micaiah then has to face the full force of Ahab's anger. Siding with Zedekiah and the 400 (vv. 26–27), Ahab orders Micaiah to be arrested and returned[26] to custody, and to be fed on scant rations "until I

---

25. See De Vries, *Prophet*, 45.
26. The use of the verb "return" hints that Micaiah may already have been in custody prior to his appearance before Ahab; De Vries, *Prophet*, 38–39.

come in peace."[27] No doubt Ahab hopes to return victorious, and to parade himself before Micaiah to rub in the fact that Micaiah had been wrong, the scant fare of bread and water being intended to humiliate Micaiah during the interim. Also, Ahab's words "Thus says the king" are perhaps intended to mock Micaiah's words. Thus far Micaiah has spoken a word from Yahweh, but nothing has happened, while Ahab now speaks a word that has immediate results, with Micaiah suffering severely.

Zedekiah and the 400 prophets appear to have won the day, despite Micaiah's claim about the lying spirit. The king has heard from Micaiah, but then has decisively sided with the others, while punishing Micaiah.

Battle Scene and Denouement (1 Kings 22:29–38)

Yet, a number of ambiguities remain concerning Ahab, despite his assertive braggadocio in verse 27. The writer allows Micaiah, who has been shouted down by everyone, to have the last word. "If, indeed, you return in peace, the word of Yahweh is not with me" (v. 28). Micaiah's words hang like a heavy cloud over the battle scene, causing the reader to ponder whether Micaiah may indeed be correct despite the consensus against him. Gradually, it becomes clear that Micaiah's words about Ahab's death were indeed accurate, and all the other prophets were wrong.

Ahab, so unambiguously assertive in verse 27, subsequently has doubts, recalling those which had plagued him earlier. To protect himself, Ahab tells Jehoshaphat (v. 30) to wear his royal robes on the battlefield, while Ahab disguises himself from the enemy. This seems a strange thing for Ahab to do if he is confident that Zedekiah and the 400 prophets are correct. Ahab is hedging his bet, taking into account Micaiah's message that Yahweh wished for Ahab to be enticed into overconfidence by the prophets and to fall at Ramoth-Gilead. By disguising himself, Ahab shows that he still takes Micaiah's words seriously, since he employs an antidote for them. He is also setting up Jehoshaphat to take the fall in his place (as vv. 31–33 indicate), in the event Micaiah is correct.

Thus, if Yahweh wishes to entrap him, Ahab counters by disguising himself, in order to escape death at the enemy's hands. Ahab plays Yahweh's game, concealing his identity just as Yahweh concealed his intentions toward Ahab. Once again the story line is ambiguous, as the Syrian chariots hotly (and mistakenly) pursue the royally attired Jehoshaphat, following the Syrian king's command that they fight with no one except the king of Israel

---

27. "Peace" in the sense of wholeness and safety. See Gray, *I and II Kings*, 404.

(v. 31). The reader briefly wonders whether Ahab may yet escape Yahweh's entrapment. However, Ahab's plan fails. Jehoshaphat reveals his identity to the Syrians and they stop pursuing him, while a random arrow strikes Ahab, causing a mortal wound. Even here there is an element of ambiguity, as the arrow that kills Ahab is not precisely zeroed in on him, but appears almost to stumble upon Ahab: "But a man drew his bow unsuspecting and smote the king of Israel in the joint between the plates of armor" (v. 34).

At this point the ambiguity regarding Ahab's fate ends, as does the ambiguity regarding which prophet was correct. It is now unmistakably clear that Yahweh indeed wants Ahab to die, and succeeds in bringing about Ahab's death, overcoming not only Ahab's (unintended) knowledge about the lying spirit, but also Ahab's plans to thwart Yahweh's intent. At the end of verse 36, after Ahab's death, a cry spreads throughout the army for each warrior to return home, just as Micaiah had anticipated in verse 17.

Another ambiguity resolved by Ahab's death revolves around 1 Kings 21:29. Even though Elijah had anticipated that dogs would one day lick up Ahab's blood in the same place they had licked up Naboth's (21:19), the words of 21:29 suggest that Yahweh might have relented in light of Ahab's penitence and humility (21:27). Indeed, the issue of whether Yahweh had turned away from his strongly negative intentions toward Ahab is the primary ambiguity driving the narrative of chapter 22. Ahab's death, and the scene in verse 38 describing the dogs licking up Ahab's blood, decisively remove that ambiguity, making it clear that Yahweh intended all along that Ahab be led to his death, just as Elijah had said. The reader now sees that 21:29 meant that Ahab's *dynasty* would not fall in his day (thereby postponing the words of 21:21–24), even though Ahab's own punishment would not be postponed.

However, another matter is left hanging: Micaiah's fate. Ahab had ordered Micaiah imprisoned until Ahab returned in peace. What Ahab did not specify was what would happen if Ahab did not return. Intriguingly, there is no further mention of Micaiah in any of the narratives after 22:28, and one is left to wonder whether Micaiah was released as a prophet whose word had proven to be true, or whether he was left in prison to rot for having brazenly anticipated the king's death.[28] However, to have Micaiah released from prison and recognized as a true prophet would be anticlimactic, since the reader already knows that he is correct, just as it would seem anticlimactic to describe the hiding and punishment of the 400 prophets. It also is appropriate that, in a narrative filled with so many ambiguities, the writer leaves the

---

28. Gray raises the intriguing possibility that Micaiah may be the actual name of the prophet who took the assumed name of Elijah; *I and II Kings,* 400. One would wonder, though, why these two names are never related elsewhere.

ambiguity concerning Micaiah's fate perpetually dangling as the narrative reaches its end. In the final analysis, it was Ahab's end, not Micaiah's, that was the writer's primary concern.

Conclusion

In 1 Kings 22, the writer uses ambiguity as a rhetorical device to argue that Ahab was so wicked that not only did Yahweh desire Ahab's death, but also saw fit to entrap Ahab, making him think he would win, when in fact he would be defeated and killed. The writer strengthens the effect of his argument about Ahab's wickedness by using ambiguity to keep the reader in suspense, guessing whether Ahab has been forgiven by Yahweh, as 21:27–29 might imply, or whether Yahweh really wants to bring about Ahab's death, as indicated in 21:19. Although Zedekiah and the 400 prophets are consistent in supporting Ahab's going to battle, all other major players vacillate, and the writer uses this vacillation to keep the reader in suspense until the truth about Yahweh's desire for Ahab's death is dramatically affirmed in 22:34–36. Thus, the writer's use of ambiguity powerfully strengthens the impact of Yahweh's negative assessment of Ahab.

PART FOUR

**RHETORICAL ARGUMENTATION
IN THE GOSPELS**

CHAPTER 9

*THE ROLE OF THE AUDIENCE
IN THE DETERMINATION OF ARGUMENTATION:
THE GOSPEL OF LUKE AND THE ACTS OF THE APOSTLES*

L. Gregory Bloomquist

The Connection between Argumentation and Audience

Following Aristotle, rhetoric has often been viewed as the process of persuasion (*Rhet.* 1.1[1354a1]). While this is broadly true, it doesn't get at the reality of most common rhetoric, that is, popular speech, which seeks primarily to communicate and only sometimes to persuade. More broadly true is the notion that underlies the "new rhetoric," namely, that rhetoric is about persuasion sometimes, but always about the consent involved in making communication work.[1] Accordingly, rhetoric not only involves argumentation, but is primarily the "science" of argumentation within the bounds of consent.

For this reason, rhetorical analysis has always incorporated a significant element of logical analysis. Since Aristotle, logical analysis in some form has been a part of rhetoric because rhetorical analysis consists, at least in part, in an attempt to reconstruct arguments as having a valid argument form (*Rhet.* 1.2[1356b1]). Such an analysis assumes the existence of logical, valid forms that permit an argument to be abstracted from the vicissitudes of the local and the individual and to be universalized. Logic allows the argument to be "independent of the situation in which the arguments happen to occur," makes "the argument independent of the participants involved, and even of people in general," presents "the argument in standard form" rather than in the language of the user, renders the language more logically formal and prominent than colloquial and "normal," substitutes logical constants for ordinary language, and finally presents individual arguments in the context of the wider constellation of argument forms, in order to arrive at a decision regarding the logical validity or invalidity of the statement.[2] All this is, of

---

1. Ch. Perelman and L. Olbrechts-Tyteca, *The New Rhetoric: A Treatise on Argumentation* (trans. John Wilkinson and Purcell Weaver; Notre Dame, Ind.: University of Notre Dame Press, 1969).
2. Frans H. van Eemeren, Rob Grootendorst, and Francisca Snoeck Henkemans, eds., *Fundamentals of Argumentation Theory: A Handbook of Historical Backgrounds and Contemporary Developments* (Mahwah, N.J.: Lawrence Erlbaum Associates, 1996), 14–15.

course, necessary to make an argument universally valid, everywhere, at all times, and for all people.

Rhetoric, however, is about making an argument work locally, not universally. For this reason, Aristotle and the western tradition that has largely followed him has not confused rhetoric with dialectic. In fact, for Aristotle the enthymeme, which is the basic element of rhetorical argumentation, "works" because it makes sense to the specific audience. For Aristotle, it was clear that "to engage in rhetoric, one needs to know the lines of reasoning used by that community" in which an address is made or to which a text is written.[3] For this reason, considerations of audience are directly pertinent to rhetoric.

So, while one does not need to go the extreme route of Peter Ramus and eliminate logic from rhetoric, in rhetoric any logical analysis must be supplemented by a pragmatic analysis wherein "the unexpressed premise that helps to make the argument logically valid is then more precisely defined on the basis of contextual information and background knowledge."[4] From a rhetorical perspective, logicians clearly miss the "great many verbal, contextual, situational and other pragmatic factors that play a part in the communication process."[5] Rhetoricians and argumentation theorists pursue these factors, since rhetoricians are interested in "the problems involved in the *production, analysis,* and *evaluation* of argumentative discourse... in the light of the actual circumstances in which it takes place."[6] And we might add, this makes the question of audience in rhetorical argumentation crucial.

But, if the audience is so crucial, are we sure that we know what the audience is? In spite of the abundant references to audience in classical and contemporary authors, James Porter asks this very pertinent question.[7]

To find an answer, Porter begins by pointing to the work by Lisa Ede and Andrea Lunsford, according to whom there are two ways in which rhetorical scholarship envisioned the audience.[8] As "audience addressed," the audience consists of real people, understood to be existing outside the text, whose attitudes, beliefs, and social dimensions can be and indeed must be known for

---

3. Alan Bilansky, "Rhetoric, Democracy, and the Deliberative Horizon," in *Rhetoric, the Polis, and the Global Village: Selected Papers from the 1998 Thirtieth Anniversary Rhetoric Society of America Conference* (C. Jan Swearingen and Dave Pruett, eds.; Mahwah, N.J.: Lawrence Erlbaum Associates, 1999), 221–29.

4. Eemeren et al., *Fundamentals of Argumentation Theory,* 14–15.

5. Ibid., 6.

6. Ibid., 12.

7. James E. Porter, *Audience and Rhetoric: An Archaeological Composition of the Discourse Community* (Englewood Cliffs, N.J.: Prentice Hall, 1992).

8. Lisa Ede and Andrea Lunsford, "Audience Addressed/Audience Involved: The Role of Audience in Composition Theory and Pedagogy," *CCC* 35 (1984): 155–71.

a correct understanding of the text and the author's intention. Alternatively, as "audience invoked," the audience is that fictive reality created by the writer, a concept in the mind of the author, since from "the purely empirical view of the writer in the act of composing, no reader yet exists."[9] Ede and Lunsford conclude that the audience is really both, as it likely was for Aristotle, for whom the audience — as local as the immediate readers or hearers or as internally local as a "constructed audience" that exists in the author's mind — is always making some kind of judgment about the logical validity of the argument at stake (*Rhet.* 2.18.1).[10]

But, there are in fact multiple audiences. Through the incorporation of earlier strands of traditions and texts or the interweaving of discourse modes, authors incorporate multiple audiences, sometimes distant in space and time, in a way that envisions audiences overlapping with other audiences, or future, distant audiences as the goal of the "movement" of the intended audience. There are also audiences that are in the "peripheral" vision of the author, audiences that might be the real "target" of the text, even though the text is "addressed" to another. We see a peripheral audience just as we see something through peripheral vision, namely, by focussing on something else, not on it.

*The Place of Argumentation and Audience
in the Determination of Modes of Discourse in Socio-Rhetorical Analysis*

The Problem

The problem of audience is particularly in focus in socio-rhetorical analysis where one is after modes of discourse that are operative in texts.[11] These modes of discourse, or "rhetorolects," as Robbins has called them, can be determined most successfully through the programmatic attention to the various textures identified by Robbins and others as present in texts. If it is the case that a rhetorical discourse mode appears when we regularly and consistently find ourselves configuring and moving through the identifiable textures in ways that differentiate such a configuration and movement from

---

9. Porter, *Audience and Rhetoric*, 6.
10. G. A. Kennedy, "Rhetoric and Culture/Rhetoric and Technology," Charles Kneupper Memorial Lecture, in *Rhetoric, the Polis, and the Global Village: Selected Papers from the 1998 Thirtieth Anniversary Rhetoric Society of America Conference* (ed. C. J. Swearingen and D. Pruett; Mahwah, N.J.: Erlbaum, 1999), 55–61. My thanks to David Amador Hester for the suggestion of the title "constructed audience."
11. Vernon K. Robbins, *The Tapestry of Early Christian Discourse: Rhetoric, Society and Ideology* (London and New York: Routledge, 1996), 170–74.

any others, we should be able to see how, within these modes of discourse, individual rhetorical "features," like argumentation, audience, and the nexus of the two, function specifically and differently. In what follows I am going to assume that there is a unique way that argumentation, audience, and their nexus "work" in two different modes of discourse: wisdom and apocalyptic. Since this is only a test case, I am going to be looking at only one body of literature, namely, Luke-Acts. Given that this is an exploratory hypothesis, I only ask that you grant me plausibility in the discussion of it, not its certainty.

Audience and Argumentation in Wisdom and Apocalyptic Rhetorical Modes of Discourse: Rhetorical Modes of Discourse or Particular Modes of Discourse?

According to Robbins, wisdom discourse is characterized by a specific sacred texture, in which the deity is viewed as acting beneficently toward humanity. This is a heuristically helpful definition but is dependent on only one texture (sacred). Furthermore, it focuses on the wisdom mode of discourse almost exclusively through consideration of Jewish, Christian, and some Greco-Roman texts. It might better be said, then, to function like a dialect or rhetorolect and thus be a particular mode of wisdom discourse rather than rhetorical wisdom mode of discourse itself. It is undeniably a foundational characteristic of Jewish and Christian wisdom discourse, but can we say more about the rhetorical form of wisdom discourse beyond the ideological and cultural boundaries of Judaism and Christianity? I would suggest that, if rhetorical discourse modes, and their consequent argumentation, "develop in a variety of linguistic, social, political, and cultural contexts," then perhaps something can be gained by going beyond the "dialectical" or "rhetorolectical" borders of particular rhetorics to see whether there are common elements in rhetorical modes of discourse themselves, making them identifiable as such. In order to do so, I will look at aspects of Asian rhetoric, not because it is the only rhetoric available, or even the most amenable, but because of certain perceived similarities with our literature, in spite of a generally acknowledged independence from it. In doing so, I do not intend to return to the "dialectical fallacy" in rhetoric (that is, to making the local universal) but to ground the modes of discourse in the textures discerned by socio-rhetorical analysis.

Asian Rhetoric: Wisdom Rhetorical Discourse

Asian rhetoric is generally considered to give pride of place to ethos and moral character, to putting one's life in order, to the importance of trustworthiness, genuineness, integrity, sincerity, goodness, humility, and respectfulness.[12] Unlike the generally understood Western, agonistic notion of "winning and its attendant pleasure,"[13] one generally reads that Asian rhetoric emphasizes complementarity and harmony, that a central tenet "embedded in the concept of *yin* and *yang*" is that "opposites are really complements," that entities like "the negative, quiescent, receptive, darkness, night, Earth, and the static" associated with *yin* and those like "positives, active, assertive, light, day, Heaven, and the dynamic" associated with *yang* "are not opposites but complementary aspects of life which maintain an equilibrium, which bring cohesion, oneness, to all of life, and which humans are to preserve."[14]

It is also generally believed that this cohesion is derived from the social philosophy that underlies Asian rhetoric, a philosophy that focuses on "an honoring of groupness, a centripetal force powerfully creating strong cohesive entities," over against individualism and separateness.[15] This centripetal force leads to cultural and ideological differentiation by caste (in India), by class (in Confucian belief), and by ethnicity (in Japan — as well as in Israel) and to the social — and sacral — characteristics of hierarchical and xenophobic behavior consequent on these differentiations. As Wu notes, this hierarchy is really the process of building within "an enlarged circle of the family": a person is important "through a reflection of one's title of position or connections in a larger circle of 'family' and one is only responsible for the interests of those within the 'family.'"[16] Not surprisingly, in Asian rhetoric, "age, rather than logic," is the guide in decision making.[17] Rephrasing this in terms of socio-rhetorical analysis, we would not say that there is no logic in Asian rhetorical argumentation, but rather a different logic, namely one that proceeds on the basis of ancient authority or antiquity, that is, "qualitative argumentation."[18] This is not less argumentation than "logical argumentation," but rather a different form of argumentation.

Asian argumentation is also characterized by argument from analogy. "Assertions are made, developed, and supported from comparisons with the lives

---

12. J. Vernon Jensen, "Values and Practices in Asian Argumentation," *Argumentation and Advocacy* 28 (Spring 1992): 157.
13. Ibid., 155.
14. Ibid., 104.
15. Ibid., 104; Hiu Wu, "The Enthymeme Examined from the Chinese Value System," in *Making and Unmaking the Prospects for Rhetoric: Papers of the 7th Rhetoric Society of America Conference, Tuscon, Arizona, 1996* (ed. Theresa Enos; Mahwah, N.J.: L. Erlbaum, 1997), 116.
16. Wu, "The Enthymeme Examined from the Chinese Value System," 116; Robert T. Oliver, *Communication and Culture in Ancient India and China* (Syracuse: Syracuse University Press, 1971), 270–71.
17. Jensen, "Values and Practices in Asian Argumentation," 158–59.
18. Vernon K. Robbins, *Exploring the Texture of Texts: A Guide to Socio-Rhetorical Interpretation* (Valley Forge: Trinity Press International, 1996), 23.

of others, both contemporaries and those who have lived before, and with aspects of nature, with which humans should identify and in many respects should emulate."[19] This observation further confirms the predominance of qualitative argumentation in Asian rhetoric, as opposed to deductive argumentation.[20] Even the so-called "rationalist rhetoricians" of China "neither evolved any syllogism nor discovered any law of thought. They expressed themselves in dialogues, aphorism, and paradoxes instead of systematic and cogent argumentation."

The emphasis on complementarity over against opposition, and on cohesion and "harmony, achieving oneness with other human beings, and indeed with nature and all of life" as opposed to struggle and winning, makes itself manifest in Asian rhetoric's clear social desire to seek to preserve harmony "by learning how to save face for another person, how to present uncomfortable truths in a non-threatening way or how to be appropriately ambiguous,"[21] what Oliver describes as "the principle of coherence that governs the natural sequence of ordinary discourse."[22] Asian rhetoric is characterized by its emphasis on the "importance of knowing and adjusting to the audience's prejudices, intelligence, emotions and desires."[23] This is the reason why some Asian rhetorical argumentation may appear disinterested in audience concerns and thus "audience-invariant."

This is not surprising. Asian rhetorical argumentation, like biblical wisdom discourse, appears to have been practiced by a coherent and homogeneous group of men, all of whom shared the same concerns within the same hierarchical structure. As such, we can see that consistency and coherence are suggestive of a static and secure, socio-economic world order. Hsüntze, who "brought the consideration of human motivation to the highest form it achieved among the ancient Chinese," believed that a rhetorician was not a dialectician, because, "far from being merely skilled in argument, so that he could speak with equal facility on any side of any question, he must be searchingly sure that his words convey only the meaning he intends — and that this be a meaning which will aid in maintaining the harmony of the state."[24]

---

19. Jensen, "Values and Practices in Asian Argumentation," 158–59; Robbins, *Exploring the Texture of Texts: A Guide to Socio-Rhetorical Interpretation*, 23.
20. Jensen, "Values and Practices in Asian Argumentation," 161–62.
21. Jensen, "Values and Practices in Asian Argumentation," 104; Wu, "The Enthymeme Examined from the Chinese Value System," 116.
22. Oliver, *Communication and Culture in Ancient India and China*, 155.
23. Jensen, "Values and Practices in Asian Argumentation," 162.
24. Oliver, *Communication and Culture in Ancient India and China*, 201.

One could continue, and should, with considerably more detail than what I have provided here, admittedly on the basis of the work of others in Asian rhetoric. Nevertheless, I believe that this brief but scholarly assessment also presents a suggestive picture that hints at a variety of points of intersection with what is often called biblical wisdom literature. I believe that this is due to both Asian and biblical texts sharing a rhetorical discourse mode that, for lack of a better term, we can call "wisdom." It is a discourse that is characterized by essentially qualitative argumentation from authority and analogy, carried out in a hierarchical, "solid-state" context of audience-invariance in which the audience and the rhetor are at the top of the hierarchy.

If this hypothesis is correct, a fuller analysis would reveal particular parallel ways in which each texture is configured, as well as particular ways in which they differ for cultural and sacred reasons (such as the biblical wisdom emphasis on the deity's beneficence). Obviously there are "local" differences from culture to culture even within Asia (e.g., from India to China),[25] but I believe that there may be enough material here to talk of a socio-rhetorically discerned mode of discourse that we call "wisdom" (cf., e.g., rabbinic commentary on the Torah,[26] and Greco-Roman cynic forms of argumentation[27]).

A Shift in Asian Rhetoric: Apocalyptic Rhetorical Discourse

Building on this hypothesis, I would suggest further that we may be able to identify a rhetorical shift when the world in which this rhetoric is practiced does not function in the consistent, solid-state way that it is intended, be it for social, cultural, sacral, or even textual reasons. What happens when, for whatever reason, an alternative rhetoric becomes better suited to the world of the speaker or audience? This is not a wild hypothesis, especially considering the social context of wisdom discourse, perhaps the predominant discourse mode in antiquity. When the connection between this discourse mode and

---

25. Ibid.
26. Brigitte (Rivka) Kern Ulmer, "The Advancement of Arguments in Exegetical Midrash Compared to the Arguments in the Greek Diatribe," paper presented at the National Endowment for the Humanities Summer Seminar, Yeshiva University, 1992.
27. Ulmer, "The Advancement of Arguments in Exegetical Midrash Compared to the Arguments in the Greek Diatribe"; L. Gregory Bloomquist, "Methodological Considerations in the Determination of the Social Context of Cynic Rhetorical Practice: Implications for Our Present Studies of the Jesus Traditions," in *The Rhetorical Analysis of Scripture: Essays from the 1995 London Conference* (ed. Stanley E. Porter and Thomas H. Olbricht; JSNTSup 146; London: Sheffield Academic Press, 1997), 200–231.

the literary elite's production of communication in "hydraulic" societies[28] is shaken, as was often the case in the fragile ancient world, whether because of experiences that could not be accounted for or because of social upheaval, we would expect new discourse modes to arise in the new situation. This is in fact just what we find.

One of the transformations that occurred is often supposed to have taken the form of what we call apocalyptic. In light of our above suggestion regarding wisdom discourse, is it possible to expand on the work of Collins[29] and see whether a phenomenon like apocalyptic rhetorical discourse exists, both localized within particular biblical texts, but also existing as a rhetorical mode of discourse itself?[30] Can we once again use Asian rhetoric here? I suggest that we can, for two areas of transformation that we know to have occurred in Asian rhetoric reveal a new phenomenon in that cultural context that overlaps in a remarkable way with the transformation of biblical wisdom into biblical apocalyptic in the eastern Mediterranean.

As noted above, Asian rhetoric, like biblical wisdom discourse, is less interested in deductive argumentation. There is, however, a development in Asian rhetoric, associated with classic Chinese rhetoric of the period 500–200 B.C.E. and with the followers of Mo-Tzu, that sees a more prominent role for deductive patterns. In Garrett's discussion of *bian,* for example, it becomes clear that this "making of fine distinctions" involves both disagreement (versus harmony) and deductive thinking from contradictories. According to Garrett, "many of the surviving examples of *bian* are characterized by an exclusive use of strict deductive reasoning, in the form of strict inferences from definitions or of chains of reasoning establishing a self-contradiction in an opponent's position."[31]

The reason for this interest is not clear, but it is possible that it derives, in part at least, from an interest and skill in geometry and science. Such an interest would find a ready home in a world of argumentation emphasizing definition (*bian*), that is, a "process of marking divisions" and "the denotations of discrimination and ever-finer drawing of distinctions." It also certainly appears clear in the later "Mohist" interest in *shuo* argumentation,

---

28. Karl A. Wittfogel, *Oriental Despotism: A Comparative Study of Total Power* (repr. ed.; New York: Vintage, 1981 [orig. 1957]).

29. J. J. Collins, "Early Jewish Apocalypticism," in *Anchor Bible Dictionary,* 1:282–88.

30. L. Gregory Bloomquist, "Methodological Criteria for Apocalyptic Rhetoric: A Suggestion for the Expanded Use of Sociorhetorical Analysis," in *Vision and Persuasion: Rhetorical Dimensions of Apocalyptic Discourse* (ed. Greg Carey and L. Gregory Bloomquist; St. Louis: Chalice, 1999), 181–203.

31. M. M. Garrett, "Classical Chinese Conceptions of Argumentation and Persuasion," *Argumentation and Advocacy* 29 (1993): 105–15 (here 107–8).

namely, explanation and "reason-giving" concerning "the reasons an event occurred, the causes of certain natural phenomena, or the suitability of a particular pattern of behavior."[32]

But, here, a biblical scholar should be very keenly interested. For there are elements of content that overlap between biblical apocalyptic and this "revisionist" approach to Asian rhetoric, for example, the "Mohist" emphasis on universalism overlaps in a striking way with the universalist concern found in biblical apocalyptic. Furthermore, this view of the origins of "Mohism" also overlaps in a striking way with the assertion by Michael Stone concerning the origins of biblical apocalyptic, namely, that it may have arisen in circles of scientific, and therefore almost assuredly, extra-canonical explorations of the divine. According to Stone, "it seems to be quite clear that the "scientific" or speculative interests that play a predominant role in these oldest parts of *1 Enoch* were beyond the pale from the tradents of biblical literature."[33] Such a genesis, he argues, would account for the interest in heavenly explorations that is so characteristic of so-called apocalyptic literature, but relatively absent in much wisdom literature. This interest is difficult to explain if we understand apocalyptic only as an attempt at theodicy or eschatology. Such a view would also suggest that the scientific exploration common to elements of late B.C.E. and early C.E. Near and Far Eastern hierarchies may have had more in common rhetorically than just sacred texture. If so, one should be hesitant to over-emphasize the definition of the rhetorical discourse of apocalyptic exclusively from the angle of sacred texture. One should see the rejection of such groups by the central hierarchies and the discourse of such groups on that rejection as significant elements of their audience-directed argumentation.

Thus, attention to the social context, as well as the scientific means of dealing with a changing social context, help us to account for the shift in Asian forms of argumentation from inductive-based, wisdom argumentation to deductive-based modifications of wisdom discourse. The "Mohists" were "a philosophical school rooted in the lower-class" and "could not argue from the authority of high position of power." Accordingly, Garrett argues, they turned to "logos" and found that their "mainly upper-class contemporaries were not especially interested in, and sometimes even expressed prejudice against, those areas in which the Mohists' forms of reasoning were more powerful, i.e., mechanics, optics, physics, and other investigations of physical reality."[34]

---

32. Ibid., 109.
33. Michael E. Stone, "The Book of Enoch and Judaism in the Third Century B.C.E.," *CBQ* 40 (1978): 488–89.
34. Mary M. Garrett, "The 'Mo-Tzu' and the 'Lu-Shih Ch'un-Ch'Iu': A Case Study of Classical

This is why another form of argumentation that Garrett finds associated with classic Chinese thinking is so important. *Shui,* nearly homophonous with *shuo,* and thus able to be distinguished from the latter only by syntax and context, emphasizes neither definition (*bian*) nor explanation (*shuo*) of the world, but persuasion of an audience. Garrett notes that *shui* is informed more by the "socio-political environment" and would be useful not in a homogeneous environment but in a "hierarchical, centralized and bureaucratized political system such as characterized China" if one is aiming to persuade "the most obviously important audience," namely, "the person at the top," on the assumption that one is not at the top or, at the least, that there are others "above oneself."[35] This shift in argumentation has moved toward audience-variance rather than the more characteristic audience-invariance that we associate with both Asian rhetoric and biblical wisdom. This would suggest that the transformation of Asian argumentation occurs as rhetorical practice becomes more widespread and more popular or, at the very least, as members of the centralized hierarchy find themselves distanced or alienated from others.

I believe that, in light of insights such as these and the work in biblical apocalyptic of Stone and others, a similar "ideological" process was at work in the formation of the rhetorical discourse of biblical apocalyptic. Following Gilles Deleuze and his work on codes, I have argued that apocalyptic is a way of inverting cultural codes.[36] This may have occurred for sacred, scientific, economic, or a variety of other reasons, possibly because the codes became "outdated." But whatever the reason, the outcome appears to have been to facilitate communication to a hierarchical audience, from which some have become distanced, of a vision of a movement away from the static cultural expression (usually associated with both a static world-order and a static way of enacting it) to another.

I would further say now that in this way the genesis of "apocalyptic rhetorical discourse" is one of our best pictures of "ideological texture" in action, if by ideology we mean that "movement" by which peoples and cultures and forms of people in culture change from one way of being or looking at the world to another.[37] Notice, for example, the original title of Jacques Ellul's "commentary" on the Book of the Revelation, namely, "architecture

---

Chinese Theory and Practice of Argument" (dissertation, University of California Berkeley, 1983); Jensen, "Values and Practices in Asian Argumentation," 162.

35. M. M. Garrett, "*Pathos* Reconsidered from the Perspective of Classical Chinese Rhetorical Theories," *QJS* 79 (1993): 114.

36. Bloomquist, "Methodological Criteria for Apocalyptic Rhetoric," 196.

37. Bloomquist, "Refining Ideological Texture," paper presented at the Rhetoric and Early Christian Discourse panel, Canadian Society of Biblical Studies and Canadian Society for the Study of Rhetoric, Edmonton, Alberta, May 27, 2000.

en mouvement."[38] Apocalyptic discourse is one of our best pictures of the very movement that is ideology (that is, a culture in movement) captured in the time and space of the narrative form.

The same question arises in a later work of Lunsford and Ede on audience.[39] In that article Lunsford and Ede saw a need to correct their original oversights in describing audience as expressed, invoked, or expressed/invoked, by noting the way "ideology" had escaped their initial description. In an attempt to redress the overly dichotomized views into which they had divided audiences, they sought to explore how traditional rhetoric had blinded them to the prominent roles of institution, discourse, and genre by causing them to focus on "successful communication" (synonymous with "persuasion" in traditional rhetoric) and "exclusionary tendencies" (in which both audiences had been viewed by them as "coherent, autonomous, and unified").[40] In the end, our analysis of transformations of discourse must engage the subsequent receptions of a speech, receptions by audiences in some cases completely disconnected from initial writer, text, or audience. It will do so not merely by looking at the subsequent encounter with the text as distortion (a limited view of the meaning of "ideology") but with how subsequent readers have "stumbled upon" this network of significance and given heed to it, even be it only in their peripheral vision. In the end, it may be the peripheral audience that is really the one we can least see clearly but most need to be able to see to do justice to the text.

Argumentation and Audience in Luke-Acts: The Examples of Wisdom and Apocalyptic Discourse

In order to illustrate the connection between audience and argumentation, I will provide two examples of wisdom discourse and two, not entirely unrelated examples of wisdom-discourse transformed into apocalyptic discourse. These examples are provided in hopes of illustrating the hypothesis and its implications. However, given that the above hypothesis cannot be judged on the basis of isolated examples, I would encourage the further exploration of this question with other examples.

---

38. *Apocalypse: The Book of Revelation* (New York: Seabury Press, 1977).
39. A. Lunsford and L. Ede, "Representing Audience: 'Successful' Discourse and Disciplinary Critique," *CCC* 47 (1996): 167–79.
40. Lunsford and Ede, "Representing Audience," 167–79; Pegeen Reichert Powell, "Facing the Audience: Reconsidering 'Audience' through the Chinese Concept of 'Face,'" in *Rhetoric, the Polis, and the Global Village* (C. Jan Swearingen and Dave Pruett, eds.; Mahwah, N.J.: Lawrence Erlbaum Associates, 1999), 140.

Wisdom Discourse

Luke. Luke 12:16–21 presents an L parable about a rich man and contrasts contentedness and wealth with the demands to use riches wisely. The uncertainty of life holds no threat to one who acts wisely; the vagaries of life are a threat only to the one who does not.

The argument here is derived from a common *topos* of wisdom discourse: the rich man in his status context. Also, the analogies from nature and the invocation of testimony from antiquity bear the look of *topoi* in wisdom discourse. Finally, the give-and-take, *yin-yang,* of being given and of having taken away, suggest the underlying coherence that gives the whole picture its consistency: this is not a teeter-tottering on the precipice but rather a harmonious fulfillment of riches given and riches taken. An audience of the rich, cultured, and self-satisfied elite would hear this story as a confirmation of elite values, not challenges, and would hear themselves called not to reform an elite lifestyle in favor of some subservient status, but to reconfirm their already existing values.

There are, of course, elements that make this particular pericope not only wisdom discourse as such but a unique local example of biblical wisdom discourse. Above all, there is a deity who keeps the cosmic harmony by overseeing one who has much and who tends to others, who presumably have nothing, through the overflow of the gifts to the rich. But, the story suggests a certain audience-invariance that is both rhetorically local and trans-sacred culture.

But, the story told on its own differs from the story told in the context of Luke-Acts. Luke has clearly woven this wisdom discourse tightly into his overall story. And while there are wisdom elements in the larger context (the extensive series of rationales that follows the parable, drawn from Luke 12:22–32, also suggest no condemnation of the rich man's wealth or an exaltation of poverty, though in their Matthean form [Matt 5:25–34] they appear to do so; cf. especially the build up to the verses in Matt 6:19–21 and 6:24), the rationales appear intended to drive home, not merely to an economically and culturally elite audience but to a now multifaceted audience, the "point" of the discourse, namely, the need to change before it is too late. Thus, there is an apocalyptic "tinge" to this interwoven discourse, which includes wisdom discourse but is not restricted to or by it. Not surprisingly, the next section (Luke 12:35–59) is configured "in the mode of apocalyptic discourse."[41] Thus, the "audience variant" (characteristic of apocalyptic) ele-

---

41. Robbins, "The Gospel of Luke," unpublished manuscript.

ment of the parable's Lukan context seems to cloud the "audience invariant" "punch" of the parable itself.

Acts. Acts 14:8–18 is another excellent example of wisdom discourse that has been modified slightly. The point of the initial story as wisdom discourse is to show both the homage paid to the Christian missionaries and the attempt of Paul and Barnabas not to dishonor the Lystrans.[42]

The scene begins with a healing that is verbally reminiscent of the healing performed by Peter and John in Acts 3:1. Though the dialogue found there concerning the request for alms and Peter's *chreia* ("I have no gold and silver, but what I have I give you: in the name of Jesus Messiah of Nazareth walk") is missing, it is likely that the passage is intended to be connected in the implied reader's mind with the "new" apostolic currency that the reader has found in Acts 3, namely, a "thaumaturgical" currency: the signs and wonders performed in the name of Jesus.

That this "wealth" is honorable is clear from the narrated reaction of the crowd (14:11; cf. Acts 3:10 for the crowd's response), but so is the fact that it is shared so generously. In this, Paul and Barnabas, like Peter and John but unlike the man in the parable we have noted (Luke 12:16–21), act wisely. So, it does not seem out of place to argue that we are presented with honorable figures, honored not by those who understand them to be equals but by those who consider that some honor is due those who are acting as truly wise rich men. The currency is different but honorable nonetheless. To put it in terms that Robbins himself might employ: the beneficence of the gods has been made real in their very midst. The thaumaturgical narrative is, then, the perfect lead up to the wisdom discourse that follows.

In that discourse that follows Paul and Barnabas express in the mode of wisdom discourse their reaction to the crowd's actions. One observes there an emphasis on the argument from the deity's beneficence and the rejection by Paul and Barnabas of their homage — which makes this wisdom literature locally Jewish, or Christian, perfectly consistent with a specifically Jewish, sacral form of wisdom discourse (acclaiming a human as a god smacks of idolatry). One notices also the general, non-deductive argumentation that is grounded on the analogous notion of cosmic sufficiency and coherence, as well as reflection on the analogous moral qualities of the deity. In this respect, this passage remarkably blends elements of a Western wisdom audience. To borrow the interpretive grid from Asian rhetoric, we could observe that in this story the "listeners are cooperative and active participants in the communica-

---

42. Robbins, *The Tapestry of Early Christian Discourse,* 201–7.

tive situation," that their "preferences help to determine the subject matter of the discourse," that their "characteristics are largely influential in shaping the style, the choice of illustrations, the kinds of proof, and the arrangement of the materials," that their "reaction is the measure of the success of the discourse," and that they as audience are subordinate (though not passive), enlightened by the speaker, because "the speaker was selected on the basis of his superiority" and "the listeners were selected on the basis of their need for his guidance."[43]

And here, as in the case of the Lukan parable, wisdom discourse is pushed toward apocalyptic; however, here thaumaturgical narrative is the medium for the apocalyptizing. And, the thaumaturgical narrative found also in Acts 3 progresses to this point, for the healing here, unlike the healing in Acts 3, is not apostolic currency shared generously with the family of Israel; it is shared with the universal family that now gains from the riches of God. While this universal sharing will not be pushed to the limits of apocalyptic discourse, Paul and Barnabas will appeal to an incipient, apocalyptic element, namely, the universality of all (cf. 14:15).

Apocalyptic Discourse

Luke. The above two examples suggest that the Lukan opus might be pointing the implied reader toward an apocalyptizing of wisdom discourse. I believe that this view is further confirmed by explicit apocalyptic discourse in the Lukan opus.

For example, in Luke 21:5 and following, the "audience" to whom Jesus speaks clearly fits the mode of apocalyptic discourse: the audience there is an ambiguous and universalizing τις, unlike the well-defined and perhaps paradoxically more wisdom-based audiences found expressed as μαθηταί in the parallels in Matthew and Mark. Distance from the Matthean and Markan identification of the audience with the disciples is also found in the use of the noun διδάσκαλος, a word that is never reported as having been used of Jesus by Jesus' inner circle in Luke/Acts. Furthermore, the code-breaking, denial on Jesus' part of a timetable or clearly identified characters or even of place, suggests that this discourse in its very ambiguity retains hallmarks of apocalyptic rhetorical discourse.

These observations are underscored by the lack of rhetorical wisdom discourse in this section. One notices, for example, the extensive "hortatory

---

43. Oliver, *Communication and Culture in Ancient India and China*, 267.

enthymemes" that characterize Jesus' speech,[44] rhetorical syllogisms that reflect prophetic modifications to wisdom discourse as we have identified it above. These syllogisms, remarkably shorn of analogy and ancient testimony, are furthermore characterized by cautions of emotion-fused activity (especially sight and trust); that is, the audience is cautioned against looking around and seeing what the world sees and to beware trusting what the world sees. The audience is to "move" to another way of seeing that transcends "wisdom" seeing.

As is clear in this section, such an event cannot leave the Jewish temple — understood not merely as a building but as a cultural network built around the elite, literate hierarchy — intact. The apocalyptic discourse here touches directly on this dismantling. The destruction of the temple surfaces explicitly or implicitly throughout the Lukan opus. It is a destruction that may happen geographically to spatially embedded objects (e.g., the temple structure) in time but that happens across periodized time to the cultural temple network and eventually to the temple itself.[45] This apocalyptic discourse is so fundamental to the work because it seeks to dismantle not first a building but rather the code by which the building has meaning: it is thus revolutionist at the level of the code, not just at the level of the visual or physical.

But, something that is revolutionist at the level of code, while it will appeal distantly to those not attuned to the code itself, only to its enactment, *will* be captured by an intellectual audience that is in charge of maintaining the code. So it is likely that the audience in the peripheral eye of Lukan apocalyptic discourse, a hierarchy detached from those generating the apocalyptic vision itself, that stands most to lose in having the code broken, that is the audience that Luke is interested in. This does not mean that Luke-Acts was written to or for them, only that the narrator keeps this audience in his peripheral vision as he narrates his story. We thus see them in a glass darkly. They are the "peripheral audience" in the encounter in the temple with Simeon — perhaps even with Zechariah. By the end of the Gospel, however, their concern, the fate of the Gentiles, is still at best understood in the context of the prophetic discourse, namely, the Gentiles will come to Jerusalem (i.e., the temple), a hope that presages even the hope of James at the end of Acts. By the end of Acts, the dark-glass audience will have become less of a reality and more of

---

44. L. Gregory Bloomquist, "Rhetorical Argumentation and the Culture of Apocalyptic: A Socio-Rhetorical Analysis of Luke 21," in *The Rhetorical Interpretation of Scripture: Essays from the 1996 Malibu Conference* (ed. Stanley E. Porter and Dennis L. Stamps; JSNTSup 180; Sheffield: Sheffield Academic Press, 1999), 173–209.

45. Ibid.

a memory. In this way the implied author suggests to the implied audience the confirmation of Jesus' initial vision.

Acts. The localized apocalyptic discourse found in Luke 21:5 and following clearly and explicitly begins to move us toward a new reality, not merely a reformed old one: the temple as a cultural network will not simply be revised and reformed; it will be undone and a new one built in its place. In Acts it becomes clear that that new cultural network is in the process of creation. It is made up of members of all nations under heaven, eating meals together and praising the one God, and it all happens not in the religious shrines of any people but in the homes of both economically wealthy and poor, in a church where there is neither Jew nor Greek (cf. Acts 2:42–47). It is a remodeling of universal proportions and it is promoted in Acts through a rhetoric that, though unique to Luke, is clearly apocalyptic.

Acts 10:34–43 is one of the clearest examples of apocalyptic discourse in this unique Lukan form. It is a form that is artfully intertwined with a variety of other discourses, including wisdom, prophetic, and thaumaturgical. The artistic intertwining is comparable to what we noted in Acts 14:1 and following, though in a different order and with a different purpose — and, I would suggest, a different audience "in mind" or "invoked."

As to setting, one notes here the clear context of a sub-cultural speaker addressing a dominant culture representative and his supporters, as well as the code-breaking elements for Jewish expectation (both sapiential and prophetic) of the deity's work in the world. It is not disconsonant with wisdom discourse, but rather modifies and transcends it. To be noted specifically are the several culturally based Old Testament allusions that, in and of themselves, do not configure the divine activity in any specific way but are clearly drawn together in the light of Peter's visionary experience and its consonance with that of Cornelius. Thus, while the echoes are of the Old Testament, they are cultural, not oral-scribal echoes, and they underscore a code-breaking shift. Note, for example, Peter's awareness of those who do the law without the law, underscored by Paul in another example of rhetorical apocalyptic discourse in Acts 13:26–43.

Conclusions

I have suggested above that audience is a fundamental feature to be considered in the determination of argumentation. There are a variety of audiences to be noted in rhetorical address (audience expressed, invoked, expressed/invoked, implied, peripheral, etc.) and these each engage particular forms of argumentation. I have further suggested that the determination of rhetorical discourse modes, which, if they are to be used in socio-rhetorical analysis, should be configured socio-rhetorically and identified generally as discourse modes and locally as specific ways of enacting the modes, will incorporate audiences and argumentation in ways that are unique to each mode. I have finally provided a couple of examples for two discourse modes, wisdom and apocalyptic, understood generally and locally, and have shown some implications for the two suggestions I have made.

CHAPTER 10

INSTRUCTIONS FOR "BROKER" APOSTLES: A SOCIO-RHETORICAL ANALYSIS OF MATTHEW'S MISSION DISCOURSE

Russell B. Sisson

At first glance, the Matthean Mission Discourse appears to lack a substantial argumentative structure. Throughout the extended discourse — a narrative introduction (9:35–38), a formal commissioning of disciples with a list of instructions (10:1–15), and a collection of sayings about the trials of discipleship (10:16–42) — we find only a few instances of argumentative language. Occasionally we find conjunctions marking either a rationale introduced to support a preceding imperative or an imperative introduced as a conclusion from a preceding statement.[1] With the majority of the imperatives in the discourse, however, there are no clearly marked statements of rationale or conclusion. The discourse seems to represent a type of rhetoric where the disciples' (or the readers') acceptance of Jesus' instructions rests simply on their acceptance of his authority. In fact, in several of the instances where argumentative language is used, attention is drawn to the speaker, Jesus. For example, Jesus instructs his disciples: "Behold, I myself send you out as sheep in the midst of wolves; so (οὖν) be wise as serpents and innocent as doves" (10:16).[2] Later he says to them: "Whenever they persecute you in one town, flee to the next; for truly I tell you (ἀμὴν γὰρ λέγω ὑμῖν), you will not have gone through all the towns of Israel before the Son of Man comes"

---

1. In several sayings from Q, imperatives and statements are linked by a post-positive γάρ or οὖν. In some instances, the conjunctions are also found in Lukan versions of the sayings, and thus are very likely in the source document: Matt 9:38/Luke 10:2; Matt 10:10/Luke 10:7; Matt 10:19/Luke 12:11; Matt 10:35/Luke 12:52. In other instances, the conjunctions are found only in Matthean versions of the Q material: Matt 10:26/Luke 12:2; Matt 10:31/Luke 12:7; Matt 10:32/Luke 12:8. Matthew may have added the conjunctions as logical markers, but we cannot be certain. In two instances, Matthew may have added to Q sayings a conclusion (10:16b) or a second supporting rationale (10:20). One saying where γάρ introduces a supporting rationale for an imperative is found only in Matthew (10:23), and it is probably a Matthean formulation because of its allusion back to Jesus' restriction of the disciples' mission to "the lost sheep of the house of Israel" (10:6), a saying found only in Matthew. It is noteworthy that those instances where Matthew *may* be introducing conjunctions to Q material occur in the sayings about the trials of discipleship (10:16–42), the section of the Mission Discourse where the writer's editorial hand is most evident.

2. The intensive use of the pronoun, ἐγὼ ἀποστέλλω, is ignored in most English translations. This is possibly a Matthean formulation of a Q saying, for the nominative singular pronoun is absent in the Lukan parallel.

(10:23). The latter saying is found only in Matthew, and the second part of the former saying is probably a Matthean expansion of Q material.[3] If neither Matthew nor his readers are inclined to question Jesus' authority, why do we view this discourse as anything more than a list of imperatives grouped thematically?

Of the five extended discourses in Matthew, the Mission Discourse poses a particular challenge for interpreters because of certain features that distinguish it from the other discourses. The Mission Discourse is interwoven into the action of the narrative, and yet it stands out from the narrative and moves the reader's attention from the narrative setting to the reader's own world. As Mark Powell observes, "Whereas Matthew usually narrates events with an economy of detail, he abandons the use of summary in reporting speeches and presents the content of these events at a pace that is more demanding of the reader's time."[4] One may reasonably suppose then that the Mission Discourse is composed to have a rhetorical effect on Matthew's readers, more than on the audience in the narrative. The methodological challenge facing interpreters is balancing attention to the discourse's function within the narrative with attention to how the discourse addresses an audience outside the text. A problem with many narrative analyses of Matthew is that exclusive attention is given to a discourse's narrative function, how action and dialogue contribute to plot and character development, thus causing certain rhetorical features of the text to be highlighted at the expense of others. That is to say, conceptions of narrative structure can become a conceptual grid imposed on a text, possibly obscuring a text's multifaceted rhetorical texture. Narrative analyses of the Mission Discourse frequently ignore the social and cultural intertexture, which is problematic if Powell's observation about the discourses in Matthew is correct. For if Matthew understands Jesus' instructions to address later itinerant disciples, not just the original twelve, then attention must be given to the ways the discourse evokes knowledge of certain social realia and cultural practices that conditions the readers' understanding of the text.

Narrative Innertexture

The introduction to the Mission Discourse in 9:35–38 establishes a connection between the mission instructions that follow and the discourse and narrative material that precede it. Here, Matthew reports Jesus going around

---

3. John S. Kloppenborg, *Q Parallels* (Sonoma, Calif.: Polebridge, 1988), 72.
4. Mark Allen Powell, "The Plot and Subplots of Matthew's Gospel," *NTS* 38 (1992): 194.

all the towns and villages "teaching in their synagogues and preaching the good news of the kingdom and healing every disease and every infirmity" (9:35). This description of Jesus' activity repeats virtually verbatim what we read earlier in 4:23. These verses, 4:23 and 9:35, bracket the Sermon on the Mount and the collection of miracle stories that follow it — a unit of discourse and narrative that establishes Jesus' authority "in word and deed." When 9:35 is read as a summary of the activity of Jesus reported in 8:1–9:34, it creates a central structural unit within the narrative. Eugene Boring observes that this "christological" unit is bracketed by "discipleship" material: the call of the disciples (4:18–22), and the Mission Discourse.[5] Boring argues for an elaborate chiastic structure centered on this christological unit that extends from 1:2 to 12:21. This is an example of the sort of conceptual grid that highlights certain rhetorical features of the narrative at the expense of others, as will soon be illustrated. Through this structure, Boring argues, Matthew relates Christology to discipleship in a manner that makes the former central: "Matthew's thinking does not begin with a community and ask about its founder or leader, but with the advent of the Christ as the representative of the kingdom of God, an event that generates a new community."[6] The Mission Discourse, as it functions within this narrative structure, illustrates how in the generation of this new community Christ is not independent of the disciples and vice versa. For example, Jesus instructs the disciples to proclaim the same good news, the message that "the kingdom of heaven is at hand" (10:7; cf. 4:17). He then instructs them to "heal the afflicted," "raise the dead," "cleanse lepers," and "cast out demons" (10:8), all of which Jesus is reported doing in 8:1–9:34.

Jesus' instruction that his disciples "cast out demons" is particularly significant because it has already been reported that an exorcism Jesus performed led Pharisees to charge, "By the ruler of demons he casts out demons" (9:34). Later in the Mission Discourse, Jesus tells his disciples: "If they have called the master of the house Beelzebul, how much more will they malign those of his household" (10:25b). This and other warnings to the disciples are introduced by the saying: "Behold, I myself send you out like sheep into the midst of wolves; so be wise as serpents and innocent as doves" (10:16). The warnings that follow address various sorts of conflicts the disciples will be drawn into because of their relationship to Jesus: trials before synagogue councils and political courts (10:17–18), and discord within households (10:21, 35–

---

5. M. Eugene Boring, "The Convergence of Source Analysis, Social History, and Literary Structure in the Gospel of Matthew," *SBL Seminar Papers,* 1994 (SBLSP 21; Atlanta: Scholars Press, 1994), 605–6. Boring notes that this A B A' chiastic structure was first worked out by Ulrich Luz.

6. Ibid., 606.

37). These conflicts do not exactly mirror the controversies we see Jesus embroiled in earlier in 9:10–17, yet there are similarities. Jesus will have his own trial before religious and political authorities later in the narrative, and his execution will provide justification for his warnings to the disciples about the possibility of death. The Mission Discourse may indeed, as Boring argues, extend to the disciples Jesus' authority "in word and deed," as it is established in 5:1–9:34, but, it does more than that. To address how the authority exercised by the disciples will lead to conflict with other authorities, the Mission Discourse looks beyond the preceding discourse and narrative sections to later episodes in the narrative, and very likely outside the narrative to conflicts which Matthew's audience experiences.

Three-Step Progression Pattern

The innertexture of the Mission Discourse is best characterized as an "opening-middle-closing" pattern of elaboration.[7] The triadic structuring of the discourse is typically Matthean. We find threefold divisions in the genealogy (1:1–18); the narration of the conception, birth, and infancy of Jesus (1:18–2:23); John's preaching and the baptism of Jesus (ch. 3); and Matthew's account of the beginning of Jesus' ministry (4:1–23). The opening, middle, and closing of the Mission Discourse are distinguished by their respective textures.[8] The lines of division are not entirely sharp because of the way material in one section builds upon material in the section that precedes it, thus making the triadic pattern progressive in nature.

The opening section of the discourse (9:35–10:4) sets the commissioning of the disciples in a narrative context. Some of the links to the preceding narrative have already been noted; there are, however, other connections. For example, Matthew describes the event that prompts Jesus to send for his disciples. Jesus, we are told, looked around at the crowd that followed him and "had compassion" for the people "because they were harassed and helpless, like sheep without a shepherd" (9:36). If read in the context of the preceding narrative, we may conclude that he pitied these people for their afflictions, like those he healed earlier. Perhaps too he pitied them for their lack of faith, as he had pitied his own disciples earlier (8:23–27). Whatever the immediate cause for Jesus' expression of compassion, he needs help in extending compassion to these people. For he says: "The harvest is great, but the laborers

---

7. This type of innertexture is named and described by Vernon Robbins, in *Exploring the Texture of Texts* (Valley Forge, Pa.: Trinity Press International, 1996), 19–21.
8. Ibid., 19.

are few; pray therefore the lord of the harvest to send out laborers into his harvest" (9:37–38). There is a tone of urgency in this saying, which might be interpreted as eschatological urgency, given that later in the discourse Jesus tells his disciples: "you will not have gone through all the towns of Israel until the Son of Man comes" (10:23). And, given the association of harvest imagery with judgment, this opening section of the Mission Discourse, while recapitulating themes of the preceding narrative material, shifts the focus to the eschatological context of Jesus' ministry and that of the disciples he is about to commission.

Concluding this opening section of the discourse is the listing of the twelve disciples by name (10:2–4), and Matthew's identification of them as "apostles." The one use of ἀπόστολος in Matthew occurs in 10:2. Even though the number twelve is symbolically significant — the mission of the disciples is restricted to Israel — the reference to the twelve as "apostles" does not necessarily historicize the discourse by making it address a closed group. Were the instructions of the discourse understood to apply only to the twelve who are named, this would clearly exclude later missionaries engaged in a mission to Gentiles, such as those besides "the eleven" who engage in the "Great Commission" (28:16–20). Later in the discourse, when Jesus speaks of disciples testifying before synagogue councils and before "governors and kings" (10:18), the warnings imply that missions to Jews and Gentiles are going on simultaneously.[9] If we understand the term simply to denote "one who is sent out," then the context of the commissioning and the instructions that follow would apply in a transparent fashion to later missionaries of Matthew's time. That is to say, the discourse connects the narrative world of the text with the world of the audience outside the text.

The middle section consists of the instructions regarding travel, receiving hospitality, and responding to rejection (10:5–15). This section, like the opening one, contains language that links the instructions with themes of the preceding discourse and narrative sections. As previously noted, Jesus authorizes the disciples to preach that "the kingdom of heaven is at hand" and to perform various acts of mercy, thus incorporating them into his own ministry of "word and deed." The itinerant disciples whom Jesus sends out represent a geographical extension of his ministry within the narrative. To Matthew and his readers, the extension of Jesus' ministry through these "apostles" is temporal as well as geographic. The travel instructions make the disciples an effective extension of Jesus' preaching and healing in two respects. First,

---

9. Ulrich Luz, in "The Disciples in the Gospel according to Matthew," *The Interpretation of Matthew* (ed. Graham Stanton; Philadelphia: Fortress; London: SPCK, 1983), 100.

the prohibitions against carrying bags, money, a staff, a second tunic, and sandals[10] allow the disciples to show their dependence on God's providential care. This evokes recollection of Jesus' teachings in the Sermon on the Mount about not being anxious about food, drink, or clothing (6:25–34). Second, the mercy the itinerant disciples show to those in need is unconditional, just like the mercy Jesus had for them in the Stilling of the Storm episode in the preceding narrative section (8:23–27). Jesus' words in 10:8b — "You received without cost, give without cost" — describe the unconditional nature of the mercy the disciples extend to others on Jesus' behalf. Matthew places this unique Matthean saying before the travel instructions. Although there are no conjunctions indicating that saying serves as a rationale for the prohibitions against carrying money or surplus provisions, Matthew may well intend the saying to function that way.

The travel instructions are followed by instructions regarding the receiving of hospitality. The implicit connection between the two sets of instructions is quite clear. The reason the itinerant disciples need not be anxious about securing sustenance is because households along the way will take them in as guests. It might reasonably be inferred that the extension of hospitality to the disciples represents a form of God's providential care, for the Jewish religion from epic times to Matthew's time and later recognized hospitality as a social institution through which God interacts with humans.[11] Twice in the preceding narrative Jesus himself is the guest of households (8:20; 9:10). The divine nature of hospitality is reflected in Jesus' instructions. As in the Q Mission Discourse (Luke 10:2–12), Matthew refers to a "peace" which will rest on households that receive disciples, but not on households that turn them away. In Matthew alone, though, the disciples are instructed to judge the "worthiness" of any household offering them hospitality. The idea that a household must prove itself "worthy" of the blessings the disciples might bestow appears to be a Matthean addition to the Q tradition. How does a household prove itself worthy? An answer is suggested in the instructions about responding to rejection that follow. Where Luke, and presumably Q, refers only to "towns" not receiving the disciples, Matthew refers to the prospect that "households" as well as "towns" might not receive them (10:14). Also, Matthew describes the rejection of the disciples as a matter of people "not receiving" them and "not hearing" their "words" (τοὺς λόγους). Earlier in the conclusion of the Sermon on the Mount, Matthew uses τοὺς λόγους in reference to the teachings of Jesus: "And when Jesus finished these sayings (τοὺς λόγους τούτους),

---

10. Among the Synoptics, Matthew's list of prohibitions is the most severe.
11. Cf. Gen 18:1–8; 19:1, 3; Heb 13:2.

the crowds were astonished at his teaching, for he taught them as one who had authority, and not as their scribes" (7:28–29). Is it possible that Matthew envisions the disciples presenting the teachings of Jesus in those households that extend them hospitality? Jesus has explicitly instructed them to "preach" and to "heal," two of the three activities mentioned in Matthew's summary of Jesus' activity in 9:35; is it implicit that they also teach? Later in Matthew, the disciples' function as teachers is affirmed (28:20). If itinerant disciples in Matthew's time are the audience for these instructions, disciples engaged in the Great Commission, then Jesus most likely is telling disciples how to act toward those who reject their teaching.

The last instructions address how the disciples should respond to rejection. Here Matthew closely parallels both Mark and Q with just a slight difference. As in Mark and Q, Matthew reports Jesus instructing the disciples to "shake off the dust of the feet" as they leave the place that has rejected them. In Mark, the gesture is said to be a "testimony" against those who do not receive or hear the disciples (6:11). In Matthew, the description of the gesture as a testimony against people is absent. Is there a reason for Matthew's omission of this explanation of what "shaking off the dust of the feet" represents? After this instruction, Jesus pronounces judgment against any city that rejects the disciples: "Truly, I tell you, it shall be more tolerable on the day of judgment for the land of Sodom and Gomorrah than for that city" (10:15). Although Jesus pronounces eschatological judgment on those who reject the disciples, it is not clear that he wants the itinerant disciples to pronounce this judgment on people. Later in the Parable of the Wheat and Weeds (13:24–30), Jesus warns against pulling weeds before the harvest, which presumably means not pronouncing eschatological condemnation on people before the day of judgment. Read in the context of the saying at the beginning of the discourse that likens the disciples to "harvest workers" (9:37–38), Matthew, it seems, envisions the disciples' mission as one of preparing people for the day of judgment, but not condemning those who reject them.

The closing section of the discourse (10:16–42) consists of sayings that elaborate on various elements of the preceding instructions. Here we find those sayings of Jesus noted earlier that call attention to his authority. First, Jesus says that he himself sends his disciples out "like sheep in the midst of wolves" (10:16), addressing the dangers of their mission. Jesus proceeds to warn that his disciples can expect to be "handed over" to religious and civil authorities on account of him (10:17–18). When this happens, Jesus tells his disciples not to be anxious about what to say. A supporting rationale is provided: The Spirit of their Father will speak for them (10:19b–20). The people who "hand over" the disciples may very well be their own families.

And again, Jesus says this persecution will happen because of the disciples' connection to him (10:21–22). The statement, "Those who endures to the end will be saved," suggests such persecutions represent eschatological tribulation. This interpretation of the persecution is strengthened by Jesus' allusion to the imminent coming of the Son of Man in 10:23, the second instance where Jesus calls attention to his authority.

Here we have two examples of case/rule/result syllogism, which Vernon Robbins identifies as a common structure of argumentation in prophetic discourse.[12] The first occurs in 10:17–23, where the order of parts is slightly altered. The case is stated first: the disciples will be handed over to religious and civil authorities where they will testify about Jesus. Then follows the result, an exhortation that the disciples should not be anxious about what to say. Last comes the supporting rule (introduced by γάρ): the Spirit will give the disciples words to speak. This rule, typical of rules in prophetic discourse, asserts that God calls certain people for special tasks and makes it possible for them to fulfill these tasks.[13] This syllogism is followed by another, and again the argument begins with a statement of the case: family members will turn against each other and people will be delivered to death. Then follows the rule: "The one who endures to the end will be saved" (10:22b). This rule is grounded in the belief that those who fulfill the responsibilities entrusted to them by God will be specially blessed by God. Enduring hardships associated with the mission is an expectation Jesus has of the disciples. The imperative "flee to the next town" does not follow as the logical result, if it means the disciples are to flee from persecution. However, if the idea is for the disciples to flee from situations where they might be killed, then they are not fleeing persecution entirely, they are simply moving to another town where they likely will encounter conflict. The eschatological saying about the nearness of the end in 10:23 implies that many or most of the itinerants, although being persecuted, will manage to survive. For this reason, we probably should not categorize these arguments as examples of suffering death discourse, another type of argumentative discourse identified by Robbins.[14] The point of these arguments is that the disciples should not be deterred in carrying out their mission by the prospect of persecution.

More prophetic argumentation follows in 10:24–31. Here the argumentation begins with a rule: "A disciple is not above the teacher, nor a slave above the master; it is enough for the disciple to be like the teacher, and the slave

---

12. Vernon K. Robbins, "Argumentative Textures in Socio-Rhetorical Interpretation," pp. 27–65 in this volume.
13. Ibid., 44.
14. Ibid., 51–54.

like the master" (10:24). Then follows what seems to be a statement of the case: "If they have called the master of the house Beelzebul, how much more will they malign those of his household" (10:25). Enthymematic reasoning is involved here. One thing not clearly stated, but clearly understood when the narrative setting of the discourse is recalled, is that Jesus has been called Beelzebul by Pharisees after casting demons from a mute man (9:32–34). Also, the reader should readily recall that Jesus has authorized his disciples to cast out demons (10:8). Thus, the unstated result that follows is that the disciples will be maligned, perhaps by the same Pharisees who maligned Jesus. The words of Jesus that follow state the appropriate response to such a situation: "Therefore (οὖν) do not fear them" (10:26). What exactly the disciples have to fear, however, is not stated. What follows is a statement (introduced by γάρ) which seems to state a further rule supporting the exhortation not to be afraid. Typical of prophetic discourse, the rule refers to the activity of God, although God is not explicitly mentioned — "For nothing is covered that will not be uncovered, and nothing is secret that will not become known." Then is stated the result: "What I say to you in the dark, tell in the light; and what you hear whispered, proclaim from housetop" (10:27), positive exhortations and counterparts of the command, "Do not fear them." A second exhortation not to be afraid follows, and here the possibility of death is addressed: "Do not fear those who kill the body but cannot kill the soul; rather fear him who can destroy both body and soul in hell" (10:28). This may be read as the statement of rule in the form of an imperative, for what is asserted here are the negative consequences of failing to satisfy God's expectations, another function of rules in prophetic discourse.[15] The imperative acknowledges the possibility of death, but, as we saw above, there are reasons why the disciples need not fear this possibility. What follows are two supporting statements of rule: "Are not two sparrows sold for a penny? Yet not one of them will fall to the ground apart from your Father. And even the hairs of your head are all counted" (10:29–30). Then follows a restatement of the previously stated result with an accompanying statement of case: "So (οὖν) do not be afraid; you are more valuable than many sparrows" (10:31). The analogy to God's care for other creatures and the argument "from the lesser to the greater" employed here are features of argumentation in wisdom discourse.[16] According to Robbins, the presence of wisdom topics in prophetic discourse shows how prophetic discourse can move out centrifugally and engage other types of

---

15. Ibid., 45.
16. Ibid., 32.

discourse, not limiting itself to rules asserting specific acts of God on behalf of specially chosen people.[17]

The saying of Jesus in 10:32–33 introduces what appears to be further support for the exhortation "Do not be afraid": "Everyone therefore (οὖν) who acknowledges me before others, I also will acknowledge before my Father in heaven; but whoever denies me before others, I also will deny before my Father in heaven." However, the saying also shifts the focus to the topic of rewards, a common topic in prophetic discourse. The fact that the saying is introduced by οὖν establishes a connection with prophetic discourse and argumentation that precedes it, for the saying indicates how God rewards those chosen individuals who fulfill their mission. This rule is then applied to the case of household discord, which the disciples will encounter, if not cause (10:34–39). Jesus here acknowledges that he himself is the cause of household discord, then warns that those who put love of family before love of him will lose their soul. Even though the itinerant disciples' activity will cause discord in some households, they may rest assured that some households will extend them hospitality, as the sayings that follow indicate. Jesus promises that those who receive prophets will receive a prophet's reward. The "receiving" of the prophets certainly refers to the extension of hospitality, as the reference to "giving a cup of cold water" signifies (10:42). However, the receiving of the prophet may also entail the acceptance of their teaching, as is implied in the earlier instruction that disciples judge the worthiness of a household based on whether or not people hear their words (10:13–14).

Social and Cultural Intertexture

The Mission Discourse in several places evokes knowledge of social codes and relationships, knowledge which all or most people in the ancient Mediterranean world would have obtained through general interaction. Hospitality codes, as just noted above, are evoked in Jesus' instructions to the disciples, the itinerants will receive the nourishment (τροφή) they are due from households in the towns where they stay (10:10b–13), and, as just noted above, hospitality codes are affirmed at the end of the discourse. Jesus' instructions to the disciples envision an exchange of goods or services between two parties. The household offers the itinerant disciples food, and the disciples offer a type of "peace" in return. But, as we have seen, the offer of peace is conditional, for Jesus tells the disciples to withdraw the gift should the household

---

17. Ibid., 37.

be "unworthy" of it. If food and a blessing of "peace" constitute reciprocal expressions of honor, then what may be envisioned is a situation where the household does something to dishonor the disciples, such as "not hearing their words" (10:14). If this is so, then the disciples' gesture of "shaking off the dust of the feet" as they exit a household or town is an act of shaming those who have dishonored them.

The blessing the disciples are authorized to bestow on any household that receives them, and the "reward" Jesus mentions at the end of the discourse (10:41–42), are spiritual gifts exchanged for material ones. The gifts exchanged are of unequal value. Let us recall here the question Paul asks the Corinthians when he defends his "right" to solicit support from them: "If we sowed spiritual goods among you, is it too much if we reap your material goods?" (1 Cor 9:11). Paul here is not defending a right he himself intends to exercise, as he subsequently indicates (9:15–18); rather, he is defending the practice of apostles in general. The rhetorical nature of the question suggests that Corinthians were not inclined to question this basic entitlement of itinerant apostles, nor were they inclined to question that the benefits of the apostles' labor were superior to the material provisions they received in return. We are possibly dealing here with specific codes of hospitality within Jewish culture. John Koenig observes that it was not uncommon for itinerant rabbis to offer Torah instruction in exchange for hospitality. He cites the teaching of Jose ben Joezer (ca. 175 B.C.E.): "Let thy house be a place of meeting for the wise and dust thyself with the dust of their feet and drink *their* words (my emphasis) with thirst' (Abot 1:4).[18] The teaching of the itinerant rabbis was viewed figuratively as an offer of hospitality, then those who receive their words are hosts on one level and guests on another. Matthew and his readers are probably familiar with this cultural understanding of hospitality as it applies to receiving religious teachers. For Matthew, "hearing the words" of the disciples is an act of "receiving" them.[19] If Matthew envisions the disciples commissioned by Jesus, or the itinerants of his own time, teaching in the households they enter, then he and his readers no doubt regarded the benefits of the disciples' teaching as superior in value to the sustenance they received in exchange.

The unequal nature of the goods and services exchanged would have created a patron-client relationship between the itinerant disciples and the households that received them. As a description of social relationship,

---

18. John Koenig, *New Testament Hospitality: Partnership with Strangers as Promise and Mission* (Philadelphia: Fortress Press, 1985), 17.

19. Matthew does this not only in 10:14, but also in 10:40, where he has δεχόμενος and δέχεται in place of Luke's (and probably Q's) ἀκούων and ἀκούει (Luke 10:16).

"patron-client" refers to a variety of open-ended relationships founded upon the reciprocal exchange of unequal goods or services. As an economic or political relationship, an inequality in power underlies the unequal exchange of goods or services. The patron, as the more powerful party, graciously offers something to the weaker client. In return the client provides the patron with some expression of loyalty or honor.[20] An extended web of patron-client relationships can be created through the use of brokers, clients chosen by a patron to serve as mediators between the patrons and other clients. As a mediator, a broker is simultaneously a client of the patron he represents and a patron in his own right to clients below him.[21] Brokers typically function as representatives for a remote patron, making possible the extension of patronage over a wide geographic area. Military commanders and "holy persons" such as teachers and priests would have been viewed as representatives of patrons in the ancient Mediterranean world. The tradition about Jesus and the centurion describes the interaction between these two types of brokers (Matt 8:5–13).[22] The centurion, who describes himself as a man under authority with men under him, recognizes Jesus as a broker for God when he petitions Jesus to heal his servant.

Patron-client relationships and the ideology behind them so thoroughly permeated ancient Mediterranean society, especially during the Empire, that conceptualizing social relationships in patron-broker-client terms would have come naturally to Matthew and his readers. Common people in ancient Mediterranean society viewed themselves and the people around them through the lenses of daily life, and patronage was a reality of everyday life. The fact that these people did not develop their own terminology for describing patronage relationships does not mean that patronage ideology did not permeate their society.[23] We may reasonably assume that Jesus was seen functioning in a broker capacity when he commissioned the disciples. In the closing unit of the discourse, Jesus alludes to what appears to be a brokerage chain: "Whoever receives you receives me, and whoever receives me receives the one

---

20. Halvor Moxnes, "Patron-Client Relations in the New Community," in *The Social World of Luke-Acts,* ed. J. Neyrey (Peabody, Mass.: Hendrickson, 1991), 242.
21. Ibid., 248–49.
22. Bruce J. Malina and Richard L. Rohrbaugh, *Social-Science Commentary on the Synoptic Gospels* (Minneapolis: Fortress Press, 1992), 70, 74–76.
23. Pertinent here is Wittgenstein's idea of reaching "bedrock" in the analysis of language, where bedrock describes the various sorts of human activity that support language, and which constitute the limit of language. Persons completely immersed in activities that constitute what Wittgenstein calls "a form of life" have no use for the terminology which those outside that form of life use to describe what they see. This concept of "bedrock" supports the distinction between etic and emic analysis, which Moxnes observes is crucial when discussing patronage in ancient societies from a modern perspective. (Cf. "Patron-Client Relations in the New Community," 251–52.)

who sent me" (10:40). Implicit here is the idea that Jesus is a broker who enlists the service of other brokers. A sense of hierarchy is also implicit in this saying and throughout the discourse. God, everyone's Father (10:20, 29, 32), stands at the head of the brokerage chain. Taking Jesus' instructions to the disciples as a whole, we see the itinerants functioning as brokers for Jesus and "the kingdom of heaven," but we also see Jesus clarifying the two dimensions of the broker relationship: the disciples relation to Jesus and their relationship to those they serve. On the one hand, the disciples have the authority to do what Jesus does; they preach the same message, they perform the same miracles, and, it is implied, they teach what he teaches. Yet, as brokers of Jesus, they are not equal to him. Jesus reminds them of their status as his clients when he says, "You received without charge, give without charge." Also, in the instructions about how to respond to rejection, Matthew envisions Jesus prohibiting the disciples from pronouncing any sort of eschatological condemnation on those who reject them. This action Jesus reserves for himself at the Parousia (Matt 25:31–46). The analogy to teacher-student and master-slave relationships in 10:24 further reinforces the idea that Jesus and his disciples remain in a patron-client relationship even while the disciples function as brokers.

Is it a concern of Matthew to clarify the disciples' role as brokers? A clue may lie in Jesus' prohibition against pronouncing eschatological condemnation, a prohibition reinforced later in the Parable of the Wheat and Weeds. Leander Keck suggests that "Spirit-authorized vigilante activity" may have been a problem in the Matthean community.[24] He observes that Matthew gives less attention to the Spirit than Luke or John. And, in the Great Commission, instead of pledging the Spirit's presence with the disciples, Jesus pledges his own presence (28:20).[25] The Mission Discourse contains one of the few instances in Matthew where some role for the Spirit is affirmed: providing words for the disciples when they testify before religious and political authorities. Matthew envisions a continued mission to Israel in spite of past rejection and the current dangers. Pronouncing eschatological condemnation on opponents would not be in harmony with mission where Jesus' disciples function as an extension of his compassion. Moreover, demanding the disciples to endure persecutions and conflicts could actually strengthen community bonds. The concept of a "household of Jesus" (cf. 10:25), which stands over against the households that rejected his servants, may well describe how the

---

24. Leander Keck, "Matthew and the Spirit," in *The Social World of the First Christians* (ed. L. Michael White and O. Larry Yarbrough; Philadelphia: Fortress, 1995), 154.
25. Ibid., 147–49.

Matthean community saw itself. The community possibly fashioned itself as a type of surrogate family[26] for those alienated from their original families.

Conclusion

The structure of argumentation and the rhetorical function of the Mission Discourse are more readily discerned when attention is given to the narrative innertexture, the three-step progression of the discourse, and the social and cultural intertexture. The discourse turns out to be a rather substantial rhetorical composition, integrally related to the surrounding narrative and other discourses in Matthew. It effectively draws the reader into the world of the narrative in a manner that illumines the status and function of a disciple of Jesus in the reader's own world. The principal aim of the discourse seems to be the encouragement of the Matthean community in its continued mission to fellow Jews.

---

26. Malina and Rohrbaugh, *Social-Science Commentary*, 92, 100–101.

CHAPTER 11

ARGUMENTATION IN JOHN 5

Harold W. Attridge

Rhetorical analysis of the New Testament, using ancient rhetorical theory and practice to illuminate scriptural texts, has inspired the reassessment of epistolary materials,[1] and the speeches in Acts.[2] Narratives have proved a less hospitable environment to this approach, although prescriptions for the elaboration of *chreiai* have illuminated certain kinds of pronouncement stories[3] and speeches of Jesus.[4] Perhaps the least likely hunting ground for rhetorical critics has been the Fourth Gospel, the subject of the current experiment,[5]

Thanks to John Fitzgerald of Miami University for helpful suggestions on a draft of this paper.

1. For developments since Hans Dieter Betz, see especially Thomas H. Olbricht, "Classical Rhetorical Criticism and Historical Reconstructions: A Critique," in *The Rhetorical Interpretation of Scripture: Essays from the 1996 Malibu Conference* (ed. Stanley E. Porter and Dennis L. Stamps; JSNTSup 180; Sheffield: Academic Press, 1999), 108–24, as well as the essays by Duane F. Watson, Stanley Porter, Dennis L. Stamps, Glenn S. Holland, Anders Eriksson, and Lauri Thurén in this volume.

2. In Porter and Stamps, *Rhetorical Interpretation,* see Kota Yamada, "The Preface to the Lukan Writings and Rhetorical Historiography," 154–72; L. Gregory Bloomquist, "Rhetorical Argumentation and the Culture of Apocalyptic: A Socio-rhetorical Analysis of Luke 21," and Ira J. Jolivet, Jr., "The Lukan Account of Paul's Conversion and Hermagorean Stasis Theory." Previous rhetorical conferences concentrated on Paul. See Stanley E. Porter and Thomas H. Olbricht, *Rhetoric and the New Testament: Essays from the 1992 Heidelberg Conference* (JSNTSup 90; Sheffield: Sheffield Academic Press, 1993); and idem, *The Rhetorical Analysis of Scripture: Essays from the 1995 London Conference* (JSNTSup 146; Sheffield: Sheffield Academic Press, 1997).

3. See Burton L. Mack and Vernon K. Robbins, *Patterns of Persuasion in the Gospels* (Minneapolis: Fortress, 1989); Burton L. Mack, *Rhetoric and the New Testament* (Minneapolis: Fortress, 1990); the essays in Vernon K. Robbins, ed., *The Rhetoric of Pronouncement, Semeia* 14 (1993), and the literature cited there. For analysis of the treatment of the subject in ancient sources, see Ronald F. Hock and Edward N. O'Neil, *The Progymnasmata* (vol. 1 of *The Chreia in Ancient Rhetoric;* SBLTT 24; Greco-Roman Religion Series 9; Atlanta: Scholars Press, 1986).

4. See C. Clifton Black, "An Oration at Olivet: Some Rhetorical Dimensions of Mark 13," in *Persuasive Artistry: Studies in New Testament Rhetoric in Honor of George A. Kennedy* (ed. Duane F. Watson; JSNTSup 50; Sheffield: Sheffield Academic Press, 1981), 66–92, and Adela Yarbro Collins, "The Apocalyptic Rhetoric of Mark 13 in Historical Context," *Biblical Research* 41 (1996): 5–36.

5. But see M. Warner, "The Fourth Gospel's Art of Rational Persuasion," in *The Bible as Rhetoric: Studies in Biblical Persuasion and Credibility* (ed. M. Warner: Warwick Studies in Philosophy and Literature; London and New York: Routledge, 1990), 153–77; Wilhelm Wuellner, "Rhetorical Criticism and Its Theory in Culture-Critical Perspective: The Narrative Rhetoric of John 11," in *Text and Interpretation: New Approaches in the Criticism of the New Testament* (ed. P. J. Martin and J. H. Petzer; NTTS 15; Leiden: Brill, 1991), 171–85, and idem, "Putting Life Back into the Lazarus Story and Its Reading: The Narrative Rhetoric of John 11 as the Narration of Faith," *Semeia* 53 (1991): 113–32; F. Thielman, "The Style of the Fourth Gospel and Ancient Literary Critical Concepts of

which focuses on the lengthy speech of Jesus in John 5. Alternatively, this paper can be construed as part of a search for an adequate method of treating the most intractable of the materials in the Fourth Gospel, the generically diverse discourses.

Literary Structure of John 5

The overall structure of the chapter is clear. A traditional miracle story provokes controversy over the legitimacy of Sabbath healing. The controversy in turn introduces a discourse which, moving beyond halakah, explores the relationship of Jesus to the Father and the evidence for that relationship.

Much previous exegetical effort focused on diachronic issues. In one scenario, the healing/controversy story, prior to incorporation in the Gospel, may have concluded with the kind of defense of Jesus' activity found in John 7:19–24, as in Synoptic counterparts.[6] The evangelist displaced this material with the discourse of chapter 5.

Redaction critics have further sensed that the substituted discourse developed over time. For Brown,[7] Jesus' initial response comprised John 5:19–25, to which was added 5:26–30, and 5:31–46. Others, like Haenchen,[8] detected a redactor's hand within the first half of the discourse, correcting the basic gos-

---

Religious Discourse," in *Persuasive Artistry,* 169–83; and Margaret Davies, *Rhetoric and Reference in the Fourth Gospel* (JSNTSup 69; Sheffield: JSOT Press, 1992), which does not deal with classical rhetoric. The survey of rhetorical studies of the New Testament by Duane F. Watson and Alan J. Hauser, *Rhetorical Criticism of the Bible: A Comparative Bibliography with Notes on History and Method* (Biblical Interpretation Series 4; Leiden: Brill, 1994), devotes only four pages to John, and many entries treat dramatic or narrative topics.

6. Mark 2:1–12; Matt 9:1–8; Luke 5:17–26 parallel the narrative of the healing. Mark 3:1–6; Matt 12:9–14; and Luke 6:6–11; 13:10–17 offer controversies over healing on the Sabbath. On the source issue, see Harold W. Attridge, "Thematic Development and Source Elaboration in John 7:1–36," *CBQ* 44 (1980): 160–70. See also Robert Fortna, *The Fourth Gospel and Its Predecessor: From Narrative Source to Present Gospel* (Studies in the New Testament and Its World; Philadelphia: Fortress, 1989), 113–17; Urban C. Van Wahlde, *The Earliest Version of John's Gospel: Recovering the Gospel of Signs* (Wilmington: Glazier, 1989), 94–97.

7. See Raymond E. Brown, *The Gospel According to John* (2 vols.; AB 29, 29a; Garden City, N.Y.: Doubleday, 1966–70), 218–19.

8. Ernst Haenchen, *John: A Commentary on the Gospel of John* (2 vols.; Philadelphia: Fortress, 1984): "These verses (scil. 22–23) introduce a completely new idea, which cannot be combined with either verses 19–21 or with verses 24–26. Up to this point it has been affirmed that the son does only what he sees the Father doing; he can do nothing of his own accord.... In these verses the complete authority for the judgment is attributed to the son;... verses 22f. contradict John 3:17f.: 'Whoever believes on him (i.e., the son), is not to be judged.' These verses also contradict what is said in 5:24.

"Moreover, the concept of 'judgment' (*krisis*), which Bultmann takes as his point of departure, is not that of the Evangelist. For him, 'the judgment,' as verse 24 indicates, is a condemnation and not a 'decision' between 'life' and 'death.' The insertions in the Johannine text, on the other hand, 'conceive the "judgment" (*krisis*) in the sense of the future judgment of the world at the end of time' (1:251–53).

pel's realized eschatology with references to future judgment and resurrection (5:22–23, 27–29). Such critics have certainly highlighted articulations of the discourse, but their analyses leave open the question of the formal coherence of the speech.

Fascinated with the dynamics of narrative, much contemporary exegesis has marginalized diachronic analysis in favor of holistic, synchronous readings.[9] Thus, recent work on John 5 has focused on the healing *tale,* its portrayal of character and its manipulation of readers' expectations.[10] Analysis of the discourse has, in contrast, suffered from comparative neglect.

Rhetorical criticism may advance the discussion by concentrating on the argumentation within the discourse and by providing another tool to assess its unity. Yet caution is required. While rhetoric deals with persuasive speech, the Gospel's rhetoric has a narrative setting, in which the primary persuasive relationship is defined by the text and its reader. Yet the rhetoric of that encounter works through the rhetoric embedded in the narrative. A full analysis of the pericope's rhetoric must consider both contexts.[11]

The Rhetoric of the Discourse on Work

Genre: The brief encounter at 5:16–18 establishes the rhetorical situation within the narrative. Having learned that Jesus instigated the paralytic's infringement of the Sabbath, "the Judeans" pursue him. Jesus responds by

---

Haenchen followed Bultmann, but departed from him in attributing 5:22–23 as well as 5:27–29 to a redactor (1:260).

9. In a fast-growing field, see R. Alan Culpepper, *Anatomy of the Fourth Gospel: A Study in Literary Design* (New Testament Foundations and Facets; Philadelphia: Fortress, 1983); Paul D. Duke, *Irony in the Fourth Gospel* (Atlanta: John Knox, 1985); Gail R. O'Day, *Revelation in the Fourth Gospel: Narrative Mode and Theological Claim* (Philadelphia: Fortress, 1986); Jeffrey Staley, *The Print's First Kiss: A Rhetorical Investigation of the Implied Reader in the Fourth Gospel* (SBLDS 82; Missoula, Mont.: Scholars Press, 1988); idem, *Reading with a Passion: Rhetoric, Autobiography, and the American West in the Gospel of John* (New York: Continuum, 1995); Francis J. Moloney, *Signs and Shadows: Reading John 5–12* (Minneapolis: Fortress, 1996); and idem, *John* (Sacra Pagina 4; Collegeville, Minn.: Liturgical Press, 1998).

10. See, e.g., John Christopher Thomas, " 'Stop Sinning Lest Something Worse Come upon You': The Man at the Pool in John 5," *JSNT* 59 (1995): 3–20; Jeffrey Staley, "Stumbling in the Dark, Reaching for the Light: Reading Character in John 5 and 9," *Semeia* 53 (1991): 55–80; R. Alan Culpepper, "John 5:1–18: A Sample of Narrative Critical Commentary," in *La communauté johannique et son histoire* (ed. J. D. Kaestli, J. M. Poffet, and J. Zumstein; Geneva: Labor et Fides, 1990), 131–51, reprinted in Mark W. G. Stibbe, ed., *The Gospel of John as Literature: An Anthology of Twentieth-Century Perspectives* (NTTS 17; Leiden: Brill, 1993), 193–207. This approach departs markedly from that of Haenchen: "The narrator is not concerned to paint a complete picture of the sick man, which is only of interest as an object of Jesus's healing act" (1:246).

11. L. Gregory Bloomquist, "The Role of the Audience in the Determination of Argumentation," makes an analogous point about the importance of the (implied) audience (see above pp. 158–63). The narrative setting here introduces further complexity.

declaring that the Father works[12] and so does he, which simply intensifies the reaction of "the Judeans," who now seek to kill Jesus on the grounds that he has made himself equal to God.[13]

The exchange establishes a forensic situation involving a complex case, in which more than one issue is adjudicated.[14] At one level, Jesus is being charged for breaking the Sabbath.[15] More importantly, his opponents allege blasphemy. Responding to the first charge, ancient defenders could mount either of two strategies, to agree to the law but dispute the facts, or to argue about the applicability of the law or the inherent quality of the act.[16] In 5:17 Jesus takes the latter course, arguing that his act did not break the law, but simply imitated what God himself does. Jesus' action, in other words, has ample precedent; therefore it was both authorized and inherently right.

A frustratingly compact argument ensues. It offers little more than a claim that might serve as the *propositio* of a fuller treatment, explaining how God works, how Jesus' actions relate to that paradigm, and why they might be exempt from strictures on Sabbath labor. Ignoring those issues, the dialogue rushes to the more serious charge, that Jesus, by claiming God as his precedent, equated himself with God.

Two possibilities remain open. Arguing on the facts, the defense might claim that the charge is inappropriate. In but *imitating* a divine paradigm, Jesus decidedly did *not* equate himself with God, and accusations that he did so are simply mistaken. That argument might allow a challenge to Jesus' appeal to divine precedent for his behavior, but it avoids the charge of blasphemy. On the other hand, the defense might argue that the accusation of blasphemy is inapplicable because Jesus *rightly* claimed equality with God. Determining which argument Jesus makes is a crucial exegetical issue.

---

12. The declaration usually elicits commentary on the treatment of divine rest and activity in Philo and Rabbinic sources. See, e.g., *Gen. Rab.* 11.12; *Exod. Rab.* 30.6, and C. K. Barrett, *The Gospel According to St. John* (2d ed.; Philadelphia: Westminster, 1978), 213; Brown, *Gospel According to John*, 1:217 and Haenchen, *John*, 1:248–49.

13. The reaction moves the plot forward. Lethal hostility from Jesus' enemies foreshadows the passion.

14. See Cicero, *Inv.*, 1.13.17.

15. For a brief treatment of the Gospel's forensic dimensions, although with little attention to classical rhetoric, see Anthony Ernest Harvey, *Jesus on Trial: A Study in the Fourth Gospel* (London: SPCK, 1976). On forensic imagery in chapter 8, see Jerome Neyrey, "Jesus the Judge: Forensic Process in John 8,21–59," *Biblica* 68 (1987): 509–42.

16. The *Rhet. Her.*, 1.14.24 calls this issue "juridical," "when there is agreement on the act, but the right or wrong of the act is in question. Of this issue there are two subtypes, one called Absolute, the other Assumptive." Cicero, *Inv.*, 2.21.62, offers a similar, but differently labeled, typology: "When it is agreed that an act has been performed and by what name it shall be called and there is no dispute about procedure, and the question is simply about the import, the nature and the essence of the occurrence, we call the issue qualitative. We have said that we think there are two divisions of it, legal and equitable."

Arrangement: Perhaps the *Rhetorica ad Herennium* may assist with its notion of an ideal or "perfect argument" (*absolutissima et perfectissima argumentatio*).[17] Such an ideal argument will consist of five parts: the proposition, the reason, the proof of the reason, the embellishment, and the resumé (propositio, ratio, rationis confirmatio, exornatio, conplexio). By comparison with such an ideal type, the apology of John 5:19–30 seems deficient, and finding the argument's structure involves arbitrary judgments. Nonetheless, comparison with the ideal type may suggest some of the argument's dynamics.[18]

Propositio: Jesus responds to the charge of blasphemy by claiming to be the *Son*. Although one could imagine other inferences drawn from that claim, the defense uses it to make a distinction between the two workers of verse 17. Because Jesus is the Son, he is *not* "equal to the Father." The propositio, however, is not clearly formulated but remains imbedded in the image that follows.

Ratio: Verses 5:19–20a depict a father and his apprentice-son, learning his trade by observation.[19] Implicitly the father symbolizes God, and the son, Jesus. Jesus thus rebuts the charge of making himself indistinguishable from God, but not without an ironic touch. As the argument leaves implicit the characters' identity, it also leaves unexplained how the Son "sees" the Father's works. A hostile reader might at first construe "sight" to mean the observation of the Father's ever present work. Behind such a construal could be a saying such as Matthew 5:44–45: as God ever casts his beneficence on humankind, even on the Sabbath, so too may his observant Son act. Yet the reader, instructed by affirmations of Jesus' heavenly origin (1:1, 3:13), may understand differently how this Son has watched his Father at work. He would have done so as the Word present with the Father "from the beginning." The reader might infer that the Son is not *indistinguishable* from the Father (modalists beware!), but he is a very special Son indeed.

Rationis confirmatio: The next verses, 5:20b–21, reinforce suspicions about the relationship of Son and Father. The language abandons the image of apprenticeship for the world of God and his emissary. What the Son has seen and done intimates what he will see and do (5:20b). He will ultimately say arise (ἔγειρε) not simply to a paralytic (5:9), but to the dead. But does Jesus mean the physically dead or the spiritually dead? The present tenses

---

17. Cf. *Ad Herennium*, 2.18.28, which notes that the structure applies to whole speeches and to their constituent arguments.
18. The model's utility is independent of its role in generating the discourse.
19. For the suggestion of an underlying parable, see C. H. Dodd, "A Hidden Parable in the Fourth Gospel," in idem, *More New Testament Studies* (Grand Rapids: Eerdmans, 1968), 30–40.

of verse 21 point in the latter direction; the hint of a future divine action in verse 20 points in the former direction; ambiguity is inescapable.

Exornatio: The discourse becomes more complex. The whole of 5:22–29 elaborates, in a neatly structured chiasm,[20] the theme of resurrection adumbrated in verse 21:

> A. Triggered by the reference to resurrection, the defense reflects on judgment, casually introduced by a γάρ in verse 22. The first step in this stage of the argument affirms that the Son, not the Father, oversees judgment. Hence, he is equal to the Father after all. He not only does whatever the Father shows him to do; he assumes the Father's role in so doing. To reinforce the point, verse 23 describes the Father's motives in assigning judgment to the Son: to ensure that the Son receives due honor, giving of which is a necessary condition of honoring the Father. Incidentally, the framework of the exornatio ties up one loose end from the initial argument. Jesus offered no obvious rationale for invoking the Father as his precedent for working on the Sabbath. The rationale offered here is simply that God explicitly authorized Jesus to do so, although the authorization here, and in verse 26, is specifically to *judge,* not to heal. Perhaps an *a fortiori* rationalization lurks beneath the surface: if Jesus was explicitly authorized to exercise a potentially destructive divine prerogative, surely he must have been authorized to exercise a beneficent function.
>
> B. At the center of the exornatio stands a pair of different reflections, 5:24–26, on what happens at the moment of "resurrection." The verses connect thematically to the confirmatio and resolve the problem that verse 21 posed. The verse's futurist eschatology is negated by a decided focus on the present confrontation of the revealer and those to whom he addresses his word. In the first solemn ("Amen, amen") affirmation (v. 24), those who hear and believe have eternal life, have escaped judgment and death, and have passed into life. The second, equally solemn affirmation (v. 25) reinforces the first. The hour is coming when the dead will hear the Son of God's voice and come to life, but it is already present as well.[21] Metaphor triumphs over apocalyptic expectation.
>
> The collocation of verse 26 is problematic, and it may serve as a transition between two phases of the argument. Its affirmation that the Son, like the Father, has "life in himself," could be part of the following scene of eschatological judgment. Or it could simply be the climactic affirmation of the Son's present power to give life. If it does serve that role, it would frame the second solemn affirmation (v. 25). More importantly, it would serve as the climax of the tendency of the "apology" to press as far as possible against the grain of its subordinationist argument. The claim, in effect, offers the defense that the charge lodged against the Son is in part correct. In status and function, he is equal to, though not identical with, God.
>
> A'. The "bookend" of the exornatio returns to the theme of judgment, from verses 22–23, with significant Christological titulature. The Son, qua Son of Man (v. 27), has

---

20. Roland Meynet's paper in this volume, "The Question at the Center," illustrates another tradition of using chiastic structures.
21. The omission of καὶ νῦν ἐστιν, limited to a few witnesses (ℵ * a b; Tertullian), eliminates the tension between the eschatological perspectives of the whole *"exornatio."*

received authorization from the Father to judge. The point at which he will exercise that judgment is a future, not present (as in v. 25), "hour" when the dead will come forth from their tombs to be assessed by their works. This is precisely what the Son of Man was traditionally expected to do.[22]

Conplexio: The apologetic exposition of the Son's works concludes (v. 30) with a tripartite[23] resumé. The conplexio significantly sounds themes from all layers of the previous speech.

> A. The first affirmation (30a) recapitulates the initial defense (5:17) against breaking the Sabbath. Jesus is not guilty because he does nothing on his own initiative; he has been authorized by divine precedent (later: appointment), to act on the Sabbath.
>
> B. The symmetry between Father and Son shifts from resurrection to judgment (5:22–23, 27–29). In tension with the denial of the believer's judgment in verse 24, the clause (v. 30b), echoing verses 22 and 27, affirms that one of the Son's works is to judge. The phrasing, "As I hear," may echo the imitatio motif of verses 19–21, although now it is not a matter of what the Son sees, but what he hears: judgment. The conplexio thus unites two rather disparate and tensive elements of the previous discourse.
>
> A'. If A and B recapitulate the elements in the previous discourse that equate Jesus and the Father, the final clause (v. 30c) returns to the initial rebuttal against the charge of blasphemy (vv. 19–21): Jesus is not guilty of blasphemy because he does not, in the end, make himself fully "equal to God." He may now and in the future exercise divine functions, but he is just doing the will of the one who sent him.

Character of the argument: Two analyses of the argumentation are possible. One, focusing on the rhetoric within the narrative world, takes its cue from the ancient taxonomy of argument into appeals inductive (per inductionem) and deductive (per ratiocinationem). The basic apology clearly exemplifies the first category. The Johannine appeal to the paradigm of a domestic apprenticeship fits closely Cicero's requirements for an inductive argument:

> Induction is a form of argument which leads the person with whom one is arguing to give assent to certain undisputed facts; through this assent it wins his approval of a doubtful proposition because this resembles the facts to which he has assented.[24]

---

22. Cf. Matthew 25; Mark 13:26–27.
23. *Rhet. Her.*, 2.30.47 advocates another tripartite conclusion, consisting of a summing up, amplification, and appeal to pity (enumeratio, amplificatio, and commiseratio).
24. *Inv.*, 1.31.51 (Loeb). Discussion of inductive argument or argument by example begins with Aristotle, *Rhet.*, 2.20 (1393a10–12): "Where we are unable to argue by enthymeme, we must try to demonstrate our point by this method of example, and to convince our hearers thereby. If we can argue by enthymeme, we should use our examples as subsequent supplementary evidence." (Translation by Jonathan Banks, *The Complete Works of Aristotle* [Bollingen Series 71,2; Princeton, N.J.: Princeton University Press, 1984], 2221).

> In arguments of this kind the first rule to lay down is that the statement which we introduce as a basis for analogy (per similitudinem) ought to be of such a kind that its truth must be granted. For a statement on the strength of which we expect a doubtful point to be conceded, ought not itself to be doubtful. In the second place, one must make sure that the statement to be proved by the induction resembles those statements which we have presented previously as indisputable, for something granted to us previously will be no help if it is unlike the statement for the proof of which we wished the first point to be conceded.[25]

John's apologetic argument works by the kind of analogy that Cicero treats. The illustration is simple, straightforward, and unobjectionable. As Cicero suggests, the argument's effectiveness depends upon the applicability of the analogy to the case. In John 5 that application is asserted, not fully argued, as Cicero suggested would usually be the case with such arguments. Yet as the analysis of the arrangement suggests, more is going on than an analogical defense. There is tension within the ratio itself and even more, within the exornatio. The tension pushes us beyond the dramatic setting and into the rhetorical situation of the text and its readers.

The first element of complexity involves the claim to "equality with God." The text throws up the opponents' accusation in order, at least in part, to refute it as a crude misunderstanding. Yet at the same time, it pushes the claims that Jesus makes for himself toward an affirmation of functional equivalency with God.[26] That thrust is clear even without those portions of the discourse, particularly in the exornatio, that highlight the role of Jesus in a future judgment after a literal resurrection (vv. 22–23, 27–29). Those elements, especially verse 23, make the point in a forceful way through the assertion that judgment has been given to the Son so that he might be honored as the Father is honored. Whether the subtle manipulations of a mature dialectical mind,[27] or the work of a redactor,[28] those elements do not change the fundamental rhetoric of the text. The speech of Jesus begins with apparent simplicity to refute a charge leveled against him, and by extension, against his followers. The defense replies that the charge is unwarranted, even though it reflects an important element of the truth. Jesus, as Son, is not the Father; he is, none-

---

25. Cicero, *Inv.*, 1.32.53.
26. Distant echoes of Philippians 2 resound. Jesus did not consider "equality with God" something to be snatched or held to, but because of his obedience to the one who sent him received honor like that of the Father.
27. For such an attempt to resolve the antinomies of the Fourth Gospel, see Paul N. Anderson, *The Christology of the Fourth Gospel: Its Unity and Disunity in the Light of John 6* (WUNT 2.77; Tübingen: Mohr [Siebeck], 1995).
28. But if so, the conplexio has been adapted to take account of the whole discourse with the insertion of 30b.

theless, for those who accept him, God's Son, and thereby authorized to act on God's behalf.

The Discourse on Witnesses

Genre: The second half of the apology (vv. 31–47) begins rather abruptly after the conplexio concluding the first half. The charge against Jesus is not explicit, but may readily be inferred from the first verse of his reply (v. 31): Jesus' claims cannot be sustained because he only makes them himself. He needs corroborating testimony.

The implicit charge might have been lodged in any case, but it responds to a weakness of the argument advanced in the first half of the defense: the fact that the relevance of the analogy is simply asserted.

Disposition: The structure of the "complete argument" does not provide even a tentative template for this stage of the discourse, although, as ever, order may be adapted to circumstances.[29] This portion of the discourse seems, in fact, to have just three parts: a propositio, proved by an apparently simple narratio of those who have witnessed. The section concludes with a confutatio, which turns the tables on the accusers and lays blame on them.

Propositio: Verse 32 offers a succinct statement of the case: there is another who bears testimony. The indefinite "other" has occasioned debate among commentators. Does it refer to John the Baptist, to the Father, to Moses?[30] Recognition of the rhetorical function of the verse clarifies the matter. The defense against the charge of self-authentication needs simply to show that there is another witness. Yet the resulting ambiguity may be deliberate.

Ratio: The proof (vv. 33–40) that there is a second witness consists of a testimonial roster: John the Baptist (vv. 33–34); the deeds of Jesus (v. 36), the Father who sent him (v. 37); and, since the Father is not directly accessible (v. 37b), the Scriptures (vv. 38–39). The conclusion (5:40) sounds a plaintive note ("You did not want to come to me to have life"), which leads to the final portion of the discourse.

Confutatio: The final stage of this portion of the discourse turns the tables on the accusers. Cicero recognizes the utility of such a move in a defensive speech (a *remotio criminis*) and urges the defendant not only to pin the blame

---

29. See especially *Rhet. Her.*, 3.9.17.
30. See, e.g., Brown, *Gospel According to John,* 1:224.

on another[31] but to "show what good will and devotion the defendant exhibited." The conclusion to Jesus' defense adopts this tactic and develops it in two parts.

The first (vv. 41–44) contrasts the attitude of Jesus with that of his adversaries through two antitheses and a concluding bit of invective. 1) The fact that Jesus loves God and accepts honor only from him contrasts with the attitude of the adversaries who have no love of God in their hearts (vv. 41–42). 2) That fact that Jesus acts in his Father's name contrasts with the work of others — various Messiahs, prophets, or revolutionaries[32] — who act in their own name and thereby win approbation (v. 43). 2) A concluding rhetorical question implies its own answer. Because the accusers seek their own glory, how can they seek God's glory (v. 44)? In contrast stands Jesus, who, as the paragraph initially stipulated, does not seek human glory.

The final stage of the confutatio also serves as a conplexio for the whole second part of the discourse. Like the preceding verses, it uses an antithesis, first contrasting Jesus and Moses (v. 45), then moving to compare Jesus and his accusers (v. 46). The introduction of a middle term, Moses, evokes the appeal to scripture as the locus of God's testimony in verses 38–40. The initial contrast between Jesus and Moses recalls a basic theme of the first half of the discourse, that Jesus does not judge/condemn (v. 24).[33] Instead, Moses, the vehicle for God's revelation of old, now stands ready to condemn those who do not understand his Messianic predictions. The accusers then are threatened with a judgment for their willful refusal to hear either of the two major testimonies to Jesus, his own and that of the Scriptures. They stand condemned, in contrast with the accused, who is the model of a faithful emissary.

Persuasive technique: The persuasive appeal in the second half of the discourse (vv. 31–47) involves two interrelated strategies, an evocation of the ethos of the accused and an ironic play on the substance of the charge.

The first half of the second speech makes a simple argument that others

---

31. This strategy appears also among epistolographers. See Pseudo-Libanius, *Epistolary Styles* 22: "The counter-accusing style is that in which we bring a countercharge against someone by accusing him of what is brought against us, thus turning the charge around upon the accuser." See Abraham J. Malherbe, *Ancient Epistolary Theorists* (Atlanta: Scholars, 1988), 70, lines 1–2.

32. The imprecise allusion may refer to various first-century figures such as Judas son of Hezekiah, Simon, Athronges, Theudas, an anonymous Egyptian, Menachem son of Judas, or Simon bar Giora, all familiar from either the pages of the New Testament (Mark 13:22 and parallels; Acts 5:6; 21:38), Josephus, or such modern treatments as Richard A. Horsley with John S. Hanson, *Bandits, Prophets, and Messiahs: Popular Movements in the Time of Jesus* (repr. ed.; Harrisburg, Pa.: Trinity Press International, 1995 [orig. 1985]).

33. This recapitulation may support redactional theories, since the verse lacks the theme of Jesus as eschatological judge, characteristic of elements of the discourse sometimes considered secondary (5:22, 27–29).

witness to Jesus apart from himself. Yet even in the midst of that argument references to Jesus figure prominently. Jesus does not accept testimony from people (v. 34), presumably because to do so would be to accept "glory" from them, which is something he neither needs nor wants (v. 41). Nonetheless, he has mentioned the Baptist as a corroborating witness "so that you might be saved" (v. 34b). One might suspect in this ambiguous acceptance of the Baptist's testimony a polemical stance against his followers. The stance of Jesus could be seen to denigrate the value of the Baptist's witness. Whatever latent polemic there may be, the most immediate rhetorical function of the verse is to show something about Jesus. Despite his exalted status and his noble independence from external human support, he has mentioned John's testimony *in order that his hearers may be saved.* He is thus a virtuous benefactor, putting the needs of his beneficiaries ahead of his own exalted status. He is *beneficent.*

The following comments on the other witnesses to be summoned in Jesus' favor (vv. 3–40) conclude with a plaintive cry, "You did not want to come to me to have life." The pathos in that comment recalls the similar sayings attributed to Jesus in Q, which may have inspired the remark.[34] The saying's pathos in turn highlights the character of the defendant, a person of compassion, who wanted only what was good for his people. The confutatio of the second discourse thus focuses heavily on the person of Jesus. His independence (v. 41) does not preclude his beneficence. His restraint in not condemning those who reject him (v. 45) attests his clemency. Here the defendant has apparently taken to heart Cicero's advice and, in shifting the blame to others, takes pains to portray his own character in the most sympathetic terms.[35]

The appeal to the ethos of Jesus involves another hint of irony. To put the matter in slightly different terms, the way in which the charge of self-testimony is handled resembles the way in which the charge of verse 18, that Jesus made himself equal to God, was deflected in the first half of the apology. There, the argument's explicit logic suggested that the charge was groundless, but elements of the defense constantly affirmed that, after all, the charge had an element of truth. The tension between the two thrusts of the discourse rested in part on the two rhetorical situations at play, that of the narrative world within the text and that of the audience of the text itself. Similarly, the second half of the discourse manifests tension between the explicit argument, that Jesus has a plethora of witnesses to substantiate his claims, and the final

---

34. Cf. Dan 7:14 and Matt 23:37–39; Luke 13:34–35.
35. On the character of the appeal here, see Jakob Wisse, *Ethos and Pathos from Aristotle to Cicero* (Amsterdam: Hakkert, 1989).

recognition that the character of Jesus most strongly validates those claims. The tension between the logos and ethos in the rhetorical situation within the text works to convince the reader of a major claim of the Gospel. The believer's focus must be on Jesus himself. The text argues, in effect, that if the person confronting Jesus can see him for what he truly is, that person will know and understand that Jesus is indeed what he claims to be, the filial agent of the Father, who fully does the Father's will. If one does see this point, no other witness, neither prophet, miracle, or scripture, is needed, however useful they may be to bring people to Christ. The one who bears testimony to himself can be recognized, for all practical purposes, as God's equal.

Rhetorical Principles and Anti-Rhetoric

The ancient handbooks have been of some use in elucidating the complexities of Johannine rhetoric, but we might pause in conclusion to reflect on the character of that utility.

This essay has not claimed that the persuasive strategies of John 5 were directly generated from the theories of ancient rhetoric, although the text does seem to play with common rhetorical conventions. Biblical models of the "divine lawsuit" may have contributed to some of the Johannine imagery.[36] Exploring that possibility would require another essay. Whatever the genetic relationship, the ancient rhetorical tradition does illuminate the structure and function of this persuasive discourse. Yet the rhetorical models in themselves do not tell the whole story, since they were not designed to explore the complexity of a persuasive discourse embedded in a narrative laced with irony. Examination of the dynamics of the speech, with its dual audience in view, reveals a more complex rhetoric than the ancient handbooks knew. This rhetoric not only develops conviction by solidifying the relationship between the reader and Jesus. It also mocks the conventions of ordinary rhetoric, subverting the surface structure of argument to push the hearer into an encounter not with words, but with the Word himself.[37]

---

36. Although Yahweh is usually the prosecutor, not the defendant!
37. The paper thus agrees with Anders Eriksson, "Enthymemes in Pauline Argumentation" (in this volume, pp. 243–59), that there is a specific form of religious rhetoric.

CHAPTER 12

THE QUESTION AT THE CENTER: A SPECIFIC DEVICE OF RHETORICAL ARGUMENTATION IN SCRIPTURE

Roland Meynet

Biblical rhetoric is quite different from Greco-Roman rhetoric. "Le Grec veut démontrer, le Juif entend montrer." A Greek imposes, a Jew proposes. Exemplum and similitudo are utilized as proofs which constrain, *mashal* and parables are narrated as invitations to personal reflection and decision. The principal tool of Greek argumentation, to convince the hearer and to force him to accept an idea, is syllogism, or at least enthymeme. The specific device of the Bible, to induce human beings to reflect by themselves, is enigma! The typical form of enigma is the question. In biblical texts, it is often a question that occupies the center, that is, the focal point, the major strategic location, within concentric constructions.

Concentric construction needs to be distinguished from "chiasmus." The latter term means a small inverted construction of four terms, for example: "For *they observed* YOUR WORD / and YOUR COVENANT *they kept* (Deut 33:9), or "IN THE HEAVEN *peace* / and *glory* IN THE HIGHEST" (Luke 19:38). The concentric construction encompasses a larger composition, which may be a pericope, a whole chapter, or even an entire book, and is always focused upon a center, which is not the case for the simple chiasmus. Chiasms may be found in many literatures. Concentric constructions are abundant in the Bible,[1] probably more than elsewhere, and in my opinion, are a principal feature of biblical and Semitic literature.[2]

---

1. In the conclusion of my analysis of Luke, I counted both parallel and concentric constructions, at the different levels of the sections and the subsections, of the sequences, the sub-sequences, and of the passages, that constitute the major units. This count demonstrates a large prevalence of the concentric construction; see R. Meynet, *L'Évangile selon saint Luc* (Rhétorique biblique 1; Paris: Les Éditions du Cerf, 1988, 2:260–61).

2. Roland Meynet, Louis Pouzet, Nayla Farouki, and Ahyaf Sinno, *Ṭarīqat al-taḥlīl al-balāġī wa-l-tafsīr. Taḥlīlāt nuṣūṣ min al-kitāb al-muqaddas wa min al-Ḥadīṯ al-nabawī* [*Méthode rhétorique et Herméneutique: Analyse de textes de la Bible et de la Tradition musulmane*] (Beyrouth: Dar el-Machreq, 1993); French ed.: *Rhétorique sémitique: Textes de la Bible et de la Tradition musulmane* (Patrimoines. Religions du Livre; Paris: Les Éditions du Cerf, 1998).

Concentric constructions were already noticed some 175 years ago, by the founders of the methodology that I, more than twenty years ago, designated "Rhetorical analysis."³ Between 1820 and 1825, two English scholars, John Jebb (1775–1833) and Thomas Boys (1792–1880), were the first to identify concentric constructions, along with parallel ones.⁴

In 1820, John Jebb called the center of Matthew 20:25–28 (namely verses 26b–27) "the key of the whole paragraph or stanza." In his second book, published in 1825, *A Key to the Book of the Psalms,* Thomas Boys said that the center of a concentric composition functions as a "keystone." Following Boys, John Forbes noted in 1854 that the function of concentric construction is to heighten the value of the center of the construction. As he likewise declared in a second publication, "the central idea may, like a heart, be the *animating center* of the whole, sending its vitalizing energy and warmth to the very extremities."⁵ Like Boys, he noted that the extremities of a unit are often in direct relation with the center. More than a century after Jebb and Boys, Nils Wilhelm Lund in 1942 developed their earlier observations, through supplying many other examples; according to him, "The center is always the turning point." This is the first of his seven "laws of chiastic structures."⁶

At the conclusion of my commentary on Luke, I set forth some observations on the nature of the center in the concentric compositions of the Third Gospel: "it can be a question, a parable, a benediction, a proverb, a prophecy. Questions, parables, proverbs have in common that they are all enigmatic." And I supplied a list of references.⁷

The simplest example of enigma is the grammatical interrogation. For example, Psalm 113 focuses upon the question, "Who is like the Lord our

---

3. Roland Meynet, *Quelle est donc cette Parole? Lecture 'rhétorique' de l'évangile de Luc (1–9 et 22–24)* (LeDiv 99 A.B.; Paris: Les Éditions du Cerf, 1979).

4. It is a great pity that the English-speaking world largely ignores its own inheritance; to give just one example, J. Breck, *The Shape of Biblical Language: Chiasmus in the Scripture and Beyond* (Crestwood, N.Y.: St. Vladimir's Seminary Press, 1994), read neither Jebb nor Boys. It is somewhat surprising that it is a French scholar who tries to make them known, by publishing, in French, then in Italian, and finally in English, some of their better texts! I hope that, with the recent English translation of my methodological book, some, especially in England and in the United States, will come back to this very promising source: see my *Rhetorical Analysis. An Introduction to Biblical Rhetoric* (JSOTSup 256; Sheffield: Sheffield Academic Press, 1998).

5. John Forbes, *Analytical Commentary on the Epistle to the Romans Tracing the Train of Thought by the Aid of Parallelism* (Edinburgh: T. & T. Clark, 1868), 82.

6. Nils W. Lund, *Chiasmus in the New Testament: A Study in Formgeschichte* (Chapel Hill: University of North Carolina Press, 1942). Repr. *Chiasmus in the New Testament: A Study in the Form and Function of Chiastic Structures* (Peabody, Mass.: Hendrickson, 1992), 40.

7. Roland Meynet, *Luc,* 2:261; Italian trans.: *Il vangelo secondo Luca* (Retorica biblica 1; Rome: Edizioni Dehoniane, 1994), 730.

God?" (v. 5a).⁸ The Song of the Sea (Exod 15) is also focused on a similar question, more developed: "Who is like you, O Lord, among the gods? Who is like you, majestic in holiness, terrible in glorious deeds, doing wonders?" (Exod 15:11).⁹ It is clear that the answer, if one reads the entire psalm, is: "There is nobody like you." In other words, the rest of the text furnishes all the necessary elements to answer the question. But the answer itself is left to the readers who are invited by the author, though indirectly, to recognize the Lord as their God and adhere to Him. The pronoun "our," as the whole question, is said both by the psalmist and those who will sing the psalm after him; its function is to cultivate inclusion, to constitute the unity of the people of God.

I cannot treat here the entire subject of "the center as a key." I shall concentrate on some examples of "the *question* at the center," and only in Luke and Amos; other aspects, such as the proverb or the parable at the center will be studied elsewhere.

The first undertaking, prior to any interpretation, is to establish the facts. In 1988, I wrote, "it is urgent not to be satisfied with intuitions, with unverified affirmations, with formulas such as 'It often happens that....' "¹⁰ A year later I noted that "The center of a concentric construction is often occupied by a question...."¹¹ "Often" is not sufficient! I will here calculate the frequency of the question at the center.

Some Data

In the Gospel of Luke

There are 19,486 words¹² in the Third Gospel; the number of words contained in questions is, according to my punctuation, 1,391. The proportion between questions and the whole text is 7.1%.

The number of literary units with questions at the center is:

9 of the 28 sequences of Luke, that is, 32%

9 of the 27 sub-sequences of Luke, that is, 33%

36 of the 120 passages of Luke, that is, 30%.

---

8. See Meynet, *Rhetorical Analysis*, 261.
9. Roland Meynet, "Le cantique de Moïse et le cantique de l'Agneau (Ap 15 et Ex 15)," *Gregorianum* 73 (1992): 19–55.
10. Meynet, *Luc*, 1:258.
11. Roland Meynet, *L'analyse rhétorique* (Paris: Les Éditions du Cerf, 1989), 288.
12. The count is based upon the 27th edition of *Novum Testamentum Graece*.

The correlation factor between 32% and 7.1% is 4.5, which is very high.

We can add that of the 158 questions in Luke, 58 are at the center of a passage and/or sub-sequence and/or sequence, that is, 36.5%.

In the Book of Amos

There are 2,037 Hebrew words in Amos; the number of words contained in questions is, according to our punctuation, 171. The proportion between questions and the whole text is 8.4%.

The number of literary units with questions at the center is:

    6 of the 15 sequences of Amos, that is, 40%

    14 of the 40 passages of Amos,[13] that is, 35%.

The correlation factor between 40% and 8.4% is 4.76.

The correlation factor between 35% and 8.4% is 4.17; these correlation factors are similar to those of Luke.

We can add that of the 171 questions of Amos, 147 are at the center of literary units, that is 86%.

All these data confirm the "intuition" that "the center of a concentric construction is often occupied by a question." Of course we are limited here to two books, and it will be necessary in the future to verify the figures in the other seventy-one books of the Bible. This will take a long time. In 1825, Thomas Boys wrote: "the subject is still in its infancy";[14] in spite of the great progress that has been made since that time, we can still say the same thing.

Some Examples

In the Book of Amos

After the "title" of the book (1:1–2), the first section of Amos (chaps. 1–2) comprises just one question. This question is located at the very center of the last sequence, the long oracle against Israel (Amos 2:6–16):[15]

---

    13. Three of these passages consist only of questions.
    14. Boys, *A Key*, 4.
    15. The translation is that of the New Revised Standard Version.

> ⁶*THUS SAYS the* Lord:
>
> For three transgressions of Israel, and for four, I will not revoke the punishment; because they sell the righteous for silver, and the needy for a pair of sandals; ⁷they who trample the head of the poor into the dust of the earth, and push the afflicted out of the way; father and son go in to the same girl, so that my holy name is profaned; ⁸they lay themselves down beside every altar on garments taken in pledge; and in the house of their God they drink wine bought with fines they imposed.

⁹Yet I destroyed the Amorite before them, whose height was like the height of cedars, and who was as strong as oaks; I destroyed his fruit above, and his roots beneath. ¹⁰Also I brought **you** up out of the land of Egypt, and led **you** forty years in the wilderness, to possess the land of the Amorite.

> ¹¹*And I raised up some of* **your** *children to be prophets,*
>   *and some of* **your** *youths to be nazirites.*
>   Is it not indeed so, O sons of Israel, *ORACLE of the* Lord?
>   ¹²*But* **you** *made the nazirites drink wine,*
> *and commanded the prophets, saying, 'You shall not prophesy.'*

¹³So, I will press **you** down in your place, just as a cart presses down when it is full of sheaves.

> ¹⁴Flight shall perish from the swift, and the strong shall not retain their strength, nor shall the mighty save their lives; ¹⁵those who handle the bow shall not stand, and those who are swift of foot shall not save themselves, nor shall those who ride horses save their lives; ¹⁶and those who are stout of heart among the mighty shall flee away naked in that day,
>
> *ORACLE of the* Lord.

For the precise analysis of this text, I turn to the commentary that Pietro Bovati and I published on the book of Amos.[16] In regard to the function of the unique question at the center, we wrote:

> The interrogation of verse 11 does not only concern what was said immediately beforehand — namely that God has sent prophets and nazirites — and is not only a request for approval by God to the reader; it concerns the whole of the text and calls for the recognition of all forms of sin denounced since the beginning, and of the just and necessary character of the consequences which shall follow.

---

16. Pietro Bovati and Roland Meynet, *Le livre du prophète Amos* (Rhétorique biblique 2; Paris: Les Éditions du Cerf, 1994), 73–92; Italian ed.: *Il libro del profeta Amos* (Retorica biblica 2; Rome: Edizioni Dehoniane, 1995), 81–103; in the next pages I refer only to the French edition. See also Roland Meynet, *Rhetorical Analysis,* 272–73.

If the center of the whole oracle is a question (11c), it also means that there is something there to discern. The effort of intelligence — of wisdom — required from the hearer, constitutes the foundation of his acquiescence. It is only if one "sees" how, in these few words, God, by the intermediary of his prophet, interprets truly the totality of a history, that one can say, "He told me all that ever I did" (John 4:39), and adhere and believe in his Word, that is to convert. What the reader is invited to understand is the relationship between crime and punishment, because the announced punishment seems disproportionate to the denounced crime. To speak straight out, it seems that the key to the interpretation of this oracle is the following: the extreme gravity of the sin of Israel is linked to the fact that its injustice is concealed; worse still, it is perverse.[17]

It should be noticed that there is a kind of progression from the extremities to the center: while at the beginning (6–9) and at the end of the passage (14–16) the Lord depicts Israel in the third person, in the central part (11–12) and also just before (10) and after (13a) he addresses them directly, in the second person. The implication for the audience culminates at the very center of the passage (11c).

We can add that the central question identifies both the one who asks it and the audience to whom it is directed. The question says that the whole oracle is not only what Amos pronounced once to a small group of people who heard it in Samaria. These words are also addressed now by "the Lord" to all "the sons of Israel." The fact that they were included in the sacred Scriptures of both Israel and Judah, and subsequently of all the Christians, means that they were recognized as the word of God and were accepted as addressed to those who preserved them. They are still heard by their true audience.

Just after this oracle against Israel (which concludes the first section of the book), as the second section (chaps. 3–6) begins, the first sequence (3:1–8) focuses on three pairs of questions.

This passage contains nine questions. In the last part (8), the two questions identify two speakers: the lion who is the enemy (8a), and God himself who sent him (8c). It also identifies the double addressees: the prophet who speaks in the name of the Lord (8d, 7), and the "sons of Israel" (1a) "who will fear" (8b). The question of verse 3 is answered in verse 7: the two who walk together are the Lord and his prophet. In between there are three pairs of questions around which the entire passage is focused.

About the central pair of questions (5) we wrote, "The double snare around which the sequence revolves is an enigma, strengthened by its interrogative

---

17. *Amos*, 87; *Rhetorical Analysis*, 275.

> ¹Hear this word that the LORD has spoken against you, O sons of Israel,
>   against the whole family   that I brought up from out of the earth of Egypt, saying:
>   ²You only have I known   of all the families of the ground;
> therefore I will punish you for all your iniquities.

³Do two walk together *without* having made an appointment?

> :: ⁴Does a lion roar in the forest,   when it has no prey?
> :: Does a young lion cry out from its den,   if it has caught nothing?
>
> + ⁵Does a bird fall into a *snare* on the earth,   when there is no trap for it?
> + Does a *snare* spring up from the ground,   when it has taken nothing?
>
> :: ⁶Is a trumpet blown in a city,   and the people are not afraid?
> :: Does disaster befall a city,   unless the LORD has done it?

⁷Surely the Lord GOD does nothing, *without* revealing his secret to his servants the prophets.

> ⁸The lion   hath roared;
>   who will not fear?
> The Lord GOD   has spoken;
>   who can but prophesy?

formulation."¹⁸ Then the title we chose for the sequence is "A snare for the Sons of Israel." As for the "interpretation" of the sequence, we organized it around two correlated ideas: "The enigma of the snare," and "The revelation of the snare." So we used the central double question of the sequence as a key for interpreting it.¹⁹ What must be underlined here is that the question at the center is an enigmatic one. As in the oracle against Israel (2:6–16), it invites the hearers to reflect. More than that, it requires them to open their eyes. In fact, the greatest danger of the snare is that it is hidden. Everybody can hear the roar of the lion (4), that is, the enemy sent by God, whose arrival is announced by "the trumpet" (6). But no one can discover the snare (5) if the Lord himself does not reveal it by the voice of his prophet. Only those who heard carefully the beginning of the oracle can understand that the snare is the election of Israel itself, behind which they try unconsciously to hide their "iniquities" (2b). What is asserted here is that the true enemy of Israel is herself.

The second section of Amos is composed of seven sequences, organized in a concentric fashion around the fourth. The fact is that all the last three sequences are focused on a question. Let us examine only the last one (6:8–14); its central passage begins with a double question:

---

18. *Amos,* 110.
19. Ibid., 101–12.

> ⁸The Lord GOD had sworn by himself, says the LORD, the God of hosts: I abhor the pride of Jacob and hate his strongholds; and I will deliver up the city and all that is in it.
> ⁹If ten people remain in one house, they shall die. ¹⁰And if a relative, one who burns the dead, shall take up the body to bring it out of the house, and shall say to someone in the innermost parts of the house, "Is anyone else with you?" the answer will come, "No." Then the relative shall say, "Hush! We must not mention the name of the LORD."
> ¹¹See, the LORD commands, and the great house shall be shattered to bits, and the little house to pieces.

¹²Do HORSES	run	on *rock?*
Does one plow	(there)	with OXEN?
For you have turned	JUSTICE	into *poison*
and the fruit of	RIGHTEOUSNESS	into *wormwood.*

> ¹³You who rejoice in Lo-debar, who say, "Have we not by our own strength taken Karnaim for ourselves?
> ¹⁴Indeed, I am raising up against you a nation, O house of Israel, says the LORD, the God of hosts, and they shall oppress you from Lebo-hamath to the Wadi Arabah.

We wrote, "The beginning of this brief passage is a proverb which is very enigmatic" (*Amos*, 218; see also 240–41; 245–46). But the second segment of it (12cd) furnishes elements for the solution of the enigma: "justice" and "righteousness" are good things, as are "horses" and "oxen," while "poison" and "wormwood" are as "rock."

We also noticed that the first and the last sequence of this second section correspond to each other: both are centered on a question "the meaning of which is not immediately transparent" (*Amos*, 256–57). Without entering into detail, all these quotations underline the enigmatic character of the central questions.

These two examples show clearly how the biblical way of argumentation functions, if we can call it "argumentation." Questions do not demonstrate or prove any proposition for the reader; they invite the audience to answer, but the hearer remains free and can answer or not. Furthermore, when the question involves an enigma or a parable, considerable reflective effort is required so as to find the solution before answering. Argumentation of this sort respects not only the freedom of the audience, but above all his dignity, allowing maximum space for his own activity. While the syllogism aspires to do all the work, the enigmatic question leaves half of it to the audience.

In the Gospel of Luke

For Luke, as for Amos, I will present only certain significant passages, subsequences, or sequences that focus on a question.

The first section of the Gospel, the Annunciation (1:28–38)[20] is focused on the unique question of the passage: "Then said Mary unto the angel: How shall this be, seeing I know not a man?" (1:34). The next passage, the Visitation (1:39–45),[21] is also centered on the unique question of the passage: "And whence is this to me, that the mother of my Lord should come to me?" (1:43).

These questions are not directed by the Gospel author to his audience,[22] as in Amos. They are addressed by characters of the narrative to other characters: Mary questions Gabriel, and Elizabeth, Mary. Also the answers are supplied by characters of the narrative: Gabriel explains to Mary how she will give birth to the Messiah, though she is a virgin. Mary does not answer the question of Elizabeth in the pericope of the Visitation itself, but the next passage, the Magnificat, can be considered her answer. Anyway, clearly the text is not simply a narrative, but also intends to involve the audience, to invite each individual reader to identify with Mary or Elizabeth, to ask the same questions they asked, and to give an answer. It is also to be noticed that these questions concern the identity of the characters (Mary is mother and virgin, she is "the mother of the Lord") and, at the same time, the action of God himself. Each believing reader is invited to recognize what the Lord has done for Mary and Elizabeth. He is then invited to become a true "Theophilus," one who loves God for what he has done for him, through these two women and their children.

The sequence which presents the ministry of John (3:1–20)[23] centers on a passage in which three different kinds of people ask the Baptist the same question.

In the central question, John is called "teacher" (*didaskale*), a title which will be often conferred upon Jesus. But these questions do not concern primarily the identity of John, but the actions of those who ask him, in other words the conditions of their conversion, at the very moment of their baptism, mentioned in the center of the passage (12a). The second thing to notice is that an answer is given for each question. This was also the case in the central passage of sequence B7 of Amos 6:8–14 (see above, p. 207). More than in

---

20. *Luc*, 15; *Luca*, 52. For Luke I give the references to the French and Italian editions of my commentary: *Luc*, for Roland Meynet, *L'Évangile selon saint Luc*, vol. 2, and *Luca*, for idem, *Il vangelo secondo Luca;* in the Italian edition I sometimes corrected and improved the analysis of the French edition.

21. *Luc*, 18; *Luca*, 67.

22. Only Luke names his audience in the Prologue: he calls him "Theophilus," in the singular, but, given the meaning of this name, he represents every reader of the Gospel.

23. *Luc*, 35; *Luca*, 117–28.

+ ¹⁰And the crowds asked him, saying,
  WHAT THEN SHOULD WE DO?
    — ¹¹In reply he said to them,
      . Whoever has two coats must share with anyone who has none;
      . whoever has food must do likewise.
+ ¹²Even tax collectors came to be baptized, and they asked him,
  TEACHER, WHAT SHOULD WE DO?
    — ¹³He said to them,
      . Collect no more than the amount prescribed for you.
+ ¹⁴Soldiers also asked him, saying,
  AND WE, WHAT SHOULD WE DO?
    — He said to them,
      . Do not extort money from anyone by threats or false accusation;
      . and be satisfied with your wages.

the Annunciation and the Visitation, it is clear that the varied audiences of Luke are invited by the narrative to identify with the different peoples who direct questions to John, to listen to and to obey his commands. Even if they are not "tax collectors" (12a) or "soldiers" (14a), they belong to "the crowds" (10a) of those who were baptized, or of those who are preparing to receive Christian baptism.

The first sequence of the second section of Luke (4:14–9:50; that is, the ministry in Galilee) consists of one passage only, the visit of Jesus to Nazareth (4:14–30).[24] The central part of this passage is composed of two parallel pieces:

+ And the eyes of all in the synagogue were fixed on him;
  — ²¹and he began to say to them,
    : "THIS DAY THIS SCRIPTURE HAS BEEN FULFILLED IN YOUR HEARING."
+ ²²All spoke well of him and were amazed at the gracious words that came from his mouth;
  — and they said,
    : "IS NOT THIS JOSEPH'S SON?"

The question at the end of the second piece (22c) is a reaction to Jesus' (very short) homily at the end of the first piece (21b). The question of the true identity of Jesus will be the leitmotiv of the whole section (Luke 4:22; 4:36; 5:21; 7:19, 20; 7:49; 8:25; 9:9).[25] In the last sequence of the section (9:1–50) the confession of Peter answers the question of Jesus. This question lies at the very center of the passage (9:18–22):[26] "He said to them, 'But who do you say that I am?' Peter answered, 'The Messiah of God'" (9:20). In the symmetric passage, the Transfiguration (9:28–36), another answer is given

---

24. *Luc*, 42; *Luca*, 162.
25. See *Luc*, 116–17; *Luca* 329–32.
26. *Luc*, 93; *Luca*, 300.

by God the Father himself: "Then from the cloud came a voice that said, 'This is my Son, my Chosen; listen to him!'" (9:35).[27]

Other passages of this last sequence are centered on specific questions. There is the question of the disciples in the passage of the multiplication of the bread (9:12–17),[28] "Should we go and buy meat for all this people?" There is also the question of Jesus in the healing of the epileptic child (9:37–43a),[29] "You faithless and perverse generation, how much longer must I be with you and bear with you?" The first sub-sequence (9:1–17) is focused on the question of Herod (9:9),[30] "John I beheaded; but who is this about whom I hear such things?" The last sub-sequence also (9:37–50) is focused on an indirect question of the disciples (9:46),[31] "An argument arose among them as to which one of them was the greatest." Finally, the central passage of the central sub-sequence (9:18–36), and then of the whole sequence, is also centered on a question (9:25):[32] "What does it profit a man if he gains the whole world, but loses or forfeits himself?" We should notice that the central questions of this last sequence of the second section concern not only the identity of Jesus, but also that of the disciples.

During the second section, partial answers are given, beginning with the visit in Nazareth (Jesus presents himself as a prophet: "No prophet is received in his own country"), but the reader has to wait till the end of the section to know the complete answer: Jesus is the Messiah, the Son of God. The function of all these interrogations about the identity of Jesus, beginning with "Is not this Joseph's son?" is to help the reader enter into the problematic of the section, to identify with the historical audience of Jesus, and finally, to give his or her personal answer, becoming more and more a true disciple. At the center of the last sequence, the reader is led, by a question, to discover that the problem is not only that of the identity of Jesus, but also of his own identity, and that he is called to identify with his teacher, who looses his life so as to save it.

For the rest of the second section we will examine only the first passage of the fourth sequence (5:17–6:11). This passage is centered on two questions of the Scribes and Pharisees to which Jesus replies by asking two additional questions:

---

27. *Luc*, 96–97; *Luca*, 307.
28. *Luca*, 289. In the Italian edition I corrected the erroneous analysis of the French edition.
29. *Luc*, 90; *Luca*, 294.
30. *Luc*, 89; *Luca*, 291.
31. *Luc*, 92; *Luca*, 299.
32. *Luc*, 95, 96–97; *Luca*, 305, 307.

+ ¹⁷One day, while he was teaching,
  Pharisees and teachers of the law were sitting near by;
  they had come from every village of Galilee and Judea and from Jerusalem:
+ and the power of the Lord was with him to heal.

> ¹⁸Just then some men came, carrying a paralyzed man on a bed. They were trying to bring him in and lay him BEFORE HIM.
> ¹⁹But finding no way to bring him in because of the crowd, they went up on the roof and let him down with his bed through the tiles into the middle of the crowd BEFORE JESUS.

²⁰When he saw their faith,   he said, "Man, **your sins are forgiven you.**"

+ ²¹Then the scribes and the Pharisees began to *question,*
  : "Who is this who is speaking blasphemies?
  : Who can **forgive sins** but God alone?"

+ ²²When Jesus perceived their *questionings,* he answered them,
  : "Why do you raise such questions in your hearts?
  : ²³Which is easier, to say, '**Your sins are forgiven you**,' or to say, 'Stand up and walk'?

²⁴But so that you may know   that the Son of Man has authority on earth **to forgive sins**,"

> he said to the one who was paralyzed: "I say to you, stand up and take your bed and go to your home." ²⁵Immediately he stood up before them, took what he had been lying on, and went to his home, GLORIFYING GOD.
> ²⁶Amazement seized all of them, and they GLORIFIED GOD and were filled with awe, saying, "We have seen strange things today."

The problem of this passage is clearly expressed by the central questions (21–23). The Scribes and the Pharisees are right when they say: "Who can forgive sins, but God alone?" (21c). Forgiving sins, like healing illnesses, is not possible for men, but only for God. Luke seems to say the same thing when he writes at the end of the introduction, "and a power of the Lord was with him to heal" (17d). Using the perfect tense and the passive voice (passivum theologicum), Jesus himself seems to agree with this opinion: "Man, your sins are forgiven you," that is, "forgiven by God" (20). However, at the very symmetric position (24a), he also says, "the Son of Man has authority on earth to forgive sins." He immediately gives a strong proof of the power he has, when he heals the man. We have, however, to remark that when they brought the sick man "before Jesus" (twice at the end of v. 18 and of v. 19) they were persuaded that Jesus had the power to heal him; but at the end, they do not "glorify" Jesus but God Himself (26), as does the paralyzed man after his healing (25). All of them think, as Luke does, that "there was a power *of the Lord* with him to heal" (17d). The resolution of the enigma is placed into the hands of the reader, that is, how to reconcile the fact that only God can forgive sins and that Jesus claims to have the power to do the same? The solution I found is that God gave his power to His Son, and also to every "son of man" who believes that he has also received the power to forgive the sins of his brother.

For the rest of the Third Gospel I will present only some of the more striking examples, just to give an idea of the extension of the phenomenon. Luke 12:22–34 is centered around the two questions of the passage, which are arranged chiastically (25–26):[33]

²²He said to his disciples, "Therefore I tell you,

DO NOT WORRY about your life, what you will eat, or about your body, what you will wear. ²³For life is more than food, and the body more than clothing.

²⁴*Consider the ravens:* they neither sow nor reap, they have neither storehouse nor barn, and yet God feeds them:
    Of how much more value are you than the birds!

²⁵And can any of you by WORRYING	*add a single hour to your span of life?*
²⁶If then you are not able to do *so small a thing as that,*	why do you WORRY about the rest?

²⁷*Consider the lilies* how they grow: they neither toil nor spin; yet I tell you, even Solomon in all his glory was not clothed like one of these. ²⁸But if God so clothes the grass of the field, which is alive today and tomorrow is thrown into the oven;
    how much more will he clothe you, you of little faith!

²⁹AND DO NOT KEEP STRIVING for what you are to eat and what you are to drink, and do not keep worrying. ³⁰For it is the nations of the world that strive after all these things, and your Father knows that you need them. ³¹Instead, STRIVE for his kingdom, and these things will be given to you as well. ³²Do not be afraid, little flock, for it is your Father's good pleasure to give you the kingdom. ³³Sell your possessions, and give alms. Make purses for yourselves that do not wear out, an unfailing treasure in heaven, where no thief comes near and no moth destroys. ³⁴For where your treasure is, there your heart will be also.

The two parables of the next passage (Luke 12:35–46) are linked with the question of Peter:[34]

---

33. *Luc,* 124; *Luca,* 403.
34. *Luc,* 133; *Luca,* 416.

> ³⁵Be dressed for action and have your lamps lit; ³⁶be like those who are waiting for their master to return from the wedding banquet, so that they may open the door for him as soon as he comes and knocks. ³⁷Blessed are those slaves whom the master finds alert when he comes:
> TRULY I TELL YOU, he will fasten his belt and have them sit down to eat,
> and he will come and serve them.
>
> ³⁸If he comes during the middle of the night, or near dawn, and finds them so, blessed are those slaves. ³⁹But know this: if the owner of the house had known at what hour the thief was coming, he would not have let his house be broken into. ⁴⁰You also must be ready, for the Son of Man is coming at an unexpected hour.

⁴¹Then Peter said:
  "Lord, are you telling this parable for us or for everyone?"
⁴²And the Lord said,

> "Who then is the faithful and prudent manager whom his master will put in charge of his slaves, to give them their allowance of food at the proper time? ⁴³Blessed is that slave whom his master will find at work when he arrives.
>
> ⁴⁴TRULY I TELL YOU, he will put that one in charge of all his possessions.
>
> ⁴⁵But if that slave says to himself, 'My master is delayed in coming,' and if he begins to beat the other slaves, men and women, and to eat and drink and get drunk, ⁴⁶the master of that slave will come on a day when he does not expect him and at an hour that he does not know, and will cut him in pieces, and put him with the unfaithful."

Another example of a double parable linked by a question is the central sub-sequence of the sixth sequence of the third section (18:1–14):³⁵

> ¹Then Jesus told them a PARABLE about their need to pray always and not to lose heart. ²He said, "In a certain city there was a judge who neither feared God nor had respect for people. ³In that city there was a widow who kept coming to him and saying, 'Grant me justice against my opponent.' ⁴For a while he refused; but later he said to himself, 'Though I have no fear of God and no respect for anyone, ⁵yet because this widow keeps bothering me, I will grant her justice, so that she may not wear me out by continually coming.'"
> ⁶And the Lord said, "Listen to what the unjust judge says. ⁷And will not God grant justice to his chosen ones who cry to him day and night? Will he delay long in helping them? ⁸I tell you, he will quickly grant justice to them.

And yet, when the Son of Man comes, will he find faith on earth?"

> ⁹He also told this parable to some who trusted in themselves that they were righteous and regarded others with contempt:
> ¹⁰"Two men went up to the temple to pray, one a Pharisee and the other a tax collector. ¹¹The Pharisee, standing by himself, was praying thus, 'God, I thank you that I am not like other people: thieves, rogues, adulterers, or even like this tax collector. ¹²I fast twice a week; I give a tenth of all my income.' ¹³But the tax collector, standing far off, would not even look up to heaven, but was beating his breast and saying, 'God, be merciful to me, a sinner!'
> ¹⁴*I tell you*, this man went down to his home justified rather than the other; for all who exalt themselves will be humbled, but all who humble themselves will be exalted."

---

35. *Luc*, 173; *Luca*, 493, 516.

This question of Jesus is then at the very center of the entire sequence. Other examples of sequences focused on a question are the first and the second sequences of the Passion narrative (22:1–53 and 22:54–23:25).[36]

To conclude this brief study on the question located at the center, the most important observation is that, for the first time, the phenomenon has been quantified in two biblical books, one in the Old Testament and the other in the New Testament, namely Amos and Luke. The few examples presented here seem sufficient to illustrate the fact. We have limited our reflection thereon to a very few observations: the function of the question at the center, which is always enigmatic, is, as it seems to me, to question the reader, who is invited to reflect for himself and to give his own answer. Finally, it is clear that "the question at the center" is but one element of a more complex phenomenon, that of the function of any center of a concentric text of the Bible, which I call "the center as a key."

---

36. See *Luc,* 208–9; *Luca,* 597, 609, 615, and *Luc,* 215; *Luca,* 650, respectively. See also Roland Meynet, *Jésus passe. Testament, Jugement, Exécution et Résurrection du Seigneur Jésus dans les évangiles synoptiques* (Rhétorique biblique 3; Rome and Paris: PUG-Editrice and Les Éditions du Cerf, 1999); my complete bibliography may be consulted at *www.unigre.it* by going to the following sections: Facoltà; Teologia; Dipart. Teol. Biblica; Bibliografie; Meynet, Roland. Consult the Internet page "Rhetorica Biblica," at *www.unigre.it* Publicazioni.

PART FIVE

**RHETORICAL ARGUMENTATION
IN THE PAULINE LETTERS**

CHAPTER 13

"TO MAKE THE WEAKER ARGUMENT DEFEAT THE STRONGER": SOPHISTICAL ARGUMENTATION IN PAUL'S LETTER TO THE ROMANS

Johan S. Vos

Genuine and Fallacious Argumentation

The Problem of Genuine and Fallacious Argumentation in Classical Rhetorical Tradition

Wherever the art of persuasion is used the problem of the legitimacy of the means of argumentation arises. In antiquity, rhetoric as a whole was sometimes rejected for its negative use.[1] Not infrequently, a distinction was made between an accepted and a rejected form of rhetoric.[2] Since Plato and Aristotle, the most common word to denote the rejected form of rhetoric has become "sophistry" or "sophistical" rhetoric. Although the word "sophist" often has a positive meaning, denoting various kinds of experts and wise men, it also frequently occurs in a negative sense to denote a quibbler, a cheat, or one who makes use of fallacious arguments. The same is true for most of its cognate words.[3]

One of the classical characteristics of the so-called sophistic rhetoric is expressed in the phrase: "τὸν ἥττω λόγον κρείττω ποιεῖν" or "τοὺς ἥττους λόγους κρείττους ποιεῖν." Often the translation of this phrase is already an interpretation. "To make the weaker argument the stronger" is a rather neutral translation. It says nothing about the true or intrinsic value of the arguments. An argument can be weaker simply because the majority do not accept it or

---

1. E.g., Sextus Empiricus, *Math.*, II (ΠΡΟΣ ΡΗΤΟΡΑΣ).
2. E.g., Plato, *Phaedr.,* 269a-272c.
3. See W. K. C. Guthrie, *The Sophists* (Cambridge: Cambridge University Press, 1971), 27–34; Carl Joachim Classen, "Einleitung," *Sophistik* (ed. C. J. Classen. WdF 187; Darmstadt: Wissenschaftliche Buchgesellschaft, 1976), 1–18, esp. 1–9; C. J. Classen, "Aristotle's Picture of the Sophists," in *The Sophists and their Legacy* (ed. G. B. Kerferd; Hermes 44; Wiesbaden: Franz Steiner Verlag, 1981), 7–24; G. B. Kerferd, *The Sophistic Movement* (Cambridge: Cambridge University Press, 1981), 24–41. The use of the word with its derivates in antiquity is well documented in the *Onomasticon* of Julius Pollux, rec. I. Bekker (Berlin: Nicolai, 1846), 152–53, which contains the synonyms for both the positive and the negative sense. For a critical evaluation of the concept of "Sophistic Rhetoric," see Edward Schiappa, *The Beginnings of Rhetorical Theory in Classical Greece* (New Haven: Yale University Press, 1999), 48–65.

because the opponent has better argumentative skills. In the translation "to make the weaker argument defeat the stronger"[4] the aspect of competition is made explicit. The rendering "to make the weaker argument seem/appear the stronger,"[5] on the other hand, implies a negative judgment about this argumentative technique. It is emphasized that the strength acquired by the weaker argument is not a real one according to those who believe they adhere to the true standard. The weakness is an internal one, be it legal, logical, or ethical. Only in this last sense is the phrase an expression of the so-called sophistic rhetoric. In classical literature the phrase is mostly used in this sense.

How the average reader understood this or similar phrases is most clearly illustrated in *The Clouds* of Aristophanes. This play presents Socrates as a leading sophist. Commenting on his school Strepsiades says to his son (112–15):[6]

> I'm told they have both Arguments (ἄμφω τὼ λόγω) there, the Better (τὸν κρείττον), whatever that may be, and the Worse (τὸν ἥττονα). And one of these Arguments, the Worse, I'm told, can plead the unjust side of a case and win.

Later, both personified λόγοι give a demonstration of their rhetorical skills. The ἥττων λόγος commends itself, stating that (1041–42):

> And it'll repay you more money than you can count, this ability to adopt the worse argument and yet win.

It is clear that Aristophanes gives a moral flavor to the terms ἥττων and κρείττων. In this discussion ἥττων does not mean "weaker" in the neutral sense of initial persuasive force, but "inferior," "worse," and thus "more unjust"[7] with an ethical connotation. In the tradition of this play, the ἥττων and the κρείττων λόγος became identified as ἄδικος and δίκαιος λόγος.

The same moral flavor is conveyed by the phrase τὸν ἥττω λόγον κρείττω ποιεῖν almost everywhere it occurs in classical literature. It is used as a mutual charge between Isocrates and his fictitious opponent, Lysimachos (*Antidosis* 15), as a charge against Socrates in his trial according to Plato (*Apol.* 19b), and

---

4. E.g., Alexander Sesonske, "To Make the Weaker Argument Defeat the Stronger," in *Plato: True and Sophistic Rhetoric* (ed. Keith V. Erickson; Studies in Classical Antiquity 3; Amsterdam: Rodopi, 1979), 90; Edward Schiappa, *Protagoras and Logos* (Studies in Rhetoric/Communication; Columbia, S.C.: University of South Carolina Press, 1991), 106.

5. E.g., the translations of John Henry Freese: Aristotle, *The "Art" of Rhetoric* (LCL; Cambridge, Mass.: Harvard University Press, 1959), 335; and Aristotle, *On Rhetoric* (ed. George A. Kennedy; New York: Oxford University Press, 1991), 210. In his *A New History of Classical Rhetoric* (Princeton, N.J.: Princeton University Press, 1994), 7, however, Kennedy's translation is: "making the weaker cause the stronger."

6. Translation: Jeffrey Henderson, *Clouds.Wasps. Peace* (LCL 488; Cambridge, Mass.: Harvard University Press, 1998).

7. W. J. M. Starkie, *The Clouds of Aristophanes* (Amsterdam: Hakkert, 1966), 37.

as a phrase used by Aristotle to disqualify the argumentation of Protagoras (*Rhet.* 1402a 24).[8] Variants of the phrase include: "to make small things appear large and large things small by the power of speech" (Plato, *Phaedr.* 267a; Sextus Empiricus, *Math.* 2.46), "to make just things appear unjust and the unjust just" (Sextus Empiricus, *Math.* 2.46), or "to defeat a just argument by an unjust" (Philostratus, *Vit. Soph.* 483).

According to Aristotle, it is the task of rhetoric to distinguish the genuine from the apparent ways of persuasion (*Rhet.* 1355b.15–21). In several passages in his works dedicated to argumentation, he tries to analyze the techniques of sophistic argumentation and to discern between fallacious and true argumentation. His *De sophisticis elenchis* is dedicated exclusively to this theme. His works have become the basis for all later work on the same topic. Although the distinction between legitimate argumentation and sophistry mostly is used by classical authors as self-evident, the term "sophistical rhetoric" always remains highly ambivalent. In the use of this label subjective factors always come into play. Even as early as Plato's and Aristotle's time, some of Socrates' argumentative techniques were unmasked as sophistical in Plato's dialogues.[9] Modern analyses of Socrates' argumentative techniques arrive at the conclusion that "in particular cases it is very hard to distinguish Socratic dialectic from sophistic eristic; in fact, they are often indistinguishable."[10] Both in his *Topica* and his *De sophisticis elenchis* Aristotle sometimes recommends the use of certain argumentative techniques which he himself identifies as sophistical (*Top.* 111b.32–33; *Soph. elench.* 172b.25–26).[11] If we were to evaluate the means of argumentation in the field of what Aristotle calls "dialectical" reasoning (which, unlike "demonstrative" reasoning, proceeds from generally accepted opinions and probabilities), we would

---

8. According to Kennedy (*New History,* 7; Aristotle, *Rhet.,* 210 fn. 254), Aristotle identifies this phrase "with the use of argument from probability . . . and says the phrase was used against the sophist Protagoras." In Kennedy's interpretation, the "declaration of Protagoras" is identical with the opening sentence of Protagoras's treatise *On the Gods* (Diogenes Laertius 9,52). Other interpreters, however, identify the "declaration of Protagoras" with the phrase, "to make the weaker argument the stronger" and ascribe it to Protagoras himself, as do authors such as E. M. Cope, "On the Sophistical Rhetoric," *The Journal of Classical and Sacred Philology* 2 (1855): 129–69; 3 (1856): 34–80, 253–88: 2,162 and 3,60–61; J. F. Dobson, *The Greek Orators* (London: Ares Publishers, 1918), 10; H. Gomperz, *Sophistik und Rhetorik* (Stuttgart: Teubner, 1965), 135; Schiappa, *Protagoras,* 103–16; Schiappa, *Beginnings,* 79–80.

9. E.g., the critical remarks of Callicles in Plato, *Gorgias,* 482c-483a, and the commentary on this passage by Aristotle, *Soph. elench.,* 173a.7–18; cf. also Aristides, *Or.,* 3.599: "Then Socrates does nothing other than use sophistic tricks on Polus, as if on a child."

10. John Beversluis, *Cross-examining Socrates* (Cambridge: Cambridge University Press, 2000), 39 and passim. On the same lines Brian Vickers, *In Defence of Rhetoric* (Oxford: Clarendon Press, 1988), 83–147, with many references to the commentaries of E. R. Dodds and T. Irwin on Plato's *Gorgias;* for further literature see Beversluis, ibid., 40, n. 13.

11. Cf. Classen, "Aristotle's Picture of the Sophists," 15.23.

notice a consistent connection between: (a) the acceptance of the positions or premises of the author, and (b) the acceptance of the means of argumentation used to make that position plausible. Means of argumentation are often regarded as acceptable as far as they can strengthen the position of the speaker on whose side the hearer or reader stands. Although a far-reaching consensus on the fallacious nature of some kinds of arguments is theoretically possible, the boundaries are vague in actual practice.

The Problem of Genuine and Fallacious Argumentation in the Letters of Paul

Paul derives the premises of his theological reasoning from several sources. In defending his position, he draws upon scripture, the sayings of Jesus, Christian tradition, and direct revelations.[12] Aside from these external proofs, he uses internal or artistic proofs for which he has an arsenal of logical and hermeneutic techniques at his disposal. All in all, his is a (Jewish)-Hellenistic common-sense logic and hermeneutic. We can find parallels in the (Jewish)-Hellenistic world to all of his logical and hermeneutic techniques.[13]

The apostle, however, is aware of the fact that there are various argumentative possibilities. More than once he rejects conclusions that could be drawn from his reasoning or were already drawn by opponents.[14] The apostle also warns against fellow missionaries who, in his opinion, are using reprehensible means of persuasion.[15] Moreover, he is aware of the possibility that he himself could try to persuade his fellow Christians with unacceptable means. At various junctures he defends himself against potential or real charges of trickery.[16] Most of the words he uses in this context occur in the list of synonyms cited by Julius Pollux in his *Onomasticon*[17] for σοφίζεσθαι and cognate words as far as they are used with negative connotations: ἐξαπατᾶν (Rom 16:18; 2 Cor 11:3), ψεύδεσθαι (2 Cor 11:31; Gal 1:20), πανουργεῖν (2 Cor 4:2; 11:3; 12:16), δολοῦν (2 Cor 4:2; 12:16; 1 Thess 2:3), καπηλεύειν (2 Cor 2:17), κολακεύειν (1 Thess 2:5), ταπεινοῦν ἑαυτόν (2 Cor 11:7). More than once, he offers us a criterion for his reliability. With regard to his verbal

---

12. E.g., 1 Cor 1:19; 7:10–11; 15:3; Gal 1:11–12.
13. Cf. Folker Siegert, *Argumentation bei Paulus* (WUNT 34; Tübingen: Mohr/Siebeck, 1985); Dieter-Alex Koch, *Die Schrift als Zeuge des Evangeliums* (BHT 69; Tübingen: Mohr/Siebeck, 1986), 199–256.
14. E.g., Rom 3:1–8; 6:1, 15; 7:7, 13; 9:14, 19.
15. 1 Cor 1:18–3:5; 3:18–23; 2 Cor 11:3–4, 13–15; Rom 16:18.
16. 2 Cor 2:17; 4:2; 11:7, 31; 12:16; 1 Thess 2:3–5; Gal 1:10, 20.
17. See above fn. 3.

communication, he makes explicit mention of the criterion of consistency in his words (2 Cor 1:17–20).

From the perspective of those readers of the Letter to the Romans who were familiar with biblical, early Jewish, and/or early Christian traditions, Paul's claim that the law outside of the realm of Christ is no more than a powerless instrument in the service of sin (7:4–25) can be regarded as the weaker position. It would not be difficult for Paul's adversaries to find the very opposite position in scripture. Neither do the traditional sayings of Jesus offer much support to Paul's arguments. It is not without reason that the apostle never invokes them in this context. In early Christianity, Paul's position with regard to the law was highly disputed, as we know from several sources.[18] Nevertheless, Paul presented his position so strongly that he convinced the majority of Christian believers from his time until the present day. Critical exegetes like Origen not infrequently discerned problems in Paul's argumentation.[19] In recent times, interest in the apostle's logic and the means of argumentation have increased. Heikki Räisänen, following up on the insights of liberal theology at the turn of the century, has presented a very critical evaluation of Paul's argumentation concerning the law.[20] His conclusion that Paul uses many inconsistent and fallacious arguments has been challenged by several scholars.[21] As in the evaluation of Socrates' logic in Plato's dialogues, different evaluations of Paul's argumentation seem to link their assessment of the "truth" of the Pauline gospel to their assessment of the means of argumentation the apostle uses to make that truth plausible. Scholars who are themselves Paulinists or at least have some affinity with his gospel have much less difficulty with his argumentative strategies than those who study Paul from a critical distance. Consensus on Paul's argumentation is difficult, if not impossible, to reach due to these differences in points of departure, as well as to Paul's own highly complex arguments, arguments subject to interpretation from numerous perspectives. In the following segment I choose one specific point of view, the position of the critical reader who considers Paul's argumentation regarding the law in the letter to the Romans largely as sophistic

---

18. E.g., Gal 1–2; Acts 21:15–36; cf. G. Lüdemann, *Paulus, der Heidenapostel*, Bd. II: *Antipaulinismus im frühen Christentum* (FRLANT 130; Göttingen: Vandenhoeck & Ruprecht, 1983).
19. E.g., *Comm. Rom.* 2.14 (*PG* 14.920B); 3.1 (*PG* 14.921C-923A); 5.1 (*PG* 14.1008B-1009A, 1013A-1014A).
20. Heikki Räisänen, *Paul and the Law* (WUNT 29; Tübingen: Mohr/Siebeck, 1983); on the same lines: E. P. Sanders, *Paul, the Law, and the Jewish People* (Philadelphia: Fortress Press, 1983).
21. E.g., James D. G. Dunn, *Romans 1–8* (WBC 38A; Waco, Tex.: Word Books, 1988), lxiii–lxxii; idem, *The Theology of Paul the Apostle* (Edinburgh: T. & T. Clark, 1998), 128–61; Joseph A. Fitzmyer, *Romans* (AB 33; New York: Doubleday, 1993), 131–35; Teunis Erik van Spanje, *Inconsistentie bij Paulus? Een confrontatie met het werk van Heikki Räisänen* (Kampen: Kok, 1996). Pages 139–40 of this work contain a short survey of the reactions to Räisänen's book.

rhetoric. Although I agree with Räisänen's conclusions on many points, my perspective is different. Whereas Räisänen focuses on the "psychological, sociological and historical factors,"[22] my purpose is to shed new light on the persuasive function of Paul's controversial arguments by adducing material from classical literature concerning sophistical strategies.[23]

Sophistical Arguments in the Letter to the Romans

Seemingly Syllogistic Arguments

According to Aristotle (*Soph. elench.* 164a.20–24) syllogisms that seem to be syllogisms but are not genuine are typical of sophistical argumentation. It can be argued that the apostle Paul makes use of these seemingly syllogistic arguments in his Letter to the Romans.

According to Johannes Piscator,[24] the basic syllogism underlying the argumentation of Romans 1–3 is:

– Aut fide iustificamur, aut operibus legis
– Non autem iustificamur operibus legis
– Iustificamur ergo fide.

In his view, the apostle omits the first sentence, the propositio, because it is "evident and certain in itself." One can object, however, that this propositio is only "evident and certain" for readers who have accepted the Pauline premises from the outset. Critical readers can find the very opposite in scripture, in Jewish literature, and in other parts of the New Testament, namely, that there is by no means any contrast between faith and obedience to the law.[25] Critical readers also would observe that the creation of binary oppositions to favor one pole and exclude the other is a commonly used weapon in the hand of orators who argue for victory rather than for truth in its complexity.[26]

To prove the second sentence, the assumptio, Paul uses, according to Piscator, the following syllogism:

---

22. Räisänen, *Paul*, 11.
23. After this paper was completed, Vernon Robbins drew my attention to a paper by Mark Given about the same subject: "True Rhetoric: Ambiguity, Cunning, and Deception in Pauline Discourse," *SBLSP,* 1997 (*http://courses.smsu.edu/mdg421f/True.htm*).
24. *Commentarii in omnes libros Novi Testamenti* (Herbornae Nassoviorum, editio tertia, 1638), 442, 451.
25. Cf., e.g., Gen 15:6 with 26:5; Sir 44:20–21; 1 Macc 2:52; Jas 2:14–26.
26. Cf. Vickers, *Defence,* 90.95.110–13. In commenting on the binary oppositions of Socrates in Plato's dialogues Vickers writes: "They may masquerade as logical or value-free categories, but they merely reflect, and enforce, a prejudice" (113).

- Nullus transgressor legis ex operibus legis iustificatur
- At omnis homo transgressor legis est
- Nullus igitur homo ex operibus legis iustificatur

According to Piscator, the propositio of this syllogism is beyond dispute and the proof of the assumptio is given in 1:18–3:20. For other readers, however, the apostle only seems to prove this point. In 3:9 Paul writes: "For we have already charged that all, Jews and Greeks alike, are under the power of sin." In reality, however, Paul hardly did so with respect to the Jews. In 2:1–11, he is accusing an imaginary interlocutor, not necessarily a Jew. In 2:17–24, he addresses an imaginary Jew, who pretends to have knowledge of the law, but, in fact, transgresses the most elementary commandments. In 2:12–16, 25–29 the apostle makes a general contrast between Gentiles, who do not possess the written law and are not circumcised but nevertheless do what the law requires, and Jews, who possess both law and circumcision, but are, in fact, transgressors of the law. The following paragraph, 3:1–9, is a discussion with a fictitious interlocutor. For the critical reader, the summary Paul gives in 3:9 comes as a surprise. What he is missing is even the rudiments of proof that one would expect from a serious prosecutor. In reality, Paul's strategy is very similar to a sophistic practice described by Aristotle (*Soph. elench.* 174b.8–12):

> Often the most sophistical of all frauds practiced by questioners produces a striking appearance of refutation, when, though they have proved nothing, they do not put the final proposition in the form of a question but state conclusively, as though they had proved it, that "such and such a thing, then, is not the case."

It is hard to avoid the conclusion that Paul here uses a sophistical strategy.[27]

Ambiguity

One of the typical sophistical tricks according to Aristotle is the use of ambiguity in speech by means of homonymy. At times Aristotle also deals with the phenomenon of homonymy without the context of sophistry, as he does in his *Topica*. There, he speaks about the topos ἐκ τοῦ ποσαχῶς, the ability to distinguish in how many different ways a particular expression is used (105a 24–25;106a 1–108b 34). Ambiguity or homonymy can, however, be used as a sophistic trick to mislead the opponent: "The kind of words useful

---

27. Räisänen, *Paul*, 99, speaks in this context of "a blatant non sequitur."

to a sophist are homonyms; by means of them he cheats [κακουργεῖ])" (*Rhet.* 1404b.37–38; cf. *Rhet.* 1401a.13–25; *Soph. elench.* 165b.30–166a.7).[28]

A sophist tries to make his opponent utter paradoxes. One way to achieve that, according to Aristotle, is to pick up a word used by the opponent and apply it in a different sense:

> Also, just as answerers, when they are being refuted, often draw a distinction, if they are on the point of being refuted, so questioners also ought sometimes, when dealing with objectors, if the objection is valid against one sense of the word but not against another, to resort to the expedient of declaring that the opponent has taken it in such and such a sense. (*Soph. elench.* 174b.23–27)

As an example Aristotle refers to the discussion between Callicles and Socrates in Plato's *Gorgias* (482E–483A) where Callicles blames Socrates for using the tricks of a demagogue and deliberately confusing "justice" according to "nature" and "justice" according to "law." In establishing a general sophistic rule Aristotle says:

> Therefore, to a man who speaks in terms of nature you must reply in terms of law, and when he speaks in terms of law you must lead the argument to terms of nature; for in both cases the result will be that he utters paradoxes (*Soph. elench.* 173a 12–15).

This is exactly what the apostle Paul seems to be doing with the word νόμος. To defend his thesis that both Jews and Gentiles know the law of God, but that outside Christ the law can only lead to sin and death and that those who believe in Christ are freed from the law, but that in Christ the law is established nonetheless (3:19–20, 27, 31; 6:14; 7:4–8:4), Paul uses the word "law" in a variety of senses:

(a) When he indicts the Jew for violating the law (2:17–29), he is referring to the written law, promulgated by Moses. The written law includes the especially distinctive laws in the relation between Jews and Gentiles, not only the commandment of circumcision, but also that of the Sabbath, the food-related laws and the cultic laws. When, however, he indicates the possibility that Gentiles do what the law requires without possessing the written law (2:12–16), he is referring to a portion of the law, the ethical commandments that Jews and Gentiles have in common. In the same way, when he maintains that the law is established in Christ and that the requirement of the law can be fulfilled (3:31; 8:4), he is thinking only of those parts of the law that are in force for the Gentile Christians.

(b) When he emphasizes that the law as such is holy, just, and good, he makes a sharp distinction between the law, on the one hand, and the human being under the law, on the other. When he tries to demonstrate, however, that the law has become a

---

28. Cf. Galen, *De Captionibus*, 2; Robert Blair Edlow, *Galen on Language and Ambiguity* (PhAnt; Leiden: Brill, 1977), 92, 11–16: "For it is by holding fast to this [namely, to vice in language] as to a first principle that the sophists deceive those who are less experienced in these matters and who do not perceive the fraud."

"law of sin and death," he tries to associate law and sin by using the same word "nomos" for the law of God and the various anthropological functions of the sinful human being, the conflicting tendencies of its mind and flesh and the inner division (7:21–23).

(c) At times, Paul makes a distinction between two forms of the law by using a genitive construction, for instance the "law of works" and the "law of faith" (3:27; 8:2). In other places, however, he speaks of "the law" in an absolute sense without making it clear that he means a specific form of the law (4:15).

Playing with homonyms or, in modern terms, making "dissociations"[29] and "persuasive definitions"[30] is not necessarily sophistic in itself. Often, it is an instrument to clarify and elaborate on complicated matters. However, this instrument can always be evaluated from different perspectives. In his dialogues, Plato makes ample use of this instrument,[31] a point on which Aristides criticizes him severely. Aristides blames Plato for the confusion he creates by claiming that there are two kinds of oratory and at the same time dismissing it as if it were only a single entity. Aristides felt that dissociating words which have already an antonym was nothing more than obfuscating the meaning of words (Or. 2.446–53 [150d–152d]).

Playing with homonyms, making dissociations, or creating persuasive definition becomes sophistical when it is used to throw the opponent into confusion and put him on the wrong track.[32] That seems to be the case in the Apostle Paul's argumentation. His juggling of words is a persuasive strategy. He invented it to defend his thesis that Jewish law cannot bring about salvation outside of Christ, either for Gentiles or for Jews, and at the same time to maintain that the same law is established in Christ. Paul can maintain both only by regularly alternating the meaning of the word νόμος. The Jewish or Jewish-Christian reader who tries to enter into a discussion with Paul is constantly put on the wrong track. When he or she, thinking of the entire law in its written form, questions Paul about setting the law aside altogether (3:31), Paul answers "on the contrary, we establish the law." At this point, Paul means the law in a reduced form. This confusion has persisted until the present day: modern interpreters have been unable to reach a consensus about what Paul means exactly with the word νόμος in Rom 3:27, 31; 7:21–23; or

---

29. Cf. Ch. Perelman and L. Olbrechts-Tyteca, Traité de l'argumentation: La nouvelle rhétorique (2d ed.; Brussels: Université Libre, 1970), 550–609.
30. Cf. C. L. Stevenson, "Persuasive Definitions," Mind 47 (1938): 331–50.
31. Cf. Vickers, Defence, 100; Beversluis, Cross-examining Socrates, 302.
32. According to John Stuart Mill, A System of Logic V, vol. VIII in Collected Works (Toronto: University of Toronto Press, 1974), 809, the use of ambiguous terms is fallacious "when something which is true if a word be used in a particular sense, is reasoned on as if it were true in another sense."

8:2–4.[33] The fact that this has occurred can be traced to the nature of the argumentation: it is essential to Paul's persuasive strategy to create ambivalence. In Greek, the Pauline strategy would be termed σοφίζεσθαι τὸν νόμον (cf. Philostratus, *Vit. Ap.* 2.40).

Inconsistency

According to Aristophanes' *Clouds,* the school of the sophists is characterized by its practice of teaching two contrasting types of arguments, the weaker and the stronger or the unjust and the just. This school teaches argument for victory rather than truth (882–85; 1336–37). According to Plato, the sophists can refute any proposition, whether true or false (*Euthyd.* 272a-b). He who possesses the art of rhetoric in this sense "can make (in law courts) the same thing appear to the same people now just, now unjust, at will," and in public harangues, "he can make the same things seem to the community now good, and now the reverse of good" (*Phaedr.* 261d).[34] From this point of view, Sextus Empiricus condemns every kind of rhetoric: "For the orator, of whatever sort he may be, must certainly practice himself in contradictory speeches, and injustice is inherent in contradictions; therefore every orator, being an advocate of injustice, is unjust" (*Math.* 2.47).[35]

Real or apparent inconsistencies typify the Apostle Paul's argumentation. In New Testament scholarship this is a highly debated subject. I will limit my discussion here to one example, namely the relationship between law, sin, and death. In Romans 5:12–13, Paul distinguishes between: (a) humankind's sin from Adam until Moses; and (b) sin after Moses. In the first period, sin and, as a consequence, death entered in the world, though "sin is not accounted in the absence of the law." After God gave Moses the law on Mount Sinai, sin was accounted. This distinction between accounted sin and sin that is not accounted is not only contradictory with other statements of Paul, but also meaningless. It contradicts Romans 1:18–3:20, where Paul demonstrates that those who do not possess the law, or who do not possess it in its written form, are accountable before God in the same sense as the Jews (2:12; 3:20).

---

33. See my article "Legem statuimus. Rhetorische Aspekte der Gesetzesdebatte zwischen Juden und Christen," in *Juden und Christen in der Antike* (ed. J. v. Amersfoort and J. v. Oort; Kampen: Kok, 1990), 44–60, esp. 44–53. For a critical evaluation of Räisänen's position, see ibid., 51–52, n. 20.

34. Translation from R. Hackforth, *Plato's Phaedrus* (Cambridge: University Press, 1972), 124; about the use of the same strategy by Socrates in Plato's dialogues, see Beversluis, *Cross-examining Socrates,* 166–67.

35. Sextus Empiricus IV: *Against the Professors* (trans. R. G. Bury; LCL; Cambridge, Mass.: Harvard University Press, 1949), 211.

Neither can this distinction be harmonized with Romans 7:7–12, where Paul asserts that before the coming of the law, sin was dead and man alive, and that through the coming of the law, sin became alive and man died. According to 5:12–13, before the coming of the law, sin was neither dead, nor was man alive. The fact that the distinction in Romans 5:12–13 also contradicts the biblical stories about humankind before the giving of the law was already noted by the earliest interpreters.[36] Apart from these contradictions, the distinction can hardly be assigned an intelligible meaning.[37] Many interpretations refer to the Jewish conception of the heavenly bookkeeping.[38] However, by this conception the distinction between sin that is not accounted, but that still leads to death, and sin that is accounted and leads to the same death is not at all clarified. Paul never makes any distinction between two kinds of death. What can be clarified, however, is the persuasive function of the distinction within its context. To prove that salvation is possible only in Christ, Paul absolutely must depict the conceivable rivals, including the law of Moses, as far as it is not integrated in the realm of Christ, as a negative force. Within the traditional conception of Adam's sin and its consequences, the picture of the law as a primal factor with regard to the origin of sin and death does not really fit. In this situation, Paul invents the distinction between sin that is accounted and sin that is not accounted. The function of the law in its relation to sin and death remains a negative one. Here, in contrast to other passages in the letter to the Romans, this function is not cognitive (3:20), causative (4:15), instrumental (7:4–12), or even additive (5:20), but rather imputative. The truth is what Paul needs it to be for the purposes of persuasion at any given time.

Distraction from the Critical Point

According to Aristotle, "there is the sophistic method, by which we lead an opponent into the sort of argumentation against which we shall have a supply of arguments" (*Top.* 111b.32–33; *Soph. elench.* 172b.25–27). When

---

36. E.g., Origen, *Comm. Rom.* 5.1 (*PG* 14.1013A-1014A).
37. Cf. Rudolf Bultmann, *Theologie des Neuen Testaments* (5th ed.; Tübingen: Mohr/Siebeck, 1965), 252: "Vollends unverständlich ist V. 13." Räisänen reasons on the same lines; *Paul*, 146, n. 91. In my opinion, later interpretations have not refuted Bultmann's dictum. Dunn (*Romans 1–8*, 274–75) challenges this view. According to him, it must be significant that Paul gives another interpretation here of the nexus between sin and law than he does in chapters 1 and 2. Yet, he himself admits that "what the significance is, however, remains unclear." The distinction he makes between death as an inescapable part of the human condition and death as a consequence of the individual's responsible transgression in no way explains the assertion that sin "is not counted" before the coming of the law.
38. E.g., Gerhard Friedrich, Ἁμαρτία οὐκ ἐλλογεῖται Röm. 5,13," in *Auf das Wort kommt es an. Gesammelte Aufsätze* (Göttingen: Vandenhoeck & Ruprecht, 1978), 123–31.

the opponent in a discussion denies some point that is useful to our thesis, then we try to steer him toward an assertion that is easy to refute. A variant of this strategy is the manipulation of the interlocutor in fictitious dialogues; the author can lead the interlocutor into a weak position. Plato often uses this strategy to bring about a victory for Socrates.[39]

Romans 3:1–9 contains an example of this strategy. The interlocutor is a creation of Paul himself. The structure of the discussion is as follows:[40]

Interlocutor	Paul
¹Then what advantage has the Jew?	
²Or what is the value of circumcision?	
	Much, in every way. For in the first place the Jews were entrusted with the oracles of God.
³What if some were unfaithful? Will their faithlessness nullify the faithfulness of God?	
⁴	By no means! Although everyone is a liar, let God be proved true, as it is written....
⁵But if our injustice serves to confirm the justice of God, what should we say? That God is unjust to inflict wrath on us?...	
⁶	By no means! For then how could God judge the world?
⁷But if through my falsehood God's truthfulness abounds to his glory, why am I still being condemned as a sinner?	
⁸And why not say..."Let us do evil so that good may come?"	
	Their condemnation is deserved!

After Paul's demonstration that Jews are in the same position as Gentiles in the matter of obedience and justification before God, the interlocutor poses the critical question: "What then is the advantage of the Jew?" The striking point

---

39. Cf. Vickers, *Defence*, 118–19.
40. Translation: New Revised Standard Version.

of the discussion that follows is that the interlocutor, after Paul's first answer ("Much in every way"), instead of sticking to his position and underpinning it with arguments from scripture, continues the discussion with sophistical questions of a sort which can easily be refuted by Paul.[41] Drawing on the thesis that "the faithlessness of some Jews does not nullify the faithfulness of God" (3–4), the interlocutor concludes that:

- "our unjustice serves to confirm the justice of God" (5a), and
- "through my falsehood God's truthfulness abounds to his glory" (7a).

The sophistical element lies in the implied shift from an actual or concessive relationship between the unrighteousness of man and the righteousness of God to a causal one: human faithlessness becomes a condition for God's faithfulness.[42] From this interim conclusion, the interlocutor draws two final conclusions. The first of these is legal, the second is ethical:

- God is unjust to inflict wrath on us (5b); there is no reason to condemn me as a sinner (7b).
- Let us do evil so that good may come (8).

For Paul, both conclusions can easily be refuted. The majority of his readers will indignantly reject them. The answer to these conclusions is much easier than the answer to the original and serious question, "What then is the advantage of the Jew? Or what is the value of circumcision?" Actually, Paul does not have a real answer to this question at this point.[43] From his weaker position, he tries to make a stronger position by putting sophistical arguments

---

41. Cf. Günther Bornkamm, "Der Römerbrief als Testament des Paulus," in *Geschichte und Glaube II, Gesammelte Aufsätze IV* (Munich: Kaiser, 1971), 120–48, esp. p. 148: "Die von Paulus leidenschaftlich abgewehrte sophistische Pseudo-Theologie des Dialogpartners...." On the same lines, see Charles H. Cosgrove, "What If Some Have Not Believed? The Occasion and Thrust of Romans 3:1–8," *ZNW* 78 (1987): 90–105. He writes, on p. 94: "Given the premises stated, none of the 'objections' is *plausible* from 'a Jewish perspective.' What Jew will dispute that the ἀπιστία of some, even the majority, of God's people calls into question God's own faithfulness (v. 3)? What Jew will contest God's justice in bringing down wrath upon the unrighteous (v. 5)? What Jew will take issue with Paul's own dismissal of the *non sequitur* in v. 7 and the antinomian inference in v. 8?"

42. Cf. Isaac Watts, *Logick, or the Right Use of Reason* (2d ed., 1796), Part III, sect. III, 7. Reprinted in *Fallacies: Classical and Contemporary Readings* (ed. H. V. Hansen and R. V. Pinto; University Park: Pennsylvania State University Press, 1995), 57–66. On p. 65 he states, "the Sophism of Composition is when we infer any thing concerning Ideas in a compounded Sense which is only true in a divided Sense.... So when the Scriptures assures us the worst of Sinners may be saved, it signifies only that they who have been the worst of Sinners may repent and be saved, not that they shall be saved in their Sins."

43. Cf. H. Räisänen, "Zum Verständnis von Röm 3:1–8," in *The Torah and Christ* (SESJ 45; Helsinki: Finnish Exegetical Society, 1986), 185–205: "Das wahre Problem hinter unserem Passus ist das heilsgeschichtliche Grundproblem, das Paulus nicht lösen konnte" (201). For a totally different interpretation, see Stanley Stowers: "Paul's Dialogue with a Fellow Jew in Romans 3:1–9," *CBQ* 46 (1984): 707–22, and idem, *A Rereading of Romans* (New Haven: Yale University Press, 1994), 159–75.

into the mouth of his interlocutor and by steering him towards assertions that are easily refuted.

Contrasting Methods of Interpretation

One of the objections against rhetoric brought forward by Sextus Empiricus is that orators use their "mal-artful arts" in opposition to the laws. Depending on their needs, they change the methods of interpretation:

> For at one time they advise us to attend to the ordinance and words of the lawgiver as being clear and needing no explanation, at another time they turn round and advise us to follow neither the ordinance nor the words but the intention. . . . And sometimes they bid us cut out bits as we read the laws, and construct a different sense from what remains. Often, too, they make distinctions in ambiguous phrases and support the signification which suits themselves; and they do thousands of other things which tend to the upsetting of the laws. Hence also, the Byzantine orator, when asked "How goes the Byzantine law?" replied: "As I choose." For just as jugglers deceive the eyes of the beholders by their sleight of hand, so the orators by their low cunning blind the minds of the judges to the law and so steal away the votes. *(Math.* 2.36–39)[44]

It is not difficult to apply these criticisms to Paul's interpretation of the law. I will focus here on just one example. In Romans 10:5–10 Paul interprets two texts from scripture: Leviticus 18:5 and Deuteronomy 30:11–14. According to him, Moses is referring in the first text ("The person who does these things shall live by them") to the "righteousness that comes from the law." The accent lies upon the verb "to do." In Paul's interpretation, the second text is the voice of the "righteousness that comes from faith." The quote, "Do not say in your heart 'Who will ascend to heaven' or 'Who will descend into the abyss,'" refers to Christ. According to the usual interpretation, however, Deuteronomy 30:11–20 and Leviticus 18:1–5 refer to the same law of Moses. Both texts emphasize the relationship between the observation of the commandments and the promise of life. In Deuteronomy 30 the accent lies on the possibility of fulfillment of the law. Paul applies two different exegetical methods. In interpreting the first text, he stresses the literal meaning of the words ("scriptum"). In the second case, he focuses on the decisiveness of the intention ("voluntas legis").[45] He ignores the fact that Deuteronomy 30:11–14 speaks in the same terms as Leviticus 18:5 about the "doing" of the "commandments." All three characteristics of the "mal-artful arts" of rhetoric

---

44. Translation of R. G. Bury.
45. See my article, "Die hermeneutische Antinomie bei Paulus (Gal 3,11–12; Röm 10,5–10)," *NTS* 38 (1992): 254–70.

mentioned by Sextus Empiricus can be found in Paul's interpretation: (a) interpreting one text according to the literal meaning and another according to the intention; (b) cutting out bits and constructing a different sense from what remains; and (c) making distinctions to support the signification which suits himself.

Obscurity

"Speaking sophistically" can be identical with "speaking in an obscure way," "creating confusion" (cf. Aristotle, *Rhet.* 1419a.14). Creating confusion is a well-known strategy of orators who are interested in victory rather than in truth.[46] For the adversaries of sophistic rhetoric, obscurity is one of the main characteristics of this art. Philo characterizes the sophistic orators as follows:

> They practice a lack of clearness (ἀσάφεια), which in speech is profound darkness (βαθὺ σκότος), and darkness is the fellow-worker of thieves. It is for this reason that Moses adorned the high priest with Manifestation and Truth (δηλώσει καὶ ἀληθείᾳ), judging that the speech of the man of worth should be transparent and true (ἀρίδηλον καὶ ἀληθῆ) (*Her.* 302–3).[47]

The effect of almost all of the above sketched characteristics of Paul's argumentation is obscurity. From the earliest church to this day, Paul's use of obscurity is proverbial. Even the author of Second Peter found certain points in Paul's letters "hard to understand" (3:15–16). Origen's first few remarks in the *praefatio* to his commentary on Paul's letter to the Romans are dedicated to the problem of its lack of clarity.[48] The many different opinions about the meaning of crucial passages in Paul's letters in modern scholarship are only a reflection of this problem. I have tried in this paper to demonstrate that the problem of the obscurity in the Letter to the Romans is an essential part of Paul's persuasive strategy, of his endeavor to make the weaker argument stronger.

---

46. Cf. the analysis of Cicero's speeches by C. J. Classen, *Recht-Rhetorik-Politik* (Darmstadt: Wissenschaftliche Buchgesellschaft, 1985), Sachregister s.v. "unklare Formulierungen bewußt."
47. Translation: F. H. Colson and G. H. Whitaker, *Philo IV* (LCL; Cambridge, Mass.: Harvard University Press, 1968), 439.
48. *PG* 14.833A; cf. *Philoc.*, 9.3.

CHAPTER 14

THE TONGUES OF MEN:
UNDERSTANDING GREEK RHETORICAL SOURCES
FOR PAUL'S LETTERS TO THE ROMANS AND 1 CORINTHIANS

C. Jan Swearingen

*The Rhetorical Lexicon, Structure, and Contexts
of Romans and 1 Corinthians:
Towards a Composite Methodology*

Paul's letters to the Romans and 1 Corinthians provide especially fitting texts for testing the viability of several forms of rhetorical analysis, particularly the much-debated relevance of classical rhetoric.[1] On three levels — lexicon, rhetorical genre, and implied audience — I shall propose, these letters cannot be wholly innocent of classical rhetorical understandings or practices on the part of Paul and the communities he addresses. The Greek audience at Corinth and the Jewish and Gentile Roman audience are addressed in terms, in genres, and through shifts in ethos that assume some familiarity with a rhetorical vocabulary, concepts, and argumentative genres. Pairs such as sophia-logos, pneuma-gramma, and nomos-agape were well-established rhetorical terms linked in a variety of paired topoi and contrastive argumentation. However, I would emphasize that this is no simple case of Paul's use of contemporary rhetorical practices. In his uses of terms, antitheses, and multiple voices Paul gives Greek rhetorical and Hellenistic Jewish terms new meanings, and crafts argumentative genres with unprecedented rhetorical purposes. Regardless of

---

1. For excellent overviews of the recent debates concerning the uses of classical rhetoric in readings of Paul's letters see Anders Eriksson, *Traditions as Rhetorical Proof: Pauline Argumentation in 1 Corinthians* (ConBNT 29; Stockholm: Almqvist & Wiksell International, 1998); Stanley E. Porter and Thomas H. Olbricht, eds., *Rhetoric and the New Testament: Essays from the 1992 Heidelberg Conference* (Sheffield: JSOT Press, 1993); Calvin Roetzel, *Paul: The Man and the Myth* (Minneapolis: Fortress, 1999); Stanley E. Stowers, *Letter Writing in Greco-Roman Antiquity* (Library of Early Christianity; Philadelphia: Westminster, 1986); idem, *A Rereading of Romans: Justice, Jews, and the Gentiles* (New Haven: Yale University Press, 1994); Dale L. Sullivan and Christian Anibile, "The Epideictic Dimension of Galatians as Formative Rhetoric: The Inscription of Early Christian Community," *Rhetorica* 18:2 (Spring 2000): 117–45; R. Dean Anderson, *Ancient Rhetorical Theory and Paul* (Kampen: Kok Pharos, 1996); and Wilhelm Wuellner, "Where Is Rhetorical Criticism Taking Us?" *CBQ* 49 (1987): 448–63; and "Der vorchristliche Paulus und die Rhetorik," in *Tempelkult und Tempelzerstörung* (70 n. Chr.): *Festschrift für Clemens Thoma zum 60. Geburtstag* (ed. Simon Lauer and H. Hernst (Bern: Peter Lang, 1995), 133–65.

direct contact with Cicero's *Paradoxa Stoicorum*, for example, Paul's cumulative series of antitheses on law, flesh, sin, and separation in Romans 7–8 are drawn in sharp chiasmatic sentences that provoke and teach through paradox.[2] Using multiple voices in Romans in a manner similar to *prosopopoieia*, Paul performs his discourses, I will suggest, as models for his auditors to emulate in two ways: by following the content of the teaching, and by repeating the teaching as spoken in the letter to other auditors. Only a revised, expanded, and more flexible use of rhetorical analyses of Paul's letters can allow us to observe the innovations Paul introduces.[3] Speakers and writers learn rhetorical styles from the usage that surrounds them as well as from formal training. Paul's "departure" from the precepts of rhetoric may be applauded as a stunningly successful rhetorical strategy that would work best among those familiar with the terms and argumentative practices upon which he builds his new terms, genres, and messages. His divergence from formal rhetorical patterns is innovative and adapted to purposes well beyond those defined in classical rhetoric. Yet in avoiding a high style he "follows" one of the oldest rhetorical precepts of all: to appear artless.[4]

To reject classical rhetorical models entirely deprives us of insights from within the culture of the pre-Christian Paul and early Christianity where for several centuries oral and written traditions mingled and shaped one another.

---

2. Classen questions Anderson's claim that "Paul departs from rhetorical theory" (*Ancient Rhetorical Theory and Paul*, 131) in his uses of popular appeals and jingly antitheses of a kind generally condemned by rhetorical theorists. See C. Joachim Classen, "Review of Anderson, *Ancient Rhetorical Theory and Paul*," *Rhetorica* 16:3 (Summer 1998). Paul's uses of antithesis and of what Anderson terms "narrative apology" (*Ancient Rhetorical Theory and Paul*, 125) and "apologetic narrative" (130), Classen observes, are expressed in a tone and style appropriate for "popular" culture, a practice observed by Cicero, among other authors of Paul's era. "The authors certainly knew the rhetorical precepts, and yet departed from them, presumably because they realized they had to do so in order to be effective in their time. This was Paul's aim too — whether he was aware of such rhetorical precepts or not" (Classen, "Review of Anderson," 327).

3. Challenging simple "matching" and influence studies of Paul's epistolary rhetoric, which hunt for handbook rhetorical devices and patterns, Roetzel proposes that "Paul enjoyed enormous freedom to appropriate, change, distort, adapt, and combine to defend himself. His obvious use of that freedom works against efforts to frame Paul's argument by a rigid set of rules laid down in books of rhetoric" (*Paul: The Man and the Myth,* 81). A. N. Wilson emphasizes chronology to defend Paul's self-aware role as progenitor of subsequent Christian rhetoric: "Paul's letters — the body of work which is authentically Paul's — are the oldest Christian documents. I Thessalonians, perhaps the oldest, probably antedates the first version of Mark by nearly twenty years"; A. N. Wilson, *Paul: The Mind of the Apostle* (New York: W. W. Norton, 1997), 257.

4. Aristotle, *Rhet.*, 3.1404b. Regarding Paul's artlessness, Roetzel traces the influence of rhetorical studies in overturning the "spell that Deissmann cast over the study of the Pauline letters.... A number of important studies of the past two decades have shown that Paul was influenced at some level by first century rhetoric and that, therefore, his letters are hardly the unsophisticated, simple, earthy products that Deissmann made them out to be" (*Paul: The Man and the Myth,* 72–73). The *atechnos* topos can be observed in Socrates' self-defense (*Apology* 17–18). Kennedy observes similar patterns in the Hebrew Scriptures, and sees them as precursors to New Testament letter-spirit and wise-foolish pairs; *Comparative Rhetoric* (New York: Oxford University Press, 1998), 133–37.

Numerous references to speech and argument in Romans, and to effective versus impotent speaking in 1 Corinthians, qualify both as letters about rhetoric in some sense. To approach Romans and 1 Corinthians as collections of precepts concerning, and practicing, Christian rhetoric is no simple matter of "historical reconstruction," but rather a process of reading for patterns, terms, and meanings distributed among discourses that rubbed shoulders in the same time and place.[5] We are presented with words for words, and rhetoric about rhetoric, in two letters that are magisterial lessons on how law, love, and language should be guided by divine love and unity with and in the Holy Spirit.

The specious, malignant, and arrogant disputations that Paul refers to directly in Romans invite us to ask whether he was practicing, on one level, what he was preaching against on another. His invectives against divisive, immoral, ineffective, and unloving speaking would almost certainly have been heard against the backdrop of familiar oral speech genres: political oratory and preaching. Within these familiar genres were long-embedded topoi directly concerning speech: the *epitaphios logos* and *logos-ergon* topoi of earlier Greek rhetoric. The *logos-sophia* and *sophia-moria* topoi in 1 Corinthians take a different turn; they denounce the wisdom and words of men to emphasize a different order of both. Like the *epitaphios logos* — the speech about the speech that begins many classical epitaphia — the introductions to Romans and Corinthians explicitly allude to multiple audiences, and in doing so "instruct" the audience regarding the manner in which they are to hear the forthcoming speech. Unlike similar references to the audience in the classical *epitaphios logos,* Paul spotlights his audiences' diversity and division as an

---

5. Wuellner observes that we have looked long and hard at the influence of Greek rhetoric upon Hellenistic Jews, but we have yet to begin looking into "the influence which Rabbis had upon rhetoric and hermeneutics." That influence begins not only with the pre-Christian Paul, but with the shaping of the oral and written record of the Rabbi Jesus. Wuellner, "Die vorchristliche Paulus" (quoted here and elsewhere in a manuscript English translation provided in correspondence by the author). In addition to re-examining how classical rhetoric or rhetorical education influenced the composition of Paul's letters, we have begun looking at how Paul's letters, including his incorporation of Jewish themes and genres, reshaped the epistolary conventions of the period, the composition and themes of the Gospels, and later Christian rhetorical theory and practice (such as Augustine's) that reshaped rhetoric by adapting it to readings of biblical texts. Rhetorical studies are increasingly attending to Paul's mingling and hybridization, borrowing and converting of terms and discourse structures. See C. Clifton Black, "Rhetorical Criticism," in *Hearing the New Testament* (ed. Joel B. Green; Grand Rapids, Mich.: Eerdmans, 1995), 256–67; Richard A. Burridge, *What Are the Gospels?* (New York: Cambridge, 1992); Joel B. Green, ed., *Between Two Horizons: Spanning New Testament Studies and Systematic Theology* (Grand Rapids, Mich.: Eerdmans, 2000); idem, ed., *Hearing the New Testament* (Grand Rapids, Mich.: Eerdmans, 1995), especially Green, "Discourse Analysis and the New Testament," pp. 175–96 of the same volume; Stanley K. Stowers, *A Rereading of Romans: Justice, Jews, and Gentiles* (New Haven: Yale University Press, 1994); N. Tom. Wright, "The Letter to the Galatians: Exegesis and Theology," in *Between Two Horizons,* 205–36.

exhortation to renounce differences, and unify through love in the all and the one of shared faith.[6]

Romans and 1 Corinthians are teacherly and epideictic, dialogue-like and hortatory: the audiences of the letters are being instructed in correct "rhetoric" in that they are given a number of warnings against composing, presenting, or tolerating certain kinds of discourse that Paul defines precisely in moral and spiritual, and not rhetorical, terms. Simultaneously, the letters perform a series of examples illustrating not only what the community should believe but also providing alternative voices to employ in different situations, with different audiences. Unlike the practice speeches of progymnasmatic *prosopopoieia*, Paul's multiple genres and voices enact examples of correct speaking, an oral script that could be copied, borrowed from, excerpted, or re-enacted. In composing and practicing his orthology, Paul laid the foundations for practices that are still in use today: sermons and liturgies today shift from the minister-speaker's voice directly into biblical quote without a metadiscursive index of the shift. We lack a text of the voices among which Paul shifted as he spoke, oral "quotations" whose style or substance or both would be readily recognized by auditors: an oral Q, in effect. However, considering the diversity of Paul's doctrines and styles we may have more traces of an oral Q in the making than we have realized. Just as *prosopopoieia*, rather than doctrinal inconsistency, is now being taken into account in understanding many

---

6. Classen and Anderson, among others, suggest that diatribe may well have been unknown to many New Testament authors. See as well Martin J. Medhurst, "Rhetorical Dimensions in Biblical Criticism: Beyond Style and Genre." *QJS* 77 (1991): 214–26; and Margaret D. Zulick, "The Active Force of Hearing: The Ancient Hebrew Language of Persuasion." *Rhetorica* 10 (1992): 367–80.

Stowers and Roetzel make equally plausible cases for Paul's education up to a level that could have included *prosopopoieia*, and, in the progymnasmata of the period, quite probably the impersonation of diatribe-style voices and styles. Roetzel compares Paul's epistolary styles with Cynic as well as Jewish letters of the period, and argues for Jewish origins of the opening salutations and closing blessing. Stowers emphasizes the importance of progymnasmata to training in reading aloud, adding the rhythms and styles appropriate to the "voice" of the text. Given the absence of punctuation in the manuscripts of Paul's time, a reader's task was heavily interpretive; kola and kommata had to be inferred and then performed. "The very concept of a paragraph or a chapter is foreign to Paul's way of writing and obscures his rhetoric. Paul wrote in dialogical exchanges, ring compositions, transitional false conclusions and rejections, various rhetorical figures, speech-in-character [prosopopoieia] and so on" (*A Rereading of Romans*, 11). To these background patterns may be added the Jewish prophetic traditions, which had rich arsenals of rebuke, judgment, exhortation, and "anti-rhetorical" speeches about speech. Yehoshua Gitay's recent work on the rhetoric of prophetic discourses in the Hebrew Scriptures identifies counterparts to the *epitaphios logos* in the "anti-rhetorical" speeches in Ezra and Jonah. Gitay defines and defends rhetorical purposes and effects of prophetic discourses, and questions many of the genre categories such as diatribe and invective that have been imported to deal with them; Yehoshua Gitay, "A Designed Anti-Rhetorical Speech: Ezra and the Question of Mixed Marriage," *JNSL* 23/2 (1997): 57–68; idem, "The Projection of the Prophet: A Rhetorical Presentation of the Prophet Jeremiah," in *Prophecy and Prophets: The Diversity of Contemporary Issues in Scholarship* (ed. Yehoshua Gitay; Atlanta, Ga.: Scholars Press/SBL Semeia Studies, 1997), 41–55; idem, "The Realm of Prophetic Rhetoric," in *Rhetoric, Scripture and Theology* (ed. Stanley E. Porter and Thomas H. Olbricht; JSNTSup 131 (Sheffield: Sheffield Academic Press, 1996), 218–29.

of Paul's multiple voices, diversity of doctrines and shifts in tone, rhetorical studies can now attend to the related diversity of Paul's audiences, including different groups within the audiences of individual letters. Many of the audiences could have been familiar with the practice of *prosopopoieia* — taking on the voice, character, and style of another person — even if they had never learned it as a precept. Conversely, rhetorical studies can learn much about the compositional practice of classical *prosopopoieia* by observing the rich infusion of Old Testament terms and phrases, concepts, and quotations, that Paul weaves through his discourses, placing them alongside Gentile doctrines of law and wisdom, conscience and obedience, love and language.

As I sketch readings of Romans and 1 Corinthians that can compass these themes, I shall also suggest that Paul's teachings on immoral, divisive, empty, and unloving speaking in Romans and 1 Corinthians can be used, if we are willing, to interrogate and reform contemporary theories and practices of rhetoric in biblical studies. We employ rhetoric to read Paul. How can Paul's letters illuminate our understanding of how our own rhetoric works, and assist in assessing contemporary rhetorical theories?

Roman Educations: Rhetoric in Paul's Letter to the Romans

Romans shares a number of terms with the judicial and deliberative rhetorical lexicon of the time, just as it is shaped by the similarly hair-splitting definitional discourses of Torah exegetes. One of its major subjects is law and legal argumentation, including dialectical investigations of religious and cultural identity: Who is a Jew? Who is a Gentile? Who is saved and how? What law should be followed? Because it addresses standard topics in both Jewish and classical rhetorical legal argumentation, Romans is an especially inviting object of rhetorical analysis. What level of education in rhetorical precepts or practice can we observe in the implied audience for Romans? How is a non-homogeneous audience directly addressed and appealed to in the text? Or is this addressed to a largely homogeneous audience as an example of how to address a more divided community? How many different educational and cultural backgrounds are suggested by the terms and forms of address used in the letter? What can the diversity of the audience for Romans help us understand about the content and development of themes in the letter?

In his initial salutation, Paul uses the familiar Greek distinction between Hellene and Barbarian (any non-Greek speaker): "I am debtor both to Greeks and to Barbarians, both to the wise and to the foolish" (Rom 1:14). Traditionally, the Greek is proud not to be a barbarian, just as the Jew is proud to be non-Gentile. But the flattery implicit in these conventional forms of salutation are undermined immediately: "Claiming to be wise, they became fools" (1:22). At least a portion of the audience is conversant with the Hebrew scriptural traditions of law, prophets, and specific textual passages that Paul invokes at different points. Allusions to non-Jews outside of the immediate Roman audience: all nations, the impending visit to Spain, suggest a teacherly mode of instruction and exhortation. As a whole, the letter admonishes Jews and non-Jews who are believers in Jesus to adopt a definition of themselves as being of one body, despite their diversity, and of one salvation based upon faith beyond any extant understandings of law (Jewish) or conscience (Gentile).

In addressing law, Romans turns to a series of discourses concerning legal language, including illegal and immoral uses of language and speech. In its conclusion, Romans effects a rhetorically powerful repudiation of law and argument: they shall be replaced by faith founded upon love. Through splicing, paradox, exegesis, and redefinition, Paul converts a range of concepts of law, justice, justification, and conscience that were held by Jews and Gentiles. Exhorting the community to be one in the Spirit, Romans juxtaposes a series of key terms that develop the themes of the letter as a whole: γράμμα, πνεῦμα, νόμος, ἀνομία, ἀδικία, πάθος, πείθω, among others. Redefining wisdom (σοφία) — emphasized in pairings as a "Greek" trait or value — and righteousness (δικία) — a "Jewish" trait — the discussion cumulatively develops meanings for grace/gifts of grace (χάρισμα) and conscience (συνείδησις) that are reworked throughout the letter in different contexts. Many short versions of the definitions could easily have been excerpted as maxims or precepts. Cumulatively, they form a series of paradoxes that would lead to further reflection, much as do the parables and beatitudes of Jesus. "When Gentiles, who do not possess the law, do instinctively what the law requires, these, though not having the law, are a law unto themselves. They show that what the law requires is written on their hearts, to which their own conscience also bears witness" (Rom 2:14–15). "For just as by one man's disobedience the many were made sinners, so by the one man's obedience the many will be made righteous. But law came in, with the result that the trespass multiplied; but where sin increased, grace abounded all the more" (Rom 5:19–20).

Conscience (συνείδησις) is presented as the Gentile counterpart to the Jewish law; both are interrogated, in a series of dialogical legal arguments, including paradoxes and preacherly invectives, concluding with a long list of teachings that splice together teachings on law from the Jewish and what would then have been early Jesus traditions. Secular notions of dues and tribute are combined with portions of the Ten Commandments, sayings from Jewish wisdom traditions, what we now know as the Lord's prayer, and segments from what are now known as the Gospels. In Paul's time, we presume, many of these combinations did not exist in the written forms that we know them: " 'You shall not murder; You shall not steal; You shall not covet,' and any other commandments are summed up in this word, namely, 'Love your neighbor as yourself.' Love does no wrong to a neighbor; therefore, love is the fulfilling of the law" (Rom 13:6–10). Love, divine and human, supersedes all laws. Accept your ministers, obey them; do not dispute among yourselves. Do not boast or malign others; do not take foolish pride in your obedience to the law of the old covenant, but rather be of good faith confident in your salvation.

Although Romans as a whole can be arranged in its entirety as an argument structured along classical rhetorical lines, it is ripe for reconsideration as an amalgam of forms and genres that, aligned with its topics, can be viewed as saying the same thing(s) in several different ways for a diverse audience.[7] Like speeches preserved in Plato's and Cicero's Dialogues, and later declamation models taught in progymnasmata, such speeches would have been read aloud, heard and "learned" in a primarily oral milieu. Similarly, in composing letters intended to be read aloud, Paul was not just propounding doctrine; he was simultaneously modeling a new vocabulary, formulating new modes of discourse, and forging proclamatory genres congregations could use in their discussions with each other and in their work of spreading the gospel.

The rhetorical role played by Romans, thus understood, very probably borrows from then-current practices of *prosopopoieia* in presenting a number of alternate voices and styles that could be learned, excerpted, and adapted in speaking to audiences with the same diversity as that of the community at Rome. The strong rebukes directed against infighting, malicious and dissembling speech, and legalistic segregation further support the overall message: the group should overcome its infighting, constitute themselves as one body in the spirit, and go forth to practice and speak the gospel message of love guaranteed by the freely given gift of grace.

---

7. See Craig Kallendorf, *Epistle of St. Paul to the Romans* (Bryn Mawr Greek Commentaries; Bryn Mawr, Pa.: Thomas Library, Bryn Mawr College, 1991), for an example of the "matching" analysis that has been until recently the most common form of classical rhetorical analysis applied to biblical texts. George Kennedy's foundational work in this area is widely recognized. Anders Eriksson's work on 1 Corinthians provides this method of analysis along with several other forms of collateral rhetorical commentary. It is encouraging to see contextualized studies emphasizing levels and kinds of education in antiquity, and community-building models that contribute new understandings of the epideictic effects of Paul's letters even if some of their audiences did not understand them as epideictic.

Sundays and Cybele: Language and Love in Corinth

If the grand topos of Romans is love and law, in 1 Corinthians it is love and language. As it makes its way toward the elegant encomium in Chapter 13, 1 Corinthians incorporates beliefs, lore, and literature about divine and human love that had permeated Greek, and therefore Corinthian, communities for centuries. Thus it is possible to observe the degree to which Paul's teachings on love and language, and their relationship to one another, diverge significantly from popular secular beliefs then and now, and from the beliefs of other religions and cultures.

Among the paired, antithetical topics of 1 Corinthians are wisdom and foolishness, earthly versus heavenly treasures, gifts of the spirit, and love and speaking. Since the audience is Greek, it is tempting to examine the letter's treatment of speaking as a Christianized treatise on rhetoric, or alternately, as an early Christian rebuttal of Greek rhetoric. But 1 Corinthians may just as fruitfully be understood as a rebuke of a rival religious practice — the worship of Aphrodite, or Cybele — one which the Corinthians may not have seen as at all contradictory to Paul's teachings on divine and human love. The strong links established between love and speech, in positive and negative definitions, form the backbone of this letter's teachings, exhortations, and rebukes. That women were well-established celebrants in that liturgy provides yet another theme: Paul's treatment of marriage, hierarchy, obedience, and modesty. Concluding a long, logical argument defining God as the head (κεφαλή) of man and man as the head of his wife: "Judge for yourselves: is it proper for a woman to pray to God with her head unveiled?" (1 Cor 11: 13). In attending to the issue of head covering, let us not slight the topic of women "praying," for the kind of liturgical language employed by women in the worship of Cybele, the very practice of liturgical speaking by women, is one of the implicit topics addressed in Paul's comments on speaking in relation to women's roles. This can be located as a subset of his definitions of speaking more generally throughout the letter: who should speak, in what spirit, and to what purpose?[8]

Like Romans, 1 Corinthians opens with references to Greeks and Jews,

---

8. For a rich range of readings of these issues see Margaret M. Mitchell, *Paul and the Rhetoric of Reconciliation: An Exegetical Investigation of the Language and Composition of 1 Corinthians* (Louisville: Westminster/John Knox, 1993); Antoinette C. Wire, *The Corinthian Women Prophets: A Reconstruction through Paul's Letters* (Minneapolis: Fortress, 1990); Elisabeth Schüssler Fiorenza, "Rhetorical Situation and Historical Reconstruction in 1 Corinthians," *NTS* 33 (1987): 386–403; and Anders Eriksson, "'Women Tongue Speakers, Be Silent': A Reconstruction Through Paul's Rhetoric," *BibInt* 6:1 (1998): 80–104. Eriksson provides a particularly illuminating discussion of the rhetoric of Paul's uses of *pneumatikos* and *lalein*.

wisdom and foolishness, the proclamation of the gospel contrasted to "eloquent wisdom, so that the cross of Christ might not be emptied of its power" (1:17). The topos of wisdom, however, is worked through at more length here than in the opening passages of Romans, possibly because sophia is the virtue valued above all others by the Greeks. Even their worship of love is subordinated by many to the notion of a love of knowledge. Let us read Paul's comments in that context, and as a backdrop for Augustine's subsequent teachings on eloquence versus wisdom. At 1:19 and following, Paul lambasts several kinds of wisdom, with direct reference to scribes and debaters, among other evil wordsmiths.

> For it is written,
>
> > "I will destroy the wisdom of the wise,
> > and the discerning of the discerning I will thwart."
>
> Where is the one who is wise? Where is the scribe? Where is the debater of this age? Has not God made foolish the wisdom of this world? For since in the wisdom of God, the world did not know God through wisdom, God decided, through the foolishness of our proclamation, to save those who believe. For Jews demand signs, and Greeks demand wisdom: but we proclaim (κήρυγμα) Christ crucified, a stumbling block to Jews, and foolishness (μωρία) to Gentliles (1:19–23).

Continuing the repudiation of human wisdom and the clever speech of this world and its "disputers," Paul begins 1 Corinthians 2, like Socrates' self-defense as recounted in Plato's *Apology*, with an anti-rhetorical *epitaphios logos:* "When I came to you, brothers and sisters, I did not come proclaiming the mystery of God to you in lofty words or wisdom.... My speech and my proclamation were not with plausible words of wisdom but with a demonstration of the Spirit and of power, so that your faith might rest not on human wisdom but on the power of God" (2:1–4).

Subsequent chapters develop variations on these themes: preaching, wisdom and witness, preaching the gospel and living the gospel, a variant on the logos-ergon topos that would be familiar to most Greeks. "If I proclaim the gospel, this gives me no ground for boasting, for an obligation (ἀνάγκη) is laid on me; and woe is to me if I do not proclaim the gospel" (9:16). Although New Testament philologists have argued that ἀνάγκη does not denote "fate" in the New Testament, it seems equally plausible that here as in other passages Paul is combining concepts and terms familiar to a Greek audience with phrasings consonant with Old Testament prophetic discourse, such as "woe to me." The longstanding Greek meaning of ἀνάγκη as fate/necessity would not have been wholly unfamiliar to the Corinthian audience. To what ends does Paul use it in this passage, with what hoped-for effect? That is the rhetorical question, and a question directed at his methods of preaching and conversion as well. Can he convert the extant understanding of "fate" or "compulsion" to instruct the Corinthian audience in how different their ways of understanding, speaking, spirit, and love are from the spirit and truth he is preaching, expressly without artifice, without "wisdom," yet accepting of an obligation wholly unlike Greek ἀνάγκη?

1 Corinthians brings these themes to a crescendo in its centerpiece and best-known chapter. Speaking in the tongues of men or of angels, without love, is like the sounding brasses and tinkling cymbals of empty worship, mere echoes. Χαλκός, κύμβαλος — the brass instruments used in Jewish and Cybele/Aphrodite liturgies alike, ἠχηεω — sound, roar, echo, speech empty of meaning. The emphasis however, rests resoundingly on speaking, language, knowledge, and even wisdom that are empty of love. Regardless of how beautiful, persuasive, wise, and in today's terms, "scientifically correct" or "politically correct" a given discourse is, it is forever without another kind of truth because it is not uttered in and through and for love. What is such love? What kind of love is this? Paul's definitions invite comparison with the doctrines of love that were current in the worship of Cybele at that time, in the celebration of the mysteries, and among competing Christian and Jewish measures of faith. Might we also ask how 1 Corinthians measures our own scholarly claims to faith, understanding, and knowledge? "If I have prophetic powers, and understand all mysteries, and all knowledge, and if I have all faith, so as to remove mountains, but do not have love, I am nothing" (13:2). These strong antitheses amplify the definition of love and speaking that take up much of the letter. Once again we can observe paradox and "diatribe" — dialectical investigations of the same topics in different voices, styles, and terms.

Greeks had long discussed love and speech; speech as the vehicle of love; eros, logos, and pathos; the beguiling sweet words of persuasive and rhetorical speech. Sappho praises Peitho as: "Aphrodite's daughter, / it is she who beguiles our mortal hearts."[9] The difference between divine and human love takes up much of the discussion in Plato's *Symposium;* impersonating the Priestess Diotima, Socrates dons the prophetess's veil as he recites — prosopopoetically — her teachings regarding divine and human love. The speeches preserved in Plato's dialogues repeatedly compare love with divine and human madness as well, asking if the speech of orators is of divine or human origin. The topoi of divine and human love, speech, and madness in

---

9. Sappho, Fragments 86, 90, in *Sappho, Poems and Fragments* (trans. Josephine Balmer; Secaucus, N.J.: Meadowland, 1988).

several guises — Aphrodite, Eros, *peitho,* pathos — had been standard topics, tropes for centuries in Greek literary culture. A close comparison of Paul's cumulative, dialectical definition of love in 1 Corinthians with these contextual sources, and particularly with the Hymn to Aphrodite that was central to the rites of Cybele, can further illuminate the subtle shifts in meaning away from eros and seduction and toward agape and volitional faith embodied in loving speech: though I speak with... and have not love.

Recent studies have emphasized that the way in which Paul builds upon Greek terms for an understanding of love is especially interesting given the prominence of women liturgists, not only in the Corinthian "church" but also in Corinthian veneration of Cybele and in relation to the gender of Cybele/Aphrodite as the Greek personification of love and object of worship. Can we glimpse a bit of humor in his bombastic repudiations of Greek liturgies of love in its own terms? "Love never ends. But as for prophecies, they will come to an end; as for tongues, they will cease, as for knowledge, it will come to an end" (13:8). The rhetoric of love, the love of rhetoric, and the renunciation of human love and rhetoric in the service of divine love: an inquiry into these themes of 1 Corinthians is far from concluded in our rhetorical hermeneutics, or in our scholarly customs, purposes, and praxis.[10]

---

10. Fiorenza ("Rhetorical," 387) proposes that we can improve our understanding of rhetoric as it "seeks to instigate a change of attitudes and motivations, it strives to persuade, to teach, and to engage the reader-hearer by eliciting reactions, emotions, convictions, and identifications. The evaluative criteria for rhetoric is not aesthetics, but praxis."

Wuellner defines expanded goals for the praxis of new rhetorical studies that focus on ethics and community building: "(1) The theoretical securing of the re-integration of the performative, pragmatic, applicative with the structural, semantic, and interpretive in exegetical work on texts. (2) The long overdue consciousness of the rhetorical character, and thereby the ethical and political responsibility, of all scientific work" ("The Pre-Christian Paul and Rhetoric," unpublished ms. 1994, personal correspondence via David Hester, 18). He concludes: "Our legitimations take place not only in the forum of scholarly organizations on national and international levels, but also in the forum of concurring arenas of our respective cultures and their claims to truth" (18). Calling for the ethical and political responsibility of hermeneutics itself asks each reader and each reading to place itself in a setting that is made clear at the outset.

In this spirit, my readings of Romans and 1 Corinthians provide a sketch, and an example, of composite rhetorical readings drawing on philology, lexicon, argumentative structure, rhetorical genre, social context, and religious practices in Paul's time, concluding with an identification of thematic and ethical values that link past and present audiences'/communities' receptions of religious rhetoric.

CHAPTER 15

ENTHYMEMES IN PAULINE ARGUMENTATION: READING BETWEEN THE LINES IN 1 CORINTHIANS

Anders Eriksson

The study of rhetorical argumentation is for many rhetorical critics tantamount to the study of enthymemes.[1] This venerable tradition goes back to Aristotle. In his treatises on logic he gave primary importance to the syllogism and he made the enthymeme, understood as the rhetorical syllogism, the cornerstone of his rhetorical system. He starts his *Rhetoric* by complaining that other teachers of rhetoric "say nothing about enthymemes, which is the 'body' of persuasion [σῶμα τῆς πίστεως]."[2] Aristotle's assertion that argumentation is concerned with enthymemes has been deemed a correct insight by those critics who have used the enthymeme in their own rhetorical analysis.

The enthymeme is studied in a number of disciplines. In her recent bibliography on the enthymeme, Carol Poster includes books and articles in fields as diverse as logic and philosophy, speech communication, composition studies, psychology, politics, literature, film, and music, as well as 35 theses.[3] Interest in the enthymeme comes and goes in various disciplines. Sometimes the interest wanes after a period of intense study. Judging from the exasperated comment from a panelist at the CCCC in Atlanta 1999, "Not another paper on the enthymeme," this is presently the case in composition studies.[4]

It seems, however, that the time for the study of the enthymeme has come

---

1. So Thomas Conley, "The Enthymeme in Perspective," *QJS* 70 (1984): 168.
2. Aristotle, *Rhet.*, 1.1.3[1354a]. Translation from George Kennedy, *Aristotle on Rhetoric: A Theory of Civic Discourse* (New York: Oxford University Press, 1991), 30.
3. *The Enthymeme: An Interdisciplinary Bibliography of Critical Studies,* available online at http://rhetjournal.uor.edu.
4. "Why Does It Matter That Classical Rhetoric Has Disappeared from CCCC?" Panel F.14, March 25, 1999 Conference on College Composition and Communication.

to New Testament interpretation. Through his keynote address at the London conference 1995, Vernon Robbins has given a strong impetus to the serious study of enthymemes. The reason the search for enthymemes is so important is that it shows the social and cultural nature of the reasoning in the text, it becomes "a gateway into early Christianity as a social and cultural movement during the first century."[5] Enthymemic analysis holds the promise of a rhetoric re-valued and reinvented in which the text must reveal its context. In the words of Wilhelm Wuellner, such rhetoric takes us to "the social aspect of language which is an instrument of communication and influence on others."[6]

Robbins has developed the role of enthymemes as a part of the argumentative texture of a text in *Exploring the Texture of Texts,* and *The Tapestry of Early Christian Discourse,* as well as articles studying enthymemes in specific texts.[7] Greg Bloomquist has incisively shown the importance of this new serious study of enthymemes, and the enthymeme has become a lively topic on our group's listserv Rhetoric-L.[8] At previous conferences, several papers have been devoted to the enthymeme.[9] This paper is a result of a promise made three years ago to contribute a listing of all the enthymemes in 1 Corinthians in a database listing all the enthymemes in the New Testament.[10]

---

5. Vernon K. Robbins, "The Present and Future of Rhetorical Analysis," in *The Rhetorical Analysis of Scripture: Essays from the 1995 London Conference* (ed. Stanley Porter and Tom Olbricht; JSNTSup 146; Sheffield: Sheffield Academic Press, 1997), 35–36.

6. "Where is Rhetorical Criticism Taking Us?" *CBQ* 49 (1987): 449. Wuellner quotes Chaim Perelman and Lucie Olbrechts-Tyteca, *The New Rhetoric: A Treatise on Argumentation* (Notre Dame, Ind.: University of Notre Dame Press, 1969), 513.

7. *Exploring the Texture of Texts: A Guide to Socio-Rhetorical Interpretation* (Valley Forge, Pa.: Trinity Press International, 1996); *The Tapestry of Early Christian Discourse: Rhetoric, Society and Ideology* (London: Routledge, 1996); "From Enthymeme to Theology in Luke 11:1–13," in *Literary Studies in Luke-Acts: A Collection of Essays in Honor of Joseph B. Tyson* (ed. R. P. Thompson and T. E. Phillips; Macon, Ga.: Mercer University Press, 1998), 191–214; "Enthymemic Texture in the Gospel of Thomas," *1998 SBLSP* (Atlanta: Scholars Press, 1998): 343–66.

8. "The Place of Enthymemes in Argumentative Texture," unpublished paper at the Rhetorical Pre-Session at the 1997 SBL in San Francisco. The Rhetoric-L can be found online at *http://groups.yahoo.com/group/rhetoric-L*.

9. In Florence 1998 the following papers dealt with enthymemes: L. Gregory Bloomquist, "A Possible Direction for Providing Programmatic Correlation of Textures in Socio-rhetorical Analysis: Who Could Ask for Anything More?"; Marc Debanné, "An Enthymemic Reading of Philippians: Towards a Typology of Pauline Arguments"; and Anders Eriksson, "Contrary Arguments in Paul." The papers will be published in *Rhetorical Criticism and the Bible: Essays from the 1998 Florence Conference* (ed. Stanley E. Porter and Dennis Stamps; JSNTSup 195; Sheffield: Sheffield Academic Press, forthcoming).

10. Robbins envisaged such a database in his London address: "Once we have an exhibit of all the assertions (theses) and premises throughout the New Testament, we are on the doorstep of serious cultural analysis of early Christianity as it reveals itself to us through these early texts," "Present and Future," 34.

Defining the Enthymeme

What then is an enthymeme?[11] Aristotle defined an enthymeme as a rhetorical syllogism.[12] The difference between a syllogism in logic and in rhetoric is that in the former the premises are unquestionable truths, in the latter opinions shared by the audience, by Aristotle called ἔνδοξα.[13] This distinction has far-reaching implications. Enthymemes are not limited to the strict rules of logic; they are arguments in everyday life.

As human beings we produce arguments all the time. As my four-year-old daughter and I were looking through her window into the backyard, we saw two cats fighting and she produced the following enthymeme: "That cat must be a girl. She is kind. And girls are more kind than boys." In this enthymeme she concludes "the cat must be a girl," and she bases this conclusion on the observation that this particular striped cat is not as aggressive as the other cat: "She is kind." The argumentative link, which makes the logical inference possible, is the generalization: "Girls are more kind than boys."

Thomas Conley explains the logical reasoning in Aristotle's enthymeme as: 1) a claim made by the speaker; 2) evidence cited in support of it; and 3) the *protasis* or premise that links them together. Such an argumentative link can be found in the many *topoi* listed in rhetoric.[14] In his *Rhetoric* Aristotle presents common topics and special topics (1.2.21 [1358a]), the latter limited to a special subject matter. In 1.4 through 1.14 he presents the available *topoi* a speaker can rely upon in the deliberative, epideictic, and legal genres. In 2.2–11 he presents the *topoi* concerning emotions, and in 2.12–17 the *topoi* concerning the "ages and fortunes" of three kinds of people.[15] An important consequence of this understanding of Aristotle's enthymeme is that it is not

---

11. Carol Poster argues that the analytic copula in the definition ought to be interpreted as "ought to be" and that interpreters should specify how different thinkers have understood the enthymeme; "Being, Time, and Definition: Toward a Semiotics of Figural Rhetoric," in *Philosophy and Rhetoric* 33 (2000): 128–130. For various understandings of the enthymeme, see the contribution by Manfred Kraus in this volume, "Theories and Practice of the Enthymeme in the First Centuries B.C.E. and C.E.," 95–111, as well as his article "Enthymem," in *Historisches Wörterbuch der Rhetorik* 2 (ed. Gert Ueding; Tübingen: Niemeyer, 1994), 1197–1222.

12. *Rhet.*, 1.2.8 [1356b]; 2.24.1 [1400b37]. On Aristotle's enthymeme, see Jürgen Sprute, *Die Enthymemtheorie der aristotelischen Rhetorik* (Göttingen: Vandenhoeck & Ruprecht, 1982).

13. In *Top.*, 1.1 [100b] Aristotle defines these ἔνδοξα as the opinions "which commend themselves to all or to the majority or to the wise — that is, to all of the wise or to the majority or to the most famous and distinguished of them." Cf. *Rhet.*, 1.1.11[1355a].

14. So Paul Slomkowski, *Aristotle's Topics* (New York and Leiden: Brill, 1997), 43–67.

15. Thomas Conley, *Rhetoric in the European Tradition* (Chicago: University of Chicago Press, 1990), 15; James McBurney, "The Place of the Enthymeme in Rhetorical Theory," in *Aristotle: The Classical Heritage of Rhetoric* (ed. K. V. Erickson; Metuchen, N.J.: The Scarecrow Press, 1974), 117–40.

limited to "rational" argumentation, since it includes *ethos* and *pathos* as *topoi* for the construction of an enthymeme.

The understanding of the enthymeme has changed throughout history. The philosophical understanding of the enthymeme as a syllogism with a suppressed premise has been the dominating view, and the alternative understanding of the enthymeme as a syllogism based on probabilities has only recently come to the fore.[16] For the modern discussion in rhetorical criticism, Thomas Conley's important article "The Enthymeme in Perspective" has been pivotal, and in speech departments Stephen Toulmin's development of the enthymeme in six parts is widely used.[17]

For my analysis I have chosen the recent adaptation of the enthymeme by Peirce and Lanigan,[18] which Vernon Robbins has adopted for the analysis of enthymemes. In this adaptation, the conclusion to the argument is called the "Result," the evidence is called the "Case," and the argumentative link is called the "Rule." As a heuristic tool for analysis of texts, these terms are less rigid than the terms from Toulmin, and they allow for enthymemes with a looser logical structure.

Male and Female Cats

My daughter's comment when she saw the two fighting cats leads me to make some quick observations.

1. She does not know Aristotle's theory about enthymemes, but she still reasons in an enthymeme. The enthymeme is a universal mode of human expression in argumentation. Finding enthymemes in actual discourse has very little to do with whether the speakers in the discourse know the theory about enthymemes. Ever since Hans Dieter Betz's important commentary on Galatians,[19] which for many interpreters introduced rhetoric into New Testament exegesis, it has been unclear whether rhetoric is the tool used for analysis or the object for the study. Rhetoric can be defined both as cultural conventions in the ancient Mediterranean world and as a theoretical tool for analysis of human communication. Historical critics are often so accustomed to assess parallels that for them the tool and the object are sometimes hard to separate, whereas rhetorical critics usually see rhetoric as a tool

---

16. Edward Madden, "The Enthymeme: Crossroads of Logic, Rhetoric, and Metaphysics," *The Philosophical Review* 61 (1952): 368–76.

17. *The Uses of Argument* (Cambridge: Cambridge University Press, 1958).

18. Richard Lanigan, "From Enthymeme to Abduction: The Classical Law of Logic and the Postmodern Rule of Rhetoric," in *Recovering Pragmatism's Voice: The Classical Tradition, Rorty, and the Philosophy of Communication* (ed. L. Langsdorf and A. R. Smith; Albany, N.Y.: SUNY Press, 1995), 49–70.

19. Hans Dieter Betz, *Galatians: A Commentary on Paul's Letter to the Churches in Galatia* (Hermeneia; Philadelphia: Fortress Press, 1979).

for analysis. As an analytical tool, Aristotle's understanding of human communication expressed in the enthymeme can be used for analysis of human communication in different cultures and different times.[20]

2. The enthymeme does not necessarily contain a suppressed premise. Hanna spelled out the argumentative link as: "Girls are more kind than boys." She could of course have left this unstated, since the enthymeme is the result of the "joint efforts of the speaker and audience."[21] I would have understood her anyway, since I am well aware of her social context. In my analysis of Paul's enthymemes in 1 Corinthians I have found that often all three parts of the enthymeme are expressed, albeit sometimes in rudimentary form.

3. Hanna started with the result of her reasoning: "That cat must be a girl." This is often the case in human reasoning. After an assertion we give the reasons why the conclusion is true. George Kennedy comments that this mode of arguing also has influenced Aristotle's expressions in the *Rhetoric*. "In Aristotle's own writing enthymemes often take the form of a statement followed by a clause introduced by the Greek particle *gar*, which gives a supporting reason or sometimes a corollary."[22]

4. My fourth observation is that in Hanna's enthymeme the reason from the observed case was not signaled by a hypotactic particle. She just said: "She is kind." When I first started looking for enthymemes, I thought they were ordinarily marked by hypotactic particles like γάρ, οὖν, ὅτι and ὥστε. Sometimes these particles are present in enthymemes, but not always. The paratactic style typical of oral culture does not necessarily lack rhetorical argumentation. Enthymemes in 1 Corinthians are not always signaled by hypotactic particles. Besides the particles stated above, the interpreter should look for clauses introduced with ἵνα and ὅπως, which often introduce the result of the reasoning, as well as conditional sentences which often contain an enthymeme with a suppressed rule (the protasis forms the case and the apodosis the result).

5. Enthymemes are true only for those audiences who accept the underlying premises. Hanna's big brother rejects the conclusion because he rejects the premise that "girls are kinder than boys," but for Hanna this premise is a truth gained from hard experience at pre-school. We might add that she is not the only one holding this premise. We sometimes hear that the world would be a much better place if there were not so many men in ruling positions. The premise in such reasoning seems to be the inherent evil of the patriarchy.

6. The truth of an enthymeme must be distinguished from the validity of the reasoning in it. Hanna's enthymeme is logically valid, the conclusion follows from the premises. Her brother David however questions the premises in saying: "just because you see two cats fighting it does not mean than one is male and the other female." In this he is absolutely correct. But in real life the enthymeme has proven to be true: we have been offered kittens from that striped "girl."

---

20. It can be universalized, so George Kennedy, *New Testament Interpretation through Rhetorical Criticism* (Chapel Hill: University of North Carolina, 1984), 10.

21. Lloyd Bitzer, "Aristotle's Enthymeme Revisited," in *Aristotle: The Classical* Heritage of *Rhetoric* (ed. K. V. Erickson; Metuchen, N.J.: The Scarecrow Press, 1974), 150, 152.

22. Kennedy, *Aristotle On Rhetoric*, xii.

Procedure for Finding Enthymemes

Enthymemes are only found in argumentative texts. A speaker or writer may assert things without giving reasons for them, such texts are declarative and not argumentative. But as soon as the speaker gives reasons for the ideas he or she engages in argumentation and tries to persuade the audience. The first step in finding enthymemes is therefore to look for assertions and rationales. Usually, but not always, the assertion comes before the rationale.

The next step is to find the argumentative link, which makes the rationale a support for this particular assertion. In Peirce's terminology the argumentative link is the rule which warrants the particular result drawn from the case.[23] The rule is sometimes suppressed. The rules in 1 Corinthians are derived from a number of different *topoi*. Some enthymemes build on common topics like "What applies to the whole applies to all of its parts." Other enthymemes build on special topics. Some special topics are cultural conventions from the ancient Mediterranean world, others are specific beliefs in the early church,[24] in socio-rhetorical interpretation known as "ideology" but more commonly known as "theology."

Typical components of the enthymemes in 1 Corinthians are analogies, examples, comparisons, contraries, and written testimonies. These components are the building blocks used for the elaboration of the *chreia* in the *progymnasmata* and they can be found at various places in the enthymeme. An example from real life can function as a case, but so can also written testimonies in the form of quotations from the Hebrew Bible (1 Cor 2:9). Quotations can also function as rules (1 Cor 3:19, 20).

Enthymemes are often found on a text's micro-level, comprising a sentence or two. Sometimes enthymemes can be linked together so that the same rule applies to a variety of cases. If there is similarity between the cases, there will also be similarity between the results; but if there is dissimilarity between the cases one should expect dissimilarity in the results as well. Alternative cases and hypothetical cases are found next to the original case. Often a contrary lies behind the reasoning in such cases.[25]

Several subordinated enthymemes can support the same point or main assertion in an enthymeme on a higher argumentative level. When analyzing enthymemes the interpreter must be careful to separate the various levels

---

[23]. For a discussion of Peirce's understanding of the rules of rhetorical argumentation, see Bloomquist, "A Possible Direction," 13–26.

[24]. Anders Eriksson, "Special Topics in 1 Corinthians 8–10," in *The Rhetorical Interpretation of Scripture: Essays from the 1996 Malibu Conference* (ed. Stanley E. Porter and Dennis L. Stamps; Sheffield: Sheffield Academic Press, 1999): 272–76.

[25]. See Eriksson, "Contrary Arguments in Paul."

from one another. A special problem is that a statement can shift place in successive enthymemes. What was a "result" in one enthymeme can become the "rule" in the next. This occurs when something has been established in one enthymeme, which is then used as the basis for the next line of reasoning. This is called a *sorites*.

Enthymemes in 1 Corinthians

Enthymemes in the Thanksgiving Section, 1 Corinthians 1:4–9

It is sometimes maintained that the thanksgiving section of a letter is not suitable for a rhetorical analysis. Two reasons for this can be given. One is a vestige from the eighties, when many interpreters attempted to cut off epistolary introductions and conclusions, which should be studied with epistolography, before the remaining part of the letter could be studied with the help of rhetoric.[26] A second reason is that many interpreters do not expect to find rhetorical argumentation in the thanksgiving section of a letter.

In 1 Corinthians 1:4 we find Paul asserting that he gives thanks to God for the Corinthians. The assertion is followed by a rationale; the reason Paul gives thanks is that they have been given the grace of God. This rationale in its turn is supported by a statement, which specifies that the grace of God has been manifested in speech and knowledge. The assertion forms the result in the enthymeme and the rationale the case. The rule is suppressed and must be gathered from the context.

RESULT: "I give thanks to my God always for you (1:4a)

CASE: because of the grace of God that has been given you in Christ Jesus" (1:4b),

SUPPORT: "for in every way you have been enriched in him,
in speech and knowledge of every kind" (1:5)

[RULE: Thanks are due the giver of gifts]

As typical for enthymemes the conclusion or result comes first in this text. The case or rationale is taken from the experience of the Corinthians. The supporting statement in 1:5 is signaled by ὅτι. The suppressed rule, that a receiver of a gift (and his friend) are obliged to thank the giver of the gift, is

---

26. This opinion is due to the dominance of the historical-critical paradigm, which sees rhetoric primarily as cultural conventions, not as a theory about human communication. For a critique, see Dennis L. Stamps, "Rhetorical Criticism of the New Testament: Ancient and Modern Evaluations of Argumentation," in *Approaches to New Testament Studies* (ed. Stanley E. Porter and David Tombs; Sheffield: Sheffield Academic Press, 1995), 157–65.

a topic taken from cultural conventions in the ancient Mediterranean world. In socio-rhetorical interpretation such a topic is classified as a "Common social and cultural topic" and belongs to the social and cultural texture of a text.[27]

This enthymeme naturally leads into the next, in which Paul asserts that the Corinthians "are not lacking in any spiritual gift." This assertion forms the result in the enthymeme and is signaled by the hypotactic particle ὥστε. It is supported by a rationale taken from the Corinthians' own experience: "the testimony of Christ has been strengthened among you." The rationale is the case in the enthymeme.

> CASE: "just as the testimony of Christ has been strengthened among you," (1:6)—
>
> RESULT: "so that you are not lacking in any spiritual gift
> as you wait for the revealing of our Lord Jesus Christ" (1:7).
>
> [RULE: When Christ is strengthened among you his spiritual gifts will be shown]

In this line of reasoning the rule is suppressed. We can infer that Paul has in mind the idea: "when Christ is strengthened among you his spiritual gifts will be shown." As to formal validity we could say that this is an argument based on the common topic that what applies to the whole also applies to all of its parts. Behind that we find a theological content where Christians' participation in Christ is presupposed, as well as the idea that such participation includes spiritual gifts.

The rendering of the next verse with a result clause in the NRSV might point to an implicit enthymeme,[28] but I see the latter part of the verse as more declarative than argumentative. The next assertion supported with a rationale is instead Paul's claim that God is faithful in 1:9. What rationale do the Corinthians and Paul have for claiming that God is faithful? The evidence adduced is taken from the Corinthians' own experience. It forms the case in the enthymeme.

> RESULT: "God is faithful" (1:9);
>
> CASE: "by him you were called into the fellowship of his Son, Jesus Christ our Lord."
>
> [RULE: God's calling supports his faithfulness]

Implicit in this line of reasoning is a belief that God's calling supports his faithfulness. Paul could probably rely on his Corinthian converts' acceptance of this premise. Election is a strong theme in the Hebrew Bible and for the

---

27. Robbins, *Tapestry*, 159–66.
28. Such an enthymeme would lead us to ask in what way God's strength makes believers "blameless on the day of our Lord Jesus Christ" (1:8).

early Christians God's faithfulness to his promises was shown by his calling of both Jews and Gentiles.

The three enthymemes above are fairly evident, and similar exegetical results can be reached without recourse to technical rhetorical terminology. My claim is that an analysis of the enthymemes in a text is a helpful tool for discovering the reasoning in a text, and especially the premises upon which this reasoning builds. The rules above are grounded in general logic, cultural conventions, and specifically Christian beliefs.

Implied Premises about Women in 1 Corinthians 11:2–16

The exegetical yield might be greater when we analyze controversial passages, usually considered to be problems of interpretation. One such passage is 1 Corinthians 11:2–16, where Paul's argument is derived from the key *topos* of headship drawn from the order of creation in Genesis 2 and a dissociation between men and women many of us today find objectionable.

The references to creation permeate the whole argument. The main *topos* can be phrased as "parent-child" or "begetter-begotten."[29] Head, κεφαλή, can be interpreted both as authority or source, but the two figurative uses become inseparable. To be the source or progenitor puts one in the place of authority. God is the "progenitor" of Christ, who is the firstborn of creation. Christ is the "progenitor" of man (Adam), from whom woman comes. Paul lays down this premise in 11:3: "Christ is the head of every man, and the husband is the head of his wife, and God is the head of Christ." That Paul here has Genesis 2 in mind is strengthened by the allusions in 11:8–9. We can summarize the argument as follows:

> RULE: *Topos* of headship drawn from creational order in Genesis 2.
>
> CASE: since man is the head of woman (11:3)
>
> RESULT: she should honor her head by wearing the head covering (11:4)

That heads should be honored is implied in the rule. The case is spelled out in 11:3 and the result for women in 11:5 and 11:10. That the particular type of honoring of heads Paul is talking about is a head covering is dependent on cultural conventions, which saw the head covering as a protection from the lust of men and a respectable status symbol.

In the next line of reasoning, the result above becomes the basis for two contrary rules for men and women.

---

29. I am thankful for comments by Rodney Duke at this point.

> RULE FOR MEN: "Any man who prays or prophesies
> with something on his head disgraces his head" (11:4)
>
> RULE FOR WOMEN: "but any woman who prays or prophesies
> with her head unveiled disgraces her head
> — it is one and the same thing as having her head shaved" (11:5)

These rules make a dissociation between men and women.[30] Women are seen not just as subordinate to men but as the contrary to men: what applies to men does not apply to women and vice versa.

Paul's argumentation continues with two alternative cases in which the rule for women in 11:5 should be supplied. The first case shows disagreement with the rule, the second agreement.

> CONTRARY CASE: "For if a woman will not veil herself"
>
> RESULT: "then she should cut off her hair"
>
> CASE 2: "but if it is disgraceful for a woman to have her hair cut off or to be shaved"
>
> RESULT 2: "she should wear a veil" (11:6)

It is presupposed that both behaviors are disgraceful for women; the argument rests on cultural conventions of honor and shame in the ancient Mediterranean world.

When elaborating on the behavior of men, Paul sees no need to clarify that the general rule about all men applies to each individual male prophet. It is evident that a male prophet does not need a head covering. Instead Paul proceeds with a supporting argument which establishes the rule.[31] The rule from 11:4 becomes the result in the next line of reasoning.

> RESULT: "For a man ought not to have his head veiled"
>
> CASE: "since he is the image and reflection of God" (11:7a, cf. 11:3)

To make this reasoning a complete enthymeme we will have to supply the unstated premise:

> [RULE: That which is the image and reflection of God does not need a veil].

This general statement seems strange and should probably not be understood as Paul's theological reflection on Genesis 1, but as an ideological underpinning of a contested premise. Since Paul needs to argue for the premise in 11:4, probably some rejected it. Theology arises out of controversy.

---

30. For dissociation as a general argumentative device, see Perelman and Olbrechts-Tyteca, *The New Rhetoric*, 411–59.

31. In Perelman's terminology this would be an argument which establishes the structure of reality, *The New Rhetoric*, 350–57.

Paul continues his argumentation with a curious twist of reasoning: an enthymeme in which just one member is clearly stated. This is a statement about women, which makes sense as a contrary case to what he has said about men.

CONTRARY CASE: "but woman is the reflection of man" (11:7b)

The implicit rule in this enthymeme is taken from contraries:

[RULE: Women are the contrary to men]

The implicit result then becomes:

[RESULT: Women are not the image and reflection of God]

If confronted with Genesis 1:26–27, Paul might have had to retract this implication (after all he never said it straight out), but the urgency of the issue and his reasoning in contraries leads him to give a theological justification to the conventional construction of gender.

The dichotomy Paul posits between men and women in this chain of arguments we would regard as a faulty premise — just because you see an aggressive cat it does not mean it is a male. As foreign as it might seem to us, it is a premise firmly based on ancient Mediterranean conceptions of gender.[32] Since the truth of an enthymeme depends on the audience accepting its premises, we can suspect that many in the Corinthian church would have accepted the conventional cultural role for women, even though others might have begun to see a new vision of equality in Christ. Such a new vision would have stirred the controversy.[33]

A Refutation in 1 Corinthians 8:7–13

As interpreters of argumentation in the New Testament we can have different opinions about how useful ancient categories are for our interpretation. For example, Lauri Thurén in his paper in this volume argues against the use of ancient rhetorical categories for interpretation.[34] I have argued that both ancient and modern conceptions of rhetoric, understood as a theory about human communication, can be used as analytical tools.[35] In this paper I use Peirce's

---

32. See Genevieve Lloyd, *The Man of Reason: "Male" and "Female" in Western Philosophy* (London: Routledge, 1993); and Anders Eriksson, "Women Tongue Speakers, Be Silent: A Reconstruction through Paul's Rhetoric," *Biblical Interpretation* 6 (1998): 80–104.

33. See Antoinette Wire, *The Corinthian Women Prophets: A Reconstruction through Paul's Rhetoric* (Minneapolis: Fortress Press, 1990).

34. "Is There Biblical Argumentation?" 77–92.

35. Anders Eriksson, *Traditions as Rhetorical Proof: Pauline Argumentation in 1 Corinthians* (ConBNT 29; Stockholm: Almqvist & Wiksell International, 1998), 23–24.

development of the enthymeme for my analysis. Since Latin is no longer the language for the scientific community, we might do well to use Peirce's label "rule" for Hanna's statement "Girls are kinder than boys" instead of the term *rationis confirmatio* used in Rhetorica ad Herennium 2.18.28 for the similar functional equivalent.[36] But there is also a sense in which, to quote Thurén, "it is not reasonable to replace ancient names for certain functional conventions with new labels as long as the former remain viable."[37] In the rhetorical canon of concepts I would like to retain the enthymeme and the various *topoi*.

The basic difference between myself and Thurén seems to be that he wants to "de-rhetorize" Paul to arrive at the theological core,[38] whereas I am more interested in analyzing the rhetorical interaction between author and audience in the original context. This historical interest leads me to be sensitive to the contextualized rhetoric of the early Christian movement. Rhetoric is not just a universalized theory about human (persuasive) communication. It is also a culture specific praxis. The ancient handbooks are both prescriptive, teaching how to write and speak, and descriptive, noting how people in the Hellenistic culture persuaded with words. Ancient conceptions of rhetoric therefore have a heuristic advantage compared to modern conceptions of rhetoric derived from our modern culture. Sharon Crowley also suggests that ancient conceptions of rhetoric have a heuristic advantage over modern conceptions in that they are not reduced to the Enlightenment view of rationality.[39] Rhetorical critics of the New Testament who are aware of rhetorical conventions in the ancient Mediterranean world have not failed to note the similarities, and the dissimilarities, between the rhetoric in the larger Hellenistic world and the rhetoric of the emerging Christian movement. It is a legitimate historical enterprise for the rhetorical critic of the New Testament to study the relationship between the two.

The different ways in which a speaker could present a thesis and support it with evidence were well known in ancient rhetorical theory. Cicero combines the Aristotelian and the Stoic theories of the enthymeme in his presentation of the fivefold syllogistic pattern called the *ratiocinatio* in which the major

---

36. One can also use Toulmin's term "warrant" or Aristotle's term "major premise" for this rhetorical function.

37. Lauri Thurén, *The Rhetorical Strategy of 1 Peter: With Special Regard to Ambiguous Expressions* (Åbo: Åbo Akademis Förlag, 1990), 54.

38. *Derhetorizing Paul: A Dynamic Perspective on Pauline Theology and the Law* (Harrisburg, Pa.: Trinity Press International, 2000). In this book Thurén uses ancient rhetorical categories for his analysis.

39. Sharon Crowley, *The Methodical Memory: Invention in Current-Traditional Rhetoric* (Carbondale: Southern Illinois University Press, 1990), 1–14.

and the minor premises were supported by separate proofs.⁴⁰ A more widely used pattern was the complete argument in which a thesis (*propositio*) is presented, supported with a reason (*ratio*), which in turn is supported by the proof of the reason (*rationis confirmatio*). The latter "corroborates by means of additional arguments the briefly presented reason."⁴¹

The Hellenistic schools taught their students various ways of presenting a thesis and how to support it with arguments. In the elaboration of a *chreia*, in the elementary rhetorical exercises called the *progymnasmata*, a student was taught to expand a thesis with arguments from the contrary, analogy, example, and authoritative witness.⁴² This pattern of elaboration is also found in the amplification of a theme in the *Rhetorica ad Herennium* 4.44.57–58.

1. The theme is expressed simply
2. The reason is added
3. The theme is expressed in a new form, with, or without, the reasons
4. The argument from the contrary
5. The argument by comparison
6. The argument from example
7. The conclusion

When we compare Paul's argumentation in 1 Corinthians 8:7–13 with the elaboration pattern found in the *Rhetorica ad Herennium*, we note certain similarities:

1. Theme: Not all have this knowledge (v. 7a)
2. Reasons:

    a) For τινές accustomed to idols, eat ὡς εἰδωλόθυτον (v. 7b)

    b) The conflict caused by your slogans testify that not all have this knowledge (v. 8)

3. Restatement of the theme: Take care so that this liberty of yours does not somehow become a stumbling block to the weak (v. 9)

4. Argument from contrary: Your behavior when at table in an idol's temple contradicts the concern for the weaker brother (v. 10)

---

40. *Inv.*, 1.34.57–41.77. For a graphic description, see Frans van Eemeren et al., *Fundamentals of Argumentation Theory: A Handbook of Historical Backgrounds and Contemporary Developments* (Mahwah, N.J.: Lawrence Erlbaum Associates, 1996), 48–49. On the background see Kraus, "Enthymem," 1207.

41. *Rhet. Her.*, 2.18.28

42. See the *progymnasmata* by Hermogenes, 7.10–8.14 [Rabe], and Aphthonius, 4.12–6.19 [Rabe]. The elaboration pattern is the same for the maxim as well.

6. Argument from example: The tradition in v. 11b is applied to the Corinthians in a double enthymeme (v. 12)

7. Conclusion: Paul refraining to eat κρέα out of concern for the weaker brother is a personal example for them to follow (v. 13)[43]

The difference compared to the standard elaboration pattern is that Paul supplies two reasons but no argument from analogy.

In this chain of arguments Paul refutes the claim by some Corinthians that "we all have knowledge" (8:1).[44] Paul begins with the assertion that not everyone has this knowledge (8:7a). The assertion is supported by two cases, which show some Corinthians' lack of knowledge. In the first case Paul reminds the "wise," who claim that all have knowledge, that there are some "weak" who still eat food ὡς εἰδωλόθυτον, 8:7b. The first case is corroborated with a supporting enthymeme.

> RESULT: "It is not everyone, however, who has this knowledge" (8:7a)
>
> CASE 1: "Since some have become so accustomed to idols until now, they still think of the food they eat as food offered to an idol" (8:7b)
>
> [RULE: One exception invalidates a general claim]

The implicit rule is a common topic in logic.

> RESULT: "and their conscience,... is defiled"
>
> CASE: "being weak" (8:7c)
>
> [RULE: Action against conscience defiles a person]

In 8:8 Paul brings in a second case which gives yet another reason for the claim that "not all have this knowledge." There is strife in the Corinthian church about whether "food will bring us close to God"; whether "we are worse off if we do not eat"; and whether "we are better off if we eat." Some "wise" in the Corinthian church might have ascribed to this ideology, some "weak" did not. Paul disagrees with the slogans by negating them.[45]

> CASE 2: "Food will" NOT "bring us close to God"
> "We are worse off if we do not eat." NO, Paul inserts
> "and better off if we do." NO (8:8). Paul disagrees

---

43. Eriksson, *Traditions*, 160.

44. Noting the similarity between Paul's argumentation and contemporary modes I have called 1 Cor 8:7-13 a *refutatio;* Eriksson, *Traditions,* 152. Thurén uses the Toulminian term "rebuttal" for the whole passage, "Is There Biblical Argumentation," 88. He thereby uses the term in a different sense than Toulmin.

45. For this interpretation of 1 Cor 8:8, see Eriksson, *Traditions,* 161.

Their behavior shows that not all have the knowledge the "wise" among them claim "all" have.

A general result in one enthymeme can be specified and applied in the next. In my analysis of the enthymemes in 1 Corinthians I have called this an exhortative result or a result rephrased. The amplification of a theme in *Rhetorica ad Herennium*, 4.43.56 labels such a step a "theme expressed in a new form." In 1 Corinthians 8:9 Paul applies the result of the enthymeme above to the Corinthians in a second person imperative: "take care that this liberty of yours does not somehow become a stumbling block to the weak." The point is not just that some fellow Christians lack "knowledge" about idol food, but the effect the "wise" Corinthians' knowledge has on the weaker brothers. In the next move Paul elaborates this concern for the weaker brother with arguments from contrary, example, and authoritative witness.[46]

In the argument from the contrary Paul points out the negative consequences of their behavior by bringing in a contrary case.

> CONTRARY CASE: "For if others see you, who possess knowledge, eating in the temple of an idol"
>
> RESULT: "might they not,"
>
> SUPPORTIVE CASE: "since their conscience is weak,"
>
> RESULT: "be encouraged to the point of eating food sacrificed to idols?" (8:10)
>
> [RULE: The behavior of leaders is imitated, for good and bad]

The implicit rule points to the "wise" Corinthians as leaders in the church. In a hierarchical society such leaders were imitated.[47] The point of the contrary argument is that if "the weak" in the Corinthian church follow the example of "the wise" (the contrary to Paul's view), the consequences will be disastrous.

The argument from example brings in the experience of the Corinthians themselves.

> CASE: "So by your knowledge those weak believers the brothers for whom Christ died"
>
> RESULT: "are destroyed" (8:11)
>
> [RULE: The behavior of leaders is imitated, for good and bad]

This argument from example also contains an argument from authoritative witness in that Paul alludes to the early Christian confession "Christ died for

---

46. Eriksson, "Special Topics," 286–93.
47. On imitation in 1 Corinthians, see Elisabeth Castelli, *Imitating Paul: A Discourse of Power* (Louisville: Westminster/John Knox Press, 1991).

us."[48] In his argumentation Paul uses this confession to redefine the "weak" Christian to the status of a Christian brother. The person Christ dies for is a brother; the weak is one for whom Christ died; therefore the weak is a Christian brother. In the next verse Paul carries this line of argumentation one step further by claiming that those who sin against the weaker brother thereby sin against Christ. We can here infer the suppressed premise that due to Christ's vicarious death Christians have been united with Christ.[49]

As interpreters cognizant of the rhetorical conventions of the ancient Mediterranean world, we have to ask whether the similarities between Paul's argumentation and the ways a student was taught to put forward a thesis in the *progymnasmata* are merely coincidental. A number of interpreters have come to the conclusion that the similarity is best explained as derived from Paul's knowledge of rhetoric. Joachim Classen concludes: "a study of some technical terms which occur in Paul's letters has led me to the conclusion that he must have had some familiarity both with the practice and theory of ancient rhetoric, perhaps through writings influenced by this theory."[50]

Reading between the Lines

Interpreters of the Bible customarily read between the lines when they fill in background information for a biblical text. Such information often concerns historical, cultural, religious, and social aspects of the ancient world from which the texts derive. The rhetorical critic interpreting the argumentation in a biblical text focuses on the argumentative links in enthymemes that join assertions with rationales. Often these argumentative links are unstated premises that need to be explained for the reasoning to become apparent.

Such premises are found in the many *topoi* discussed in rhetoric. Some of these *topoi* are the common topics of logical inference found in all human rational discourse. If the understanding of Aristotle's enthymeme here advanced is accepted, *ethos* and *pathos* also are *topoi* for enthymemes. Appeals to authority and emotions can then be interpreted as enthymemic, which opens the speaker's ethos and relationship to his audience for rhetorical analysis. Interpreters with a more limited view of rationality probably would consider many such enthymemes as irrational.[51]

---

48. On the vicarious death formula as a confession in early Christianity and as a premise shared by the Corinthians, see Eriksson, *Traditions*, 97–99.
49. Ibid., 163–64.
50. "Review of R. Dean Anderson, *Ancient Rhetorical Theory and Paul*," *Rhetorica* 16 (1998): 328.
51. For example David Hellholm ("Enthymemic Argumentation in Paul: The Case of Romans 6,"

Many of the *topoi* used in early Christian discourse are different than the *topoi* we ordinarily use. Paul's argumentation differs from other forms of argumentation by the special topics used to substantiate the assertions made.[52] Paul's discussion partners of early Christians share a common pool of beliefs; many of these beliefs are specific to the Christian group. The later developments of these beliefs can be found in the history of theology. Paul's argumentation also differs from modern modes of argumentation due to its cultural location. In community with other people in the ancient Mediterranean world, the early Christians share a set of cultural conventions about values like honor and shame that marks the argumentation as quite peculiar to us modern people. Without an awareness of these cultural conventions biblical interpreters risk misinterpreting the text.

---

in *Paul in His Hellenistic Context* [ed. Troels Engberg-Pedersen; Minneapolis: Fortress, 1995], 119–79) claims that *ethos*-arguments are non-logical (136), and John Moores (*Wrestling with Rationality in Paul: Romans 1–8 in a New Perspective* [Cambridge: Cambridge University Press, 1995], 10) divorces appeals to Scripture from appeals to reason.

52. Together with the strong prophetic appeal to authority, derived from the need to create a new Christian *paideia*, the special topics are a distinctive trait of early Christian rhetoric; see Eriksson, "Special Topics," 272–76.

CHAPTER 16

PAUL'S BOASTING IN 2 CORINTHIANS 10–13 AS DEFENSE OF HIS HONOR: A SOCIO-RHETORICAL ANALYSIS

Duane F. Watson

Paul's boasting in 2 Corinthians 10–13 has long been a source of difficulty for the professional interpreter and the casual reader alike. How can Paul be so arrogant as to boast about his exploits and accomplishments as an apostle? Such a question cannot be answered by merely imposing our modern concepts of boasting upon Paul's letters and measuring Paul by our moral ruler. It can be answered only by placing Paul's boasting within its first-century Mediterranean context and judging his boasting by standards of the Greco-Roman world. Is boasting ever appropriate? If so, in what context is it acceptable? What was the appropriate content of boasting in each context? When these questions are answered, we find Paul defending his honor and authority against the derision and challenge of others. We see a man who works within the conventions of his time, but in new and often surprising ways proffered by his new Christian perspective and values.

What situation arose in Corinth that prompted Paul to resort to boasting? Paul supported himself at Corinth by tentmaking or leatherworking. This support was supplemented by contributions from the newly established church of Philippi (11:9; Phil 4:10–20). In the course of his ministry some wealthy Corinthians wanted to become Paul's benefactors, that is, they would pay Paul to become their own private apostle. It had been Paul's position to freely preach the gospel to the Gentiles. He did not want to accept support for his preaching and become a burden to his congregations (11:7–9, 20–21; 12:16; 1 Cor 9:15–18). More importantly, acceptance of a gift from a benefactor or patron would have changed his status to that of a client and he would have been considered a member of the household of the patron extending the benefaction. This dependent status could have become a hindrance to his freely preaching the gospel.[1]

---

1. Ronald F. Hock, *The Social Context of Paul's Ministry* (Philadelphia: Fortress Press, 1980), 50–65. For further discussion of the patron-client relationship in antiquity, and an excellent bibli-

In the Greco-Roman honor culture, to refuse such benefaction was a social affront to those extending it. This was especially true when the refusal was coming from a social inferior, as was the case here. Paul was a tentmaker and thus of the artisan class, near the bottom of society. The Corinthians offering the benefaction were likely of the upper class. Paul had alienated a wealthy portion of the Corinthian church by refusing their benefaction. These alienated patrons found willing recipients of their benefaction in a group of itinerant preachers who came to Corinth (11:4) claiming to be apostles, workers, and ministers of Christ (11:13, 23).[2] They supported their apostolic status with claims of visions and revelations (12:1). They treated Paul as a rival religious teacher or philosopher. As was often the case among teachers and philosophers of the day, they compared themselves to their rival, and found Paul and his claims unfounded and abilities lacking (10:12; 11:12). Their comparison involved self-praise and accusations launched against Paul (see specific accusations below), and ultimately denied his apostolic authority.

Paul therefore engages in an apology or self-defense. Boasting was part of the apologist's hortatory arsenal at that time (cf. 12:19). As we will discover below, Quintilian and Plutarch would say that, like anyone else, Paul is justified in boasting in self-defense against those who denounce his actions as discreditable and question his honor. Not only is Paul's situation one in which boasting is regularly prescribed, but his boasting has the standard content and exhibits the usual techniques for mitigating self-praise with the audience. However, Paul does not slavishly follow social conventions, but in light of the Christ event, radically transforms their content and shifts their emphases to create rightful boasting.

We will employ socio-rhetorical criticism as proposed by Vernon Robbins to analyze Paul's use of inner texture, intertexture, and social-cultural texture in 2 Corinthians 10–13 to defend his honor, modify the values of the Corinthians, and regain their allegiance.[3] Space limitations preclude thorough treatment of all of these textures, so the discussion will focus on those aspects that best suit the explication of Paul's boasting.

---

ography, see John H. Elliott, "Patronage and Clientage," in *The Social Sciences and New Testament Interpretation* (ed. Richard Rohrbaugh; Peabody, Mass.: Hendrickson, 1996), 144–56.

2. For extensive discussion of the opponents in these chapters, see, among many others, Dieter Georgi, *The Opponents of Paul in Second Corinthians* (Philadelphia: Fortress Press, 1986).

3. Robbins, *The Tapestry of Early Christian Discourse: Rhetoric, Society and Ideology* (New York: Routledge, 1996); idem, *Exploring the Texture of Texts: A Guide to Socio-Rhetorical Interpretation* (Valley Forge, Pa.: Trinity Press International, 1996).

Honor-Shame, Challenge-Riposte:
Insight from Social and Cultural Texture

Central to 2 Corinthians 10–13 are the interrelated common social and cultural topics of honor and challenge-response (riposte).[4] Paul's honor has been challenged by the opponents and not defended by the Corinthians (12:11; 13:3). "The *challenge* is a claim to enter the social space of another. This claim may be positive or negative. A negative reason would be to dislodge another from his social space, either temporarily or permanently."[5] Paul's opponents acquire honor by comparing themselves with one another and with Paul and by finding him lacking (10:18; 11:12), as well as by making claims to Paul's work in Corinth (10:13–16). Paul never defends his gospel in these chapters. The issue is not the content of his teaching and preaching, but a challenge to his honor as an apostle by those who claim to be his superiors.

Paul's opponents challenge his honor and authority with accusations on several fronts.[6] Paul needs to respond to the challenge in order to reestablish his honor. Challenge-response (riposte) within an honor culture has three parts: 1) the challenge in word and/or deed by a challenger; 2) the perception of the challenge by the one challenged and the public; and 3) the reaction of the one challenged and the public's evaluation of the reaction.[7]

The Challenge to Paul's Honor

Paul's opponents have come to minister in what Paul defines as his missionary field assigned by God (10:13–16). They claim that Paul acts according to human standards, and is worldly (10:2), perhaps meaning he is not spiritual. They claim that he is humble or timid when present, but bold when away (10:1). He is weak in person but strong in letter (10:10). They have compared their rhetorical abilities and personal presence with that of Paul and found

---

4. For more on honor and shame, see Halvor Moxnes, "Honor and Shame," in *The Social Sciences and New Testament Interpretation* (ed. Richard Rohrbaugh; Peabody, Mass.: Hendrickson, 1996), 19–40; Bruce J. Malina and Jerome H. Neyrey, "Honor and Shame in Luke-Acts: Pivotal Values of the Mediterranean World," in *The Social World of Luke-Acts: Models for Interpretation* (ed. Jerome H. Neyrey; Peabody, Mass.: Hendrickson, 1991), 25–65; Bruce J. Malina, *The New Testament World: Insights from Cultural Anthropology* (rev. ed.; Louisville, Ky.: Westminster/John Knox, Press 1993), 28–62; David A. deSilva, *The Hope of Glory: Honor Discourse and New Testament Interpretation* (Collegeville, Minn.: Michael Glazier, 1999).

5. Robbins, *Exploring*, 80.

6. For full identification of Paul's opponents in this section and careful reconstruction of their challenge and claims, see Jerry Sumney, *Identifying Paul's Opponents: The Question of Method in 2 Corinthians* (JSNTSup 40; Sheffield: Sheffield Academic Press, 1990), 149–79.

7. Malina, *New Testament World*, 42–45; Malina and Neyrey, "Honor and Shame in Luke-Acts," 29–32; Moxnes, "Honor and Shame," 20–21.

his wanting (10:1, 10, 12; 11:5), perhaps to the point of claiming that he does not manifest the gifts of an apostle. The Corinthians themselves have challenged Paul to prove that Christ speaks through him. The opponents have accused him of being socially dishonorable for not taking support from members of the Corinthian congregation and entering into a patron/client relationship. He is inconsistent for not taking money from the Corinthians while accepting contributions from the Philippians. His actions demonstrate a lack of love (11:7–11; 12:14–18). Financial support is one mark of an apostle; Paul is not a true apostle because he refuses support (12:12–13). Perhaps they even accuse Paul of cunningly using the collection for Jerusalem as a ruse for gaining support while claiming to refuse such support (12:13–18). Based on the inconsistency between Paul's strong letters and weak presence, and his acceptance of support from Philippi but not from Corinth, Paul is a flatterer (*kolax*). This charge could be supported by Paul's own words in 1 Corinthians 4:12–13: "When reviled, we bless; when persecuted, we endure; when slandered, we speak kindly."[8]

The Perception of the Challenge by Paul and the Corinthians

"The interaction over honor, the challenge-response game, is meant to take place only among equals. The receiver must judge whether he is equal to the challenger, whether the challenger honors him by regarding him as an equal, as is implicit in the challenge, or whether the challenger dishonors him by implying equality when there is none, either because the receiver is of a higher level or a lower level."[9] Claiming to be messengers for Christ, Paul's opponents are socially his equals on one level. However, by comparison they have flaunted their abilities, especially rhetorical, as superior (10:12, 18; 11:5), and condemned his presence as weak and contemptible (10:10). They want to be Paul's equals (if not superiors) in what they boast about (11:12). Even though said with a tinge of irony, Paul reestablishes equality (if not superiority) with the opponents. He says, "I am not in the least inferior to these super-apostles" (11:5; 12:11), and claims to be a better minister of Christ (11:23), with exceptional revelations (12:7). Paul's riposte will be given in detail below.

The public, the Corinthians, did not come to the defense of Paul's honor (12:11). They even asked for proof that Christ was speaking in him (13:3). Malina states, "the right to truth and the right to withhold the truth belong

---

8. Christopher Forbes, "Comparison, Self-Praise and Irony: Paul's Boasting and the Conventions of Hellenistic Rhetoric," *NTS* 32 (1986): 10.
9. Robbins, *Exploring*, 81.

to the 'man of honor' and to contest these rights is to place a person's honor in jeopardy, to challenge that person."[10] The reaction of the audience further amplifies the negative challenge to Paul's honor posed by the opponents.

The Reaction to the Challenge by Paul and the Corinthians

The public scrutinizes the reaction of the one challenged. The public can remove honor and give it to the challenger, or once more affirm the honor of the one challenged. The challenge is a threat to the reputation of the one challenged; he or she must respond to retain the reputation that has been threatened. No response is a forfeiture of honor and reputation.[11] This perspective on an honor challenge explains Paul's motivation; he must reestablish his honor, reputation, and the authority of his message.

Paul's Approach to Defending His Honor

Insight from Inner Texture and Further Insight from Social and Cultural Texture

A riposte to a challenge to honor can take many forms, ranging from direct affront to indirect and ambiguous responses.[12] Paul chooses to respond with boasting in an ironic mode, an indirect approach.[13]

Why an Indirect Approach? Inner texture shows that 2 Corinthians 10–13 is framed by an important, complex inclusio that explains both Paul's rhetorical approach in these chapters and a central issue that he seeks to address. I have not found commentators taking full advantage of the insights this inclusio offers. Paul has been accused of being weak in person and strong in his letters (10:1, 10). The inclusio shows Paul's intention is not just to be stronger in person, thereby removing the inconsistency between his letters and his person. His intention is to refute his opponents' accusation by being both stronger in person and weaker in his letters. On the one hand, he is ready to punish every disobedience when he arrives in person (10:6). What he says by letter he will do when present (10:11). When he comes he will not be lenient, but will deal with opposition in the power of God (13:2, 4).

---

10. *New Testament World*, 43.
11. Robbins, *Exploring*, 81.
12. Malina, *New Testament World*, 42.
13. Quintilian, *Institutio oratoria* (trans. H. E. Butler; 4 vols.; LCL 124–27; Cambridge: Harvard University Press, 1976–80), 9.1.2a.

He hopes that he will not have to be severe in using his authority when he comes (13:10). On the other hand, his letters have been strong, but he does not want to frighten the Corinthians in this letter (10:9). His letter is for building up rather than tearing down (13:10; 12:19). Paul's approach in the letter is a refutation of the "weak in person" and "strong in letter" accusation of his opponents. The inclusio shows that Paul's intention is to refute this accusation by being stronger in person and weaker in his letter.

Why Boasting? This inclusio also indicates the reason for Paul's use of irony and boasting like a fool. Such an approach is not severe and frightening, but one of self-praise that keeps him vulnerable to ridicule throughout. Defending his honor against accusations and asserting his authority through boasting, no matter if he overdoes it, will prevent him from frightening the Corinthians (10:8–9). It will refute the accusation that he lobs strong letters from a safe distance. If Paul attacks the opponents directly and strongly, it only reinforces the perception that the strength of his presence and the strength of his letters are incongruent, that he is a flatterer. He has yet to prove that he can be as strong in person as he is in his letters.

Why Irony? In the first and second centuries C.E. irony was appropriately used in situations requiring invective and forensic oratory. For example, you could use irony to ridicule your opponents for things they prided themselves.[14] Irony was often used when speakers were badly treated and their achievements were credited to others and their honor imperiled.

> The quality of *barytes,* "indignation," was seen as particularly appropriate to a speaker who had been badly treated; whose achievements were being credited to others, and whose good name had been traduced. This was especially true if the value of his actual achievements was being disputed. Straightforward irony was perhaps the most common method of producing the effect, though other methods, including comparison, and ironically calling into question matters that would be universally conceded, were used. Straightforwardly and forcefully answering one's own rhetorical questions could also reflect indignation.[15]

The situations for which irony was appropriate certainly include the one in which Paul found himself at Corinth. Paul's honor has been challenged

---

14. *Rhet. Alex.,* 35.1441b.23–24, in [Aristotle], *Rhetorica ad Alexandrum* (trans. H. Rackham; LCL 317; Cambridge: Harvard University Press, 1983), in the volume with Aristotle, *Problems,* 35.1441b.23–24.

15. Forbes ("Comparison, Self-Praise and Irony," 13), summarizing an extensive quotation from Hermogenes, *On Rhetorical Forms,* 2.8, in L. Spengel, *Rhetores Graeci* (3 vols.; Leipzig: B. G. Teubner, 1853–56), 2:384ff.

through the invective of his opponents. His achievements have been minimized and the credit taken by others. Irony is an appropriate part of his response to express his indignation. It is noteworthy that throughout this section Paul aligns his irony with rhetorical questions that he answers himself, further underscoring his indignation.

Why Weakness? The irony is that Paul boasts of the opposite of what his culture and his opponents accept as occasions for boasting. He boasts not of strength, recommendations, speaking ability, physical presence, or benefactors, but of weakness. His irony is used in typical self-praise, but not in an expected offensive way. Rather it is in a surprising, value-reversing way. Paul's entire ironic stress on God's use of weakness for God's power stands as a silent challenge that God does not praise the opponents' comparison and self-congratulation based on what the world deems to be strength. For those who accept it, the emphasis on weakness supports Paul's honor and undermines the honor of those who base their honor on strength.

One aspect of Paul's weakness is central. Even though he has had visions and revelations, he cannot use their content to support his authority in a powerful way. Having a thorn in the flesh, a messenger from Satan, prevents him from being boastful (12:6–10). In this context the thorn can be both a physical malady and the opponents themselves, for the opponents are ministers of Satan (11:15). Paul has incorporated the very presence of the opponents and their degradation as part of God's plan to keep him humble and able to boast in weakness. But the physical emphasis suggested by the "thorn" is also present. Paul says he must contend with "weaknesses, insults, hardships, persecutions, and calamities for the sake of Christ" (12:10). Notice the cultural, intertextural allusion to Job. God used Satan to further God's purposes with Job, and now God does so again with Paul. Just as in Job's case, God's plan for Paul involves physical weakness, insults from others, hardships, persecution from those deemed friends, and calamities (11:23–33).

Ascription of Divine Honor. In his riposte, Paul ascribes himself divine honor and authority, an acceptable part of an honor defense.[16] Paul wields divine power to destroy strongholds raised against the knowledge of God (10:4); the Lord gave him authority to build up the Corinthians (10:8); he works as an apostle in the field God has assigned to him (10:13–16); he

---

16. Malina and Neyrey, "Honor and Shame in Luke-Acts," 28.

is the father who prepares the Corinthians to be the bride of Christ (11:2); he is trained in knowledge (11:6); the truth of Christ is in him (11:10); he is a minister of Christ (11:23); he has been given exceptional visions and revelations (12:1–7); he speaks in Christ before God (12:19); he lives with Christ in the power of God (13:4); and Christ gave him authority to build up the church (13:10). Paul does not attempt to demonstrate acquired divine honor with any formal proofs. However he does conclude the fool's speech with a proof of eyewitness testimony. He points to the signs, wonders, and mighty works he performed in Corinth as part of his ministry (12:12) as if to say, "if all this boasting has not convinced you that I am a God-appointed apostle, eyewitness testimony should."

The opponents are denying Paul's God-given authority on the grounds that he does not speak well, have a strong presence, or accept deserved support from a benefactor. The Corinthians are in agreement (12:11; 13:3). Paul cannot prove he deserves honor through these traditional means. He must regain his honor and authority through shaming the Corinthians into realizing that all he has done for them has been God working through his weakness to build them up. Their existence as a church and strength as a congregation, which came from Paul's weakness, are proof of his God-given authority as an apostle.

Paul's Self-Praise (Periautologia), *Boasting*

Insight from Social and Cultural Intertexture

There were conventions for self-praise as early as 100 B.C.E. Popular philosophers and sophists were known for their self-praise. This self-praise could take the form of comparison, as it did for Paul's opponents.[17] Self-praise was generally considered repugnant,[18] and appropriately used in only a few well-defined circumstances: "the educated Hellenistic world in which Paul moved knew of conventions of self-praise, but believed that they required great delicacy if they were not to be misused."[19] We will examine the conventions in place in Paul's time as discussed by Dio Chrysostom, Quintilian, and Plutarch.

---

17. Forbes, "Comparison, Self-Praise and Irony," 9–10.
18. Ibid., 8.
19. Ibid., 10.

Dio Chrysostom. In his *Fifty-Seventh Discourse*[20] Dio Chrysostom defends Nestor's self-praise in the context of trying to stop a quarrel between Agamemnon and Achilles (*Iliad*, 1.260–68, 273–74). Nestor's references to the deference paid to him by important men are intended to convince Agamemnon and Achilles that his words of advice are worthy of attention and obedience and will benefit them (3–5). Also, by praising these important men above Agamemnon and Achilles Nestor humbles these two and shows them the folly of not emulating such important men who were willing to listen to him (6–9). Self-praise is acceptable if it secures the audience's attention, compliance, and imitation (10).

Quintilian. Quintilian describes self-praise in his *Institutio oratoria* (11.1. 15–28).[21] He observes that boasting generally disgusts and depreciates the audience (11.1.15–17). However, drawing on the example of Cicero, he does allow for boasting in specific instances: defending others who have assisted you, speaking in self-defense against those who accuse you out of envy (11.1.17–18), and speaking against enemies and detractors who denounce your actions as discreditable (11.1.23). Quintilian's advice condones Paul speaking in self-defense against those accusing him out of envy and denouncing his actions as discreditable, that is, challenging his honor.

Quintilian despises indirect boasting by denial of the opposite. He states, "And yet I am not sure that open boasting is not more tolerable, owing to its sheer straightforwardness, than that perverted form of self-praise, which makes the millionaire say that he is not a poor man, the man of mark describe himself as obscure, the powerful pose as weak, and the eloquent as unskilled and even inarticulate. But the most ostentatious kind of boasting takes the form of actual self-derision" (11.1.21–22). At first glance Paul's approach in these chapters appears to be indirect boasting by denial of the opposite. While Paul denies rhetorical power (11:5–6), he proceeds to demonstrate it in the fool's speech (11:16–12:13). However, since his audience does not appreciate his oratory (10:1, 10), what may be a denial of the opposite for him is a demonstration of irony and rhetoric meant to convince his audience of his rhetorical skill. Also, Paul could be understood as a powerful person posing as weak, another of Quintilian's pet peeves. Paul assumes he exercises divine power, yet stresses his weakness. Again, since his audience does not grant him strength and authority (10:1, 9–10), he is not perceived as a powerful

---

20. Dio Chrysostom, *Disc.*, 37–60 (trans. H. Lamar Cosby; LCL 376; Cambridge: Harvard University Press, 1962).

21. Quintilianus, *Inst.*, 11.1.15–28.

person posing as weak. Rather Paul has turned this on its head: he is powerful because he is weak.

Boasting about yourself can be tempered by presenting it indirectly as quotes of others (11.1.21), demonstrating that the necessity of boasting was made by another (11.1.22), and attributing success in part to others and the providence of the gods (11.1.23). Paul stresses that the Corinthians provided the necessity of boasting: "I have been a fool! You forced me to it" (12:11). They were not acknowledging his obvious apostolic status — a status demonstrated by knowledge (11:5), and signs, wonders, and mighty works (12:12). Paul does not attribute his success to others, but completely to the providence of God who works through his weakness. His boasting can only be in the Lord (10:17–18) and Christ's power is made perfect in Paul's weakness (12:9–10; 13:4).

Plutarch. One of the most important works about boasting from the first century C.E. is Plutarch's *On Praising Oneself Inoffensively* (*De Se Ipsum Citra Invidiam Laudando*).[22] Plutarch outlines for statesmen what situations and purposes are appropriate for boasting, and the content and devices to use to make such boasting acceptable to the audience. Plutarch argues that in general self-praise is deplorable and shameless. The boaster is assigning to himself what others should bestow, forcing others to agree with him in a public setting when they may not really agree (539 D). However, he finds self-glorification acceptable under the circumstances outlined below, which I am relating to Paul's practice.

Contexts for Boasting

When self-glorification works to upbuild the reputation of the speaker in order to facilitate some greater good, it is acceptable (539 E-F). Paul's boasting has a greater good as its focus. He deals with the Corinthians in the power of God (10:4; 12:9; 13:4). The Corinthian church is part of his God-given mission (10:13–16) and God has given him authority for building it up (10:8; 12:19; 13:10). It is his responsibility to present the church to Christ free from corruption (11:3), but the Corinthians are being corrupted by another gospel (11:4) that may prevent them from living in the faith and meeting the test (13:5–7). To address this danger Paul must reestablish his authority. The Corinthians may not perceive the necessity of his boasting, but he has

---

22. Plutarch, *Moralia* (trans. Phillip H. De Lacy and Benedict Einarson; 15 vols.; LCL; Cambridge: Harvard University Press, 1958).

included statements about their mistreatment by his opponents (11:20) and the opponents' association with Satan (11:3, 13–15) which the Corinthians can compare to what Paul says about himself and his relationship with them.

Self-praise is also acceptable when "you are defending your good name or answering a charge" (540 C). As outlined above, many accusations and charges have been made against Paul that challenge his honor. These provide ample warrant for his boasting.

The unfortunate can use self-praise and boasting, for it attests to their ambition and courage in struggling to reach beyond circumstance and ill-fortune, and casts aside pity (541 A–C). Paul certainly makes it clear that he has been struggling with ill-fortune, as seen in his list of hardships and sufferings (11:23–33) and the revelation about his thorn in the flesh (12:7–10). The latter ends with the expression, "Therefore I am content with weaknesses, insults, hardships, persecutions, and calamities for the sake of Christ; for whenever I am weak, then I am strong" (12:10). Paul is attempting to reach beyond his circumstances and ill-fortune, but presenting the state in which he revels and finds his strength. He is not trying to overcome these circumstances for something better, but something better — the power of Christ — arises out of this ill-fortune. Paul is also casting aside pity, for he may not have power and prestige as the opposition defines them, but he certainly cannot be pitied because his sorry circumstances work for the sake of Christ and the gospel.

Boasting is also permissible when pleading for justice to those who have dealt harshly with you (541C–F). Plutarch's examples are prominent citizens who have given some great benefit to those speaking harshly or turning their backs on them. These prominent citizens point to the benefits they have given their detractors in the past in hopes of changing their attitudes. Compare the Corinthians who are following Paul's opponents and forgetting all he had done for them in the Lord. Paul mentions that he was the first to bring the gospel to them (10:14). He did not charge them for his ministry among them (11:7–11; 12:13–18). Although he has been their benefactor, they accuse him of being sinful (11:7) and crafty (12:16). Even though he has left them a great benefit, he has to stress that not charging them is an expression of his love (11:10–11, 20–21; 12:15) and of building them up (12:19; cf. 10:8; 13:10). His need for boasting is necessary because his benefaction has been misrepresented as malefaction.

Closely related to this pleading for justice is the use of self-glorification in contrasts to show that "the opposite of what one is charged with would have been shameful and base" (541 F; 541 F–542 A). Paul contrasts his choice of not accepting support from the Corinthians with his opponents' choice to do so. He emphasizes that his behavior stemmed from love (11:11; 12:15), and aimed at building them up (12:19), but his opponents' behavior burdens (11:9; 12:16), preys upon, and takes advantage of them (11:20–21).

A speaker can also make it clear that self-praise has some advantage and further end in view, like inspiring the audience with emulation and ambition (544 D–F). Paul does not explicitly emphasize that his self-praise has an advantage or further end in view. His self-praise is aimed at reestablishing his honor, authority, and the respect of the Corinthians. Allegiance to Paul and his teaching has the effect of building up the Corinthians (10:8; 12:19; 13:10) and rescuing them from the cunning and oppression of the opponents (11:3–4, 20–21), but Paul does not make this explicit. Neither does Paul ask the Corinthians to emulate him. He discusses behavior that he expects to see from the Corinthians (12:19–13:10), but it is in obedience to what he has taught them rather than in emulation.

Self-praise can be used "to overawe and restrain the hearer and to humble and subdue the headstrong and rash" (544 F; 544 F–545 C). Plutarch cites how Aristotle told Alexander that those who have true opinions about the gods have the right to be proud and use it against their enemies (545 A). Certainly true opinions about God are Paul's basis for boasting. He has been given visions and revelations (12:1–4), the Lord has given him authority (10:8; 13:10), divine power works through him (10:4; 12:9; 13:4), he is trained in knowledge (11:6), and "the truth of Christ is in me" (11:10). Certainly these components of his boasting are meant to overawe and restrain the headstrong opposition.

When evil or unsound policy is being praised in matters of important issues, and the audience is being corrupted and swayed to adopt it, self-praise is acceptable to show the unsound policy for what it is and to divert the audience to a better course (545 D–546 A). Paul is boasting in part to sway the Corinthians from giving allegiance to what his opponents boast about: strength according to human standards (11:18), including trust in social conventions of benefaction, rhetorical finesse, recounting of visions and revelations, and comparison with others for self-promotion. He argues that it is not strength as society defines it, but weakness that is true strength and the working of the power of Christ (11:23–33). True boasting is in the Lord and in weakness (10:17; 12:9). His opponents' way is one of cunning that draws the church away from Christ (11:3) to enslavement and dishonor (11:20–21) and immoral behavior (12:19–13:2).

When people have made claims for themselves that are undeserved, these should be refuted and the claims shown to be pointless. Self-praise should not be used to undermine their claims. "If we hold them undeserving and of little worth, let us not strip them of their praise by presenting our own, but plainly refute their claim and show their reputation to be groundless" (540 C). Paul does not directly refute his opponents' claims by praising himself. Rather, through irony he demonstrates the futility of their grounding praise in boastful comparison, undermining their claims without directly refuting them. He uses an ironic point-by-point comparison in the fool's speech based on the criteria of weakness, demonstrating that the comparison of the opponents with Paul is completely groundless (11:16–12:13). The comparison begins with standard points of ascribed honor derived from family and kinship (11:22), moves to atypical points of acquired honor (e.g., hardships, 11:23–33), and returns to a standard point of comparison in the ascribed honor of religious experience (which Paul cannot utilize fully because of physical infirmity, 12:1–10). Paul demonstrates that he could have boasted on the highest levels of ascribed and acquired honor, but rather focuses his boasting in weakness. This subtle and ironic comparison demonstrates that there really are no grounds of comparison between him and the opponents since their honor is not based on weakness.

Self-glorification is not acceptable when bestowed upon oneself to gratify ambition and an appetite for fame (540 A). Self-praise is particularly inappropriate when done in comparison to others whose praise you wish to usurp. "But when they do not even seek to be praised simply and in themselves, but try to rival the honour that belongs to others and set against it their own accomplishments and acts in the hope of dimming the glory of another, their conduct is not only frivolous, but envious and spiteful as well" (540 B). This warning illumines Paul's statement about his opponents' comparison with one another and himself as "not showing good sense" (10:12), his reference to them working in his sphere of ministry and trying to oust him (10:13–16), as well as his feigned reluctance to boast in comparison with his opponents (11:16–21).

Moderating Boasting

The danger of self-praise becoming offensive and arousing envy is always present, but Plutarch advises that these dangers can be lessened by several techniques. Boasting can be mixed with the praise of the audience (542 B–C). Paul never praises the Corinthians in these chapters. His focus is on reestablishing his honor at the expense of the opponents' honor. Perhaps praise would have reinforced the Corinthians' assessment that Paul was a flatterer (10:1, 10). Also, using and amending the praise of others can moderate boasting

(543 A–F). In this situation Paul has no praise from his audience or opponents to use.

Some of the honor for what is praised can be ascribed to chance or God (542 E–543 A). Note that Paul uses this technique and gives all honor to God. He boasts of the authority the Lord gave him (10:8; 12:19; 13:10) and boasts only in the Lord (10:17; 12:9). He can boast in his human weakness because God has chosen it as the means of manifesting his power (11:21–12:10).

Mention can be made to some shortcomings of your own that are not degrading or ignoble: "So some do not present their own praise in all its brilliance and undimmed, but throw in certain minor shortcomings, failures, or faults, thus obviating any effect of displeasure or disapproval" (543 F). These shortcomings can be mistakes, ambitions, lack of information, or mention of poverty and low birth (544 A–B). In light of his countercultural values, Paul does just the opposite of this advice. He boasts of what is degrading and ignoble: his imprisonments, floggings, whippings, beatings with rods, and being hungry, cold, and naked. Brushes with the law and lack of necessities were not virtues in his culture. Paul uses these degrading and ignoble items, not to lessen the arousal of envy or offense in his boasting, but to surprise the Corinthians that what they devalue is what Paul and God value: weakness. So although these countercultural values lessen any boasting Paul is making, they become a proper boast in the Lord that furthers the glory of Christ (12:9).

Mentioning the hardships inherent in the items for which people are praising you also moderates boasting. "For it is with reputation and character as with a house or an estate: the multitude envy those thought to have acquired them at no cost or trouble; they do not envy those who have purchased them with much hardship and peril" (544 D). The Corinthians are not praising Paul, so he cannot obviate his boasting using this technique. However, those convinced of Paul's authority and the content of his boasting could be less offended or envious because Paul obtained his authority through great hardships and a thorn in the flesh (11:22–33; 12:6–10).

Conclusion

In his honor defense in 2 Corinthians 10–13, Paul utilizes the conventions of the dominant Greco-Roman culture. In light of the charge that he hurls strong letters at them from a safe distance but cannot demonstrate such strength in person, he has to respond with an honor defense that is not perceived as confrontational and "strong." To do this he takes an indirect approach using boasting in an ironic mode, stressing his weakness and ascribed honor from God. With this indirect approach he can defend his honor without leaving himself vulnerable to further criticism regarding the discrepancy between his strong letters and weak presence. At the same time it enables Paul to defend his honor and shame the Corinthians into seeing that he has been wrongly dishonored.

Although generally repugnant, boasting is permitted in certain situations, and in these situations there is an acceptable content and way of approaching boasting that minimizes the dangers always present in it. Boasting is acceptable when speakers must tell the truth about themselves and their accomplishments in order to achieve some good, defend their name against charges due to envy, speak against enemies or detractors who denounce their actions as discreditable, discuss their unfortunate circumstances and how they overcame them, plead their case for justice with those that have mistreated them, demonstrate that the opposite of the conduct that is criticized would have been shameful, show an advantage or further purpose like inspiring the audience to emulation and ambition, subdue the headstrong, sway the audience from unsound policy, or refute the unfounded claims of others against them.

In his boasting Paul has worked within these conventions, but has modified his approach to suit his needs to reestablish his authority and honor and realign the value system of the Corinthians. He discusses himself in terms of his work with the Corinthians and his mission and authority from God in order to achieve a greater good: to counter opposition that he fears corrupts and takes advantage of the Corinthians. He boasts about his sufferings and hardships, but not to demonstrate his moral character in overcoming them, but to boast in the reality that in his suffering Christ's power is realized. He pleads for justice by reminding the Corinthians of all that he has done for them, because his benefaction has been misinterpreted as malefaction. He shows that the opposite of his action — to have accepted support from the Corinthians as his opponents did — would have been shameful and base. His boasting is meant to regain his honor and the allegiance of the Corinthians, strongly implying that his ministry has the advantage of building up the Corinthians and rescuing them from the cunning of the opponents. His boasting is meant to subdue the headstrong and rash among the Corinthians and return their allegiance to him as one having true opinions and knowledge about God. His boasting is aimed at swaying the Corinthians from an unsound policy to a better course of action. His boasting refutes the claims of others, but not explicitly. Rather it shows that their comparison with Paul is pointless when it is understood that weakness provides the grounds for legitimate comparison.

Paul tempers his boasting according to convention. The Corinthians and their comparison of apostles necessitate his boasting. In accord with his theology in which his weakness is the conduit of the strength of God, Paul attributes his success, through weakness, to God. He does not temper his boasting by praising the audience, perhaps so as not to appear even more the flatterer. He roots his boasting in the God who uses his weakness for God's strength. Paul lists his hardships and things degrading and ignoble, not to temper his boasting, but to surprise the Corinthians that such ignoble "weak" things are in fact noble. Paul tempers boasting by mention of his hardships that brought him to the point for which he boasts: his weakness.

Given the situation of challenge-riposte, Paul's honor defense conforms to the conventions prescribed by notables of his day. However, there is also a counter-cultural thread running throughout the honor defense. In keeping with countercultural groups, Paul rejects the dominant culture's criteria for honor, and offers a different set of criteria that he hopes will be its replacement.[23] Even while working within the fabric of social conventions, he surprises the Corinthians by boasting with non-conventional values. His emphasis upon weakness in the midst of an honor challenge to his strength and truthfulness would have been surprising if not "foolish." Reversing the values of the Corinthians so that they see weakness as strength is undergirded by Paul's self-ascription of divine honor and the very working of Paul in weakness among the Corinthians which successfully created their churches. True honor is honor acquired from God as he works through weakness. Honor challenges based on matters of strength "do not make good sense."

---

23. Robbins, *Exploring,* 87; *Tapestry,* 169–70.

CHAPTER 17

RE-READING 2 CORINTHIANS: A RHETORICAL APPROACH

J. David Hester (Amador)

Continuing the Discussion

In arguing for a coherent reading of 2 Corinthians, two important steps must be taken. First, it is incumbent upon the scholar who argues for the thesis of compositional integrity to fulfill an essentially negative task, namely, to address and refute the arguments offered on behalf of the composite model. In addition to the numerous, standard introductions that support or propose from two up to six separate sources behind the canonical version of the letter,[1] monographs specifically addressing the Corinthian correspondence,[2] as well as rhetorical treatments of 2 Corinthians itself,[3] present a formidable array of arguments on behalf of the multi-source hypothesis. The scholar who supports the compositional integrity of the letter must consider three important issues: the relationship of the arguments in chapters 1–9 to that in chapters 10–13, the question of the presence of sources and/or interpolations in chapters 1–9, and the relationship of chapters 8 and 9. Elsewhere[4] I have sought to meet these questions directly by means of a rhetorical approach that appreciates

---

1. Cf. Helmut Koester, *Introduction to the New Testament: History and Literature of Early Christianity* (Berlin: Walter de Gruyter, 1987), 2:53–54; Steven L. Davies, *New Testament Fundamentals* (Sonoma, Calif.: Polebridge, 1994), 89; Dennis Duling and Norman Perrin, *The New Testament: Proclamation and Paraenesis: Myth and History* (3d ed.; Fort Worth, Tex.: Harcourt Brace College, 1994), 178–83; David Barr, *New Testament Story* (2d ed.; Belmont, Calif.: Wadsworth, 1995), 115–17; Edwin Freed, *The New Testament: A Critical Introduction* (Belmont, Calif.: Wadsworth, 1991), 263–65; Bart Ehrman, *The New Testament: A Historical Introduction to the Early Christian Writings* (Oxford: Oxford University Press, 1997), 280–85; Stephen Harris, *The New Testament: A Student's Introduction* (2d ed.; Mountain View, Calif.: Mayfield, 1995), 260–62.

2. Victor P. Furnish, *II Corinthians* (AB 32A; Garden City, N.Y.: Doubleday, 1985); Walter Schmithals, *Die Gnosis in Korinth* (2d rev. ed.; Göttingen: Vandenhoeck & Ruprecht, 1965); G. Bornkamm, *Paul* (New York: Harper and Row, 1960); J. C. Hurd, *The Origin of 1 Corinthians* (Macon: Mercer, 1983), 43–47; C. K. Barrett, *A Commentary on the Second Epistle to the Corinthians* (HNTC; New York: Harper Row, 1973). For an additional review of major English commentaries on 2 Corinthians, cf. Gordon Dutile, "An Annotated Bibliography for 2 Corinthians," *Southwestern Journal of Theology* 32/1 (1989): 41–43.

3. Hans Dieter Betz, *2 Corinthians 8 and 9* (Hermeneia; Philadelphia: Fortress Press, 1985).

4. J. D. H. Amador, "Revisiting 2 Corinthians: Rhetoric and the Case for Unity," *NTS* 46 (2000): 92–111.

the impact of *inventio* upon the persuasive and communicative function of the letter in order to undermine and overturn the assertions of those who espouse the multi-source hypothesis.[5]

The second, complementary task, in contrast, is a predominantly positive one: to outline through a "re-discovered and re-invented rhetoric"[6] the argumentative units, postures, methods, and dynamics of the letter as a whole. To be specific: it is the task of this paper to pick up from the argument that shows why the letter is *not* a composite of independent sources, and to move to the issue of why and how it *is* compositionally an integral unit. In order to do this, I return to a model of rhetorical analysis sufficiently complex to address the intricate and dynamic argumentative situations, strategies, and audiences of this correspondence. The result will be a rhetorical analysis of the letter that can discern and describe the nuances of the relationships among and trajectories within its various arguments, and of its argumentative dynamics.

In this fashion, using both negative and positive responses to construct a case for the unity of 2 Corinthians, I hope not only to demonstrate the potential impact of rhetorical studies upon source criticism of Pauline letters, but to provide an opportunity for further inquiry into our understanding of Paul's rhetoric.[7]

The Model

With a slight reconfiguration of the original model, the following steps are offered as a means by which to analyze the argumentation in 2 Corinthians:

1. Rhetorical Unit: the rhetorical unit might be a literary unit, but the dominant factor in rhetorical analysis is its argumentative dimension. It's size and relationship to other rhetorical units and contexts must be considered in order to avoid falsely delimiting and isolating its function and contextuality.

2. Relational Posture of the Rhetorical Unit(s): One must discern the ways in which the relationships between the audience(s) and the text are generated, particularly

---

5. Carol Poster's cautionary notes to me in numerous conversations (Lund, Summer 2000) regarding many factors (including material) impacting upon the composition of letters in the ancient world offer an important reminder for us to avoid importing the kind of rationalist presumptions that often accompany the multi-source hypothesis. Such presumptions seek to reorder and reconstruct the letter's composition according to modernist rules of reasonability and persuasion. A descriptive approach that seeks to discern the rhetorical trajectories and shifting argumentative situations in the letter as it stands is more likely to avoid such cultural and anachronistic impositions.

6. Cf. James D. Hester (Amador), "Re-discovering and Re-inventing Rhetoric," *Scriptura* 50 (1994): 1–22.

7. For an important new reading of 2 Corinthians which also takes into consideration a unitary hypothesis of composition, cf. Jerry W. McCant, *2 Corinthians* (Readings: A New Biblical Commentary; Sheffield: Sheffield Academic Press, 1999).

(but not exclusively) by exploration into the argumentative function of modalities and deictic indicators.

3. Method of Argumentation: By turning to Perelman/Olbrechts-Tyteca's theory of argumentation,[8] categories of *loci* (quantity, quality, preferable) and argumentative strategies (associative, dissociative) are considered within and between argumentative units.

4. Dynamics of the Argumentative Situations: Several argumentative shifts might be made in the course of a larger rhetorical unit as a result of the influence of earlier stages of the discussion prior to and during the course of the argument. Identification of their function and relationship to one another through the trajectory of argumentation helps to discern changes in approach and inventional moves, making it possible to consider their overall function and relationship to one another.

Application to 2 Corinthians

Rhetorical Units

The greater rhetorical unit is the letter of 2 Corinthians as a whole. Within this unit are the following major argumentative units and their divisions:[9]

2 Cor 1:1–14	Introductory Unit
2 Cor 1:1–2	Letter opening
2 Cor 1:3–11	Argument developing the *topos* of "affliction," with disclosure formula in 1:8–11 (which might also be seen as the start of the letter's *narratio*)
2 Cor 1:12–14	Letter *causa* or *propositio* concerning "boasting,"[10] "sincerity," and "frankness"
2 Cor 1:15–2:13	Unit 1 (plans for Corinth and Achaia as they relate *to the past*)
2 Cor 1:15–16	*Narratio* concerning the rhetor's trip to Macedonia.[11]
2 Cor 1:17–22	Justification through dissociation of human from divine standards of judging the ministry

---

8. Chaim Perelman and Lucie Olbrechts-Tyteca, *The New Rhetoric* (Notre Dame, Ind.: University of Notre Dame Press, 1979).

9. This outline was first proposed in Amador, "Revisiting 2 Corinthians," 19–20.

10. For a discussion of the function of boasting in Hellenistic letters, see Stanley Olson, "Epistolary Uses of Expressions of Self-Confidence," *JBL* 103/4 (1984): 585–97. See also Scott Hafemann, " 'Self-Commendation' and Apostolic Legitimacy in 2 Corinthians: A Pauline Dialectic?" *NTS* 36/1 (1990): 66–88.

11. Benjamin Fiore, "Root Metaphors in Paul — Pauline Comings and Goings: The Travel Image," in *Proceedings (Eastern Great Lakes Biblical Society)* 11 (1991): 174–84, explores the function of the travel references as a means by which the redactor brought the letters together.

2 Cor 1:23–2:11		Previous visit "with grief" and decision, based on "confidence," to write "that I might know the results of your testing, whether you are obedient in everything"
2 Cor 2:12–13		*Narratio*
2 Cor 2:14–7:4		Unit 2 (purpose of the ministry as related *to the present*)
	2 Cor 2:14–17	Recap and variation of *causa* ("sincerity" in 2:17)[12]
	2 Cor 3:1–4:6	*Topos* of "confidence" through Christ to God in a new covenant proclaiming Jesus Christ as Lord[13]
	2 Cor 4:7–6:10	Dissociation of earthly weakness, with *topoi* of "confidence," "building up" (5:1) related to "affliction" through the promise of salvation brought about through the ministry of reconciliation *to God*
	2 Cor 6:11–7:4	Peroration and extension of object of "sincerity" and "boasting" in "affliction" elaborated through an argument for separation based on the notion of righteousness in which the believer participates[14]
2 Cor 7:5–9:15		Unit 3 (plans for Corinth and Achaia *for the future*)
	2 Cor 7:5	*Narratio* (from 2:12–13)
	2 Cor 7:6–16	Letter reception, with themes of "affliction," "proof," "boasting," and "confidence"
	2 Cor 8:1–2	*Narratio* (from 7:5)
	2 Cor 8:3–24	Argument from sharing and reciprocity, defining the relationship of the churches to the missionaries with respect to Macedonia

---

12. For arguments contrary to the fragmentary hypothesis which sees 2:14 as the beginning of a new letter, see Jerome Murphy-O'Connor, "Paul and Macedonia: The Connection Between 2 Corinthians 2:13 and 2:14," *JSNT* 25 (1985): 99–103.

13. Regarding the literary unity of 3:12–18, cf. W. C. Van Unnik, "'With Unveiled Face,' an Exegesis of 2 Corinthians 12–18," *NovT* 6 (1963): 153–69. Theological, social, and metaphorical issues regarding this section are addressed in a number of works, e.g., J. D. G. Dunn, "2 Corinthians 3.17 — 'The Lord is the Spirit'," *JTS* 21/2 (1970): 309–20; D. Greenwood, "The Lord Is the Spirit: Some Considerations of 2 Corinthians 3:17," *CBQ* 34/4 (1972): 467–72; C. J. A. Hickling, "The Sequence of Thought in 2 Corinthians, Chapter 3," *NTS* 21/3 (1974): 380–95; Martin Schalemann, "Of Surpassing Splendor: An Exegetical Study of 2 Corinthians 3:4–18," *Concordia Journal* 4/3 (1978): 108–17; A. T. Hanson, "The Midrash in 2 Corinthians 3: A Reconsideration," *JSNT* 9 (1980): 2–28; Thomas Provence, "'Who is Sufficient for These Things?' An Exegesis of 2 Corinthians 2:15–3:18," *NovT* 24/1 (1982): 54–81; P. Grelot, "Note sur 2 Corinthiens 3:14," *NTS* 33/1 (1987):135–44.

14. Many commentators believe this unit contains an interpolation of some kind. David deSilva, "Recasting the Moment of Decision: 2 Corinthians 6:14–7:1 in its Literary Context," *Andrews University Seminary Studies* 31/1 (1993): 3–16, rejects the thesis that this section is an interpolation, while Paul Brooks Duff, "The Mind of the Redactor: 2 Corinthians 6:14–8:1 in its Secondary Context," *NovT* 35/2 (1993): 160–80, sees this passage as a later insertion which helped bring together the various Pauline fragments. James Scott, "The Uses of Scripture in 2 Corinthians 6:16c-18," *JSNT* 56 (1994): 73–99, also argues for the theological unity of the argument from 2 Cor 2:14–7:4. See also J. A. Fitzmyer's well known, but problematic article, "Qumran and the Interpolated Paragraph in 2 Corinthian 6:14–7:1," *CBQ* 23 (1961): 271–80.

2 Cor 9:1	*Narratio* (from 8:2)
2 Cor 9:2–24	Argument from abundance and return "with many thanksgivings *to God*" as patron
2 Cor 10:1–13:4	Unit 4 (apostolic apologia)
2 Cor 10:1–18	Boasting no longer in "you," but in "me" and "my authority"
2 Cor 11:1–12:13	Fool's Speech
2 Cor 12:14–13:4	Apostolic parousia
2 Cor 13:5–13	Concluding Remarks
2 Cor 13:5–9	Closing appeal ("testing," "examination," and weakness-for-strength)
2 Cor 13:10	Appeal to authority based on "building up"
2 Cor 13:11–13	Final appeals and salutations

Relational Posture

This is the most theoretically complex step in the analytical model herein presented. It is complex because so many different aspects of the text can be noted, discussed, and evaluated. Wilhelm Wuellner has provided an example of such an analysis on the text of Romans,[15] and elsewhere I have done so on the text of 1 Corinthians.[16] For the sake of brevity and utility, the relational posture of the text can be explored under two major subheadings: the text's *modality* and the text's *deixis*. Both modality and deixis are aspects of an argument's generative context, the relationality argumentatively created between rhetor, argument, and audience. Through them the multiplicity of possible contextualities is encountered, adapted or rejected.

Modalities refer to the presentation of an argument, the certainty and importance of its claims.[17] Modalities operate not only within the intentionalities of the text and rhetor, but also reflect the impact and strategic positioning of the audience as well. For modalities to function, there must be a set of conditions provided by background or context, this being determined by natural possibilities (the rhetor's and audience's skill in communication), norms, social values and desires, as well as the communicants' beliefs and knowledge.[18]

The three major modalities predominant throughout the several argumentative units can be identified as *assertive, volitional*, and *ironic*. With respect

---

15. Wilhelm Wuellner, "Reading Romans in Context," unpublished SNTS seminar paper (Göttingen Conference, 1987).
16. Hester (Amador), "Re-discovering and Re-inventing Rhetoric."
17. Perelman/Olbrechts-Tyteca, *The New Rhetoric*, 154.
18. Wuellner, "Reading Romans in Context," 13, 19.

to the assertive modality, it is clear that little appeal is made to the hypothetical or conditional nature of certain important argumentative *topoi* used throughout the letter. Instead, direct definitional (e.g., 1:12–14; 2:15), quasi-logical (e.g., 3:6–12) and "factual" evidence (e.g., the *narratio* throughout the unit, list of afflictions in 11:23–33, vision in 12:2–4) are dominant modal strategies made use of at key moments in the argumentative trajectory. This modal strategy gives shape to the role of *volitional* appeal that makes its presence felt in Unit 1 with respect to the one who has caused pain (2:5–11), and in Unit 3 in the collection appeal (cf. 8:8 and 9:13). Namely, upon the basis of the relationship developed through *assertive* argumentation, the *volitional* can be carried out under the *topos* "not as a command, but as a test." This in turn puts the audience(s) in a particular hierarchy between themselves and the rhetor, so that the *ironic* modality of Unit 4 can shift from defensiveness to a growing presence of authoritative appeal and command. The combination of these modalities is to effect a particular relationship between rhetor(s) and audience(s) within the context of ministry and with particular respect to the question of authority. How this is so, and how modalities contribute to the argumentative strategies of the letter, will be explored in greater detail below.

Deixis orients the content of a sentence in temporal, intonational, and spatial relations. Indexical expressions are used to construct contexts of utterance and reference, relating both text and audience to a cultural, social, and historical context in which people interact through language reflecting their social roles, perceptions, and positions. The basic function of deixis is to relate the actors and concerns referred to in an argument "to the spatiotemporal . . . here-and-now of the context of utterance."[19]

Personal deixis includes the use of personal and demonstrative pronouns, proper names, appellatives and substantives, and in this regard profound changes take place in the personal relationality between the various argumentative units. First person singular and plural dominates the *narratio* of 1:15–16; 2:1, 12–13; 7:5; 8:1; 9:2; 11:9 that tie the argumentative units together by reference to a historical series of events occasioning the relationship between rhetors and audiences. This relationship goes through multiple adaptations throughout the argumentative units. "We"[20] (with reference to "I" in 1:15–2:12) is set up in a *positive* relation to "you," in both Units 1 and 2, that is premised upon and culminates in a relationship of inclusion and mutuality.[21]

---

19. Wuellner, "Reading Romans in Context," 14.
20. For another study on the function of the first person plural, see M. Carrez, "Le 'Nous' en 2 Corinthiens," *NTS* 26/4 (1980): 474–86.
21. Note the appeal to the universal audience in the extension of "we" to include all Christians (including the Corinthians and Achaians) in 4:15–5:10 and 6:14–7:1

This allows for a seemingly benign shift, however, in Unit 3 where "I," now in distinction from "you," can make a personal, individual effort at persuasion concerning the collection by appeal to "your" reputation in "my" boasting and to "your" future reward. This distinction, while premised on mutuality, nevertheless allows for a partition between rhetor(s) and audiences(s), so that in Unit 4, "I" (with only occasional reference to "we" in 10:3–6, 12–18; 12:18–19) am now set up in a relationship to "you" as over against "they/them" (10:10, 11:12–15), with "you" now becoming the reason for "my" excesses and the need to boast. By the conclusion, "I" and "you" are now in a new hierarchical (and ironic) relationship, with "we" weak and "you" strong, but "I" in a position to threaten to use "my" authority with severity (13:10).

In this respect, the universal audience plays an important role in the argument, shifting from that construct of which the addressees are a part in Unit 2, to that which judges the addressees by the end of the letter for their failure to adhere to the norms argumentatively presented in Unit 4.[22] This is just one of the ways in which the audiences of this letter are continually being immersed in broad argumentative contexts.

Other ways include the function of three other deixes of interest when considering the relationship between rhetor(s) and audience(s): The *spatial* deixis of the letter shows an interesting inventional choice wherein the rhetor is always *coming* (in distinction from "going") to "you." In that respect, only once (1:16) are the Corinthian and Achaian communities addressed in terms of a stop-over point, near the beginning of the *narratio* wherein this spatial relationship becomes the cause of trouble. In every other case, the reference to "you" is spatially described as a *terminus,* the destination of the rhetors' travels and the object of their intentions. Also of prominence throughout the letter is the place of Macedonia; it is referred to in relationship to the rhetors and Corinth/Achaia six times (in Units 1, 3, and 4; 2 Cor 1:16, 2:13, 7:5, 8:1, 9:2, 11:9). Clearly, Macedonia is a rhetorical space of great importance to the argument and indicates, again, a situation of greater (now geographical) context that keeps the audience continually pondering its relationship to others outside themselves and the rhetor(s).

---

22. Personal deixis also can be explored with respect to a number of other aspects of the argument, all of which serve to create specific relationships and contexts within which and through which the argument is performed. Note, for example, that the readership is addressed not just as "the church of God in Corinth," but to the broader (therefore multiple, and even mixed) audience of "together with all the saints in all of Achaia" in 1:2. Note also that the authorship of the letter is ascribed not only to Paul ("an apostle of Christ Jesus by the will of God"), but also to Timothy "our" brother (thus a multiple, and perhaps therefore mixed, authorship). Note also the function of proper names and substantives (Silvanus, Titus, "famous" brother, Satan, "super apostles," "fool"). All these function rhetorically to situate the rhetor(s), and thereby also the audience(s), in broader personal, subcultural, cultural, ideological, missionary contexts.

Temporal deixis also plays an integral role in the argumentative relationship between rhetor(s) and audience(s). It begins out of a concern with plans for Corinth and Achaia and the missionary activity of the rhetor (but also Silvanus and Timothy) predominantly in the past ("I wanted to come," "I did not come," "I judged," "I wrote") in Unit 1. It next shifts to their working out in the present in Unit 2 ("we have confidence," "we are afflicted," "we are persecuted," "we do not lose heart") and the working out of past plans in the present in Unit 3 ("for this is to your advantage, who not only last year began to do something but even to desire to do it — now finish doing it"; 8:10). However, in Unit 3 there is a shift to future promise ("the one sowing bountifully will also reap bountifully"; 13:6). By Unit 4 and the conclusion, both the present (with respect to "boasting" and "building up") and the past (with respect to the "affliction") contribute to the impact of the shift to the future plans to "come" to Corinth and Achaia with authority: all three aspects function together in the argumentative climax of 13:2, "I have warned and give warning to those having sinned previously and to all the rest, as when present the second time and absent now, that if I come I will not be lenient again." Argumentatively, by the end, the audience(s) has been immersed in a complex chronological context culminating in the future advent of the rhetor(s) who will come with authority.

Finally, the *intonational deixis* is dominated by a sense of confidence, first in "us" (Unit 1), "through Christ for God" (Unit 2), in "you" (Unit 3), and, finally, in "me" (Unit 4). This is complemented by the prevalence of boasting, first in "us" and "you," but always "in the Lord," which allows for the eventual boasting in "my weakness" (Unit 4). These shifts prepare for the culmination of the intonation of authority with a hint of threat that is reached by the conclusion. The sense of affection that began in Unit 1, and is used as the basis of "confidence" in the volitional appeal in Unit 3, is transformed by a threatened potential of division by the end of the letter that is premised upon the very affection and confidence it threatens.

In short, modality and deictic indicators show a strategic argumentative development through a variety of relationships that secure, again and again, the audience in a particular (broad) context, and secure the relationship of the audience(s) under the rhetor(s)' authority in light of that context.

Methods of Argumentation

The letter opens with multiple attestations to both its authors and its audiences: Paul and Timothy (identified as "brother," a term used of several of the missionaries referred to throughout the letter) address not just the church that is in Corinth, but include "all the saints in all of Achaia" (1:1). This address begins a dynamic, argumentative process of immersing the addressees in a relational and geographical context beyond their immediate environs, a process that will contribute to the complex dynamics of the letter's strategies. These strategies are directed at shaping and developing a relationship between rhetor(s) and audience(s) through the argumentation.

When the declaration of praise is offered (1:3, a modified "thanksgiving" section), it is with a specific definitional strategy leading to building a mutuality between rhetor(s) and audience(s). Beginning with the argumentative label of "the Father of mercies" and "God of all consolation, the one consoling us in all our afflictions," the argumentative implications of the *topos* of affliction begin their extensive development here: through a quasi-logical connection, both sufferings and consolation are causally related (1:5). The rhetor's experience of "affliction" and "consolation" are then related directly to the addressees: our affliction is for your consolation and salvation; our consolation is also your consolation (1:4–6), so that "as you are partners in (our) suffering, so also in (our) consolation" (1:7). This experience of "affliction" then becomes the cause for boasting. That is, the causes of this "affliction," as described in the disclosure formula of 1:8–11, are argumentatively connected to "frankness and godly sincerity, not in earthly wisdom but in the grace of God" (1:12). This connection helps to reinforce and extend a relationship with the Achaian communities: it is a "frankness," "sincerity," and "boasting" "all the more towards you" (1:12) that allows a shared reciprocity in boasting ("we are your boast just as you are ours" — 1:14).

Therefore, by the time we reach the letter's *causa* in 1:12–14, all of the major argumentative themes found throughout the rest of the letter have been introduced and intertwined. "Affliction," "consolation," "suffering," "frankness" and "sincerity," and "boasting" will resonate throughout the correspondence, weave throughout the tapestry of argumentation, and provide the argumentatively developed shared ground and mutual relationship for both the audience(s) and the author(s) of the letter.

Unit 1 is framed by the *narratio* of the missionary activities *in the past* and their relationship to the Achaian communities. In 1:15 we meet the *narratio* that will be distributed throughout the letter. It becomes an important framework that ties together not only the various argumentative units (2:12–13, 7:5, 8:1, 9:2, and 11:9), but also allows for the continuation of some *topoi* outlined in the introduction ("affliction" in 7:5 and 8:1, "boasting" in 9:2). It also serves to prepare for the introduction of a new *topos* ("burden" in 11:9, elaborated in 12:14–18). The division of the *narratio* is not to be seen as evidence of interpolations breaking up the narrative (for example, 11:9 is a report of events prior to the storyline beginning in 1:15, but sets up its continuation in 12:14–18 with the sending of Titus), but as a device by which argumentation is simultaneously driven forward and integrated.

The story is set up by 1:15–16, "And from this confidence I wanted first to come to you, so that you might have double grace: to come to you (on my way) to Macedonia, and again from Macedonia to come to you and to be sent from you to Judea." Then comes a *digressio* (1:17–22) defending the rhetor's decision not to visit them on the way to Macedonia. This sets up the reason "sparing you I no longer went to Corinth" through a dissociative argument that is consistent according to divine standards ("God is faithful," 1:18; "but in him everything is 'Yes,'" 1:19), even if it appears inconsistent according to human standards. The argument gets to the heart of a difference between the rhetor and the audiences, namely a question of a hierarchy of values. The Achaian communities are accused of judging the ministry and the rhetor according to human "appearances," whereas the divine "reality" is the one by which they should understand and judge. They are thereby placed in a position of having "misunderstood" the nature of ministry. This dissociative strategy first introduced here will be an important strategy employed throughout the letter.[23]

Interestingly, the implication of rejection (by not visiting the communities on the way to Macedonia) becomes the argumentative means by which the rhetor (note the dominance of first person singular deixis) seeks to reinforce the bond between himself and the audiences. His choice to "refrain from coming to Corinth" (1:23) was premised on the effort to avoid inflicting pain. However, contrary to the interpretation of most commentators, the argument describes the pain as being *the rhetor's,* rather than the community's: "And I wrote as I did, so that coming *I* might not have pain from those who should give me joy, confident about all of you that my joy is the joy of all of you" (2:3). The source of pain should therefore *not* be seen as the previous letter that the rhetor wrote, written out of love (2:4) and confidence in "you" (2:3). Instead, the source of pain is the unnamed individual who is being punished by the majority and should now be forgiven and consoled. The previous

---

23. Jerry McCant, "Second Corinthians as Parodic Apologia," *Rhetorics and Hermeneutics: Conference in Honor of Wilhelm Wuellner* (Claremont, Calif.: March 2000), suggests the whole letter, not just chapters 10–13, should be read as an apologetic parody similar to that of Socrates' apology before than Athenian *Symbulion*. "Parody in 2 Corinthians subverts the anticipation of judicial rhetoric and Paul becomes the prosecutor rather than the defendant in much the same way Socrates does.... Each major argument in 2 Corinthians concludes with a subversion of anticipation." While I do not necessarily ascribe an apologetic function to the whole letter, the notion of "subversion" seems to be a useful way to consider several aspects of the argumentation, including the dissociative strategies found throughout the argumentation.

letter is therefore to be seen as a "test" of "obedience" on the part of the community of Corinth (in particular; 1:23), another important *topos* that will be employed later.

However, the relationship being built here, while apparently described in terms of mutual reciprocity ("Not that we lord it over your faith, but that we are workers for your joy, because you stand (firm) in the faith," 1:24; "whom you forgive, I also," 2:10), has been surreptitiously defined in the argument in terms of a hierarchy. Both the *topoi* of "testing" and "obedience," and the caveat "for what I have forgiven, *if I have forgiven anything*, (is) on account of you in the presence of Christ" in 2:10, allow the rhetor a certain freedom in decision-making power and some authority over the communities. It is a particular argumentative development of the relationship between rhetor and audiences — initially reciprocal, it is now also hierarchical.

Therefore, it is clear how this unit serves the important function of confronting problems with and rebuilding the rhetor(s)' ethos among the community, thereby providing the foundation for the argumentative work and development to follow. Beginning with an "apology" regarding the rhetor's decision not to "pass through" Corinth, a mutuality is argumentatively generated in an effort to secure the rhetor's status with the audience by means of dissociative argumentation. Once the relationship is secured and so defined/clarified, however, it is also carefully shaped according to a specific relationship of authority that develops through the trajectory of the argument.[24]

The Unit is rounded off with the *narratio* in 2:12–13 which both picks up the story in 1:15–16 and presages the next installment in 7:5. Some scholars suggest that the argument beginning at 2:14 (Unit 2) represents an insertion of an independent source, as evidenced by the break in the *narratio* at this point. Rather, the purpose of this unit is to develop an argument that anticipates, by speaking of the purpose of the ministry as it relates to the present, the "affliction" experienced by the rhetors in Macedonia. That is, while the audiences have been told about afflictions in Asia (1:8), they have not yet been told about any afflictions in Macedonia (7:5). The *narratio,* therefore, frames Unit 2, whose purpose is to explain how the "triumphal procession" in 2:14 is to be understood in terms of the experiences of "affliction" which meet with the missionaries wherever they go, including Macedonia by 7:5.

---

24. Questions concerning the reasons for waiting to address the question of ethos at the end of the letter in chapters 10–13 presuppose no such ethical argumentation has taken place in the previous chapters. Clearly, Units 1 and 2 address precisely this issue: the rhetor(s)' standing, allowing him to speak to the community. Indeed, Units 1 and 2, as we shall see below, help provide the foundation upon which the further ethical argumentation of Unit 4 can take place.

This, in turn, will provide a foundation for the collection appeal, providing a background for the generous gift of the churches in Macedonia made in spite of the "great trial of affliction" confronting them found in Unit 3.

Unit 2 is concerned with the plans for the ministry as related *to the present*. It begins by describing the ministry in terms of "odor" (2:14) and "fragrance" (2:15). These are rhetorical allusions to terms of ritual and sacrifice, perhaps in reference to Roman triumphal processions (e.g., God "leading us"; 2:14) after successful warfare. As such, it helps to build a connection between sacrifice/procession and the *topos* of affliction personified in "us" as persons "of sincerity" (2:17). This definitional argument serves two functions: First, on the basis of "sincerity," it is not necessary for "us" to need "a letter from you or for you" (3:1), since we are the sacrifice/procession of God leading from life to life, but also for others from death to death (2:16). Rather, "you" are now "a letter from Christ delivered by us, written not with ink but with the Spirit of the living God, not on tablets of stone but on tablets of human hearts" (3:3). Once again, an argumentative relationship is being defined between rhetor and audiences, this one now of mutuality.

Second, it allows a claim of "confidence" in the ministry as stemming, not from "us," but from the Spirit. This definition becomes the foundation of a series dissociations: new covenant/old covenant, letter-death/Spirit-life, veiled/unveiled (3:4–4:6). These are argumentative elaborations of the theme introduced in 2:16, "from death to death," "from life to life." In addition to this, and premised upon it, the "confidence" of ministry is based upon the refusal "to practice cunning or to falsify the word of God, but rather commending ourselves to the conscience of everyone before God by the open statement of truth" (4:2). However, the "confidence" is not *self*-commendation, since what is being proclaimed is not "ourselves," but "Jesus Christ as Lord, and ourselves as your slaves through Jesus." (4:5).

This anticipates the dissociation carefully prepared for since 3:3: the "power (which) belongs to God" is made to shine in the ministry through "weakness" and "affliction." Rather than marks of shame, the issues of "weakness" and "affliction" become the reason for boasting ("you" in "us," "so that you might have [an answer] for those boasting in appearance and not in the heart"; 5:12, cf. 10:12–18). Through the dissociative argument the universal audience (from 4:16 to 5:10 the address "we" becomes a universal address, as explicitly emphasized in the phrase "all of us") participates in a rhetorical reconstitution of reality: "the old things have passed away, see, they have become new" from God through Christ (5:17f.).

In other words, a certain redistribution of authority and power continues to be shaped through dissociating the worldly "appearance" of weakness from the "reality" that afflictions represent a "true" measure of power. "Confidence" can now be expressed ("we do not lose heart"; cf. 4:16) in spite of afflictions. The dissociation also informs the division of "our earthly tent" (appearance of weakness) from "the building from God" (5:1). It explains how when "we are beside ourselves" for God (appearance of foolishness), we are nevertheless "in our right mind" for "you" (5:13). It also explains the basis of the claim that we "in all things understand ourselves as ministers of God," namely by reference to a catalogue of afflictions, hardships, calamities, etc. (6:4–10).

Finally, this dissociative move also anticipates and grounds the peroration in 6:11–7:4. Up to this point, the entreaty to be reconciled to God (5:20), the urgent ("now"; 6:2) request not to accept the grace of God in vain (6:1), the frankness and openness of "our" affections, have been set within *convincing* argumentation. Once the argument reaches 6:11–7:4, they are herein given practical and *persuasive* application to enact these principles. In other words, an ethos has been developed, a relationship in which the rhetors have proven themselves not to be "self-commending" by reference to human standards. They are not cunning or shameful, nor could they be blamed for putting obstacles in anyone's way, nor have they been restricted in their affections: "We wronged no one, corrupted no one, took advantage of no one" (7:2). At this point, and on the basis of a shared status in Christ (e.g., "reconciliation" in 5:18–20,[25] but also note back at 2:16 the ministry being "from life to life") a *persuasive* appeal is made to adopt concrete action: "do not be mismatched[26] with unbelievers" (6:14).[27] This appeal culminates a long and complex argument concerning the nature, function, and characteristics of the ministry of the rhetors, and is premised upon the division reflected in the ministry being an odor for some "from death to death," but for others "from life to life." It offers a pathos appeal for the audiences to enact the values they have been presented up to this point. The suggestion is made not out of a desire to condemn/fault them (7:3), but to "make room for us" (7:2), that is, to build

---

25. Note: the ministry of reconciliation is not concerned with Paul's reconciliation to the community, but with the community's reconciliation *to God*. It does not at all represent a separate source referring to a phase of "reconciliation" wrought after the fallout of the "letter of tears."

26. For a discussion of the possible understandings of "unequal yoke," see William Webb, "Unequally Yoked Together with Unbelievers: Part 2 (of 2 parts) What Is the Unequal Yoke (*heterozugountes*) in 2 Corinthians 6:14?" *BSac* 149 (1992): 162–79.

27. Scholarly appeals for later source insertion on the basis of "inauthentic" vocabulary, premised as they are upon a predetermined notion of "authentic" letters, themes, vocabulary, and theology, simply ignore the inventional dynamic at work in this text. The "insider/outsider," "saved/condemned," "righteous/lawless" divisions are part of Paul's rhetorical vision, acting as fantasy theme dynamics throughout his letters, particularly 1 Corinthians (e.g., the vocabulary shared in this section and 1 Cor 3:16, 6:6, 6:19, 9:21), but also 1 Thessalonians, Romans, and elsewhere.

a relationship between rhetor and audiences that prepares for the practical issues to follow.

When the third unit begins, which itself is a two-part structure employing two distinct but related strategic approaches to persuade the Achaian communities to complete the task of collection, the persuasive groundwork has been laid. It is tied to the foregoing by means of picking up the thread of the *narratio* in 7:5, 8:1-2, and 9:2. Shifting from concerns with present experiences of the ministry, it is the relationship of the Achaian communities to the *future* plans of the ministry that is the driving impetus of this unit. Thus, the *narratio* serves as the means of bringing all the argumentative units together. It returns to the letter reception mentioned in 1:23-2:12, but can now introduce the argumentative *topos* of "affliction" into the story (experienced by both the missionaries in Macedonia in 7:5 and by the church in Macedonia in 8:1-2). It also draws from the *topoi* of "boasting" (in "you"), "confidence" (in "you"), and "consolation," all of which have been elaborated in the previous argumentative units. It is in particular with respect to "consolation" that the transition is made (7:5-16) from the second unit through the *narratio* to the collection appeal in the third unit. It is significant that the basis of the consolation is the justification of the rhetor's (first person singular) "boasting" about and "confidence" in the communities, on account of the obedience shown to Titus. The confidence the rhetor ("I" in 7:16) has in the communities because of their obedience becomes the standard against which they are being tested. The first argumentative strategy builds upon this and appeals to a consistency of action: "Just as you excel in everything, in faith and word and knowledge and all eagerness and in your love of us, so also you should excel in this gift" (8:7). The collection appeal is not a command, but a test of their own reputation, a volitional strategy. Appealing to "the grace of our Lord Jesus Christ" (8:9), and to fairness in the distribution of abundance to those in need (8:14-15), the audiences should finish what they started (8:11). Titus, sent specifically as "my" partner and co-worker in this task (8:23), along with the brother "who is famous among all the churches for proclaiming the good news" (8:18) and the brothers/sisters who are "apostles of the churches" are to be shown "proof of your love and of our boasting about you" (8:24). They must live up to the test of their own consistency, but also to the boasting on their behalf. Here is particularly (but not exclusively) where the mixed audiences of the introductory section come into play importantly.

The second strategy is an argument from a promise for future abundance. It moves from the previous argument from fairness by means of a *paralepsis* figure, drawing once again from the *narratio* of 8:1-2 and 9:1-2. The paralepsis ("now it's superfluous for me to write to you about the ministry of the saints") functions to downplay the rhetor's concerns just mentioned (it is "superfluous") by playing up the confidence he feels ("for I know your eagerness"). It also draws from the *topoi* of "boasting" and "zeal" mentioned in the previous argument. But, while it may be "superfluous" for him, the rhetor nevertheless returns to the *topos* of testing, this time in order to avoid a potentially "shameful" circumstance (of lack of preparation or willingness). The avoidance of such a situation is identified as the purpose for sending the brothers/sisters ahead to prepare for Paul and the Macedonians' arrival. The intention of the visit, once again specifically stated, is to encourage the offering as a voluntary gift, *not* an extortion.

In other words, it is a volitional, direct appeal outlining the benefits of giving cheerfully, not reluctantly, with the knowledge of the promise of a return. Through the "testing" of this ministry "you" glorify God "by your obedience to the confession of the good news of Christ and by the sincerity of the partnership with them and with everyone" (9:13). In turn, "they will pray for you while longing for you on account of the exceeding grace of God for you" (9:14), the implication being that this is the first fruits of the bountiful harvest (9:6).[28]

Both of the strategies in this unit, therefore, share a modality of volition in order to secure a commitment to action. This volitional appeal, however, is subtly reinforced by two intriguing strategies that suggest a specific relationship between rhetor and audiences. The first, while appealing to mutual dependence and deliberative freedom, also sets the congregation under obligation. This is made clear not only through the specific rhetorical *topoi* of "testing" and "obedience," but also through the presence of Paul's representatives (who are there to ensure that the congregation recognizes its obligation to "live up to the boast"), as well as its relationship under God's patronage. It is an appeal that combines persuasion and praise with obligation and reinforcement.

The second rhetorical strategy is to direct the thanksgiving for their participation in the collection not back to them, but *to God*. This move subverts any potential assumption on the part of the audience that they are the patrons of this missionary effort. Rather, they are set under obligation to the rhetors, who are acting as brokers for their patron, *God*.[29]

When the fourth unit begins in 10:1, it is with a distinct change of tone. An ironic modality gives shape to the argument; tones of defensiveness enter into the discourse. Yet, while the argumentative situation has certainly changed,

---

28. See David deSilva, "Investigation of the Integrity and Argumentation of 2 Corinthians," *JSNT* 52 (1993): 41–70, for an alternative rhetorical reading of this section of the argument.

29. Cf. McCant, "Second Corinthians as Parodic Apologia," 23–24.

and with it the inventional strategies to address it, it is by no means isolated from the previous argumentation, as we shall see.

The unit begins in 10:1–18 with a return to "confidence" and "boasting," but now it is no longer in "you" or "your obedience," but rather a question of "me." It derives from the argumentative groundwork in Unit 2. As before, the issue is addressed through a dissociative move that shifts the foundation upon which to judge boldness and weakness from human standards to a divine one. Pleading "through the meekness and gentleness of Christ" (10:1) not to be forced into a game whose rules he rejects, the rhetor turns the table on those who judge him "strong while absent/weak when present" (cf. 10:10). He does so not only by arguing for a consistency between speech and action (10:11), but also by accusing the accusers of a faulty standard of judgment: "But they, classifying and comparing themselves to themselves, do not show good sense" (10:12). This proposition was already grounded in both 10:2–5 (not according to human standards, etc.) and in the argument of Unit 2 leading to the statement, "we do not again commend ourselves to you but, giving you an opportunity to boast about us, you might have (an answer) for those boasting in outward appearance and not in the heart" (5:12). The rhetor has taken the moral high ground from those with whom he feels in competition.

Also note the relational twist that takes place in this argument: it is not merely a question of arguing over standards by which to judge the rhetors, but one of standing vis-à-vis Paul and the communities. The moral high ground is linked to the issue of authority over the communities. This is not new. "Obedience" was already introduced into the discourse with respect to the letter reception in 2:9, 6:11, and 9:13. But it is particularly with regard to "punish[ment]" in 10:6 that the stakes are raised. This intensification is noted immediately. It is not denied, but is defined in as positive a fashion as possible: making use of the previous philosophical pair of "earthly tent/building from God," it is an authority derived from the Lord "for building up and not for tearing you down" (10:8) which had been clearly identified in Unit 2. It is this particular argumentative understanding of the ministry to the Achaian churches that will become the defining argumentative context out of which and toward which the rest of this unit is shaped.[30]

The communities are warned away from possible infidelity (the marital metaphor of 11:2). The rhetor is concerned to address his apparent inferiority to the so-called "super apostles" whose activities (and boasting!) he goes on to equate with the actions of Satan (11:14–15). An apparent misunderstanding

---

30. See Georg Strecker, "Die Legitimatät des paulinischen Apostolates nach 2 Korintherbrief 10–13," *NTS* 38/4 (1992): 566–86.

of the rules of hospitality seems to impact upon the rhetor's standing (11:7–11). Out of this the issue of "boasting" arises, and it is very interesting that it is set up within the argumentative context of the division of human/divine standards: "I will boast" *as a fool according to human standards* (11:16–18). And accordingly, it is with deep irony that the boasting is of "my" weakness: Are they Hebrews? Israelites? Ministers of Christ? "I am a better one" by witness to all the afflictions "I" have suffered (11:23–12:10). Note even how the exceptional character of the revelation is tempered by the "thorn in the flesh" in 12:7. The strategy is made clear: based on the proposition, "So I will boast all the more in my weakness that the power of Christ might dwell on me" (12:9), the argument drives toward the conclusion, "for whenever I am weak, then I am strong" (12:10). On *this* basis it is "clear" that "I ought to be *commended* by you, for I am not inferior to these 'super-apostles,' even though I am nothing" (12:11). This argument is the fulfillment of the dissociative strategy first introduced in Unit 2 (4:7–6:10).

Additionally, a rhetorical effort is being directed in this argument with respect to "the limits" of boasting. The standard is, set in 10:15–17: "We do not boast beyond the limits, that is, *in other people's works*.... 'Let the one boasting boast in the Lord.'" The limits, as defined here, will not be trespassed. But the boasting of the "fool's speech" is indeed "beyond the limits." That is, it is a boasting in which the rhetor is perhaps best described as being "beside himself" in the visions reported in 12:1–4 (reminiscent of being "beside ourselves for God" in 5:13; note also in 11:23: "I am talking like a madman"). The limits are far beyond the limits (i.e., they are "mad"), but are not inconsistent with the claim (i.e., they are for Christ; cf. 12:10–11). This is not an unanticipated argumentative move, but is given clear justification both by the groundwork laid in the affliction notices and catalogues (1:8–10, 4:8–11, and chapters 5 and 6) and in the dissociative argumentation of human/divine wisdom in Unit 2. But it is also a move which was "forced" upon the rhetor by the communities (12:11).

So when the rhetor reports that "I am ready to come" in 12:14–13:4, the hierarchical metaphor of "parent/child" can be extended not only to justify previous and current action as based in "love," but can also allow for the rhetor's authority to be extended. It is an authority which has been argumentatively tied to the power of God (13:4), and whose purpose is consistently "for the sake of your building up" (12:19; cf. 13:10). The rhetor places the responsibility for his response on the communities (10:1–2; 12:20–21; 13:2, 5–7), once again making appeal to the notion of "testing," this time testing "yourselves" (13:5).

By the time of the final salutation, therefore, the relationship between rhetor(s) and audience(s) are clearly delineated and the resulting expectations imperatively described. "Put things in order, encourage each other, think the same thing, live in peace, and the God of love and peace will be with you" (13:11). Here, at the end, the full force of the impact of the rhetor's standing vis-à-vis the audience(s) stakes its argumentative claim upon his authority, albeit an authority which is carefully, argumentatively delineated in the strategies previously developed throughout the whole letter.

Dynamics of the Argumentative Situations

Taking a step back from the detailed analysis, it is clear that the complex argumentative dynamics of this letter display shifts, both subtle and profound, in the argumentative situation as encountered through the reading of the letter. Units 1 and 2 represent an effort to rebuild and then elaborate upon the rhetor(s)' standing with/in the community by quasi-logical, definitional appeals, assertive (not conditional) modalities, and relations postures of mutual upbuilding, consolation, and boasting under the explicit (if only casually mentioned) rubric of a hierarchy of "testing" and "obedience." By the time Unit 3 is encountered, this mutuality can be shaped through arguments from justice and the promise of future return set within a modality of volition that is premised upon the values of honor/shame and on living up to the audience's consistency and reputation. However, relationally, the hierarchy is reinforced by reference to God's patronage of the audience, allowing the rhetors to position themselves as brokers *of God*.

Once these pragmatic and relational matters have been settled, saving the "most important" ethos argumentation for last, the rhetor finally returns to his relationship to the audience with respect to "outsiders" ("they"), "super-apostles," and the constellation of values that "they" represent as a threat to the relationship. It is clear that this final unit and concluding section show an integral relationship to the rest of the argumentation. Throughout it, the *topoi* of "confidence," "boasting," "obedience," "building up," "affliction," the dissociation of human versus divine standards of judging the ministry, the development of the *narratio,* love (affection), even "Satan," continue their argumentative function from out of the previous units. By the end of the letter, the transformation of what was originally an approach of a sometime affectionate intonation and volitional modality into a modality of irony and intensity of apologetics does not suggest a separate source. Rather, it suggests a strategic inventional choice with respect to the way in which to address what is clearly an important issue. Having "saved this for last," the rhetor can build upon and draw from all the complex relational and strategic work found throughout the correspondence.[31]

It is clear that the many argumentative shifts need not at all represent independent sources. To the contrary, they display a complex web of modalities, deictic relations, and argumentative strategies that build upon one another, presage, fulfill, and develop threads according to the presumed and anticipated reception of the letter. Apologetic, deliberative, and epideictic approaches within the correspondence (to revert to traditional Aristotelian genres) all make their argumentative presence felt in a concerted effort of convincing and persuasive appeal premised upon the ministerial "needs" addressed in the letter. Setting aside preconceived notions of how a relationship between rhetor and audience ought to develop, and how a trajectory of reasoning ought to take place, we see instead a number of interrelated strategies that work together to culminate in an argumentative gestalt. They function to secure a certain understanding of ministry and the hierarchical relationships this understanding entails between rhetor(s) and audience(s), both of which are subsumed under God whose power is demonstrated through weakness and affliction.

Conclusion

Our model, a rhetorical theory of dynamic argumentation, has successfully explained the developing inventional strategies and argumentative moves made throughout 2 Corinthians. The result is an awareness of the careful integration of topics, an improved understanding of modalities and deictic indicators, and an appreciation of the changing argumentative situations. The argumentative significance of the *topoi* of "affliction," "boasting," and "confidence," the dissociative strategies of "weak/strong," the use of narrative threads within the argumentative units, and relational developments between rhetors and audiences all weave together into a complex and interactive whole in which arguments presage later developments and help provide important foundational moves to "subversive" argumentative ventures.

The results, when considered in relationship to previous argumentative efforts to undermine the partition theory, suggest that the multi-source hypothesis of 2 Corinthians can be radically undermined by means of an appreciation of the complexity of rhetorical strategies exhibited in the letter.

---

31. Contra Niels Hyldahl, "Die Frage nach der literarischen Einheit des Zweiten Korintherbriefs," *ZNW* 64/3–4 (1973): 289–306.

This insight frees us up to begin considering the implications of the correspondence as a whole, not piecemeal as a series of letters in response to a series of reconstructed "events" predetermined by the historian's desire to set events within a developmental scheme.

It is now up to rhetorical critics and others to take up the challenge of exploring several potential fields of inquiry: Pauline rhetorical compositional techniques and *inventio,* the dynamics of and appeal to power and authority in Pauline rhetoric, the ramifications of our interpretative results upon Pauline chronology and early church history, the relationship of authority to the rhetoric of the "sublime," the history of interpretation of the letter, the problematization of its reception as a unified letter at a certain moment in the discipline of Pauline studies, and its on-going reception and message of faith (the rhetoric of religion).

Now that the letter has been reunited through rhetorical analytics that present a formidable challenge to traditional Pauline historical reception of the text, the fullness of its rhetorical power can finally be critically explored and assessed.

CHAPTER 18

GALATIANS:
RED-HOT RHETORIC

Michael R. Cosby

When Paul dictated Galatians, he was under attack. His honor had been challenged. His feelings were hurt, and he responded like an erupting volcano. We should not expect a polished, logical explanation of theological concepts from a man in this frame of mind. We should expect to see fiery hyperbole directed against his opponents and their beliefs, and defensive overstatements when he describes his own gospel message. Nevertheless, down through the centuries commentators have read Galatians primarily as a carefully reasoned treatise contrasting salvation by faith with futile and arrogant human efforts to earn salvation by good works. Superlatives abound as both ancient and modern scholars praise what they perceive as Paul's brilliantly reasoned explanation of theological truths.

During the Reformation, Martin Luther said of Galatians, "So Paul goeth about to establish the doctrine of faith, grace, forgiveness of sins,... to the end that we may have a perfect knowledge and difference between Christian righteousness, and all other kinds of righteousness."[1] C. K. Barrett uses the theology of Galatians as the cornerstone of his book on Pauline theology, and he is not unusual in taking this view.[2] Richard Longenecker's summary well expresses the importance of this epistle:

> Historically, Galatians has been foundational for many forms of Christian doctrine, proclamation, and practice. And it remains true today to say that how one understands the issues and teaching of Galatians determines in large measure what kind of theology is espoused, what kind of message is proclaimed, and what kind of lifestyle is practiced.[3]

With such weight placed on understanding the theology of Galatians, scholars naturally seek to determine the logical development of Paul's thought. When they go looking for theological precision, however, most either miss or dilute the significance of Paul's use of hyperbole. In so doing they not only misread

---

1. *A Commentary on St. Paul's Epistle to the Galatians* (trans. P. S. Watson; London: James Clark, 1953), 21.
2. *Paul: An Introduction to His Thought* (Louisville: Westminster John Knox, 1994).
3. *Galatians* (WBC 41; Waco, Tex.: Word Books, 1990), xliii.

Paul's theology but also err in their reconstructions of the identity of his opponents.

Galatians has long played a central role in Gentile Christianity's self-understanding as compared with Jewish beliefs. Marcion placed it first in his truncated list of Pauline letters, the *Apostolikon* (Tertullian, *Marc.* 5:2–21), and it served as his key for interpreting Christian faith in contrast with Judaism. Though Tertullian derided Marcion's beliefs, he agreed with him on the importance of Galatians for renouncing Jewish laws (*Marc.* 5.2.1). Luther so loved Galatians that he called it his Katie von Bora (his wife). It is "my own epistle," said Luther, "to which I have plighted my troth" (*Werke* 40.2), and the influence of the letter on his theology was immense. Since Luther's time, scholars have mined every sentence of Galatians, digging for doctrine, refining every word for specific truths. However, Galatians is not the super-enriched, high-grade ore that so many think. It is hot lava, which — to be sure — contains precious minerals, but in a mixture of various other kinds of molten rock.

The emotional intensity in Galatians is obvious, and usually mentioned in books on the letter, yet scholars frequently are so focused on finding Paul's theology that they do not adequately deal with the implications of Paul's wrath in his choice of words. Until recently commentators also tended to refer to his anger as a righteous response to what they perceived as wicked Jewish-Christian heretics who were subverting the pure gospel.[4] By taking every detail of Paul's criticisms at face value for reconstructing his foes' beliefs and practices, scholars have missed the significance of his hyperbolic language. Only a few have avoided this pitfall to any extent. Hans Dieter Betz, for example, says

> Not everything that Paul... accuses his opponents of doing or thinking represents their actual goals and intentions. Paul's references must be interpreted in terms of their rhetorical origin and function before they can be used as the basis for conclusions about the opponents.[5]

Betz does not mean by this that Paul was semantically careless. He believes that Paul carefully composed Galatians to follow the form of a judicial speech.[6] Thus, he finds care and precision in the apostle's composition of

---

4. Some, in asserting how evil Paul's opponents were, almost improve on the apostle's own rhetoric; see, e.g., Calvin, *Calvin's New Testament Commentaries* (ed. D. W. and T. F. Torrance, vol. 11; Grand Rapids: Eerdmans, 1965), 5; and E. DeWitt Burton, *A Critical and Exegetical Commentary on the Epistle to the Galatians* (ICC; Edinburgh: T. & T. Clark, 1921), lv–lvi.

5. *Galatians: A Commentary on Paul's Letter to the Churches in Galatia* (Hermeneia; Philadelphia: Fortress, 1979), 6.

6. Betz's attempt to force the contents of Galatians into Greco-Roman rhetorical structures has rightly been criticized. See the book reviews by Wayne A. Meeks, *JBL* 100 (1981): 304–7, and

the supposed *exordium, narratio, propositio, probatio,* and *exhortatio*. In this model, Paul's words become intelligible when we become aware of their rhetorical origin and function. Betz, like many before him, sees intricacy, but he locates it in a different way. However, such complexity is more imagined than real — more wishful thinking than truly descriptive.

We should hesitate to impose order and sophistication where there is a superabundance of emotional heat. The apostle is not carefully conforming each part of an "apologetic letter" to the guidelines of forensic rhetoric. He is not functioning like a professional orator, plotting every move of a speech (e.g., "I will cause the audience to feel emotions at this point in my peroratio by..."). Betz makes Paul overly precise in his structuring of the contents of Galatians and dismisses some semantic problems by appealing to rhetorical strategies.

> In fact, for the rhetoricians of Paul's time, there could be nothing more boring than a perfect product of rhetorical technology.... The arguments were to be presented in a lively way.... Extremely perfected logic was thought to create suspicion and boredom, not credibility, while a carefully prepared mixture of some logic, some emotional appeal, some wisdom, some beauty, and some entertainment was thought to conform to human nature and to the ways in which human beings accept arguments as true.[7]

A number of recent publications follow Betz's basic philosophy but disagree with him on the type of speech form that Galatians represents.

Ben Witherington III argues that Galatians is deliberative rhetoric instead of judicial, but like Betz he believes that Paul's seemingly emotional outbursts are actually calculated use of feigned emotion. From his perspective, Paul uses the "more bombastic style of Asiatic rhetoric [rather] than the measured and restrained tones of the more scholarly and upper-class Attic rhetoric."[8] All through his commentary, Witherington downplays Paul's barrages by calling them deliberately designed, rhetorical techniques, each calculated to bring about certain responses from his audience. In his view Paul is not so emotional as his words would seem to indicate. He is merely following prescribed, deliberative rhetoric.

David Aune, *RSR* 7 (1981): 323–28; C. Joachim Classen's analysis in "St. Paul and Ancient Greek and Roman Rhetoric," *Rhetorica* 10 (1992): 319–44; George Kennedy's critique in *New Testament Interpretation through Rhetorical Criticism* (Chapel Hill: University of North Carolina Press, 1984), 144–52; Longenecker's comments in *Galatians*, ciii–cxix; and Philip Kern's analysis in *Rhetoric and Galatians: Assessing an Approach to Paul's Epistle* (SNTSMS 101; Cambridge University Press, 1998), 4–5, 29, 32–35, 52–59, 92–111, 113–18, 131–41, etc.

7. Betz, *Galatians*, 129.

8. Ben Witherington III, *Grace in Galatia: A Commentary on Paul's Letter to the Galatians* (Grand Rapids: Eerdmans, 1998), 32.

Similarly, Lauri Thurén argues that Galatians is "a stylistic and rhetorical masterpiece, and there is no reason to doubt that the same applies to its theology."[9] According to Thurén, Galatians tells us little or nothing about Paul's emotions, but it reveals a great deal about his rhetorical skills. From Thurén's perspective, commentators have fallen for Paul's rhetoric when they think the apostle was angry. Thus, when readers are fooled in this way, it proves how effective Paul was in making it sound like he was highly agitated.

> The speech of a trained orator hardly happens to reveal something about his heart, nor does a carefully prepared letter...the *ethos* of the author is boosted and the reader is to be emotionally affected by the author's implied emotions. Most commentators seem to have neatly fallen victim to this strategy.[10]

Using this approach, Thurén postulates a rhetorical strategy behind every emotional sounding outburst in Galatians, and in so doing he seeks to understand the true theological intent of the letter by stripping away the rhetorical language, or, as he would say, "derhetorizing" the epistle.

Although I agree with Thurén's desire to understand the meaning of Paul's message by deciphering his use of hyperbole, I disagree with his view that we cannot know that the apostle was angry. I am *not* claiming that Paul was out of control and merely ranting and raving. I *am* claiming that the harsh language in Galatians reveals much about Paul's emotional response to the challenge from Galatia. He was not so angry that what he says completely distorts his theological viewpoint, but his fury affects the wording of the letter in very significant ways.

To relegate Paul's emotional language to calculated use of rhetorical techniques, or to force it to conform to a Greco-Roman speech form, is to miss a vital source of the letter's power. Besides, if he wrote Galatians according to a set speech form, is it not remarkable that no two scholars who seek to determine the structure of this "speech" can agree on their outlines? From Betz to Kennedy to Smit to Longenecker to Witherington, no two outlines are the same. Philip Kern exposes the weaknesses of this approach in a probing analysis, showing in detail the methodological inconsistencies of those who evaluate Galatians according to the ancient rhetorical handbooks.[11] And J. Louis Martyn is correct when he says that insisting on Galatians conforming to the directives of ancient rhetoricians places the letter into a straightjacket.[12]

---

9. "Was Paul Angry? Derhetorizing Galatians," in *The Rhetorical Interpretation of Scripture, Essays from the 1996 Malibu Conference* (ed. S. Porter and D. Stamps; JSNTSup 180; Sheffield: Sheffield Academic Press, 1999), 320.
10. Thurén, "Angry," 309.
11. Kern, *Rhetoric and Galatians*, 1–166.
12. *Galatians: A New Translation with Introduction and Commentary* (AB 33A; New York: Doubleday, 1997), 21.

Early Christian Assessment of Galatians as Crudely Written

If Galatians were a forensic, deliberative, or epideictic speech, surely early Christian writers who were trained in rhetoric would have recognized this. Yet, as Kern demonstrates, Christian leaders who were experts in classical rhetoric evaluated Paul's writing quite differently than do Betz, Witherington, Thurén et al. For example, Origen responds to Celsus's criticism that biblical writings are "corrupted by poor literary style" by admitting stylistic poverty but arguing that Paul's lesser style explains the truth to the many, whereas more refined writings are understandable only to the elite (*Cels.* 7.62).

Celsus finds Christian writings to be crude, stupid, and illiterate, and Origen's defense is to say that the apostles were indeed simple folks who depended on God's power instead of "ordered narrative by the standards of Greek dialectical or rhetorical arts."[13] He appeals to Paul's words in 1 Corinthians 2:4–5: "My speech and my proclamation were not with plausible words of wisdom, but with a demonstration of the Spirit and of power, so that your faith might not rest on human wisdom but on the power of God." Origen criticizes "the pernicious sophistry of the Greeks, which has great plausibility and cleverness" and says that the apostles "knew nothing of the rhetoric prevalent in the law-courts" (*Cels.* 3.39). He obviously does not consider Paul an orator. "He also does not seem to think that all writers who have their origin in the Graeco-Roman world 'breathe the air of rhetoric' in such a way that it necessarily determines the shape and strategy of their discourse."[14]

Chrysostom studied under Libanius, a leading orator of his day, and later taught rhetoric himself. This significant Christian orator freely admits Paul's lack of training and asserts that the apostle possessed "a greater power by far than power of speech" (*De sacerdotio* 4.6). Indeed, he contrasts Paul's rudeness of speech with "the tricks of profane oratory," the same techniques that Betz, Witherington, Thurén et al. argue that the apostle consciously used. And as Kern shows, by analyzing a number of other early Christian writers (and non-Christian critics), who were trained in the very Greco-Roman rhetoric to which modern scholars appeal, these people who actually used the skills of oratory did not believe that Paul possessed them.[15]

Their evaluation does not mean that Paul lacked persuasive ability (e.g., see Chrysostom's commentary on Galatians); it means that his persuasion did not follow the higher-level canons of oratory. There are, of course, parallels

---

13. Kern, *Rhetoric and Galatians*, 171–72.
14. Ibid., 175.
15. Ibid., 167–203.

between parts of Paul's letters and techniques used in the speeches of rhetoricians. Effective speech is not the select domain of orators who are trained to sway the emotions of their audiences by feigning emotion and implementing other manipulation techniques. One of history's ironies is that Paul's letters exerted a much more profound influence on the world than did the polished orations of those who would have considered his language crude and uneducated. Authentic emotion is also persuasive. When Paul wrote Galatians, his anger was genuine, not contrived for fitting into a set rhetorical structure. His words reverberate with emotional intensity. As Chrysostom said, "[Gal. 1:1] is full of great passion and strong sentiment; and not the prologue only but, as it were, the whole letter. For always to speak mildly to those who are being taught, even when they need vehemence, is not the part of a teacher but of a corrupter and an enemy" (*Hom. Gal.* 1:1–3).

Winning Honor through Defaming Opponents

Paul's spirited defense of himself and his gospel responds forcefully to the attack launched by Jewish-Christian missionaries who were telling the Gentile Christians of Galatia that they needed to obey the laws of Moses in order to be fully devoted to God.[16] They have challenged his apostolic credibility, and he vigorously seeks to retain his honor in a heated reply to their charges. Paul's descriptions of these opponents and his explanation of his own theological position are part of a contest of honor.

A number of biblical scholars have argued persuasively that Mediterraneans live in honor/shame societies,[17] and a variety of scholars from other disciplines have documented this cultural mindset.[18] Paul did not seek merely

---

16. These people are explicitly mentioned in 1:6–9; 3:1–2, 5; 4:17; 5:7–12; 6:12–14. For a detailed investigation of these teachers, see Martyn, *Galatians,* 117–26.

17. For descriptions of honor as an important Mediterranean virtue, see Victor H. Matthews and Don C. Benjamin, eds., *Honor and Shame in the World of the Bible* (*Semeia* 68; Atlanta: Scholars Press, 1996); Barth L. Campbell, *Honor, Shame, and the Rhetoric of 1 Peter* (SBLDS 160; Atlanta: Scholars Press, 1998); Bruce Malina, *The New Testament World: Insights from Cultural Anthropology* (rev. ed.; Louisville: Westminster John Knox, 1993), 28–62; Bruce Malina and Jerome Neyrey, "Honor and Shame in Luke-Acts: Pivotal Values of the Mediterranean World," in *The Social World of Luke-Acts: Models for Interpretation* (ed. J. Neyrey; Peabody, Mass.: Hendrickson, 1991), 25–65; and Malina and Neyrey, *Portraits of Paul: An Archaeology of Ancient Personality* (Louisville: Westminster John Knox, 1996), 176–82.

18. E.g., David D. Gilmore, ed., *Honor and Shame and the Unity of the Mediterranean* (Washington, D.C.: American Anthropological Association Special Publication No. 22, 1987); John George Peristiany, ed., *Honour and Shame: The Values of Mediterranean Society* (Chicago: University of Chicago Press, 1966); Julian Pitt-Rivers, *The Fate of Shechem or the Politics of Sex: Essays in the Anthropology of the Mediterranean* (Cambridge: Cambridge University Press, 1977); Raphael Patai, *The Arab Mind* (New York: Scribner, 1973), 90–96, 119–27. Thomas L. Friedman gives a great

to present the unembellished truth about Christ and salvation. He competed in what we might call the "Missionary Games" against opponents whose physical presence and rhetorical skills surpassed his own, yet he emerged the winner in the church's longer historical perspective. In Corinth, for example, missionary rivals considered the apostle Paul's physical presence to be unimpressive, and they called his public speaking skills pathetic. He admits this while defending himself against attack when he says,

> I do not want to seem as though I am trying to frighten you with my letters. For they say, "His letters are weighty and strong, but his bodily presence is weak, and his speech contemptible...." I think that I am not in the least inferior to these super-apostles. I may be untrained in speech, but not in knowledge. (2 Cor 10:9; 11:5–6)

His opponents challenged his intellect. They challenged his message. They challenged his spirituality. They challenged his honor. They lost.

In the bruising world of challenge/riposte contests, Paul's accusations are actually somewhat sedate when compared with many other examples of name-calling. Luke T. Johnson provides an important analysis of how ancient Mediterraneans used vitriolic hyperbole when castigating opponents.[19] Describing the polemics of philosophers, he gives an example of Dio of Prusa, who viciously criticized those belonging to his former occupation of rhetorician.

> He calls the *sophistai:* "ignorant, boastful, self-deceived" (*Or.* 4.33)... "unlearned and deceiving by their words" (4.37)... "evil-spirited" (4.38)... "impious" (11.14) ... "liars and deceivers" (12.12)... "preaching for the sake of gain and glory and only their own benefit" (32.30). They are flatterers, charlatans and sophists (23.11)... they profit nothing (33.4–5)... they are mindless (54.1), boastful and shameless (55.7), deceiving others and themselves (70.10), demagogues (77/78.27). He can say all this though he grudgingly admits that some sophists act for good (35.9–10). In other words, the polemic has nothing to do with specific actions, but typical ones.[20]

Johnson's study also reveals the penchant of ancient authors to defame opponents who were part of their own cultural subgroups even more than they verbally attacked complete outsiders. He observes that "Plutarch, a priest of Apollo at Delphi, was the most urbane of ancient philosophers, encyclopedic in learning, vast in sympathy." This liberal-minded man exhibited considerable generosity when describing the Jews, and this, says Johnson, proves that "*their* version of philosophy was unimportant to him." Against rival

---

example of the problems incurred with failure to restore honor when he recounts the legend of the turkey, *From Beirut to Jerusalem* (New York: Doubleday, 1989), 89.

19. "The New Testament's Anti-Jewish Slander and the Conventions of Ancient Polemic," *JBL* 108 (1989): 419–41.

20. Johnson, "Polemic," 430.

schools that Plutarch took seriously, however, the urbane philosopher heaped scorn and personal attacks. When Colotes, a disciple of Epicurus, attacked Plutarch's heroes by calling them "buffoons, charlatans, assassins, prostitutes, nincompoops," he responded by calling them charlatans whose "eminent men write with such shameless arrogance" (*Mor.* 1124C).[21] Similarly, the Stoic philosopher Epictetus attacked Epicureans, saying, "your doctrines are bad, subversive of the state, destructive of the family, not even fit for women" (*Diss.* 3.7.21). Such slander indicated that the author saw a certain group as a threat, and typically he wrote his harangue to be read by members of his own group (those who agree, not opponents).

Jewish polemic, although sometimes directed with blistering heat toward Gentiles who were hostile toward Jews,[22] more often attacked competing Jewish groups. Josephus thoroughly castigates the zealots in *Bellum judaicum*, 4.6.3, and calls the Sicarii "imposters and brigands" (2.8.6), "slaves, the dregs of society, and the bastard scum of the nation" (5.8.5) who are more wicked than Sodom in being godless (5.13.6) and "outdo each other in acts of impiety toward God and injustice to their neighbors ... no word unspoken to insult, no deed untried to ruin" (7.8.1).[23] Johnson illustrates slander directed toward various Jewish opponents with quotations from the Mishnah, *Psalms of Solomon*, Dead Sea Scrolls, and other texts. For example, 1QS 4.9–14 asserts that Jews outside the group are characterized by "greed and ... wickedness and lies, haughtiness and pride, falseness and deceit, cruelty and abundant evil, ... abominable deeds committed in a spirit of lust."

Johnson concludes by saying that New Testament polemic against Jewish groups seems inappropriate to many people today only because so few first-century Jewish vilifications of Christians have survived. All sides in such debates ordinarily used slanderous descriptions of one's opponents. Johnson's study is valuable for sensitizing us to the nature of polemical language and helping us to avoid interpreting such caustic comments as literal descriptions of precisely what an ancient author believed to be true about all members of opposing groups.[24] Such denunciations were so widespread in Mediterranean

---

21. Ibid., 431.
22. Johnson ("Polemic," 434–36), gives excellent examples of such attacks on Gentiles in the writings of Josephus and Philo and in the Wisdom of Solomon. E.g., in Wisdom 14, after condemning the perversions of Gentiles, the author says, "all is a raging riot of blood and murder, theft and deceit, corruption, faithlessness, tumult, perjury, confusion over what is good, forgetfulness of favors, defiling of souls, sexual perversion, disorder in marriages, adultery, and debauchery," 14:25–26.
23. Johnson, "Polemic," 437.
24. J. Roger Dunkle shows similar tendencies among the Romans, "The Greek Tyrant and Roman Political Invective of the Late Republic," *TAPA* 98 (1967): 151–71.

cultures that we may reasonably assume that Paul would be aggressive when defending himself and his theology against attack.

Indeed, Paul's desire to restore his honor in Galatians is visible even in the defensive way he begins the epistle. He asserts that God appointed him to apostolic office; no human being had any say in this divine decision (1:1). So indignant is he that, after his initial greeting (1:1–5), he skips entirely his normal thanksgiving section and begins the body of the letter by launching directly into his counterattack. Gone are the polite, flattering statements that characterize thanksgiving sections in his other letters. He moves immediately into his assault with an exaggerated assessment of the Galatians' apostasy from God: "I am astonished that so quickly you are deserting the one who called you [i.e., God; see 5:8] in the grace of Christ" (1:6).

Although Paul's readers likely believe that they are acting in good faith on the knowledge they have available, his words do not even hint at this possibility. Paul's language is all or nothing: they are committing apostasy against God by turning away from the gospel that he taught. He does not present a literal description of the situation in Galatia. He verbally accosts his audience with highly confrontational language. Then he proceeds to blast those who are turning the Galatian Christians against him.

Paul accuses the intruding teachers of confusing the Galatians and perverting the gospel of Christ (1:7). He indicates that they exalt the law of Moses (e.g., 2:15–18), have bewitched the Galatians (3:1), rely on the law (3:10–12), and prevent the Galatian Christians from obeying the truth (5:7). Yet these people may not be so terrible as his words indicate. They are probably respected leaders who have sufficient stature to challenge Paul's theology persuasively, for he obviously considers them to be a significant threat. Nevertheless, Paul's confrontational language dismisses them as evil. To make his point he hyperbolically asserts: "But even if we or an angel from heaven preach a gospel differing from the one we preached to you, let him be accursed!" (1:8). He feels so strongly about this that he repeats the curse formula in verse 9. By indicating that he is ready to pronounce a curse on himself or even on an angel for having the audacity to challenge his gospel proclamation, Paul dramatically increases the force of his assertion.

Unfortunately, many scholars are so committed to finding exact correspondences in Paul's words that they conclude that his opponents in Galatia were proclaiming some sort of gospel message involving angels. Their diverse attempts at reconstruction fail to recognize that Paul is exaggerating. His polemical words function more to defame than to define.

When Paul refers to the "false brothers" in 2:4, he defames Jewish Christians who strongly believed that Gentiles should be required to undergo circumcision as a means of fulfilling the covenant with God.[25] They were not peripheral extremists. The meeting that Paul describes in 2:2 was not open to the general Christian public; he calls it a "private meeting" to discuss important matters with the Jerusalem apostles. Therefore, the opponents' presence at this meeting indicates that they had access to the apostles and were allowed to make their case. However, when describing them Paul says they are "false brothers *secretly brought in,* who *snuck in to spy out* our freedom which we have in Christ Jesus, in order to *enslave* us" (2:4). His choice of words portrays them as devious and deceptive, sneaking in to destroy the gospel and enslave Christians. Respected members of the Christian community held a different opinion, but Paul viewed them as a serious threat.

Paul was not averse to slander. His sensitivities would have been closer to Martin Luther's, who could be quite graphic when attacking theological adversaries. In 1511 Luther wrote in *Wider Hans Worst* the following polemic against Duke Heinrich von Braunschweig-Wolfenbüttel:

> You shouldn't have written a book, unless you had heard a fart from an old sow, when you should have opened your mouth wide to it and said, "Thank you very much, beautiful nightingale, that will make good text for me."[26]

Paul's object was to win, to defeat his opponents and reclaim his honorable position. His language, while colorful, would be quite acceptable in the verbally rough and tumble societies in which he ministered.

Overstating the Contrast between Law and Faith

Sensitivity to Paul's tendency to overstate his descriptions of opponents also helps us to understand his theology. His defensive rebuttal carries over into his explanation of justification by faith. He does not suddenly change from defending himself to giving a calmly logical treatise designed to impress post-Enlightenment scholars. His identity as apostle to the Gentiles is bound up with the message he proclaims, and when he defends his gospel he defends his own honor. To try to separate the message from the man is foolish.

When Paul equates living under the law of Moses with slavery in Galatians 3–4, his stark assertions overstate his true attitude toward the law. Does this former Pharisee, who in another rhetorical context proudly claims that his righteousness under the law was blameless (Phil 3:6), literally believe

---

25. See Carol Schlueter, *Filling Up the Measure: Polemical Hyperbole in 1 Thessalonians 2.14–16* (JSNTSup 98; Sheffield: Sheffield Academic Press, 1994), 161.
26. Quotation from Gerhard Ebeling, *Luther: An Introduction to his Thought* (Philadelphia: Fortress, 1970), 54.

that living under the law is living under a curse (Gal 3:10, 13)? Or is this an overstatement to emphasize his point about justification coming through faith? Does Paul actually believe that the law was merely *added* because of sin and has only the temporary role of revealing sinfulness and slavishly leading people to faith in Christ (3:19, 23–26)? Or does he believe that the law plays a more constructive role in God's dealings with humans?

Paul's attitude toward the law is more clearly visible in Romans, where, although still on the defensive (e.g., Rom 3:8) and still overstating for persuasive effect, he expresses himself more calmly. There he refers to the scriptures as "the oracles of God" (3:2) and says that he does not overthrow the law with his teaching of justification by faith but rather upholds it (3:31). He appeals to scripture for teaching about righteousness (4:1–25) and says that "the law is holy, and the commandment is holy and just and good" (7:12) and "the law is spiritual" (7:14). When speaking to the issue of Israel's place in God's purpose, he quotes scripture profusely in Romans 9–11. When urging Christians not to avenge themselves in 12:19–20, he quotes Deuteronomy 32:35 and Proverbs 12:19–20. When teaching in 14:11 that all Christians will stand before God's judgment seat, he quotes Isaiah 45:23 as a proof text. The relevance of scripture is further emphasized in 15:4: "For whatever was written in former days was written for our instruction, so that by steadfastness and by the encouragement of the scriptures we might have hope." And when Paul stresses that Jewish and Gentile Christians should welcome each other, he strings together four Old Testament proof texts in 15:9–12 in order to demonstrate the correctness of his teaching about unity in the church.

In Galatians Paul defends his honor with greater intensity than he does in Romans, and exaggeration increases the force of his words for convincing his audience to maintain his viewpoint and reject the teachings of the opponents who challenged his gospel message. His heated counterattack boils with emotion as he strikes back, and his readers feel the sting of his words. By assailing their intelligence in 3:1, he transfers the focus of criticism from himself to them: "O foolish Galatians, who bewitched you?"[27] With frustrated sarcasm he asks, "Are you so foolish, that, having begun with the spirit, now you are

---

27. Betz calls 3:1 "biting and aggressive" but adds, "This insult, however, should not be taken too seriously. Such addresses were commonplace among the diatribe preachers of Paul's day" (*Galatians*, 130, citing Bultmann, *Der Stil der paulinischen Predigt und die kynisch-stoische Diatribe* [Göttingen: Vandenhoeck & Ruprecht, 1910], 13f., 32f., 55, 60ff., 85ff.). J. H. Neyrey interprets the message in light of the Mediterranean concept of the evil eye, claiming that Paul believes his converts have come under a spell cast by his opponents at Galatia, "Bewitched in Galatia: Paul and Cultural Anthropology," *CBQ* 50 (1988): 72–100. For further information on the evil eye, see also John H. Elliott, "Matthew 20:1–15: A Parable of Invidious Comparison and Evil Eye Accusation," *BTB* 22 (1992): 52–65. Such investigations, while illuminating, fail to recognize overstatement in Paul's criticisms of his opponents. They focus on one aspect of his cultural setting and overlook another.

ending with the flesh?" (3:3). The questions that follow focus on Paul's point that keeping the law is a move backward to immaturity, not forward to spiritual maturity. So strongly and emotionally does he seek to make this point that he exaggerates his comments on the problems of living under the law.

When Paul equates living under the law with being enslaved to the *stoicheia* (Gal 4:1–3), he intends through passionate overstatement to sway his readers by contrasting freedom under his gospel with the Mosaic slavery that his opponents seek to impose on Gentiles. He does not associate the law with slavery so much as he views his foes' teaching as leading to bondage, and he ups the stakes by escalating the rhetoric.

What do his converts have to gain from embracing the law? *Nothing!* What do they have to lose? *Everything!* Although these Gentile Christians are probably seeking to be obedient to Christ by yielding to the law as they are being taught by Paul's opponents, he states the matter in absolute terms to scare them away from such an action. He himself is circumcised, and in 5:6 he states that it does not matter whether or not one is circumcised. Yet in the same passage he asserts, "if you let yourself be circumcised, Christ will not benefit you *at all!* . . . You who want to be justified by the law were *cut off* (nice word play) from Christ; you have fallen away from grace" (5:2, 4). His overstatement creates a sense of momentous decision between faithfulness and apostasy. And the depth of the emotional intensity with which he writes becomes even more visible in the outburst in 5:12: "I wish that those who are troubling you would castrate themselves!"

Although most commentators recognize the sarcasm here,[28] some are so troubled by Paul's blunt assertion that they seek to explain it away. W. M. Ramsey, for example, resists understanding Paul's use of *apokoptō* as having the "foul" meaning of castration or mutilation, because such a "scornful expression would be a pure insult, as irrational as it is disgusting."[29] However, what many modern readers consider "disgusting" Paul considered persuasive. Denigrating opponents was, after all, a stock rhetorical technique. Dunn

---

28. Heikki Räisänen uses 5:12 to evaluate Paul's attitude toward the Jewish community. He observes that "the sarcastic comment in 'obscene language' (Betz, *Galatians,* 270 n. 164) on circumcision in Gal 5.12 (cf. Phil 3.2) reveals in a flash to what degree Paul had become alienated from a piety centered around the Torah. To use four-letter-words about sacred tradition, as Paul does in Phil 3.8 shows that one has really become an outsider with respect to that tradition" (*Paul and the Law* [Philadelphia: Fortress, 1983], 76–77). Dunn states, "There is something shocking about the vehemence of Paul's language.... For eunuchs were among the most despised groups of men in the ancient world (Josephus, *A. J.* 4.290–91; Lucian, *Eunuch* 6). And self-castration was a feature of the cult of Cybele which had its home in Galatia; so that Paul's wish in effect was for the other missionaries to lapse into a form of paganism which could not but be thoroughly despised by Jews" (*Galatians,* 283).

29. *A Historical Commentary on St. Paul's Epistle to the Galatians* (2d ed.; London: Hodder & Stoughton, 1900), 438.

partially recognizes this when he says that "Paul in the heat of the moment lapses into an earthiness which he elsewhere normally avoids."[30] He goes on to say that "such coarse humour... is the sort of joking remark which might be tossed off lightly, without serious intent (he could hardly have expected it to happen or to be taken seriously), perhaps even to lighten the seriousness of the appeal in this most crucial section of the letter."[31] However, in the midst of recognizing exaggerated language, Dunn quickly gets back to the "serious" theological matters at hand. Scholars are hesitant to see that Paul's exaggerated language extends into the heart of his theological claims.

Important in this regard is Paul's allegory of Sarah and Hagar in 4:22–31, by which he argues that his opponents, by insisting on keeping the law of the old covenant, are in slavery themselves and want to enslave Gentiles along with them. Paul's depth of emotion is clear when he states that scripture commands, "Drive out the slave girl and her son!" (4:30).[32] He not only wants restored loyalty, but he also wants the opposing teachers out of Galatia. He wants to regain the respect given to him by the Jerusalem apostles, who acknowledged that, as Peter had received a commission to preach to the circumcised, so Paul had been appointed by God to preach to the Gentiles (2:7–10). Paul's opponents in Galatia have no business on his turf. He is God's apostle to the Gentiles. They are out of line in criticizing him.

Summary

When Paul dictates Galatians he is like a volcano, spewing red-hot rhetoric. His fury is inspired by formidable challenges against his position as an apostle of Christ, and it is directed toward both the antagonists who speak against him and his converts who are coming under their influence. Galatians is not a logically eloquent explanation of salvation by faith in contrast with futile human efforts to earn salvation by works. Neither is it a speech written to conform to the dictates of Greco-Roman oratory, with artificial emotion designed for desired audience response. An angry apostle Paul condemns his opponents and gives fear-inspiring warnings to his converts of the consequences of following what he considers to be heresy. As he seeks to undermine the credibility of his opponents, he employs hyperbole to make

---

30. Dunn, *Galatians*, 283.
31. Ibid., 283.
32. Betz takes the wording literally to stress a difference between Galatians and Romans. "In Galatians there is no room or possibility for an eschatological salvation of Judaism as in Rom 11:25–34. Romans 9–11, therefore, means that Paul had revised his ideas as compared with Galatians. According to Galatians, Judaism is excluded from salvation altogether" (*Galatians,* 251).

them look completely evil, although they are probably respected missionary teachers. And to deter his Gentile converts from embracing the law of Moses as his foes are teaching them is necessary, he exaggerates the implications of capitulating to their demands. When we recognize where and why Paul uses hyperbole, we will be in a much better position to understand his theology in Galatians.

CHAPTER 19

RHETORICAL ARGUMENTATION IN THE LETTER TO THE EPHESIANS

Roy R. Jeal

To even speak of an argument in Ephesians is immediately problematic. Perusal of the scholarly interpretation of the letter indicates broad variation of opinion regarding what Ephesians is about, how it functions, and whether it actually has an argument at all. While Ephesians is prima facie a letter, ostensibly written by Paul (1:1; 3:1) and addressed to ἅγιοι (1:1), it is clearly distinctive among the letters of the Pauline Corpus structurally, theologically, and rhetorically. When the obviously epistolary elements in 1:1–2 (prescript) and 6:21–24 (postscript) are isolated from the document, Ephesians no longer looks so much like a letter. Where an introductory thanksgiving might be expected, Ephesians has a long introductory eulogy (1:3–14). This praise language is followed by a thanksgiving and description of the author's prayer wishes for the audience (1:15–19a) which in turn blends into a description of the christological basis for the growth and strengthening in mind for the audience (1:19b–23). Chapter 2 is comprised of two anamneses (2:1–10 and 2:11–22) where the audience members are reminded of the implications of their pre-Christian past and their Christian present by means of a "then"/"now," ποτέ/νῦν structure and the employment of highly realized eschatological language and vivid metaphor. The anamneses are followed, in 3:2–13, with a digression describing the nature of the ministry of Paul and then with more language of praise, prayer wishes, and doxology (3:1, 14–21). Chapters 4 to 6 form a lengthy paraenesis calling the audience to some specifics of Christian behavior.

On the ground of the formal epistolary views held by scholars who would eliminate thanksgiving, supplication, and paraenesis in order to locate the letter body, Ephesians would appear to have either no body at all, or the body is to be found between the first thanksgiving and supplication section (1:15–23) and the second supplication and doxology section (3:1, 14–21). If the letter body is thus seen to be comprised only of the anamneses of 2:1–22, it becomes extremely difficult to determine what, if anything, is actually being argued and why the language of remembrance is employed. Epistolary

310

analysis is useful for describing how a letter is structured, but in the case of Ephesians, where definition of the letter body is so tenuous, it offers little help for describing the argument. As a kind of form criticism it does not work well as a determinative interpretive tool.[1] Epistolary analysis does not, in itself, explain what the author of Ephesians wanted to accomplish.

To further complicate things, a distinctive of Ephesians is that it does not explicate the circumstances that occasioned its composition. Unlike other New Testament letters where there is an issue or ἀγῶν being discussed, Ephesians does not address a pastoral or theological problem. No controversy is handled by either author or recipients. Ephesians does not have a section that provides direct, formal argumentation of a case.[2]

These observations about Ephesians raise some interesting questions. What is it arguing for or against, or does it make any consistent or complete argument at all? What message was the author attempting to convey? How does Ephesians influence its audience? Taking into account the oral/aural and rhetorical nature and context of New Testament texts, how does Ephesians present a rhetorical argument?[3] What rhetorical situation or exigence gave rise to Ephesians, and what rhetorical strategy does it employ?

In an attempt to answer these questions it is necessary to determine if Ephesians actually has an argument, whether it seeks to gain audience support for an understanding that is likely to cause change of thinking relative to a perceived need.[4] This essay aims to describe the purpose or intention of Ephesians as it is indicated in the text, and proceeds to describe and explain how that purpose is argued rhetorically. Explaining the rhetorical argument will involve more than tracking the flow of thought. It will mean explaining how the argument is made and how it is effective, examining some features of "inner texture"[5] as a way of observing how the language of Ephesians works to influence the thinking and emotions of the audience members.

---

1. Cf. Bruce C. Johanson, *To All the Brethren* (ConBNT 16; Uppsala: Almqvist & Wiksell, 1987), 61–65; Charles B. Cousar, *The Letters of Paul* (Nashville: Abingdon Press, 1996), 33.

2. On this see Roy R. Jeal, *Integrating Theology and Ethics in Ephesians: The Ethos of Communication* (Lewiston: Mellen, 2000), 62–67.

3. In his recent commentary, Peter T. O'Brien, *The Letter to the Ephesians* (Pillar NT Commentary; Grand Rapids: Eerdmans; Leicester: Apollos, 1999), 73–82, discounts a rhetorical approach to studying Ephesians. However, O'Brien uses a narrow definition of rhetorical criticism and does not mention recent developments in socio-rhetorical interpretation.

4. Cf. the description of argumentation in Lauri Thurén, "On Studying Ethical Argumentation and Persuasion in the New Testament," in *Rhetoric and the New Testament: Essays from the 1992 Heidelberg Conference* (ed. S. E. Porter and T. H. Olbricht; Sheffield: Sheffield Academic Press, 1993), 466 n. 7, 468.

5. Vernon K. Robbins, *The Tapestry of Early Christian Discourse* (London: Routledge, 1996), 44–95.

Purpose of Writing

The scope of theories regarding the purpose of Ephesians proposed by interpreters ranges from the extremely speculative[6] to the view that purpose cannot be known with certainty.[7] A major barrier to attaining a satisfactory understanding has been scholarship's attempt at historical reconstruction of the audience situation rather than close examination of what the text itself actually says about its intention. Fischer suggests that Gentile Christians had withdrawn from Jewish Christians in the church, with the result that unity became the main idea addressed.[8] Schnackenburg suggests that Ephesians' purpose is to address a spiritual crisis in the church.[9] Chadwick proposes that Ephesians was written to deal with embarrassment on the part of Gentile Christians over the supposed late arrival of the Christian message. Ephesians supposedly answers this embarrassment by explaining the continuity of the church with Judaism, by emphasizing the universality of the church, and by indicating that the church is a metaphysical body that encompasses all generations.[10] Kitchen sees purpose in a need to vindicate Paul, after his death, as one appointed by God to proclaim the gospel to the Gentiles.[11] Kirby finds the purpose in recalling the audience members' baptism.[12] Lindemann speculates about a situation during the reign of Domitian where the recipients of Ephesians may have been in need of encouragement in the face of persecution.[13]

Lincoln submits that Ephesians is "intended to reinforce its readers identity as participants in the Church and to underline their distinctive role and conduct in the world."[14] Some authors think that Ephesians was written to combat a sense of alienation Gentile Christians felt from Jewish Christians

---

6. E.g., the conjectures of Edgar J. Goodspeed, *The Key to Ephesians* (Chicago: University of Chicago Press, 1956).

7. J. Paul Sampley, "The Letter to the Ephesians," in *Ephesians, Colossians, 2 Thessalonians, The Pastoral Epistles* (ed. Gerhard Krodel; Proclamation Commentaries; Philadelphia: Fortress, 1978), 9. For a recent survey of views see Ernest Best, *A Critical and Exegetical Commentary on Ephesians* (ICC; Edinburgh: T. & T. Clark, 1998), 63–75.

8. Karl Martin Fischer, *Tendenz und Absicht des Epheserbriefes* (FRLANT 111; Göttingen: Vandenhoeck & Ruprecht, 1973), 201–2.

9. Rudolf Schnackenburg, *The Epistle to the Ephesians* (trans. H. Heron; Edinburgh: T. & T. Clark, 1991), 35.

10. Henry Chadwick, "Die Absicht des Epheserbriefes," *ZNW* 51 (1960): 148–49.

11. Martin Kitchen, *Ephesians* (London/New York: Routledge, 1994), 129.

12. John L. Kirby, *Ephesians, Baptism and Pentecost* (Montreal: McGill University Press, 1968), 145, 159.

13. Andreas Lindemann, "Bemerkungen zu den Addressaten und zum Anlaß des Epheserbriefes," *ZNW* 67 (1976): 242–43.

14. Andrew T. Lincoln, *Ephesians* (WBC 42; Waco, Tex.: Word Books, 1990), lxxxvi.

and the Jewish roots of Christianity.[15] This distancing of peoples from each other is supposedly combated by reminders of Jewish and Gentile Christian solidarity in one body (2:11–22), and by appeal for the maintenance of unity in 4:1–16. Mitton claims that Ephesians was intended to be a restatement of the gospel preached by Paul.[16] Arnold, in his treatment of Ephesians' relationship to "powers" and magical practices that were current in western Asia Minor at the time of composition, suggests that Ephesians was written to address the needs of Christians "who perceived themselves as oppressed by the demonic realm."[17]

Among the authors of more recent studies, Best is willing to "hazard a guess" that the audience of Ephesians, having recently come out of paganism, needed to recognize the nature of the church and the behavior required in it.[18] Kittredge claims that Ephesians' "primary purpose is to persuade the audience to correct their view of ekklesia in favor of another view based upon the model of the kyriarchal family."[19] She sees the *Haustafel,* particularly 5:22–33 addressing wives and husbands, as being the core message of Ephesians, instructing the audience to be unified around a hierarchy where the inferior are linked to superiors through obedience to them.[20] O'Brien views Ephesians as a remodeling of Colossians that has a view to "identity formation" through assuring the audience members of their place in God's purpose, and by urging them to conform to God's plan to sum up all things in Christ (1:10). To O'Brien, the message of Ephesians is thus about "cosmic reconciliation and unity in Christ."[21]

Rather than attempting a reconstruction of the largely unknowable circumstances that may have occasioned the composition of Ephesians, this discussion of the (rhetorical) purpose of Ephesians is based on a simple assumption: the author intended to communicate intelligibly and persuasively to an audience (whose members heard the letter read aloud rather than read it individually), addressing what would be beneficial to them in their situation. Considered below are passages that bear most directly on the purpose of writing by indicating what the author desired for the benefit of the audience.

---

15. E.g., Ralph P. Martin, "An Epistle in Search of a Life-Setting," *ExpT* 79 (1968): 296–302.
16. C. Leslie Mitton, *The Epistle to the Ephesians: Its Authorship, Origin and Purpose* (Oxford: Clarendon Press, 1951), 266.
17. Clinton E. Arnold, *Ephesians: Power and Magic* (SNTSMS 63; Cambridge: Cambridge University Press, 1989), 123–24, 171.
18. Best, *Ephesians,* 75.
19. Cynthia Briggs Kittredge, *Community and Authority: The Rhetoric of Obedience in the Pauline Tradition* (Harrisburg, Pa.: Trinity Press International, 1998), 146.
20. Ibid., 148.
21. O'Brien, *Ephesians,* 57–58.

Ephesians 1:17–19a. Having completed the introductory eulogy of 1:3–14 and the thanksgiving of 1:15–16, the author proceeds to indicate his request to God on behalf of the audience. While clearly aware that the audience has attained some level of Christian understanding and practice (they possess both faith and love; 1:15), the author's concern is that they reach a greater knowledge of the blessings given to believers than they have at the time of writing. This greater knowledge is particularized in three τίς statements (1:18b–19a) where an enhanced appreciation of the salvation that has been in view from 1:3 onward is expressed in terms of the hope of God's calling, the riches of the glory of God's inheritance among the saints, and the greatness of God's power among believers.

Ephesians 2:19–22. The anamnesis of 2:11–22 has frequently been understood to indicate division between Jewish and Gentile Christians, or as an argument for the unity of disparate peoples who have been reconciled by the blood of Christ, or as a clarification of the place of Gentiles in salvation history. Analysis shows, however, that the pericope presents a comparison of the Gentile audience's past relative to Israel, with their present existence in the church, so that the audience will have a deeper appreciation of the value of their salvation.[22] The before and after (ποτέ/νῦν) contrast of 2:1–10 continues in 2:11–22, reminding the audience that they possess salvation and continuity with Judaism on the basis of the reconciling work of Christ. The comparison of "then" with "now" leads to the conclusion that the audience members, who are now συμπολῖται τῶν ἁγίων καὶ οἰκεῖοι τοῦ θεοῦ (2:19), are moving together toward maturity as the new temple of God (2:21–22). On this reading of 2:11–22, it follows that 2:19–22 has directly to do with the author's purpose of writing, that is, that the audience is addressed as a "building" (οἰκοδομή) that is growing εἰς ναὸν ἅγιον ἐν κυρίῳ (2:21). The author is vividly emphasizing that the Gentiles who listen to Ephesians are growing toward greater Christian maturity.

Ephesians 3:14–19. Here again the author expresses a wish for deep Christian maturity. The focus of the author's desire for the audience is found in the prayer offered to "the Father" that believers be strengthened in the "inner person," that Christ dwell in their hearts, that they understand the dimensions of the love of Christ, and that they be filled "into all the fullness of God." Clearly this shows that the author wants the audience to come to full growth.

Ephesians 4:13–16. The goal of the gifts given by Christ (4:7–12), and indeed of the unity-promoting behavior encouraged in 4:1–6, is encapsulated in the three prepositional (εἰς) statements of 4:13. The goal to be attained is

---

22. Lincoln, *Ephesians*, 132–34.

full, adult, Christian maturity, in contrast to the immaturity of νήπιοι (4:14), and the instability that goes along with such immaturity. The author explicitly has in mind the growth of the body of Christ as each member of it functions to benefit the maturity of all members. The references to false teaching and crafty, deceitful people (4:14) do not presuppose their actual existence among the audience members, but only that the author wants the audience to be fully mature in order to face such teaching and people, if and when they appear.

Ephesians 6:10–17. In this final section the audience members are encouraged to clothe themselves with the "armor" of God in order to stand firmly in the cosmic battle in the heavenlies. The battle is fought not by the audience's own power, but in the power of the Lord (6:10). Believers are to be adequately armed so as to be able to stand against the attacks of cosmic forces without being defeated. Although the imagery has changed from that of "building" in 2:19–22 and "body" in 4:15–16 to that of "battle" in 6:10–17, the notion of strength and maturity remains as the author wants the audience to be fully armed in order to withstand "the schemes of the devil" (6:11).

Other passages can be understood to point to a concern for the benefit of the audience. The behavioral exhortations of the paraenesis demonstrate the concern that the audience practice a mature Christian lifestyle. At 3:4 the author wants the audience to comprehend Paul's understanding of the mystery of Christ, and, at 3:13, expresses concern that the letter's recipients not be dismayed at Paul's tribulations. These verses add to the description of the author's concern for the level of understanding the audience members have of significant factors in Paul's life, and of the effect of them on their behalf. An allusion to the behavior of Christians is present from the opening lines of Ephesians: believers were "chosen ... to be holy and blameless ... in love" (1:4). The notion of Christian conduct was thus in the author's mind from the beginning of Ephesians.

The foregoing provides cumulative evidence indicating the author's concern for audience growth and maturity. There is no explicit statement such as "My purpose for writing to you is ...," but the author's prayers, as revealed in 1:16 and 3:14–15, function as an equivalent to explications of purpose. Certainly the prayers point out the author's desires for the benefit of the audience (cf. Rom 1:9; 1 Thess 1:2–3; Phlm 4–6). Taken together, these verses lead to the conclusion that the desire for the maturation of the audience was at the heart of the author's purpose.

From the introductory eulogy through to the doxology of 3:20–21, the language of worship provides a context in which the author attempts to achieve his purpose for writing. Underlying the praise language is the author's view of God's great salvation planned from before creation (1:4). This thematic trajectory, along with the recognition that God calls people to participate in new community and new existence, reminds the audience members that God, in Christ, has provided a salvation, unity, and peace that would not otherwise be part of their experience.

The Object of Rhetorical Argumentation in Ephesians

What happens in Ephesians is that the author's concern for the growth, maturation, and Christian behavior of the audience members is encouraged through a rhetorical argument that is designed to shape their thinking. The audience members become so reminded of their status and of the blessings of their salvation that they are likely to be moved toward the maturity that the author has in mind. The rhetorical argument has an ethical goal in mature Christian faith (cf. 4:13) that is expressed behaviorally.

Rhetoric and Audience Identification

Receptivity to the rhetorical argument would have been unlikely if the audience members of Ephesians were not already the Christian people they are described as being (e.g., 1:13–14, 15). "People can neither understand, accept, nor appreciate lucid, logical, or impassioned utterances that have no bearing on their status in the community and the environment."[23] In other words, while it is appropriate for people to be receptive to any "important" concepts or events, they are generally receptive only to things which provoke their interest or are significant to their lives. An audience must, therefore, have a sense of identification with the subject matter about which someone wishes to expound. Since the audience members had already attained some level of Christian awareness, they were likely to have been receptive to a message that reminded them of it.

Burke[24] and Mouat[25] have discussed the rhetorical effect of identification. Burke claims that "You persuade a man only insofar as you talk his language by speech, gesture, tonality, order, image, attitude, idea, identifying your ways with his [sic]."[26] Identification involves using ideas in such a way that the

---

23. Lawrence H. Mouat, "An Approach to Rhetorical Criticism," in *The Rhetorical Idiom* (ed. D. C. Bryant; New York: Russel & Russel, 1966), 167.
24. Kenneth Burke, *A Rhetoric of Motives* (Berkeley/Los Angeles: University of California Press, 1969), passim.
25. Mouat, "Approach," 171–77.
26. Burke, *Rhetoric*, 55.

content of a rhetorical presentation is identified with the beliefs and wishes of the audience,[27] that is, the audience members find themselves in agreement with the statements made. If audience members identify with the subject matter presented, then assent to the argument (and consequent behavior) is likely to occur. By producing identification among audience members, a sense of order and continuity reinforces their beliefs about the subject, and draws them to assent to the actions the author/speaker has in mind for them and to the actual performance of the activities.

In Ephesians, identification plays an important role in the overall rhetorical effect. The author has used language that enables the audience members to identify with what they already know about themselves. The result or effect of the rhetorical use of identification is that the audience members are reminded of their personal involvement in the Christian faith. They are impressed again with the value of salvation and its implications. When people are impressed in this way they are more likely to be moved to become personally involved in behavior that will lead them to deeper Christian maturity. Ephesians employs this rhetorical effect to present its argument so that the audience would move toward maturity by practicing the behavior encouraged in the paraenesis.

How the Rhetorical Argument Functions

A full description of how the rhetorical argument of Ephesians functions is not possible here. Some samples from the major rhetorical units must suffice to indicate how the argument operates.[28]

Ephesians is arranged in such a way that the audience is immediately drawn into a rhetoric of praise and worship (1:3–14). This exordium-like material, which reflects the strong influence of Jewish berakah statements on early Christianity, begins by placing God as the object of praise (1:3) in a clause employing words from the same stem as the initial εὐλογητός. Reduplication of the like-sounding εὐλογητός, εὐλογήσας, and εὐλογίᾳ serves to impress the notion of blessing on the mind of the audience.[29] This introductory statement sets the stage for the rest of the eulogy by establishing the theme of praise to God in the minds of the audience members. The theme is explicit again in 1:6, 12, 14 (εἰς ἔπαινον [τῆς] δόξης αὐτοῦ). There is a

---

27. Cf. Mouat, "Approach," 172.
28. For a full description of the rhetorical features used in the argument, see Jeal, *Integrating*, 73–175.
29. The device of reduplication "is the repetition of one or more words for the purpose of Amplification or Appeal to Pity.... The reiteration of the same word makes a deep impression on the hearer" (*Rhet. Her.*, 4.28.38).

powerful rhetorical effect in the words of praise in 1:3 by means of identification. The audience of Ephesians was comprised of people who were already participants in salvation and cognizant of the fact that God was worthy of praise. Ephesians treats with esteem a theme held in esteem by the audience members, sharing their perspective, moving them to share in the praise (cf. Aristotle, *Rhet.* 1.9.30; 3.14.11). The author is thus using pathos (*Rhet.* 1.2.5), that is, he begins the eulogy by arousing a sense of praise in the audience.

A recurring feature of the eulogy is the use of ἐν phrases. The preposition ἐν is coupled with Χριστός (or equivalent pronoun), and several other words (ἐν πάσῃ εὐλογίᾳ πνευματικῇ; ἐν τοῖς ἐπουρανίοις; ἐν ἀγάπῃ; ἐν τῷ ἠγαπημένῳ; ἐν πάσῃ σοφίᾳ καὶ φρονήσει). A rhetorical effect of the repeated ἐν is evident in the rhythmic pattern in 1:3: ὁ εὐλογήσας ἡμᾶς ἐν πάσῃ εὐλογίᾳ πνευματικῇ ἐν τοῖς ἐπουρανίοις ἐν Χριστῷ. Burke indicates how such patterns can "awaken an attitude of collaborative expectancy in us." By this he means that awareness of a word pattern "invites participation regardless of the subject matter."[30] Yielding to a pattern leads to audience assent to the matters identified with it. When an audience is confronted with word patterns the tendency is to collaborate with the pattern to make a complete utterance. A similar effect occurs when a speaker uses the "body language" of nodding the head, stimulating head-nodding among the audience members, thus obtaining the audience's tacit agreement with the speaker's words. The word pattern based on ἐν in 1:3 is an example of *epanaphora* (*Rhet. Her.* 4.13.19), the repetition of the same word at the beginning of successive phrases. The resultant rhetorical effect is the tendency of the audience to assent to the praise of God and to the proposition that God is the one who blessed them "in every spiritual blessing in the heavenlies in Christ." The epanaphoric use of ἐν is repeated in 1:4, 6–7, 10–11, 12–13, sustaining heightened awareness of the thought of 1:3 and focusing attention on the actions of God in Christ.

Perhaps the most powerful rhetorical feature in the eulogy occurs in 1:13 where the second person pronoun ὑμεῖς is employed rather than the first person ἡμεῖς used in 1:3–12. This change of pronoun indicates that 1:13 is aimed directly at the inclusion of the audience of Ephesians in the praise and blessings of the eulogy.[31] This inclusion of the audience has great rhetorical

---

30. Burke, *Rhetoric*, 58–59.
31. Scholars are divided over whether the change from ἡμεῖς to ὑμεῖς has Jewish Christians (ἡμεῖς) and the Gentile Christian audience (ὑμεῖς) as referents, or if ἡμεῖς refers to Christians in general, with ὑμεῖς referring specifically to the recipients of Ephesians. The most straightforward understanding is that "we who hoped first" (1:12) indicates a contrast between the author and others who were Christians prior to the audience, and the audience members (ὑμεῖς, 1:13). The audience members were not excluded from the discussion of 1:3–12, but in 1:13 they are explicitly included.

force because it stresses audience participation and identification with the theological concepts of Ephesians 1–3. While the audience should have felt a sense of participation in the praise of 1:3–12, their participation is emphasized and impressed upon them in 1:13. They are full participants in the salvation spoken of in 1:3–12 and are full participants in the praise of God (1:14). This rhetoric is likely to gain the audience members' goodwill and persuade them to agree with the ideas and themes being presented. The power of this language of identification and involvement will encourage the audience to be moved in the direction the author desires and to practice behavior perceived to accord with it.[32] By persuading the audience members to identify with and be included in the thought flow of the eulogy, they are likely to participate in praise and in the blessings given by God, and in the implications of those salvific blessings, e.g., holiness, blamelessness, and love (1:4).

The eulogy/berakah is followed by the thanksgiving and prayer of 1:15–23, which continues to include the audience in the flow of thought, encouraging them to collaborate with the author. The recipients' faith and love provide a foundation for the author's action. Because of the inclusion and participation of the recipients in the blessings described in 1:3–14, and because word of their faith and love has reached the author (ἀκούσας τὴν καθ' ὑμᾶς πίστιν...καὶ τὴν ἀγάπην...), he is motivated to offer thanksgiving and prayer for their growth and maturity.

Recognition of the audience has a strong rhetorical and emotional effect because it tends to build up self-esteem through the praise that it implicitly directs toward them, evoking receptivity to the author's concerns. Thanksgiving and supplication are founded on the author's estimation of the value of the audience's participation and potential in Christian faith.[33] The recognition given to the audience, coupled with the knowledge of the author's unceasing thanksgiving and supplication on their behalf, demonstrates the author's sincere concern for the welfare of the audience. By yielding to the feelings of the audience members in this way the author identifies himself with them. This sort of identification is persuasive because deference to an audience secures the favor of its members and moves them to a willingness to accept suggestions, conclusions, or exhortations. Thankfulness for the recipients' faith and love would elicit pleasure and acceptance of the author's words. Rhetorically,

---

32. See Donald D. Evans, *The Logic of Self-Involvement* (London: SCM Press, 1963), 139: "Insofar as I actually look on x as y in my daily life, it becomes true that x is y. For example, if I look on my suffering as a means to moral growth, it is likely that my suffering will be a means to moral growth.... In general, people tend to conform to the roles which they see themselves as playing."

33. Indicated by the διά, "on account of," "because of."

this is *philophronesis*, the attempt to mitigate by means of gentle speech and submission.[34]

The content and purpose of the author's prayer for the recipients is detailed in 1:17–19a. The author's concern for the welfare and growth of the audience members becomes very specific and elicits identification among the audience members by another interchange of the pronouns ἡμεῖς and ὑμεῖς. While intercession addresses "the God of our (ἡμῶν) Lord Jesus Christ," the request is that God "give to you (ὑμῖν) a spirit of wisdom and revelation in the knowledge of him." The author's concern for the audience is nearly palpable.

The anamneses of 2:1–10 and 2:11–22 remind the audience of many of the basic facts of their salvation and status as Christians. The overarching rhetorical feature in 2:1–10 (and equally in 2:11–22) is the ποτέ/νῦν, "then"/"now" motif.[35] The dramatic antithesis between the pre-Christian (ποτέ) status of "death," with its corresponding sinful behavior, and the Christian (νῦν) status of life with Christ, and its corresponding behavior of "good works," is the vehicle used to convey the idea of the place and status of Christians in God's salvific actions. The dramatic movement from death to life has an obvious emotional effect because it arouses the deepest feelings of finality, loss and deprivation (death), contrasted with a sense of continuity, security, progress, and privilege (life). These themes engender a sense of identification because the reminder of the pre-Christian past reapprises the recipients of who they are. They are made to feel that they are a part of the narrative. Their consequent collaboration with the narrative would tend to the development of a frame of mind receptive to the author's goal.

An outstanding feature of 2:4–10 is its highly realized eschatology. This is most evident in 2:5–6 where σῴζω appears in the perfect tense, and the resurrection and seating of believers in heaven are described as past events. Rhetorically, the realized eschatology functions as part of the then/now contrast between pre-Christian and Christian states. Under the influence of the language of 1:20–22, 2:4–10 impresses the notion that God's actions in Christ have saved the audience members completely. They are now very much alive. Salvation described in such a highly realized way stands in striking contrast to the former existence of death. Rather than having their functional purpose in the promotion of a new or different theology of eschatological salvation, these verses are intended to make an emotional (pathos: Aristotle, *Rhet.* 1.2.5;

---

34. See Richard A. Lanham, *A Handlist of Rhetorical Terms* (Berkeley: University of California Press, 1968), 77.

35. On the "then"/"now" motif in the New Testament see Peter Tachau, *"Einst" und "Jetzt" im Neuen Testament. Beobachtungen zu einem urchristlichen Predigt-schema in der neutestamentlichen Briefliteratur und zu seiner Vorgeschichte* (FRLANT 105; Göttingen: Vandenhoeck & Ruprecht, 1972), 79–96.

Quintilian, *Inst.*, 6.1.51; 6.2.2–8) impression that elicits an understanding of the nature and scope of salvation distinguished from unsaved existence. Existence has been transferred from lowest depth to greatest height. The practical function of the language is to emphasize the contrast between "then" and "now" so strongly that the audience members will be imbued with thinking appropriate to the rhetorical purpose. The realized eschatology presses home the concept of the dramatic change from death to life with Christ so forcefully that it sensitizes the audience members to their state as Christians, thus generating a mindset that makes them susceptible to moral exhortation and to the author's concern for their growth.

The second anamnesis (διὸ μνημονεύετε ὅτι…; 2:11–22) again contrasts the pre-Christian past and the Christian present. The reconciliation and unity of Jew and Gentile in one body is not the subject of concern in 2:11–22, but is used to illustrate, emphasize, and explain the author's thought. The guiding feature is, again, the ποτέ/νῦν schema. There are two very significant rhetorical effects. First, because the then/now motif has been used in 2:1–10, its repetition in 2:11–22 reinforces a thought pattern with which the audience is familiar. Since they are already thinking in terms of "then" and "now," the parallel language of 2:11–22 invites them to continue to cooperate in the contrast and share the author's perspective on their situation. Second, the anamnesis has a particular rhetorical function. The remembrance of things past is inherent in the then/now schema, and is made explicit by the word μνημονεύω in 2:11. The anamnesis is not employed simply as a recollection, ἀνακεφαλαίωσις or enumeratio of facts, but as a recordatio[36] that impresses the reality of the past on the mind in such a way that an appreciation of the blessings of the present is instilled in the audience. Because the language calls for the Gentile audience members to remember their personal past and compare it with their present status the passage has pathos appeal. It has a psychological effect by deepening the awareness and meaning of salvation, and effectively prepares the recipients to be receptive to the author's thoughts and concerns for movement toward growth (2:21–22).

The most significant rhetorical feature in 2:19–22 is the elaborate paronomasia based on the word οἶκος. From the initial past versus present contrast of πάροικοι and οἰκεῖοι in 2:19, the word play progresses through the verses by means of the words ἐποικοδομηθέντες (2:20), οἰκοδομή (2:21), συνοικοδομεῖσθε (2:22), and κατοικητήριον (2:22). While the then/now contrast has brought out the value of the saved condition against the background of the unsaved state, the movement described by the words using the οἰκ-

---

36. Lanham, *Handlist*, 7, 85: "Recalling matters of the past; ideas events, persons."

root changes the focus toward the author's concern for the maturation of the recipients. The anamnesis has highlighted salvation, but verses 20-22 direct the memory of salvation to the growth of the community. The architectural metaphor begins in 2:19 with πάροικοι, literally "those beside a house," who have become οἰκεῖοι, "those who belong to a house" (family members). In 2:20 there is a shift of imagery from viewing the recipients as members of the household of God to viewing them as the house itself. They have been built on a foundation (ἐποικοδομηθέντες, 2:20), they are a building (οἰκοδομή, 2:21), and they are being built together (συνοικοδομεῖσθε, 2:22) as a dwelling (κατοικητήριον, 2:22) of God. Tied closely to those words is the sacral image of the ναὸν ἅγιον (2:21). Christians constitute a building that is a holy temple where God dwells.

Seen together, the rhetorical features of 2:19-22 function in a way that presses home the understanding that the Christian status of the audience members transcends the former pre-Christian state. As Christians, the audience members are being "framed together" as a growing dwelling place of God. The rhetorical effect of the language is such that it elicits identification with the concepts and images described so that the audience members will see themselves as the growing temple of God, and, subsequently, participate in the behavior deemed to accord with the goal of growth and maturity.

Ephesians returns to the language of praise, prayer, and worship in 3:1, 14-21. The portrayal of action in 3:14 grasps audience attention by the way it expresses emotion and devotion to God. The descriptive statement κάμπτω τὰ γόνατά μου πρὸς τὸν πατέρα is capable of producing a deep sense of pathos as the audience visualizes Paul bowing in prayer. Such an action, while symbolic, indicates an attitude of worship and respect that audience members, who have been hearing the language of worship and praise since 1:3, can be reasonably expected to appreciate and with which they can identify. Observing such an emotional scene as the "bowing of knees" is conducive to an emotional collaboration on the part of an audience.

The features of 3:20 are particularly remarkable. The most obvious is the piling up of comparative language describing the ability of God. The comparative terms ὑπὲρ πάντα and ὑπερεκπερισσοῦ are paronomastic and synonymous.[37] The ability of God to supply superabundantly above all ὧν αἰτούμεθα ἢ νοοῦμεν indicates that his blessings surpass human comprehension. The rhetorical effect of these words suggests the enhanced rendering "above all that we ask or even think." The κατά-clause of 3:20 clarifies the nature of God's ability to bless beyond human comprehension by asserting

---

37. Schnackenburg, *Ephesians*, 155.

that it is in conformity with "the power which works in us." The synonyms (δύναμις and the participle of ἐνεργέω) intensify the theme. The use of first person forms in the doxology, changed from the second person in the prayer, should be taken in an inclusive sense, that is, that the author includes all Christians among those who are blessed in superabundance. The rhetoric of 3:20 produces a clear identification of God as the one who is to be praised. This is likely to persuade the audience members to collaborate with the praise following in verse 21. The final ἀμήν adds a note of solemnity and confirmation, possibly uttered as suggestive of a congregational response (cf. 1 Cor 14:16), thereby encouraging participation in the worship. The doxology has reiterated the praise of God and presented an emotional and climactic appeal to worship God who can provide blessings. Such language stimulates acquiescence and a sense of obligation to join in praise, and sharing in subsequent thought and action.

Ephesians 3:2–13 is a digression in the sequence of thought that provides additional rhetorical force, even if the additions are not crucial to the logic of the epistle. Prompted by the assertion of 3:1, this digressio functions as a description of the source and nature of Paul's ministry to the Gentiles ("for you," 3:1, 2, 13) that dispels possible dismay over his sufferings on behalf of the audience. The author is primarily concerned to demonstrate that Paul's ministry, and even his sufferings, were for their (Gentile) benefit, that Paul's ministry is God-given, that Paul accepts and appreciates it as God-given, and that they should not lose heart at the thought of Paul's circumstances. The passage portrays Paul as a legitimate and authoritative figure, but does so without detracting from the gospel message which he received and preached. At the same time, the digression explains the meaning of the "mystery," generates sympathy for Paul, elicits pathos among the audience members along with a sense of their collective security as Christians, and drives home the knowledge that Gentiles are joint-participants (with Jews) in the gospel (3:6). The pericope acts as a reinforcement of the meaning of the gospel (as received and proclaimed by Paul) for the audience. The goal of the author's statement of these concerns is, rhetorically speaking, that the audience members will be persuaded to accept the authority of Paul to speak, and consequently will be stimulated to be receptive to the letter's exhortations to maturity and growth.

The paraenesis of chapters 4–6 encourages the audience to practice the behavior considered necessary for the growth and maturity for which Ephesians argues. The paraenesis presents its own self-contained argumentation for behavioral practice based on theological, pragmatic, rhetorical, or social (church community) foundations. Acceptance and practice of the behavior encouraged is the goal of the rhetorical argumentation of Ephesians.

Conclusion

Ephesians fundamentally has in view the Christian growth, maturity, and appropriate behavior of its audience members. It argues to obtain the agreement and elicit the participation of its audience in growth, maturity, and specific behaviors, not by addressing a particular early Christian ἀγῶν but by engaging with their Christian consciousness. Ephesians does not employ direct argumentation to attain its purpose. Rather, its rhetorical argument aims to impress, to arouse a sense of identification with the gospel and salvation, and to use an emotional style so as to generate receptivity to the notion of Christian growth and maturity (cf. 4:13–16) and the exhortations of the paraenesis (4:1–6:20). Ephesians has employed a remarkable amount of language that employs evocative, extra-verbal, and very human sensibilities to persuade effectively.[38]

The specific behavior of the paraenesis is not directly derived from the more theological description of Ephesians 1–3. Ephesians builds a rapport with its audience through praise and worship, through prayer, through reminders of compelling facts from the past that stand in contrast to the present, through highly realized eschatological language, and through suggestions that growth toward maturity is to be expected. These features are used rhetorically to produce a sense of identification and personal involvement that moves the audience to collaborate with the author's goal. By the time the audience members come to the paraenesis they have heard so many things with which they agree that the exhortations are likely to seem natural and acceptable. Their subsequent active response leading to Christian maturity is what the author intended to encourage from the outset of the letter.

---

38. Cf. the notion of "tone color" (Klangenfarben) described by Oliver Sacks, *The Man Who Mistook His Wife for a Hat* (New York: Summit Books, 1985), 76–77.

CHAPTER 20

LIVING AND DYING, LIVING IS DYING (PHILIPPIANS 1:21): PAUL'S MAXIM AND EXEMPLARY ARGUMENTATION IN PHILIPPIANS

Rollin A. Ramsaran

New Testament scholarship has vigorously analyzed and debated the genre and structure of Paul's letter to the Philippians. Three major perspectives that inform the discussion are rhetorical analysis, epistolary analysis, and oral/aural analysis.[1] Consensus is beginning to take shape with regard to larger structural details and indications of genre. It is generally recognized that Philippians 1:27–30 marks an important imperatival exhortation (epistolary; oral/aural) or functions as the letter's propositio or propositional statement (rhetorical).[2] Most hold that Paul's use of πολιτεύεσθε in 1:27

---

1. The following list should be considered sufficient though not exhaustive. Rhetorical: Duane F. Watson, "A Rhetorical Analysis of Philippians and Its Implications for the Unity Question," *NovT* 30 (1988): 57–88; L. Gregory Bloomquist, *The Function of Suffering in Philippians* (JSNTSup 78; Sheffield: JSOT, 1993); Timothy C. Geoffrion, *The Rhetorical Purpose and the Political and Military Character of Philippians: A Call to Stand Firm* (Lewiston, N.Y.: Mellon, 1993); Ben Witherington III, *Friendship and Finances in Philippi: The Letter of Paul to the Philippians* (Valley Forge, Pa.: Trinity Press International, 1994). Epistolary: L. Michael White, "Morality Between Two Worlds: A Paradigm of Friendship in Philippians," in *Greeks, Romans, and Christians: Essays in Honor of Abraham J. Malherbe* (ed. David L. Balch, Everett Ferguson, and Wayne A. Meeks; Minneapolis: Fortress, 1990), 201–15; Stanley K. Stowers, "Friends and Enemies in the Politics of Heaven," in *Pauline Theology, Volume 1: Thessalonians, Philippians, Galatians, Philemon* (ed. Jouette M. Bassler; Minneapolis: Fortress, 1991), 105–21; Gordon D. Fee, *Paul's Letter to the Philippians* (NICNT; Grand Rapids: Eerdmans, 1995); Jeffrey T. Reed, *A Discourse Analysis of Philippians: Method and Rhetoric in the Debate over Literary Integrity* (JSNTSup 136; Sheffield: Sheffield Academic Press, 1997). Oral/Aural: Casey W. Davis, *Oral Biblical Criticism: The Influence of the Principles of Orality on the Literary Structure of Paul's Epistle to the Philippians* (JSNTSup 172; Sheffield: Sheffield Academic Press, 1999); John D. Harvey, *Listening to the Text: Oral Patterning in Paul's Letters* (Grand Rapids: Baker, 1998), 231–58.

2. Fee, *Philippians*, 159–61; Harvey, *Listening to the Text*, 236–43; Davis, *Oral Biblical Criticism*, 111. Reed (*Discourse Analysis*, 216–18) strongly objects, however, to raising 1:27–30 above the other exhortations in the letter. As a rhetorical propositio, see Watson, "Rhetorical Analysis," 66–67; Geoffrion, *Rhetorical Purpose*, 179; Witherington, *Friendship and Finances*, 50–55.

and πολίτευμα in 3:20 forms a ring device around 1:27–3:21,³ and Paul's argumentation within the smaller sections is built on key examples (Christ, Timothy, Epaphroditus, Paul).⁴ Finally, a number of rhetorical and epistolary approaches show marked appreciation for the friendship motifs that abound in Philippians.⁵ Hence, one finds a growing appreciation for the complementary nature and necessity of these various approaches in interpreting Paul's letters.⁶

In this paper, I make a sustained argument for Paul's use of a rhetorically effective maxim in chapter 1:19–26. This device and the accompanying personal example are often overlooked and seldom commented upon at length.⁷ Paul's maxim and personal example in 1:19–26, however, set the parameters for his propositio in 1:27–30. A series of exempla then shape the response to Paul's propositional statement in a way pertinent to the imperial context of the Philippian believers. Finally, a second maxim (4:13), offered at the close of the letter, forms a fitting inclusio to Paul's maxim argumentation.

---

3. D. E. Garland, "The Composition and Unity of Philippians: Some Neglected Literary Factors," *NovT* 27 (1985): 160; David A. Black, "The Discourse Structure of Philippians: A Study in Textlinguistics," *NovT* 37 (1995): 34. Cf. Fee, *Philippians*, 162, 378–9; Andrew T. Lincoln, *Paradise Now and Not Yet: Studies in the Role of the Heavenly Dimension in Paul's Thought with Special Reference to His Eschatology* (Cambridge: Cambridge University Press, 1981), 97–101; Geoffrion, *Rhetorical Purpose*, 227.

4. Peter T. O'Brien, "The Gospel and Godly Models in Philippians," in *Worship, Theology and Ministry in the Early Church: Essays in Honor of Ralph P. Martin* (ed. Michael J. Wilkins and Terence Paige; JSNTSup 87; Sheffield: JSOT, 1992), 273–84; Stowers, "Friends and Enemies," 115–16; Geoffrion, *Rhetorical Purpose*, 125–58; Witherington, *Friendship and Finances*, 56–103.

5. White, "Morality Between Two Worlds," 211–15; Stowers, "Friends and Enemies," 105–21; Fee, *Philippians*, 12–13, 20; Witherington, *Friendship*, 118–21; James L. Jaquette, "A Not-So-Noble Death: Figured Speech, Friendship and Suicide in Philippians 1:21–26," *Neot* 28 (1994): 184–88.

6. I find Paul to be an eclectic figure and letter-writer. When pushed strongly by the Corinthians, Paul can take up and emphasize the role of the rhetor. At other times (e.g., 1 Thessalonians, Philippians), Paul prefers the role of moral philosopher and his writings reflect epistolary forms in that style. Regardless of genre descriptions, it is evident that Paul uses Greco-Roman rhetorical conventions in a world that recognizes and responds to persuasion by those very forms. Hence, both epistolary and rhetorical analyses are helpful in interpreting Paul's letters. Cf. Duane F. Watson, "The Integration of Epistolary and Rhetorical Analysis of Philippians," in *The Rhetorical Analysis of Scripture: Essays from the 1995 London Conference* (ed. Stanley E. Porter and Thomas H. Olbricht; JSNTSup 146; Sheffield: Sheffield Academic Press, 1997), 398–426.

7. Mention is made by Bloomquist, *Function of Suffering*, 126 and Troels Engberg-Pedersen, "Stoicism in Philippians," in *Paul in His Hellenistic Context* (ed. idem.; Minneapolis: Fortress, 1995), 274–76. Notable for some commentary are J. Paul Sampley, "Reasoning from the Horizons of Paul's Thought World: A Comparison of Galatians and Philippians," in *Theology and Ethics in Paul and His Interpreters: Essays in Honor of Victor Paul Furnish* (ed. Eugene H. Lovering, Jr., and Jerry L. Sumney; Nashville: Abingdon, 1996), 127–28; Geoffrion, *Rhetorical Purpose*, 129–33, 172–78; Jaquette, "Not-So-Noble Death," 188–90 and Fee, *Philippians*, 126–55. With regards to Paul's maxim at 1:21, only Fee, *Philippians*, 140–42, gives special attention.

Analyzing Paul's Maxim (Philippians 1:21)

Maxim Forms during Paul's Time

The rhetorical maxim[8] had a long history of development and usage from the Greek classical period to the early empire.[9] The use of maxims as a whole, and the moral sententia (see below) in particular, was intensified in the time of Paul with the rise of declamation exhibitions. Following Quintilian's counsel on maxims in *Institutio oratoria* 8.5.3–34, we can posit that Paul had access to three different maxim forms: the gnomic maxim, the gnomic sentence, and the moral sententia.[10]

The gnomic maxim was encapsulated wisdom taken from poetical or prose genres as an expression of general, traditional, and moral truth. The truth of the gnomic maxim was generally thought to be universal and indisputable. An example of a gnomic maxim is "The chances of war are the same for both."[11] Compare 1 Corinthians 4:2: "Moreover, it is required of stewards that they be found trustworthy."[12]

The gnomic sentence was an individual's spoken expression of recognized wisdom based on general observations or decrees of judgment, *applied to particular circumstances of the moment*. Rather than simply being considered indisputable (cf. the gnomic maxim), the gnomic sentence could be affirmed or refuted. As a move from the universal to the particular, the gnomic sentence is not simply traditional, but it is rhetorical. It brings recognized wisdom to bear in a deliberative context and as such must be framed in light of one's stature, one's ability to move the audience, and the coherency of the counsel given with the particulars of the situation. An example of the gnomic sentence is "There is no man who is really free, for he is the slave of either wealth

---

8. A maxim is a concisely expressed, stylized, and memorable principle or rule of conduct. Greeks called such sayings γνῶμαι; Romans called them *sententiae*. The content of these maxims is drawn largely from recurrent, observable, and taken-for-granted experiences common to the world of the intended hearers. As a rhetorical device, the maxim at the time of Paul was particularly valued for its persuasive power and its character-building qualities. For a complete analysis of maxims at the time of Paul, see Rollin A. Ramsaran, *Liberating Words: Paul's Use of Rhetorical Maxims in 1 Corinthians 1–10* (Valley Forge, Pa.: Trinity Press International, 1996).

9. Note that with Quintilian the two generic terms for "maxim" (Greek: γνώμη and Latin: sententia) form descriptive *subcategories* as the two cultures move together. For a complete discussion, see ibid., 5–29.

10. The following discussion of the three maxim forms follows closely the more detailed investigation in ibid., 9–17.

11. Aristotle, *Rhet.*, 2.21.11. All translations from classical sources are from the LCL unless otherwise specified.

12. All translations are from the NRSV unless otherwise specified.

or fortune."[13] Compare 1 Corinthians 1:25: "For God's foolishness is wiser than human wisdom, and God's weakness is stronger than human strength."

According to Quintilian (*Inst.* 8.5.9–34), moral general truth could be shaped in the form of a "newer" sententia: that is, a statement that is brief, well-rounded, memorable, employing a striking figure, having an aesthetic-emotional appeal, and often placed as a clausula (conclusion). The use of stylish and proper sententiae increased the ethos of the speaker. An example of the moral sententia is "All happiness is unstable and uncertain."[14] Compare 1 Corinthians 10:23: "All things are permissible" (my translation).

Maxim Identification

Rhetoricians and philosophic moralists considered it a sign of maturity and stature to compose maxims for proper living, commonly neither citing their sources nor prefacing their created wisdom outright. The placement of maxims in Paul's letters may be roughly divided into two sets: embedded maxims, and maxim stacks. Embedded maxims denote those maxims that stand independently in a written text as an important part of argumentation. Maxim stacks or γνωμολογία are collections or anthologies of gnomic sayings written in succession. Paul uses stacks at the end of some of his letters for the didactic purpose of "painting pictures" of proper community relationships.[15]

The identification of embedded maxims of any of the three types (moral sententia, gnomic sentence, or gnomic maxim) begins with three factors.[16] First, one establishes that a proposed maxim contains *traditional moral content* derived from either (1) the social stock of knowledge recognizable in the wider Greco-Roman society or (2) the common (in-group) social stock of knowledge recognizable to a participant in a Pauline community. Second, one considers the *brevity* or *conciseness* of the statement. Moral sententiae are usually brief. Gnomic sentences, while concise, tend to be longer, with the addition of particularizing characteristics such as the supplement or reason. Gnomic maxims vary with the types of stylistic features chosen. Third, maxims have a *figured form.* One or more figures or stylistic markers (e.g., comparison, antithesis, interrogation, or even brevity itself) attract the hearer's attention and distinguish the maxim from everyday speech.

Two supporting factors for maxim identification are argumentation and

---

13. Aristotle, *Rhet.*, 2.21.2.
14. Seneca the Elder, *Controv.*, 1.1.3.
15. See J. Paul Sampley, *Walking Between the Times: Paul's Moral Reasoning* (Minneapolis: Fortress, 1991), 96–97.
16. The following two paragraphs closely follow Ramsaran, *Liberating Words,* 23–25.

recurrence. Rhetorical handbooks provide known argumentative patterns for maxim usage: establishment of the rhetorician's character, refutation of another maxim, detailed elaboration, and inclusion in diatribal style. Recurrence of a maxim within the same Pauline letter or within the grouping of Paul's letters also strengthens identification. Rhetoricians to some degree treated their moral maxims as commonplaces.[17]

"For to Me to Live Is Christ and to Die Is Gain"[18]

Given the above background on rhetorical maxims, it now remains to evaluate Paul's statement in 1:21 with regard to maxim features. First, the statement includes *traditional moral content*. The phrase "to live is Christ" does not indicate simple existence but rather the "quality and influence" of that life, namely to be marked by "fruitful labor" (1:22) and the Philippians' "progress" (1:25). The statement is placed in the context of moral deliberation ("Yet which I shall choose I cannot tell"), using the life and death topos common among moral philosophers of the time (see below).

Second, the statement core, as well as the full statement, is marked by *brevity*. Three elements are present in succession: (1) a personalizing element (ἐμοὶ; indirect object); (2) the postpositive transitional marker (γάρ; causal conjunction); and (3) the statement core (τὸ ζῆν Χριστὸς καὶ τὸ ἀποθανεῖν κέρδος). Brevity is accomplished (1) by compressing the verbal and nominal aspects of sense into each of the two infinitives, (2) by the ellipsis of the verb (ἐστίν) following each infinitive, and (3) by the avoidance of constructing a more lengthy conditional sentence.[19]

Third, certain stylistic features (in addition to brevity as discussed) mark out this statement core from ordinary speech:

τὸ ζῆν Χριστὸς καὶ τὸ ἀποθανεῖν κέρδος

The same structure of nearly equal length (*isocolon*[20]) stands on both sides of the καὶ ("and"), with the repetition of τὸ at the beginning of each clause

---

17. See The Elder Seneca, *Controv.*, 1.pr.24, and the discussion in Ramsaran, *Liberating Words*, 14.
18. RSV.
19. The conditional sense of the statement might have been expressed along the following lines: "If having been given a life I continue to live, then this is Christ, and if having been given a life I die, then this is gain."
20. *Rhet Her.*, 4.20.27. The *isocolon* is the figure made up of two or more cola — a colon or clause being a part of a sentence that is brief and complete but needing another colon to complete the entire thought — that "consist of a virtually equal number of syllables."

producing *epanaphora*.²¹ In addition, each clause ends with the same sound/ syllable -ος, thereby producing *homoeoptoton*.²² There is also a striking correspondence between the sounds within each clause, especially with respect to the X/κ and τ/δ of Χριστὸς and κέρδος and the long vowel sounds of ζῆν and the final syllable of ἀποθανεῖν. The result is a striking *paromoiosis*.²³ With the addition of ἐμοὶ γάρ to round out the completed statement, one obtains an equality of length (seven syllables) on each side of the καὶ.

This analysis demonstrates that this statement is indeed a maxim. In a fashion that sets it apart from normal speech, Philippians 1:21 provides traditional moral content, brevity, balance, and stylistic features in a form that is memorable.²⁴ Paul has created a moral sententia that has been shaped, like a gnomic sentence, to fit the contour of his argument.

There is no recurrence of this or a similar maxim in Paul's letters. The maxim, however, does occur within the topos of life and death, which is a recurrent subject in Paul's reasoning from *adiaphora*.²⁵ Paul creates maxims within certain topoi and often chooses to express them in *adiaphora* form.²⁶ Hence, this may also add weight to the recognition of Philippians 1:21 as a maxim.

Looking for "Gain": The Maxim, Proposition, and Examples

The Maxim as Introduction to a Proposition

Information on the relationship of the maxim to a thesis, hypothesis, or *propositio* is limited, entirely lacking in the rhetorical handbooks of the time. There

---

21. *Rhet Her.*, 4.13.19: "*Epanaphora* occurs when one and the same word forms successive beginnings for phrases expressing like and different ideas."

22. *Rhet Her.*, 4.20.28: "*Homoeoptoton* occurs when in the same period two or more words appear in the same case, and with like terminations."

23. *Paromoiosis* is a "parallelism of sound between the words of two clauses either approximately or exactly equal in size. This similarity in sound may appear at the beginning, at the end (*homoioteleuton*), in the interior, or it may pervade the whole." Richard A. Lanham (*A Handbook of Rhetorical Terms* [2d ed.; Berkeley: University of California Press, 1991], 109), quoting from Smyth's *Greek Grammar*. See Aristotle, *Rhet.*, 3.9.9. Cf. Demetrius, *On Style*, 3.154.

24. Cf. the discussion in Fee, *Philippians,* 140, with n. 8.

25. Moralists in Paul's world, particularly those connected with Stoicism, shaped their moral reasoning on the basis of virtues, vices, and things of indifference (*adiaphora*). The flourishing life was achieved by focusing on what was important, i.e., virtue; by laying aside vice; and by setting indifferent things aside or using them rightly. In addition to our present text, see 1 Thess 5:10 and Rom 14:7–9.

26. This is argued in detail in Rollin A. Ramsaran, "Getting to the Point: Maxims in Paul's Moral Reasoning," in *Paul in His Greco-Roman World* (ed. J. Paul Sampley; Harrisburg, Pa.: Trinity Press International, forthcoming).

is, however, important counsel in Theon's rhetorical exercise handbook: "We will get the introductions of theses (θέσεις) by confirming the thesis with a maxim, a proverb, a chreia, a useful saying, a story, an encomium, or a denunciation of the subject matter which the investigation concerns."[27] On analogy with Theon's counsel concerning the thesis, Paul's maxim in 1:21 (with its accompanying personal example) precedes his propositio in 1:27–30 as introduction,[28] provides criteria for behavior, and supplies key terms ("living" and "dying") for the string of examples that follow the statement itself.

If Paul's maxim is an introduction for his propositio in 1:27–30, there must be a close and intentional connection between the sections of text. Is it appropriate to couple the earlier section of 1:12–26[29] together with the tight inclusio structure of 1:27–4:1?[30] Can 1:12–4:1 be identified as a larger unit? The following three observations indicate an affirmative answer. First, one must notice that Paul's maxim speaks of "gain" (κέρδος), also a key term in 3:7–8 ("whatever gain [κέρδη] I had"; "that I may gain [κερδήσω] Christ"). Second, the idea of "gain" is reinforced by a cluster of other topics common to both 1:12–26 and 3:2–4:1: σάρξ (1:22, 23; 3:3, 4), πίστις/πιστεύω (1:25; 3:9), πεποιθὼς/πεποιθότες/πεποίθησιν (1:25; 3:3, 4), θάνατος (1:20; 3:10), σῶμα (1:20; 3:21, 21), and σωτηρία/σωτήρ (1:19; 3:20).[31] Third, the juxtaposition of negative examples with Paul's own personal example stand as bookends to the larger section of 1:12–4:1: those who preach Christ from envy and rivalry (1:15), enemies with minds set on earthly things (3:18–19).

When Paul directs the Philippians to "live as citizens worthy of the gospel of Christ" (1:27), he is specifying a behavioral stance that must take its cue from the larger context. He is not referring simply to the military metaphor of standing firm in battle formation, as important as that is to the letter's background.[32] Paul is referring to how the Philippians make proper decisions and treat one another in community. While Paul's directive in 1:27–30 surely

---

27. Quoted from James R. Butts, "The 'Progymnasmata' of Theon: A New Text with Translation and Commentary" (Ph.D. diss., Claremont Graduate School, 1987), 515.
28. This line of argument can only proceed by analogy, not by directly (and incorrectly) relating a θέσις (general question at issue) with ὑπόθεσις (specific question at issue) and *propositio*. My thanks to R. Dean Anderson for reminding me of this point. See his discussion in *Ancient Rhetorical Theory and Paul* (rev. ed.; Leuven: Peeters, 1998), 56–59; 193–94.
29. 1:12–26 is marked as a section by Paul's use of προκοπή ("progress") in v. 12 and v. 25, thus forming an inclusio. See Davis, *Oral Biblical Criticism*, 107.
30. See note 3, above.
31. Davis, *Oral Biblical Criticism*, 155.
32. On the use of the military language and metaphor, see Edgar R. Krentz, "Military Language and Metaphors in Philippians" in *Origins and Method: Towards a New Understanding of Judaism and Christianity. Essays in Honour of John C. Hurd* (ed. Bradley H. McLean; JSNTSup 86; Sheffield: JSOT, 1993), 105–27 and Geoffrion, *Rhetorical Purpose*, 35–81.

looks forward to 2:1–4, it also reinforces the moral paradigm put forward in Paul's example in 1:19–26. For both 1:19–26 and 2:1–4 bear the same weight: not allowing one's own interests to crowd out service to others (1:23–25; 2:4).[33]

A careful and attentive reading of 1:12–4:1 identifies the theme of life and death as central to the series of examples contained therein (see below). "For to me to live is Christ and to die is gain." Paul's maxim in 1:21 as interpreted by his personal example are related to his propositio (1:27) and its restatement (3:20) as a charter for "the commonwealth directed from heaven":[34] live life in a cruciform manner of self-giving on behalf of others.

Paul's Exemplary Argumentation

Exemplary argumentation was common to both rhetoricians and moralists at the time of Paul. As a means of establishing proof in the realm of oratory, examples of past (and sometimes present) revered figures were employed. Examples were thought to be advantageous in that they were more easily comprehended than the enthymeme.[35] In deliberative discourse good examples as well as bad were offered as guidance for proper moral action. In the case of good examples, deliberative discourse often included a call to imitation (cf. Phil 3:17).[36] In philosophical circles, moralists (often with rhetorical training) advocated a strong relationship between teacher and student(s) based on the personal example of the teacher.[37] Such relationships were reinforced or maintained at a distance through hortatory letters.[38]

Paul's argumentation may be structured as a series of examples with three exhortations interspersed among them:

Paul's example (1:12–26)

Counter-Imperial exhortation (1:27–2:4)

Jesus' example (2:5–11)

---

33. Paul's thanksgiving/prayer also prepares his readers for this type of moral reckoning: "that your love may overflow more and more with knowledge and full insight to help you determine what is best" (1:9).

34. This phrase is borrowed from Stowers, "Friends and Enemies," 117.

35. For a complete review and analysis of the rhetorical sources, see Benjamin Fiore, *The Function of Personal Example in the Socratic and Pastoral Epistles* (Rome: Biblical Institute Press, 1986), 26–44.

36. Margaret M. Mitchell, *Paul and the Rhetoric of Reconciliation: An Exegetical Investigation of the Language and Composition of 1 Corinthians* (HUT 28; Tübingen: Mohr/Siebeck, 1991), 42–46.

37. Abraham J. Malherbe, *Paul and the Thessalonians: The Philosophic Tradition of Pastoral Care* (Philadelphia: Fortress, 1987), 53–60.

38. Fiore, *The Function of Personal Example*, 84–100.

Counter-Imperial exhortation (2:12–18)
Timothy and Epaphroditus's examples (2:19–30)
Paul's example (3:1–16)
Counter-Imperial exhortation (3:17–21)

Space considerations dictate that most attention be given to the examples. It should be noted, however, that the counter-imperial exhortations form a strong background for the letter and, therefore, Paul's use of examples. They represent the Philippian community as an alternative society/polis within a dominant Roman context. The exhortations subvert imperial words and images to legitimate this alternative society: e.g., σωτηρία, σωτήρ, κύριος, πολίτευμα.[39] They appropriate apocalyptic language (1:28b–29; 2:15–16; 4:20–21) as a means to legitimate the community's hope in God's ongoing and imminent final overthrow of imperial powers and the community's place within the cosmic renewal. The exhortations advocate a lifestyle contrary and despicable to the ruling powers' pattern of honor and shame and their inherent power structures.[40] Therefore, the "firm stance" produces suffering for Paul and the Philippians from a common source (1:30): the patronal network of Roman imperial power. Ironically, however, it is through the cross (symbolizing death and dying) that the ruling powers are being undone (Phil 2:5–11; cf. 1 Cor 2:6–8).

Paul's exemplification begins boldly. He brings forth his own work and circumstances as exemplary for faithful believers in his location (1:12–14), and for the Philippians as well. Then he notes the poor example of some of his detractors and the good work of those following his confident example (1:15–17). In Philippians 1:19–26, Paul returns to his example and artfully casts it in the form of suicide contemplation.[41] Such reflection signals Paul's intention to do serious moral reckoning; his use of a maxim suggests that his audience would recognize his position as an accomplished moral teacher. Certainly a segment of Paul's "Roman" audience at Philippi would have resonated with the Stoic moral reasoning from *adiaphora* (indifferences), here with respect to the theme of life and death. Paul's maxim and example are not set up as contrastive in terms of right and wrong, rather they present two choices and ask which is to be preferred? Which of the two *adiaphora* (life or death) most

---

39. See Dieter Georgi, *Theocracy in Paul's Praxis and Theology* (Minneapolis: Fortress, 1991), 72–78.

40. See "God Turned Upside Down," in ibid., 79–104. For extensive discussion of the issue, see Richard A. Horsley, ed., *Paul and Empire: Religion and Power in Roman Imperial Society* (Valley Forge, Pa.: Trinity Press International, 1997).

41. Jaquette, "Not-So-Noble Death," 177–83, refining the position of Arthur J. Droge, "*Mori Lucrum:* Paul and Ancient Theories of Suicide," *NovT* 30 (1988): 263–86.

fully supports God's telos (ultimate goal), the proclamation of the good news that restores a faithful people of God.[42]

Because the question and contemplation of suicide was controversial and somewhat unsavory, Paul brings it forward in covert/figured speech.[43] Paul draws in his audience to consider the choice with him. Proper judgment weighs desire, relational friendship and loyalty, and rational thought. Notably, either life or death leads to Christ.[44] Paul, however, formulates the "dying" to emphasize an existential *immediacy* of being with Christ! How great Paul's love for the Philippians to have set this relational immediacy with Christ aside to be with them for service! No doubt Paul expects them to respond to one another in kind and give up items of self-interest in order to love and serve others. Paul's *adiaphora* reasoning demands that the hearers make a choice according to the circumstances of the situation based on its relationship to an ultimate goal or truth — is choosing life or death to be preferred? Because a maxim also demands a hearer's engagement in moral reckoning according to circumstances,[45] it is appropriate that Paul uses a maxim within this argument.[46]

Strikingly Paul chooses life to serve the Philippians, while he presents Jesus as one who chooses death to serve all believers (2:5–11). Both Paul and Jesus share the same mind, humbly looking after the interests of others (2:3). Yet the "preferred" selected by each differs with their respective situations: one lives, one dies (to live again). Furthermore, Paul is ever mindful that his choice for life may not overrule death's claim (2:17); yet even then, dying leads to gain.

Paul's commendation of Timothy (2:19–24) follows the pattern he recommends for members of Philippi's alternative community, namely, be in "full accord" (σύμψυχοι) and "look after the interests of others" (2:2–4). Paul

---

42. *Adiaphora*, or indifferent things, were regarded as largely neutral in nature; however, in Stoic circles, a division between those indifferent things "preferred" and "unpreferred" was based on whether they helped or hindered the individual along the path to virtue. For a complete discussion, see Glen Lesses, "Virtue and the Goods of Fortune in Stoic Moral Theory," *Oxford Studies in Ancient Philosophy* 7 (1989): 95–128. See note 25, above.

43. For a review of the problem with literature and a strong rhetorical argument for this view, see Jaquette, "A Not-So-Noble Death," 177–92.

44. To live means "fruitful labor" on Christ's behalf among Christ's community (1:22); to die means "to depart and be with Christ" (1:23).

45. Ramsaran, *Liberating Words*, 10–12.

46. Here, Paul's argument fits best into a "Christian prophetic discourse about suffering and death: one who suffers fulfilling God's calling is following the example of Christ." See Vernon K. Robbins, "Argumentative Textures in Socio-Rhetorical Interpretation," 51, in this volume. Cast in Robbins's analytical model, Paul's ensuing argument moves forward to develop the following syllogism: *Rule:* Believers follow Christ's example of serving others. *Case:* Paul may take his life and be removed from serving the Philippians or he may live and be with them. *Result:* Following Christ's dying example, Paul remains to serve the Philippians.

testifies that Timothy relates to Paul with "equal accord" (ἰσόψυχοι). And unlike others, Timothy does not "look after [his] own interests," but those of the Philippians, which are "those of Christ" (2:20–21)! For Timothy, "To live is Christ."

The strength of Paul's endorsement of Epaphroditus (2:25–30) may possibly betray some sense of disappointment on the part of the Philippians.[47] Whatever the case, Paul makes use of the situation to shape Epaphroditus's misfortune as exemplary ("honor such men"; 2:29b). Epaphroditus "longs" for the Philippians as Paul does (1:8; 2:26). His life (commissioned on behalf of the partnered Philippians; 2:25b) is given over to supporting Paul's affairs and not his own (2:30b). Living in a manner risking death for "the work of Christ" is "dying for gain" (2:30).

Paul's last example in our section aptly demonstrates the fluid movement of his maxim and its exemplary application throughout this larger section. After parading his own list of status symbols (3:4–6), Paul denounces them all as loss (ζημία) in order that he may gain Christ.[48] Paul does this so that his relationship to God and others might be grounded in the power stemming from the example of Christ's faithfulness[49] and not in his own interpretation of Torah. Hence, Paul's "living" is to share in Christ's sufferings by becoming like Jesus in his "dying praxis" or death (συμμορφιζόμενος τῷ θανάτῳ αὐτοῦ; 3:10b).

While Paul's "dying praxis" is, to some extent, motivated by the resurrection from the dead, Paul makes clear that this "dying" is not grounded in the "immediacy" claimed when he first uttered his maxim in chapter 1. In 3:12–16, Paul says that this living that becomes like Jesus in his death ("living as dying") is the moral race to maturity through a lived-out existence ("I press on toward the goal"); it only finds its accomplished and final reward in the resurrection of the dead.

Hence, it is clear that Paul's maxim has provided a thematic and structural plan for his exemplary argument of living as an alternative commonwealth directed by the living Lord in heaven (1:27 with 3:20). Paul introduces his maxim at 1:21 in a specific context: contemplation of suicide. Paul solidly

---

47. See the discussion in Fee, *Philippians*, 272–73.
48. Paul's example here is in figured/covert speech. Drawn into Paul's past historical example, the Philippian believers, *in their present situation,* are challenged to reject any coercion to, siding with, or longing for *imperial status connections* that would negate full allegiance to their "commonwealth directed by Christ from heaven." See Frederick W. Weidmann, "An (Un)Accomplished Model: Paul and the Rhetorical Strategy of Philippians 3:3–17," in *Putting Body and Soul Together: Essays in Honor of Robin Scroggs* (ed. Virginia Wiles, Alexandra Brown, and Graydon F. Snyder; Valley Forge, Pa.: Trinity Press International, 1997), 245–57 (without the imperial connection).
49. Following the interpretation of M. D. Hooker, *"PISTIS CHRISTOU,"* NTS 35 (1989): 331–33.

grounds the first half of his maxim, "to live is Christ," as promoting God's work of intervention in the world by advancing "individual communities over against the dominant society."[50] Paul, however, exploits the final telos of a believer's destiny to portray artificially a sense of immediacy to the latter part of his maxim — to die is gain (i.e., the gain of being in Christ's "immediate" presence). But as Paul continues, his examples begin to demonstrate the truth of each side of his maxim from the perspective of life rather than death as a means of personal gain:

> Paul's choice — *willingness to live* in this life for the welfare of believers
>
> Jesus' choice — *willingness to die* in this life in service to believers
>
> Timothy — *willingness to live* in this life for the welfare of believers
>
> Epaphroditus — *willingness to die* in this life in service to believers
>
> Paul — *willingness to die to self-directed things* in this life so he might live by Christ's direction in this life and the life to come

"To live is Christ" means promoting the power of God's present intervention over ruling powers through new communities. "To die is gain" means practicing a cruciform love of self-giving to others in the midst of and in conflict with imperial structures and oppression. Living is dying. This is to say that Paul's maxim and exemplary argumentation forces one to consider the power of God as cruciform in shape.

It is fair to ask whether Paul's audience in Philippi would have naturally followed Paul's exemplary refinement of the maxim in 1:21. I imagine that the refinement was probably their primary context into which Paul slipped his figurative example in 1:19–26. Possibly, contrary to what many have thought, there were some heads turned in Philippi at the way in which Paul collapses the lived life and the eschatological paradigm into the "immediacy" of his presence with Christ.[51] Much of what Paul says in the Philippian letter is by way of reminder, especially his most explicit personal example in 3:1–16 ("Moreover,... to write the *same* things to you; 3:1). "Living as dying" or "living in the fashion of dying" is part of Paul's gospel proclamation and a moral foundation from which he constantly appeals: Galatians 6:14 ("by which the world has been crucified to me, and I to the world"); 1 Corinthians 15:31c

---

50. Richard Horsley, "1 Corinthians: A Case Study of Paul's Assembly as an Alternative Society," in *Paul and Empire: Religion and Power in Roman Imperial Society* (ed. idem; Harrisburg, Pa.: Trinity Press International, 1997), 251.

51. If Paul collapsed his normal eschatological paradigm (Christ "coming" and the resurrection of the living and the dead *at that point*) for rhetorical effect, then the strong tension between 1:23 and the more nuanced Pauline passages such as 1 Thess 4:13–18 and 1 Cor 15:23–28 begins to fade. The problem has a long history. See Ben F. Meyer, "Did Paul's View of the Resurrection of the Dead Undergo Development?" *TS* 47 (1986): 363–82.

("I die daily"; my trans.); 2 Corinthians 4:10 ("always carrying in the body the death of Jesus"), 6:9b ("as dying, and see — we are alive"; cf. Rom 6).

Paul concludes 1:12–4:1 by encouraging the community to imitate the common example of him, Timothy, and Epaphroditus ("as you have an example in us"; 3:17), their example being patterned by the "living as dying" modeled in Jesus. The mindset of Jesus that focuses self-giving love on behalf of others is antithetical to the mindset that navigates by "earthly things" and that is to be associated with the reigning Roman commonwealth from which the community is summoned to stand apart (3:20). Worthy of the good news proclamation of God's intervention and ultimate victory in Christ, its pattern of citizenship as cruciform love, and its present guidance from the living Lord, the community is called to "stand firm" (1:27; 4:1).

Paul, Moral Teacher and Rhetorician

Paul's statement in 1:21 ("For to me to live is Christ and to die is gain") is a moral maxim. It functions within the letter to introduce the propositional statement in 1:27–30. The maxim, along with Paul's personal example in 1:19–26, introduces the key themes of gain/loss and life/death. In the string of examples that follows, Paul refines his maxim from its immediate context ("which to choose, life or death?") to the more concrete ("how shall we *live* in present circumstances?"). In this way, Paul's maxim in 1:21 becomes applicable to the entire Philippian community. To live is life directed by Christ, to die is to disavow status, power, and protective indicators that most assuredly tie into the imperial context. The believer's life this side of Christ's parousia is a combination of both perspectives at once; living is dying.

In my estimation, Philippians 1:21 is only one of two isolated embedded maxims used by Paul in the letter. While 2:4 significantly reiterates 1:21 and is translated with gnomic quality into English, its Greek grammatical structure speaks against the intent of Paul to coin a maxim here.[52] In 4:4–7, Paul seems to have begun a maxim stack (4:4–5a; cf. 1 Thess 5:15–16; Rom 12:15–18) only to have broken off into general paraenesis (4:5b–7), a virtue list (4:8), and a further call to imitation (4:9). Hence, Paul's singular early use of a maxim in chapter 1 supports a strong ethos and speaks to his confidence as their moral guide. The texture of Paul's rhetoric includes strong praise and confidence in the exordium/thanksgiving; a low number of maxims used;

---

52. The negative participial clause that makes up verse 4 is dependent on the main verb πληρώσατε and the ἵνα construction in verse 2:2. As written by Paul, the verse is not easily transferred to another context, as is the usual case with maxims.

multiple examples focused on one theme (steadfastness in meeting the needs of others while maintaining imperial non-identification); friendship language; and a lack of a "maxim stack" at the conclusion of the letter. This texture supports a perception of the Philippians as a mature community with minor problems, not a community besieged by great divisiveness.[53] Paul's counsel comes to partners and friends by way of a reminder to stand firm as an alternative commonwealth entrenched in the imperial context.[54]

But how does one maintain moral consistency, inward calm, and control in a world subjected by imperial control? Following the tightly crafted section of 1:12–4:1, Paul emphasizes the theme of "contentment" amidst all circumstances (4:2–20).[55] In philosophical style, reminiscent of 1:19–26, Paul identifies with his Roman audience at Philippi by picking up Stoic aims (that which is true, noble, righteous, pure, pleasing, admirable, praiseworthy) and themes (ἀρετή, moral virtue; αὐτάρκης, sufficiency). Paul, however, argues for "God-sufficiency" (4:7, 9, 13, 19) as opposed to self-sufficiency.[56] Hence, the power of Paul's maxim, "living is dying," can only be grounded in the apprehension of God's present power, believers' apprehension of that power as present control, and God's imminent victory. Once again, after reflecting on recent events (reception of the Philippians' gift), Paul, moral teacher and rhetorician, crafts a response using his personal example of contentment and a second concluding maxim: "I can do all things through him who strengthens me" (4:13).[57] Taken together, Paul's two maxims sum up his entire Philippian message and exhortation in a memorable way:

- For me to live is Christ and to die is gain.
- I can do all things through him who strengthens me.

---

53. Sampley, "Comparison of Galatians and Philippians," 121–23, 127–31 and Fee, *Philippians*, 32–34.

54. Geoffrion (*Rhetorical Purpose*) has correctly and substantially demonstrated the importance of this overarching theme in Philippians.

55. Cf. Sampley, "Comparison of Galatians and Philippians," 129.

56. Or "Christ-sufficiency," based on the weight of the whole letter rather than this specific section. So Fee, *Philippians*, 426–36.

57. πάντα ἰσχύω ἐν τῷ ἐνδυναμοῦντί με. The following factors contribute to the identification of 4:13 as a sententia: (1) The statement contains moral direction and its motivational source. (2) Note the brevity of the statement. Later text-critical questions arise from the need to clarify the antecedent for "the one strengthening." (3) Paul is fond of creating maxims with πάντα. Note the first position of πάντα in 4:13. Cf. the πάντα maxims in 1 Corinthians and their first position in eight of ten examples, in Ramsaran, *Liberating Words*, 66; 141, nn. 6–7. (4) The sentence reads gracefully: opening and closing with short vowels, πάντα ... -ντί με; moving through an extended section of predominantly long vowels, ἰσχύω ἐν τῷ ἐνδυναμοῦ-, while centering on a resonant alternation of -ω ἐν τῷ ἐν- (also cf. χύ/ω/ἐν/τῷ/ἐν/δυ). (5) Because Paul personalized his first maxim in 1:21 by casting it in the first person singular, it is appropriate that he has done the same here. Paul usually puts forward his πάντα maxims in third person singular direct or indirect form. My thanks are due to Joop Smit for inquiring into a more careful identification of the maxim form.

CHAPTER 21

THE ARGUMENT OF COLOSSIANS

Jerry L. Sumney

Hans Hübner asserts that Colossians' reliance on the authentic Pauline letters renders rhetorical analysis of this letter useless.[1] This essay will test that supposition. Aristotle envisioned rhetoric being used in written compositions,[2] as well as by speakers, sees it drawing on various persuasive tactics to convince the audience.[3] It seems especially appropriate to use ancient rhetoric as a heuristic device to aid our understanding of Colossians because most literate people of the first century had at least a minimal acquaintance with rhetorical practice. I do not assume the author of Colossians had formal rhetorical training, only a basic Hellenistic education, and that he was an observant member of society who saw what worked for orators and employed those tactics.

I construe "argumentation" broadly enough to include the mutually reinforcing elements of pathos, ethos, and logos.[4] Since invention was versatile,[5] identifying the rhetorical species is not as useful for helping us understand the flow of an argument as is identifying the stasis. Since the basic facts (e.g., its Christology) that Colossians relies upon for its argument are not being questioned, the stasis seems to be one of quality. According to Hermogenes, this stasis explores what is just or advantageous and their opposites,[6] and whether

---

1. Hans Hübner, in *An Philemon, An die Kolosser, An die Epheser* (HNT 12; Tübingen: Mohr [Siebeck], 1997), 22–23.
2. See *Rhet.* 3.12.2.
3. Quintilian says that the orator's most important gift is "a wise adaptability since he is called upon to meet the most varied emergencies" (2.13.2; cited by Malcolm Heath, *Hermogenes On Issues; Strategies of Argument in Later Greek Rhetoric* [Oxford: Clarendon Press, 1995], 4 n. 6).
4. Richard Young, "Invention," in *Encyclopedia of Rhetoric and Composition: Communication from Ancient Times to the Information Age* (ed. T. Enos; New York: Garland, 1996), 351. Thomas Conley, "Πάθη and πίστεις: Aristotle 'Rhet'. II 2–11," *Hermes* 110 (1982/3): 310, 305–6, defines an argument as the proper relating of claim, evidence, and προτάσεις (propositions or premises), and notes that for Aristotle pathos was among those premises from which one could argue.
5. See Thomas H. Olbricht, "The Stoicheia and the Rhetoric of Colossians: Then and Now," in *Rhetoric, Scripture and Theology; Essays from the 1994 Pretoria Conference* (ed. Stanley E. Porter and Thomas H. Olbricht; JSNTSup 131; Sheffield: Sheffield Academic Press, 1996), 310–11, on how little help identifying the species is. Lionel Pearson (*The Art of Demosthenes* [Chico, Calif.: Scholars, 1981], 20) comments that the more successful deliberative speeches of Demosthenes are constructed in a forensic manner. Quintilian (2.13.2) also says that the rules of rhetoric "are liable to be altered by the nature of the case, circumstances of time and place, and by hard necessity itself."
6. See Hermogenes, *On Issues*, 37.15ff.

the debated thing should or should not happen or be granted. Similarly Cicero and Quintilian discuss the stasis of quality as one concerned with the nature or import of something.[7] This is the sort of question Colossians treats when it exhorts the readers to remain faithful to the received gospel rather than adopting the new teaching.[8] We may formulate the question as: What advantages does one gain by being "in Christ" and what might the advantages (or disadvantages) be to adopting the new teaching?

Ethos

Ancient rhetoricians recognized that the ethos of the speaker was an important "source of conviction,"[9] even if it did not affect the audience's ability to make a decision in the ways that pathos did.[10] Cicero says one should make known the client's merits, achievements, and reputable life and paint the client as upright, conscientious, and long-suffering under injustice.[11] Aristotle asserted that the speaker needed to present himself as "a trustworthy, intelligent, and well-intentioned person" to gain the assent of the hearers.[12] Aristotle did not limit such characterizations to the narratio, because speaking of the opponents' reputation is a part of the proofs (3.13.4).[13] Developing a particular ethos showed the hearers that the speaker held the same values they did,[14] and thus could be trusted to have their interests at heart.[15]

Colossians 1:24–2:5 is devoted to ethos. Here Paul is described as one who suffers for the sake of the Colossians and struggles mightily for them (even

---

7. See Duane F. Watson, "The Rhetoric of James 3:1–12 and a Classical Pattern of Argumentation," *NovT* 35 (1993): 54, and the references in n. 29.

8. Harold Van Broekhoven ("Persuasion and Praise in Colossians," in *Proceedings: Eastern Great Lakes and Midwest Biblical Societies* 15 [1995], 68–69) also finds the stasis of Colossians to be one of quality.

9. See Eugene E. Ryan, *Aristotle's Theory of Rhetorical Argumentation* (Collection Noêl; Montreal: Bellarmin, 1984), 173.

10. See William W. Fortenbaugh, "Quintilian 6.2.8–9: *Ethos* and *Pathos* and the Ancient Tradition," in *Peripatetic Rhetoric after Aristotle* (ed. W. W. Fortenbaugh and D. C. Mirhady; Rutgers University Studies in the Classical Humanities 6; New Brunswick, N.J.: Transaction Publishers, 1994), 189.

11. *De Oratore*, 2.43.182–84.

12. John M. Cooper, "Rhetoric, Dialectic, and the Passions," *Oxford Studies in Ancient Philosophy* 11 (1993): 177.

13. See also Cicero, *De or.*, 2.311–12, where he discusses interspersing sections which bear on ethos (and pathos) throughout a speech.

14. Ryan, *Aristotle's Theory*, 175.

15. George Kennedy (*The Art of Rhetoric in the Roman World, 300 B.C.–A.D. 300* [Princeton, N.J.: Princeton University Press, 1972], 78) notes that by the second century C.E. Roman orators recognized that people are motivated by self-interest and began to draw on it. In doing so they drew on earlier Greek oratory.

though he has never met them), as one commissioned by God and empowered by Christ, and as one who is confident in them. So Paul is upright, reputable, and working in the best interest of the readers. He is just the sort of person one is inclined to listen to and be persuaded by. Paul's suffering of "the afflictions of Christ" for them performs a philophronetic function,[16] and brings Paul's character into the proofs.

DeLuca notes that bodies may be used as a crucial part of public argumentation. His analysis of the tactics of some modern protest movements indicates that people's views are sometimes changed through the observation of bodies being put at risk rather than through rational argumentation.[17] This placing of bodies at risk is a mode of argument less focused on abstract reasoning than are other forms of argumentation.[18] Recognizing the argumentative value of placing oneself at risk helps us understand the function of the description given of Paul's suffering and the reminder of his status as a prisoner in 4:10. That bodies function as instruments of persuasion would not have been news to Paul, or before him, to Diogenes of Sinope or the ancient rhetoricians who recognized that mentioning the suffering of a just person was a useful element in establishing his or her ethos.[19]

Colossians further enhances Paul's ethos by associating him with known and reliable people: Epaphras, Onesimus, and Nymphia.[20] But the most important claim about Paul's status is made in the greeting; he is an apostle of Christ Jesus. This alone might have been sufficient to require the recipients to take the letter seriously, but its authority is enhanced by these other associations.

In the midst of establishing a favorable ethos for Paul, the author mentions some who defraud or delude with specious arguments (πιθανολογία, 2:4). Then in 2:23 they espouse things which have the reputation of wisdom but really are of no value. So the other teachers are presented as the sort of people one should not trust.

Thus, Colossians creates a strong favorable ethos for Paul and gives pass-

---

16. Thomas J. Sappington (*Revelation and Redemption at Colossae* [JSNTSup 53; Sheffield: JSOT Press, 1991], 143) sees the demonstration of *philophronesis* as one of the main purposes of 1:24–2:5.
17. Kevin Michael DeLuca, "Unruly Arguments: The Body Rhetoric of Earth First!, Act Up, and Queer Nation," *Argument and Advocacy* 36 (1999), 10–11.
18. Ibid., 15–16.
19. This use of the body as an instrument of persuasion is seen in many episodes in the life of Diogenes, as told by Diogenes Laertius (*Lives of the Eminent Philosophers*). In fact, the life of Diogenes of Sinope was in large part such a use of the body. Also see, e.g., Cicero, *De or.*, 2.47.195, for the displaying of the client's scars to produce pity in the audience.
20. If Colossians is pseudonymous, these characters may be known by reputation in the community (or communities) which initially received this letter.

ing attention to establishing an unfavorable ethos for those who advocate the other teaching. From the amount of attention given to it, establishing and supporting a particular image of Paul is important for the argument of Colossians.

Pathos

Arguments from pathos play only a small role in Colossians. Still the writer portrays Paul as one who works for (2:1) and suffers for the Colossians (1:24, 29), recognized ways of evoking love and pity.[21] The writer also arouses fear of the other teachers, saying they want to take the Colossians captive (2:8), and may imply that they try to shame the Colossians by claiming something which others with the same status (i.e., Christians) do not have but could have (2:18).

Logos and Invention

A preponderance of readers see a major break at 3:1, identifying it as the beginning of a relatively separate hortatory section.[22] Others see the hortatory material in chapters 3 and 4 as more integral to the letter's argument.[23] How one views 3:1–4:6 significantly influences how the argument of the letter works. Though most interpreters read Colossians as polemical, others argue that it is more admonitory,[24] and that its primary intention is to shape the readers' "moral dispositions and behavior."[25] Olbricht argues that the basic strategy of Colossians is to give an overarching understanding of Christian

---

21. See Cicero, *De or.*, 2.51.206, and *Rhet. Her.*, 2.31.
22. E.g., Eduard Lohse, *Colossians and Philemon* (ed. H. Koester; trans. W. R. Poehlmann and R. J. Karris; Hermeneia; Philadelphia: Fortress, 1971), 3; Eduard Schweizer, *The Letter to the Colossians; A Commentary* (trans. A. Chester; Minneapolis: Augsburg, 1982), 171; Petr Pokorny, *Colossians: A Commentary* (trans. S. S. Schatzmann; Peabody: Hendrickson, 1991), 26; Andreas Lindemann, *Der Kolosserbrief* (ZBK; Zürich: Theologischer Verlag, 1983), 14; James D. G. Dunn, *The Epistles to the Colossians and to Philemon* (NIGTC; Grand Rapids: Eerdmans, 1996), 136.
23. Jean-Noël Aletti, *Saint Paul Épitre aux Colossiens; Introduction, traduction et commentaire* (EB, new series; Paris: Gabalda, 1993), 37; David M. Hay, *Colossians* (ANTC; Nashville: Abingdon, 2000), 28.
24. Olbricht, "The Stoicheia," 310–12.
25. Wayne A. Meeks, "'To Walk Worthily of the Lord': Moral Formation in the Pauline School Exemplified by the Letter to Colossians," in *Hermes and Athens: Biblical Exegesis and Philosophical Theology* (ed. Eleonore Stump and Thomas P. Flint; University of Notre Dame Studies in the Philosophy of Religion 7; Notre Dame, Ind.: University of Notre Dame Press, 1993), 39. See also Walter Wilson, *The Hope of Glory: Education and Exhortation in the Epistle to the Colossians* (NovTSup 88; Leiden: Brill, 1997), 6–12, which identifies it as a letter of paraenesis.

existence that is different from that being proposed by the other teaching.[26] Similarly Meeks asserts that Colossians creates an alternative symbolic universe and describes what living in it means for Christians.[27] The little time Colossians spends directly opposing the other teaching makes a good prima facie case for such an understanding of its overall approach. If correct, chapters 3–4 may be important to the letter's argument.

While the emphasis of this letter is "continuational" rather than polemical,[28] its admonishment is achieved in part by countering the false teachers. These teachers are mildly ascetic visionaries who observe and perhaps participate in angelic worship. The Colossian author probably does not oppose the mystical experience itself, because Paul had such experiences. What Colossians opposes is the imposition of this experience on all Christians, the claim of superiority of the visionaries, and especially the assertion that those without these experiences are still in sin.[29]

In the face of such teaching Colossians sets out its alternative understanding of the cosmos and of Christian existence. To do this, the author works, as all good rhetors must, from what he and the audience agree on — and in this case that is much. The writer's task, then, is to show the readers how their commonly held assumptions mean that they must not adopt the new teaching, but should continue in the formerly received teaching.

Since it is the judgment the visionaries pass on those without such experiences which Colossians finds unacceptable, the main thesis of the letter is probably related to this element of their teaching. Some interpreters find this thesis in 2:6–7,[30] where the readers are exhorted to hold firmly to the way of life and teaching they had already received. This prepares the way for the rejection of the other teaching in 2.8–23.

However, Lähnemann and Aletti find the basic thesis statement of Colossians in 1:21–23.[31] Lähnemann notes that 1:20–23 prepares for the polemic by assuring the Colossians that they already have salvation.[32] Lähnemann's

---

26. Olbricht, "The Stoicheia," 319.
27. Meeks, "To Walk Worthily of the Lord," 44–46.
28. Olbricht, "The Stoicheia," 311; followed by Hay, *Colossians,* 28–29. See also George E. Cannon, *The Use of Traditional Materials in Colossians* (Macon: Mercer University Press, 1983), 167; Van Broekhoven, "Persuasion and Praise in Colossians," 68–71.
29. See the more detailed description and my argument in *Servants of Satan, False Brothers, and Other Opponents of Paul* (JSNTSup 188; Sheffield: Sheffield Academic Press, 1999), 188–213.
30. E.g., Hay, *Colossians,* 28. Meeks ("To Walk Worthily of the Lord," 45–46) finds the theme of the letter in 2:6. Similarly, Peter T. O'Brien *Colossians, Philemon* (WBC; Waco, Tex.: Word, 1982), 102.
31. Johannes Lähnemann, *Der Kolosserbrief; Komposition, Situation und Argumentation* (Gütersloh: Gütersloher Verlagshaus [Gerd Mohn], 1971), 42–43; Aletti, *Épitre aux Colossiens,* 39, 52, 120. Similarly, Lindemann, *Kolosserbrief,* 31.
32. Lähnemann, *Komposition, Situation und Argumentation,* 43.

remark focuses our attention on the correct issue, soteriology. Aletti finds 1:21–23 to be the *partitio*, the announcement of the themes of the treatise. The three themes he finds are: 1) they have received the effect of the work of Christ for believers; 2) they are to be faithful to the received gospel; and 3) this gospel is the one proclaimed by Paul. These three themes designate, in reverse order, the three main divisions of the letter (1:24–2:5; 2:6–23; 3:1–4:1), which take us to the final exhortations and epistolary frame.[33]

Noting that 2:6–7 summarizes the first part of the letter[34] does not cast doubt on this analysis. Rather, as Eriksson notes, the amplification of a theme often calls for the theme to be restated so that it bears more directly on the matter at hand.[35] Thus, 2:6–7 refocuses the preceding themes in preparation for the direct attack on the other teaching in 2:8ff. Colossians 1:12–14 foreshadows the thesis of 1:20–23, with references to forgiveness of sins and reconciliation in Christ. Additionally, 3:1[36] and 4:2[37] restate the basic thesis, showing that the primary concern is to assure the readers of their salvation/reconciliation/forgiveness by holding to the teaching they had already received.

Having identified the basic thesis, we may analyze the flow of the argument and the strategies it employs.[38] Colossians 1:3–8 begins the exordium, praising the addressees and proclaiming the universal validity of the gospel. This *insinuatio* establishes good relations between the author and the readers even if the letter is pseudonymous, because the actual readers are to identify with the implied readers through their acceptance of the same gospel. The mention of Epaphras advances the ethos-building function of the section. These verses also raise topics central to the letter: the hope that is already theirs in heaven, and the truth and effectiveness of the previously received apostolic gospel.

Verses 9–11(12) use the topos of the antecedent and its consequent. The writer asserts in verse 9 that the readers had received the gospel and its blessings, and that Paul prays for them, asking that they be filled with knowledge of God's will "with all wisdom and spiritual understanding." These assertions are the antecedent for "that you might live worthily of the Lord" (v. 10). This consequent is then defined by the four prepositional phrases that follow in

---

33. Aletti, *Épitre aux Colossiens*, 39, 52.
34. As does Lähnemann, *Komposition, Situation und Argumentation*, 49.
35. Anders Eriksson, *Traditions as Rhetorical Proof: Pauline Argumentation in 1 Corinthians* (ConBNT 29; Stockholm: Almqvist & Wiksell, 1998), 59.
36. Lähnemann, *Komposition, Situation und Argumentation*, 59
37. Olbricht, "The Stoicheia," 313.
38. See David Hellholm, "Enthymemic Argumentation in Paul: The Case of Romans 6," in *Paul and His Hellenistic Context* (ed. T. Engberg-Pedersen; Minneapolis: Fortress, 1995), 139, for the relationship between the thesis and the argument.

verses 10–11. The sentence begun in 1:3 may end after μακροθυμίαν in verse 11, as the United Bible Society's fourth edition and Nestle-Aland twenty-sixth edition indicate. Dunn and Hay, however, assert that all of verses 9–20 form a single sentence.[39] If the sentence ends in verse 11, the following sentence has no main verb. Even if a new sentence does not begin here, there is a clear break before μετὰ χαρᾶς because verses 10–11 contain a series of four prepositional phrases, the first and last beginning with εἰς and the two middle beginning with ἐν. These four prepositional phrases are the species listed within the genus of "living worthily." By defining "living worthily" as it does, Colossians inches the reader toward rejecting the other teaching, while still building a good relationship with them.

Verse 11d introduces a second consequent from the antecedent of their having accepted the gospel: God has made them fit to share in the inheritance of τῶν ἁγίων.[40] This assertion may stand in direct opposition to the visionaries' teaching. Verses 13–20 support 1:11d–12 with a series of citations of authorities. Most commentators acknowledge that verses 13–14 make use of traditional material.[41] Known liturgical or confessional material qualifies as ἔνδοξα for early Christians, and so serves as proof of the preceding assertion.[42] Since ἔνδοξα are accepted by the audience as true, they serve as an undisputed basis for an argument.

The confessional material in verse 13 may be taken from a baptismal context.[43] If so, the writer has introduced a theme that is central to the letter's argument. Use of the aorist (ἐρρύσατο) indicates that the Colossians already possess the blessings associated with their transfer into the "kingdom of his beloved Son." Verse 14, the second citation supporting the assertion of verse 12, again asserts that they already possess the blessing, and amplifies the transfer assertion of verse 13 by defining redemption as forgiveness of sins.

The hymn of verses 15–20 is the third authority cited to support the claim that God has made them sufficient to share in the heavenly inheritance. It defines the one through whom they receive forgiveness as the one through whom all was created and is sustained. Through this same Christ all things are reconciled, including all cosmic powers and especially the members of his body. The space allotted this hymn indicates that it was expected to sway

---

39. Hay, *Colossians*, 44. Dunn (*Colossians and Philemon*, 75) notes that the sentence continues in v. 12 and describes vv. 13–14 as a series of clauses. It seems unlikely that Dunn would see the hymn as the beginning of a new sentence.
40. For this study no decision about whether this means angels or saints is necessary.
41. E.g. Lohse, *Colossians and Philemon*, 32–33; Hübner, *An die Kolosser*, 52; Hay, *Colossians*, 48.
42. See Hellholm, "Enthymemic Argumentation in Paul," 128, also 128–30.
43. See Cannon, *Traditional Materials*, 12–15, 19.

the readers significantly.[44] This third citation ends the exordium by establishing Christ as the one in whom God has reconciled all things and identifying those who adhere to Paul's gospel as those "in Christ." The full implications of this identification have yet to be drawn, but the readers get an inkling of its implications through the assurances of their possession of the heavenly blessings. Thus 1:3–20 has introduced main topics and important arguments, has introduced and undergirded a sympathetic ethos for Paul, and has established a relationship between Paul and the Colossians.

While 1:21–23 returns to and refines the themes found in 1:12–14 in light of the hymn of verses 15–20,[45] it also sets out the thesis of Colossians, along with the supporting plan of argumentation for the whole letter. The basic thesis is in verse 22:[46] the Colossians are now reconciled to God and so are holy, spotless, and blameless before God. The supporting theses (that they must remain faithful to the received gospel and that this gospel is the one preached by Paul) are presented in reverse order, so that the end of verse 23 makes a smooth transition to the presentation of Paul's ethos in 1:24–2:5.

Verses 21–22 include the Colossians among those who have been reconciled through the cross of Christ with an exercise of definition. Verses 22 and 23 are an inverted form of the cause and effect topos. The cause, in the argumentative (not theological) sense, of their reconciliation is their holding fast to the gospel they had come to earlier. Thus there are overlapping topoi in this section: in verses 21–22 the Colossians are included among the reconciled through definition, and verse 22 also serves as the effect of the cause of maintaining the faith they received earlier.

The first argument in the body of the letter is one from ethos. Since I discussed this section above, I note only that the primary aim of 1:24–2:5 is not so much to establish Paul's authority as to present him as one to whom the readers will listen. The presentation of Paul given here produces a stark contrast with the visionaries: he brings knowledge from God, they deceive with specious arguments.

Verses 2:6–7 reprise the main thesis of the letter; they must retain the faith they have in Christ. This statement draws on both Paul's ethos and the assertions about the place of Christ in 1:12–20, refocusing the main thesis to bear directly on the question of whether to accept or reject the other teachers.

---

44. Stephen Fowl (*The Story of Christ in the Ethics of Paul; An Analysis of the Function of the Hymnic Material in the Pauline Corpus* [JSNTSup 36; Sheffield: Sheffield Academic Press, 1990], 131) comments that Paul assumes that the hymn is uncontestable. However, in discussion at the Lund Conference, Dean Anderson pointed out that the Patristic writers do not use liturgical material as authoritative sources.

45. Wilson, *Hope of Glory*, 235–6. Cf. Lohse, *Colossians and Philemon*, 3; Hay, *Colossians*, 40.

46. Lindemann (*Kolosserbrief*, 31) also sees v. 22 as the place where the main proposition begins.

Verse 8 opens the *refutatio* (2:8–15), which is an elaborated argument from the contrary. Being "taken captive" (v. 8) is the contrary of remaining firm in the faith (vv. 6–7). This is supported by the use of the topos of contradiction (according to human tradition and the στοιχεῖα and not according to Christ) in the second half of the verse.

The ὅτι clause of verses 9–10 provides a ground for not allowing anyone to take them captive. This use of the antecedent/consequent topos is reversed so that the consequent comes first. The antecedent is that the Colossians are "in" Christ in whom the fullness of deity dwells. As a consequence they must reject the visionaries' teaching as incompatible with their position in Christ. Whether verses 9–10 echo the hymn of chapter 1[47] or draw on another preformed piece,[48] the author is providing proof by citing material that has the ring of authority. Through the expression "in him," which appears seven times in 2:6–15, the author ties his assertions about Christ to those about Christians.[49] The assertion that Christians are "in Christ," and the exposition of the meaning of that assertion, are central argumentative goals of verses 6–15.

At 2:11–15 the focus turns to the effects of the Colossians' conversion, and the acts of God and Christ that made those things possible. The diverse metaphors for baptism[50] (circumcision, death, life, and resurrection) and the initial reception of the gospel affirm that they already possess all blessings because they are "in Christ." The writer uses the topos of assimilation here. He is making a comparison or connection between two things that is not explicit and asserting there is no difference between them.[51] It was not explicit in their baptism that being "in Christ" meant that they were being granted all the fullness. But all three metaphors in verses 11–13 make baptism and fullness inseparable.[52] Perhaps this bringing together of baptism and fullness is a counterdefinition for baptism.[53]

---

47. Schweizer (*Colossians*, 137) says that this verse picks up and interprets 1:19.
48. Dunn, *Colossians and Philemon*, 146.
49. Lindemann, *Der Kolosserbrief*, 38.
50. Cannon (*Traditional Materials*, 39–41) argues that the liturgical material found in vv. 11–13 is probably not all from a single hymn or confession.
51. See the discussion of Hermogenes, *On Issues*, 88.4–11.
52. Hübner (*An die Kolosser*, 84) notes that the author uses the συν- compounds in these verses to express a desirable self-understanding.
53. Harold W. Attridge ("On Becoming an Angel: Rival Baptismal Theologies at Colossae," in *Religious Propaganda and Missionary Competition in the New Testament World; Essays Honoring Dieter Georgi* [ed. L. Borman, K. Del Tredici, A. Standinger; NovTSup 74; Leiden: Brill, 1994], 481–98) has proposed that they possess an understanding of baptism something like that found in Zostrianos. Zostrianos may represent a later point on a trajectory similar to that on which Colossian visionaries also are found.

Verse 13 returns to the topic of forgiveness of sins, reaffirming that forgiveness is a central issue. Verses 14–15 identify the means through which forgiveness is achieved: Christ's death on the cross.[54] Since this death "for us" entailed the defeat and humiliation of the principalities and powers, being "in Christ" means that one is freed from them and their accusations. Additionally, those "in Christ" possess the superior fullness of Christ. The writer uses preformed material to make these assertions about the work of Christ,[55] and so they may be used as an authority.

The flow of the argument so far approximates the pattern Aphthonius gives for the elaboration of a chreia. We have no chreia but if we take 1:20–23, the letter's thesis statement, as our starting point, 1:24–2:15 parallels the pattern Aphthonius says is standard. The first six parts of this elaboration[56] with the corresponding sections in Colossians are: praise of the character, 1:24–2:5; paraphrase of the saying or action, 2:6–8; giving a rationale, 2:11–13; giving its converse, 2:9–10; corroboration by an analogy, 2:11–13; and an historical example, 2:14–15. This is not to suggest that the writer of Colossians knew the work of Aphthonius (who was not even born for another 200 years) or that this pattern existed earlier and was known by our author. Indeed, the flow of Colossians could also be seen as compatible with the different order of parts for the amplification of a theme found in *Rhetorica ad Herennium*.[57] Though the fit is not as neat, beginning at 1:12 there is significant correspondence. The Colossian writer is not following a prescribed order of types of arguments, he is drawing on well-known means of persuasion in ways that were recognized as effective.[58] Thus his argument has a good chance of carrying the day.

To this point I have identified no enthymemes. Colossians does not use deductive argumentation as a main strategy. Eriksson has noted that the words

---

54. For discussion of the difficulties of interpreting vv. 14–15 see Sappington, *Revelation and Redemption at Colossae*, 205–23.

55. See, e.g., Cannon, *Traditional Materials*, 46–47; Dunn, *Colossians and Philemon*, 146.

56. As cited by Ronald F. Hock, "General Introduction to Volume I," in *The Progymnasmata* (vol. 1 of *The Chreia in Ancient Rhetoric;* ed. R. F. Hock and E. N. O'Neil; Atlanta: Scholars, 1986), 35. The final two elements of the elaboration are an ancient testimony and a concluding epilogue. The same first six elements are found as early as Hermogenes' *Progymnasmata*. See the discussion and text in Burton L. Mack and Edward N. O'Neal, "The Chreia Discussion of Hermogenes of Tarsus," in Hock and O'Neil, eds., *The Progymnasmata*, 160–61, 174–77.

57. Its parts and the corresponding parts of Colossians are: theme expressed simply, 1:12–14; a reason added, 1:15–20; theme in a new form, 1:21–23 and 2:6–7; argument from the contrary, 2:8a-c; argument by comparison, 2:8d–9; argument from example, 1:24–2:5.

58. Burton Mack (*Rhetoric and the New Testament* [GBS; Minneapolis: Fortress, 1990], 31) notes that all those influenced by Hellenistic culture had "ears trained for the rhetoric of speech. Rhetoric provided the rules for making critical judgments in the course of all forms of social discourse."

ὅτι, γάρ, and οὖν are indicators that a writer is using an enthymeme.[59] Γάρ and ὅτι (and ὥστε) are extremely scarce in Colossians in comparison with their appearances in other Pauline letters of similar length.[60] While ἵνα, another word that might indicate a deductive argument, appears at about the same rate in Colossians as in other shorter Paulines, it is not found at all in 2:6–23. This section, which most directly addresses the other teaching, contains no uses of γάρ, only one of ὅτι (2:9), and only 2 of οὖν: one introduces the whole section by tying it to the ethos of Paul (2:6), and the other is found in 2:16. So this author relies heavily on means of argumentation other than deductive reasoning to be persuasive.

Verse 2:16 may indeed provide an instance of deductive argumentation. If so, its premises extend throughout verses 9–15. The major premise is: you are in Christ. The minor premise is: those in Christ receive forgiveness and participate in the triumph over the powers accomplished through the cross. The conclusion then is: those in Christ are not judged by the visionaries' regulations that come from those powers. The author bolsters this conclusion with a comparison of degree, asserting that those regulations are the shadow, not the substance,[61] which the gospel they originally heard offers. Verses 18–19 restate the conclusion from verses 8–15 drawn in verses 16–17 and make the visionaries' condemnation of the Colossians the contrary of holding fast to Christ, the head. Thus, verses 16–19 provide two supporting arguments for rejecting the visionaries' unfavorable evaluation of the Colossians.

Verse 2:20 starts a new subsection, which takes us at least through 3:4 and perhaps through 3:17. Though it has clearly distinct parts, language associated with baptism (dying with Christ [2:20], being raised with Christ [3:1], and the entailed imperatives of put to death [3:5] and put on [3:12]) holds the section together.

Verses 20–23 connect argumentatively with 2:(8)12–15 rather than the immediately preceding section, and so contain a second conclusion built on 2:8–15.[62] This second conclusion introduces a line of thought that assimilates

---

59. Eriksson, *Traditions*, 43. His essay in this volume adds ὥστε and ὅπως.

60. Γάρ appears only 6 times in Colossians but 39 in Galatians, 15 in Ephesians, 13 in Philippians, 25 in 1 Thessalonians, and 5 in 2 Thessalonians. Ὅτι appears 6 times in Colossians but 29 times in Galatians, 13 in Ephesians, 21 in Philippians, 13 in 1 Thessalonians, and 11 in 2 Thessalonians. Οὖν appears 5 (or the second corrector of ℵ adds another) in Colossians but 6 times in Galatians, 7 in Ephesians, 6 in Philippians, 2 in 1 Thessalonians, and 1 in 2 Thessalonians. Ὥστε is not used at all in Colossians, while it appears 5 times in Galatians, 3 in Philippians and 1 Thessalonians, and 2 in 2 Thessalonians.

61. The different interpretations of "the body of Christ" do not affect our identification of the argumentative topos employed.

62. Verses 2:20–23 and 2:16–19 are parallel in several ways. Both give a list of the opponents' regulations (vv. 16, 21) and of what they attain (vv. 18, 23), in both the regulations and the attainments are rejected, and both distinguish between appearance and reality (vv. 17, 23).

yet more things into baptism. But the basic strategy within 2:20–23 seems to be counterdefinition. In verses 21–22, the regulations the teachers advocate as a means to attain visions are called merely human commandments. Then in verse 23 what is perceived as wise is defined as without value. Verse 20 also makes "obeying instructions as though living in the world" the contrary of dying with Christ. So their status as the baptized precludes adopting the visionaries' regulations.

While 3:1–4 introduces and gives the foundation for the hortatory material in 3:5ff.,[63] it is also clearly the counterpart of 2:20–23. Verse 2:20 speaks of their having died with Christ; 3:1 refers to their having been raised with Christ. Similarly the imagery of 3:5 corresponds with that of 2:20 and the imagery of 3:12 with 3:1.[64] So, while 2:20–23 concludes direct opposition to the visionaries,[65] the transition to 3:1 and following is seamless, and the instructions of 3:5 and following are an inextricable part of the argument against the other teaching[66] and for continuing in the received gospel.

Verses 3:1–4 continue the argument by setting out the appropriate manner of life in contrast to that advocated by the visionaries. The exhortation in 3:1, "Seek the things above," must have come as a shock to the initial readers of Colossians. Beginning in 2:6 (and perhaps earlier) there is a sustained argument against seeking visionary experiences and what is necessary to attain them. Now they are told to "seek the things above," but this is connected with their baptism through the image of "being raised with Christ." This introduces a startling counterdefinition of "seeking the things above" which 3:5–4:1 fills with new content. The language of deduction reappears here with οὖν, γάρ, and ὅτι all being found in 3:1–4. So the manner of life prescribed in 3:5 and following is presented as the logical consequence of their having died with Christ, being raised with him, and looking forward to being made manifest with him. The οὖν of 3:1 gives a conclusion built on the premises of the meaning of baptism (2:12ff.) and Christians' participation in that reality. The γάρ of verse 3 shows that baptismal death with Christ is also a basis of the exhortation to think about things above in verse 2,[67]

---

63. So, e.g., Lohse, *Colossians and Philemon*, 132. Aletti (*Épitre aux Colossiens*, 215) argues that 3:1–4 is the *partitio* for 3:5–4:6 with the topics announced in reverse order.

64. O'Brien (*Colossians, Philemon*, 195) calls 3:5 and 3:12 contrasting parallels, as not only the language but also the contrasting lists show, vv. 5–11 begin with a five member vice list and vv. 12–17 begin with a five member virtue catalog.

65. Though it is too much to say with Hübner (*An die Kolosser*, 94) and many others that the argument against the opponents ends in 2:20–23.

66. Lindemann (*Kolosserbrief*, 52) calls 3:1–4 the hub of the letter.

67. The premises in v. 2 being (minor) those who die with Christ have their lives hidden with God and (major) you died with Christ.

which is a restatement of the theme of verse 1.[68] The language of baptism and admission into a new realm dominates 3:1–4. Verse 3:1 also vigorously renews the argument of assimilation; the way of life prescribed in what follows becomes part of what it means to be baptized. Baptismal language is so prevalent in Colossians because through expounding, really expanding, its meaning the author proscribes the visionaries' teachings and prescribes a way of "seeking the things above" which is compatible with the previously received gospel.[69]

Assimilation often included offering a definition for what one was arguing as one of the elements of its elaboration. This is used extensively throughout 3:1–10, as well as other common elements of assimilation, the constant presentation of the fact (here of their baptism), and discussing the lawgiver's (here God's) intention (in their baptism).[70] Verses 9–10 pick up baptismal and eschatological language, making "putting on" the new person a consequent of no longer being the object of God's wrath (vv. 6–8) and making participation in the vices incompatible with their present existence.

Verses 3:12–4:1 describes the manner of conduct appropriate for the baptized. This is the life in which they receive forgiveness, possess richness in Christ, and exercise wisdom (v. 16). The *Haustafel* is part of the writer's instruction about the proper manner of life for those "seeking the things above."

Verses 4:2–17 concludes the argument by giving attention to Paul's ethos.[71] He asks them to pray for him, establishing his humility (a distinctly Christian virtue), and reminds them of his commitment to the already received gospel (vv. 2–4). The final greetings in 4:7–17 both enhance Paul's ethos by associating him with these honored people and supply examples for the Colossians to imitate. So the letter ends with a final support for Paul and his ministry through supporting his ethos. If his ethos and his desire to proclaim his gospel are supported, then the readers are being called to remain faithful to that gospel Paul proclaims. Additionally, verse 12 refers to how Epaphras prays that they may "stand mature and fully assured." Perhaps this is a reference to the confidence they should have because of their place in Christ, if they remain faithful (1:20–23). Thus, important themes of the letter emerge in this concluding section.

---

68. Verse 2b gives the opposite of that theme.
69. Meeks ("To Walk Worthily of the Lord," 46) comments that in Colossians baptism points to the "whole process of resocialization into the Christian community of which baptism is the symbolic center."
70. See Hermogenes, *On Issues,* 88.4–11.
71. Cf. Van Broekhoven, "Persuasion and Praise in Colossians," 73, who identifies 4:12 as part of the epilogue.

Conclusions

Rather than simply copying the pattern of Pauline letters, the writer of Colossians puts together an impressive argument using means that were known to be persuasive in Hellenistic rhetoric. Not only does the writer use recognized means to make the central point within various sections, but he sometimes arranges them in ways that the writers of handbooks came to see as persuasive. Interestingly, deductive reasoning plays almost no part in the argument when the author engages the visionaries more directly. Rather, other means of argumentation dominate. The writer constantly draws on traditional material and elaborates themes found in it to make his case. Traditions surrounding baptism are central to the argument. Colossians assimilates into baptism the whole range of the life of the Christian as a life in Christ. This allows him to reject the visionaries' judgment on those who do not adhere to their regulations, and to promote a manner of life he labels "seeking the things above." Thus the argument of Colossians does not stop at 2:23, where the letter becomes more hortatory. Rather, the instructions of 3:1 and following are an important part of the argument for his understanding of what it means to be "in Christ." By requiring this manner of life he does not mean that the forgiveness they have received is in jeopardy. He assures them of their place in Christ and focuses on what they possess now rather than on the future reception of eschatological blessings, even as he prescribes the proper manner of life (e.g., 3:1, 3, 7–8, 12, 15). Thus, the Colossians' response to the stasis question of what advantages one receives in Christ is that the baptized receive forgiveness and reconciliation to God, and so securely possess all the fullness. The visionaries' teaching adds nothing to this fullness.

From beginning to end this letter encourages its readers to remain faithful to the apostolic gospel that Paul preaches as the way to retain their place in Christ, their forgiveness of sins, and their part in the heavenly realms and blessings. Since the figure of Paul is important, significant attention is given to matters of ethos. Thus, through its presentation of Paul (and others) and its drawing on preformed traditions which function as ἔνδοξα, Colossians calls its readers to remain faithful to the gospel they had received by rejecting the teaching of the visionaries. The letter's arguments, while not enthymemic or deductive, seem to have persuasively argued that being in Christ through baptism bestows forgiveness, access to the heavenly blessings, and a new existence even in the present.

PART SIX

RHETORICAL ARGUMENTATION IN HEBREWS

CHAPTER 22

ANTICIPATING AND PRESENTING THE CASE FOR CHRIST AS HIGH PRIEST IN HEBREWS

Thomas H. Olbricht

Hebrews contains some of the most rigorously argued positions in the New Testament. The detailed arguments for Christ as high priest are found in Hebrews 5–7. Following the recommendations of the rhetoricians, the Hebrews author anticipates his contentions in the introduction 1:3, and in 2:11, 17–18, 4:14–16.[1] I will first comment on the overall argument of Hebrews, then scrutinize how these anticipatory remarks work rhetorically. The major affirmations for the high priesthood (5–7) are carefully crafted upon commonly accepted outlooks (that is, enthymemic propositions), and proofs that depend mostly upon Scripture, except in the exhortatory materials. The end result is a contribution toward understanding the contours of argumentation in the Scriptures, especially Hebrews.

I argued in a previous essay that Hebrews employs amplification as recommended by Aristotle.[2] "And you must compare him with illustrious personages, for it affords ground for amplification and is noble, if he can be proved better than men of worth."[3] The author of Hebrews compared Jesus with such renowned personages as angels, Moses, Joshua, the Levitical priests, and Melchizedek. He also compared the sacrifice of Christ's blood with the respected blood of bulls and goats. He set out to prove that Jesus was superior, thereby establishing his higher status.

The argument in regard to Christ's superiority is reflected in the structure.[4] We must first take seriously the author's declaration that Hebrews is a "word of exhortation" (13:22). In what manner did exhortation inform his argu-

---

1. Aristotle, *Rhet.*, 3.14.6; Cicero, *Inv.*, 1.16.23; Quintilianus, *Inst.*, 4.1.5.
2. Thomas H. Olbricht, "Hebrews as Amplification," in *Rhetoric and the New Testament: Essays from the 1992 Heidelberg Conference* (ed. Stanley E. Porter and Thomas H. Olbricht; Sheffield: Sheffield Academic Press, 1993), 375–87.
3. Aristotle, *Rhet.* 1.9.38–39.
4. Harold W. Attridge (*The Epistle to the Hebrews* [Philadelphia: Fortress Press, 1989], 16, 17) correctly observes that it is difficult to fit everything into a structure for Hebrews even employing the cues offered by the author.

ment and arrangement?[5] Some of those to whom the document is addressed have become negligent (10:25) as well as lethargic in regard to recondite understanding (5:11). The author is adamant that recovery will come about through in-depth theological reflection upon Christ's achievements as sacrificer and sacrifice. "Therefore let us go on to perfection, leaving behind the basic teaching about Christ" (6:1). His strategy, therefore, is to set forth complicated instruction or theology, followed by exhortation, that is, a charge to action.[6] He reveals his basic concerns in 1:2-4 in which he proclaims Jesus as Son, creator, and the very imprint of God's being, the purification for sins (that is, the sacrifice), and the one sitting at the right hand of God as priest forever (that is, as sacrificer).

I propose the following as the skeletal arrangement of his strategy:

I. Christ is Son (1:1-14)

    A. Above prophets (1:1-4)

    B. Above angels (1:5-14)

First Exhortation (2:1-4) Obey his words because of his status

    C. For a time he was lower than angels; now he has resumed his former status, lifting up believers (2:5-18)

II. Christ is superior to Moses (3:1-6)

Second Exhortation (3:7-4:16) Hold faith firmly because of the great high priest

---

5. George H. Guthrie (*The Structure of Hebrews: A Text-Linguistic Analysis* [Leiden: E. J. Brill, 1994]), in a detailed independent analysis, came to much the same conclusion. His outline is almost identical (p. 144) with the one I proposed in 1992.

6. I am indebted to Floyd V. Filson, *"Yesterday": A Study of Hebrews in the Light of Chapter 13* (London: SCM Press, 1967), 27-30, for the insights in regard to exhortation. In an impressive study, Walter G. Übelacker (*Der Hebräerbrief als Appell* [ConBNT 21; Stockholm: Almqvist & Wiksell International, 1989]) argued that the writer employed the model of a deliberative speech. Hebrews 1:1-4 is an exordium; 1:5-2:18, the narratio; with 2:17-18 as the propositio. Hebrews 13:22-25 is the postscriptum (214-29; cf. 110ff., n. 161). While I agree that these items are useful in description, they do not help us understand the rhetorical structure of the body, especially in regard to amplification. I agree that in many ways Hebrews has deliberative elements. I conclude, as does David A. deSilva that "Hebrews, like many orations, utilizes elements of both epideictic and deliberative oratory"; David Arthur deSilva, *Perseverance in Gratitude: A Socio-Rhetorical Commentary on the Epistle "to the Hebrews"* (Grand Rapids: Eerdmans, 2000), 48. In regard to the structure I argued in "Hebrews as Amplification" that another way of looking at the arrangement in Hebrews is after the fashion of ancient funeral orations or eulogies (p. 378). I think, therefore, that the model is epideictic in arrangement, while specific arguments take on more the genre of deliberative speaking. But I am not sure that either designation helps us much to track the arguments in Hebrews. I have questioned the usefulness of rigid delineation according to the three genres in "An Aristotelian Rhetorical Analysis of 1 Thessalonians," *Greeks, Romans, and Christians: Essays in Honor of Abraham J. Malherbe* (eds. David L. Balch, Everett Ferguson, and Wayne A. Meeks; Minneapolis: Fortress Press, 1990), 216-36.

III. Christ is a superior high priest and sacrifice (5:1–10:18)

    A. As priest (5:1–7:28)

[Third Exhortation (5:11–6:12) This is an exhortation regarding the need to pay close attention to the argument for Christ as high priest, but also to the whole discourse regarding going on to perfection]

    B. As sacrifice (8:1–10:18)

Fourth Exhortation (10:19–39) Be bold, recover commitment, endure

IV. Christ as the pioneer of a better faith completed by fulfilled promises (11:1–40)

Fifth Exhortation (12:1–13:17) Follow the road of Jesus' suffering

V. Glory to Jesus Christ forever, concluding remarks (13:18–25)

In-depth Christological reflection is therefore the path to spiritual renewal, accompanied by encouragement to commitment and action. Several rhetorical agendas are played out in Hebrews, but the chief end is to enhance Christological understanding as well as incite the hearers to move on out, empowered by the newly gained understanding. Comparison is a strategy employed within this larger framework to prove "that [Christ] is better than men of worth."

The Anticipatory Remarks in Regard to Priesthood

The priesthood of Christ as a focus in Hebrews is set out in Hebrews 1:3. In regard to exordia, Aristotle wrote:

> But in speeches and epic poems the exordia provide a sample of the subject, in order that the hearers may know beforehand what it is about, and that the mind may not be kept in suspense, for that which is undefined leads astray; so then he who puts the beginning, so to say, into the hearer's hand enables him, if he holds fast to it, to follow the story.[7]

Übelacker identifies Hebrews 1:1–4 as the exordium in which the topics for the whole discourse are set forth.[8] The first two verses declare who it is who sat down at the right hand of the majesty on high, that is, the Son who is the heir of all things and through whom the worlds were created. It is he who made purification for sins and sat down at the right hand of God. By this succinct introduction the author clues in his audience to the fact that before the discourse is over he will set out the role of the Son as both sacrifice and

---

7. *Rhet.*, 3.14.6.
8. Übelacker, *Der Hebräerbrief,* 224–28, also 66–138.

sacrificer.[9] As R. McL. Wilson wrote, "It is one of the author's characteristics that he quite often introduces a theme casually, almost in passing, only to return to it later and give it a fuller development."[10] The writer will also take up the superiority of Christ over the angels (1:4). Interestingly, he takes up the items set out in 1:2-4 in reverse order, first Christ above the angels (1:5-2:18), then Christ as priest (4:14-7:28), and finally, Christ as sacrifice (8:1-10:24).[11]

That Christ is seated at the right hand of God obviously declares his ascension after his death. In being situated at the right hand of God he is in a position to fully serve humans as a mediating priest (4:14-16).[12] He is appropriate for this high calling on behalf of humankind, since he became human in every way (4:14) and experienced every human temptation (4:15). He was therefore perfected to this priesthood through his suffering and obedience.[13] Humans, as the result, have one of their own seated at the right hand of God, speaking a word on their behalf.

The second intimation of Christ as high priest is found in Hebrews 2:17:

> Therefore he had to become like his brothers and sisters in every respect, so that he might be a merciful and faithful high priest in the service of God, to make a sacrifice of atonement for the sins of the people.

The declaration at this point is not an isolated one. The ground has been prepared for it.

---

9. William R. G. Loader, *Sohn und Hoherpriester: Eine traditionsgeschichtliche Untersuchung zur Christologie des Hebräerbriefes* (WMANT 53; Neukirchen: Neukirchener Verlag, 1981).

10. R. McL. Wilson, *Hebrews* (NCBC; Grand Rapids: Eerdmans, 1987), 33.

11. The ancient rhetorians (see: Aristotle, *Rhet.*, 3.13-19, *Rhet. Her.*, 3.10, Quintilianus, *Inst.*, 7.1) do not comment on this chiastic phenomenon. For comments on the chiastic structure of Hebrews, see Übelacker, *Der Hebräerbrief*, 90ff., also John P. Meier, "Structure and Theology in Heb 1,1-14," *Biblica* 66 (1985): 504-33. Wilson (*Hebrews*, 93) observes, in regard to 5:1-4, "The first four verses of this section set out three criteria which require to be fulfilled by any true high priest, then verse 5 begins the demonstration that they are met by Jesus, characteristically starting with the last." It may be that the author thinks that the topic mentioned last should be taken up first because it is probably that item upon which the auditor centers his attention at that point. See also Robert H. Smith, *Hebrews* (Minneapolis: Augsburg, 1984), 71, commenting on 5:5.

12. Juliana Casey, *Hebrews* (Wilmington: Michael Glazer, 1980), 10-11.

13. DeSilva (*Perseverance in Gratitude*) concludes that the statements about Christ's perfection (2:10, 5:9, 7:28) are related to the perfecting of believers and not simply to his vocation as a priest. But he concludes, "In sum, the perfecting of Christ signifies chiefly his arrival at his heavenly destiny (as, in one sense, it will also mean for the 'many sons and daughters,' " while the path through which he has passed toward that destiny is certainly seen by the author to fit him for the ministry he performs "on the other side." See also David Peterson, *Hebrews and Perfection: An Examination of the Concept of Perfection in the "Epistle to the Hebrews"* (Cambridge: Cambridge University Press, 1982). Also, Barnabus Lindars, *The Theology of the Letter to the Hebrews* (Cambridge: Cambridge University Press, 1991), 42-55. I tend to think the perfection is more closely identified with Christ's human experiences perfecting him for his role as high priest, though not limited to that.

The overarching claim is that the Son is prior to and superior to the angels, and that in his death as human in every respect he opened up for humankind a new relationship with God as eternal high priest and sacrifice. He seeks to establish the superiority of Christ over angels on a basis, not so much of accepted commonplaces (the ground for enthymemes), but of Scripture texts.[14] Of course, the conclusions, established from the Scripture texts, now form propositions for enthymemes.[15] The Hebrews writer's propensity to move from one proposition (or enthymeme) to another defies in some sense the recommendation of the rhetoricians. Aristotle wrote:

> The function of Rhetoric, then, is to deal with things about which we deliberate, but for which we have no systematic rules; and in the presence of such hearers as are unable to take a general view of many stages, or to follow a lengthy chain of argument.[16]

We may demur by proposing a difference between oral presentation and the leisurely reading of documents, but the manner in which most ancients apprehended Hebrews was through hearing it read aloud.

Not only then is the Son higher than the angels, his work on behalf of humanity elevates humans in the age to come even higher than the angels. In that age, all things will be subject to humans (Heb 2:8). In two places then, the author argues that the auditors need to be amazed over what the Son accomplished for humankind so as to assign to themselves a higher status than the angels (Heb 2:5, 16).[17] In order, therefore, for the Son to be a high priest for humankind, "he had to become like his brothers and sisters in every respect" (2:17). It was as a human that the death of Jesus became efficacious for humans.

The author's argument, therefore, runs as follows:

The Son was the exact imprint of God's very being.
He was above the angels, as attested in Scripture.
He became for a time fully human.

---

14. Attridge, *The Epistle to the Hebrews,* 49–62.

15. The classical rhetoricians did not adequately reflect on the rhetorical function of Scripture texts because their three genres or rhetorical situations did not conceive of audiences which assigned a privileged status to "revealed" documents. The use of Scripture falls, it seems, into the category of what Aristotle identifies as "inartificial proofs" employed mostly in forensic rhetoric consisting of: laws, witnesses, contracts, torture and oaths (*Rhet.*, 1.15.1–3).

16. *Rhet.*, 1.2.12.

17. I agree with the sense of the NRSV translation of 2:8, employing the plural rather than the singular and thus focusing on humans rather than the Son: "Now in subjecting all things to them, God left nothing outside their control." Attridge (*The Epistle to the Hebrews,* 72) leaves open the possibility that the writer has in mind the prospect that the world to come will be subject to humans. DeSilva (*Perseverance in Gratitude,* 109–11) thinks that the author may be fostering a double meaning, first that the future will be subject to the Son, but not only to him, but to those who, because of his death on their behalf, have become his brothers and sisters.

He was tested in life and suffered in death as a human.
He gave his life as a once-for-all sacrifice for humankind.
He returned to the right hand of God, to take up his station above the angels, as attested in Scripture.
In that station he is a high priest who officiates on their behalf forever.
Because he suffered as a human he is able to help humans.

These foundational propositions complete the major theological affirmations in the document.[18] However, it remains for the author to advance the larger arguments from which he adduces specific warrants for Jesus' role as high priest. The initial observations or propositions above pave the way. Attridge correctly reflects on the statement in 2:17–18 as a harbinger for the fuller argument to follow.

> The incarnation and suffering of Christ took place so that he might be a High Priest characterized by mercy and fidelity.
>
> The introduction of the title High Priest is abrupt, although the exordium (1:3) had alluded to Christ's priestly act. This abruptness may indicate that the title was familiar to the addressees. The title, in any case, announces for the first time the theme that will dominate the rest of Hebrews' christological exposition. (Cf. 4:14–5:10; 6:20–7:28 on Christ as High Priest "according to the order of Melchizedek"; and 9:11–10:18 on Christ's priestly act).[19]

Before taking up the details of Christ's high priesthood the author continues to show how Jesus stands above revered religious authorities from the past. This Jesus, who is "the apostle and high priest of our confession" (3:1), is worthy of more glory than Moses (3:3). He is able to bring about the rest of which Joshua spoke but could not bring to fruition (4:8–11).

Finally, the author sums up Jesus' role as high priest in 4:14–16 before launching upon the detailed argument in chapters 5–7. Jesus, as high priest, occupies a status higher than all who preceded him since he, the Son of God, has passed through the heavens (4:14). Though he is Son of God (Heb 4:14, 6:6, 7:3, 10:24) and is now seated at the right hand of God, he was human in every respect, suffering what humans suffered and being tested as humans are tested (4:15). Therefore he is the ideal high priest, for he is able to sympathize with human weaknesses. The outcome is that believers should constantly approach his throne of grace (4:16). The character of 4:14–16 is exhortation. The exhortation is crafted upon previously laid out claims.[20] We will take up the character of argument contained in exhortation when discussing Hebrews

---

18. One could label this run of propositions a sorites, that is, a series of syllogisms, the conclusion of one forming a proposition for the next.

19. Attridge, *The Epistle to the Hebrews*, 95.

20. Keijo Nissilä, *Das Hohepriestermotiv im Hebräerbrief: Eine exegetische Untersuchung* (SFEG 33, Helsinki: Oy Liiton Kirjapaino, 1979), 55–78; discusses these characteristics.

5:11–6:12. Clearly the readers have been alerted in advance that the author plans to launch into a major exposition of Jesus as high priest.

Hebrews 5:1–7:28 is an integral unit, including the exhortation section 5:11–6:12, detailing Christ's office and function as high priest. Guthrie observed:

> The central term καθίστημι, used in 5:1 and 7:28, finds no intervening expression. Whereas Heb. 5:1–3 presents a general picture of old covenant priests, the second embodies a comparison of those priests with the Son — the ultimate high priest appointed by God's oath. Thus, the author crafts an *inclusio* which brackets the section running from 5:1–7:28.[21]

The Argument in Hebrews 5

In chapter 5 the author identifies aspects of the Aaronic high priesthood to show how the Son is to be perceived in that light, yet is superior to his priestly predecessors. His argument is therefore based upon Old Testament views of the priesthood, and possibly upon the personal knowledge of some of his readers regarding an incumbent high priest. First, every human high priest administers sacrifices for forgiveness of sins as provided by God (5:1). The writer offers no warrant for this claim, under the assumption that it is common knowledge.[22] He may well have in mind not only Jewish priestly assumptions, but also Hellenistic.[23] Second, the priest is appropriate for the task of dealing with the ignorant and wayward because he himself is inadequate (5:2). The proof of the priest's sinfulness is established by the fact that he must offer sacrifices for his own sins as well as for those of the people (5:3) as declared in Leviticus 16:6–14 (though he does not cite the text). Finally, the high priest was appointed by God, a prime example being Aaron, perhaps based upon Exodus 28:1–3. In this regard Attridge observed,

> As in the description of the high priest's moderation, Hebrews does not rehearse an explicit scriptural stipulation, although the remark conforms to the accounts of Aaron's priestly designation by God.[24]

---

21. Guthrie, *The Structure of Hebrews*, 82. Übelacker (*Der Hebräerbrief*, 224) argues that 3:1–5:10 is an integral unit.
22. I employ here the language of Stephen Toulmin, which I consider helpful, though not the only manner for discerning argument in discourse. See discussions of Toulmin in this volume: Frans H. van Eemeren, "Argumentation Theory: An Overview of Approaches and Research Themes," pp. 12–13, and Lauri Thurén, "Is There Biblical Argumentation?" pp. 83–89.
23. For example, Numbers 8:6–13. See especially John M. Scholer, *Proleptic Priests: Priesthood in the Epistle to the Hebrews* (Sheffield: Sheffield Academic Press, 1991), 13–81. Also, deSilva, *Perseverance in Gratitude*, 186–87.
24. Attridge, *The Epistle to the Hebrews*, 145.

The Hebrews author therefore sets forth three declarations, establishing the second with a reasoned warrant and the last with an example. His approach to argumentation conforms with Aristotle's observation regarding enthymemes, that they are

> deduced from few premises, often from fewer than the regular syllogism; for if any one of these is well known, there is no need to mention it, for the hearer can add it.[25]

The same dictum may be brought to bear in regard to premises in which Scripture is cited.

The author in 5:1–3 has, as noted, identified three ways in which Christ's priesthood is superior to that of the Levitical priests. In 5:5–10 he offers added observations on the three, taking them up in the reverse order as he set them out in 5:1–3.[26] It is interesting that, as in the case for his claim about the angels, he thinks the case for his last point of Christ's divine appointment can be clinched by citing Scriptures. It could be that he commenced with the argument which he believed was most susceptible to proof because of the Scripture warrants. First, Christ did not assume the high priesthood on his own, but was appointed by God (5:5–6). As warrants he offered statements from two psalms. The first is from Psalm 2:7, "You are my Son...." This text, as such, does not explicitly mention the high priesthood, so he cites additionally Psalm 110:4. Psalm 110:4 declares that the one who received the appointment is distinct from other priests (1:5):[27] "You are a priest forever according to the order of Melchizedek." Not only has the Son been uniquely appointed priest, but the appointment is forever. At this juncture the author wishes to press ahead with the argument at hand, so he does not stop to comment on Melchizedek. He will do that in some detail later (chapter 7). He therefore elaborates upon how Christ can sympathize because of what he himself experienced. He has already declared that, though tested, Christ was without sin (4:15). All the signs were that Christ died as other humans. The author's warrant for this claim is that he "offered up prayers and supplications with loud cries and tears" (5:7) to God. The source of this allusion is not

---

25. *Rhet.*, 1.2.13.
26. See comments on 1:2–4. In this case (5:1–4) the author's development also somewhat conforms to the reverse order. Hebrews first takes up the appointment of Christ (5:5–6), the point of 5:4. Second, he discusses Christ's suffering as a human (5:7–10), the point of 5:2–3. Third, he returns to the appointment of Christ with an oath (6:13–30), the point of 5:4. Fourth, he discusses the eternal appointment of Melchizedek and one time sacrifice of Christ and how these are greater than the appointments of the Levitical priests, which entailed continual sacrifices and ended with their death (7:1–22), the point of 5:1.
27. The grammar and other features of the text are discussed by James Kurianal, *Jesus Our High Priest: Psalm 110,4 as the Substructure of Heb 5,1–7,28* (Frankfurt: Peter Lang, 1999), 63–68.

certain. Many commentators have seen it as a reference to Gethsemane.[28] If so, the source is the Gospels. Attridge argues, however, that it is difficult to find this exact phraseology in the Gospels and concludes that the declarations are more reflective of traditional views in regard to a righteous person's prayers.[29] Whatever the origin, the author apparently sees these actions of Jesus as recognizable by his auditors and therefore adequate warrant for his claim that Jesus suffered. Because of his submission, the Son experienced obedience. In his obedience he was made perfect (5:8). His perfection was not that of moral perfection, rather he is prepared to serve as a high priest in behalf of humans, because he now knows what it is like to live as a human.

The writer has already declared that it was through suffering that God made Christ perfect for his role in respect to humans (2:10). He will repeat the same assertion as he closes his observations on Christ as forever perfected in his role as high priest (7:28). Therefore he is the one who, unlike the human high priests, is an eternal source of salvation (5:7, cf. 5:1). In 5:1–10, the author argues his premises through the use of Scriptures, conclusions drawn from them, and commonly accepted viewpoints. His modus operandi is therefore moving from one enthymeme to another, the foundations being laid in the prior enthymemes.

We may put his chain of arguments in syllogistic form as follows:

God appoints all human high priests to offer sacrifices.
Jesus has been appointed a human high priest.
Jesus has therefore been appointed to offer a sacrifice on behalf of humankind.

Priests subject to weakness and sin can deal gently with the ignorant and wayward.
The high priests are subject to weakness and sin.
Therefore they can deal gently with the ignorant and wayward.

Those who offer sacrifices for their own sins as well as for the people are weak and sinful.
The high priest offers sacrifices for his own sins and those of the people.
Therefore the high priests are weak and sinful.

According to Scripture, all high priests are appointed by God.
Jesus was a high priest.

---

28. James Moffatt, *The Epistle to the Hebrews* (New York: Harper & Brothers, 1933), 63–65; Frederick F. Bruce, *The Epistle to the Hebrews* (Grand Rapids: Eerdmans, 1964), 97–102.

29. Attridge, *The Epistle to the Hebrews,* 148–53.

Jesus was appointed by God, according to the Scriptures, and therefore is High Priest as Melchizedek.

The perfect high priest for humans suffers as a human for humans once for all.
Jesus suffered as a human for humans once for all.
Therefore Jesus is a perfect high priest for humans.

The high priest who is Son of God exists forever and serves as high priest forever.
Jesus was the Son of God.
Therefore Jesus exists forever and serves as high priest forever.

The Exhortation of 5:11–6:12

A major exhortatory section now appears to interrupt the flow of the high priest argument. But actually the exposition is integrated into the larger argument of 5:1–7:28 in that the author is challenging his readers to give careful attention to the claim that Jesus is a high priest after the order of Melchizedek, since the reasoning, as it turns out, is quite complicated. This exhortatory interlude may be appraised as a classical rhetorical *digressio,* but its function is not, as the *digressios* characterized by the rhetoricians, to delight or give relief, but to persuade the auditors of the weightiness and seriousness of the argument now underway.[30] It connects two distinct parts: 3:1–4:16 (or 3:1–5:10, as Übelacker argues), and 7:1–10:18. As deSilva observed,

> The first four paragraphs of this "digression" (which is nevertheless central to the author's rhetorical purpose) are held together by an *inclusio* formed by the words "you have become sluggish" (νωθροὶ γεγόνατε, 5:11) and "in order that you not become sluggish" (νωθροὶ γένησθε, 6:12). The transitional character of 6:12–20 is borne out structurally.[31]

Exhortatory rhetoric is expressly designed to incite response from the auditors. The Hebrews writer inserts exhortation in appropriate places after having set out explicit arguments for the priestly role of Christ, as noted in the proposed outline of the discourse. Although these exhortatory sections

---

30. Cicero, *Inv.*, 1.51.97, denounces the injection of a *digressio* since it is unconnected with the matter at hand such as the praise of self or abuse of the opponent, or amplification rather than argument. Quintilianus, *Inst.*, 4.3.1–2, wrote that certain rhetoricians recommended that the orator, after the statement of facts, should digress "to some pleasant and attractive topic with a view to securing the utmost amount of favour from their audience." He considered digression of this sort appropriate in certain cases but not in all.

31. DeSilva, *Perseverance in Gratitude,* 210.

are designed to provoke response, nevertheless exhortation normally entails arguments.

First, in respect to Hebrews 5:11–6:3, the author declares that many in-depth insights are to be drawn from the implications of Christ being a high priest after the order of Melchizedek, but that the auditors have not pushed ahead toward perfection and are therefore unprepared to track the complexities involved (5:11). The language is direct and in the second person. In this regard his exhortation is unlike most moral discourse in Greco-Roman documents in which the author addresses his auditors in the third person as a general audience, not a specific one, though the diatribe may be an exception.[32] Attridge observes, "The structure of this section, much like that which follows (6:4–12), develops from a more negative to a more positive stance and does so through an image that is set in the center of the pericope."[33] The author's first warrant for his charge is that whereas the auditors should be teachers, they need to be taught (5:12). His second warrant is a typical ancient analogy that they need milk, not solid food (5:12–14).[34] His third move is to challenge the listeners to build on the fundamentals so as to move beyond them (6:1). He then lists, by way of explaining his challenge, a number of the fundamentals that they should have now mastered (6:1–2). He closes the first exhortatory pericope by expressing the confidence that they will, in fact, take this step (6:3).

In the next section (6:4–12), the author declares the necessity for going on toward perfection, since, if they fail, they are doomed (6:4). The warrant for this claim is that it is impossible to restore to repentance persons who have been enlightened, shared the Holy Spirit, and tasted the goodness of the word of God and the powers of the age to come, when they have fallen away (6:4–6).[35] This warrant itself comprises an enthymeme.[36] Another argument ensues in that not only do they endanger their own future by the failure to grow, they crucify "again the Son of God and are holding him up to contempt" (6:6). Their action belies the fact that the death of Christ was once for all, a point the author will develop in more depth later (9:23–28). To illustrate the result of failing to move toward perfection, the author employs the

---

32. I have examined all the documents found in Abraham J. Malherbe, *Moral Exhortation: A Greco-Roman Sourcebook* (Philadelphia: Westminster, 1986), and Stanley K. Stowers, *Letter Writing in Greco-Roman Antiquity* (Philadelphia: Westminster, 1986).

33. Attridge, *The Epistle to the Hebrews,* 156.

34. See James W. Thompson, *The Beginnings of Christian Philosophy: The Epistle to the Hebrews* (CBQMS 13; Washington, D.C.: Catholic Biblical Association, 1982), 17–40, for a discussion of similar Greco-Roman and Jewish Hellenistic uses of these metaphors.

35. Earlier the author argued that those accompanying Moses fell in the wilderness because of hardened hearts (3:7–19).

36. DeSilva, *Perseverance in Gratitude,* 219–21.

analogy of farm land continually drinking up the rain, that receives a blessing from God if it produces a useful crop but that is cursed if it produces thorns and thistles (6:7–8). Though Jesus spoke of bountiful and unproductive harvests, Attridge believes that the sources for this metaphor are commonplaces in Jewish and Hellenistic materials.[37] The writer therefore employs conventional observations — which, as the rhetoricians noted, were the mainstays of discourses.

The author ends the exhortation on a positive note. He expresses confidence that the auditors will, in fact, overcome their lethargy and be productive (6:9).[38] His warrant for this conclusion is: first, that God will act on their behalf (6:10); second, that because of his urging they will take up the challenge (6:11); and third, that they will imitate those "who through faith and patience inherit the promise" (6:12). The latter foreshadows his exposition of an extended list of such persons in chapter 11.

The rhetorical features of the exhortations differ from those of the rest of the discourse. In the first place, the language is pressing and interlaced with second person pronouns. Second, the warrants do not depend upon texts from Scripture as they do in the rest of Hebrews. Third, the author depends much more on widespread metaphors to give credence to his points. Fourth, his enthymematic premises therefore mirror the commonplaces observed by the classical rhetoricians.

The rhetoric of exhortation in Hebrews has affinity with Greco-Roman moral suasion. Since the rhetoricians did not, by and large, focus upon the moral rhetoric of the popular philosophers, the contours of a new genre are in order, not only in assessing Hebrews, but also the discourses of the moral philosophers.[39] More work needs to be done on exhortation in Greco-Roman moral discourse, as well as in synagogue sermons. Perhaps the best analogy for the rhetoric of exhortation found in Hebrews is Deuteronomy (e.g., Deut 4; 8) and the Deuteronomic prophets (e.g., Jer 2; 11).[40] From such assessments the features of exhortatory rhetoric can be delineated. I am inclined to agree with the conclusion of George H. Guthrie:

---

37. Attridge, *The Epistle to the Hebrews*, 172.
38. Cf. the same point in Hebrews 13:20–21.
39. Quintilian, discussing whether there are three genres or more, concluded that the "classical three" are essentially exhaustive. He does, however, point out that others in the history of Greco-Roman oratory reached different conclusions (*Inst.*, 3.4).
40. Ernst Käsemann (*The Wandering People of God: An Investigation of the Letter to the Hebrews* [Minneapolis: Augsburg, 1984], 184–94) asserts that Hebrews 5:11–6:12 reflect an effort to awaken the listener's Gnostic style to a new life. But I would argue that it reflects more traditional efforts at moral suasion.

> Hebrews is not easily categorized according to any one speech form of ancient Greek rhetoric.... While the speech forms in the classical handbooks were crafted in the judicial and political spheres, the book of Hebrews has the characteristics of the Hellenistic synagogue homily. This form, while containing a wide range of rhetorical features described in the Greek handbooks, cannot be forced into the mold of a classical speech. Rather, the Author's means of argument follow the rhetoric and exegetical skills of the rabbis.[41]

In fact, I question the helpfulness of the classical three genre rhetorical categories in effectively analyzing the rhetoric of Hebrews. For example, in moral discourse the focus is not the past as in forensic rhetoric, nor the future as in deliberative, nor the present as in epideictic, but contains all three.[42] A statement in Hebrews 13:8 sums up the multiple character of time in Hebrews. "Jesus Christ is the same yesterday and today and forever."[43] The basis for understanding life's foundation is what God did yesterday in the death and ascension of Christ. The implications for human ethics and morality are obvious for the present, and the ramifications of the work of Christ as sacrificer and sacrifice are forever. The rhetorical features of these exhortations are similar to those of moral discourse among the Greek philosophers, but the grounding (ontology) is based upon what God did, not what is endemic in nature and life. Malherbe, in observing these differences, wrote:

> This all having been said, it is yet possible to venture some generalizations on pagan philosophical and Christian ethics. From the first century B.C., philosophy became increasingly open to religion. The way in which Stoics of the period speak of the divine frequently suits a conception of a personal god better than it does Stoic pantheism. And the Neopythagorean motivation for ethics is religious in the sense that it aims at purifying the person of the material body so that after death he might return to the nonmaterial world. Yet the philosophers retained their stress on reason and reliance on self in striving for virtue. Christians, on the other hand, stressed reliance on God, Christ, and the Holy Spirit, and considered the moral life a corollary to their knowledge of God and the divine will. They therefore very seldom spoke of virtue, did not share the Greek notion of character development, and did not define happiness as their goal. The major differences between the philosophers and Christians therefore reside in the way religion was thought to be related to ethics and in the different views of human nature that they held.[44]

These differences in fundamental beginnings also influence the rhetorical features of Jewish and Christian discourses.

---

41. George H. Guthrie, *The Structure of Hebrews*, 32. But this judgment itself bears more investigation inasmuch as Guthrie does not cite the basis for his conclusion and I myself have not examined the synagogue sermons.
42. Aristotle, *Rhet.*, 1.2.4.
43. Cf. Hebrews 1:8, 12.
44. Malherbe, *Moral Exhortation*, 15.

Hebrews 6:13-20

The author has now prepared his hearers through exhortation (paraenesis) to give closer attention to the implications that Christ is a high priest after the order of Melchizedek. He both chides his listeners and expresses confidence in their steadfastness of conviction and action (6:9–12), and is now ready to return to his assertions and Scripture warrants concerning the high priesthood of Christ after the order of Melchizedek. The believers can have great confidence in Christ's status as priest because God made a promise and accompanied it by an oath. He noted that when God made a promise to Abraham he did so through an oath. Since God had no being greater than himself to swear by, he swore by himself (6:13). Human beings, in contrast, must swear by someone greater than themselves (6:16). God, likewise, in the case of Jesus' assignment as high priest, provided the appointment with an assured and unchangeable promise (6:17). Not only did God make the promise, he did so with an oath, so that by two unbreakable means God guaranteed Christ's priesthood (6:18). Believers therefore need to seize upon this hope, which serves as a sure anchor (6:18, 19). Just as did the human high priest, Jesus entered the inner shrine behind the curtain, having become a high priest forever after the order of Melchizedek. God's past action in Christ has provided those who believe with a sure foundation for both the present and the future. The author therefore in 5:11 through 6:20 exhorted his auditors to take up with great vigor the implications of God's work in Christ. This section is a bridge and a reminder of some of the points made in chapter 5, especially that Christ is a high priest of the order of Melchizedek (noted especially in 6:20).[45]

Christ after the Order of Melchizedek (Hebrews 7)

In chapter seven the author plunges into the heart of his argument in regard to Jesus as high priest. He has alerted his audience by charging them to listen intently so that they may inherit the promises (6:12). He has already carefully laid the foundations for launching the epicenter.[46] Jesus stands heads and shoulders above the Aaronic (Levitical) priests because he is of a different order. His order is that of Melchizedek, and whereas the service of the Levitical priests was only for their lifetime, the service of Melchizedek and

---

45. DeSilva (*Perseverance in Gratitude,* 248–53) notes these features of this material.
46. So also Käsemann, *The Wandering People of God,* 187, though I do not agree with his "gnostic" reason for making it central."

hence of Christ is forever. The author has already alluded to these aspects twice (5:6; 6:20). He is now ready to buttress his assertions with proofs and warrants.

The writer begins with comments upon Melchizedek and what is known about him in both Scripture and in tradition. He is basically dependent upon Genesis 14:17–20 and Psalm 110:4b.[47] Melchizedek was superior to Abraham: **first warrant**, Melchizedek blessed Abraham (7:1); **second warrant**, Abraham gave Melchizedek a tenth of everything (7:2). Next he sets out the etymology of the name Melchizedek, that is, king of righteousness and peace, apparently to suggest messianic attributes, adding to the loftiness of Melchizedek's position as well as Christ's.[48] Third, Melchizedek was without father or mother and therefore his priesthood had no beginning or end.[49] What is the warrant for this claim? Clearly the absence of information regarding his birth or death in the Genesis account (Genesis 14:18–20).[50]

From these observations in regard to Abraham, the author went on to set out specific proofs for Melchizedek's superiority. Melchizedek was greater than Abraham; **warrant**, Abraham gave him a tenth. Second, the Levitical priests collected tithes from the descendants of Abraham (7:5). Third, Melchizedek is superior to the Levitical priests; **warrant** (1) The superior blesses the inferior, and Melchizedek blessed Abraham and his descendants, that is, the Levitical priests (7:7). The Hebrews writer declares such a blessing a commonly accepted proposition (enthymeme) even though biblical evidence erodes it as an absolute rule (see, e.g., Job 31:20; 2 Sam 14:22; 1 Kgs 1:47).[51] **Warrant** (2) The inferior pays tithes to the superior, and Abraham [and through him his descendants] paid tithes to Melchizedek (7:8). It is of interest to note that the warrants the author sets out in 7:6 are tithes and promises. But as previously, when he takes them up specifically, he reverses the order to promises first, then tithes (7:7–8). An additional warrant is now offered in that the Levites who received tithes are mortal, that is, finite, while Melchizedek lives (7:8). What is the significance of "he lives"? This is a warrant from Scripture. He lives because of the fact that his death is not

---

47. Kurianal, *Jesus Our High Priest,* 85–138, analyzes 7:1–25 as a midrash on Ps 110:4b.

48. So deSilva, *Perseverance in Gratitude,* 266. Kurianal, *Jesus Our High Priest,* 91–92, disputes this claim.

49. Thompson (*The Beginnings of Christian Philosophy,* 116–27) discusses Hebrews 7 as a midrash. He concludes that affinities with the exegetical approach of Philo may be found and points out that Philo entertained the prospect of a heavenly high priest (124).

50. Some, for example, Käsemann (*The Wandering People of God,* 208) think that in certain quarters Melchizedek was perceived of as a heavenly priest. Harold Attridge, *The Epistle to the Hebrews,* discussed the matter at length in an excursus (192–95) and concluded that the author must have known of such views available in his time.

51. Attridge, *The Epistle to the Hebrews,* 196.

recorded in Scripture.[52] But that he is eternal may also depend upon contemporary speculation regarding Melchizedek as a divine or heavenly being. The author then goes on to claim that Levi paid tithes to Melchizedek because he was in the loins of Abraham when Abraham presented the tithes (7:10).

We now can set out the author's claims in syllogistic form so as to reveal the unstated nature of some of the propositions, hence qualifying, in rhetorical terminology, as enthymemes.

> The greater blesses the lesser.
> Melchizedek blessed Abraham.
> Therefore, Melchizedek is the greater of the two.

> The lesser pays tithes to the superior.
> Abraham paid tithes to Melchizedek.
> Therefore, Melchizedek was superior to Abraham.

> The Levitical priests are the descendants of Abraham.
> Melchizedek was greater than Abraham.
> Therefore, Melchizedek was superior to the Levitical priests.[53]

The conclusion in each case, though clearly implied, is unstated, supporting Aristotle's observation that in normal discourses authors do not set out arguments in a formal syllogistic manner.

Having laid this groundwork, the author now goes on to present other **warrants** for the inferiority of the Levitical priesthood. The Levitical priesthood, he alleges, did not attain perfection.[54] As warrants he declares that (1) the law was received under their priesthood (7:11; the author plans to present a detailed case for the insufficiency of the law later, in chapter 8). (2) A different order of priesthood was identified, that of Melchizedek (Psalm 110). He therefore concluded that another priesthood would not have been predicted had the Levitical priesthood exhibited perfection. (3) A change in priesthood, he further argued, requires a change in the law. Although the writer brings up at this point the insufficiency of the law, he is actually going to explicate the superior priesthood of Christ before he sets out detailed proofs (warrants) for the insufficiency of the law. (4) Christ's high priesthood is different in that no human has before or since served at the altar of Melchizedek's priesthood (7:13). Finally, Christ himself did not become a priest by Levitic decent; **warrant**, he is descended from David. Moses does not say anything about a

---

52. So Attridge, *The Epistle to the Hebrews*, 196.
53. Walter Übelacker has presented an almost identical analysis in "Hebr 7:1–10 –dess struktur och funktion i författarens retoriska argumentation," in *Mellan tid och evighet: Festskrift till Bo Johnson* (ed. S. Hidal, L. Haikol, S. Norin [Religio 42]; Teologiska institution i Lund, 1994), 215–32; see especially p. 229.
54. Scholer, *Proleptic Priests,* 198–200, argues for the general use of "perfect."

priest coming from the tribe of Judah (7:14), and since the Son is declared a priest, he must be of a different order.[55]

The writer is now ready to develop the superiority of the priesthood of the order of Melchizedek. First, such a priesthood is not authorized by a legal statute, but because of an indestructible and never-ending life. The author has already presented his warrants for this claim: (1) that genealogy is irrelevant in regard to Melchizedek (7:3), and (2) the priesthood of Melchizedek is forever according to Psalm 110 (5:6), which text he quotes again (7:17). Second, the legal basis or command for the Levitical priesthood has been rescinded because it did not result in perfection (a claim yet to be supported). Third, the legally established priesthood is superseded by a better hope, namely, the priesthood of Jesus Christ (7:19). As warrant for this new priesthood, the author repeats what he has already asserted in regard to an oath from God, that is, Psalm 110:4, "The Lord has sworn and will not change his mind." For these three reasons, with attendant warrants, "Jesus has also become the guarantee of a better covenant" (Heb 7:22).

The author is now prepared to make additional claims about the superiority of Jesus' priesthood. In regard to the Levitical high priests one followed another from age to age because of death (7:23). But in the case of Jesus, he alone is sufficient, since he continues forever (7:24). The Son is the only priest to whom the believer is obliged to turn, since he "always lives to make intercession for them" (7:25).

The author ends his main comments on the high priesthood by summing up his claims.[56] It is appropriate that God supplied through Christ such a high priest: (1) Christ is superior in every way; "blameless, undefiled, separated from sinners and exalted above the heavens" (7:26, a claim made also in 4:14–16). (2) Christ does not need to offer daily sacrifices for his own sins, or for those of humans, as did the Levitical priests (7:27, cf. 5:3). (3) The law appoints priests who are subject to weakness (7:7, cf. 5:2). (4) The oath declaring Christ's priesthood came later than the law (7:28, cf. 6:17; 7:20). (5) Through the oath the Son became High Priest, having been perfected for this role, and his tenure is forever.[57] As a result Jesus occupies an eternal priestly role (5:9–10; 7:23).

The author now has completed his claims as to the grounds for Jesus' superior priesthood. The warrants for these claims are based upon the Scriptures, and conclusions drawn from them. Several of the interpretations are commonplace, thus providing the grist for enthymemes. The Hebrews writer

---

55. Wilson, *Hebrews*, 124.
56. DeSilva (*Perseverance in Gratitude*, 266) identifies it as a recapitulation.
57. On "perfected," see 2:10; 5:9.

is now ready to make a case for the superiority of Christ's sacrifice. His claim is that Jesus is at the same time both sacrificer and sacrifice forever.

Conclusion

Now that we have scrutinized the Hebrews writer's argument regarding Jesus as high priest, what have we contributed to the understanding of his discourse? First, we noticed how the writer clearly anticipated the detailed arguments of 5–7 in earlier affirmations. Second, we pointed out that the author often reversed the declared order of the arguments. Third, we determined that the exhortatory materials are integral to the overall argument of the document. Fourth, we discovered that the author's warrants in the theological sections are almost altogether from the Scriptures or commonly accepted interpretations of those Scriptures. In this manner, though the common interpretations reflect the enthymemes of the rhetoricians, the rhetoricians provided no insights as to the rhetorical power of scriptural warrants. Fifth, we concluded that the warrants in the exhortatory or paraenetic sections employed the sorts of commonplaces identified by the rhetoricians, but that the bases are different enough so that exhortatory materials should be studied in more detail so as to determine their rhetorical features. Sixth, we discovered that our concentrated attention upon arguments in Hebrews resulted in delineating in bold relief the claims advanced by the author. Even though all the nuances of his assertions were not thereby ferreted out, nevertheless the basic lines of his arguments were clarified.

PART SEVEN

**THE RHETORIC OF
APOCALYPTIC AND ROMANCE**

CHAPTER 23

*REVELATION AND ROMANCE:
GENRE BENDING IN THE SHEPHERD OF HERMAS
AND THE ACTS OF PETER*

John W. Marshall

Introduction

What has Athens to do with Jerusalem? Tertullian's question on philosophy has provided a trope for organizing the study of Paganism, Christianity, and Judaism in the ancient world and the answers have rarely been as simple as the "absolutely nothing" that Tertullian's rhetoric implies. What has romance to do with apocalyptic or Chariton with Enoch? Perhaps surprisingly, the two genres exhibit a web of connections that includes the rhetorical strategies most suited to the genres as a whole, namely ethical and pathetic appeals. The phenomenon under consideration is a slippery one: the interpenetration of two genres usually thought to be quite disparate, apocalyptic and romance. The task is difficult not only because of the uncommon combination of genres, but also because of rhetorical theory's inadequate account of the persuasive power of genre,[1] and its even sparser attention to the generic digression.[2] Intertwining romance and apocalyptic provides the writers of the *Shepherd of Hermas* and of the *Acts of Peter* a means to round out their rhetorical appeals and, in the latter case, to move the plot forward. These ancient writers are in control, if not cognizant, of a rhetoric of genre.

The New Testament provides a number of compelling examples of the rhetorical power of genre. The transformation of sermons and sayings collections apparent in the letter of James and in 1 John illustrates not only the rhetorical power of persona (essentially a dimension of ἦθος) through pseudepigraphy, but also persuasive power of genre through the artificial assumption of the form of the letter. With reference to apocalyptic literature, John J. Collins has

---

1. The three-fold genus division — deliberative, forensic, and epideictic — has almost nothing to do with the wide concept that needs to operate in a treatment of literary works. Modern studies such as that of Chaïm Perelman and Lucie Olbrechts-Tyteca, *The New Rhetoric: A Treatise on Argumentation* (Notre Dame, Ind.: University of Notre Dame Press, 1971), make little focused treatment of genre.

2. Quintilianus (*Inst.*, 4.3) treats digression within narrative, but his discussion is largely limited to formal speech contexts and is of little help in analyzing literary works. It is noteworthy, however, that Quintilian sees emotional and ethical appeals as the opportune functions for digression.

examined the interleaving of that genre with wisdom modes of discourse.[3] Genre is a persuasive tool which ancient writers did employ, even if rhetorical theory in the ancient world did not attend to this mode of persuasion.[4]

Neither the *Shepherd of Hermas* nor the *Acts of Peter* are usually held up as ideal types of their genre, but this is actually an asset addressing the questions under examination here: how does genre and generic digression contribute to persuasion? How does an apocalyptic mode (either as macrogenre or sub-genre) undertake persuasion? What features of romance and apocalypse enable these two genres to mix? Precisely because the *Shepherd of Hermas* and the *Acts of Peter* are generically mixed rather than the ideal, they illustrate in high relief the presence of the genres they comprehend and the interactions of those genres.

The Trials of Hermas

The *Shepherd of Hermas*[5] stands on the edge of the apocalyptic tradition. Some have disputed whether it ought to be considered an Apocalypse at all, or as a whole.[6] Yarbro Collins emphasizes, however, its consistent use of a visionary framework and its ongoing eschatological concern.[7] John J. Collins classes it as "Type Ib, An Apocalypse with Cosmic and/or Political Eschatology (which has neither historical review nor otherworldly journey)."[8] The romantic dimensions the *Shepherd of Hermas* have received less attention in discussions of its genre, though commentators remark on them during spe-

---

3. John J. Collins, "Wisdom, Apocalypticism, and Generic Compatibility," in *In Search of Wisdom: Essays in Memory of John G. Gammie* (ed. Leo G. Perdue, Bernard Brandon Scott, and William Johnston Wiseman; Louisville: Westminster/John Knox, 1993): 165–85.

4. Treatments of style in ancient rhetorical theory approach the subject of genre to some degree, but style is late in the theoretical process and is also assumed to be largely a matter distinct from content, whereas genres are partially constituted through coherences of content.

5. Although the provenance of *The Shepherd of Hermas* is generally fixed in Rome, opinions on the date range from 60 C.E. for part of the work (W. Coleborne, "The *Shepherd of Hermas*: A Case for Multiple Authorship and Some Implications," *StPatr* 10 [1970]: 65–70) to 140 C.E. for the work as a whole (Graydon F. Snyder, *The Shepherd of Hermas* [vol. 6 of *The Apostolic Fathers: A New Translation and Commentary;* ed. Robert McQueen Grant; New York: T. Nelson, 1964], 24). Carolyn Osiek (*Shepherd of Hermas: A Commentary* [Hermeneia; Minneapolis: Fortress Press, 1999], 20) suggests roughly 95–140 C.E.

6. E.g., Philipp Vielhauer and Georg Strecker, "Apocalyptic in Early Christianity," in *New Testament Apocrypha* (ed. Edgar Hennecke and Wilhelm Schneemelcher; trans. R. McL. Wilson; Louisville: Westminster/John Knox, 1991), 563–99.

7. Adela Yarbro Collins, "Introduction: Early Christian Apocalypticism," *Semeia* 36 (1986): 9. Cf. Osiek, *Shepherd of Hermas* and "The Genre and Function of the Shepherd of Hermas," *Semeia* 36 (1986): 113–21.

8. John J. Collins, "Introduction: Towards the Morphology of a Genre," *Semeia* 14 (1979): 14.

cific discussions.[9] Two parts of the text especially seem to invite a romantic appreciation from the audience. First, the interactions with Rhoda that begin the first vision and continue as a topic of anxiety for the first four visions. Second, the contest of chastity that the recipient of revelation[10] undergoes when he is forced to spend the night with twelve "merry and gracious" maidens is a clear analogue of the contests of chastity in the Greek romances. As filters for episodes within the more traditional apocalyptic form, these romantic elements perform several rhetorical functions for the *Shepherd of Hermas:* they broaden the applicability of the paranesis, build the *ethos* of the recipient of the revelation, and, not least, stimulate an emotional investment in the story and an adherence to its values intensified by that emotional response.

Visions

The Visions of Hermas seem very clearly to be an independent document.[11] Understood as an independent product, the work evinces a consistent play on the tropes of romance beginning in the "recognition" scene that initiates the first vision.[12] Hermas encounters his former mistress as she bathes in the

---

9. Osiek, *Shepherd of Hermas;* Snyder, *Shepherd of Hermas;* Norbert Brox, *Der Hirt des Hermas* (Kommentar zu den Apostolischen Vätern 7; Göttingen: Vandenhoeck & Ruprecht, 1991). Cf. Otto Luschnat, "Die Jungfrauenszene in der Arkadienvision des Hermas," *ThViat* 12 (1973–74): 53– 70. Ton Hilhorst ("Erotic Elements in the Shepherd of Hermas," in *Groningen Colloquia on the Novel* [vol. 9, ed. H. Hofmann and M. Zimmermann; Groningen: Forsten, 1998], 193–204) focuses specifically on "erotic elements," but does so within a context of an assumption that there is a correspondence with a biography of Hermas. Hilhorst details the three episodes helpfully — including *Vis.*, 1.1.7, in addition to the two I have emphasized — and provides helpful bibliography.

10. Traditionally named as "Hermas," though the name is not mentioned after *Vis.*, 4.1.7.

11. Osiek, *Shepherd of Hermas,* 3. The basic and standard arguments are the manuscript evidence that *Vis.*, 1–4 and *Vis.*, 5 – *Sim.*, 10 each circulated alone (Antonio Carlini et al., eds., *Il pastore* [*Ia– IIIa visione*]); Papyrus Bodmer 38; Cologne and Geneva: Fondation Martin Bodmer, 1991), 12, and Campbell Bonner, ed., *A Papyrus Codex of the Shepherd of Hermas (Similitudes 2–9) with a Fragment of the Mandates* (University of Michigan Studies 22; Humanistic Series; Ann Arbor: University of Michigan Press, 1934, 8–9), the change in superscription between *Vis.*, 4 and *Vis.*, 5 (from Ὅρασις to Ἀποκάλυψις), the clear function of *Vis.*, 5.5–7 as an introductory device for the Mandates and Similitudes which follow, and the observation that the Shepherd's mention of a previous "handing over" of the recipient of the vision to the Shepherd has no previous referent in *Vis.*, 1–4 (Kirsopp Lake, ed., *The Apostolic Fathers* [2 vols.; Cambridge: Harvard University Press, 1912–13], 2:69, n. 2). I would also add the characterological observation that "Hermas" and "the Shepherd" never meet. The former's last appearance is in *Vis.*, 4.1.7, and the latter first comes onto the scene in *Vis.*, 5.1. To me this suggests serial authorship: the persona of Hermas is the device of the author of *Vis.*, 1–4, and "the Shepherd" is a character introduced by a later author (or authors) who continues the basic persona of the bumbling recipient of visions, but does not go so far as to write in the name of Hermas. If this is so, it makes an interesting case of pseudepigraphy not quite consummated.

12. *Vis.*, 1.1.1–2, "The one who raised me sold me to a certain Rhoda at Rome. After many years I recognized her, and began to love her as a sister (Ὁ θρέψας με πέπρακέν με Ῥόδῃ τινὶ εἰς Ῥώμην· μετὰ πολλὰ ἔτη ταύτην ἀνεγνωρισάμην καὶ ἠρξάμην αὐτὴν ἀγαπᾶν ὡς ἀδελφήν). See Bryan P. Reardon, *The Form of the Greek Romance* (Princeton, N.J.: Princeton University Press, 1991), 51, and Shadi Bartsch, *Decoding the Ancient Novel: The Reader and the Role of Description in Heliodorus and*

Tiber and he looks upon her and says to himself, "I should be happy if I had a wife of such beauty and character."[13] Hermas, however, already has a wife and family (*Vis.* 2.3). His reflection is immediately followed by a denial that such thoughts had any untoward connotation (*Vis.* 1.2), but the accusation made by God's representative suggests a sin nonetheless.[14] Hermas is caught enjoying not any pleasures of adultery, but the pleasures of fantasy. Still, the heavenly Rhoda accuses Hermas of the "desire of wickedness,"[15] and this is generalized as the sin which dominates not only the visions, but the *Shepherd of Hermas* as a whole: double-mindedness.[16]

In the visions that follow, Hermas continues to struggle with double-mindedness, especially, though not exclusively (*Vis.* 4.1.4; 4.2.6), in his relation to the female revealers. He finds himself preparing to meet one in a field on a sumptuous couch and he panics (*Vis.* 3.1.4–5); when the revealer takes a young and beautiful form (though with old hair) and awaits him joyfully on a couch, he is deeply grieved (*Vis.* 3.10.5–6). The romantic motifs pervade the visions and both highlight the topic of double-mindedness and draw the audience into the plot.

Virgins

While the sections of the *Shepherd of Hermas* in which "the Shepherd" appears do not have the same concentration of romantic motifs as the visions, the ninth similitude contains an interlude that has been the object of much speculation with regard to the possible or probable erotic dimensions of the passage.[17] Hermas, to his shame, is confined for the night in the company of twelve virgins (παρθένοι). After the maidens assure Hermas that the arrangements will be strictly fraternal, the principal maiden leads the others in kissing and embracing Hermas. A feeling of youthfulness and rejuvenation comes upon Hermas and he begins to reciprocate their playful affection. He spends the night in prayer beside the tower with the maidens and when the Shepherd returns, Hermas testifies to their collective virtue (*Sim.* 9.11.1–9).

Achilles Tatius (Princeton, N.J.: Princeton University Press, 1989), 132, for examples and discussion of the recognition scene in the ancient novel. Note also one of the traditional titles of the Clementine romance — *Recognitions*.

13. *Vis.*, 1.2: Μακάριος ἤμην εἰ τοιαύτην γυναῖκα εἶχον καὶ τῷ κάλλει καὶ τῷ τρόπῳ.

14. When Hermas's "sin" of desire is not brought to the foreground, it functions as a sort of divine sting operation in order to grab his attention and then direct it towards the various sins of his family and his lack of patriarchal responsibility on these issues (*Vis.*, 1.3.1; 2.2.1; 2.3.1).

15. *Vis.*, 1.1.8: Ἐπὶ τὴν καρδίαν σου ἀνέβη ἡ ἐπιθυμία τῆς πονηρίας.

16. Oscar J. F. Seitz, "Antecedents and Signification of the Term ΔΙΨΥΧΟΣ," *JBL* 63 (1944): 131–40.

17. See note 9.

The maidens "are" the virtues, as *Similitudes,* 9.15.1–3 makes clear. They are matched by the twelve loose-haired, bare-shouldered, beautiful women that remove stones from the tower in *Similitudes,* 9.9.5–6. The Shepherd explains that these loose women seduce those who were once attended by the maidens and remove them from the tower (*Sim.* 9.13.8–9.14.2). These women "are" the vices (*Sim.* 9.15.1–4).

Osiek downplays the erotic reference of these sections by taking the virgins' assurance of a fraternal disposition as determinative for her interpretation.[18] Other factors, however, such as the loose women who seduce members of the tower, point toward the romantic genre. Reardon notes the common denominator of *femmes fatales* in the Greek romances, "sexually passionate creatures, who are in the story only to pursue the hero."[19] We have in a single scene in *Similitudes,* 9.11 a theme familiar in the Greek romances, the contest of chastity. Like the formative and chaste interactions of Anthia and Habrocomes, the contest of chastity takes place in a religious setting — for Hermas, in the shadow of the tower; for the Ephesian lovers, in the temple of Artemis.[20] Caught literally between the dual appearances of the twelve viragos, Hermas finds that he can maintain his chastity by cleaving to the twelve virgins, even if things look worrisome for a little while.

Romance in the Shepherd

The episodes under discussion clearly resemble the content and conventions of the Greek romance. Within the *Shepherd* as a whole these generic digressions make three contributions. First, and perhaps most important, within a work that even the major commentator has described yawn provoking, monotonous, and pedantic,[21] the romantic digressions call the audience to attention by the most simple means: exciting subject matter and a plot fraught with danger. Will Hermas be punished for his thoughts? Will he maintain his chastity? These are perennially popular subjects. Second, and not unrelated, the romantic interludes provide an apt forum for the *Shepherd*'s teaching on its two favorite themes: double-mindedness and post-baptismal sin. The substantially internal qualities of emotion and desire bring διψυχία to the foreground and are the most difficult to control and to monitor in the long

---

18. And by other means, such as interpreting Hermas's rejuvenation solely as an "image of conversion"; Osiek, *Shepherd of Hermas,* 229.

19. Reardon, *Form,* 82.

20. *Ephesiaca,* 1.5. It is also worth noting that the woman clothed as if she has just come from the bridal chamber in *Vis.,* 3.2.1 has its counterpart in the Ephesian virgins "dressed as if to receive a lover" (*Ephesiaca,* 1.2).

21. Osiek, "Genre and Function," 113.

interlude between baptism and the eschatological completion of the tower. Third, the romantic interludes function like parody. They constitute a polemic against the values that found the Greek romance, but they do so by playing with them and utilizing their attractiveness. Parody integrates attraction and repulsion and this combination is obvious both in Hermas the character and in the reaction to the scene into which the work invites the audience. Richard Pervo uses Horace's phrase "profit with delight" as an entré into the entertaining side of the canonical Acts.[22] The *Shepherd*'s romantic scenes go much further in "delight" than anything Pervo chronicles with Acts, and are part of a Christian culture-building exercise. The *Shepherd*'s delights offer a certain vicarious enjoyment of the very sins from which the work dissuades its audience. To name this as compensatory conjures a movement much more desultory than it need be.

The Visions of Peter

The connections of canonical *Acts* and other early Christian acts of apostles to the prose narrative tradition seen in the Greek romances have long been recognized. The *Acts of Peter*[23] exhibits all the appropriate themes. The prose narrative is episodic, sinusoidal, oriented to travel and especially sea-voyages, filled with court episodes, and of course it contains, in some measure, the erotic tension that marks Christian transformations of the romantic tradition. In the *Acts of Peter,* the apostle's daughter's tempting beauty would be a trial to him and others if not for the paralysis from which he will give her only the most temporary respite.[24] The troubles begin when Peter's daughter is seen bathing — like Rhoda is by Hermas.[25] And in a standard trope of the acts tradition, Peter lures the wives and concubines of the elite away from their marriages and into the Christian community.[26] In contrast to his rival Simon, who seduces women to himself, Peter seduces women to the Lord. The plot centers on this rivalry between Simon and Peter rather than the

---

22. Richard I. Pervo, *Profit with Delight: The Literary Genre of the Acts of the Apostles* (Philadelphia: Fortress, 1987).
23. Wilhelm Schneemelcher ("The Acts of Peter: Introduction," in Hennecke et al., eds., *New Testament Apocrypha,* 283) suggests that the *Acts of Peter* was composed around 180–190 c.e. in Rome or Asia Minor.
24. *Acts Pet.*, Berlin Coptic Papyrus 8502, pp. 128–32 (Hennecke et al., eds., *New Testament Apocrypha,* 285).
25. *Acts Pet.*, Berlin Coptic Papyrus 8502, p. 132 (Hennecke et al., eds., *New Testament Apocrypha,* 286). Cf. *Vis.*, 1.1.
26. *Acts Pet.*, 33, 34; Hennecke et al., eds., *New Testament Apocrypha,* 313.

struggle of two lovers against fate.[27] Within this romance, visions pepper the narrative, pushing the plot forward, confirming the authority of Peter over that of Simon, and making complete the Christian adaptation of the adventure-romance genre. Three examples illustrate the complementary functions of apocalyptic discourse within the romantic *Acts of Peter*.

Visionary Guidance

The first and most obvious function of apocalyptic motifs in the *Acts of Peter* is visionary guidance that moves the plot forward. Peter justifies his seemingly cruel treatment of his daughter by recourse to a vision.[28] By a vision, Paul makes plans to leave Rome, thus setting the stage for Simon's corrupting influence on the community of believers there.[29] In *Acts of Peter*, 2.2.5, Peter receives a vision from God warning him of Simon's infiltration of the community of believers in Rome. God commands Peter to sail to Rome and there confront Simon. In Italy, outside Rome, Peter's host Ariston claims to have had a vision of Paul instructing him to leave Rome.[30] The climax of the narrative is scheduled by Jesus appearing to Peter in a vision and telling him that the great contest with Simon will take place on the coming Sabbath.[31] In all these cases the content of the vision is pretty thin, but the authority of the vision adds a logic of sorts to the movement of the plot. Things happen not by caprice, fate, or fortune, but by the will of God expressed through his legitimate revealers.

Marcellus's vision on the eve of Peter's contest with Simon, however, presents substantial links with the romantic genre and actually shows a sort of fusion of apocalypse and romance. After a prayer session with old blind widows to whom the Lord appears as a young lad, Peter and Marcellus retire to "attend to the virgins of the Lord and to rest until morning."[32] The *Acts of Peter* does not demonstrate the same intensity of play with the erotic potential of such a scene as does the *Shepherd of Hermas*, but similarly they pray and fast all night. Peter's companion Marcellus has a prophetic dream that encourages Peter in preparation for the contest. The dream-vision is quite lurid and its action would fit well within the most sensational of

---

27. A closer correspondence in the romantic tradition might be found in *The Life of Apollonius of Tyana*. See Reardon, *Form*, 5.
28. *Acts Pet.*, Berlin Coptic Papyrus 8502, pp. 131–32 (Hennecke, *New Testament Apocrypha*, 285).
29. *Acts Pet.*, 1 (Hennecke et al., eds., *New Testament Apocrypha*, 287).
30. *Acts Pet.*, 6 (Hennecke et al., eds., *New Testament Apocrypha*, 292).
31. *Acts Pet.*, 16 (Hennecke et al., eds., *New Testament Apocrypha*, 300).
32. *Acts Pet.*, 21–22 (Hennecke et al., eds., *New Testament Apocrypha*, 304–5).

the Romances: *The Golden Ass,* the *Babylonica,* or *The Wonders Beyond Thule.*[33] In his dream, Marcellus sees two figures: Peter, and a demon in the appearance of a female Ethiopian dancer in chains. Peter calls upon Jesus to kill the demon who is the power of Simon, but instead a *Doppelgänger* of Peter appears and dismembers the demon.[34] The wakened Marcellus calls these images "signs of Christ" and Peter is cheered and refreshed by them.[35]

The correspondences between the *Acts of Peter* and Hermas's contest of chastity and the romantic literature are striking. Juxtaposed good and evil women support and afflict the hero. The motif of blackness, in clothing and skin, is used to emphasize moral character. And the exoticism of Ethiopia — note Heliodorus's *Aethiopica* — is characteristic of the romances. Rhetorically, Marcellus's vision confirms Peter's authority not only by recourse to the authority behind revelation, but by combining that source of authority with the portrayal of Peter as a romantic hero.

Simon's Abortive Ascent

After a series of resurrections and striking people dead, Peter seems to have bested Simon in the Forum, but Simon promises that on the next day he will offer conclusive proof of his power: he will ascend to heaven. Ascent is — as a substantial array of apocalyptic literature witnesses — that action that corresponds to the vision which is fundamental to an apocalyptic worldview.[36] And Simon does begin to ascend to the heavens in front of numerous witnesses. Peter, however, who has been guided to the site by a vision,[37] curses Simon so that he falls from his ascent and breaks his leg in three places.[38] Simon subsequently dies on the operating table.

---

33. *The Wonders Beyond Thule* apparently contained a tour of hell. Photius's summary (*Bibliotheca,*166.109a [Bryan P. Reardon, *Collected Ancient Greek Novels* (Berkeley: University of California Press, 1989), 778]) mentions that while among the Cimmerians, Dercyllis "saw Hades and learned much about it." Cf. also the discussion of descents to the underworld in the epic predecessors of the Greco-Roman novel — the *Nekyia* of the Odyssey (Book 11) and Aeneas's descent to the underworld (*Aenead* 6) — in Hubert Cancik, "The End of the World, of History, and of the Individual in Greek and Roman Antiquity," in *The Encyclopedia of Apocalypticism* (ed. John J. Collins; New York: Continuum, 1998), 92, 119.

34. Note also the (false) disembowelment of Leucippe (*Leucippe and Clitophon* 3.15.4–6).

35. *Acts Pet.*, 22; (Hennecke et al., eds., *New Testament Apocrypha,* 305).

36. See Collins, "Introduction," 6; Martha Himmelfarb, *Tours of Hell: An Apocalyptic Form in Jewish and Christian Literature* (Philadelphia: University of Pennsylvania Press, 1983); and idem, *Ascent to Heaven in Jewish and Christian Apocalypses* (Oxford: Oxford University Press, 1993). The otherworldly journey is much more elaborately developed in some apocalypses than in others. Adela Yarbro Collins, "Early Christian Apocalyptic Literature," *ANRW* 25.6: 4683–4687, treats several apocalypses in which this manner of attaining revelation is central, but compare also the mode of revelation in, for example, Revelation and *4 Ezra.*

37. *Acts Pet.*, 3.7.32; (Hennecke et al., eds., *New Testament Apocrypha,* 305).

38. Ibid.

This description of an abortive ascent seems not only to resolve the contest between Peter and Simon, but to do so in a way that de-vulgarizes the apocalyptic tradition. Visions are fine; physical ascents are untrustworthy. The anonymous anti-Montanist source employed by Eusebius shows this to be a narrative motif of heresiological writing.[39] Just like Simon, the Montanist Theodotus starts an ascent to heaven that eventually goes awry and ends in a fatal crash landing. Thus Peter, the recipient of visions, bests Simon, the misguided practitioner of merely physical ascent and angel of the Devil.

Revelation in the Acts of Peter

The rhetorical function of visions in the *Acts of Peter* is primarily an appeal to authority. When God authorizes the vision, what question can there be of the persuasiveness of the injunctions within the vision, the authority of the receiver, or the rightness of his program? In a sealed system of faith, there can be no such questions, but the *Acts of Peter* makes it clear that the system of faith, and likewise the community of faith, is not quite sealed. Visions appear to Simon, but they are not, according to the narrator, from God. God is not the only source of visions. And this functions not only negatively, undermining the authority of visions not from God, but also positively, as when Peter or Paul are the revealers of visions seen by lesser believers.[40] At the same time as control is exercised over the veracity of visions, figures such as Peter and Paul become authoritative sources for visionary guidance. This exercises some power to corral the scope of "authentic" visions within proto-orthodoxy and the range of thought and practice authorized under the names of those apostles. Conversely, overt practice of visionary ascent, a process with scarcely predictable results, receives censure in the narrative.

Rhetoric and Relations of Genre

As I have indicated, apocalypses and romantic narratives are, as a whole, unsuited to most practices of rhetorical criticism.[41] Considering the novel,

---

39. Eusebius, *Hist. Eccl.*, 5.16.14.
40. Paul: *Acts Pet.*, 6; (Hennecke et al., eds., *New Testament Apocrypha*, 292–93); Peter: *Acts Pet.*, 40; (Hennecke et al., eds., *New Testament Apocrypha*, 316–17). David Frankfurter, "Early Christian Apocalypticism: Literature and Social World," in *The Encyclopedia of Apocalypticism* (ed. John J. Collins; New York: Continuum, 1998), 432, notes this function also in full-blown literary apocalypses.
41. This is true of the texts as a whole even if certain rhetorical units can be isolated within the texts for discrete analysis. See for example Ronald F. Hock, "The Rhetoric of Romance," in

M. Bakhtin declares "the utter inadequacy of literary theory is exposed when it is forced to deal with the novel."[42] Mutatis mutandis, this is true also of rhetorical theory: when faced with narrative prose or visionary accounts, it has little to offer. It is no revelation that the wide agreement on three means of appeal — logical, ethical, and emotional — does not lead to equally rich treatments of those three means in any ancient or modern theorist. Romance and apocalypse intertwine so profitably, and are so resistant to conventional rhetorical analysis, precisely because they feed on each other's strengths: the Christian romantic text draws upon the authority of revelation and the serial apocalypse exploits the emotional appeal of romance.

Emotion and Ethos

B. P. Reardon attempts to elucidate the rhetoric of romance by noting Plato's insight that dramatic forms affect the audience's emotions the most directly.[43] Though overtly rhetorical forms such as speeches or laments may be set within a romance, the genre as a whole tugs on the audience's emotions because of their investment in and identification with the fate and feelings of the hero and heroine. The romantic digressions within the *Shepherd* assert that something is actually at stake in the otherwise stultifying work; Hermas, with whom the audience is invited to identify, risks damnation, risks his status as a member of God's church. And he does it in a (relatively) exciting manner. The digression to romance is a gesture to identification at least with the audience's tastes, if not to their ideals.[44] The incorporation of romance is also a transformation of the pleasures of pagan entertainment and a subsumption of those forms into a more hallowed genre. The digression to revelation, on the other hand, is nearly always a gesture to authority, not only moving the plot forward and validating the authority of the protagonist, but in some cases even allowing the protagonist to become the revealer and thus to channel the social practice of receiving visions.

Handbook of Classical Rhetoric in the Hellenistic Period, 330 B.C.–A.D. 400 (ed. Stanley E. Porter; Leiden: Brill, 1997), 445–65.

42. Mikhail Mikhailovich Bakhtin, *The Dialogic Imagination: Four Essays* (trans. Caryl Emerson and Michael Holquist; Austin: University of Texas Press, 1981), 8.

43. Reardon, *Form,* 69, citing *Republic,* 392–98.

44. That is to say it subsists in the relationship of the audience to the subject matter of the text. With dependence on Kenneth Burke, I have developed this notion more extensively in John W. Marshall, "Paul's Ethical Appeal in Philippians," in *Rhetoric and the New Testament: Essays from the 1992 Heidelberg Conference* (ed. Stanley E. Porter and Thomas H. Olbricht; JSNTSup 90; Sheffield: Sheffield Academic Press, 1993), 357–74.

Genre Relations

This commerce of ethos and pathos between revelation and romance builds upon certain intersections between the two genres. Two common features of the genres facilitate their mutual deployment for persuasive purpose: sex in apocalypses, and dreams in romance. In the apocalyptic literary tradition, the problems associated with sexual relations appear at the beginning in *1 Enoch*, where the congress of the Watchers and the women of the earth generates the basic problem of evil. It may function as a minor trope of censure, as in the Apocalypse of John. Or, as in the *Shepherd*, it may function in the *Testament of Reuben* as a sin on the part of the visionary that sets the agenda for revelation and associated paranaesis (as in the *Shepherd*, Reuben's occasion for sin is the sight of a woman bathing).[45]

There is also precedent for mixing romantic and apocalyptic genres in the Jewish novelistic texts — e.g., Daniel's combination of court-tale and vision, the erotic addition of Susannah and the Elders, the dream reports in the Greek additions to Esther, etc.[46] Neither the *Shepherd* nor the *Acts of Peter* shows much acquaintance or interaction with those texts, but the scale at which the genres are intertwined is very similar.[47]

Conversely, the Greek romances make extensive use of dream visions and oracles as a means of plot movement.[48] Callirhoe's hope in the continued safety of Chaereas is buttressed by a dream in which she saves him (*Chaereas and Callirhoe*, 4.1). An oracle of Apollo sets the program of the whole *Ephesiaca* (1.6–7). Pantheia's dream of the violation of her daughter by bandits (*Leucippe and Clitophon*, 2.23.5) is an oblique foreshadowing of Leucippe's falsified disembowelment. Thyamis receives a dream-oracle combination that riddles the future of his kidnapping of Charicleia (*Aethiopica*, 1.18.4). These are but a few examples of a narrative device that is strewn all over the ro-

---

45. *T. Reu.*, 3.11. Hilhorst, "Erotic Elements," 195, provides a wide and helpful catalogue of erotic bathing scenes in ancient literature, though he does not include the *Testament of Reuben*.

46. See Lawrence Wills, *The Jewish Novel in the Ancient World* (Ithaca, N.Y.: Cornell University Press, 1995), on Jewish novelistic literature as well as Erich S. Gruen, *Heritage and Hellenism: The Reinvention of Jewish Tradition* (Hellenistic Culture and Society 30; Berkeley: University of California Press, 1998).

47. Note again Collins, "Wisdom," 174–81. Vernon K. Robbins's work in this volume (pp. 27–65), which configures wisdom and apocalyptic among six elemental "discourses" of early Christianity, begins to examine, more generally and with greater theoretical acumen, the rhetorical force of what I have treated as generic interludes.

48. See Cancik, "End of the World," 91, on signs and divination in Greco-Roman religion. The dream and vision actually converge in Scipio's dream, in which the dreamer/visionary sees the heavens (Cancik, "End of the World," 91, treating Macrobius's *Commentary on Somnius Scipionis*, 1.3).

mantic tradition.[49] Though misinterpretation is quite common (*pace* Bartsch), Hermas is likewise a quite ineffective interpreter of his own visions.

It is obvious, however, that the whole character of the Greek novels that dominate the formulation of the ancient romantic genre[50] and the major apocalypses that influence the formulation of that genre[51] are substantially different. There are, however, similarities of structure that make the bridge between the genres possible. Reardon's[52] description of the sinusoidal pattern of romance evokes the language of apocalyptic: "it is a pattern of ascent and descent, of alternate triumph and tragedy, danger and salvation." More systematically, Reardon's synthesis of the paradigms of romance proposed by Northrop Frye and others[53] begs for comparison with the basic structures of apocalypses.

Table 1. Patterns in the Greek Novel and the Apocalypses[54]

	Setting	Initial Condition	Activity	Experience	Final Condition
Frye	dream world	alienation	quest	circumstance brings descent and ascent	identity
Perry/ Reardon	big world	isolation	travel	adventure brings trials, love sustains	salvation
Kerényi/ Merkelbach	life	vulnerability	search	evil forces bring death, resuscitation	eternal life
Apocalypses	problem in life	ignorance	cognition, often travel	trials, new contexts, knowledge	beatitude

The character of this table is so schematic as to be dangerously distorting and the addition of "Apocalypses" to Reardon's table begs for an extensive

---

49. Bartsch, *Decoding*, 80–108, in particular treats the varied functions of dreams and oracles in *Leucippe and Clitophon* and the *Aethiopica* in much more detail.

50. See Niklas Holzberg, *The Ancient Novel: An Introduction* (London: Routledge, 1995), 1–9, 26–27.

51. See Collins, "Introduction."

52. Reardon, *Form*, 174.

53. Reardon, *Form*, 174, drawing upon Northrop Frye, *The Secular Scripture: A Study of the Structure of Romance* (Cambridge: Harvard University Press, 1976); B. E. Perry, *The Ancient Romances: A Literary-Historical Account of their Origins* (Berkeley: University of California Press, 1967); Karl Kerényi, *Die griechisch-orientalische Romanliteratur in religionsgeschichtlicher Beleuchtung: Ein Versuch mit Nachbetrachtungen* (3d ed.; Darmstadt: Wissenschaftliche Buchgesellschaft, 1973), and Reinhold Merkelbach, *Roman und Mysterium in der Antike* (Munich: C. H. Beck, 1962).

54. The structure of this table and the first three rows are taken directly from Reardon, *Form*, 1974. The bottom row is a synthesis of patterns in apocalyptic literature indebted especially to Collins, "Introduction."

explanation that is beyond the scope of this paper. Nevertheless, the summaries that scholars offer of the romantic genre can apply with little or no modification to the apocalyptic genre. This similarity of narrative pattern, and especially its episodic structure, is what makes apocalypse and romance so receptive to each other.[55]

Genre Development

Bakhtin, again, offers a comment on the development of the novel that can invigorate the question of its relationship to the apocalyptic tradition:

> The ancient period of the novel is enormously significant for a proper understanding of the genre. But in ancient times the novel could not really develop all its potential; this potential came to light only in the modern world. We indicated that in several works of antiquity, the inconclusive present begins to sense greater proximity to the future than to the past. The absence of a temporal perspective in ancient society assured that this process of reorientation toward a real future could not complete itself; after all there was no real concept of a future. Such a reorientation occurred for the first time during the Renaissance.[56]

Bakhtin's comment, with its gap yawning between Heliodorus and the Renaissance, has an apocalypse-shaped hole in its center. Though he notes the affinity between the ancient novel and the Christian martyrological and hagiographical literature, the relationship is not simply a linear development. The martyrdom, especially with its characteristic visionary interlude as death approaches, depends on the apocalyptic as well as on the novelistic tradition. And the eschatological concern that is elaborated in so many apocalypses, and there integrated with prose narrative, begins the process of orientation to the future (though probably not the "real" future) that Bakhtin indicates is essential to the modern novel. Thus, once we have seen a bridge between romance and apocalypse (via Reardon), we are in a better position to understand the development from (ancient) romance to (modern) novel (via Bakhtin).

Conclusions

Rhetorical understanding of the reciprocal digressions of apocalyptic and romantic texts wends a circuitous path, not unlike the progress of the *Shepherd* or of a Greek novel. Instead of comparison of the romance or the apocalypse with a prescriptive handbook tradition against which its construction could

---

55. Reardon, *Form,* 161, characterizes romance as a receptive genre.
56. Bakhtin, *Dialogic Imagination,* 39–40.

be explicated, it has been necessary to tease out commonalities and deduce effects. Instead of employing a theoretical treatise devoted to the rhetoric of these genres, and their intersections, it has been necessary to build from modern accounts of their genres in order to describe the less theorized, yet no less rhetorical, workings of apocalyptic and romantic motifs. The romantic digressions in the visionary text vivify the otherwise moribund apocalypse and appropriate the power of the romance while still vilifying its moral framework. The apocalyptic digressions in the romantic text conversely sanctify and impart a (religious) logic to the otherwise bewildering movement of the romantic plot. This deployment of apocalyptic scenes concentrates authority not only in the Christian God, but in specific representatives of that God, drawing it away from the rivals of the apostles and from the gods of the non-Christian world. Complementary means of rhetorical appeal, common narrative patterns, common, though distinct, concern with sexual attraction and practice, and related motifs of dream and vision, facilitate the amalgamation of the romantic and apocalyptic genres we see in the *Shepherd* and the *Acts of Peter* and thus facilitate the persuasion those texts undertake.

BIBLIOGRAPHY

Papyri (including Tablets):

Abbreviations in *BASP* Suppl. 7 (1992).
P. Abinn.=*The Abinnaeus Archive: Papers of a Roman Officer in the Reign of Constantius II.* Edited by H. I. Bell et al. Oxford: The Clarendon Press, 1962.
P. Cair. Isid.=*The Archive of Aurelius Isidorus in the Egyptian Museum, Cairo and the University of Michigan (P. Cair. Isidor.).* Edited by Arthur E. R. Boak and Herbert Chayyim Youtie. Ann Arbor: University of Michigan Press, 1960.
P. Lond. VII=*Greek Papyri in the British Museum,* Vol. VII: *The Zenon Archive.* Edited by T. C. Skeat. London: British Museum Publications Ltd., 1974.
P. Mich. VIII=*Michigan Papyri.* Vol. VIII. *Papyri and Ostraca from Karanis.* 2d series, nos. 464–521. Edited by H. C. Youtie and J. G. Winter. Ann Arbor: University of Michigan Press, 1951.
P. Oxy. IV=*The Oxyrynchus Papyri.* Vol. IV, nos. 654–839. Edited by B. P. Grenfell and A. S. Hunt. London: Egypt Exploration Fund, 1904.
P. Oxy. XII=*The Oxyrynchus Papyri.* Vol. XII, nos. 1405–1593. Edited by B. P. Grenfell and A. S. Hunt. London: Egypt Exploration Fund, 1916.
P. Petaus=*Das Archiv des Petaus.* Edited by U. Hagedorn et al. Cologne and Opladen: Westdeutscher Verl., 1969.
P. Ryl. II=*Catalogue of the Greek Papyri in the John Rylands Library, Manchester, Vol. 2: Documents of the Ptolemaic and Roman Periods, Nos. 62–456.* Edited by J. de M. Johnson, V. Martin, and A. S. Hunt. Manchester University Press, 1915.
P. Ups. Frid.=*Ten Uppsala Papyri.* Edited by Bo Frid. Ph.D. Dissertation. Lund, Sweden, 1980.
T. Vindol.=*Vindolanda: The Latin Writing Tablets.* Edited by A. K. Bowman and J. D. Thomas. London: Brittania Monograph Series No. 4, 1983.
Zenon Archive of Greek Papyri in the British Museum, The. Vol. 7. Edited by Theodore C. Skeat. London: British Museum Publications, 1974.

Primary Sources

Acts of Peter. Pages 128–32 and 135–41. Berlin Coptic Papyrus 8502. Reprinted as pages 285–317 in Hennecke et al., eds., *New Testament Apocrypha II.* Louisville: Westminster/John Knox, 1992.
Aphthonius. *Aphthonii Progymnasmata.* Edited by Hugo Rabe. Rhetores Graeci 10. Leipzig: Teubner, 1926.
Apostolic Fathers, The. Translated by Kirsopp Lake. 2 vols. LCL 24–25. Cambridge: Harvard University Press, 1912–1913.
Aristides, Aelius. *Aristides.* 4 vols. LCL. Cambridge, Mass.: Harvard University Press, 1973–

Aristophanes. *The Clouds of Aristophanes*. Translated, with critical notes and commentary by W. J. M. Starkie. Amsterdam: Hakkert, 1966.
Aristophanes. *Clouds-Wasps-Peace*. Translated by Jeffrey Henderson. LCL 488. Cambridge, Mass.: Harvard University Press, 1998.
Aristotle. *Ars Rhetorica*. Edited by W. D. Ross. OCT. Oxford: Oxford University Press, 1959.
Aristotle. *The "Art" of Rhetoric*. Translated by John Henry Freese. LCL 193. Cambridge, Mass.: Harvard University Press, 1959.
Aristotle. *On Rhetoric*. Translated by George A. Kennedy. New York and Oxford: Oxford University Press, 1991.
Aristotle, *Rhetoric*. Pages 1317–1451 in *The Basic Works of Aristotle*. Translated by W. Rhys Roberts. Edited by R. McKeon. New York: Random House, 1941.
Aristotle, *Rhetoric*. Translated by Jonathan Banks in *The Complete Works of Aristotle*. Bollingen Series 71,2. Princeton: Princeton University Press, 1984.
Aristotle. *Rhetorica*. Edited by Robert McKeon. Translated by W. Rhys Roberts. Pages 1317–1451 in *The Basic Works of Aristotle*. New York: Random House, 1941.
Aristotle. *On Sophistical Refutations*. Translated by E. S. Forster. LCL. Cambridge, Mass.: Harvard University Press, 1955.
Aristotle. "Topica." Edited and translated by E. S. Forster. Vol. 2 of *Aristotle in twenty-three volumes*. LCL. Cambridge, Mass.: Harvard University Press, 1960.
[Aristotle]. *Rhetorica ad Alexandrum*. Translated by N. Rackham. Pages 257–449 LCL 317. Cambridge: Harvard University Press, 1983.
Augustine. *On Christian Doctrine*. Translated by D. W. Robertson, Jr. New York: Macmillan/Library of Liberal Arts, 1986.
Cassiodorus. *Varie*. Translated, with notes and introduction by S. J. B. Barnish. Liverpool: Liverpool University Press, 1992.
Cassius Dio. *Historiae Romanae*. Edited by E. Cary. LCL. Cambridge, Mass.: Harvard University Press, 1914–26.
Chrysostom, Dio. *Discourses XXXVII–LX*. Translated by H. Lamar Cosby. LCL 376. Cambridge, Mass.: Harvard University Press, 1962.
Cicero. *The Letters to His Friends*. Translated by W. Glynn Williams. 3 vols. LCL 205, 216, 230. Cambridge, Mass.: Harvard University Press, 1927–29.
Cicero, Marcus Tullius. "De oratore." Vols. 3 and 4 of *Cicero in twenty-eight volumes*. Translated by E. W. Sutton. LCL. Cambridge, Mass.: Harvard University Press, 1942.
Cicero, Marcus Tullius. *Letters to Atticus*. Edited and translated by E. O. Winstedt. 3 vols. LCL 97. Cambridge, Mass.: Harvard University Press, 1962–1984.
Cicero. *Rhetorica ad Herennium*. Translated by Harry Caplan. LCL 403. Cambridge: Harvard University Press, 1954.
Cornificus. *Rhetorica ad C. Herennium*. Edited by G. Calboli. 2d ed. Bologna: Pàtron, 1993.
Demetrius. "On style." Edited and translated by Doreen C. Innes based on W. Rhys Roberts. In the volume with Aristotle's *Poetics*. LCL. 2d ed. Cambridge, Mass.: Harvard University Press, 1995.
Demetrius. "On style." Pages 16–19 in *Ancient Epistolary Theorists*. Edited and translated by Abraham Malherbe. Atlanta: Scholars Press, 1988.
Diodorus of Sicily. *Works*. Translated by R. M. Geer. 10 vols. LCL. Cambridge, Mass.: Harvard University Press, 1963.

Diogenes Laertius. *Lives of the Eminent Philosophers.* 2 vols. Translated by R. D. Hicks. LCL. Cambridge: Harvard University Press, 1925-.
Galen, *De Captionibus.* In Robert Blair Edlow, *Galen on Language and Ambiguity.* Philosophia antiqua 31. Leiden: Brill, 1977.
Hermogenes. *On Issues: Strategies of Argument in Later Greek Rhetoric.* Translated by Malcolm Heath. Oxford Clarendon Press, 1995.
Hermogenes. *Progymnasmata.* Pages 1–27 in *Hermogenis Opera.* Edited by Hugo Rabe. Rhetores Graeci 6. Leipzig: Teubner, 1913.
Libanius. *Autobiography and Selected Letters.* Edited and translated by A. F. Norman. 2 vols. LCL. Cambridge, Mass.: Harvard University Press, 1992.
Libanius. *Imaginary Speeches.* Translated by D. A. Russell. London: Duckworth, 1996.
Libanius. *Selected Works.* Introduction and translation by A. F. Norman. 3 vols. LCL. Cambridge, Mass.: Harvard University Press, 1969.
Livy. *The History of Rome.* Translated by D. Spillan and C. Edmonds. 2 vols. Harper's Classical Library. New York: Harper & Brothers, 1875–1881.
Lucian. *Lucian.* Translated by A. M. Harmon et al. 8 vols. LCL. Cambridge, Mass.: Harvard University Press, 1913.
Lydus, Ioannes. *On Powers or the Magistracies of the Roman State.* Edited and translated by Anastasius C. Bandy. Philadelphia: The American Philosophical Society, 1983.
Origen. *Commentarii in Romanos.* PG 14.831–1294.
Philo. With an English Translation by F. H. Colson and G. H. Whitaker. 10 vols. LCL. Cambridge, Mass.: Harvard University Press, 1932–62.
Philostratus and Eunapius. *Lives of the Sophists.* Translated by Wilmer C. Wright. LCL. Cambridge, Mass.: Harvard University Press, 1989.
Plato. "Apology." Vol. 1 of *Plato in twelve volumes.* Translated by Harold North Fowler. LCL. Cambridge, Mass.: Harvard University Press, 1914.
Plato. *Opera.* Edited by I. Burnet. 5 vols. OCT. Oxford: Oxford University Press, 1900–1907.
Plato *Plato's Phaedrus.* Translated with commentary by R. Hackforth. Cambridge: University Press, 1972.
Pliny. *Letters and Panegyricus.* Edited and translated by Betty Radice. 2 vols. LCL. Cambridge, Mass.: Harvard University Press, 1969.
Plutarch. *Moralia.* Translated by Phillip H. De Lacy and Benedict Einarson. 15 vols. LCL. Cambridge, Mass.: Harvard University Press, 1958.
Quintilianus. *Institutio Oratoria.* Translated by H. E. Butler. 4 vols. LCL 124–27. Cambridge, Mass.: Harvard University Press, 1976–80.
Rhetores Graeci. Edited by L. Spengel. 3 vols. Leipzig: B. G. Teubner, 1853–56.
Scriptores Historiae Augustae. *Lives of the Later Caesars.* New York: Penguin, 1976.
Seneca, Lucius Annaeus. *Declamations.* Translated by Michael Winterbottom. 2 vols. Cambridge, Mass.: Harvard University Press, 1974.
Sextus Empiricus. *Adversus Mathematicos.* Translated by R. G. Bury. LCL. Cambridge, Mass.: Harvard University Press, 1949.
Suetonius. *Suetonius.* Translated by J. C. Rolfe. 2 vols. LCL. Cambridge, Mass.: Harvard University Press, 1944.
Symmachus. *Prefect and Emperor: The Relationes of Symmachus A.D. 394.* Translated, with introduction and notes by R. H. Barrow. Oxford: Clarendon Press, 1973.

Tertullian. *Adversus Marcionem*, vol. 2. Translated by Ernest Evans. Oxford: Clarendon Press, 1972.
Théon, Aelius. *Progymnasmata*. Edited by Michel Patillon. Collection des Universités de France. Paris: Les Belles Lettres, 1997.
Thrax, Dionysius. *Tekhnê Grammatikê*. Translated by Alan Kemp. Pages 169–90 in *The History of Linguistics in the Classical Period*. Edited by Daniel J. Taylor. Amsterdam: John Benjamins Publishing Company, 1987.
Thucydides. *History of the Peloponnesian War*. Translated by R. Warner. Penguin Classics 139. Baltimore: Penguin Books, 1954.
Tragicorum Romanorum Fragmenta. Edited by Otto Ribbeck. Leipzig: B. G. Teubner, 1871. nos. 110; 107; 108.

Secondary Sources

Aletti, Jean-Noël. *Saint Paul Épitre aux Colossiens; Introduction, traduction et commentaire*. EB, new series. Paris: Gabalda, 1993.
Alexandre, Manuel. *Rhetorical Argumentation in Philo of Alexandria*. Brown Judaic Studies 322, SPhil 2; Atlanta: Scholars, 1999.
Alter, Robert. *The Art of Biblical Narrative*. New York: Basic Books, 1981.
Alter, Robert. *The Art of Biblical Poetry*. New York: Basic Books, 1985.
Amador, J. David Hester. "Revisiting 2 Corinthians: Rhetoric and the Case for Unity." *NTS* 46 (2000): 92–111.
Anderson, Paul N. *The Christology of the Fourth Gospel: Its Unity and Disunity in the Light of John 6*. WUNT 2.77. Tübingen: Mohr (Siebeck), 1995.
Anderson, R. Dean. *Ancient Rhetorical Theory and Paul*. Kampen: Kok Pharos Publishing House, 1996.
Anderson, R. Dean. *Ancient Rhetorical Theory and Paul*. Rev. ed. Leuven: Peeters, 1998.
Anderson, R. Dean. *Glossary of Greek Rhetorical Terms Connected to Methods of Argumentation, Figures and Tropes from Anaximenes to Quintilian*. Leuven: Peeters, 2000.
Anscombre, Jean-Claude, and Oswald Ducrot. *L'argumentation dans la langue*. Brussels: Mardaga, 1983.
Arens, Arnold. "In memoriam Heinrich Lausberg," in *Archiv für das Studium der neueren Sprachen und Literaturen* 230 (1993): 1–5.
Arnold, Clinton E. *Ephesians: Power and Magic*. SNTSMS 63. Cambridge: Cambridge University Press, 1989.
Attridge, Harold W. *The Epistle to the Hebrews*. Philadelphia: Fortress Press, 1989.
Attridge, Harold W. "On Becoming an Angel: Rival Baptismal Theologies at Colossae." Pages 481–98 in *Religious Propaganda and Missionary Competition in the New Testament World; Essays Honoring Dieter Georgi*. Edited by L. Borman, K. Del Tredici, A. Standinger. NovTSup 74. Leiden: Brill, 1994.
Attridge, Harold W. "Thematic Development and Source Elaboration in John 7:1–36," *CBQ* 44 (1980): 160–70.
Aubert, Jean-Jacques. *Business Managers in Ancient Rome*. Leiden: E. J. Brill, 1994.
Auerbach, Erich. *Mimesis: The Representation of Reality in Western Literature*. Princeton, N.J.: Princeton University Press, 1968.

Aune, David E. "Review of Hans-Dieter Betz, *Galatians: A Commentary on Paul's Letter to the Churches in Galatia.*" *Religious Studies Review* 7 (1981): 323–28.
Bakhtin, Mikhail Mikhailovich. *The Dialogic Imagination: Four Essays.* Translated by Caryl Emerson and Michael Holquist. Austin: University of Texas Press, 1981.
Baldwin, Charles S. *Ancient Rhetoric and Poetic: Interpreted From Representative Works.* New York: Macmillan, 1924.
Bar-Efrat, Shimon. *Narrative Art in the Bible.* Sheffield: Almond Press, 1989.
Barr, David. *New Testament Story.* 2d ed. Belmont, Calif.: Wadsworth Publishing Co., 1995.
Barrett, Charles K. *A Commentary on the Second Epistle to the Corinthians.* HNTC. New York: Harper Row, 1973.
Barrett, Charles. *The Gospel According to St. John.* 2d ed. Philadelphia: Westminster; London: SPCK, 1978.
Barrett, Charles K. *Paul: An Introduction to His Thought.* Louisville: Westminster John Knox, 1994.
Barthand, Else M., and Erik C. W. Krabbe. *From Axiom to Dialogue: A Philosophical Study of Logics and Argumentation.* Berlin/New York: de Gruyter, 1982.
Bartsch, Shadi. *Decoding the Ancient Novel: The Reader and the Role of Description in Heliodorus and Achilles Tatius.* Princeton, N.J.: Princeton University Press, 1989.
Benner, Margareta. *The Emperor Says: Studies in the Rhetorical Style in Edicts of the Early Empire.* Göteborg: Acta Universitatis Gothoburgensis, 1975.
Berlin, Adele. *Poetics and the Interpretation of Biblical Narrative.* Sheffield: Almond Press, 1983.
Best, Ernest. *A Critical and Exegetical Commentary on Ephesians.* ICC. Edinburgh: T. & T. Clark, 1998.
Betz, Hans Dieter. *Galatians: A Commentary on Paul's Letter to the Churches in Galatia.* Hermeneia. Philadelphia: Fortress, 1979.
Betz, Hans Dieter. *2 Corinthians 8 and 9.* Hermeneia. Philadelphia: Fortress Press, 1985.
Beversluis, John. *Cross-examining Socrates.* Cambridge: Cambridge University Press, 2000.
Bilansky, Alan. "Rhetoric, Democracy, and the Deliberative Horizon." Pages 221–29 in *Rhetoric, the Polis, and the Global Village.* Selected papers from the 1998 Thirtieth Anniversary Rhetoric Society of America Conference. Edited by C. Jan Swearingen and Dave Pruett. Mahwah, N.J.: Lawrence Erlbaum Associates, 1999.
Bitzer, Lloyd F. "Aristotle's Enthymeme Revisited." Pages 141–55 in *Aristotle: The Classical Heritage of Rhetoric.* Edited by K. V. Erickson. Metuchen, N.J.: The Scarecrow Press, 1974.
Bizzell, Patricia, and Bruce Herzberg, eds. *The Rhetorical Tradition: Readings from Classical Times to the Present.* Boston: Bedford Books of St. Martin's Press, 1990.
Black, C. Clifton. "An Oration at Olivet: Some Rhetorical Dimensions of Mark 13." Pages 66–92 in *Persuasive Artistry: Studies in New Testament Rhetoric in Honor of George A. Kennedy.* Edited by Duane F. Watson. JSNTSup 50. Sheffield: Sheffield Academic Press, 1981.
Black, C. Clifton. "Rhetorical Criticism." Pages 256–77 in *Hearing the New Testament.* Edited by Joel B. Green. Grand Rapids, Mich.: Eerdmans, 1995.
Black, David A. "The Discourse Structure of Philippians: A Study in Textlinguistics." *NovT* 37 (1995): 16–49.

Blair, J. Anthony, and Ralph H. Johnson. "Argumentation as Dialectical." *Argumentation* 1 (1987): 41–56.
Bloomquist, L. Gregory. *The Function of Suffering in Philippians.* JSNTSup 78. Sheffield: JSOT, 1993.
Bloomquist, L. Gregory. "Methodological Considerations in the Determination of the Social Context of Cynic Rhetorical Practice: Implications for our Present Studies of the Jesus Traditions." Pages 200–231 in *The Rhetorical Analysis of Scripture: Essays from the 1995 London Conference.* Edited by Stanley E. Porter and Thomas H. Olbricht. JSNTSup 146. London: Sheffield Academic Press, 1997.
Bloomquist, L. Gregory. "Methodological Criteria for Apocalyptic Rhetoric: A Suggestion for the Expanded Use of Sociorhetorical Analysis. Pages 181–203 in *Vision and Persuasion: Rhetorical Dimensions of Apocalyptic Discourse.* Edited by Greg Carey and L. Gregory Bloomquist. St. Louis: Chalice, 1999.
Bloomquist, L. Gregory. "The Place of Enthymemes in Argumentative Texture." Paper read at Rhetorical Pre-Session at the 1997 SBL in San Francisco.
Bloomquist, L. Gregory. "A Possible Direction for Providing Programmatic Correlation of Textures in Socio-rhetorical Analysis: Who Could Ask for Anything More?" In *Rhetorical Criticism and the Bible: Essays from the 1998 Florence Conference.* Edited by Stanley E. Porter and Dennis Stamps. JSNTSup 195. Sheffield: Sheffield Academic Press, forthcoming.
Bloomquist, L. Gregory. "Rhetorical Argumentation and the Culture of Apocalyptic: A Socio-rhetorical Analysis of Luke 21." Pages 173–209 in *The Rhetorical Interpretation of Scripture: Essays from the 1996 Malibu Conference.* Edited by Stanley E. Porter and Dennis L. Stamps. JSNTSup 180. Sheffield: Sheffield Academic Press, 1999.
Bonner, Campbell, ed. *A Papyrus Codex of the Shepherd of Hermas (Similitudes 2–9) with a Fragment of the Mandates.* University of Michigan Studies. Humanistic Series 22. Ann Arbor: University of Michigan Press, 1934.
Booth, Alan D. "The Schooling of Slaves in First Century Rome." In *TAPA* 109 (1979): 11–20.
Boring, Eugene M. "The Convergence of Source Analysis, Social History, and Literary Structure in the Gospel of Matthew." Pages 587–611 in *SBLSP 1994.* Atlanta: Scholars Press, 1994.
Bornkamm, Günther. *Paul.* New York: Harper & Row, 1960.
Bornkamm, Günther. "Der Römerbrief als Testament des Paulus." Pages 120–48 in *Geschichte und Glaube II, Gesammelte Aufsätze IV.* Munich: Kaiser, 1971.
Bovati, Pietro, and Roland Meynet. *Le livre du prophète Amos.* Rhétorique biblique 2. Paris: Les Éditions du Cerf, 1994; Italian ed.: *Il libro del profeta Amos.* Retorica biblica 2. Rome: Edizioni Dehoniane.
Bowersock, Glen W. *Greek Sophists in the Roman Empire.* Oxford: Oxford University Press, 1969.
Boyarin, Daniel. *Dying for God: Martyrdom and the Making of Christianity and Judaism (Figurae: Reading Medieval Culture).* Stanford: Stanford University Press, 1999.
Boys, Thomas. *A Key to the Book of the Psalms.* London: L. B. Seeley & Sons, 1825.
Braun, Roddy L. "The Significance of 1 Chronicles 22, 28, and 29 for the Structure and Theology of the Work of the Chronicler." Th.D. diss., Concordia Seminary, 1971.

Braun, Willi. *Feasting and Social Rhetoric in Luke 14.* SNTSMS 85. Cambridge: Cambridge University Press, 1995.
Braund, David, ed. *The Administration of the Roman Empire.* Exeter: University of Exeter Press, 1988.
Breck, John. *The Shape of Biblical Language: Chiasmus in the Scripture and Beyond.* Crestwood, N.Y.: St. Vladimir's Seminary Press, 1994.
Brown, H. Stephen. "The Martyrs on Trial: A Socio-Rhetorical Analysis of Second Century Christian Court Narrative." Ph.D. diss. Temple University, 1999.
Brown, Peter. *The Making of Late Antiquity.* Cambridge, Mass.: Harvard University Press, 1978.
Brown, Peter. *Power and Persuasion in Late Antiquity: Towards a Christian Empire.* Madison: University of Wisconsin Press, 1992.
Brown, Raymond E. *The Gospel According to John.* 2 vols. AB 29, 29a. Garden City, N.Y.: Doubleday, 1966–70.
Brox, Norbert. *Der Hirt des Hermas.* Kommentar zu den Apostolischen Vätern 7. Göttingen: Vandenhoeck & Ruprecht, 1991.
Bruce, Frederick F. *The Epistle to the Hebrews.* NICNT. Grand Rapids: Eerdmans, 1964.
Brueggemann, Walter. *Theology of the Old Testament: Testimony, Dispute, Advocacy.* Minneapolis: Fortress, 1997.
Bultmann, Rudolf. *Der Stil der paulinischen Predigt und die kynisch-stoische Diatribe.* Göttingen: Vandenhoeck & Ruprecht, 1910.
Bultmann, Rudolf. *Theologie des Neuen Testaments.* 5th ed. Tübingen: Mohr/Siebeck, 1965.
Bünker, Michael. *Briefformular und rhetorische Disposition im 1. Korintherbrief.* GTA 28. Göttingen: Vandenhoeck & Ruprecht, 1984.
Burke, Kenneth. *A Rhetoric of Motives.* Berkeley/Los Angeles: University of California Press, 1969.
Burnyeat, Myles F. "Enthymeme: Aristotle on the Logic of Persuasion." Pages 3–55 in *Aristotle's Rhetoric: Philosophical Essays.* Edited by D. J. Furley and A. Nehamas. Princeton, N.J.: Princeton University Press, 1994.
Burridge, Richard A. *What Are the Gospels?* New York: Cambridge, 1992.
Burton, E. DeWitt. *A Critical and Exegetical Commentary on the Epistle to the Galatians.* ICC. Edinburgh: T. & T. Clark, 1921.
Butts, James R. "The 'Progymnasmata' of Theon: A New Text with Translation and Commentary." Ph.D. Dissertation, Claremont Graduate School, 1987.
Calvin, John. *Calvin's New Testament Commentaries.* Edited by D. W. and T. F. Torrance. Vol. 11. Grand Rapids: Eerdmans, 1965.
Campbell, Barth L. *Honor, Shame, and the Rhetoric of 1 Peter.* SBLDS 160. Atlanta: Scholars Press, 1998.
Cancik, Hubert. "The End of the World, of History, and of the Individual in Greek and Roman Antiquity." Pages 84–125 in *The Encyclopedia of Apocalypticism,* vol. 1. Edited by John J. Collins. New York: Continuum, 1998.
Cannon, George E. *The Use of Traditional Materials in Colossians.* Macon: Mercer University Press, 1983.
Carey, Gregory, and L. Gregory Bloomquist. *Vision and Persuasion: Rhetorical Dimensions of Apocalyptic Discourse.* St. Louis: Chalice, 1999.

Carlini, Antonio, Luigi Giaccone, Rodolphe Kasser, Guglielmo Cavallo, and Joseph van Haelst, eds. *Il pastore (Ia–IIIa visione)*. Papyrus Bodmer. Vol. 38. Cologne and Geneva: Fondation Martin Bodmer, 1991.

Carrez, M. "Le 'Nous' en 2 Corinthiens." *NTS* 26/4 (1980): 474–86.

Casey, Juliana. *Hebrews*. Wilmington: Michael Glazer, 1980.

Castelli, Elisabeth A. *Imitating Paul: A Discourse of Power*. Literary Currents in Biblical Interpretation. Louisville: Westminster/John Knox Press, 1991.

Cavallo, G., and H. Maehler. *Greek Bookhands of the Early Byzantine Period, A.D. 300–800*. Institute of Classical Studies Bulletin Suppl. 47, 1987.

Chadwick, Henry. "Die Absicht des Epheserbriefes." *ZNW* 51 (1960): 145–53.

Classen, Carl Joachim. "Aristotle's Picture of the Sophists." Pages 7–24 in *The Sophists and their Legacy*. Edited by G. B. Kerferd. Hermes 44. Wiesbaden: Franz Steiner Verlag, 1981.

Classen, Carl Joachim. *Recht-Rhetorik-Politik*. Darmstadt: Wissenschaftliche Buchgesellschaft, 1985.

Classen, Carl Joachim. "Review of R. Dean Anderson, *Ancient Rhetorical Theory and Paul*." *Rhetorica* 16:3 (1998): 324–29.

Classen, Carl Joachim. "St. Paul and Ancient Greek and Roman Rhetoric," *Rhetorica* 10 (1992): 319–44.

Classen, Carl Joachim. "St. Paul's Epistles and Ancient Greek and Roman Rhetoric." Pages 265–91 in *Rhetoric and the New Testament: Essays from the 1992 Heidelberg Conference*. Edited by Stanley Porter and Thomas Olbricht. JSNTSup 90. Sheffield: JSOT Press, 1993.

Classen, Carl Joachim, ed. *Sophistik*. WdF 187. Darmstadt: Wissenschaftliche Buchgesellschaft, 1976.

Coleborne, W. "The *Shepherd of Hermas:* A Case for Multiple Authorship." *StPatr* 10 (1970): 65–70.

Collins, Adela Yarbro. "The Apocalyptic Rhetoric of Mark 13 in Historical Context." *Biblical Research* 41 (1996): 5–36.

Collins, Adela Yarbro. "Early Christian Apocalyptic Literature." *ANRW* 25.6, Part 2 Principat, 25.6.4665–4711. Edited by H. Temporini and W. Haase. New York: de Gruyter, 1988.

Collins, Adela Yarbro. "Introduction: Early Christian Apocalypticism." *Semeia* 36 (1986): 2–11.

Collins, John J. *The Apocalyptic Imagination: An Introduction to Jewish Apocalyptic Literature*. 2d ed. Grand Rapids: Eerdmans, 1998.

Collins, John J. "Early Jewish Apocalypticism." *Anchor Bible Dictionary* 1 (1992): 282–88.

Collins, John J. "Introduction: Towards the Morphology of a Genre." *Semeia* 14 (1979): 1–19.

Collins, John J. *Jewish Wisdom in the Hellenistic Age*. Louisville: Westminster John Knox, 1997.

Collins, John J. "Wisdom, Apocalypticism, and Generic Compatibility." Pages 165–185 in *In Search of Wisdom: Essays in Memory of John G. Gammie*. Edited by Leo G. Perdue, Bernard Brandon Scott, and William Johnston Wiseman. Louisville: Westminster/John Knox Press, 1993.

Collins, John J., ed. *Apocalypse: The Morphology of a Genre*. Semeia 14. Chico, Calif.: Scholars Press, 1979.
Collins, John J., ed. *The Encyclopedia of Apocalypticism*. Vol. 1 of *The Origins of Apocalypticism in Judaism and Christianity*. New York: Continuum, 1998.
Conley, Thomas M. "The Enthymeme in Perspective." *QJS* 70 (1984): 168–87.
Conley, Thomas M. *Rhetoric in the European Tradition*. Chicago: University of Chicago Press, 1990.
Conley, Thomas. "Πάθη and πίστεις: Aristotle 'Rhet'. II 2–11." *Hermes* 110 (1982/3): 300–315.
Cooper, John M. "Rhetoric, Dialectic, and the Passions." *Oxford Studies in Ancient Philosophy* 11 (1993): 175–98.
Cope, E. M. "On the Sophistical Rhetoric." *The Journal of Classical and Sacred Philology* 2 (1855): 129–69; 3 (1856): 34–80, 253–88.
Cosgrove, Charles H. "What If Some Have Not Believed? The Occasion and Thrust of Romans 3:1–8." *ZNW* 78 (1987): 90–115.
Cotter, Wendy. *Miracles in Greco-Roman Antiquity: A Sourcebook*. London: Routledge, 1999.
Cousar, Charles B. *The Letters of Paul*. Nashville: Abingdon Press, 1996.
Cranfield, C. E. B. "St. Paul and the Law." *SJT* 17 (1964): 43–68.
Crawshay-Williams, R. *The Comforts of Unreason*. London: Routledge & Kegan Paul, 1947.
Crawshay-Williams, R. *Methods and Criteria for Reasoning: An Inquiry into the Structure of Controversy*. London: Routledge & Kegan Paul, 1957.
Crenshaw, James L. *Old Testament Wisdom*. Atlanta: John Knox, 1981.
Crenshaw, James L. "Prolegomenon." Pages 1–45 in *Studies in Ancient Israelite Wisdom*. Edited by J. L. Crenshaw. New Work: KTAV, 1976.
Crenshaw, James L. *Urgent Advice and Probing Questions: Collected Writings on Old Testament Wisdom*. Macon: Mercer University Press, 1995.
Crenshaw, James L. "Wisdom and Authority: Sapiential Rhetoric and Its Warrants." Pages 10–29 in *Congress Volume: Vienna, 1980*. Edited by J. A. Emerton. VTSup 32. Leiden: Brill, 1981.
Cribiore, Raffaella. *Writing, Teachers, and Students in Graeco-Roman Egypt*. American Studies in Papyrology 36. Atlanta: Scholars Press, 1996.
Crowley, Sharon. *The Methodical Memory: Invention in Current-Traditional Rhetoric*. Carbondale: Southern Illinois University Press, 1990.
Culpepper, R. Alan. *Anatomy of the Fourth Gospel: A Study in Literary Design*. NTFF. Philadelphia: Fortress, 1983.
Culpepper, R. Alan. "John 5:1–18: A Sample of Narrative Critical Commentary," in *La communauté johannique et son histoire*. Edited by J. D. Kaestli, J. M. Poffet, and J. Zumstein. Geneva: Labor et Fides, 1990, 131–51. Reprinted in Mark W. G. Stibbe, ed., *The Gospel of John as Literature: An Anthology of Twentieth-Century Perspectives*. NTTS 17. Leiden: Brill, 1993, 193–207.
Davies, Margaret. *Rhetoric and Reference in the Fourth Gospel*. JSNTSup 69. Sheffield: JSOT Press, 1992.
Davies, Steven L. *New Testament Fundamentals*. Sonoma, Calif.: Polebridge Press, 1994.

Davis, Casey W. *Oral Biblical Criticism: The Influence of the Principles of Orality on the Literary Structure of Paul's Epistle to the Philippians.* JSNTSup 172. Sheffield: Sheffield Academic Press, 1999.

De Quincey, Thomas. "Elements of Rhetoric." *Blackwood's Edinburgh Magazine* 24 (1838).

De Vries, Simon. *Prophet Against Prophet: The Role of the Micaiah Narrative (1 Kings 22) in the Development of Early Prophetic Tradition.* Grand Rapids: Eerdmans, 1978.

Debanné, Marc. "An Enthymemic Reading of Philippians: Towards a Typology of Pauline Arguments." In *Rhetorical Criticism and the Bible: Essays from the 1998 Florence Conference.* Edited by Stanley E. Porter and Dennis Stamps. JSNTSup 195. Sheffield: Sheffield Academic Press, forthcoming.

DeLuca, Kevin Michael. "Unruly Arguments: The Body Rhetoric of Earth First!, Act Up, and Queer Nation." *Argument and Advocacy* 36 (1999): 9–21.

Derda, Tomasz. "Necropolis Workers in Graeco-Roman Egypt in the Light of Greek Papyri." *Journal of Juristic Papyrology* 21 (1991): 13–36.

deSilva, David A. *The Hope of Glory: Honor Discourse and New Testament Interpretation.* Collegeville, Minn.: Michael Glazier, 1999.

deSilva, David. "Investigation of the Integrity and Argumentation of 2 Corinthians." *JSNT* 52 (1993): 41–70.

deSilva, David A. *Perseverance in Gratitude: A Socio-Rhetorical Commentary on the Epistle "to the Hebrews."* Grand Rapids: Eerdmans, 2000.

deSilva, David A. "The Persuasive Strategy of the Apocalypse: A Socio-Rhetorical Investigation of Revelation 14:6–13." Pages 785–806 in *SBLSP*, 1998. Atlanta: Scholars Press, 1998.

deSilva, David. "Recasting the Moment of Decision: 2 Corinthians 6:14–7:1 in its Literary Context." *Andrews University Seminary Studies* 31/1 (1993): 3–16.

deSilva, David A. "A Socio-Rhetorical Investigation of Revelation 14:6–13: A Call to Act Justly toward the Just and Judging God." *BBR* 9 (1999): 65–117.

Dillard, Raymond B. "Reward and Punishment in Chronicles: The Theology of Immediate Retribution." *WTJ* 46 (1984): 164–72.

Dobson, J. F. *The Greek Orators.* London: Ares Publishers, 1918.

Dodd, C. H. "A Hidden Parable in the Fourth Gospel." Pages 30–40 in *More New Testament Studies.* Grand Rapids: Eerdmans, 1968.

Donelson, Lewis R. *Pseudepigraphy and Ethical Argument in the Pastoral Epistles.* HUT 22. Tübingen: Mohr, 1986.

Dowd, Sharyn E. *Prayer, Power, and The Problem of Suffering.* SBLDS 105. Atlanta: Scholars Press, 1988.

Droge, Arthur J. "*Mori Lucrum*: Paul and Ancient Theories of Suicide." *NovT* 30 (1988): 263–86.

Droge, Arthur J. *A Noble Death: Suicide and Martyrdom among Christians and Jews in Antiquity.* San Francisco: HarperSanFrancisco, 1991.

Duff, Paul Brooks. "The Mind of the Redactor: 2 Corinthians 6:14–8:1 in its Secondary Context." *NovT* 35/2 (1993): 160–80.

Duke, Paul D. *Irony in the Fourth Gospel.* Atlanta: John Knox, 1985.

Duke, Rodney K. *The Persuasive Appeal of the Chronicler: A Rhetorical Analysis.* Bible and Literature Series 25. Sheffield: Almond, 1990.

Duke, Rodney K. "A Rhetorical Approach to Appreciating the Books of Chronicles." Pages 100–135 in *The Chronicler as Author: Studies in Text and Texture.* Edited by M. Patrick Graham and Steven L. McKenzie. JSOTSup 263. Sheffield: Sheffield Academic Press, 1999.

Duling, Dennis, and Norman Perrin. *The New Testament: Proclamation & Parenesis, Myth & History.* 3rd ed. Fort Worth, Tex.: Harcourt Brace College, 1994.

Dunkle, J. R. "The Greek Tyrant and Roman Political Invective of the Late Republic." *TAPA* 98 (1967): 151–71.

Dunn, James D. G. *The Epistles to the Colossians and to Philemon.* NIGTC. Grand Rapids: Eerdmans, 1996.

Dunn, James D. G. *The Epistle to the Galatians.* BNTC. Peabody, Mass.: Hendrickson, 1993.

Dunn, James D. G. *Romans 1–8.* WBC 38A. Dallas: Word Books, 1988.

Dunn, James D. G. "2 Corinthians 3.17 – 'The Lord is the Spirit'." *JTS* 21/2 (1970): 309–20.

Dunn, James D. G. *The Theology of Paul the Apostle.* Edinburgh: T. & T. Clark, 1998.

Dutile, Gordon. "An Annotated Bibliography for 2 Corinthians." *Southwestern Journal of Theology* 32/1 (1989): 41–43.

DuToit, A. B. "Hyperbolic Contrasts: A Neglected Aspect of Paul's Style." Pages 178–86 in *A South African Perspective on the New Testament.* Edited by J. H. Petzer and P. J. Hartin. Leiden: E. J. Brill, 1986.

Ede, Lisa, and Andrea Lunsford. "Audience Addressed/Audience Invoked: The Role of Audience in Composition Theory and Pedagogy. *CCC* 35 (1984):155–71.

Edelstein, Emma J., and Ludwig Edelstein. *Asclepius.* 2 vols. Baltimore: Johns Hopkins Press, 1945.

Eemeren, Frans H. van, et al. *Fundamentals of Argumentation Theory: A Handbook of Historical Backgrounds and Contemporary Developments.* Mahwah, N.J.: Erlbaum, 1996.

Eemeren, Frans H. van, and Rob Grootendorst. "*Argumentum ad hominem*: A Pragma dialectical Case in Point." Pages 223–28 in *Fallacies: Classical and Contemporary Readings.* Edited by Hans V. Hansen and Robert C. Pinto. University Park, Pa.: Pennsylvania State University Press, 1995.

Eemeren, Frans H. van, and Rob Grootendorst. *Argumentation, Communication, and Fallacies.* Hillsdale, N.J.: Lawrence Erlbaum, 1984.

Eemeren, Frans van, and Rob Grootendorst. *Handbook of Argumentation Theory: A Critical Survey of Classical Backgrounds and Modern Studies.* Dordrecht: Foris, 1987.

Eemeren, Frans H. van, and Rob Grootendorst. "The Pragma-dialectical Approach to Fallacies." Pages 130–44 in *Fallacies: Classical and Contemporary Readings.* Edited by Hans V. Hansen and Robert C. Pinto. University Park, Pa.: Pennsylvania State University Press, 1995.

Eemeren, Frans H. van, and Rob Grootendorst. *Speech Acts in Argumentative Discussions.* Berlin: De Gruyter; Dordrecht: Foris, 1984.

Eemeren, Frans H. van, and Peter Houtlosser. "Strategic manoeuvering in argumentative discourse." *Discourse Studies 1* (1999): no. 4, 479–97.

Eemeren, Frans H. van, Rob Grootendorst, Sally Jackson, and Scott Jacobs. "Argumentation." Pages 208–29 in *Discourse as Structure and Process. Discourse Studies.* Edited by Teun A. van Dijk. Vol. I. London: Sage, 1997.

Eemeren, Frans H. van, Rob Grootendorst, Sally Jackson, and Scott Jacobs. *Reconstructing Argumentative Discourse.* Tuscaloosa: University of Alabama Press, 1993.

Eemeren, Frans H. van, Bert Meuffels, and Mariël Verburg. "The (Un)reasonableness of ad hominem Fallacies." *Language and Social Psychology 19* (2000): 416–35.

Eemeren, Frans H. van, Rob Grootendorst, J. Anthony Blair, and Charles A. Willard, eds. *Argumentation Illuminated.* Amsterdam: Sic Sat/ISSA, 1992.

Ehrman, Bart. *The New Testament: A Historical Introduction to the Early Christian Writings.* Oxford: Oxford University Press, 1997.

Elliott, James K., ed. *The Apocryphal New Testament: A Collection of Apocryphal Christian Literature in an English Translation based on M. R. James.* Oxford: Oxford University Press, 1993.

Elliott, John H. "Matthew 20:1–15: A Parable of Invidious Comparison and Evil Eye Accusation." *BTB* 22 (1992): 52–65.

Elliott, John H. "Review of Thurén, Argument and Theology in 1 Peter." *CBQ* 59 (1997): 597–98.

Elliott, John H. "Patronage and Clientage." Pages 144–56 in *The Social Sciences and New Testament Interpretation.* Edited by Richard Rohrbaugh. Peabody, Mass.: Hendrickson, 1996.

Ellul, Jacques. *Apocalypse: The Book of Revelation.* Originally published as *L'apocalypse, architecture en mouvement.* Translated by G. W. Shreiner. New York: Seabury Press, 1977.

Engberg-Pedersen, Troels. "Stoicism in Philippians." Pages 256–90 in *Paul in His Hellenistic Context.* Edited by Troels Engberg-Pedersen. Minneapolis: Fortress, 1995.

Eriksson, Anders. "Contrary Arguments in Paul." In *Rhetorical Criticism and the Bible: Essays from the 1998 Florence Conference.* Edited by Stanley E. Porter and Dennis Stamps. JSNTSup 195; Sheffield: Sheffield Academic Press, forthcoming.

Eriksson, Anders. "Special Topics in 1 Corinthians 8–10." Pages 272–301 in *The Rhetorical Interpretation of Scripture: Essays from the 1996 Malibu Conference.* Edited by Stanley E. Porter and Dennis Stamps. JSNTSup 180. Sheffield: Sheffield Academic Press, 1999.

Eriksson, Anders. *Traditions as Rhetorical Proof: Pauline Argumentation in 1 Corinthians.* ConBNT 29. Stockholm: Almqvist & Wiksell International, 1998.

Eriksson, Anders. "'Women Tongue Speakers, Be Silent': A Reconstruction Through Paul's Rhetoric." *BibInt* 6:1 (1998): 80–104.

Evans, Donald D. *The Logic of Self-Involvement.* London: SCM Press, 1963.

Fee, Gordon. *The First Epistle to the Corinthians.* NICNT. Grand Rapids: Eerdmans, 1987.

Fee, Gordon D. *Paul's Letter to the Philippians.* NICNT. Grand Rapids: Eerdmans, 1995.

Filson, Floyd V. *"Yesterday": A Study of Hebrews in the Light of Chapter 13.* London: SCM Press, 1967.

Fiore, Benjamin. *The Function of Personal Example in the Socratic and Pastoral Epistles.* Rome: Biblical Institute Press, 1986.

Fiore, Benjamin. "Root Metaphors in Paul — Pauline Comings and Goings: The Travel Image." *Proceedings (Eastern Great Lakes Biblical Society)* 11 (1991): 174–84.

Fischer, Karl Martin. *Tendenz und Absicht des Epheserbriefes*. FRLANT 111. Göttingen: Vandenhoeck & Ruprecht, 1973.
Fisher, Alec. "Suppositions in Argumentation." *Argumentation 3* (1989): 4: 401–13.
Fitzgerald, John T. *Cracks in an Earthen Vessel: An Examination of the Catalogues of Hardship in the Corinthian Correspondence*. SBLDS 99. Atlanta: Scholars Press, 1988.
Fitzmyer, Joseph. "Qumran and the Interpolated Paragraph in 2 Corinthian 6:14–7:1." *CBQ* 23 (1961): 271–80.
Fitzmyer, Joseph A. *Romans*. AB 33. New York: Doubleday, 1993.
Fohrer, Georg. *Introduction to the Old Testament*. Nashville: Abingdon, 1968.
Fokkelman, J. P. *Narrative Art and Poetry in the Books of Samuel: A Full Interpretation Based on Stylistic and Structural Analysis*. 4 vols. Assen: Van Gorcum, 1981, 1986, 1990, 1993.
Forbes, Christopher. "Comparison, Self-Praise and Irony: Paul's Boasting and the Conventions of Hellenistic Rhetoric." *NTS* 32 (1986): 1–30.
Forbes, Clarence. "The Education and Training of Slaves in Antiquity." *TAPA* 86 (1955): 321–60.
Forbes, John. *Analytical Commentary on the Epistle to the Romans Tracing the Train of Thought by the Aid of Parallelism*. Edinburgh: T. & T. Clark, 1868.
Fortenbaugh, William W. "Quintilian 6.2.8–9: *Ethos* and *Pathos* and the Ancient Tradition." Pages 183–91 in *Peripatetic Rhetoric after Aristotle*. Edited by W. W. Fortenbaugh and D. C. Mirhady. Rutgers University Studies in the Classical Humanities 6. New Brunswick, N.J.: Transaction Publishers, 1994.
Fortna, Robert. *The Fourth Gospel and Its Predecessor: From Narrative Source to Present Gospel*. Studies in the New Testament and Its World. Edinburgh: Clark; Philadelphia: Fortress, 1989.
Fowl, Stephen. *The Story of Christ in the Ethics of Paul: An Analysis of the Function of the Hymnic Material in the Pauline Corpus*. JSNTSup 36. Sheffield: Sheffield Academic Press, 1990.
Frankfurter, David. "Early Christian Apocalypticism: Literature and Social World." Pages 415–53 in *The Encyclopedia of Apocalypticism*, vol. 1. Edited by John J. Collins. New York: Continuum, 1998.
Freed, Edwin. *The New Testament: A Critical Introduction*. Belmont, Calif.: Wadsworth Publishing Co., 1991.
Freeman, J. B. "Relevance, Warrants, Backing, Inductive Support." *Argumentation* 6 (1992): 219–35.
Freeman, James B. *Dialectics and the Macrostructure of Arguments*. Berlin: Walter de Gruyter; Dordrecht: Foris, 1991.
Friedman, Thomas L. *From Beirut to Jerusalem*. New York: Doubleday, 1989.
Friedrich, Gerhard. "Ἁμαρτία οὐκ ἐλλογεῖται Röm. 5,13." Pages 123–31 in *Auf das Wort kommt es an: Gesammelte Aufsätze*. Göttingen: Vandenhoeck & Ruprecht, 1978.
Frye, Northrop. *The Secular Scripture: A Study of the Structure of Romance*. Cambridge, Mass.: Harvard University Press, 1976.
Furnish, Victor P. *II Corinthians*. AB 32A. Garden City, N.Y.: Doubleday & Co., 1985.
Garland, D. E. "The Composition and Unity of Philippians: Some Neglected Literary Factors." *NovT* 27 (1985): 141–73.

Garrett, Mary M. "The 'Mo-Tzu' and the 'Lu-Shih Ch'un-Ch'iu': A Case Study of Classical Chinese Theory and Practice of Argument." Dissertation, University of California Berkeley, 1983.

Garrett, Mary M. "*Pathos* Reconsidered from the Perspective of Classical Chinese Rhetorical Theories." *QJS* 79 (1993): 19–39.

Geoffrion, Timothy C. *The Rhetorical Purpose and the Political and Military Character of Philippians: A Call to Stand Firm.* Lewiston, N.Y.: Mellon, 1993.

Georgi, Dieter. *The Opponents of Paul in Second Corinthians.* Philadelphia: Fortress Press, 1986.

Georgi, Dieter. *Theocracy in Paul's Praxis and Theology.* Minneapolis: Fortress, 1991.

Gilmore, David D., ed. *Honor and Shame and the Unity of the Mediterranean.* Washington, D.C.: American Anthropological Association Special Publication No. 22, 1987.

Gitay, Yehoshua. "A Designed Anti-Rhetorical Speech: Ezra and the Question of Mixed Marriage." *JNSL* 23/2 (1997): 57–68.

Gitay, Yehoshua. "The Projection of the Prophet: A Rhetorical Presentation of the Prophet Jeremiah." Pages 41–55 in *Prophecy and Prophets: The Diversity of Contemporary Issues In Scholarship.* Edited by Yehoshua Gitay. Atlanta: Scholars Press/SBL Semeia Studies, 1997.

Gitay, Yehoshua. *Prophecy and Persuasion.* Bonn: Linguistica Biblica, 1981.

Gitay, Yehoshua, ed. *Prophecy and Prophets: The Diversity of Contemporary Issues in Scholarship.* Atlanta: Scholars Press/SBL Semeia Studies, 1997.

Gitay, Yehoshua. "The Realm of Prophetic Rhetoric." Pages 218–29 in *Rhetoric, Scripture and Theology: Essays from the 1994 Pretoria Conference.* Edited by Stanley E. Porter and Thomas H. Olbricht. JSNTSup 131. Sheffield: Sheffield Academic Press, 1996.

Gitay, Yehoshua. "Rhetorical Criticism and the Prophetic Discourse." Pages 13–24 in *Persuasive Artistry.* Edited by D. F. Watson. Sheffield: JSOT Press, 1991.

Given, Mark. "True Rhetoric: Ambiguity, Cunning, and Deception in Pauline Discourse." *SBLSP*, 1997 (*http://courses.smsu.edu/mdg421f/True.htm*).

Gomperz, Heinrich. *Sophistik und Rhetorik.* Stuttgart: Teubner, 1965.

Goodspeed, Edgar J. *The Key to Ephesians.* Chicago: University of Chicago Press, 1956.

Göttert, Karl-Heinz. *Argumentation. Grundzüge ihrer Theorie im Bereich theoretischen Wissens und praktischen Handelns.* Tübingen: Niemeyer, 1978.

Govier, Trudy. *A Practical Study of Argument.* Belmont, Calif.: Wadsworth, 1985.

Govier, Trudy. *Problems in Argument Analysis and Evaluation.* Dordrecht: Foris, 1987.

Gray, John. *I and II Kings: A Commentary.* OTL. Philadelphia: Westminster, 1963.

Green, Joel B. "Discourse Analysis and the New Testament." Pages 175–96 in *Hearing the New Testament.* Edited by Joel B. Green. Grand Rapids: Eerdmans, 1995.

Green, Joel B., ed. *Between Two Horizons: Spanning New Testament Studies and Systematic Theology.* Grand Rapids: Eerdmans, 2000.

Green, Joel B., ed. *Hearing the New Testament.* Grand Rapids: Eerdmans, 1995.

Greenwood, D. "The Lord is the Spirit: Some Considerations of 2 Corinthians 3:17." *CBQ* 34/4 (1972): 467–72.

Grelot, P. "Note sur 2 Corinthiens 3:14." *NTS* 33/1 (1987): 135–44.

Gressmann, Hugo. *Die Schriften des Alten Testaments in Auswahl, II,* 2d edition. Göttingen: Vandenhoeck & Ruprecht, 1921.

Groarke, Leo. "In Defense of Deductivism: Replying to Govier." Pages 113–21 in *Argumentation Illuminated*. Edited by Frans H. van Eemeren et al. Amsterdam: Sic Sat/ISSA, 1992.

Gruen, Erich S. *Heritage and Hellenism: The Reinvention of Jewish Tradition*. Hellenistic Culture and Society 30. Berkeley: University of California Press, 1998.

Gunn, David M., and Dana Nolan Fewell. *Narrative in the Hebrew Bible*. Oxford: Oxford University Press, 1993.

Guthrie, George H. *The Structure of Hebrews: A Text-Linguistic Analysis*. Leiden: E. J. Brill, 1994.

Guthrie, William K. C. *The Sophists*. Cambridge: Cambridge University Press, 1971.

Haenchen, Ernst. *John: A Commentary on the Gospel of John*. 2 vols. Philadelphia: Fortress, 1984.

Hafemann, Scott. "'Self-Commendation' and Apostolic Legitimacy in 2 Corinthians: A Pauline Dialectic?" *NTS* 36/1 (1990): 66–88.

Hamblin, Charles L. *Fallacies*. London: Methuen, 1970.

Hansen, Hans V., and Robert C. Pinto, eds. *Fallacies: Classical and Contemporary Readings*. University Park, Pa.: Pennsylvania State University Press, 1995.

Hanson, Anthony T. "The Midrash in 2 Corinthians 3: A Reconsideration." *JSNT* 9 (1980): 2–28.

Harris, Stephen. *The New Testament: A Student's Introduction*. 2d ed. Mountain View, Calif.: Mayfield Publishing Co., 1995.

Harris, William V. *Ancient Literacy*. Cambridge, Mass.: Harvard University Press, 1989.

Harvey, Anthony Ernest. *Jesus on Trial: A Study in the Fourth Gospel*. London: SPCK, 1976.

Harvey, John D. *Listening to the Text: Oral Patterning in Paul's Letters*. Grand Rapids: Baker, 1998.

Hauser, Alan J. "Judges 5: Parataxis in Hebrew Poetry." *JBL* 99 (1980): 23–41.

Hawking, Stephen W. *A Brief History of Time: From the Big Bang to Black Holes*. Toronto: Bantam, 1988.

Hay, David M. *Colossians*. ANTC. Nashville: Abingdon, 2000.

Hays, Richard B. "Three Dramatic Roles: The Law in Romans 3–4." Pages 151–64 in *Paul and the Mosaic Law*. Edited by James D. G. Dunn. Tübingen: J. C. B. Mohr, 1995.

Hays, Richard B. *The Faith of Jesus Christ: An Investigation of the Narrative Substructure of Galatians 3:1–4:11*. SBLDS 56. Chico, Calif.: Scholars Press, 1983.

Heath, Malcolm. *Hermogenes On Issues; Strategies of Argument in Later Greek Rhetoric*. Oxford: Clarendon Press, 1995.

Hellholm, David. "Enthymemic Argumentation in Paul: The Case of Romans 6." Pages 119–79 in *Paul and His Hellenistic Context*. Edited by T. Engberg-Pedersen. Minneapolis: Fortress, 1995.

Hengel, Martin. *Atonement: The Origins of the Doctrine in the New Testament*. Philadelphia: Fortress, 1981.

Hennecke, Edgar. *New Testament Apocrypha*. Edited by W. Schneemelcher. Translated and edited by R. McL. Wilson. 2 vols. Philadelphia: Westminster, 1963 and 1965.

Hennecke, Edgar, Wilhelm Schneemelcher, and R. McL. Wilson. *New Testament Apocrypha*. Vol. 2. Rev. ed. Louisville, Ky.: Westminster/John Knox Press, 1992.

Hester (Amador), James D. "Re-discovering and Re-inventing Rhetoric." *Scriptura* 50 (1994): 1–22.
Hickling, C. J. A. "The Sequence of Thought in 2 Corinthians, Chapter 3." *NTS* 21/3 (1974): 380–95.
Hilhorst, Ton. "Erotic Elements in the Shepherd of Hermas." Pages 193–204 in *Groningen Colloquia on the Novel*. Volume IX. Edited by H. Hofmann and M. Zimmermann. Groningen: Forsten, 1998.
Himmelfarb, Martha. *Ascent to Heaven in Jewish and Christian Apocalypses*. Oxford: Oxford University Press, 1993.
Himmelfarb, Martha. *Tours of Hell: An Apocalyptic Form in Jewish and Christian Literature*. Philadelphia: University of Pennsylvania Press, 1983.
Hock, Ronald F. "General Introduction to Volume I." Pages 1–60 in *The Chreia in Ancient Rhetoric*. Vol. I. *The Progymnasmata*. Edited by R. F. Hock and E. N. O'Neil. Texts and Translations 27. Atlanta: Scholars, 1986.
Hock, Ronald F., and Edward N. O'Neil, eds. *The Chreia in Ancient Rhetoric*. Vol. 1: *The Progymnasmata*. SBLTT 24. Greco-Roman Religion Series 9. Atlanta: Scholars Press, 1986.
Hock, Ronald F. *The Social Context of Paul's Ministry*. Philadelphia: Fortress Press, 1980.
Hock, Ronald F. "The Rhetoric of Romance." Pages 445–65 in *Handbook of Classical Rhetoric in the Hellenistic Period, 330 B.C.–A.D. 400*. Edited by Stanley E. Porter. Leiden: Brill, 1997.
Holzberg, Niklas. *The Ancient Novel: An Introduction*. London: Routledge, 1995.
Hooker, Mona D. *"PISTIS CHRISTOU."* *NTS* 35 (1989): 321–42.
Horsfall, Nicholas. "Rome Without Spectacles." *Greece and Rome* 42 (1995): 49–56.
Horsfall, Nicholas. "Statistics or State of Mind?" *Journal of Roman Archeology* Suppl. 3: Literacy in the Roman World. Ann Arbor, Mich.: Department of Classical Studies, University of Michigan, 1991: 59–76.
Horsley, Richard A., with John S. Hanson. *Bandits, Prophets, and Messiahs: Popular Movements in the Time of Jesus*. Reprint ed.; Harrisburg, Pa.: Trinity Press International, 1995 [1985].
Horsley, Richard A., ed. *Paul and Empire: Religion and Power in Roman Imperial Society*. Harrisburg, Pa.: Trinity Press International, 1997.
Hübner, Hans. *An Philemon, An die Kolosser, An die Epheser*. HNT 12. Tübingen: J. C. B. Mohr (Siebeck), 1997.
Hurd, John C. *The Origin of 1 Corinthians*. Macon: Mercer, 1983.
Hyldahl, Niels. "Die Frage nach der literarischen Einheit des zweiten Korintherbriefs." *ZNW* 64/3-4 (1973): 289–306.
Japhet, Sara. *I & II Chronicles: A Commentary*. London: SCM, 1993.
Jaquette, James L. "A Not-So-Noble Death: Figured Speech, Friendship and Suicide in Philippians 1:21–26." *Neot* 28 (1994): 177–92.
Jeal, Roy R. *Integrating Theology and Ethics in Ephesians: The Ethos of Communication*. Lewiston: Mellen, 2000.
Jensen, J. Vernon. "Values and Practices in Asian Argumentation." *Argumentation and Advocacy* 28 (1992): 153–166.
Johanson, Bruce C. *To All the Brethren: A Text-Linguistic and Rhetorical Approach*. ConBNTS 16; Uppsala: Almqvist & Wiksell, 1987.

Johnson, E. Elizabeth. *She Who Is: The Mystery of God in Feminist Theological Discourse*. New York: Crossroad, 1992.
Johnson, E. Elizabeth. *The Function of Apocalyptic and Wisdom Traditions in Romans 9–11*. SBLDS 109. Atlanta: Scholars Press, 1989.
Johnson, Luke T. "The New Testament's Anti-Jewish Slander and the Conventions of Ancient Polemic." *JBL* 108 (1989): 419–41.
Johnson, Ralph H. "The Impact of the Continuum Hypothesis on Theories of Evaluation." Pages 148–58 in *Argumentation Illuminated*. Edited by Frans H. van Eemeren et al. Amsterdam: Sic Sat/ISSA, 1992.
Johnson, Ralph H., and J. Anthony Blair. *Logical Self-defense*. 1st ed. Toronto: McGraw-Hill Ryerson, 1977. (3rd ed. 1993).
Johnstone, William. "Guilt and Atonement: The Theme of 1 and 2 Chronicles." Pages 113–38 in *A Word in Season*. Edited by J. D. Martin and P. R. Davies. JSOTSup 42. Sheffield: JSOT Press, 1986.
Jolivet, Ira J., Jr. "The Lukan Account of Paul's Conversion and Hermagorean Stasis Theory." Pages 210–220 in *The Rhetorical Interpretation of Scripture: Essays from the 1996 Malibu Conference*. Edited by Stanley E. Porter and Dennis L. Stamps. JSNTSup 180. Sheffield: Academic Press, 1999.
Jost, Walter, and Wendy Olmstead, eds. *Rhetorical Invention and Religious Inquiry*. New Haven: Yale University Press, 2000.
Judge, Edwin A. "Paul's Boasting in Relation to Contemporary Professional Practice." *ABR* 10 (1968): 37–50.
Judge, Edwin A. "St Paul and Classical Society." *JAC* 15 (1972): 19–36.
Kallendorf, Craig. *Epistle of St. Paul to the Romans*. Bryn Mawr Greek Commentaries. Bryn Mawr, Pa.: Thomas Library, Bryn Mawr College, 1991.
Käsemann, Ernst. *The Wandering People of God: An Investigation of the Letter to the Hebrews*. Minneapolis: Augsburg, 1984.
Keck, Leander E. "Matthew and the Spirit." Pages 145–55 in *The Social World of the First Christians*. Edited by L. Michael White and O. Larry Yarbrough. Philadelphia: Fortress, 1995.
Kennedy, George A. *Aristotle On Rhetoric: A Theory of Civic Discourse*. New York: Oxford University Press, 1991.
Kennedy, George A. *The Art of Persuasion in Greece*. Princeton, N.J.: Princeton University Press, 1963.
Kennedy, George A. *The Art of Rhetoric in the Roman World, 300 B.C.–A.D. 300*. Princeton, N.J.: Princeton University Press, 1972.
Kennedy, George A. "Historical Survey of Rhetoric." Pages 3–50 in *Handbook of Classical Rhetoric in the Hellenistic Period (330 B.C.–A.D. 400)*. Edited by Stanley E. Porter. Leiden: Brill 1997.
Kennedy, George A. *A New History of Classical Rhetoric*. Princeton, N.J.: Princeton University Press, 1994.
Kennedy, George A. *New Testament Interpretation through Rhetorical Criticism*. Studies in Religion. Chapel Hill: University of North Carolina Press, 1984.
Kennedy, George A. *Progymnasmata: Greek Textbooks of Prose Composition Introductory to the Study of Rhetoric: Writings by or Attributed to Theon, Hermogenes, Aphthonius, Nicolaus, Together with an Anonymous Prolegomenon to Aphthonius, Selections from the Commentary Attributed to John of Sardis, and Fragments of the Progymnasmata*

of Sopatros Translated into English, with Introductions and Notes. Fort Collins, Colo.: Chez l'auteur, 1999.

Kerényi, Karl. *Die griechisch-orientalische Romanliteratur in religionsgeschichtlicher Beleuchtung: Ein Versuch mit Nachbetrachtungen.* 3d ed. Darmstadt: Wissenschaftliche Buchgesellschaft, 1973.

Kerferd, George B. *The Sophistic Movement.* Cambridge: Cambridge University Press, 1981.

Kern, Philip H. *Rhetoric and Galatians: Assessing an Approach to Paul's Epistle.* SNTSMS 101. Cambridge: Cambridge University Press, 1998

Kienpointner, Manfred. *Alltagslogik.* Stuttgart: Frommann-Holzboog, 1992.

Kinneavy, James L. *Greek Rhetorical Origins of Christian Faith.* New York: Oxford, 1987.

Kirby, John L. *Ephesians, Baptism and Pentecost.* Montreal: McGill University Press, 1968.

Kitchen, Martin. *Ephesians.* London/New York: Routledge, 1994.

Kittredge, Cynthia Briggs. *Community and Authority: The Rhetoric of Obedience in the Pauline Tradition.* Harrisburg, Pa.: Trinity Press International, 1998.

Kloppenborg, John S. *Q Parallels.* Sonoma, Calif.: Polebridge, 1988.

Koch, Dieter-Alex. *Die Schrift als Zeuge des Evangeliums.* BHT 69. Tübingen: Mohr/Siebeck, 1986.

Koenig, John. *New Testament Hospitality: Partnership with Strangers as Promise and Mission.* Philadelphia: Fortress, 1985.

Koester, Helmut. *Introduction to the New Testament: History and Literature of Early Christianity.* Vol. 2. Berlin: Walter de Gruyter, 1987.

Kopperschmidt, Josef. *Methodik der Argumentationsanalyse.* Stuttgart-Bad Cannstatt: Frommann-Holzboog, 1989.

Koskenniemi, Heikki. *Studien zur Idee und Phraseologie des griechischen Briefes bis 400 n. Chr.* Helsinki: Suomalainen Tiedeakatemia, 1956.

Kraus, Manfred. "Enthymem." Pages 1197–1222 in *Historisches Wörterbuch der Rhetorik.* Vol. 2. Edited by Gert Ueding. Tübingen: Niemeyer, 1994.

Krentz, Edgar R. "Military Language and Metaphors in Philippians." Pages 105–27 in *Origins and Method: Towards a New Understanding of Judaism and Christianity: Essays in Honour of John C. Hurd.* Edited by Bradley H. McLean. JSNTSup 86. Sheffield: JSOT, 1993.

Kurianal, James. *Jesus Our High Priest: Psalm 110,4 as the Substructure of Heb 5,1–7,28.* Frankfurt: Peter Lang, 1999.

Lähnemann, Johannes. *Der Kolosserbrief: Komposition, Situation, und Argumentation.* Gütersloh: Gütersloher Verlagshaus (Gerd Mohn), 1971.

Lake, Kirsopp, ed. *The Apostolic Fathers.* 2 vols. Cambridge, Mass.: Harvard University Press, 1912–13.

Lanham, Richard A. *A Handbook of Rhetorical Terms.* 2d ed. Berkeley: University of California Press, 1991.

Lanham, Richard A. *A Handlist of Rhetorical Terms.* Berkeley: University of California Press, 1968.

Lanigan, Richard L. "From Enthymeme to Abduction: The Classical Law of Logic and the Postmodern Rule of Rhetoric." Pages 49–70 in *Recovering Pragmatisms's Voice: The Classical Tradition, Rorty, and the Philosophy of Communication.* Edited by Lenore Langsdorf and Andrew R. Smith. Albany, N.Y.: SUNY Press, 1995.

Lausberg, Heinrich. *Handbuch der literarischen Rhetorik: Eine Grundlegung der Literaturwissenschaft*, 2d ed. Munich: Max Hueber, 1973.
Lausberg, Heinrich. *Handbook of Literary Rhetoric: A Foundation for Literary Study*. Edited by David E. Orton, R. Dean Anderson. Translated by Matthew T. Bliss, Annemiek Jansen, and David E. Orton. Leiden: E. J. Brill, 1998.
Leeman, A. D. and A. C. Braet. *Klassieke retorica: haar inhoud, functie en betekenis*. Groningen: Wolters-Noordhoff/Forsten, 1987.
Leroux, Neil R. "Luther's Use of Doublets." *Rhetoric Society Quarterly* (Summer 2000): 35–54.
Lesses, Glen. "Virtue and the Goods of Fortune in Stoic Moral Theory." *Oxford Studies in Ancient Philosophy* 7 (1989): 95–128.
Lewis, Naphtali. *The Compulsory Public Services of Roman Egypt*. 2d ed. Florence: Edizioni Gonnelli, 1997.
Lewis, Naphtali. *Life in Egypt Under Roman Rule*. Oxford: Clarendon Press, 1983.
Lewis, Naphtali. "Literati in the Service of Roman Emperors: Politics Before Culture." In *Coins, Culture, and History in the Ancient World: Numismatic and Other Studies in Honor of Bluma L. Trell*. Edited by Lionel Casson and Martin Price. Detroit: Wayne State University Press, 1981.
Lincoln, Andrew T. *Ephesians*. WBC 42. Dallas: Word Books, 1990.
Lincoln, Andrew T. *Paradise Now and Not Yet: Studies in the Role of the Heavenly Dimension in Paul's Thought with Special Reference to His Eschatology*. Cambridge: Cambridge University Press, 1981.
Lindars, Barnabas. *The Theology of the Letter to the Hebrews*. Cambridge: Cambridge University Press, 1991.
Lindemann, Andreas. "Bemerkungen zu den Addressaten und zum Anlaß des Epheserbriefes." *ZNW* 67 (1976): 235–51.
Lindemann, Andreas. *Der Kolosserbrief*. ZBK. Zürich: Theologischer Verlag, 1983.
Lindsay, Hugh. "Suetonius as *ab epistulis* to Hadrian and the Early History of Imperial Correspondence." *Historia* 43, no. 4 (1994): 454–68.
Lloyd, Genevieve. *The Man of Reason: "Male" and "Female" in Western Philosophy*. 2d ed. London: Routledge, 1993.
Loader, William R. G. *Sohn und Hoherpriester: Eine traditionsgeschichtliche Untersuchung zur Christologie des Hebräerbriefes*. WMANT 53. Neukirchen: Neukirchener Verlag, 1981.
Lohse, Eduard. *Colossians and Philemon*. Edited by H. Koester. Translated by W. R. Poehlmann and R. J. Karris. Hermeneia. Philadelphia: Fortress, 1971.
Longenecker, Richard N. *Galatians*. WBC 41. Dallas: Word Books, 1990.
Lotman, J. M. *The Structure of the Artistic Text*. Ann Arbor: University of Michigan Press, 1977.
Lüdemann, Gert. *Paulus, der Heidenapostel*, Bd. II: *Antipaulinismus im frühen Christentum*. FRLANT 130. Göttingen: Vandenhoeck & Ruprecht, 1983.
Lund, Nils W. *Chiasmus in the New Testament: A Study in Formgeschichte*. Chapel Hill: University of North Carolina Press, 1942. Reprint ed. *Chiasmus in the New Testament: A Study in the Form and Function of Chiastic Structures*. Peabody, Mass.: Hendrickson, 1992.

    item Lunsford, Andrea, and Lisa Ede. "Representing Audience: 'Successful' Discourse and Disciplinary Critique. *CCC* 47 (1996):167–79.

Luschnat, Otto. "Die Jungfrauenszene in der Arkadienvision des Hermas." *Theologia Viatorum* 12 (1973–74): 53–70.
Luther, Martin. *A Commentary on St. Paul's Epistle to the Galatians*. Translated by P. S. Watson. London: James Clark, 1953.
Luz, Ulrich. "The Disciples in the Gospel according to Matthew." Pages 98–128 in *The Interpretation of Matthew*. Edited by Graham Stanton. Philadelphia: Fortress; London: SPCK, 1983.
Mack, Burton. *Rhetoric and the New Testament*. GBS. Minneapolis: Fortress, 1990.
Mack, Burton L. *Who Wrote the New Testament?* San Francisco: Harper, 1995.
Mack, Burton L., and Vernon K. Robbins. *Patterns of Persuasion in the Gospels*. Sonoma, Calif.: Polebridge, 1989.
Madden, Edward H. "The Enthymeme: Crossroads of Logic, Rhetoric, and Metaphysics." *Philosophical Review* 61 (1952): 368–76.
Malherbe, Abraham J. "Ancient Epistolary Theorists." *Ohio Journal of Religious Studies* 5 (1977): 3–77. Reprint ed. Atlanta: Scholars Press, 1988.
Malherbe, Abraham J. *Moral Exhortation: A Greco-Roman Sourcebook*. LEC 4. Philadelphia: Westminster Press, 1986.
Malherbe, Abraham J. *Paul and the Thessalonians: The Philosophic Tradition of Pastoral Care*. Philadelphia: Fortress, 1987.
Malina, Bruce J. *The New Testament World: Insights from Cultural Anthropology*. Rev. ed. Louisville, Ky.: Westminster/John Knox Press, 1993.
Malina, Bruce J., and Jerome Neyrey. "Honor and Shame in Luke-Acts: Pivotal Values of the Mediterranean World." Pages 25–65 in *The Social World of Luke-Acts: Models for Interpretation*. Edited by J. Neyrey. Peabody, Mass.: Hendrickson, 1991.
Malina, Bruce J., and Jerome Neyrey. *Portraits of Paul: An Archaeology of Ancient Personality*. Louisville: Westminster John Knox, 1996.
Malina, Bruce J., and Richard L. Rohrbaugh. *Social-Science Commentary on the Synoptic Gospels*. Minneapolis: Fortress, 1992.
Marshall, John W. "Paul's Ethical Appeal in Philippians." Pages 357–74 in *Rhetoric and the New Testament: Essays from the 1992 Heidelberg Conference*. Edited by Stanley E. Porter and Thomas H. Olbricht. JSNTSup 90. Sheffield: Sheffield Academic Press, 1993.
Martin, Ralph P. "An Epistle in Search of a Life-Setting." *ExpT* 79 (1968): 296–302.
Martyn, J. Louis. *Galatians: A New Translation with Introduction and Commentary*. Anchor Bible 33A. New York: Doubleday, 1997.
Matthews, Victor H., and Don C. Benjamin, eds. *Honor and Shame in the World of the Bible*. Semeia 68. Atlanta: Scholars Press, 1996.
McBurney, James H. "The Place of the Enthymeme in Rhetorical Theory." Pages 117–40 in *Aristotle: The Classical Heritage of Rhetoric*. Edited by K. V. Erickson. Metuchen, N.J.: The Scarecrow Press, 1974.
McCant, Jerry W. "Second Corinthians as Parodic Apologia." Paper presented at *Rhetorics and Hermeneutics: Conference in Honor of Wilhelm Wuellner* (Claremont, Calif.: March 2000).
McCant, Jerry W. *2 Corinthians*. Readings: A New Biblical Commentary. Sheffield: Sheffield Academic Press, 1999.
McClelland, Scott E. " 'Super-Apostles, Servants of Christ, Servants of Satan': A Response." *JSNT* 14 (1982): 82–87.

Medhurst, Martin J. "Rhetorical Dimensions in Biblical Criticism: Beyond Style and Genre." *QJS* 77 (1991): 214–26.

Meeks, Wayne A. "Review of Hans-Dieter Betz, *Galatians: A Commentary on Paul's Letter to the Churches in Galatia.*" *JBL* 100 (1981): 304–307.

Meeks, Wayne A. "'To Walk Worthily of the Lord': Moral Formation in the Pauline School Exemplified by the Letter to Colossians." Pages 37–58 in *Hermes and Athens: Biblical Exegesis and Philosophical Theology*. Edited by Eleonore Stump and Thomas P. Flint. University of Notre Dame Studies in the Philosophy of Religion 7. Notre Dame: University of Notre Dame Press, 1993.

Meier, John P. "Structure and Theology in Heb 1,1–14." *Biblica* 66 (1985): 504–33.

Merkelbach, Reinhold. *Roman und Mysterium in der Antike*. Munich: C. H. Beck, 1962.

Meyer, Ben F. "Did Paul's View of the Resurrection of the Dead Undergo Development?" *TS* 47 (1986): 363–82.

Meynet, Roland. *L'analyse rhétorique*. Paris: Les Éditions du Cerf, 1989. Italian ed. *L'analisi retorica*. Biblioteca biblica 8. Brescia: Queriniana, 1992. English ed. *Rhetorical Analysis: An Introduction to Biblical Rhetoric*. JSOTSup 256. Sheffield: Sheffield Academic Press, 1998.

Meynet, Roland. "Le cantique de Moïse et le cantique de l'Agneau (Ap 15 et Ex 15)," *Gregorianum* 73 (1992): 19–55.

Meynet, Roland. *L'Évangile selon saint Luc*. Rhétorique biblique 1. Paris: Les Éditions du Cerf, 1988, I-II. Italian ed. *Il vangelo secondo Luca*. Retorica biblica 1. Rome: Edizioni Dehoniane, 1994.

Meynet, Roland. *Jésus passe: Testament, Jugement, Exécution et Résurrection du Seigneur Jésus dans les évangiles synoptiques*. Rhétorique biblique 3. Rome and Paris; PUG-Editrice and Les Éditions du Cerf, 1999.

Meynet, Roland. *Quelle est donc cette Parole? Lecture "rhétorique" de l'évangile de Luc (1–9 et 22–24)*. LeDiv 99 A.B. Paris: Les Éditions du Cerf, 1979.

Meynet, Roland, Pouzet Louis, Farouki Nayla, and Sinno Ahyaf, *Ṭarīqat al-taḥlīl al-balāġī wa-l-tafsīr. Taḥlīlāt nuṣūṣ min al-kitāb al-muqaddas wa min al-Ḥadīṯ al-nabawī* [*Méthode rhétorique et Herméneutique: Analyse de textes de la Bible et de la Tradition musulmane*] Beyrouth: Dar el-Machreq, 1993. French ed. *Rhétorique sémitique: Textes de la Bible et de la Tradition musulmane*. Patrimoines. Religions du Livre. Paris: Les Éditions du Cerf, 1998.

Mill, John Stuart. *A System of Logic Book* V. Vol. VIII in *Collected Works*. Toronto: University of Toronto Press, 1974.

Millar, Fergus. *The Emperor in the Roman World*. Ithaca, N.Y.: Cornell University Press, 1977.

Mitchell, Margaret M. *Paul and the Rhetoric of Reconciliation: An Exegetical Investigation of the Language and Composition of 1 Corinthians*. Louisville: Westminster/John Knox, 1993.

Mitton, C. Leslie. *The Epistle to the Ephesians: Its Authorship, Origin and Purpose*. Oxford: Clarendon Press, 1951.

Moffatt, James. *The Epistle to the Hebrews*. New York: Harper & Brothers, 1933.

Moloney, Francis J. *John*. Sacra Pagina 4. Collegeville, Minn.: Liturgical Press, 1998.

Moloney, Francis J. *Signs and Shadows: Reading John 5–12*. Minneapolis: Fortress, 1996.

Montgomery, James A. *A Critical and Exegetical Commentary on the Books of Kings*. ICC. Edinburgh: T. & T. Clark, 1967.

Moores, John D. *Wrestling with Rationality in Paul: Romans 1–8 in a New Perspective.* Cambridge: Cambridge University Press, 1995.

Mouat, Lawrence H. "An Approach to Rhetorical Criticism." Pages 161–77 in *The Rhetorical Idiom.* Edited by Donald C. Bryant. New York: Russel & Russel, 1966.

Moxnes, Halvor. "Honor and Shame." Pages 19–40 in *The Social Sciences and New Testament Interpretation.* Edited by Richard Rohrbaugh. Peabody, Mass.: Hendrickson, 1996.

Moxnes, Halvor. "Patron-Client Relations in the New Community." Pages 241–68 in *The Social World of Luke-Acts.* Edited by Jerome H. Neyrey. Peabody, Mass.: Hendrickson, 1991.

Murphy-O'Connor, Jerome. "Paul and Macedonia: The Connection Between 2 Corinthians 2:13 and 2:14." *JSNT* 25 (1985): 99–103.

Næss, Arne. *En del elementære logiske emner.* Oslo: Universitetsforlaget, 1947.

Næss, Arne. *Interpretation and Preciseness: A Contribution to the Theory of Communication,* Oslo: Det Norske videnskaps-akademi, 1953.

Neyrey, Jerome H. "Bewitched in Galatia: Paul and Cultural Anthropology." *CBQ* 50 (1988): 72–100.

Neyrey, Jerome H. "Jesus the Judge: Forensic Process in John 8,21–59." *Biblica* 68 (1987): 509–42.

Nissilä, Keijo. *Das Hohepriestermotiv im Hebräerbrief: Eine exegetische Untersuchung.* SFEG 33. Helsinki: Oy Liiton Kirjapaino, 1979.

Nølke, Henning. "Semantic Constraints on Argumentation: From Polyphonic Microstructure to Argumentative Macro-structure." Pages 189–200 in *Argumentation Illuminated.* Edited by Frans H. van Eemeren et al. Amsterdam: Sic Sat/ISSA, 1992.

O'Banion, J. D. "Narration and Argumentation: Quintilian on Narratio as the Heart of Rhetorical Thinking." *Rhetorica* (1987): 325–51.

O'Brien, Peter T. "The Gospel and Godly Models in Philippians." Pages 273–84 in *Worship, Theology, and Ministry in the Early Church: Essays in Honor of Ralph P. Martin* Edited by Michael J. Wilkins and Terence Paige. JSNTSup 87. Sheffield: JSOT Press, 1992.

O'Brien, Peter T. *Colossians, Philemon.* WBC. Waco, Tex.: Word, 1982.

O'Brien, Peter T. *The Letter to the Ephesians.* Pillar NT Commentary. Grand Rapids: Eerdmans; Leicester: Apollos, 1999.

O'Day, Gail R. *Revelation in the Fourth Gospel: Narrative Mode and Theological Claim.* Philadelphia: Fortress, 1986.

Olbricht, Thomas H. "An Aristotelian Rhetorical Analysis of 1 Thessalonians." Pages 216–36 in *Greeks, Romans, and Christians: Essays in Honor of Abraham J. Malherbe.* Edited by David L. Balch, Everett Ferguson, and Wayne A. Meeks. Minneapolis: Fortress Press, 1990.

Olbricht, Thomas H. "Classical Rhetorical Criticism and Historical Reconstructions: A Critique." Pages 109–24 in *The Rhetorical Interpretation of Scripture: Essays from the 1996 Malibu Conference.* Edited by Stanley E. Porter and Dennis L. Stamps. JSNTSup 180. Sheffield: Academic Press, 1999.

Olbricht, Thomas H. "Hebrews as Amplification." Pages 375–87 in *Rhetoric and the New Testament: Essays from the 1992 Heidelberg Conference.* Edited by Stanley E. Porter and Thomas H. Olbricht. JSNTSup 90. Sheffield: Sheffield Academic Press, 1993.

Olbricht, Thomas H. "The Stoicheia and the Rhetoric of Colossians: Then and Now." Pages 308–28 in *Rhetoric, Scripture and Theology: Essays from the 1994 Pretoria Conference*. Edited by Stanley E. Porter and Thomas H. Olbricht. JSNTSup 131. Sheffield: Sheffield Academic Press, 1996.

Oliver, Robert T. *Communication and Culture in Ancient India and China*. Syracuse: Syracuse University Press, 1971.

Olson, Stanley. "Epistolary Uses of Expressions of Self-Confidence." *JBL* 103/4 (1984): 585–97.

Ong, Walter. *Orality and Literacy: The Technologizing of the Word*. London: Methuen, 1982.

Osiek, Carolyn. "The Genre and Function of the Shepherd of Hermas." *Semeia* 36 (1986): 113–21.

Osiek, Carolyn. *Shepherd of Hermas: A Commentary*. Hermeneia. Minneapolis: Fortress Press, 1999.

Patai, Raphael. *The Arab Mind*. New York: Scribner, 1973.

Pearson, Lionel. *The Art of Demosthenes*. Chico, Calif.: Scholars, 1981.

Pedersen, Fritz Saaby. *Late Roman Professionalism*. Odense, Denmark: Odense University Press, 1976.

Perdue, Leo G. *Wisdom and Creation: The Theology of Wisdom Literature*. Nashville: Abingdon, 1992.

Perelman, Chaim, and Lucie Olbrechts-Tyteca. *Traité de l'argumentation: La nouvelle rhétorique*. 2d ed. Brussels: Université Libre, 1970.

Perelman, Chaim, and Lucie Olbrechts-Tyteca. *La nouvelle rhétorique: traité de l'argumentation*. Bruxelles: l'Université de Bruxelles, 1958. English trans.: *The New Rhetoric: A Treatise on Argumentation*. Translated by John Wilkinson and Purcell Weaver. Notre Dame, Ind.: University of Notre Dame Press, 1969, 1971.

Peristiany, J. G., ed. *Honour and Shame: The Values of Mediterranean Society*. Chicago: University of Chicago Press, 1966.

Perkins, Judith. *The Suffering Self: Pain and Narrative Representation in the Early Christian Era*. London: Routledge, 1995.

Perry, Benjamin E. *The Ancient Romances: A Literary-Historical Account of Their Origins*. Berkeley: University of California Press, 1967.

Pervo, Richard I. *Profit with Delight: The Literary Genre of the Acts of the Apostles*. Philadelphia: Fortress, 1987.

Peterson, David. *Hebrews and Perfection: An Examination of the Concept of Perfection in the "Epistle to the Hebrews."* Cambridge: Cambridge University Press, 1982.

Piscator, Johannes. *Commentarii in omnes libros Novi Testamenti*. 3d ed. Herborn, 1638.

Pitt-Rivers, Julian. *The Fate of Shechem or the Politics of Sex: Essays in the Anthropology of the Mediterranean*. Cambridge: Cambridge University Press, 1977.

Plank, K. A. *Paul and the Irony of Affliction*. Atlanta: Scholars Press, 1987.

Pokorny, P. *Colossians: A Commentary*. Translated by S. S. Schatzmann. Peabody, Mass.: Hendrickson, 1991.

Pollux, Julius. *Onomasticon*. Edited by J. Bekker. Berlin: Nicolai, 1846.

Porter, James E. *Audience and Rhetoric: An Archaeological Composition of the Discourse Community*. Prentice Hall Studies in Writing and Culture. Englewood Cliffs, N.J.: Prentice-Hall, 1992.

Porter, Stanley E. "Paul as Epistolographer *and* Rhetorician." Pages 222–48 in *The Rhetorical Interpretation of Scripture*. Edited by Stanley E. Porter and Dennis L. Stamps. JSNTSup 180. Sheffield: Sheffield Academic Press, 1999.

Porter, Stanley E. "The Theoretical Justification for Application of Rhetorical Categories to Pauline Epistolary Literature." Pages 100–122 in *Rhetoric and the New Testament: Essays from the 1992 Heidelberg Conference*. Edited by Stanley E. Porter and Thomas H. Olbricht. JSNTSup 90. Sheffield: Sheffield Academic Press, 1993.

Porter, Stanley E., and Thomas H. Olbricht. *Rhetoric and the New Testament: Essays from the 1992 Heidelberg Conference*. JSNTSup 90; Sheffield: JSOT, 1993.

Porter, Stanley E., and Thomas H. Olbricht. *The Rhetorical Analysis of Scripture: Essays from the 1995 London Conference*. JSNTSup 146. Sheffield: Sheffield Academic Press, 1997.

Poster, Carol. "Being, Time, and Definition: Toward a Semiotics of Figural Rhetoric." *Philosophy and Rhetoric* 33 (2000): 116–36.

Poster, Carol. "The Enthymeme: An Interdisciplinary Bibliography of Critical Studies." http://rhetjournal.uor.edu.

Powell, Mark Allen. "The Plot and Subplots of Matthew's Gospel." *NTS* 38 (1992): 187–204.

Powell, Pegeen Reichert. "Facing the Audience: Reconsidering 'Audience' through the Chinese Concept Of 'Face.' " In *Rhetoric, the Polis, and the Global Village: Selected Papers from the 1998 Thirtieth Anniversary Rhetoric Society of America Conference*. C. Jan Swearingen and Dave Pruett, eds.; Mahwah, N.J.: Lawrence Erlbaum Associates, 1999.

Preiswerk, Rudolph. *De inventione orationum Ciceronianarum*. Basel: Friedrich Reinhardt, 1905.

Prickett, Stephen. " 'Gospel Stories': Review of Douglas Templeton *The New Testament as True Fiction.*" *Times Literary Supplement* (March 3, 2000): 30.

Provence, Thomas. " 'Who is Sufficient for These Things?' An Exegesis of 2 Corinthians 2:15–3:18." *NovT* 24/1 (1982): 54–81.

Räisänen, Heikki. *Paul and the Law*. WUNT 29. Tübingen: Mohr/Siebeck; Philadelphia: Fortress Press, 1983.

Räisänen, Heikki. "Zum Verständnis von Röm 3:1–8." Pages 185–205 in *The Torah and Christ*. SESJ 45. Helsinki: Finnish Exegetical Society, 1986.

Ramsaran, Rollin A. "Getting to the Point: Maxims in Paul's Moral Reasoning." In *Paul in the Greco-Roman World*. Edited by J. Paul Sampley. Harrisburg, Pa.: Trinity Press International, forthcoming.

Ramsaran, Rollin A. *Liberating Words: Paul's Use of Rhetorical Maxims in 1 Corinthians 1–10*. Valley Forge: Trinity Press International, 1996.

Ramsey, W. M. *A Historical Commentary on St. Paul's Epistle to the Galatians*. 2d ed. London: Hodder & Stoughton, 1900.

Reardon, Bryan P. *Collected Ancient Greek Novels*. Berkeley: University of California Press, 1989.

Reardon, Bryan P. *The Form of the Greek Romance*. Princeton, N.J.: Princeton University Press, 1991.

Reboul, Olivier. "Rhétorique et dialectique chez Aristote." *Argumentation* 4 (1990): no. 1, 35–52.

Reed, Jeffrey T. *A Discourse Analysis of Philippians: Method and Rhetoric in the Debate over Literary Integrity.* JSNTSup 136. Sheffield: Sheffield Academic Press, 1997.
Richards, E. Randolph. *The Secretary in the Letters of Paul.* WUNT II:42. Tübingen: J. C. B. Mohr, 1990.
Ricoeur, Paul. *Essays on Biblical Interpretation.* Philadelphia: Fortress, 1980.
Rimmon, Shlomith. *The Concept of Ambiguity — the Example of James.* Chicago: University of Chicago Press, 1977.
Robbins, Vernon K. "The Dialectical Nature of Early Christian Discourse," *Scriptura* 59 (1996): 353–62. Online at *www.emory.edu/COLLEGE/RELIGION/faculty/robbins/dialect/dialect353.html.*
Robbins, Vernon K. "Enthymemic Texture in the Gospel of Thomas." Pages 343–66 in *SBLSP, 1998.* Atlanta: Scholars Press, 1998. Online at *www.emory.edu/COLLEGE/RELIGION/faculty/robbins/enthymeme/enthymeme343.html.*
Robbins, Vernon K. *Exploring the Texture of Texts: A Guide to Socio-Rhetorical Interpretation.* Valley Forge: Trinity Press International, 1996.
Robbins, Vernon K. "From Enthymeme to Theology in Luke 11:1–13." Pages 191–214 in *Literary Studies in Luke-Acts: A Collection of Essays in Honor of Joseph B. Tyson.* Edited by R. P. Thompson and T. E. Phillips. Macon, Ga.: Mercer University Press, 1998. Online at *www.emory.edu/COLLEGE/RELIGION/faculty/robbins/Theology/theology191.html.*
Robbins, Vernon K. "Interpreting Miracle Culture and Parable Culture in Mark 4–11." *SEÅ* 59 (1994): 59–81.
Robbins, Vernon K. "The Present and Future of Rhetorical Analysis." Pages 24–52 in *The Rhetorical Analysis of Scripture: Essays from the 1995 London Conference.* Edited by Stanley E. Porter and Thomas H. Olbricht. JSNTSup 146. Sheffield: Sheffield Academic Press, 1997.
Robbins, Vernon K. "Progymnastic Rhetorical Composition and Pre-Gospel Traditions: A New Approach." Pages 111–47 in *The Synoptic Gospels: Source Criticism and the New Literary Criticism.* Edited by Camille Focant. BETL 110. Leuven: Leuven University Press, 1993.
Robbins, Vernon K. "Rhetorical Ritual: Apocalyptic Discourse in Mark 13." Pages 95–121 in *Vision and Persuasion: Rhetorical Dimensions of Apocalyptic Discourse.* Edited by Gregory Carey and L. Gregory Bloomquist. St. Louis: Chalice, 1999.
Robbins, Vernon K. *The Tapestry of Early Christian Discourse: Rhetoric, Society and Ideology.* London: Routledge, 1996.
Robbins, Vernon K. "The Woman Who Touched Jesus' Garment: Socio-Rhetorical Analysis of the Synoptic Accounts." *NTS* 33 (1987): 502–15. Repr. pages 185–200 in *New Boundaries in Old Territory: Form and Social Rhetoric in Mark.* ESEC 3. Edited by David B. Gowler. New York: Peter Lang, 1994.
Robbins, Vernon K, ed. *The Rhetoric of Pronouncement.* Semeia 14. 1993.
Roetzel, Calvin. *Paul: The Man and the Myth.* Minneapolis: Fortress, 1999.
Rudolph, Wilhelm. *Chronikbücher.* HAT 21. Tübingen: J. C. B. Mohr (Paul Siebeck), 1955.
Ryan, Eugene E. *Aristotle's Theory of Rhetorical Argumentation.* Collection Noël. Montreal: Bellarmin, 1984.
Sacks, Oliver. *The Man Who Mistook His Wife for a Hat.* New York: Summit Books, 1985.

Sampley, J. Paul. "The Letter to the Ephesians." Pages 9–39 in *Ephesians, Colossians, 2 Thessalonians, The Pastoral Epistles*. Proclamation Commentaries. Edited by Gerhard Krodel. Philadelphia: Fortress, 1978.

Sampley, J. Paul. "Reasoning from the Horizons of Paul's Thought World: A Comparison of Galatians and Philippians." Pages 114–31 in *Theology and Ethics in Paul and His Interpreters: Essays in Honor of Victor Paul Furnish*. Edited by Eugene H. Lovering, Jr. and Jerry L. Sumney. Nashville: Abingdon, 1996.

Sampley, J. Paul. *Walking between the Times: Paul's Moral Reasoning*. Minneapolis: Fortress, 1991.

Sanders, Ed P. *Paul, the Law, and the Jewish People*. Philadelphia: Fortress Press, 1983.

Sanders, Ed P. *Paul and Palestinian Judaism: A Comparison of Patterns of Religion*. Philadelphia: Fortress, 1977.

Sappington, Thomas J. *Revelation and Redemption at Colossae*. JSNTSup 53. Sheffield: JSOT, 1991.

Schaefer, Glenn E. "The Significance of Seeking God in the Purpose of the Chronicler." Th.D. diss., Southern Baptist Theological Seminary, 1972.

Schalemann, Martin. "Of Surpassing Splendor: An Exegetical Study of 2 Corinthians 3:4–18." *Concordia Journal* 4/3 (1978): 108–17.

Schiappa, Edward. *The Beginnings of Rhetorical Theory in Classical Greece*. New Haven: Yale University Press, 1999.

Schiappa, Edward. *Protagoras and Logos*. Studies in Rhetoric/Communication. Columbia, S.C.: University of South Carolina Press, 1991.

Schlueter, Carol J. *Filling up the Measure: Polemical Hyperbole in 1 Thessalonians 2.14–16*. JSNTSup 98. Sheffield: Sheffield Academic Press, 1994.

Schmithals, Walter. *Die Gnosis in Korinth*. 2d rev. ed. Göttingen: Vandenhoeck & Ruprecht, 1965.

Schnackenburg, Rudolf. *The Epistle to the Ephesians*. Translated by Helen Heron. Edinburgh: T. & T. Clark, 1991.

Schneemelcher, Wilhelm. "The Acts of Peter: Introduction." Pages 271–85. In *New Testament Apocrypha*. Vol. II. Edited by Edgar Hennecke et al. Louisville: Westminster/John Knox, 1992.

Scholer, John M. *Proleptic Priests: Priesthood in the Epistle to the Hebrews*. JSNTSup 49. Sheffield: Sheffield Academic Press, 1991.

Schüssler Fiorenza, Elisabeth. "Rhetorical Situation and Historical Reconstruction in 1 Corinthians." *NTS* 33 (1987): 386–403.

Schüssler Fiorenza, Elisabeth. *In Memory of Her: A Feminist Theological Reconstruction of Christian Origins*. New York: Crossroad, 1984.

Schüssler Fiorenza, Elisabeth. *Miriam's Child, Sophia's Prophet*. New York: Continuum, 1994.

Schwally, Friedrich. "Zur Geschichte der historischen Bücher." *ZAW* 12 (1892): 153–61.

Schweizer, Eduard. *The Letter to the Colossians; A Commentary*. Translated by A. Chester. Minneapolis: Augsburg, 1982.

Scott, James. "The Uses of Scripture in 2 Corinthians 6:16c-18." *JSNT* 56 (1994): 73–99.

Seeley, David. *The Noble Death: Graeco-Roman Martyrology and Paul's Concept of Salvation*. JSNTSup 28. Sheffield: Sheffield Academic Press, 1990.

Seitz, Oscar J. F. "Antecedents and Signification of the Term ΔΙΨΥΧΟΣ." *JBL* 63 (1944): 131–40.

Sesonske, Alexander. "To Make the Weaker Argument Defeat the Stronger." Pages 71–90 in *Plato: True and Sophistic Rhetoric.* Edited by Keith V. Erickson. Studies in Classical Antiquity 3. Amsterdam: Rodopi, 1979.

Siegert, Folker. *Argumentation bei Paulus: Gezeigt an Röm 9–11.* WUNT 34. Tübingen: Mohr Siebeck, 1985.

Slomkowski, Paul. *Aristotle's Topics.* New York and Leiden: Brill, 1997.

Smith, Jonathan Z. *To Take Place: Toward Theory in Ritual.* Chicago: University of Chicago Press, 1987.

Smith, Robert H. *Hebrews.* Minneapolis: Augsburg Press, 1984.

Snaith, Norman. "Introduction and Exegesis on The First and Second Books of Kings." Pages 3–338 in *The Interpreter's Bible.* Edited by George Arthur Buttrick. Vol. 3. New York and Nashville: Abingdon Press, 1954.

Snoeck Henkemans, A. Francisca. *Analysing Complex Argumentation: The Reconstruction of Multiple and Coordinatively Compound Argumentation in a Critical Discussion.* Amsterdam: Sic Sat, 1992.

Snyder, Graydon F. *The Shepherd of Hermas.* Vol. 6 of *The Apostolic Fathers: A New Translation and Commentary.* Edited by Robert McQueen Grant. New York: T. Nelson, 1964.

Spanje, Teunis Erik van. *Inconsistentie bij Paulus? Een confrontatie met het werk van Heikki Räisänen.* Kampen: Kok, 1996.

Sprute, Jürgen. *Die Enthymemtheorie der aristotelischen Rhetorik.* Abhandlungen der Akademie der Wissenschaften in Göttingen: Philologisch-Historische Klasse 3:124. Göttingen: Vandenhoeck & Ruprecht, 1982.

Staley, Jeffrey. *The Print's First Kiss: A Rhetorical Investigation of the Implied Reader in the Fourth Gospel.* SBLDS 82. Missoula, Mont.: Scholars Press, 1988.

Staley, Jeffrey. *Reading with a Passion: Rhetoric, Autobiography, and the American West in the Gospel of John.* New York: Continuum, 1995.

Staley, Jeffrey. "Stumbling in the Dark, Reaching for the Light: Reading Character in John 5 and 9," *Semeia* 53 (1991): 55–80.

Stamps, Dennis L. "Rhetorical Criticism of the New Testament: Ancient and Modern Evaluations of Argumentation." Pages 129–69 in *Approaches to New Testament Studies.* Edited by Stanley E. Porter and David Tombs. JSNTSup 120. Sheffield: Sheffield Academic Press, 1995.

Sternberg, Meir. *The Poetics of Biblical Narrative.* Bloomington: Indiana University Press, 1985.

Stevenson, C. L. "Persuasive Definitions." *Mind* 47 (1938): 331–50.

Stone, Michael E. "The Book of Enoch and Judaism in the Third Century B.C.E." *CBQ* 40 (1978): 479–92.

Stowers, Stanley K. *The Diatribe and Paul's Letter to the Romans.* SBLDS 57. Chico, Calif.: Scholars Press, 1982.

Stowers, Stanley K. "Friends and Enemies in the Politics of Heaven." Pages 105–21 in *Pauline Theology, Volume 1: Thessalonians, Philippians, Galatians, Philemon.* Edited by Jouette M. Bassler. Minneapolis: Fortress, 1991.

Stowers, Stanley K. *Letter Writing in Greco-Roman Antiquity.* LEC 5. Philadelphia: Westminster Press, 1986.

Stowers, Stanley K. "Paul's Dialogue with a Fellow Jew in Romans 3:1–9." *CBQ* 46 (1984): 707–22.

Stowers, Stanley K. *A Rereading of Romans: Justice, Jews, and Gentiles.* New Haven: Yale University Press, 1994.

Strecker, Georg. "Die Legitimität des paulinischen Apostolates nach 2 Korintherbrief 10–13." *NTS* 38/4 (1992): 566–86.

Sullivan, Dale L., and Christian Anibile. "The Epideictic Dimension of Galatians as Formative Rhetoric: The Inscription of Early Christian Community." *Rhetorica* 18:2 (2000): 117–45.

Sumney, Jerry. *Identifying Paul's Opponents: The Question of Method in 2 Corinthians.* JSNTSup 40. Sheffield: Sheffield Academic Press, 1990.

Sumney, Jerry L. *Servants of Satan, False Brothers, and Other Opponents of Paul.* JSNTSup 188. Sheffield: Sheffield Academic Press, 1999.

Swearingen, C. Jan. "*Ethos:* Imitation, Impersonation, and Voice." Pages 115–48 in *Ethos: New Esays in Rhetorical and Critical Theory.* Edited by James S. Baumlin and Tita F. Baumlin. Dallas, Tex.: Southern Methodist University Press, 1994.

Tachau, Peter. *"Einst" und "Jetzt" im Neuen Testament: Beobachtungen zu einem urchristlichen Predigtschema in der neutestamentlichen Briefliteratur und zu seiner Vorgeschichte.* FRLANT 105. Göttingen: Vandenhoeck & Ruprecht, 1972.

Teitler, Hans C. *Notarii and Exceptores.* J. C. Gieben: Amsterdam, 1985.

Templeton, Douglas A. *The New Testament as True Fiction.* Sheffield: Sheffield Academic Press, 1999.

Theissen, Gerd. *The Gospels in Context: Social and Political History in the Synoptic Tradition.* Minneapolis: Fortress, 1991.

Theissen, Gerd. *The Miracle Stories of the Early Christian Tradition.* Philadelphia: Fortress, 1983.

Thielman, Frank. "The Style of the Fourth Gospel and Ancient Literary Critical Concepts of Religious Discourse." Pages 169–83 in *Persuasive Artistry: Studies in New Testament Rhetoric in Honor of George A. Kennedy.* Edited by Duane F. Watson. JSNTSup 50. Sheffield: Sheffield Academic Press, 1991.

Thomas, John Christopher. " 'Stop Sinning Lest Something Worse Come upon You': The Man at the Pool in John 5." *JSNT* 59 (1995): 3–20.

Thomas, Stephen N. *Practical Reasoning in Natural Language.* 3d ed. Englewood Cliffs, N.J.: Prentice-Hall, 1986. [1973].

Thompson, James W. *The Beginnings of Christian Philosophy: The Epistle to the Hebrews.* CBQMS 13. Washington, D.C.: Catholic Biblical Association, 1982.

Throntveit, Mark A. *When Kings Speak: Royal Speech and Royal Prayer in Chronicles.* SBLDS 93. Atlanta: Scholars, 1987.

Thurén, Lauri. *Argument and Theology in 1 Peter: The Origins of Christian Paraenesis.* JSNTSup 114. Sheffield: Sheffield Academic Press, 1995.

Thurén, Lauri. *Derhetorizing Paul: A Dynamic Perspective on Pauline Theology and the Law.* WUNT 124. Tübingen: Mohr Siebeck, 2000.

Thurén, Lauri. "On Studying Ethical Argumentation and Persuasion in the New Testament." Pages 464–78 in *Rhetoric and the New Testament: Essays from the 1992 Heidelberg Conference.* Edited by Stanley E. Porter and Thomas H. Olbricht. JSNTSup 90. Sheffield: Sheffield Academic Press, 1993.

Thurén, Lauri. *The Rhetorical Strategy of 1 Peter: With Special Regard to Ambiguous Expressions.* Åbo: Åbo Akademis Förlag, 1990.

Thurén, Lauri, "Style Never Goes out of Fashion — 2 Peter Re-evaluated." Pages 329–47 in *Rhetoric, Scripture and Theology*. Edited by Stanley E. Porter and Thomas H. Olbricht. JSNTSup 131. Sheffield: Sheffield Academic Press, 1996.

Thurén, Lauri. "Was Paul Angry? Derhetorizing Galatians." Pages 302–20 in *The Rhetorical Interpretation of Scripture: Essays from the 1996 Malibu Conference*. Edited by Stanley E. Porter and Dennis L. Stamps. JSNTSup 180. Sheffield: Sheffield Academic Press, 1999.

Thurén, Lauri. "Was Paul Sincere? Questioning the Apostle's Ethos." *Scriptura* 65 (1998): 95–98.

Thurman, Robert. Email-Interview on Indo-Tibetan Reasoning, June 2, 2000.

Torjesen, Karen Jo. "You Are the Christ: Five Portraits of Jesus from the Early Church." Pages 73–88 in *Jesus at 2000*. Edited by Marcus J. Borg. Boulder, Colo.: Westview, 1997.

Toulmin, Stephen, R. Rieke, and A. Janik. *An Introduction to Reasoning*. 2d ed. New York: Macmillan, 1984.

Toulmin, Stephen E. *The Uses of Argument*. Cambridge: Cambridge University Press, 1958.

Townend, G. B. "The Post of *ab epistulis* in the Second Century." *Historia* 10 (1961): 375–81.

Tracy, Stephen W. *Attic Letter-Cutters of 229 to 86 B.C.* Berkeley: University of California Press, 1990.

Trible, Phyllis. *Texts of Terror: Literary Feminist Readings of Biblical Narrative*. Philadelphia: Fortress Press, 1984.

Turner, E. G. *Greek Manuscripts of the Ancient World*. 2d ed. Revised by P. J. Parsons. Institute of Classical Studies Bulletin Supplement 46. London, 1987.

Turner, Max. "Modern Linguistics and the New Testament." *Hearing the New Testament*. Edited by Joel B. Green. 175–96.

Turretini, J. A. *De Sacrae Scripturae interpretandi methodo tractatus bipartitus*. Dordrecht, 1728.

Übelacker, Walter G. *Der Hebräerbrief als Appell: I. Untersuchungen zu* exordium, narratio *und* postscriptum *((Hebr 1–2 und 13,22–25)*. ConBNT 21. Stockholm. Almqvist & Wiksell International, 1989.

Übelacker, Walter. "Hebr 7:1–10 – dess struktur och funktion i författarens retoriska argumentation." Pages 215–32 in *Mellan tid och evighet: Festskrift till Bo Johnson*. Edited by Sten Hidal, Lars Haikol, Stig Norin. Religio 42. Lund: Teologiska institution, 1994.

Ulmer, Rivka Kern. "The Advancement of Arguments in Exegetical Midrash Compared to the Arguments in the Greek Diatribe." Paper presented at NEH Seminar, Yeshiva University, 1992.

Van Broekhoven, Harold. "Persuasion and Praise in Colossians." *Proceedings: Eastern Great Lakes and Midwest Biblical Societies* 15 (1995): 65–78.

Van Unnik, W. C. "'With Unveiled Face,' an Exegesis of 2 Corinthians 12–18." *NovT* 6 (1963): 153–69.

Van Wahlde, Urban C. *The Earliest Version of John's Gospel: Recovering the Gospel of Signs*. Wilmington: Glazier, 1989.

Verhoot, A. M. F. W. *Menches, Komogrammateus of Kerkosiris*. Leiden: Brill, 1998.

Vickers, Brian. *In Defence of Rhetoric*. Oxford: Clarendon, 1988.

Vidén, Gunhild. *The Roman Chancery Tradition: Studies in the Language of Codex Theodosianus and Cassiodorus' Variae*. Göteborg: Acta Universitatis Gothoburgensis, 1984.

Vielhauer, Philipp, and Georg Strecker. "Introduction to Apocalyptic in Early Christianity." Pages 569–602 in *New Testament Apocrypha*. Vol. 2. Edited by Edgar Hennecke and Wilhelm Schneemelcher. English translation by Robert McL. Wilson. Louisville: Westminster/John Knox, 1991.

Viertel, W. *The Hermeneutics of Paul*. Waco, Tex., 1976 (unpublished).

Vos, Johannes Sijko. "Die hermeneutische Antinomie bei Paulus (Gal 3,11–12; Röm 10,5–10)." *NTS* 38 (1992): 254–70.

Vos, Johannes Sijko. "Legem statuimus: Rhetorische Aspekte der Gesetzesdebatte zwischen Juden und Christen." Pages 44–60 in *Juden und Christen in der Antike*. Edited by J. van Amersfoort and J. van Oort. Kampen: Kok, 1990.

Wachob, Wesley H. *The Voice of Jesus in the Social Rhetoric of James*. SNTSMS 106. Cambridge: Cambridge University Press, 2000.

Walton, Douglas N. *Arguer's Position*. Westport, Conn.: Greenwood Press, 1985.

Walton, Douglas N. *Argumentation Schemes for Presumptive Reasoning*. Mahwah, N.J.: Lawrence Erlbaum, 1996.

Walton, Douglas N. *Informal Fallacies*. Amsterdam: John Benjamins, 1987.

Walton, Douglas N. *A Pragmatic Theory of Fallacy*. Tuscaloosa, Ala.: University of Alabama Press, 1995.

Walton, Douglas N., and Erik C. W. Krabbe. *Commitment and Dialogue*. Albany, N.Y.: SUNY Press, 1995.

Warner, M. "The Fourth Gospel's Art of Rational Persuasion." Pages 153–77 in *The Bible as Rhetoric: Studies in Biblical Persuasion and Credibility*. Edited by M. Warner. Warwick Studies in Philosophy and Literature. London and New York: Routledge, 1990.

Watson, Duane F. "A Rhetorical Analysis of Philippians and Its Implications for the Unity Question." *NovT* 30 (1988): 57–88.

Watson, Duane F. "The Integration of Epistolary and Rhetorical Analysis of Philippians." Pages 398–426 in *The Rhetorical Analysis of Scripture: Essays from the 1995 London Conference*. Edited by Stanley E. Porter and Thomas H. Olbricht. JSNTSup 146. Sheffield: Sheffield Academic Press, 1997.

Watson, Duane F. "The Rhetoric of James 3:1–12 and a Classical Pattern of Argumentation." *NovT* 35 (1993): 48–64.

Watson, Duane F., and Alan J. Hauser. *Rhetorical Criticism of the Bible: A Comparative Bibliography with Notes on History and Method*. Biblical Interpretation Series 4. Leiden: Brill, 1994.

Watts, Isaac. *Logick, or the Right Use of Reason* (2d ed. 1796). Reprinted in *Fallacies: Classical and Contemporary Readings*. Edited by H. V. Hansen and R. V. Pinto. University Park: Pennsylvania State University Press, 1995.

Webb, William. "Unequally Yoked Together with Unbelievers. Part 2 (of 2 parts): What is the Unequal Yoke (*heterozugountes*) in 2 Corinthians 6:14?" *BSac* 149 (1992): 162–79.

Weidmann, Frederick W. "An (Un)Accomplished Model: Paul and the Rhetorical Strategy of Philippians 3:3–17." Pages 245–57 in *Putting Body and Soul Together: Essays in*

Honor of Robin Scroggs. Edited by Virginia Wiles, Alexandra Brown, and Graydon F. Snyder. Valley Forge: Trinity Press International, 1997.

Weinstein, M. "Toward an Account of Argumentation in Science." *Argumentation* 4 (1990): 269–98.

Wellhausen, Julius. *Die Composition des Hexateuchs und der historischen Bücher des Alten Testaments*. 4th ed. Berlin: Georg Reimer, 1963.

Welten, Peter. *Geschichte und Geschichtsdarstellung in den Chronikbüchern*. WMANT 42. Neukirchen-Vluyn: Neukirchener Verlag, 1973.

Wenzel, Joseph W. "Perspectives on Argument." In *Proceedings of the 1979 Summer Conference on Argument*. Edited by Jack Rhodes and Sarah Newell. Falls Church, Va.: SCA, 1980.

Wenzel, Joseph W. "The Rhetorical Perspective on Argument." Pages 101–9 in *Argumentation: Across the Lines*. Edited by Frans H. van Eemeren et al. Dordrecht: Foris, 1987.

White, Hayden. *Metahistory: The Historical Imagination in Nineteenth-Century Europe*. Baltimore: Johns Hopkins University Press, 1973.

White, Hayden. "Rhetoric and History." Pages 3–24 in *Theories of History*. Edited by Hayden White and F. E. Manuel. Los Angeles: University of California Press, 1978.

White, Michael L. "Morality Between Two Worlds: A Paradigm of Friendship in Philippians." Pages 201–15 in *Greeks, Romans, and Christians: Essays in Honor of Abraham J. Malherbe*. Edited by David L. Balch, Everett Ferguson, and Wayne A. Meeks. Minneapolis: Fortress, 1990.

Williams, Sam K. *Jesus' Death as Saving Event: The Origin of a Concept*. HDR 2. Missoula, Mont.: Scholars Press, 1975.

Wills, Lawrence. *The Jewish Novel in the Ancient World*. Ithaca, N.Y.: Cornell University Press, 1995.

Wilson, Andrew N. *Paul: The Mind of the Apostle*. New York: W. W. Norton, 1997.

Wilson, R. McL. *Hebrews*. NCBC. Grand Rapids: W. B. Eerdmans, 1987.

Wilson, Walter. *The Hope of Glory: Education and Exhortation in the Epistle to the Colossians*. NovTSup 88. Leiden: Brill, 1997.

Wire, Antoinette Clark. *The Corinthian Women Prophets: A Reconstruction through Paul's Rhetoric*. Minneapolis: Fortress Press, 1990.

Wisse, Jakob. *Ethos and Pathos from Aristotle to Cicero*. Amsterdam: Hakkert, 1989.

Witherington, Ben, III. *Friendship and Finances in Philippi: The Letter of Paul to the Philippians*. Valley Forge: Trinity Press International, 1994.

Witherington, Ben, III. *Grace in Galatia: A Commentary on Paul's Letter to the Galatians*. Grand Rapids: Eerdmans, 1998.

Wittfogel, Karl A. *Oriental Despotism: A Comparative Study of Total Power*. New York: Vintage, 1981.

Woods, John, and Douglas Walton. *Argument: The Logic of the Fallacies*. Toronto: McGraw-Hill Ryerson, 1982.

Woods, John, and Douglas Walton. *Fallacies*. Dordrecht: Foris, 1989.

Wright, N. T. "The Letter to the Galatians: Exegesis and Theology." Pages 205–36 in *Between Two Horizons: Spanning New Testament Studies and Systematic Theology*. Ed. Joel B. Green. Grand Rapids, Mich.: Eerdmans, 2000.

Wright, N. T. "The Law in Romans 2." Pages 131–50 in *Paul and the Mosaic Law*. Edited by James D. G. Dunn. Tübingen: J. C. B. Mohr, 1995.

Wu, Hiu. "The Enthymeme Examined from the Chinese Value System." Pages 115–122 in *Making and Unmaking the Prospects for Rhetoric*. Edited by Theresa Enos. Mahwah, N.J.: L. Erlbaum, 1997.
Wuellner, Wilhelm. "Putting Life Back into the Lazarus Story and Its Reading: The Narrative Rhetoric of John 11 as the Narration of Faith." *Semeia* 53 (1991): 113–32.
Wuellner, Wilhelm. "The Pre-Christian Paul and Rhetoric." Unpublished ms. 1994, personal correspondence via David Hester.
Wuellner, Wilhelm. "Reading Romans in Context," unpublished paper presented to SNTS, Göttingen, 1986.
Wuellner, Wilhelm. "Rhetorical Criticism and its Theory in Culture-Critical Perspective: The Narrative Rhetoric of John 11." Pages 171–85 in *Text and Interpretation: New Approaches in the Criticism of the New Testament*. Edited by P. J. Martin and J. H. Petzer. NTTS 15. Leiden: Brill, 1991.
Wuellner, Wilhelm. "Der vorchristliche Paulus und die Rhetorik." Pages 133–65 in *Tempelkult und Tempelzerstörung: Festschrift für Clemens Thoma zum 60. Geburtstag*. Edited by Simon Lauer and H. Hernst. Bern: Peter Lang, 1995.
Wuellner, Wilhelm H. "Where Is Rhetorical Criticism Taking Us?" *CBQ* 49 (1987): 448–63.
Würthwein, Ernst. "Zur Composition von I Reg 22:1–38." Pages 245–54 in *Das ferne und nahe Wort: Festschrift L. Rost*. BZAW 105. Edited by F. Maass. Berlin: A. Töpelmann, 1967.
Yamada, Kota. "The Preface to the Lukan Writings and Rhetorical Historiography." Pages 154–72 in *The Rhetorical Interpretation of Scripture: Essays from the 1996 Malibu Conference*. Edited by Stanley E. Porter and Dennis L. Stamps. JSNTSup 180. Sheffield: Academic Press, 1999.
Young, Richard. "Invention." Pages 349–55 in *Encyclopedia of Rhetoric and Composition: Communication from Ancient Times to the Information Age*. Edited by T. Enos; New York: Garland, 1996.
Youtie, H. C. "AGRAMMATOS: An Aspect of Greek Society in Egypt." *Harvard Studies in Classical Philology* 75 (1971): 161–76.
Youtie, H. C. "Because They Do Not Know Letters." *Zeitschrift für Papyrologie und Epigraphik* 19 (1975): 101–8.
Youtie, H. C. "Βραδέως γράφων: Between Literacy and Illiteracy." *Greek, Roman, and Byzantine Studies* 12 (1971): 239–61.
Youtie, H. C. "Pétaus, fils de Pétaus, ou le scribe qui ne savait pas écrire." *Chronique d'Egypte* 41 (1966): 127–43.
Zappel, K. "Argumentation and Literary Texts." Page 217 in *Argumentation: Analysis and Practices*. Edited by Frans H. van Eemeren et al. Dordrecht: Foris, 1987.
Zulick, Margaret. "The Active Force of Hearing: The Ancient Hebrew Language of Persuasion." *Rhetorica* 10 (1992): 367–80.
Zulick, Margaret. "The Agon of Jeremiah: On the Dialogic Invention of Prophetic Ethos." *QJS* (1992): 125–48.

Index of Ancient Texts

OLD TESTAMENT

Leviticus
18:1–5	*230*

Deuteronomy
30:11–20	*230*

1 Kings
22:1–8	*145–47*
22:9–12	*147*
22:13–23	*147–51*
22:24–28	*151–52*
22:29–38	*152–54*

1 Chronicles
1–9	*132*
1:11–20	*60–61*
10	*133–35*
13:10	*133, 136*
15:25–26	*136*
17	*137*
21:8	*137*
22:11–13	*137*
22:18–19	*138*
28	*138*

2 Chronicles
10–36	*139*

Amos
1:1–2	*203*
2:6–16	*203–4*
6:8–14	*206–7*

OLD TESTAMENT PSEUDEPIGRAPHA

First Enoch
100:1–6	*55–56*
100:4–6	*56*

NEW TESTAMENT

Matthew
5:3–12	*45–47*
9:35–10:4	*177–78*
9:35–38	*175–76*
10	*176–77*
10–13	*183–84*
10:5–15	*178–80*
10:10–13	*183–84*
10:16–42	*180–83*
10:25	*186–87*
10:40	*185–86*
10:41–42	*184*
23:1–15	*47–50*

Mark
1:32–34	*38*
5:21–34	*39–41*
9:23	*41*
11:22–25	*41–42*

Luke
1:28–38	*208–9*
4:14–9:50	*209–10*
5:17–6:11	*210–12*
11:1–13	*388*
12:16–21	*168*
12:22–32	*168*
12:22–34	*212*
12:35–46	*212–13*
18:1–14	*213*
21:5	*172*

John
1:1–18	*61–62*
5:16–18	*190–91*
5:19–30	*192*
5:20b–21	*192–93*
5:22–29	*193–94*
31–47	*196–98*

Acts
10:34–43	*172*
14:8–18	*169–70*

Romans
1:14	*236*
1:18–3:20	*226*
2:14–15	*237*
3:1–9	*228–30*
5:12–13	*226, 227*
5:19–20	*237*
7:7–12	*227*
10:5–10	*230*
13:6–10	*238*

1 Corinthians
1:4–9	*249–51*
6:9–11	*110–11*
8:4–12	*87–89*
8:7–13	*255–58*
11:2–16	*251–53*
11:29–30	*110*

2 Corinthians
1:17–22	*285*
2:12–13	*286*
6:11–7	*288*
7–8	*288–89*
9	*290*
10	*290–91*
10–13	*262–73*
11	*291–92*
12–13	*292–93*

Ephesians
1:1–2	*310*
1:3–14	*310, 317–20*
2:1–20	*320–21*
2:11–22	*314, 320–21*
2:19–22	*314, 321–22*
3:2–13	*323*
3:20	*322–23*
3:20–21	*315–16*
4:13–16	*314–15*
6:21–24	*310*

Philippians
1:12–14	*333*
1:19–26	*333*
1:21	*330, 335–36, 337*
1:22	*329*
1:25	*329*
1:27–30	*331–32*
2:19–24	*334–35*
2:25–30	*335*

Colossians
1:3–8	*344*
1:9–12	*344–45*
1:11–20	*60–61*
1:15–20	*345–46*
1:20–23	*343–44*
1:21–23	*346*
1:24–2:5	*340–41*
2:6–10	*346–47*
2:11–15	*347–48*
2:16	*349*
2:20–23	*349–50*
3:1–4	*342, 350–51*
4:2–17	*351*

1 Timothy
4:6–11	*85–86*

Hebrews
1:1–4	*357*
1:2–4	*356*
2:17	*358–59*
4:14–16	*360*
5	*360–64*
5:11–6:12	*364–66*
6:13–20	*368*
7	*368–72*

James
2:1–13	*34–35*
2:10–11	*37*
2:1–4	*35–36*
2:8	*36*
2:12–13	*37*
2:14–15	*42–43*
5:14–17	*42–43*

1 Peter

2:18–25	*51–52*
2:21	*52*
2:22–25	*53*

Revelation

4:2–11	*57–58*
4:6–13	*58–59*

OTHER ANCIENT TEXTS

Acts of Peter	*376, 380–83*
Clouds (Aristophanes)	*218, 226*
Gorgias (Plato)	*224*
De Inventione (Cicero)	*70, 97–98*
Letters to Lucilius (Younger Seneca)	*109–10*
Rhetoric (Aristotle)	*128*
Rhetoric ad Herennium (anonymous)	*74, 76, 97–98, 101, 102, 192, 255, 257*
Shepherd of Hermas	*375, 376–80, 384, 385*

Index of Subjects and Authors

Abductive reasoning, 60, 63
Acceptability, 15
Adiaphora, 330, 333–34
Administrators, letter-writing, 120
Adversative formulation, 40–41, 48
Affliction, 284, 286, 287, 347
Aletti, Jean-Noël, 343, 344
Ambiguity, 144–54, 223–26
American Forensic Association (AFA), 25
American National Communication Association (NCA), 25
Amplificatio methodology, 73–74, 355
Amplification, 73–74, 355
Analogy, 256, 365–66
  apocalyptic discourse, 56
  Asian argumentation, 161–62, 163
  Fourth Gospel, 195, 196
  Matthean Mission Discourse, 186
  wisdom discourse, 31, 63
Analytic component of the study of argumentation, 11
Anamneses, 314, 320–21
Ancient rhetoric
  amplification, 73–74
  deliberative speeches, 713
  Paul's letters and, 232–33, 234, 236–38
  sentence construction, 74–75
  techniques, 90–91
  textbook on, 66–68, 70, 75–76
  variance within, 70–71
  See also Greco-Roman rhetorical tradition; Sophistic rhetoric
Ancient rhetorical theory
  amplificatio methodology, 73–74, 355
  as analytical tool, 68–69, 253–55

Book of Chronicles and, 128–29
  vs. modern, 68, 77, 78, 79–82, 83–92
  purposes, 68–70
  stasis theory, 71–72, 339–40
Anderson, R. Dean, 2, 66
Anscombre, Jean-Claude, 15–16
Antecedent/consequent topos, 347
Anticipation of arguments, 132
Antithesis, 100
Apocalyptic rhetoric
  in *Acts of Peter*, 381–83
  Asian, 163–67
  early Christian, 54–59, 63, 64
  literary form, 28, 375, 385–87
  wisdom discourse and, 167–69, 170–72
Apology, 261
Appeal to authority, 90–91
Argument
  of assimilation, 347, 351
  character of, 194, 194–96
  complete and perfect, 97–98
  contrary, from the, 257
  deductive, 348–49, 350
  seeking, 132, 133, 135–39
  schemes, 13–14, 22–23
Argumentation
  analysis, 19–26, 84–85, 89–90
  audience and, connection between, 157–59, 172–73
  convincing, 288
  deductive, 348–49, 350
  defined, 10
  definitional, 287
  dissociative, 285, 287–88
  dynamic, 283–84
  exemplary, 332–37

425

Argumentation (continued)
  general aims of, 10
  genuine and fallacious, 220–23
  influential approaches, 12–19
  legitimate vs. sophistic, 219
  method, 278, 283–93
  point of departure of, 9–10
  persuasive, 288–90
  religious, 90–91
  research program for, 10–12
  vs. rhetoric, 82–83
  in small units, 141
Argumentation and Advocacy, 25
Argument technique
  ambiguity, 144–54
  audience and, 13–14
  Colossians, 344–51, 352
  2 Corinthians, 283–93
  sophistical, 217–20
Argumentum ad hominem, 19
Arrangement, 192, 195, 356–57
Aristophanes, 218, 226
Aristotle, 69
  on audience, 158
  enthymemes and, 85–86, 96, 98, 99, 100, 106, 107–8, 133, 243, 245–46, 362
  on ethos, 340
  on exordia, 357
  fallacious argumentation and, 219
  on function of rhetoric, 359
  on homonymy, 223–24
  influence of, 128
  rhetorical techniques, 80, 81
  sentence construction, 74, 75
  terminology used by, 80
Arrangement, 192
Asian rhetoric, 160–67
Assertions, 249, 250, 256, 258, 259
Assertive modality, 280–81
Assimilation, 347, 351

Association for Informal Logical and Critical Thinking (AILACT), 25
Attridge, Harold W., 3, 44, 188, 361, 363, 366
Audience
  apocalyptic discourse and, 166–67, 170–72
  argumentation and, connection between, 157–59, 172–73
  Asian rhetoric and, 162, 166
  concern for growth of, 314–16
  deixis and, 282, 283
  enthymemes and, 99–100, 133–34
  identification, 316–20, 322, 323, 324, 384
  multiple, 234–36, 238
  question at the center and, 205, 207, 208
  relationship between rhetor and, 284, 285–86, 292–93
  soundness of argumentation techniques and, 13–14
  universal, 13, 282, 287
  wisdom discourse and, 168–70
Authority
  appeal to, Early Christian reasoning and, 90–91
  Asian argumentation, 161, 163
  enthymemes and, 136–37, 140
  Matthean Mission Discourse, 174, 175, 176, 177, 180, 181, 186
  Pauline argumentation, 251, 260, 261, 262, 264–65, 266–67, 283, 287, 291, 292–93
  visions and, 381, 382, 384
Autograph, 115, 122–23

Backing, 12–13, 83
Bakhtin, M., 383–84, 387
Barrett, C. K., 296
Barth, Else M., 17
Begging the question, 24–25

INDEX OF SUBJECTS AND AUTHORS 427

Behavior
  Asian argumentation and, 252, 255, 257
  Christian audience and, 314–17, 319, 320, 322, 323, 324
  Pauline argumentation and, 271
benefaction, 260–61, 271
Betz, Hans Dieter, 297–98
Bian, 164
Biographical history, 28, 29, 30, 32, 44, 64
Blair, J. Anthony, 15
Bloomquist, Greg, 244
Boasting
  benefaction and, 260–61
  contexts for, 269–72
  defense of Paul's honor and, 262–67, 273–74
  moderating, 272–73
  social/cultural conventions and, 267–69, 272, 274–75
  topos of, 284, 289, 291–92
Body language, 318
Boring, Eugene, 176
Bovati, Pietro, 204
Boys, Thomas, 201
Braun, Willi, 44
Brevity, 328, 329–30
Broker, 185–87
Brueggemann, Walter, 28–29
Bünker, Michael, 78
Burke, Kenneth, 316
Burnyeat, Myles, 108
Business managers/agents, 118–19

Calligraphers, 116
Causal argumentation, 22
"center as key," 202, 214
Centrifugal rhetorical movement
  defined, 27
  miracle discourse, 42
  prophetic discourse, 50, 182–83
  wisdom discourse, 37

Centripetal rhetorical movement
  apocalyptic discourse, 59
  Asian discourse, 161
  defined, 27
  miracle discourse, 42, 44
  pre-creation discourse, 60, 62–63
  prophetic discourse, 50
  suffering death discourse, 53, 54
  wisdom discourse, 37
Challenge/riposte, 262, 263–67, 275
Chiasmus, 200–202
Chreiai, 188, 255, 348
Chrysostom, Dio, 268, 300–301
Cicero
  enthymemes and, 97, 98, 100–105
  on ethos, 340
  on inductive argument, 194–95
Claim, 12, 83
Classical rhetoric. *See* Ancient rhetoric
Clerks, 117–18, 119
Codes of hospitality, 183–84
Collins, John J., 375–76
Collins, Yarbro, 376
Commonplaces, 329, 359, 366
Comparison, argumentation by, 22
Complex inclusio, 264
Complexio, 97–98, 194, 197
Concentric construction, 200–2
Conciseness, 328
Conferences for the study of argumentation, 25
Confirmatio, 192–93
Confutatio, 196–97
Conley, Thomas, 95, 245, 246
Conplexio, 97–98, 194
Consequents, 105–7
Contradiction, topos of, 347
Contrary, 32, 48, 136
  enthymemes and, 50, 52, 62, 248
  Pauline argumentation, 255, 257, 347, 349

Contrasting methods of interpretation, 230–31
Contrarium, 98, 99, 100
Convergent argumentation, 23
Coordinative argumentation, 23, 24
Copyists, 116
Cosby, Michael R., 5, 296
Counterdefinition, 350
Crowley, Sharon, 254
Cultural codes, 166

Data, 12, 83, 84
Deceiving, 149, 302
Deductive argumentation, 97–98, 140, 164, 348–49, 350, 352
Deductive validity, 20–22
Definitional argument, 287
Deictic enthymeme, 106
Deixis, 280, 281–83
Deleuze, Gilles, 166
Deliberative rhetoric, 71–73, 245, 294, 298, 300, 332, 367
DeLuca, Kevin Michael, 341
Demetrius, 74–75
Demonstrative enthymeme, 106
Descriptive goal of research programs, 10, 91
Descriptive, 10, 15, 90, 91, 128, 254
DeSilva, David A., 58
Diachronic analysis, 189–90
Dialectical reasoning, 219–20
Dialectics
  modern approaches, 17–19
  vs. rhetoric, 16–17, 158
Dialogue, 17–18, 24, 25, 142, 169, 175
Dictation, 113, 115, 116, 120, 122
Digressio, 285, 364
digression, 379, 384, 387, 388
Dio Chrysostom, 268, 300–301
Dio of Prusa, 302
Discourse, moral, 365, 366, 367
  See also Rhetorical discourse modes

Disposition, 196
Dissociations, 225
Dissociative argument, 285, 287–88
Distraction from the critical point, 227–30
Divergent argumentation, 23
Divine honor, 266–67
Donelson, Lewis R., 85
Ducrot, Oswald, 15–16
Duke, Rodney K., 3, 69, 127
Dunn, James D. G., 307–8, 345
Dynamic argumentation, 283–84, 293–94
Dynamics of argumentative situations, 278, 293–94

Ede, Lisa, 158, 167
Education, epistolary, 120–23
Eemeren, Frans H. van, 9, 10, 17, 18, 20, 78–79
Elaboration, rhetorical, 32, 34, 255–56
Elenctic enthymeme, 106
Elliptic enthymeme, 109–11
Ellul, Jacques, 166–67
Embedded maxims, 328
Emic, 185*n*. 3
Empirical component of study of argumentation, 11
Enigma, 200, 201–2, 205–6, 207
Enthymemes, 42, 43, 46–47
  apocalyptic discourse, 58
  Aristotelian, 80, 85, 98, 99, 100, 106, 243, 245–46
  in Book of Chronicles, 127–28
  case/result/rule, 50
  Ciceronian, 97–98, 100–105
  in Colossians, 348–49
  from consequents, 105–7
  in Corinthians 1, 249–53, 255–58
  defining, 95–97, 245–46
  development through, 136–39
  deictic vs. elenctic, 106

elaboration and, 255–56
elliptic, 109–11
  as a figure of speech, 98–100
  finding, 248–49
  in Hebrews, 359, 362, 363–64, 365, 370
  hortatory, 170–71
  as imperfect syllogism, 108–9
  from incompatibles, 101, 106, 107
  miracle discourse, 41
  observations on, 246–47
  procedures for finding, 248–49
  rationales and, 32–35
  refutative, 106
  Roman rhetoric and, 97–98, 100
  study of, 243–44
  three part, 35–36, 40–42, 48–50, 246, 249–50
  wisdom discourse and, 31, 32
  See also Syllogisms
Entice, 149, 150, 152
Enumeratio, 321
Epanaphora, 318, 329–30
Epicheireme, 13, 98
Epideictic
  genre, 245, 294, 367
  speeches, 72–73
  rhetoric, 40, 45, 71, 2, 73, 235, 367
Epistolarity, 112, 113, 115, 123
Epistolary
  analysis, 310–11, 325
  contextualizing, 123–24
  economics of, 113–14
  education, 120–23
  functions, 114–20
  enthymeme in, 109–10
  literary form, 28
  techniques and skills, 123
  texts, 112, 113
  theory, 112, 123
Epistolography, 112, 113, 123
Epitaphios logos, 234

Eriksson, Anders, 1, 4, 87, 243, 348–49
Eschatological salvation, 320–21
Ethos, 197–98, 199, 258, 340–42, 351, 377
Exaggeration, 304, 306
Example, 131–32, 135–36, 200, 326, 338
Exemplary argumentation, 332–37
Exhortations, 332–33, 355–57, 360–61, 364–68
Exhortative result, 257
Exordium, 357
Exornatio, 97, 193–94

Fallacy, 24–26, 90, 219–23
Fallacy *argumentum ad hominem,* 19
Figure of speech, 98–100
Figured form, 328
Forbes, John, 201
Forensic rhetoric, 300, 367
Formal dialectic procedure, 17–18
Formal logic, 14, 20–22
Freeman, James B., 24
Function at the center, 204–5, 207, 210, 214

Garrett, M. M., 164
Generic digression, 375, 376, 379
Genre
  apocalyptic, 376, 381–84
  deliberative, 71–73, 245, 298, 300, 332, 367
  development, 387
  emotions and, 384
  epideictic, 245, 294, 367
  epistolary. *See* Epistolary
  forensic, 300, 367
  in Fourth Gospel, 5, 90–91, 196
  persuasive power of, 375–76
  relations, 385–87
  romance, 375, 380–81, 383–84
Gnomic maxim, 327
Gnomic sentence, 327–28

Govier, Trudy, 21
Greco-Roman rhetorical tradition
  vs. biblical rhetoric, 200
  enthymemes and, 96–98, 100, 103, 106, 107
  exhortation and, 366
  on Galatians, 300–301
  Paul's rhetoric and, 239–42
  See also Ancient rhetorical theory; Mediterranean world
Greek romances, 379, 385–86
Green, Lawrence D., 108
Groarke, Leo, 21
Grootendorst, Rob, 10, 18, 20
Guthrie, George H., 361, 366–67

Hauser, Alan J., 3, 141
Hay, David M., 345
Henkemans, Snoeck, 23, 24
Hermeneutic techniques, 220
Hester, J. David, 276
Hierarchical relationship of audience to rhetor, 163, 166, 285–86, 292–93
Historical narrative, 128–29
Historical rhetorical criticism. *See* Ancient rhetorical theory
Homoeoptoton, 330
Homonymy, 223–26
Honor, 262–67, 273–74, 301–5
Hortatory, 342–43, 350, 352
Hortatory enthymemes, 170–71
Hospitality codes, 183–84
Houtlosser, Peter, 17
Hübner, Hans, 339
Hymnic discourse, 28
Hyperbole, 296, 299, 302, 308–9

Identification, audience, 208–10, 316–20, 322, 323, 324, 384
Implicit reasons, 19–20
Implied premises, 251–53
Inclusio, 138, 264, 265, 331, 361, 364

Inclusion, 202, 318–19, 329
Incompatibles, 103–4, 105, 107
Inconsistency, 226–27
Inductive reasoning, 63, 131, 132, 140, 194–95
Informal logic, 14–15, 21
Informal Logic, 25
Innertexture, narrative, 175–83, 264–65
International Society for the Study of Argumentation (ISSA), 25
Intertexture, narrative, 175, 183–87, 267–72, 274–75
Intonational deixis, 283
Invalid argument forms, 9
Inventio, 276–77, 295
Ironic modality, 281, 290–91, 293
Irony, 198, 199, 265–66

Jeal, Roy R., 5, 310
Jebb, John, 201
Johnson, Luke T., 302, 303
Johnson, Ralph H., 15, 21
Journals for the study of argumentation, 25
Judicial speech, 297

Keck, Leander, 186
Kennedy, George, 128
Kern, Philip, 299
Koenig, John, 184
Kopperschmidt, Josef, 17
Krabbe, Erik C. W., 17
Kraus, Manfred, 2, 95

Lähnemann, Johannes, 343–44
Language, discourse on, 237–38, 239–42
Lanigan, Richard, 246
Lausberg, Heinrich, 66–68, 70, 71–75
Law
  Jewish, 237–38
  of Moses, 305–7
Lectors, 117

Letter-cutters, 116
Letter-delivery, 117
Letter formulae, 112, 118, 123
Letter-writing, 113–15, 120–23
Linked argumentation, 23
Literacy, 117, 118, 120–21, 122–23
Literary modes of discourse, 27, 28
　See also Genre
Literates, 113, 115, 116, 118, 122, 123
Loci communes, 74
Logic
　vs. argumentation, 82–83
　dialogue, 17–18
　formal, 20–22
　informal, 14–15, 21
　rhetorical analysis and, 14, 157–58
　Stoic, 100, 101, 108–9
Logical analysis, 157–58
Logos, 199, 342
Logos-sophia, 234
Longenecker, Richard, 296
Love, discourse on, 239–42
Lunsford, Andrea, 158, 167
Luther, Martin, 296, 297, 305
Lying spirits, 148, 149–50, 151, 153

Malherbe, Abraham J., 367
Marshall, John W., 6, 375
Martyn, J. Louis, 299
Martyrdom, 29, 387
Mashal, 200
Maxim, 326, 335–36
　defined, 133
　embedded, 328
　forms, 327–28
　identification, 328–30
　as introduction to proposition, 330–32
Maxim stacks, 328–38
Maxims, moral, 333–34, 337–38
Mediterranean world
　honor/shame in, 301
　hospitality codes in, 183–84

　letter-writing in, 113–23
　Paul's boasting and, 260–61
　polemics and, 303–4
　patron-client relationship in, 184–87
　rhetorical conventions in, 254
Meshalim, 31
Messengers, 117
Metaphors, 141, 292, 310, 322, 331, 347, 366
Meynet, Roland, 4, 200
Military clerks, 119
Miracle discourse, 36–44, 47, 50, 63, 64
Modalities, 280–81, 290–91, 293
Modern dialectical approaches, 17–19
Modern rhetorical analysis
　as analytical tool, 253, 254
　disregard for, over ancient methods, 77, 78, 79–82
　objectives, 89–90
　religious argumentation, 90–92
　studies on, 78–79
　Toulmin's model, 83–84
　vs. ancient approach, 68–71, 84–89
Modern rhetorical approaches, 16–17
Modus ponens, 20–21
Mohism, 164–5
Moral
　content, 327, 328
　discourse, 365, 366, 367
　maxim, 337–38
Moses, law of, 305–7
Mouat, Lawrence, 316–17
Muilenburg, James, 2–3
Multiple argumentation, 23

Narratio, 51, 286–87
Narrative criticism, 142–43
Narrative discourse, 28
　enthymemes and, 131, 136–39
　as less direct, 142
　seeking argument and, 132–36
　thaumaturgical, 170

Narrator, 134, 171
  See also Ethos; Narrative discourse
New rhetoric, 12–14, 157
Normative purposes of research program, 10, 90, 91

Obscurity, 231
Office of *ab epistulis*, 119
Olbrechts-Tyteca, Lucie, 13–14
Olbricht, Thomas H., 1, 5–6, 355
Ontario Society for the Study of Argumentation (OSSA), 25
Opinions, preconceived, 100, 103
Opposites, 16, 32, 98–99, 161
Oracle, 203, 204–5, 306, 385
Oral/aural analysis, 325
Organization of argumentation, 9
Organizations for the study of argumentation, 25
Ornatus, 73
Osiek, Carolyn, 379
Overstatement, 296, 306, 307

Papyrus, 121
Parable, 168–69, 180, 186, 200, 201, 202, 212–13
Paraenesis, 323, 324, 377
  See also Exhortation
Paraenetic, 29, 372
Paralepsis, 289–90
Paralepsis figure, 289–90
Paromoiosis, 330
Participation, audience, 318, 322, 323, 324
Pathos, 1, 5, 91, 198
  audience appeal and, 318, 321, 322, 323
  Colossians, 342
  enthymeme and, 245–46, 258
  love and, 241
  romance and, 385
Patron-client relationship, 184–87

Patterns of reasoning, 9
Patronage, 185, 186
Peirce, Charles S., 246, 253–54
Peitho, 242
Perelman, Chaim, 12, 13–14, 84
Peroratio, 73, 279, 288, 298
Persecution-death discourse. *See* Suffering-death discourse
Personal deixis, 281–82
Persuasion, 82, 83, 155, 197–99, 288–90, 352
Persuasive definitions, 225
Persuasive power of genre, 375–76
Petitio principii, 24–25
Philophronesis, 319–20
Philosophical component of the study of argumentation, 10–11
Piscator, Johannes, 222
Pistis, 335n.49
Plot, 143, 144–45, 147, 175, 379, 380–81
Plutarch, 269
Point of departure, 9–10, 12, 13, 18–19
Polemics, 302–5, 342–43, 380
Porter, James, 158
Poster, Carol, 2, 112, 243
Powell, Mark, 175
Power, 185, 266–70, 273, 287–88
Practical component of the study of argumentation, 11–12
Pragma-dialectics, 18–19, 23
Pragmatic factors influencing argumentation, 9–10
Praxis, 242, 254, 335
Preconceived opinions, 100, 103
Pre-creation discourse, 59–63, 64
Premises
  faulty, 253
  implied, 251–53
  minor and major, 80
  unexpressed, 19–20, 158
Procedural form of argumentation, 12–13
Progymnasmata, 255

Prophetic discourse, 28, 38, 44–54, 63, 63–64, 64, 181–82, 182–83
Propositio, 97, 192, 196, 222, 223, 255, 326, 330–32
Propositions, 96–97, 101, 330–31, 337, 359, 360
Prosopopoieia, 233, 235–36
Proverb, 201, 202, 207
Purpose
  boasting, 269, 274
  Books of Chronicles, 129–31
  Ephesians, 312–16, 324
  exhortation, 364–65
  Lausberg's handbook, 66–70

Qualifier, 83
Qualitative argumentation, 162
Question
  at the center, 201–14
  rhetorical, 99, 102, 104, 105, 197
Quintilian
  amplificatio and, 73
  enthymemes and, 96, 105–7, 109
  rhetorical techniques, 81
  on self-praise, 268
  stasis theory and, 72

Radical argumentativism, 15–16
Räisänen, Heikki, 221
Ramsaran, Rollin A., 5, 325
Ramsey, W. M., 307
Ratio, 97, 192, 196, 255
Ratiocinatio, 254–55
Rationales, 249, 250
  apocalyptic discourse, 55, 57–58
  miracle discourse, 39–40
  prophetic discourse, 46–50
  suffering-death argumentation, 51–52
  wisdom discourse, 33, 34–35
Rationis confirmatio, 97, 192–93, 255
Reardon, Bryan P., 379, 384, 386
Research programs, 10–12

Reasoning
  abductive, 60, 63
  deductive, 97–98, 140, 164, 348–49, 350, 352
  dialectical, 219–20
  inductive, 63, 131, 132, 140, 194–95
Reboul, Olivier, 16
Rebuttal, 83, 88
Re-invented rhetoric, 277
Relational posture, 277–78, 280–83
Relevance, 15
Religious argumentation, 90–91
Repetition, 91, 318
Research, descriptive, 90
Research program, components of, 10–12
Result rephrased, 257
Rhetoric
  argumentation not equated with, 82–83
  defined, 157
  deliberative, 367
  descriptive works on, 128
  epideictic, 40, 45, 72–73, 367
  forensic, 367
  function of, 359
  modern, 16–17
  See also Ancient rhetoric
Rhetorical argumentation. *See Argumentation*
Rhetorical analysis. *See* Rhetorical criticism
Rhetorical criticism, 325
  2 Corinthians, 277–78
  defined, 157–58
  Fourth Gospel, 188–89
  historical vs. modern, 68–71, 79–82, 84–90
  limitations of Lausberg's work for, 71–76
  logic and, 157–58
  Paul's letters and, 232, 233, 236
  of romance and apocalypse genres, 383–84

INDEX OF SUBJECTS AND AUTHORS

Rhetorical discourse modes
  apocalyptic, 54–59, 163–67, 170–72
  audience and, 159–60
  in Hebrew Bible, 27–28
  literary forms, 28, 29
  miracle discourse, 37–44
  New Testament literature, 29–30
  pre-creation, 59–63
  prophetic discourse, 181–83
  suffering-death, 51–54
  wisdom, 31–37, 160–67, 168–70, 375–76
Rhetorical interpretation, 30
  See also Socio-historical interpretation
Rhetorical maxims. *See* Maxims
Rhetorical method, 68, 69, 70, 76
Rhetorical movement
  apocalyptic discourse, 59
  miracle discourse, 42, 44
  pre-creation discourse, 60, 62–63
  prophetic discourse and, 50
  suffering death discourse, 53, 54
  wisdom, 37
Rhetorical process, 27
Rhetorical theology, 28–29
Rhetorical theory, 67, 77, 78, 79–82
  See also Ancient rhetorical theory
Rhetorical units, 277–80
Rhetoric of genre, 375
Rhetorolect, 65, 159, 160
Ricoeur, Paul, 27–28
Robbins, Vernon K., 1–2, 27, 160, 181, 243–44, 246
Romance genre, 375, 380–81, 382, 383–84, 385–87
Roman rhetoric. *See* Greco-Roman rhetorical tradition

Salutation, 236–37
Sarcasm, 307
School rhetoric, 70, 71, 75, 76
Scribe, 118, 240

Secretaries, 119
Semitic rhetoric, 200
Sententia, 327, 328
Serial argumentation, 23
Shaefer, G. E., 130
Shorthand, 113, 116
Shui, 166
Shuo argumentation, 164–65
Sign, 22, 133, 134
Similitudo, 200
Sisson, Russel B., 3, 174
Slander, 302–4, 305
Slave(s), 113, 115, 116–18, 120, 122, 185–86
Snoeck Henkemans, A Francisca, 24
Socio-rhetorical analysis, 30, 34
  Asian argumentation, 160–67
  audience and, 159–60, 167–73
  enthymemes and, 250
  Paul's boasting and, 261, 264–73
  social codes and relationships, 183–87
Socio-rhetorical interpretation, 32, 54, 63, 248, 250
Socio-rhetorical strategies, 58
Socrates, 219
Sophia-moria, 234
Sophistic rhetoric
  ambiguity in, 223–25
  distraction from critical point in, 227–30
  fallacious nature of, 219–20
  inconsistency in, 226–27
  obscurity in, 231
  Pauline gospels, 220–22
  syllogisms, 222–23
  "to make the weaker argument the stronger" and, 217–18
Sorites, 249
Source criticism, 142–43, 277
Spatial deixis, 282
Speech material, 136–39, 241–42
Stasis theory, 71–73, 339–40

Stoics, 98
Stoic logic, 100, 101, 108–9
Stoic syllogisms, 100–101, 106–7, 108–9
Stone, Michael, 165, 166
Street scribes, 118
Structure of argumentation, 19, 23–24, 181, 187, 189
Subordinative argumentation, 23, 24
Suffering-death discourse, 51–54, 63
Sufficiency, 15
Sumney, Jerry L., 5, 339
Swearingen, Jan, 4
Syllogisms
  apocalyptic discourse, 55–56, 57–58
  case/result/rule, 38, 50
  case/rule/result, 40, 43, 52, 53, 181
  in Hebrews, 363–64
  imperfect, 108–9
  incomplete, 95, 96–97
  in Matthean Mission Discourse, 181
  pre-creation discourse, 60–62
  rationales and, 40, 41, 42
  sophistical argumentation and, 222–23
  stoic, 100–101, 106–7, 108–9
  three part, 36–37, 42, 47, 48–49, 52, 55–56
  truncated, 95, 96–97
  wisdom discourse and, 31
  See also Enthymemes
Syllogistic argumentation, 53, 83, 84–86, 87–89
Syllogistic reasoning, 36–37, 41, 56
Symptomatic argumentation, 22
Synonymy, 220, 322–23

Tachygraphers, 116–17
Teleological argumentation, 22
Telika kephalaia, 72
Temporal deixis, 283
Tertullian, 375
Thaumaturgical narrative, 170

Theology, 248, 252
  Galatians and, 296–97, 299, 305
  rhetorical, 28–29
Theoretical component of research program, 11
Thesis, 17–8, 31–32, 254–55, 330–31, 343–44, 346
Thomas, Stephen N., 23
Threats, 91
Thurén, Lauri, 2, 69, 77, 253, 254, 299
Topoi, 16
  enthymemes and, 245–46, 248, 254, 258–59
  Greek literary culture, 241–42
  Pauline, 234, 259, 346
  See also Topos
Topos, 16, 347
  of affliction, 284, 286–88, 289, 347
  antecedent/consequent, 347
  of assimilation, 347
  of boasting, 284, 289, 291–92
  of consolation, 284, 289, 293
  of contradiction, 347
  of frankness, 284, 288
  of obedience, 286, 290
  of sincerity, 284, 287, 290
  of testing, 286, 290
  See also Topoi
Torjesen, Karen Jo, 29
Toulmin, Stephen, 12–13, 83
Toulmin model of argumentation, 12–13, 83–84, 88
Traditional moral content, 328, 329
Translators, 118
Truth, 148–49, 221, 226
  of enthymeme, 247, 253
  of maxims, 327, 328, 336

Übelacker, Walter, 1, 357

Vagueness, 144
Valid argument forms, 9

Validity, deductive, 20–22
Van Eemeren, Frans H., 1, 9
Virgins, 378–79
Visions, 377–78, 381, 383, 385–86
Vitriolic hyperbole, 302
Volitional modality, 281, 290, 293
Vos, Johan S., 4, 217

Wachob, Wesley H., 34, 36
Walton, Douglas, 25
Warrant, 12, 83, 84, 365, 366, 369–71
Watson, Duane F., 4–5, 260
Weakness, 266, 267, 287
Wenzel, Joseph W., 16
White, Hayden, 128–29
Wilson, R. McL., 358

Wisdom, 234, 236, 237, 239–41, 327–28
Wisdom discourse, 28, 63, 64
  apocalyptic discourse and, 56–57, 375–76
  Asian rhetoric, 160–67
  argumentation and early Christian, 31–37
  audience and, 168–70
  miracle discourse and, 43, 44
  pre-creation discourse and, 29–30
  prophetic discourse and, 38, 47, 50, 182–83
  suffering-death discourse and, 51
Witherington, Ben, 298
Woods, John, 25
Word patterns, 318
Wuellner, Wilhelm, 280

BS
1199
.R5
R54
2002